Cruising French Waterways

4TH EDITION

Hugh McKnight

ADLARD COLES NAUTICAL
LONDON

To the people who helped ensure the safe future of French inland waterways

Roger Pilkington, 1915–2003
Michael Streat, 1924–1993
Pierre Zivy, 1929–2001

Published by Adlard Coles Nautical
an imprint of A & C Black Publishers Ltd
37 Soho Square, London W1D 3QZ
www.adlardcoles.com

First published by Stanford Maritime Ltd 1984
Reprinted 1985, 1988
Second edition published by Adlard Coles
Nautical 1991
Third edition 1999
Fourth edition 2005

Typeset in Meridian 9/11pt
Printed and bound in Great Britain by
Martins the Printers, Berwick-upon-Tweed

Winner of the Thomas Cook
Guide Book Award

TITLE PAGE: The centre of Metz

Note: Whilst every effort has been taken to ensure the accuracy of this book, neither the Author nor the Publishers can take responsibility for any accident or damage arising out of any error of commission or omission.

Also by Hugh McKnight

Canal and River Craft in Pictures, 1969
A Source Book of Canals, Locks and Canal Boats, 1974
The Guinness Guide to Waterways of Western Europe, 1978
The Shell Book of Inland Waterways, Second edition, 1981
Waterways Postcards 1900–1930, 1983
Slow Boat Through France, 1991
Slow Boat Through Germany, 1993

FOREWORD ∼

In 1977 my family and I enjoyed a wonderful holiday on the Canal du Midi, joining it at Castelnaudary and ending up at Marseillan. I had no idea at the time that my great grandfather Linley Sambourne, the political cartoonist on "Punch", had experienced the same pleasure 104 years before. His sketches were published shortly afterwards in a book called "Our Autumn Holiday on French Rivers". Although I too spent most of the time sketching the views, bridges and locks, mine were of such an inferior quality, they remain in a bottom drawer.

Like him, I was excited to discover this amazing survival of 17th century engineering and architecture. Water transport pre-dates the age of steam: yet in France inland waterways are still used by commerce. They are not just a reconstruction job for tourists, but are very much used for industry as well as for pleasure.

The speed is slow and ideal for sketch book or camera. You stop when and where you want. And if you take off on the boat's bicycles for shopping or sight seeing, the towpaths and quiet lanes have none of the fumes and dangers of the main roads.

Among my companions on that journey was the author, Hugh McKnight. With this book to guide them, I am sure that many more people will be encouraged to discover these hidden highways.

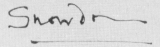

CONTENTS ∽

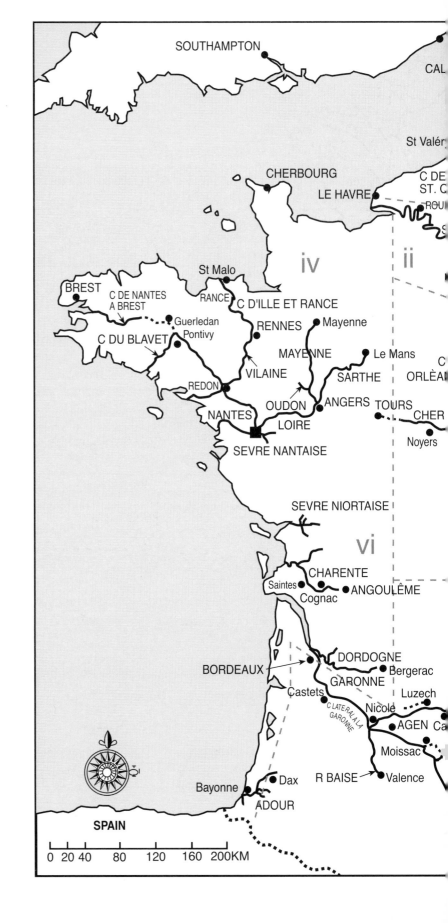

INTRODUCTION ～

'Madame reminded her husband of an Englishman who had come up this canal in a steamer.

"'Perhaps Mr Moens in the *Ytene*," I suggested.

"'That's it," assented the husband. "He had his wife and family with him, and servants. He came ashore at all the locks and asked the name of all the villages, whether from boatmen or lock keepers; and then he wrote, wrote them down. Oh, he wrote enormously! I suppose it was a wager."'

Robert Louis Stevenson, *An Inland Voyage*, 1878.

Equipped with camera and tape recorder, I have often felt like William Moens, attempting to describe waterways in a foreign land whose language he could speak only with difficulty. Yet 20 years after the first edition of this book I am delighted to find that it remains in demand as new generations of navigators set out to discover French rivers and canals. It has appeared in American editions and translations into German and French.

It all began in the late 1950s, when as a 14-year-old I travelled abroad for the first time to stay with a French family in Lyon. Already an enthusiastic Thames boater, I would watch barges gliding peacefully down the Saône to the confluence with a then untamed Rhône. There, the green and wild water picked them up and hurled them out of sight on their voyage to the South and the Mediterranean. Some day, I thought, it would make a great adventure to explore the canals and rivers of France.

But Britain came first. For the next decade the waterways of England and Wales absorbed all my spare time. Then in the autumn of 1968 I accepted an invitation from John Liley of *Motor Boat & Yachting* to join a party of friends on a Saint Line cruiser, making a circuit from the Canal du Nivernais. It was pure magic! Horse barges were not quite extinct and we must have met all that remained in service, an evocative link with freight transport as practised in the 19th century. The following spring I was among a group of 30 British people who took part in a 5-day publicity cruise from Bordeaux to Toulouse at the inauguration of France's second hire boat company, Blue Line Cruisers. Since

then I have returned to the French waterways annually, in everything from an inflatable dinghy to passenger vessels, hire cruisers and private motor yachts. This culminated in my keeping my own motor cruiser on the waterways of mainland Europe for some 18 years, and in 2004 moving to a house whose *parc* is bordered by the River Lot.

There are about 8,800km of navigable canals and rivers in France, a figure that grows annually as further sections of derelict routes are reopened to traffic. Yet the total distance remains far short of the 12,467km total that was recorded in 1879. Nonetheless, the aquatic tourist can penetrate almost every region of the country: from the Ardennes to Picardy, Provence to the Ile de France, Burgundy to the Vosges. Developed over the centuries, the network has regularly been modernised and extended. Recent years have seen new lines opened up for 2,000 tonne barges; many other canals are now fitted with automated locks and swing bridges controlled by radar beams, switches suspended from pylons or *télécommandes* (portable push button devices); flights of locks have been replaced by boat lifts, reducing hours of effort to a matter of minutes.

In spite of massive investment during the last 40 years, commercial freight carriage continues to decline, largely because of unfair subsidies available to alternative transport systems. It is worth remembering that the *smallest* working boats remaining in commission in France load around 350 tonnes, so in theory water transport should be highly competitive with road vehicles. Perhaps one third of the system carries substantial quantities of freight; another third is used less and less for transport; the remainder is now devoted entirely to pleasure boating.

Leisure use of French canals (and to a lesser extent the rivers) is relatively new. Such developments came to France several decades after Britain. True, sea-going craft have long used inland routes between the English Channel, the Rhine and the Mediterranean, or taken a short-cut from the Atlantic across the sun-drenched country of Languedoc. But now inland boating is firmly established as an activity in its own right. For the solitary traveller or family group alike, there can be no more peaceful way to explore this beautiful land, seeking out ancient towns and villages, drinking local wines and eating in waterside *auberges*. The key to fullest enjoyment is to avoid being hurried: 30km and 10 locks each day ought to be a target ambitious enough for anyone.

Safety and peace are prime characteristics of French inland boating. In thousands of kilometres of cruising I have had few anxious moments, with the possible exception of the time when the yacht on which I was a guest caught fire in a lock near St-Dizier. By comparison, the world of dry land is infinitely more dangerous and long-remembered hazards include my being thrown from the pillion of the ship's motorcycle into the path of a lorry on the hilly approach to Langres; being surrounded by gangs of hostile youths in the early hours of the morning as I tried to sleep in a tent on the banks of the Marne; and having my car broken into twice in one year while boating by inflatable; parking sites were subsequently chosen with a greater regard for security. Coastal cruising can introduce elements of danger from which canals and rivers are generally free. After travelling the Lower Seine from Paris to Honfleur, I agreed to stay aboard the boat for a further day's run by sea to Cherbourg. Many hours after our estimated arrival time we were enveloped in a dense fog with faulty steering, one of two engines defunct and a rapidly dwindling fuel supply. Thanks to the radio telephone, a rescue tug pulled us into the safety of the harbour in the early hours of the morning. I then decided that inland waters, complete with the hazards introduced by flood and drought, were more trustworthy.

Waterways are in a constant state of change. Information which is accurate at the time of writing may well have altered by the time you read this book. Shops come and go, restaurants change owners, lock opening times are adjusted and even the physical layout of some canals may alter. I have attempted to update this fourth edition to 2004, but I freely admit that this is a nearly impossible task: inevitably, there are some routes that I will not have travelled for some time. I strongly suggest, therefore, that this book is used in conjunction with the appropriate *Carte Guides*, where it is possible to note revisions with greater frequency. My greatest concern has been to add new entries for those routes recently brought back into full use from utter dereliction. These include the River Baïse, River Cher and connected portion of the Canal de Berry, the lower River Lot, the Canal de Roubaix, a major section of the Canal du Rhône au Rhin long superseded by the hectic Grand Canal d'Alsace and a score of small arms and branches which every true waterways enthusiast will wish to explore. While every effort has been made to ensure that statements in this book were correct as it went to press, neither I nor my publishers can accept responsibility for any consequential difficulties arising from material contained in it.

Cruising French Waterways was the first and remains the only descriptive account of the entire French network. It is designed to inform readers exactly what they can expect of each waterway in terms of historical development, scenery, places to visit, suitable moorings and – to a more limited extent, for here the *Carte Guides* are designed to provide the fullest information – other facilities. One quandary was to decide which end of a canal or river should start the description. Inevitably, some users will be making their journey in the opposite direction. But, where possible, through routes or circuits have been dealt with as a continuous sequence. **Rather than adopt the convention of making references to the left bank or right bank when moving downstream (this works well enough on rivers but is most confusing on canals), left and right refer to the direction of travel.**

I hope that British and American readers will accept my use of metric measurements throughout. It is helpful to remember that metres and yards are roughly interchangeable. A kilometre is five-eighths of a mile (50 miles = 80km). For practicable purposes, I find that conversion from kilometres to miles is easily achieved by dividing by 2 and adding 'a bit'. Use of a dual system in this book would have complicated the issue. In any event France has been metric for two hundred years and all publications such as the *Carte Guides* quote the native units. For those used to thinking in miles, the kilometre is a surprisingly optimistic form of measurement, 30km being a reasonable day's cruising distance while 30 miles could constitute a daunting prospect.

This book has been designed to be used in conjunction with the excellent series of *Carte Guides* listed in the Bibliography. The appropriate volume is identified at the start of each chapter. These map/guides, regularly updated, contain text in French, English and German and include full details of facilities en route such as fuel, water points, moorings, repairs, shopping and restaurants. For planning purposes a large-scale map of the waterways system is also very useful. Signals for traffic control and between vessels, navigational and other marks are explained either in the *Carte Guides* or on a small self adhesive panel which can be sited alongside the steering position for instant reference.

Many friends have assisted me with compilation and I am extremely grateful to them. First, June and John

Humphries, whose enthusiasm for French waterways has been boundless. I began exploring waterways with them and their daughters 35 years ago. That we acquired in 1983 the jointly-owned sea-going motor yacht *Avonbay* for Continental use was an indication of our combined involvement with the subject. Their assistance has taken numerous practical forms, not least the encouragement I have received throughout the life of this book. My friend and wife Marjory has shared much of the boating research. I am very fortunate that she loves France and the French waterways quite as much as I do; moreover, she tolerates the occasional patches of cold and wet weather with extraordinarily good humour. Most people complain when they get wet: Marjory habitually reminds me that 'it's only water'.

The late Lord and Lady Harvington regularly invited me to travel on their charming motor cruisers *Melita* and *Melitina*. These voyages generally featured a rapid and sometimes exciting progress through France. There were few yachtsmen who explored Continental waterways so extensively and with such perennial enthusiasm: Grant Harvington was to take delivery of his final vessel when well into his 80s in spite of by then being increasingly reliant on an electric wheelchair.

John Liley, a former editor of *Motor Boat & Yachting* and subsequently a French hotel barge proprietor, was responsible for my very first French canal travels. The cruiser was owned by pioneer the late Pierre Zivy, then of Saint Line: he introduced hire craft to France and as a result saved the ravishingly beautiful Canal du Nivernais and quite possibly many other equally important routes from certain closure. Pierre Zivy was a 20th century hero of the French waterways and must never be forgotten.

By launching Blue Line Cruisers (France) Ltd, the late Michael Streat instigated many of my fluvial forays and on one memorable occasion spent a week on board *Avonbay*. Those who today enjoy the waterways of France owe Michael a huge debt. Blue Line's original president, the late Gerald Norman, francophile, was a source of great inspiration, instilling in me a love of France, its history and people. The late Professor David Horsfall, wit, world expert on coal washing and fellow collector of rare waterways literature, shared a small but invaluable part of the practical cruising research. The executives, base managers and staff of Blue Line Cruisers (now Crown Blue Line) past and present and especially Charles Gérard (now of H$_2$O, St-Jean de Losne), John Riddel and former Managing Director Keith Gregory, all provided services, facilities and hospitality. So did Jimmy Hoseason and his colleagues of Hoseason's Holidays, Andrew Brock of French Country Cruises, Messrs Locoboat Plaisance and the staff of the French Government Tourist Office in London.

Many readers of the first three editions were kind enough to write to me saying how much this book had added to their cruising enjoyment. A number of them went to considerable trouble to provide additional information, all of which I have tried to incorporate into the present updated version. These include Sir Timothy Bevan, Denise Closier, Robert Cowley, John Cruse, Mike and Tania Herniman, Carrie and Mike Hofman, J R Liney, Marshall Long, Vernon Marchant, Jim Marshall, D C Minett, the late Tony Paris, Karen and Morvyn Phillips, John Riddel, Sefton Sandford, Bob van Gulik and the Rev Ricky Yates.

Two fellow waterways authors (both long-standing friends) must be credited: David Edwards-May for answering questions and keeping me up to date with new developments, and the much lamented late Dr Roger Pilkington, whose *Small Boat* books have been a massive source of inspiration. I know that without Roger's writing, many routes that we now take for granted, both in France and in other parts of Western Europe, would have been utterly lost to dereliction.

My original editor, Phoebe Mason, viewed the gestation of this book with remarkable patience and good humour – a rare combination in a publisher. This excellent relationship continues under Janet Murphy. Lastly, I salute the lock keepers and people of France who (almost without exception) have accepted my invasion of their country with real kindness. Thank you to all.

Unless otherwise credited, all photographs are my own, with historical material drawn from the Hugh McKnight Photography Collection.

If, during the course of their French cruises, readers should discover information which might enhance future editions of this book, I shall be delighted to hear from them. Fellow waterways enthusiasts travelling on the Lower River Lot are invited make contact with us at our new home, on the left bank 2km upstream of the lock at Aiguillon.

Hugh McKnight,
Cul de l'Ilot, 47190 Aiguillon, France

AFLOAT IN FRANCE ∽

Some years ago, France, in common with a number of other European nations, decided that those in charge of pleasure craft should be examined in the theory and practice of boating techniques. When it was realised that such legislation would bring the fast-growing and economically important hire cruiser industry to its abrupt destruction, a typically Gallic solution decreed that hire boat clients could be exempted on the grounds of having been given a few minutes of basic instruction at the start of their holidays, resulting in their being given a temporary *Carte de Plaisance*. Owners of private boats, whose skills will almost always be superior, would still be subject to an official test. The implications of this are startling: the owner of a motor cruiser who has admirably demonstrated his skills by navigating the Channel to France from the River Thames, cannot legally enter the French canals and rivers unless they are in possession of the required certification. Their British friend, with no previous knowledge of boats, is permitted to arrive in France by car, drive to his chosen hire cruiser base and enjoy a fortnight afloat without any official form of licence. This foolish situation remains and is unlikely to be changed. Consequently, conscientious private boat owners with years of experience gained (for example) on British waterways must acquire an acceptable qualification to use French navigations. Exceptions are made for very small, low-powered vessels, such as might be used by anglers.

For British nationals, the required document is the International Certificate of Competence (ICC) issued by the Royal Yachting Association, RYA House, Ensign Way, Hamble, Southampton, Hampshire SO31 4YA. Tel 0845 345 0375. The RYA will provide the syllabus, together with a list of approved boating school test centres, where a practical exam can be taken. All the information needed for the theory test is contained in *The ACN Book of EuroRegs for Inland Waterways* by Marian Martin, published by Adlard Coles Nautical. Fees are charged both by the Association and by the examiners. The ICC is now only available to British subjects, meaning that American, Australian and other English-speaking yachtsmen must either obtain equivalent qualifications in their own countries or opt to take a test in France, where use of an interpreter is permitted. Larger craft, between 15m and 39m in length, require a category PP licence (*Péniches de*

Plaisance) or equivalent recognised by the French authorities. For details, contact the RYA. Alternatively, consult the Barge Association, of which membership is much recommended, if only to receive the excellent magazine, *Blue Flag*. This covers a wide range of topics of interest to barge owners, especially those travelling in France. Details from: Les Gibson, Hon Secretary, The Barge Association, 2 Church Lane, Uxbridge, Middlesex UB8 2XD. Tel 01895 847440. Always, a copy of the CEVNI rules must be carried on board. The *ACN EuroRegs* (see above) is an acceptable substitute.

While the test for inland waters is not especially difficult, the fact that it is required at all is, to say the least, irksome, in view of the situation relating to boat hirers.

British subjects or those from nations within the European Community are entitled to use and keep a boat in French waters with exactly the same freedom that you can cruise in your home country, although it is necessary to carry documentary evidence that Value Added Tax has been paid on your vessel. An exception is boats built before 1985 or which were in use on EU waters on or before the last day of 1992. It would be wise to check the latest situation with the RYA or the British Customs and Excise.

The situation is more complicated for non-European Community nationals, where, if they are to avoid payment of 18.6% French tax on the estimated value of their boat, it may only be used in France for up to 18 months in a 2 year period. After this time, it appears that it is possible to export the vessel from France, obtain documentary proof that this has been done, and commence a new 2 year period! It would be wise to check with the French Embassy in your home country, although it is unlikely that the staff will be able to provide instant confirmation.

Insurance (especially third party) and a VHF ship's radio licences (both for the installation and for the operator) are needed for private craft. All non-French passengers should of course carry passports. Finally, the boat should be registered. This is similar to a boat's passport and serves as proof of ownership. For UK vessels, this can either be the Small Ships Register or the rather more complicated Registration Part 1. Both are available from the Registry of Shipping and Seamen in Cardiff. Tel 02920 448 800.

The intention of this book is to describe the waterways themselves rather than such matters as what equipment to take, working through locks, or organising shopping expeditions in unknown towns. In many respects, inland cruising in France is much the same as anywhere: provided your boat is well fendered, furnished with adequate lines and preferably has one or more bicycles aboard (useful for sight-seeing, shopping and travelling up canal towpaths to help keepers prepare manual locks), you should encounter few difficulties.

These days, many canal locks are automated and worked by boat crews using various ingenious methods. A large number of locks, however, remain manned by resident or mobile keepers. You are expected to help them, under their direction. Locks on the larger waterways may be contacted before you arrive via VHF radio telephone. Much waiting time can be saved in this way. Appropriate channel numbers appear in the *Carte Guides*.

One important difference between smaller UK locks, which are normally operated by the boater, and the great majority of manual French locks and mobile bridges, which can only be negotiated when accompanied by a keeper, is that it is not possible to make totally independent travelling plans. French keepers work certain hours only with a short break for their midday meal. Where they are responsible for more than one lock (in some cases for an extended flight of locks) you cannot stop on a whim as and when you please and expect the keeper to resume his duties when it suits you. When prevented from further progress by evening closure of locks, a keeper will frequently ask at what time you wish to move on next morning. You will be expected to present yourself with boat at the following lock at the promised time. As can be imagined, this system can be frustrating if you encounter an unexpected attraction that demands you stop and investigate knowing that a mobile keeper may not be able to resume working for you until hours later or even the next day.

Until 1991, French waterways were available to pleasure craft free of charge. Since then, a licence (*vignette*) has been necessary for each boat. Currently, these may be purchased for one day or 16 days, start and finishing dates to be specified; 30 days, not necessarily consecutive, a 'day' being counted only when the boat is moving; or for a year, terminating 31 December following date of purchase. Various price categories depend on the total area of the vessel (length x beam). A discount is available on the annual licence where application is made before a specified date early in the year. Very small and low powered craft are exempt, while no charge is made for using certain

Springtime on a canal in Central France.

routes which are under local rather than national control: these include the Canal du Nivernais, rivers and canals in Brittany and the French canalised Rhine.

It is preferable to buy a *vignette* by post, well in advance of the start of a cruise, as the various regional offices of the navigation authority appear to open at irregular hours. The completed application form should be accompanied by payment in Euros and photocopies of your personal helmsman's certificate and the boat's registration document. Details are available from Voies Navigables de France (VNF), rue Ludovic Boutleux, BP 820, 62408 Béthune. Tel 03 21 63 24 24. There is also an English language web site, www.vnf.fr, which at the time of writing is unfortunately neither exciting or particularly easy to use. However improvements are promised.

Lock opening hours vary with the time of the year and between one navigation and another. Broadly speaking, keepers are generally on duty from 06.00–19.30h in the summer, with a break for the midday meal. Occasionally, some routes are closed on a particular day of the week. Extraordinary as it is, many locks are closed throughout certain public holidays – often the very days when pleasure traffic might be expected to be at a peak! Stoppages (*chômages*) for planned repairs normally avoid the most popular boating months. A list, published around late March each year, is available from the VNF or the French Government Tourist Office in London.

A lock keeper waits as this towering barge slowly leaves the chamber.

Several methods are used to actuate automatic locks. These include bankside sensors, manually operated switches suspended over the water or 'zappers' lent to the boat when entering a relevant section. Printed instructions are normally issued to craft before the first such lock. A small number of locks are worked manually by boaters (Rivers Charente and Upper Lot) or by special 'smart card' (River Baïse).

Boatyards and marinas are moderately prolific in most areas (they remain rare in the extreme north west of the country). Drinking water supplies are sometimes few and far between, so it is best to top up whenever possible, especially if your boat's tank capacity is limited. The same applies to diesel supplies (*gas oil*), where it should be noted that red (tax-free) fuel bought in France may not be used to propel craft, although it is permitted for central heating purposes. Imported red diesel may be used in engines, but you are strongly advised to keep accurate details of consumption/distances travelled etc, as French Customs are known to carry out spot checks. Penalties are very severe and there appears to be no appeal against their rulings. Waterside petrol pumps (*essence*) chiefly of interest to users of outboard motors, are virtually non-existent: here, fuel must be carried in cans from roadside garages.

Bottled gas (propane or butane, often used for cooking, water heating and refrigeration) is widely available throughout France from marinas, garages and supermarkets. Empty 'foreign' cylinders are not exchangeable for French brands. It is best to select the two types that are distributed in most regions: Primagaz and Butagaz. Note that the fittings differ from those used in the UK: French chandleries and hardware shops stock suitable replacements.

Although living costs for British holiday makers are no longer as favourable as during the late 1990s, at the time of writing they are generally similar to or slightly cheaper than in the UK. Locally produced alcohol is perhaps the best bargain, while market stalls offer good value in fruit and local vegetables. Careful research will reveal restaurants where a four-course meal, inclusive of house wine, can still be bought for well under £10! My golden rule is to select the more ambitious menu at an inexpensive village restaurant, where you will always obtain better value than by attempting to economise at a smart establishment. Watch where the lock keepers, *pénichiers* and truck drivers are eating and do likewise. Supermarket shopping is less fun than visiting village stores, but they do provide really fresh food without any language barrier. Sometimes, country lock keepers will sell you their own produce, from eggs, rabbits, chickens and wine to vegetables and fruit. I like to buy from such places rather than offering tips which can appear a little patronising and, on a long journey become very expensive.

Try not to antagonise the people who make their living on the waterways. Earn the respect of the barge families who work there 12 months of the year. Never race working boats to a lock unless you are certain that you will be out of their way before they are ready to pass through. It can be infuriating to have the same barge stern in view, lock after lock, as when I once crawled up the Canal de l'Est for three days behind a convoy of slow-moving laden *péniches*, none of the pounds being long enough to allow overtaking. But in compensation you may have the opportunity to really get to know these working-boat people, exchange bottles of wine and finally end up enjoying an open-air dinner with them under the towpath plane trees. Equally, while almost all of the lock keepers are charming, the odd sour example will be encountered. Always reflect that you are a foreigner in someone else's territory and remain patient.

Speed limits are imposed for the safety of other craft and to protect canal and river banks from erosion. They are usually 6kph on small canals, 8–10kph on larger artificial waterways and 20–25kph on river navigations. But if, even within these speeds you are creating a breaking wave, you should slow down. Never endanger those in canoes or rowing boats and do try to be considerate to fishermen (this is sometimes impossible to achieve, judging from the comments you will receive). Notice boards inform where reduced speed is demanded. Certain river reaches are classified for water-skiing, with limits as high at 40kph. Never be tempted to emulate the disgraceful behaviour of certain power boaters, whose passage can cause far more disturbance than a 1,350-tonne barge. Sadly, not everyone afloat is blessed with either common sense or good manners! Almost nothing annoys waterways authorities and lock keepers as much as boats tearing along a canal creating a massive bow wave with wash crashing onto the banks. If the boat happens to be capable of being described as a floating gin palace, the offence is compounded! It is no excuse to claim urgent business elsewhere, or that your vessel handles badly at slow speeds. The worst offenders are generally sea-going yachts using the waterways as a coast-to-coast short-cut. They can give a bad name to all pleasure craft. Unless you are willing to slow down to conventional canal and river speeds and enjoy inland waterways boating as an experience in its own right, it is better to stick to the sea.

You should be familiar with all forms of navigation markers, signals and instruction panels: these are explained in the *Carte Guides* in colour. All but the shortest tunnels (where a strong torch is adequate) require a powerful headlight, with one or more handheld torches ready for use. Many tunnels are now lit. Additional illumination can be provided by turning the cabin lights on, but not so as to impair the helmsman's vision.

Other necessary equipment includes a loud horn to alert lock keepers of your approach. An excellent and inexpensive type is a portable device working on a can of compressed gas: these will not be confused with car hooters. Acquire a really long water hose (25m or more): mine folds flat on a reel and occupies far less space than the conventional type. French taps with threaded outlets occur in several diameters. Most French hardware stores stock adapters, although a rubber compression fitting with a butterfly clip is often the best solution. A French courtesy flag to fly in addition to your national ensign, clothes pegs, plastic rubbish sacks, large fuel can for emergency use where bankside pumps are not available, a medical kit, plenty of spare mooring lines and as long a shaft (boat hook) as you can easily handle and stow are all items you should not forget to take.

Where a trans-France passage with a substantial motor sailing boat is proposed, mast and spars will need to be unstepped and stored on deck in order to clear the bridges. If the mast greatly overhangs the hull, there will be anxious moments when passing through locks. Some owners prefer to have the mast sent ahead by road on a passage between the Rhône Delta and Le Havre or vice-versa. One firm who will under take this service is Port Napoléon, 13230 Port Saint Louis du Rhône.

Choosing a Boat

There is no such thing as the ideal vessel for exploring French rivers and canals. Even if money is no object what is suitable for you may be quite wrong for someone else. I know from experience that given good company, an outfit costing less than £1,000 can provide more pleasure than a luxury cruiser priced at £250,000.

Starting at the bottom end of the scale, in order to carry out research for part of this book, I spent six thoroughly enjoyable weeks mainly in a quality 9ft (2.70m) inflatable dinghy, with a low-powered outboard motor with clutch. This took me safely down the Upper Seine to Paris, along much of the Saône, the Seille, part of the Canal du Midi and Canal latéral à la Garonne, the Charente and the Sèvre Niortaise. Some of the time I was single-handed, but elsewhere I was joined by a friend. Our combined weights left space for little beyond fuel, tent, stove, bedding and cameras. We survived superbly in the (mainly) brilliant sunshine of early summer, buying food as required or eating ashore. The huge advantage of using tiny craft like this is that one-way boating becomes possible. Leaving equipment in safekeeping, it is easy to recover the car by public transport and drive on to the next waterway location. Twice, we resorted to packing the whole outfit into taxis: to return from the head of navigation on the Seille to the Saône, and to bypass a series of locks near Toulouse, which were closed by an emergency stoppage. On another occasion, having arrived at a lock just on closing time, we spent 20 minutes portaging everything from one end to the other and enjoyed a further two hours of evening boating on the long pound that followed. Disadvantages were susceptibility to wash – not from commercial traffic but from thoughtless speedboats: here, we no more than shipped some water. Another problem was that nobody would believe that we had come farther than from the nearest town. After all, it did appear to be a frail and insignificant little boat.

Similar considerations apply to canoes, especially collapsible versions than can be carried by train; and the range of usable waters is greatly increased. However, even travelling with the current, I regard unpowered canoeing as rather too much like hard work. Many of the 19th century explorers of French canals travelled by rowing boat. George Waring and his wife drifted 200 miles (321km) down the Moselle, employing an oarsman for much of the time. Rather later, in the 1920s, Mr and Mrs C S Forester spent three months in a camping dinghy fitted with an outboard which they never managed to fully understand. Their contemporaries may have lived on steam yachts with paid hands, but it is evident from their respective narratives which form of transport was the more enjoyable.

Still remembering that small can be beautiful, in 1998, one of my friends bought a very cheap, elderly and frankly worn-out timber motorised sailing cruiser in Cornwall, took her to France by car ferry and spent an enjoyable summer slowly travelling down to the Mediterranean. On reaching the port of Sète, he literally gave the boat to the first local who showed any interest. (I must emphasise that the vessel's condition was such that it presented no danger to either user or other craft.) Some years ago, I spent three days on the Canal de l'Est, locking in company with a Dutch carpenter who had put a cabin on his little wooden lifeboat and had passed an entire season voyaging on the cheap from the Netherlands to the Mediterranean and back. He wore the most colourful hand-knitted socks ever seen and was accompanied by a young lady who generally declined to appear except at dusk, when she exercised her black cat on the towpath.

One of my favourite waterways stories is Weston Martyr's *The £200 Millionaire*, first published in 1932. It tells of an English doctor who retired early with £4,000 capital of which he spent £200 on a small cabin cruiser fitted with sails and an engine. Investing his

A small freight barge (which once worked on Shakespeare's Avon) now converted for pleasure use on French waterways.

remaining money brought him an annual income of just £200, then more than sufficient to live aboard for 12 months of the year, wintering in the warmer climes of the Mediterranean and ranging throughout Europe's rivers and canals for the rest of the time. He had seen waterways in Denmark, Sweden, Germany, France, the Netherlands and down the Danube to the Black Sea. He would stock up with cheap wine where prices were low in French villages, find free wood for the stove, and buy food from lock keepers – all at trifling expense: this wandering life continued for 10 years at an average cost of £150 a year. Seventy years later, the finances have changed but the principle remains good. Waterway travel is not the sole preserve of the rich.

One advance in the quest for mobility is the trailed cruiser. Here, you are restricted to a boat no more than about 20ft (6m) long, which can be towed by a moderately powerful car. (Check with the RYA on the regulations regarding maximum weights that can be towed legally by vehicles of a specific power.) Often, there need be no winter mooring fees: you park at home in the front garden. Driving from England (or wherever) the boat becomes a private hotel, parked overnight in camping sites or the excellent French *autoroute* services areas, where showers, loos and restaurants are at hand. Arriving at your chosen waterway, you consult the appropriate *Carte Guide* for a suitable slipway or boatyard with lifting facilities – and the voyage begins. As with an inflatable there is no need to return by water to the starting points: public transport to collect car and trailer solves that problem. In the summer of 2001, two of us spent a month boating in France with a 14ft (4.27m) trailed day boat and tent, managing to re-explore several Brittany navigations, and the Rivers Charente and Upper Lot. It was a great success, although we did discover that slipways are not officially recorded in the appropriate publications with the accuracy we had expected.

So much for the really mobile rig, which in the view of some readers involves a degree of discomfort. If you have a large family, like to sleep in real beds and hate to sever your links with civilisation, something bigger is called for. Many choose to hire, a more convenient (and in the long term cheaper) approach unless you intend to go boating often. However, this can no longer be described as a budget holiday as was once the case. In 1969, I was involved with establishment of the second hire cruiser company in France. Much has changed since. Now, most parts of the French network – and all the beautiful lengths – are well served by self-drive cabin boats, sleeping from two to ten. For a long time British firms led the market, drawing on experience gained in the UK over several decades; many of their boats remain the best in terms of looks and equipment. But today most French-owned cruisers are quite as good, with full-sized cookers, refrigerators and reliable engines as standard fitments. One of the nicest types, aesthetically, is the fibreglass *pénichette*, produced by a French company in the form of a scaled-down working barge.

GRP (glass reinforced plastic or 'fibreglass') is now an almost ubiquitous material for hulls and super-structures of inland cruisers and, thanks to mass pro-duction techniques, generally offers the best value. Maintenance is negligible and most repairs can be carried out without much difficulty if you are unlucky to suffer damage. I have owned several elderly wooden boats and cannot recommend them to anyone but a real enthusiast or a very wealthy person. This is my realistic opinion and I would be the first to agree that a classic timber-built boat can be an object of great beauty.

Another suitable material is steel. Properly pro-tected against rust, it is strong: indeed an inland boat needs to be. There will be frequent contact with lock walls, quays and even commercial barges at moorings. Visit a boatyard in the Netherlands, and you will find that many of the best-looking craft are made of steel.

Anything primarily designed for inland boating should be capable of ranging throughout the whole network (with the possible exception of certain less important sub-standard sections). Sizes must be within the dimensions that are listed later in this section. Length is very rarely critical: but you must pay close attention to beam, draft and most vitally air draft. Far too many boat builders produce craft that are useless in France when you consider bridge clearances. Routes used by large freight-carriers are not ideal boating territory for very tiny craft. Yet I have used an inflatable successfully on the quite busy Upper Seine, it would not take much to persuade me to do the same on the now tamed Rhône (at least during times of feeble summer flow), and I have witnessed canoes taking their chances with 2,000-tonne ships on the hectic French Rhine near Strasbourg. But a degree of caution must be wise: do not be tempted to tackle waters for which you are your boat are not fitted.

If you buy an inland boat in the UK (where there is generally a wider choice than in France) it will normally have to reach mainland Europe via a car ferry on a trailer or low-loader; the latter can be expensive: upwards of £1,500 in 2004 for a 14m narrow boat between London and Calais. One firm with considerable experience in such operations is Ray Bowern, Streethay Wharf, Streethay, Lichfield, Staffs. Tel 01543 414808, or mobile 0860 729522. Little craft regularly cross the Channel under their own power. My 11m twin-engined motor yacht did so several times without undue alarm or difficulty. You will know, or should take advice, whether this course is open to you. If your boat is suitable, but you do not feel competent at marine navigation, a professional delivery skipper can take it across.

Outboard motors are ideal for the very smallest craft. My own (admittedly basic) British Seagull performed on the back of the inflatable for six weeks without even a hint of temperamental behaviour. More modern outboards are even more reliable. But inboard diesels will cause you less trouble still and are considerably more economical to run. I would recommend that a diesel should be installed in any cruiser over 20ft (6m). Now that numerous varieties of small diesels are available, petrol (*gasoline*) inboard engines are best avoided on safety grounds, although I have noted that the American boating industry appears to disagree.

So far, I have considered inland cruisers to the exclusion of sea-going boats or converted barges. Normally, the bigger the vessel the greater the expense of initial purchase and running. However, this is not invariably true. Rarely does anything smaller than the 38m/350-tonne capacity *péniche* carry cargo today. But many lesser working boats remain in service as pleasure craft. In many instances, the smaller they are (and consequently the easier to handle and maintain), the higher the value. A traditional hunting ground for would be purchasers is the Netherlands, where the authorities offered cash benefits to encourage owners to withdraw small capacity barges from freight use. Enter this world warily; although good examples upwards of 100 years old can be found, there are obvious pitfalls. Equipped with a single engine and boatman's accommodation, but otherwise unconverted, an 80 footer (24m) might cost £30,000 (41,000 Euros). Add at least as much again for the conversion (or several times as much, depending on the equipment you require) and you should have a luxurious vessel, able to roam throughout Europe and capable of making short sea passages under good weather conditions. Fully converted barges are advertised in the British and French boating press at prices from around £40,000 (55,000 Euros) upwards. Anything much cheaper will almost certainly require major renovation and refitting. Probably nothing is better suited or looks so well on river or canals, but you should not underestimate the responsibilities that barge ownership entails. Running costs, maintenance, mooring charges and ease of handling are all rather different than with a cruiser. Often, when travelling, marinas will be encountered were large barges are not welcome and you will have to use public quays used by working craft. As an initial step, arrange to look over as many privately owned examples as possible and book a cabin for a week aboard one of the many hotel boats of this type so as to

get an accurate impression of what is involved. Better still, from boating magazine classified advertisements, locate an enthusiast-owned barge that takes paying guests or offers practical barge handling courses in France. See the Bibliography for books about barges. Join the Barge Association (see below) for an introduction to owners prepared to share their expertise.

Boats of all types, suitable for French waterways, are advertised in the following British monthlies: *Boats for Sale, Canal Boat & Inland Waterways, Motor Boat & Yachting, Motor Boats Monthly* and *Waterways World*. Try also *Blue Flag*, the journal of the Barge Association (available only to members) and the French monthly waterways magazine *Fluvial*. Postal subscriptions available from 48 rue de Provence, 75009 Paris, France.

Barge brokers/builders include Bourgogne Marine (Central France), tel 03 80 39 25 63, fax 03 80 29 11 49. Bowcrest Marine (English south coast), tel/fax 02392 550263, mobile 07711 006766. Delta Marine Services (English Midlands), tel 01926 499337, fax 01926 498331. Enkhuizen Maritiem (Netherlands), tel 02280 17279, fax 02280 18297. Friesland Boating (Netherlands), tel 05142 2607, fax 05142 2620. H_2O (Central France), tel 03 80 39 23 00, fax 03 80 29 04 67. The London Tideway Harbour Co (West London), tel 020 8748 2715, fax 020 8748 5237. New Holland Steel Barges (Cambridgeshire), tel 01945 871077. Pickwell & Arnold (Yorkshire), tel 01706 812411. Sagar Marine (Yorkshire), tel 01484 714541, fax 01484 400683. Virginia Currer Marine (West London), tel 01753 832312, fax 01753 830130. Staff at all these companies speak English.

It is very ill-advised to buy any but the most basic boat without using the services of a qualified specialist surveyor. Consult the classified advertisements in British boating magazines for details of such experts who regularly work throughout the UK and on the Continent.

A few words are in order about using the very popular variety of English 'barge' on French waterways: the narrow boat, either converted from freight vessels or purpose-built for pleasure. In earlier editions of this book, I advised against their use in mainland Europe on grounds of the restricted accommodation offered by their 7ft (2.10m) beam and a possible lack of stability resulting from the length:beam ratio. In recent years, many such vessels have been transported to the French waterways – a few have even made the journey by sea. I have since felt it necessary to revise my views. If you already own one and do not wish to part with it, I now see no reason why they should not be used successfully. Fitted with a suitably powerful engine and provided your insurer is happy to give cover, narrow boats in the hands of experienced skippers should be able to navigate all French waterways, the Rhine included. But I continue to maintain that a narrow boat is not ideal if purchased specifically for France.

Now to sea-going craft: if you live outside France, this may be the ultimate answer. I admit to being slightly biased, having owned a succession of small craft, all exclusively used on British inland waters. Between 1983 and 2000 I owned the twin-engined steel motor yacht *Avonbay*. Measuring 37ft (11.3m) long x 11ft (3.40m) beam x 4ft 3ins (1.30m) draft x 7ft 10ins (2.40m) air draft, she was chosen specifically for her ability to travel *almost* everywhere in France, while being able to put to sea for coastal or cross-Channel passages. Some of my French cruising had already been on this type of vessel, in the late Lord Harvington's 58ft (17.70m) *Melita* and his subsequent 42ft (12.80m) Nelson *Melitina*. Only on rare occasions did the ample draft and headroom present problems.

Craft Dimensions

French rivers and canals are generously proportioned compared with many routes in the UK. Equally, there are plenty of large motor cruisers or sailing vessels whose excessive draft or air draft restricts use to the larger river navigations. In such cases, coast-to-coast voyages across France will not be possible. Nevertheless, dimensions are as large as they are thanks only to the enlightened decision taken by Charles Louis de Saulces de Freycinet, Minister of Public Works 1877–79. The Freycinet Act of 1879 classified waterways as (a) principal lines and (b) routes of secondary importance. At this time only 1,467km of a total of 12,467 were sufficiently large to admit Flemish barges loading 300 tonnes. Enlarging the principal lines to this size involved a massive programme of deepening channels, increasing the capacity of locks and raising bridges. Certain navigations such as the Canal de Briare were almost totally reconstructed and other quite recently opened waterways like the Canal de la Marne à la Saône were subjected to far-reaching structural changes. By 1892, no fewer than 4,123km had been improved to the Freycinet standard. Certain routes remain navigable where infrequent use in the late 19th century made enlargement hardly worthwhile. Details of these substandard waterways appear later in this section. Many other little-used waterways were allowed to become derelict during the first half of the 20th century, although in recent years substantial portions have been returned to navigation and further lengths are surely destined to follow. Some navigations are of course able to pass craft very considerably larger than the standard *péniche*, although it is doubtful if many more waterways will in future be enlarged for the benefit of the declining commercial freight traffic. Increasingly, the future of French rivers and canals lies with pleasure boating, an extraordinary transformation that has taken place only since the 1960s. For fullest details of maximum permitted boat dimensions, consult the *Carte Guides* or the latest edition of *Inland Waterways of France* by David Edwards-May (Imray). Always remember that headroom on rivers may be reduced in times of flood. If your boat appears to be close to the limits, check with *local* canal authorities (addresses in the above publications), enclosing a dimensioned sketch of the boat's superstructure. Obviously craft with superstructures that are nearly square in cross section will have greater difficulty at round arched bridges than those whose maximum air draft rapidly reduces towards the vessel's sides. In recent years, available water draft on some smaller canals such as the Midi and the Bourgogne has decreased. This partly results from a complete disappearance of laden freight vessels which once maintained a deep channel; it is also the consequence of a general reduction of dredging. Figures given in the table that follows are reliable when water levels are at the designed height. Deep drafted boats must expect difficulties after prolonged rain-free periods. Finally, it should be realised that a flat-bottomed barge drawing 1.30m across its entire beam is likely to have problems whereas a v-hulled cruiser drawing 1.30m only under its keel will be able to navigate unimpeded.

Useful Addresses

◆ The Royal Yachting Association, RYA House, Ensign Way, Hamble, Southampton, Hampshire SO31 4YA. Tel 0845 345 0374/5.

◆ The Barge Association, Les Gibson, Hon Sec, 2 Church Lane, Uxbridge, Middlesex UB8 2XD. Tel 01895 847440.

◆ Voies Navigables de France (VNF), rue Ludovic Boutleux, BP 820, 62408 Béthune, France. Tel 03 21 63 24 24.

◆ The French Government Tourist Office, 178 Piccadilly, London, W1V OAL.

◆ Registry of Shipping and Seamen, MCA Regional Headquarters Cardiff, Wales & West of England Region, Anchor Court, Keen Road, Cardiff CF24 5JW. Tel 02920 448 800.

CRAFT DIMENSIONS

FREYCINET WATERWAYS	Length	Beam	Draft	Air draft	Centre	Sides
	38.5m	5.00m	1.80m	3.50m		

SMALLER WATERWAYS

	Length	Beam	Draft	Air draft	Centre	Sides
Canal de Berry						
(Noyers–Selles)	28.65m	2.70m	0.80m	2.60m		
R Baïse						
(Éc S Leger)	40.50m	5.20m	1.50m	3.50m		
(Buzet Branch)	30.65m	5.20m	1.50m	3.75m		
(Buzet–Lavardac)	32.00m	5.20m	1.50m	3.50m		
(Éc St Crabary–Éc Nérac)	30.80m	4.15m	1.00m	3.50m		
(Éc Nazareth–Valence)	30.80m	4.15m	1.00m	3.00m		
R Blavet	26.30m	4.70m	1.40m	2.40m		
Canal de Bourgogne	39.00m	5.00m	1.60m		3.40m	2.20m
R Boutonne	30.50m	5.50m	0.80m	2.30m		
R Charente	34.00m	6.30m	0.80m	3.55m		
R Cher (Vallet–Noyers)	35.00m	5.20m	0.80m	3.90m		
R Ill	34.50m	5.10m	1.40m	2.25m		
Canal d'Ille et Rance	27.10m	4.70m	1.40m		2.50m	2.30m
R Lot						
(Nicole–Fumel)	30.00m	5.00m	1.00m	4.40m		
(Luzech–St-Cirq)	30.00m	5.00m	1.00m	3.70m		
R Mayenne						
(to Laval)	31.00m	5.20m	1.40m	4.10m		
(Laval–Mayenne)	31.00m	5.20m	1.40m	2.80m		
Canal du Midi						
(W of the Grand Bief)	30.00m	5.25m	1.60m		3.25m	3.00m
Canal de Nantes à Brest						
(Nantes–Redon)	26.50m	4.70m	1.50m	3.90m		
(N of Redon)	25.70m	4.65m	1.50m	3.15m		
(Rohan–Pontivy)	25.70m	4.65m	0.80m	3.15m		
Canal du Nivernais						
(Cercy–Sardy)	30.15m	5.10m	1.30m	2.71m		
(Sardy–Clamecy)	38.50m	5.20m	1.30m	2.97m		
R Oudon	30.00m	5.00m	1.50m	4.10m		
Canal de l'Ourcq						
(smaller section)	58.8m	3.70m	0.80m	2.40m		
R Sarthe	30.85m	5.15m	1.10m	3.40m		
R Seille	30.40m	5.20m	1.30m	4.70m		
R Sèvre Nantaise	31.50m	5.50m	1.20m	5.50m		
R Sèvre Niortaise	31.50m	5.20m	1.20m	2.20m		
Canal Transaquitain	18.00m	3.00m	1.20m	2.00m	(approx)	
River Vilaine	26.60m	4.70m	1.20m	3.20m		

Note: Drafts given above should be reliable under normal water supply conditions. However, in times of drought the Bourgogne, Midi, Nivernais and Vilaine are likely to be shallower than quoted above.

Hire Craft, Hotel Boats and Passenger Vessels

Until 1969 there was just a single hire cruiser company on French inland waters: now most regions are well served, with numerous vessels available on the most popular rivers and canals (Midi, Nivernais, Bourgogne, Brittany, Alsace etc). At the time of writing there were about 140 hire bases operated by 90 individual companies, between them providing around 2,000 boats for self drive rental. Aquatic tourism is big business.

Owned both by French and British firms, cruisers range from 2-berth cabin boats to large craft sleeping ten people and equipped with every luxury such as three *en suite* bathrooms. Most operators appear to welcome clients with no previous boat handling experience and provide basic tuition on arrival. It is claimed that anyone familiar with driving a car will be able to handle a 40ft (12m) cabin cruiser possibly worth up to £150,000 (210,000 Euros).

English-speaking readers may prefer to book through one of a series of reservation offices which represent a number of operators or in some cases are an individual firm with a range of bases. All publish annual brochures with price lists. The season normally begins in late March and continues to October. Costs increase to a peak in July and August. These include: Blakes International Travel Ltd, Wroxham, Norfolk NR12 8DH, tel 01603 739456. Connoisseur Cruisers, Ile Sauzay, 70100 Gray, France, tel 03 84 64 95 20. Crown Blue Line, The Port House, Port Solent, Portsmouth, Hampshire PO6 4TH, tel 0870 240 8393. French Country Cruises, Andrew Brock Travel Ltd, 54 High Street East, Uppingham, Rutland LE15 9PZ, tel 01572 821330. Hoseasons Holidays, Sunway House, Lowestoft, Suffolk NR32 2LW, tel 01502 502 602. Nicols Locations, 1 rue Denis Papin, 49300 Cholet, France, tel 02 41 62 00 45. Otherwise, request a list of cruiser hirers from the French Government Tourist Office in London. Details of many smaller hire cruiser companies, including those offering boats on less frequented routes, can be gleaned from advertisements in British inland waterways magazines or the French *Fluvial*. Other possibilities exist, such as hiring a canoe on the fast-flowing scenic River Ardèche (make local enquiries).

Many of the most attractive waterways are served by luxury hotel boats, generally converted barges, but sometimes purpose built. Passenger numbers are similar to a moderate-sized house party. They are fully crewed, usually provide catering to a very high standard and frequently attract American clients. Such luxury is only available at a high price. As a more reasonably priced but less intimate alternative, rather larger vessels, the size of small ships, also operate hotel-style cruises on rivers such as the Seine, Saône, Rhône and Rhine. Details from the French Government Tourist Office, above. Less pretentious alternatives, generally aboard owner/operator barges, can be found among the classified advertisements of British waterways magazines or may be obtained on request from the Barge Association (see above).

A large number of passenger vessels provide excursions on canals and rivers throughout the summer season. Journey times range from an hour to a full day. Information and timetables will gladly be supplied by tourist offices serving main towns in any chosen area.

Waterways Museums

There is, as yet, no collection of inland vessels and other historical relics which can compare with the British waterways museums of Gloucester and Ellesmere Port. During the 1970s and 1980s, numerous fascinating and important French vessels, especially those of timber construction, were broken up or allowed to decay. Other waterways 'antiques', among them a variety of bank towing locomotives, similarly deserve rescue and preservation. A start to reverse this trend seems likely at the Alsatian Navigation Museum in the city of Strasbourg. However, establishment of a truly national boat collection is urgently required while potential exhibits are still capable of preservation. Additionally, mention is made in the text of this book of several restored historic vessels.

For further details and opening times (always subject to change), contact the tourist office in the nearest town.

River Adour Display of local river vessels. Musée Basque, 1 rue Marengo, 64100 Bayonne.

Canal de Berry Museum at Le Port de Magnette at Reugny, 15km from Montluçon. Here are two original *berrichons* (freight craft) with many artefacts, records and photographs of this fascinating narrow canal system. Normally open weekends only, 15 July–15 September. Also the Musée du Canal de Berry, Place du Châtelet, 18130 Dun-sur-Auron. Several items associated with local barges will be found in the Musée de Berry, Hôtel de Cujas, 4–6 rue des Arènes, Bourges.

Canal de Bourgogne Various ancient offerings from the headwaters of the Seine are displayed in the former Abbaye Sainte-Bénigne, 5 rue du Docteur Maret, 21000 Dijon.

Haulage team of boatman and his bourriques *(she asses). Note the wooden clogs. Early 20th century.*

Canal de Briare There is a worthwhile waterways section in the Municipal Museum in the town of Briare.

Canal du Centre A *péniche*, boat models, documents, objects and pictures all relevant to the development of the waterway and its effect on the area. Eco-Musée de la Communauté Le Creusot/Montceau-les-Mines, Maison Écluse No 6, 71860 Ecuisses.

River Dordogne Relics of transport by water of wine, timber for barrels, gravel extraction and salmon-fishing boats. Musée Municipal, 507 rue des Con-férences, 24100 Bergerac.

Étang de Thau A good collection devoted to jousting boats from French regions and elsewhere. Musée Paul Valéry, 75 Voie Communale, 34200 Sète.

Canal d'Ille et Rance Museum of Breton waterways at the Écluse de la Madeleine, Hédé.

River Gironde Musée de la Marine, 33000 Bordeaux. Includes some material relating to river vessels.

Liaison au Grand Gabarit Upwards of 50 waterways objects, including barge models, locks and bridges. Musée des Arts et Traditions Populaires, 6 rue du Tribunal, 62400 Béthune. A selection of waterways exhibits and models of a lock and lift bridge are displayed in the Musée Municipal d'Ethnographie, 6 rue du Tribunal, Béthune. Barges of the northern waterways and the transport of coal are recalled in a museum at the Tour de l'Ostrevant, Bouchain; similar material is contained in the Musée Municipal, Place Verte, Condé-sur-l'Escaut.

River Loire Many artefacts concerning Loire barges are displayed in the Musée Municipal, Le Château, 45110 Châteauneuf-sur-Loire. Similar collections are to be found in the Musée du Vieux Chinon, 47 rue Haute St-Maurice, 37500 Chinon; and at the Musée Municipal, Bibliothèque Palais de Justice, 58200 Cosne-sur-Loire. Freshwater fishing has its own display in the Musée de la Pêche, Château de la Bussière, 45500 Gien (10km from Gien). Material relating to the lower river and the estuary is conserved in the Musée des Salorges, Château des Ducs de Bretagne, 44000 Nantes. The life of the Loire boatmen is commemorated in the Musée

Municipal, 16 rue St-Genest, 58000 Nantes, with another similar collection in the Musée du Prieuré, 42170 St-Just/St-Rambert.

Canal de la Marne au Rhin Exhibition aboard a dryland *péniche*, *Sophie-Marie*, by the Arzvillers Inclined Plane.

Canal Marseille-Rhône Relics of barges and fishing boats. Musée Municipal du Vieux Martigues à Ferrrières, rue du Colonel Denfert-Rochereau, 13500 Martigues.

Canal du Midi A splendid complex of modern buildings, on an island site, house an exhibition devoted to Riquet and his canal; between Écluses 16 and 17 (west of the summit pound) and also reached via the *Autoroute* A61 service area. Centre Cultural Riquet à Port Lauragais, 32190 Villefranche du Lauragais. *Marie-Thérèse*, a timber-built barque of the Canal du Midi dating back to 1855, is preserved by the Conservatoire Maritime et Fluvial des Pays Narbonnais on the Narbonne Branch at Domaine de Grand Castelou – Mandirac, 11100 Narbonne.

Canal de Nantes à Brest Relics of Brittany barge life are assembled in the Musée de la Batellerie de l'Ouest, 2 bis faubourg St-Julien, Malestroit. Life on the canal is recalled aboard barge/museum *Brise de Nuit*, located at Plumeliau.

Canal du Nivernais Relics of *flottage* (timber rafting) on the River Yonne. Musée Municipal, Hôtel de Bellegarde, 58500 Clamecy.

Canal d'Orléans Les Amis du Canal d'Orléans have a preserved *berrichon* barge equipped as a waterways museum on the canal at Donnery.

Canal de Roanne à Digoin Memories of Loire barge life, Musée Joseph Déchelette, 22 rue A.-France, Roanne.

River Rhine Musée Alsacien de la Navigation is housed in the Strasbourg Docks at l'Ancienne Commanderie de St-Jean. Numerous historic barges and tugs can be seen on the water with other exhibits in a large covered display area. On the banks of the river 20km north of Strasbourg at Offendorf there is a waterways museum aboard the *péniche Cabro*.

River Rhône Relics of barge traffic at the Musée Vivarois César Filhol, 15 rue Bechetoil, 07100 Annonay. Religious crosses of Rhône bargemen can be seen in the Musée Théodore Aubanel, Quartier St-Pierre, Avignon. Objects associated with the Great Fair of Beaucaire, which attracted large numbers of barges, are on view in the

18th century barge traffic depicted on a faïence *plate in the Waterways Museum by the Seine at Conflans-Ste-Honorine.*

Musée du Vieux Beaucaire, 30300 Beaucaire. Religious barge crosses, boatmen's costumes and boat models are contained in the Ancienne Chapelle St-Sornin, Quartier St-Sornin, 07340 Serrières (between Tournon and Vienne). The construction of the first (1825) large suspension bridge over the Rhône at Tournon, designed by engineer Marc Seguin, is recalled in a display at the Château de Tournon, quai Marc Seguin, 07300 Tournon. Several models of river barges can be seen in the Musée Arlaten, Rue de la République, Arles.

Canal de St-Quentin An original tunnel tug is preserved and serves as a canal museum close to the great Riqueval tunnel.

River Saône An exhibit on river freight traffic can be found in the Musée Municipal Denon, Place de l'Hôtel de Ville, 71100 Chalon-sur-Saône. A small but enthusiastic waterways museum has been established close to the town bridge in St-Jean de-Losne, junction with the Canal de Bourgogne. The Eco-Musée du Val de la Saône has objects of waterways interest: Maison Bossuet, Seurre.

River Sarthe Maison de la Rivière, 49330 Châteauneuf-sur-Sarthe.

River Seine The leading French waterways collection is the Musée de la Batellerie, Place Gévelot, 78700 Conflans-Ste-Honorine. On display are portions of real barges, haulage tractors, models, various artefacts and a large number of photographs and items of paper ephemera. Sea-going and inland craft are represented at the Musée Maritime Fluvial et Portuaire de Rouen, Quai Émile Duchemin, 76000 Rouen. Inland barge traditions are preserved with two boats at the Musée de la Batellerie, 135 rue des Masures, 27740 Poses.

River Vilaine Marine and inland boat traditions can be studied at Le Musée de la Vilaine Maritime, Château des Basses Fosses, Rue Ruicard, 56130 La Roche Bernard. At Redon is the Eco-Musée de la Batellerie Bretonne, Quai Jean-Bart.

1 ~ La Liaison au Grand Gabarit ~ Dunkerque to Belgium via Valenciennes

Carte Guide: *Nord Pas-de-Calais*
Also known as the Dunkerque-Escaut Waterway, it comprises a series of individual waterways, much enlarged in recent decades in order to accommodate massive barges, the Canal au Grand Gabarit ('Large Gauge Waterway') comprises the Canal de Bourbourg, River Aa, Canal de Neuffossé, Canal d'Aire, Canal de la Deûle, Canal de la Sensée and River Escaut. Through distance, Dunkerque to Belgium, is 187km with 14 locks. The many connections with other waterways are indicated on the accompanying map.

Before attempting even to plan a route, it is essential to study the *Carte Guide Nord Pas-de-Calais* (see Bibliography) and battle with the maze of interconnecting navigations of this north-west corner of France until they begin to make some kind of geographical sense. In practice, it is all much easier to understand when you are actually boating.

It is worth mentioning that while almost every inland waterway has some points of interest, this can never be included among the most attractive regions of France: the competition is fierce when you consider the ravishing beauty of Burgundy or the Midi. Further, widespread canal improvements and the tendency for the new through navigation to bypass places of historic interest and beauty have introduced much concrete into a sometimes bleak area. The *Carte Guide* claims that 'industry and extensive agriculture co-exist in complete harmony': I detect a note of wishful thinking. Having accepted this warning, these waterways do have plenty to offer the pleasure traveller. This may take the form of encounters with large cargo vessels (other waterways now devoid of commercial traffic have lost some of their original appeal); equally, there are opportunities to discover a series of historic towns and villages.

Possibilities for hiring pleasure cruisers in the region are limited. The route is, however, well used by sea-going motor yachts and barges from SE England and the Thames. The London-Ramsgate-Dover-Calais crossing is quite the quickest way of reaching the French inland waterways; and, while I would never want to advocate that unsuitable boats or inexperienced boaters should attempt a Channel crossing, this 'short' hop may well be practicable where the longer run from England across to the Somme or Seine Estuary at Le Havre is not. For information on how I tackled my first small boat voyage from London to Calais, see my *Small Boat Through France* (David & Charles, 1991). Although otherwise out of print, I can supply copies on application to the address at the end of my Introduction.

As implied by its ponderous name, all this route is big-gauge, accepting push-tows up to 3,000 tonnes capacity. Additionally, standard 38m *péniches* are widespread. Commercial traffic in recent years appears to have decreased, a sad situation that also applies to many other French routes. This is the Frank country, dreadfully damaged in both world wars but now rebuilt in a blend of old and new. Buildings are mostly of brick with distinct Flemish influences in the architecture of town squares and *Hôtels de Ville*. Flanders (Flandre) is a name synonymous with World War I trench fighting, but in places there is an unexpected quiet beauty. Coming inland from the sea, the first region with its own identity is the Audomarais, 3,400 hectares of marshland near St-Omer, intersected by many small watercourses and intensively cultivated with vegetables. Around Valenciennes is France's first regional and natural park of St-Amand-Raismes, designated in 1968 and devoted to a carefully managed blend of sporting activities and wildlife conservation. Festivals such as the Fishermen's Carnival of Dunkerque are held in most of the leading towns. Food owes much to immigrants from other parts of Europe. Do not be surprised where classic French *cuisine* and wines have sometimes been replaced by black puddings (*boudin noir*) and beer!

Brief history The region is well served by natural rivers flowing through flattish country. From the 12th century the Counts of Flanders began to make them suitable for barge traffic and cities started to develop along the banks of the new transport network. Thus, towns like St-Omer, Béthune, La Bassée, Lille, Douai, Valenciennes, Dunkerque and Calais were able to grow with a trading advantage and direct access to the coast. Mainly artificial parts of the through route include the Canal de Bourbourg, Dunkerque to the River Aa, built in the 17th century under Louis XIV; the Canal de

Neuffossé, St-Omer to Aire, started by Vauban and finished shortly before the Revolution, it largely followed the line of a 13th century defensive channel, dividing Flanders and the Artois; the Canal d'Aire, connecting the River Lys and Canal de Neufossé with the Canal de Deûle, 40km SE: opened in 1825, it provides a direct route from the River Escaut to the ports of Calais and Dunkerque; the Canal de la Deûle, joining the River Lys with the River Scarpe and originally constructed in the 13th century; and the 25km Canal de la Sensée, from the River Scarpe to the River Escaut, finished in 1819.

Some of the earliest attempts to replace the barge horse appeared in this area, with 77km of steam railway laid on the towpaths of the Aire, Neufossé and Deûle (Fontinettes to Douai) between about 1880 and 1886. It was not judged to be a great success, partly because of interference with traditional towpath users and also because the locomotive drivers could not be persuaded to work the long hours generally associated with horse towage. After trials on the Canal de Bourgogne, Denefle et Cie introduced electric bank traction on the Aire and Deûle in the 1890s. By 1900 there were 120 towing units, steered rather than mounted on rails. Four years later, a similar electric horse using 1m gauge rails was successfully put through trials on the Canal de la Sensée and the Escaut. All lengths were absorbed into the system of the *Compagnie Général de Traction sur les Voies Navigables* (CGTVN) in 1940. This type of haulage was to last until the 1960s, when new track was laid on the Canal de la Deûle; by then, diesel engines had mostly taken over from electric ones. To the very end, CCTVN maintained that one horsepower on the bank was worth four in a barge.

A significant development on the line was the erection of the great vertical boat lift at Les Fontinettes in 1888; it replaced five locks. Although itself now replaced by a single deep lock, it is preserved as a non-operational example of the marvels of 19th century engineering.

After World War II barge traffic had reached saturation point and consequently industry throughout the region was under serious threat. Far-reaching improvements were begun in 1959, converting a *péniche*-sized navigation into one suited for 1,350-tonners and 3,000 tonne push-tows. New locks were constructed 144.6m x 12m, each with intermediate sets of gates offering a 45m chamber for two *péniches* side by side; or alternatively, one 91.6m long for four *péniches* or one 1,350-tonner. The full length locks will pass six *péniches* or a single 3,000 tonne push-tow unit. Each Liaison lock is equipped with one pair of closely spaced bollards, suitable for use by small pleasure craft.

More than 25 new high-level bridges were necessary with extensive bank protection and deepening and straightening of the channel. All this work allowed the route to carry an annual 13 million tonnes by the mid 1960s. Sadly, in common with most modern waterways in Western Europe (with the exception of the Rhine and other major German routes) traffic levels have since fallen sharply. Pleasure craft should not therefore find the barge movements especially intimidating. Overnight moorings are best arranged in basins or old branches away from the disturbing wash produced by commercial traffic on the main line. Around 2002 works were completed to enlarge the waterway from Lille to Deûlémont, making that section suitable for 1,350-tonners.

For entry to the network from the English Channel at **Dunkerque**, use Marine Chart 1010 (Éditions Grafocarte). Here is a maze of dockland waterways, with fuel, water, showers and lifting facilities at the Yacht Club de la Mer du Nord situated in an arm SE of the Outer Harbour. Non-tidal waters are reached by working through the nearby Écluse Trystram; otherwise, through either Écluse Maritime Wattier or Écluse Maritime Charles de Gaulle, both of which connect directly with the Outer Harbour. The normal route inland is along the Bassin Maritime, running westwards parallel with the coast, and then via the huge Bassin de Mardyke which links with the Canal de Bourbourg, start of La Liaison au Grand Gabarit. Dunkerque (Dunkirk) has its origins in a little fishing port near a church: over the centuries, French ships would leave here on raiding expeditions into the Channel. More than three-quarters of the town was destroyed early in World War II and the beaches witnessed perhaps the biggest rescue operation of the 20th century, when 500,000 British and Allied troops were ferried to the safety of England in a flotilla of small craft, among them the famous Dunkirk Little Ships, many of which included cabin cruisers from the Upper Thames. The town has since grown into the third largest port in France, with car ferry links to the UK.

Two additional waterways may be joined in the centre of Dunkerque: the **Canal de Furnes** follows a 13.2km course parallel with the coast and crosses the Belgian border, destination **Furnes** (**Veurne**). Opened in 1638, it has a lock at each end. The one in Dunkerque and several swing bridges are closed on Sundays and public holidays unless advance notice is given. For updated details, consult the *Carte Guide*. A pleasure boat pontoon mooring, close to most urban facilities, is established on the **Canal de Jonction** (between the Canal de Furnes and the Canal de Bergues); 8.1km of the lock-free **Canal de Bergues** connect Dunkerque with **Bergues**, a place of Flemish buildings and a notable star-shaped fortress designed by Vauban. It was of great use during the French defence of Dunkerque in 1940. The canal, originally in use in the 9th century and rebuilt in the 18th, is now a dead end; but until closure of the **Canal de la Haute Colme** and the **Canal de Bergues à Furnes** there were links with the Canal de Bourbourg (at Lynck, providing a more agreeable way through to La Liaison au Grand Gabarit, avoiding the docks and industrial zone of Dunkerque) and with Furnes, to the east. There are pleasure craft moorings on the Canal de Bergues in Dunkerque and in the terminal basin at Bergues (water, electricity and slipway).

At Dunkerque's **Bassin de Mardyke**, we enter the start of the Liaison au Grand Gabarit, via Écluse de Mardyke (K143, distances being measured from Le Bassin Rond, junction with the River Escaut). Railway sidings, fuel storage depots and barge wharves (K140) are followed by a junction, left, with a Freycinet gauge section of the **Canal de Bourbourg** (K137.5) leading back into the centre of Dunkerque and providing

access to the Canal de Furnes and the Canal de Bergues, mentioned above: there is one lock on this length, Écluse Jeu-de-Mail, with water point and fuelling station. At K135.2 we leave a short section of shared Canal de Bourbourg, which itself continues SW for 8.3km, through one lock at **Bourbourg** (two lifting bridges, good shopping and garage) to join the River Aa at Écluse le Guindal (Chapter 3).

One general characteristic of La Liaison is that widening and improvement with consequent concrete banks and a fairly violent wash from passing traffic makes for uncomfortable moorings. In some cases town centres have poor access from the new route. Where possible, moor (subject to hazards from barges) near lock approaches or better still in the various side arms that better serve points of civilisation.

After a left-hand junction with the closed **Canal de la Haute Colme** at Lynck (K127.9) there is little of note until Écluse 1, **Watten** (K121.5). A little beyond, the River Aa can be entered on the right, providing access to the coast at Gravelines (see Chapter 3); this in turn has a connection with the Canal de Calais, perhaps the

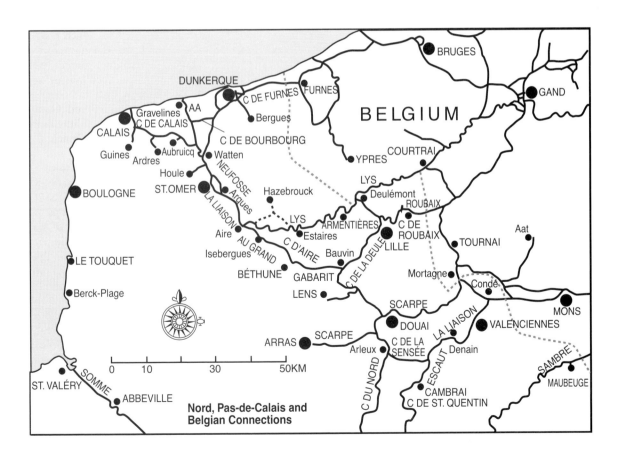

Nord, Pas-de-Calais and Belgian Connections

most convenient of all routes from the English Channel (see Chapter 2). Shopping, restaurants and garages may be visited in Watten village, where broad views over the Forêt d'Éperlecques are obtained from a hill. 6km SW, via the D207, is a massive World War II blockhouse, designed by the Nazis as a launching site from which to rain V2 rockets on England, although it was never put into service. Open to the public Easter–11 Nov from 14.30h, or 10.30h, July and August. A pleasure boat harbour, *Port de l'Ermitage* (K119.4) offers various facilities including a slipway. Alternatively, escape from the turmoil of the large canal lies in the little **River Houlle**, fully navigable for about 4km. Restaurant and butcher are located near the entrance in **Cité des Tuileries**, with another restaurant and shops near the head of navigation at **Houlle**.

Starting first on the right and then spreading like veins on both sides of the waterway is an astonishingly complex network of small canals, known as the **Audomarais**. Total length could be several hundred km. Some portions are navigable by motor craft and offer excellent prospects for peaceful overnight moorings. Elsewhere, powered boats will not be welcomed, although no one is likely to object to random exploration by dinghy. On the SW fringe is the fine old city of **St-Omer**, with a first-rate pedestrianised shopping street and a huge 12–15th century basilica. A road runs eastwards from the railway station towards **Clairmarais**, lined for several km by vendors of fresh local vegetables (especially cauliflowers) brought in from the marshland market gardens by small boat. In celebration of this notable local produce, marzipan vegetables are widely available in the cake shops. Two points for waterways enthusiasts travelling by car: small craft trips are run through the vegetable gardens in summer (watch for signs on the vegetable-sellers' road); and 6km NW of the town on the N43 at **Tilques** is a superbly different hotel, *Le Château Tilques* established in a 19th century mansion with excellent restaurant in the stable block. As it is a short drive from the Channel Ports, I have often spent my first or last nights in France here. A special welcome seems to be reserved for British clients: at any rate the proprietor always radiated happiness when our elderly green Bentley used to sweep up his gravel drive! Another equally attractive and less commercial *château-hôtel* that we have regularly visited is the beautiful 18th century *Château de Cocove* at Recques-sur-Hem, a little north of the A26 Calais *autoroute* (junction 2).

Approaching St-Omer, the waterway adopts a new course from K112 and avoids the town altogether. It is no longer possible to navigate a disused section of the Aa through Écluse Haut-Pont to reach St-Omer. This is a tragedy for the town as the navigation could readily be restored and become a tourist attraction. Until action is taken, you must stay on the main line, passing a public mooring basin with water point (K108) immediately before Écluse Flandre. After locking, take the first turning on the right (mooring point) and so enter part of the old Canal de Neufossé. 3km with one lock, Écluse St-Bertin, lead into the city centre where you can tie up not far from the cathedral. This diversion is well worth the effort. The layout of the area is clearly shown in the *Carte Guide*.

Arques (K107) is situated just beyond the St-Omer junction on the right bank and is useful for shopping. Local industries include glass, metal, paper and cement products. On the left bank is the splendid twin-caisson vertical boat lift of **Les Fontinettes** which replaced a series of five 18th century locks. These could be negotiated in 70 minutes by a descending boat, while uphill craft took 95 minutes. In order to pass the maximum number of vessels, three days of each week were devoted to downhillers and four to uphillers, enabling 40–50 craft to work through every day. Waiting time sometimes amounted to an amazing five or six days! In 1875 it was decided to duplicate the flight: the scheme was abandoned when in 1879 the Freycinet Act established 38.5m locks on all principal navigations; the old Fontinettes locks were only 35m long. Relying on experience gained with the Anderton vertical lift in England, which since 1875 had provided communication between the River Weaver and the Trent & Mersey Canal, vertical lift designs were prepared by Anderton's engineer Edwin Clark and

The preserved Les Fontinettes boat lift at Arques.

Sidengham Duer. Clark's less expensive hydraulic machinery was selected in 1881, although following an accident at Anderton it was subsequently modified. There can be few other instances of French waterways being based on British engineering! Building took place during 1883–7, with official inauguration in July 1888. Working as a double hydraulic press, one caisson virtually balanced the other, regardless of whether both chambers were occupied by barges or not. Six men were employed to work the machinery and control the safety gates at the upper end. Difference in levels is 13.13m.

When in 1959 it was decided to enlarge the canal for much bigger vessels, the working days of the lift were numbered. A new single lock, 13.3m rise and fall, Écluse des Fontinettes (K106, water point) was constructed a little farther down the canal. When it was completed in August 1967 both vertical lift and the old locks of 1760 (which had remained in occasional use) were worked for the last time. While able to pass 3,000 tonnes of freight, the new lock consumes no less than 25,000m³, compared with the 400m³ used during operation of the lift. For several years after its closure the great structure lay derelict. It was later refurbished as an outstanding example of industrial archaeology and is open for public inspection. (It has to be admitted that my most recent visit showed that there were serious arrears of maintenance.) Spikily elegant, with green-painted ironwork and towers of brick and stone, one raised tank is permanently occupied by a *péniche*. The design is unique, although similar structures can be seen in service in Belgium, Germany, England, Canada and, since 2003, on the Chinese Yangtze River.

Quiet moorings will be found in the truncated arm once leading to the lift's upper level and entered from above the Écluse des Fontinettes. The same freedom from wash is rarely to be obtained in the next section, where you might otherwise wish to stop for shopping in **Wardrecques** (K102.5, right bank) or at a public mooring by the bridge of **Pont d'Asquin** (K101.2, right bank, baker, butcher, grocer, restaurant). Similar facilities exist in **Blaringhem** (K98.3) with a public quay immediately before the bridge (right bank). A complicated junction of watercourses at **Aire-sur-la-Lys** (K93) includes a left-hand turn into the canalised River Lys, leading via Armentières to the Belgian border and Ghent (Gand). (See Chapter 4.) Pleasure boats may moor just before the first of two bridges spanning La Liaison; otherwise, continue under the second bridge and turn back along a channel serving quays in the town. Aire was an important city during the Spanish occupation of the 16th and 17th centuries and has a notable large square, surrounded mainly by 18th century buildings. Its *Église Collégiale St-Pierre* is among the best examples of the Renaissance style in Flanders. Navigation now continues via the Canal d'Aire.

In order to visit **Isbergues** (K89), it is advised to pass under a road, railway and two further road bridges before reaching a *port public* on the right. All facilities are within a moderate distance. The leading local industry is a steelworks. Pilgrims come to visit the shrine of Ste-Isbergues, sister of Charlemagne, in the 15th century church. Several villages in the next reach, all with basic shops include **Busnes** 1.8km south of a bridge at K83.7; **Robecq** (K81); and **Hinges**, right of bridges at K75.7 or K74.5 (shops within 1km). We have now entered a thickly populated area noted for its coal mines and heavy industry. **Béthune**, home the national headquarters of the inland waterways authority *Voies Navigables de France*, is inappropriately bypassed by the through route. VNF's offices are in a modern structure said to have drawn its architectural inspiration from the shape of a barge hull. The nearest approach by water to the city centre is found by entering an old portion of the Canal d'Aire (right, K72.5) just before a bridge preceding an aqueduct over the River Lawe. The Béthune boat harbour and public park have been created at the entrance to a former coal loading basin. This is a stylish town with a lovely central square surrounded by Flemish-type buildings mostly constructed after the holocaust of World War I. Among them is an art deco *Hôtel de Ville* of 1928, while at the centre rises a 14th century bell-tower with carillon. Excellent food is served with unaccustomed speed in a large restaurant opposite.

While there is a public mooring in **Gorre** (K68, left bank), it is preferable to continue for 1km to the right-hand junction with the **Canal de Beuvry**. Now that coal mining has finished, the surviving 0.6km fragment of this small waterway is very pleasant. (Café at the present terminus.) But for a fixed lift bridge it would be possible to travel 2.5km almost to Beuvry itself. Garage and all shops will be found in **Cuinchy** (K64.2) not long before the Écluse de Cuinchy (water point). Alternative places to buy food are **Auchy-les-Mines** (K61.3, right bank) and **La Bassée** (K60), where a 2.6km *péniche*-sized remnant of the former waterway offers a detour. Here are pontoon moorings for visitors, close to a supermarket, shops and restaurants and, importantly, freedom from wash. Useful moorings will also be found in a basin on the downstream side of the railway bridge with a barge repair yard opposite (baker, butcher, restaurant and garage).

Transfer to the Canal de la Deûle takes place at a triangular junction with an island, near **Bauvin** (K54). At K50 is a *Relais Nautique*, with further mooring possible on a quay a short distance up the Deûle. The

A delightful Belle Époque *keeper's cabin at Cuinchy locks.*

left fork, of Freycinet gauge, leads to Lille, the Canal de Roubaix and on to Belgium (see Chapters 5 and 6). The through route of La Liaison now runs due south through a succession of small towns of limited interest, but facilities are widespread. **Meurchin** (K51, left bank) has a public mooring on the opposite side of the canal. After the Dambrain barge yard in a basin (K49.6), shops will be found in **Pont à Vendin** (K48.4) with public mooring opposite, right bank. Restaurant and barge yard in Estevelles (K47) are followed by safe moorings (K46, right bank). **Carvin**, reached from a road bridge (K44.2), is perhaps rather far to be of much use at 3km. A right-hand junction (K43.8) marks the confluence with the **Canal de Lens**. Of an original 11.3km, only 8.6km remains, the waterway now ending abruptly well before it reaches Lens. Opened in 1886, the branch utilised the bed of the River Souchez and was intended mainly as a coal carrier. It cannot be described as attractive boating water. Shopping is possible from the quay in **Harnes** while there are further shops and a restaurant not far from the penultimate bridge at **Loison-sous-Lens**.

Dreary scenery continues past **Dourges** (K38, limited shopping) and **Noyelle Godault** (K36.1), with a useful escape from working boats in a 'leisure basin', right bank at **Courcelles** (K35.4). While there are pleasant wooded banks, K36–34, elsewhere there is much evidence of (former) coal traffic in the form of loading basins and spoil tips. Commercial traffic intensifies at **Dorignies** (K30.6) where La Liaison skirts the city of **Douai** by 'borrowing' a portion of the River Scarpe navigation. There are fuelling depots for boats near the junction with the eastern part of the Scarpe: this offers communication with Belgium, and the Haut Escaut

near Tournai (see Chapter 7). Twin locks (Écluses Douai, K28, water point) are the main line's closest approach to the city centre, with moorings on quays. Until completion of the Scarpe *dérivation*, the waterway followed a course through three locks into the heart of the city. A lock-free portion of this remains navigable: see the *Carte Guide*. Further closed but intact sections of canal feature pleasant quays lined with old houses somewhat in the manner of Amsterdam or Utrecht, with a bascule bridge and paddle gear worked by giant spoked wheels. Local coal mines (now a nearly dead industry) have inspired several original souvenirs including reproduction miners' lamps and rich chocolates wrapped in shiny black cellophane and packed in tiny hessian coal sacks. Douai's most celebrated feature is the bell-tower, an imposing 64m Gothic structure built at the end of the 14th century. Topped by pinnacles, it can be ascended via 192 steps. The view is memorable.

Beyond the southern city limits a further pair of locks, Écluses de **Courchelettes** (K24, water point), mark the junction (restaurant) with the Upper Scarpe: this continues to a terminus in Arras (see Chapter 7). Shopping and a garage can easily be reached in Courchelettes, perhaps mooring in the entrance to the abandoned old course of the Scarpe. We now join the **Canal de la Sensée** and negotiate Écluses de Goeulzin, with duplicated chambers (K20.3, water point). Water, canalside diesel and basic shopping are available at the **Arleux** bridge (K15.4) near a junction with the Canal

This attractive waterway in the centre of Douai is now bypassed by the through route.

du Nord (see Chapter 8). At this very wide intersection is a well-known barge chandlery of the sort that was once widespread throughout the network: it offers moorings, supermarket, bar, fuel and water in addition to such necessities as industrial clothing, rope and tar. As with other similar facilities mentioned in these pages, check with the latest **Carte Guide** that they remain in business: even the most active and prosperous firms have been known to suddenly disappear. Part of the Sensée is bordered by a chain of marshland lakes, introducing a much needed impression of real countryside. Beyond the Marais de **Brunémont** (K12.3) is a village grocer and restaurant, while the next lake, Marais d'Aubigny-au-Bec, close to the canal bank has been landscaped with swimming beach and other recreational features. Limited shops are in **Aubencheul-au-Bec** (K11, right-hand side) while a fuller range of stores is located opposite in **Aubigny-au-Bec, Fressies** (K8, right), **Féchain**, reached from bridges at K8 or K6.2, **Hem-Lenglet** (K6.2, public mooring), and **Wasnes-au-Bac** (K3.5), beyond another water-based leisure park.

A choice of routes now presents itself: you can either stay with La Liaison for 2.5km or take a slightly longer and much more pleasant course to the right through **Paillencourt** (most shops) and **Le Bassin Rond**. This agreeable basin, up to 100m in width, has a boatyard offering some facilities and suitable places to moor. Beyond the next bridge, turn left to rejoin La Liaison and the **River Escaut**, large-gauge section, with water point at Écluse Port Malin (K0), or right into the **Upper Escaut** (Freycinet gauge) connecting with the Canal St-Quentin.

The Upper Escaut, 12km from Le Bassin Rond to Cambrai, has five locks, each with duplicated and mechanised chambers. These are 5, **Iwuy** (K2.1 from the Canal de la Sensée); 4, **Tun-l'Evêque** (K4.2); 3, Erre (K8.3, water point); 2, Selles (K11.1); and 1, Camtimpré (K11.9, water point). Although you are likely to encounter some commercial traffic, the wooded fringes of the waterway, passing through a region of cornfields, are much more intimate and agreeable than the main line of La Liaison. Lock cottages are of brownish brick and some of the keepers sell garden produce. **Cambrai** is a long established barge port with repair yards, diesel pump at the far end of a basin entered from below Écluse 2, and a pleasure craft harbour reached from the lower end of Écluse 1 near the junction with the Canal de St-Quentin (see Chapter 10). In spite of the infamous pounding received during World War I, Cambrai still possesses many old buildings, not least of which is the early 18th century cathedral of Notre-Dame. In the church of St-Géry is an Entombment, painted by Rubens. Traditionally and still a centre of linen manufacture (cambric), the city boasts an important art museum and there are traces of Vauban fortifications in public gardens. Food specialities are *andouillettes* (sausages made from pork or veal tripe), *tripes* (mainly ox tripe), *friandises à la menthe 'betises de Cambrai'* (mint sweets) and *boulette de Cambrai* (a white farm cheese, flavoured with herbs).

We now return to the Escaut section of La Liaison, at Écluse 6, Port Malin (K0, distances now being measured from here to the Belgian frontier). Now the surroundings gradually become more industrial. Both the River Sambre and the River Meuse provide more agreeable ways of reaching Belgium. **Bouchain** (K1) is a useful shopping halt with garage, while there are similar facilities in **Lourches** (K5) and **Denain** (K7). Just before Écluse 8, Denain (K8), is a chandlery with diesel and water points. Fuel refineries and factories abound. Hurrying past **Wavrechain-sous-Denain**, shops can be visited in either **Thiant** or **Prouvy** (K13), close to an airport and the A2 *autoroute*. Now follow the right-hand channel for Écluse 10, **Trith-St-Léger** (K15, shopping). Not long after, we arrive in the city of **Valenciennes**, with Écluse 12, Folien (K22) near the centre. One place that offers moorings out of the reach of passing traffic is in the upper end of the weir stream (obviously not to be attempted if there is a strong current). Once known as the 'Athens of the North' because of the artistic talent which flourished here, Valenciennes is a thriving industrial city with an impressive and bustling modern square at its heart. Two educational visits might be planned: for culture, to the huge *Musée des Beaux-Arts* on the far side of town. It has outstanding collections of the Flemish School as well as paintings by leading French artists of the 18th and 19th centuries. Another, more prosaic, tour would be to the *Musée des Charbonnages et de la Métallurgie* (coal mining and metal working) on the opposite side of the waterway in **Anzin**.

Scenery is sometimes reminiscent of the more squalid portions of Yorkshire's Aire & Calder Navigation in the 1960s. Écluse 13, La Folie (K26), lies between Valenciennes and a junction with the **Canal de Pommeroeul à Condé** at **Fresnes-sur-Escaut** (K32, shopping). Only 5km of this 12km waterway lies within France. It was completed for 1,350-tonne vessels in 1982 and at the time of writing was undergoing a comprehensive dredging and improvement programme. The little town of **Condé-sur-Escaut** (K33) could no longer be reached by water after the 1982 works and a new channel is planned to rectify the situation. Condé provides all facilities with the remains of Vauban fortifications, an 18th century *Hôtel de Ville* and a 15th century *château*. Good shopping will be found in

Hergnies (K37). Écluse 16, **Rodignies** (K42), was removed in the early 1980s, and there is now a level run through a drawbridge at **Flines-les-Mortagne** (K44) to a junction with the River Scarpe from Douai (see Chapter 7). Shops and restaurants are near this point on the right bank with several more shops on the opposite bank in **Maulde**. Ahead, lies the Belgian frontier and routes to the Haut Escaut (Schelde), Tournai and Gent.

2 ⌁ Canal de Calais

Carte Guide: *Nord Pas-de-Calais*
From the English Channel at Calais to the canalised River Aa near Watten, 29.5km with 1 lock. There are three lock-free branches: the Canal de Guînes, from the main line near Coulogne to a terminus in Guînes, 6.2km; the Canal d'Ardres, from the main line at Le Pont d'Ardres to Ardres, 4.8km; and the Audruicq branch, from the main line near Hennuin to Audruicq, 2.3km. The latter pair are available to non-motorised craft only.

Calais harbour is quite the easiest entry to French inland waterways for sea-going pleasure craft from England. The canal, although it continues to carry some commercial traffic, is something of a backwater, in stark contrast to many km of large-tonnage waterway that must be followed once La Liaison is joined at Watten. Many of the typical elements of French canals are present, but with fairly undemanding conditions the Canal de Calais provides an easy introduction.

One problem that has affected the canal for many years is the build-up of very large quantities of duckweed, especially towards the end of summer. This curse can choke the propellers of smaller boats, or worse, block the intakes of water-cooled engines. If encountered, keep a close watch on temperature gauges.

Mainly completed under Louis XIV in 1681, the canal is fed by water supplies at Ardres and Guînes. In addition to linking Calais with the interior, it serves a useful drainage function. During the 1990s, the waterway was enlarged to accept 600-tonne barges, its single lock and several opening bridges being converted to automatic operation.

For many British visitors France starts at **Calais**, a town I have tried hard to like, fully aware that the inhabitants doubtless judge all visitors from the UK by the behaviour of some of the day-trippers. Closeness to England accounts for an atmosphere rather less than

totally French. But as a refuge from the open sea or a place to await settled weather before putting to sea, the safe, still water of Calais can seem like paradise. There is a choice of three restaurants that are both good and deservedly popular (with the locals): they face the Bassin de l'Ouest.

Near the harbour entrance is the Bassin de l'Ouest, on the right when coming in from the sea and opposite the very busy car ferry terminal. Moorings, clubhouse, water, fuel, crane and repairs are all available. This is easily the safest place to leave a boat after or before a Channel crossing; gates provide access for a short period at high water. Otherwise, buoys in the tidal outer harbour offer (very disturbed) moorings. For the Canal de Calais route, continue up the harbour to lock gates leading to the non-tidal Bassin Carnot. See the *Carte Guide* for lock operating times or consult the Bassin de l'Ouest harbour master. As wharves may well be occupied by shipping within the Bassin Carnot, it is preferable to pass through the Écluse de la Batellerie at the far end and use a visitor's pontoon sited round the right-angled corner. This is the most convenient place from which to visit the town.

Calais has recovered well from extensive damage suffered in World War II, although there is much unremarkable architecture dating from the 1950s and 60s. Its most memorable building is the great red brick and stone *Hôtel de Ville* with 75m high bell-tower. A stained glass window depicts the departure of the English in 1558 after the town had been occupied for 210 years. Nearby beaches such as **Blériot Plage** are agreeable sandy resorts.

One peculiarity of the canal is that surplus water is sometimes drained off to the sea via sluices, with a strong attendant current. Red flashing lights warn of this operation. A useful restaurant will be found on the right by the **Coulogne** lift bridge (K4) with shopping and garage in the town (left bank). Soon afterwards, the **Guînes** branch forks away to the right. As its lift bridges are no longer opened, navigation now stops after 900m. This and the other branches are also badly silted. Near to Guînes was the Field of the Cloth of Gold where in 1520 François I of France and Henry VIII of England vied with each other, displaying a magnificent court and entourage.

The main line offers shops and a garage in **Les Attaques** (K9) by a lift bridge. At the intersection of the Canal de Calais, Canal des Trois Cornets and **Canal d'Ardres** (K12), the waterway is spanned by the Pont Sans Pareil, a curious X-shaped concrete replacement for a very fine 18th century stone bridge. The structure prevented boats longer than 28m from turning into the Ardres branch; this no longer matters as motorised craft

The magnificent Hôtel de Ville *in Calais.*

are forbidden to navigate. Really keen waterways enthusiasts may feel compelled to travel to Ardres by rowing boat, where the town offers all services.

The Canal de Calais continues through rather featureless marshland until the short branch to Audruicq (K22, closed to motor boats). Grocer and restaurant are alongside a lift bridge just before the canal's only lock at **Hennuin** (K24, water point, restaurant). Loneliness of the surroundings is correctly suggested by the name of a waterside hamlet: **Le Coin Perdu** (Lost Corner). Shops and a restaurant are on the right bank at **Ruminghem** (K27.5). Several curious red brick structures, seen here and elsewhere along the canal, are not (as might initially be supposed) old fortifications: they are houses for the forcing of chicory. The River Aa is reached at an isolated junction by the Pont-du-West (K29.5): turn right for Watten and La Liaison au Grand Gabarit, leading to a series of important connections (see Chapter 1). The other direction heads back to the English Channel at Gravelines.

3 ~ River Aa

Carte Guide: *Nord Pas-de-Calais*
From the English Channel near Gravelines to St-Omer, junction with the Canal de Neuffossé. 28.7km with 1 lock and a sea lock at the estuary. 10km between Watten and St-Omer form part of La Liaison au Grand Gabarit and are described in Chapter 1. There are junctions with the Canal de Bourbourg and the Canal de Calais.

A less well known approach to the French waterways network from the coast, the River Aa follows a straight course through one-time marshland which was drained by creating a complex series of channels in the 18th century. The scenery is very flat and is rather lacking in features. The Gravelines lock and several opening bridges are available at certain times by advance notice only. For further information, consult the *Carte Guide* or contact the Gravelines Port Office: tel 03 28 23 13 42. All navigation is banned when flood prevention measures entail pumping water out of the river: under these circumstances flashing lights provide a warning at Le Guindal and the La Bistade bridge. From the sea to Watten is of standard Freycinet gauge; Watten to St-Omer is much larger.

Originally made navigable under Philip III of Spain in the 16th century, the Aa was further improved in 1737 during the reign of Louis XV with more work carried out twelve years later. The uppermost 10km were substantially enlarged in recent years as part of the creation of La Liaison au Grand Gabarit.

Approach from the English Channel is via a tideway whose entrance is guarded by fortifications known as **Grand Fort Philippe** and **Petit Fort Philippe**. The latter is now a fishing port and small holiday resort, with a slipway. Still water is reached after passing through the Écluse Maritime at **Gravelines** (K0), which is available for 1½hr either side of HW. Adequate pontoon moorings will be found in the tideway with a range of facilities located in the basin upstream of the tidal lock (boatyards, chandleries, moorings, crane, repairs and water point). Shopping is close at hand in the town, where extensive fortifications remain, encircled by a moat. They played a leading rôle in the defence of Dunkerque early in World War II. Between the lock and an opening railway bridge is a commercial barge repair yard. Main points of interest are a junction with the Canal de Bourbourg (K5.9, see Chapter 1) at **Le Guindal**, providing a link with La Liaison au Grand Gabarit and Dunkerque; a restaurant (right bank) beyond the next opening bridge at **St-Nicholas** (K8.2); limited shops in **St-Pierre-Brouck** (K11.2); and a right-hand junction with the Canal de Calais (K13.5, see Chapter 2) at **Pont-du-West**. La Liaison au Grand Gabarit is joined near **Watten** (K18.4). This route continues in Chapter 1.

4 ~ River Lys

Carte Guide: *Nord Pas-de-Calais*
From La Liaison au Grand Gabarit at Aire to the Belgian frontier at Halluin, 65km with 7 locks. There is a junction with the Canal de la Deûle at Deûlémont.

The canalised Lys, although lacking the ravishing beauty of Burgundy or the Midi, is surprisingly attractive over much of its course. Somehow, you do not expect to find such a treat in this northern part of France. For the greater part it runs through agreeable farming country; its valley, however, is littered with cemeteries recalling the slaughter of World War I. About 24km onwards from Armentières it forms the boundary with Belgium, and it eventually flows into the River Escaut (Schelde) at Gent (Gand). The frontier section, Armentières to Halluin/Menin, has been enlarged and carries regular commercial traffic. The remaining French reaches are smaller, up to 300-tonne capacity.

Used by freight craft over many centuries, the Lys was canalised and straightened in the 1870s. By 1936 half of the annual 773,000 tonnes of goods carried consisted of coal.

Aire-sur-la-Lys (K0, see Chapter 1) marks the junction of the Liaison au Grand Gabarit and the canalised River Lys. We soon pass through Écluse 1, Fort Gassion (K0.6). 1km after a mobile bridge at **Thiennes** (K3.7) will be seen a junction, left, with the **Canal de la Nieppe**, part of the **Hazebrouck Canals**, a 23km network in the shape of an inverted Y and making another connection with the Lys at Merville (K19). There were 4 locks, 38.5m x 3.5m, although the regular freight craft were just 27m long, loading 90 tonnes. Closure appears to have taken place around 1970. The route and its structures remain largely intact and it is to be hoped that restoration for pleasure cruising may eventually take place. Écluse 2, Cense à Witz, follows at K6.7 with the third lock near the centre of **St-Venant** (K12.6, shops close by). Mobile bridges span each end of Écluse 4 at **Merville** (K19.3) by the junction with the disused **River Bourre** (see above). Water point and shopping. At K19.9 an 800m navigable arm leads into Merville.

Another lost navigation once joined the Lys at **La Gorgue** (K24.4, shopping). This was the canalised River Lawe, running 18km from the Lys to Béthune, where it linked with the Canal d'Aire. It remained in use at least until 1921, when the *Guide Officiel de la Navigation Intérieure* unusually noted that the waterway with three locks was open to traffic only on Tuesdays, Thursdays and Fridays.

The flat landscape requires no further locks until No 5, **Bac de St-Maur** (K32.5), convenient shopping places en route including **Estaires** (K25.7) and **Sailly-sur-la-Lys** (K30.2). **Armentières** (K41.6), a name well known from the World War I British song, saw repeated action between 1914 and 1917. During an early bombardment the *Hôtel de Ville* clock was damaged, giving rise to the popular name 'Eleven o'Clock Square'. Completely rebuilt, Armentières now flourishes with brewing and linen interests. Lakes on the old course of the Lys have been landscaped as the Base des Pres du Hem. On the NE side of this water park is a pleasure boat harbour with pontoon moorings for 100 craft up to 20m, water, electricity and showers, launching and trailer parking. Such facilities are otherwise rare in this part of France. Nearby activities include dinghy sailing and wind surfing, a sandy beach with a long water-filled children's slide known as a *toboggan nautique*, a miniature farm and a bird sanctuary. Armentières stages an annual *Fête de la Lys* over the first weekend of July.

For a short distance above Écluse 6, Armentières (K42.7, water point), the river lies entirely within Belgium; it then briefly returns to France and for the next 24km serves as the boundary between the two countries.

Deûlémont (K48.9, shopping) stands by a right-hand junction with the Canal de la Deûle, connecting with Lille and the Liaison au Grand Gabarit at Bauvin. The final French lock, No 7 at **Comines** (K56.2), actually lies within Belgium. Close by was the start of the **Canal de Comines à Ypres**, effectively destroyed in World War I and never rebuilt. There is shopping here, in **Wervick-Sud** (K59.8) and at **Halluin** (K65). Onwards from this point, the Lys flows entirely through Belgium.

5 ∿ Canal de la Deûle

Carte Guide: *Nord Pas-de-Calais*
Part of this waterway, from the River Scarpe at Douai to Bauvin, forms a portion of La Liaison au Grand Gabarit and is described in Chapter 1. The remainder runs from La Liaison at Bauvin to a junction with the River Lys at Deûlémont, on the Belgian border. 36km with 4 locks. A junction is made with the Canal de Roubaix at Marquette-lez-Lille.

This section of the Deûle is mainly notable for serving the great industrial region centred on Lille, capital of French Flanders. Scenically, the waterway holds few attractions for the pleasure boater and its chief interest lies in providing a rapid transit between Ghent (Gand) and the Belgian Schelde and the main network of northern France.

Portions of the Deûle were first made navigable for barges as long ago as the 13th century; it was linked with the Scarpe in the 17th century and with the Lys in the middle of the 18th century. Widespread use of electric tractors to haul *péniches*, using vehicles both on rails and running on pneumatic tyres, lasted into the 1960s; one of the final developments in this field was the introduction of lengths of welded rail, each more than 1km. The whole line of the waterway, Bauvin to Lille, has been enlarged from Freycinet gauge to *grand gabarit*, enabling use by 1,350-tonne barges.

A triangular island marks the start of the Canal de la Deûle at **Bauvin** (moorings at a gravel barge quay). At K3 a disused portion of canal once served the town of **Don** which now has a 144,6m lock (K3.5) with water point a short distance into a parallel channel leading to the disused Freycinet lock. Most town facilities will be found in nearby **Sainghin-en-Weppes**. If you stop at a bridge following a disused power station on the left bank, the town of **Wavrin** is within 2.5km. More limited shopping is available by the next bridge at **Bac-de-Wavrin**. This is situated a little before a 4.5km branch canal (right bank, K8) leading to **Seclin**, noted for its *Hôpital* founded in the 13th century and built mainly in a Flemish Baroque style.

The main line continues through the heart of a heavily industrialised area with many commercial barge quays. Suburbs include **Emmerin**, **Hambourdin**, **Sequedin** and **Loos** with a dead end portion of old canal on the right at K13.4. Various channels and docks serve the busy harbour area of **Lille** (K18.5). The most promising city moorings will be found by turning right, out of the through navigation and heading towards the disued Freycinet lock, Écluse de la Barre. Alternatively, canal enthusiasts may wish to make a left turn off the main line to discover the 2km **Canteleu Branch** which offers a circular voyage and a return back to the southern outskirts of the city. Lille's massive *Citadelle*, built in the 17th century by Vauban and constructed of 60 million bricks, occupies an island site, encircled by old and new waterways. It is the most impressive and best preserved of all such structures in France. There are no public visits to the interior. Although Lille is very much an industrial city it has also developed in recent years as a tourist destination, partly thanks to the London-Paris high-speed rail link which passes through the centre. A huge *brocante* fair is staged annually in early September, attracting collectors of junk and antiques from all over Europe. Lille boasts one of the country's best art collections in its *Musée* and a fascinating Old Quarter near the Place Général de Gaulle. The leading historic building is the 17th century Flemish Baroque *Bourse* (Stock Exchange), with a magnificent galleried courtyard. Keeping the *Citadelle* on your right, the Écluse du Grand Carré will be seen ahead (K19.7, water point). Soon afterwards the canal ceases to be of 1,350 tonne standard, although it has lately been enlarged from 300 to 600 tonne capacity.

Shortly before a right-hand junction with the Canal de Roubaix at **Marquette-lez-Lille** (K24), there is a waterside fuel point on the left. Extensive works have seen removal of a lock at **Wambrechies** (K26, shopping), where the former cut has allowed creation of a very welcome pleasure boat harbour. A new lock is situated at **Quesnoy-sur-Deûle** (K28.4) with a mooring quay in the town centre, K29.9. Basic facilities at **Deûlémont** (K33.9) are within 1500m of a *relais nautique*. Beyond lies a junction with the River Lys (K34.8) which marks the border between France and Belgium (see Chapter 4).

6 ~ Canal de Roubaix

Carte Guide: *Nord Pas-de-Calais*
From a junction with the Canal de la Deûle at Marquette-lez-Lille to Roubaix, border with Belgium and start of the Canal de l'Espierres. 20km with 12 locks. Part of the course is the canalised River Marque. There are two navigable branches: Embranchement de Croix, 0.6km; and Embranchement de Tourcoing, 0.9km.

Densely urban for all of its central portion, this link with Belgium's Haut Escaut and the Bovenschelde climbs from each terminus to a summit level at Roubaix/Tourcoing. Although planned in 1825, the Canal de Roubaix was not opened throughout until 1877. The locks are very slightly larger than the Freycinet standard.

For many years the waterway was effectively abandoned, partly resulting from operational failure of the magnificent 19th century hydraulic lift bridges in the centre of Roubaix. A vigorous campaign fought at local and national levels eventually resulted in the decision to carry out a full restoration. As has frequently been the case in the UK, experience here proves that it is invariably cheaper to keep a waterway in operation than to allow it to decay and then to undertake the massive required rescue. Work commenced in 2000 and continues at the time of writing. Estimated costs are £16 million (including dredging and disposal of massive quantities of contaminated mud), with a further £13 million for landscaping. For information on progress and a likely completion date, contact Direction Régionale de la Navigation, 113 ave Max Dormoy, Bâtiment 1, BP 56, 59004 Lille. Tel 03 20 17 06 12.

Écluse 1, de **Marquette-lez-Lille** (K0.4), and 2, **Marcq-en-Barœul** (K3.7), are followed by a winding section that leads to the **Croix Branch**. It is planned only to restore the first 0.6km (of an original 2km) to the town of Croix, with the Port du Dragon pleasure boat harbour at the new terminus at **Wasquehal**. A former lock here is no longer necessary, as the levels have been changed. A flight of five locks raises the canal its summit. The **Tourcoing Branch**, now shortened from 1.5km to 0.9km, is situated in a deep landscaped cutting, forming part of an urban park. **Roubaix** (K12) is a flourishing centre for textiles and engineering. 5km south is an outstanding modern chapel at **Hem**, completed in 1958. On the canal's left bank **Tourcoing** specialises in woollen thread, producing 40 per cent of French output. Both towns are well served by shops and other urban facilities. Navigationally, the most notable features are several historic lift bridges which, it is hoped, will be restored rather than replaced. Locks 9–12 lower craft through **Wattrelos** (K15). By a lift bridge with public quay (K18.7) is a waterside restaurant. Beyond, at K20 is the Belgian frontier and the start of the Belgian **Canal de l'Espierres**. Comprising 8km with three locks, this waterway is also undergoing restoration to complete the link with the canalised Belgian River Escaut.

7 ~ River Scarpe

Carte Guide: *Nord Pas-de-Calais*
From a terminus in Arras to the Belgian frontier at Mortagne-du-Nord, junction with the Escaut. 66km with 17 locks. 8km of the line around Douai has been replaced by the Scarpe *dérivation* and forms part of La Liaison au Grand Gabarit (see Chapter 1). The upper section, Arras-Douai, is known as the 'Scarpe Supérieure', the middle part around Douai as the 'Scarpe Moyenne', and the lower portion down to the Escaut as the 'Scarpe Inférieure'.

The navigable Scarpe passes through a sometimes densely populated area but, with the exception of Douai, generally manages to avoid centres of thickest industry. Much of the course is set in very pleasing countryside, with meadows and woodland. With the exception of the enlarged portion near Douai, the waterway is designed for 38m *péniches*, the five locks nearest Arras being arranged as an automatic series. For operating guidance, see the *Carte Guide*.

Historical information on the development of the Scarpe is infuriatingly elusive. It would appear that parts have been used by barges over the centuries while most of the present infrastructure is 19th century.

Navigation starts at an agreeable landscaped basin 600m from the centre of **Arras**, with good moorings on a floating pontoon. In spite of quantities of duckweed in late summer, this is an exceptionally pleasant part of the waterway and many towns now have basic mooring facilities. Being a river, there can sometimes be a strong flow. Keep clear of weirs when coming downstream. Arras recovered magnificently from the appalling destruction of World War I, the twin squares of the Places des Héros and the Grand Place being almost without equal in the whole of France. Although dating from the 11th century, they are now surrounded by extremely fine gabled buildings in the Flemish style, erected in the 17th and 18th centuries. Here there is a laudable and remarkable absence of inappropriate street furniture, even the telephone kiosks being placed underground and out of sight. From the Middles Ages, tapestry was produced, and in English 'arras' was once the word used to describe woven pictures. The great 15th century *Hôtel de Ville* with 75m belfry overlooks a colourful Saturday market. This region was fiercely fought over throughout the Great War. Nowhere are the battles more eloquently recalled than at **Vimy Ridge**, 11km to the north. Parkland planted with 75,000 trees in memory of that number of Canadian soldiers who died here in 1917 fails to mask the tortured landscape, where bomb craters and trenches are preserved in such a way as to provide graphic understanding of just what happened. Visits are possible to underground tunnels wriggling throughout the front line. To go there is a moving yet fascinating experience.

Écluse 1, St-Nicholas (K0.5), is the first of a sequence of automatic locks on the edge of Arras. Beware of silting below the lock, where the river enters the navigation for the first time. Soon comes another lock, No 2, **St-Laurent-Blangy** (K2.3, good shopping in the village). Onwards from here is a series of further villages, mostly at lock sites and all offering shopping possibilities. They include **Athies** (K4.9, Écluse 3); **Fampoux** (K7.3, Écluse 4); **Rœux** (K10.1, fishing lakes); **Pelvès** (K11.1); and **Biache-St-Vaast**, (K14.2, Écluse 5). Two locks in **Brébières** are Écluse 7, Haute-Tenue (K20.1) and 8, Basse-Tenue (K20.6) with shops and a garage. On my last visit to this part of the Scarpe, the automatic radar operation of locks was unreliable and we arranged for personal lock keepers to come and help. (See the *Carte Guide* for the appropriate VHF channel number.)

After Écluse 9, **Corbehem**, below which is a very sharp bend (K22.4, all shops), we reach La Liaison. Turn right for Cambrai and Valenciennes, or left along the *dérivation de la Scarpe* past Douai (see Chapter 1). The river assumes its own true identity close to a boatmen's chapel at **Dorignies** junction (K29), often a hectic place with large barges manoeuvring between the two waterways.

Now clear of Douai, the river assumes more of a village character, even if these villages have developed as a result of coal mining. Always, food and fuel supplies are never far away. Locks are renumbered from 1, de Fort de Scarpe (K30), with adequate shopping by a mobile bridge either in **Frais-Marais** or **Râches** (K33.3). Equally convenient is **Lallaing**, near Écluse 2 (K36.8). Four bridges on at **Vred** (K41.5, shops and garage), lies the former abbey of Anchin, a Benedictine house of great antiquity and partly ruined during the Revolution. I well remember during an August heat wave how the Vred swing bridge became inoperable through heat expansion (it was 33°C!); the keeper requested that we wait overnight and pass through early in the morning. *Halte nautique* with water and electricity.

Marchiennes-Ville (K45.3) at Écluse 3 has a public quay and a very pleasant pleasure craft mooring with a good range of all shopping facilities. Remains of an abbey founded in the 7th century may be visited on summer Sundays. 2km N is the 800 hectare Forêt de Marchiennes, a popular destination for walks, picnics, riding and fishing. Limited shopping near Écluse 4, **Warlaing** (K49.7).

A long pound extends to **St-Amand-les-Eaux** and Écluse 5 (K59.3), well known for a 7th century abbey founded by St Amand. Most of the buildings that remain date from the 17th century. These include an impressive Baroque façade, an 82m tower with carillon which provides daily concerts and a museum. The final lock, Écluse 6, Thun (K64.8), is near shops in **Mortagne-du-Nord**, with a commercial barge yard and the possibility of diesel delivery by tanker. Extensive dredging and the total rebuilding of the lock in 1990 were indicative of a desire to encourage pleasure boats to use this under-publicised but very pleasant route. Beyond, the Scarpe flows into the Escaut near the Belgian border.

8 ⁓ Canal du Nord

Carte Guide: *Picardie*

From a junction with the Canal latéral à l'Oise near Pont-l'Evêque to a junction with the Canal de la Sensée (Liaison au Grand Gabarit) at Arleux, 95km with 19 locks. There are two tunnels: Ruyaulcourt, 4,350m and Panneterie, 1,061m. 20km of the central part of the canal shares an improved channel with the older Canal de la Somme (Béthencourt-sur-Somme to Biaches, near Péronne), described in Chapter 9.

Much the more convenient and quickest route between the Seine and the Channel Ports, the Canal du Nord is probably the most important totally new navigation of the 20th century. Locks are 91.9m long x 6m wide and were designed to take a pair of pushed *péniches* with a total payload of 700 tonnes. Operated by hydraulics from a central control cabin, chambers are fitted with lifting tail gates and side ponds which save one third of the quantity of water used at each locking. Two new locks on the improved central section, shared with the Canal de la Somme, are of a different design. With the exception of this pair, all have pumping stations enabling more than 100,000m³ of water to be lifted to the two summit levels each day.

Both tunnels are worked one-way with the aid of traffic lights, closed circuit television and microphone/loudspeaker communication between boat crews and keeper. Barges normally enter the longer tunnel, Ruyaulcourt, in groups of four starting simultaneously from each end. At the centre there is a two-way 1,150m long passing point. The Panneterie tunnel is worked one-way. On this important route, commercial traffic is heavy. There is a plan to further enlarge or

duplicate the waterway as a link between the Seine and NW France, but no starting date has yet been announced.

Large, modern canals obviously lack the intimacy of older, smaller navigations and the Canal du Nord is in parts rather bleak with severe concrete banks. Most canal enthusiasts will prefer a passage through the smaller, more historic Canal de St-Quentin, running parallel to the Canal du Nord. But devotees of commercial water transport will enjoy a journey along this quicker and more efficient route before they too start to pine for more bucolic byways such as the Canal de Bourgogne. It has to be said that the engineering is impressive, while a landscape of expansive cornfield is not without its own attractions.

Brief history Heavy congestion on the Canal de St-Quentin, then the sole link between the Seine Basin and the north, prompted the government to launch the Flamant Project in 1878, to create a totally new waterway. Construction started at the northern, Arleux, end just before the turn of the century and in spite of widespread disquiet at the large costs involved, a four month emergency stoppage on the Canal de St-Quentin at Jussy in 1900 with consequent disruption of all traffic was a major factor in carrying on with ever greater speed. Three-quarters of the excavations, 11 locks and all the bridges were finished and work was well advanced on the tunnels when war broke out in 1914. The canal itself at the very heart of the battlefields and destruction was widespread. Nothing came of attempts to resume building before World War II.

Under the Third Plan of 1959 it was decided to begin again, following substantially the same design but increasing the length of locks from 85m to 91.9m. Work started in 1960 and the new waterway was opened to traffic late in 1965. Banks almost throughout are of concrete or concrete and bitumen. Two new ports were laid out at Péronne and Noyon with numerous unloading quays at other locations. The Canal du Nord was used by no fewer than 7,000 craft in the first six months of operation and traffic has been heavy ever since. Most of the locks have water points.

The Canal du Nord leaves the Canal latéral à l'Oise at **Pont-l'Evêque** (for facilities, see Chapter 17), and passes through two locks, 19, Pont-l'Evêque (K0.6) and 18, **Noyon** (K1.6), with recommended public moorings beyond the centre of Noyon on the right bank. The city supports various industries from brewing to printing and furniture making; as an ecclesiastical town it has an ancient history. Charlemagne was crowned King of Normandy here in 768 and Hughes Capet King of

France in 987. Fully restored after severe World War I damage, the 12–13th century cathedral is a splendid example of the early Gothic. Calvin was born in the town in 1509 and his entirely rebuilt birthplace house is now a museum of his work. There are extensive shopping and eating possibilities.

Between Noyon and Péronne there are no nearby towns of any great size but several of the villages will be able to supply basic food needs. After **Beaurains-lès-Noyon** (K6) we pass through Écluse 17, **Sermaize-Haudival** (K7.3) followed in turn by **Catigny** (K11) and Écluse 16, **Campagne** (K13.1). Panneterie tunnel, one-way and controlled by lights, presents no unusual problems. This is the first of two summit levels, as the waterway crosses the divide between the Rivers Oise and Somme. Shortly before a bridge (K20), public moorings will be seen in a small basin on the right. Such sites are of greater importance to pleasure craft than on most canals as the banks of sloping concrete are generally unsuitable as well as being subject to wash from passing barges. Through the bridge at **Breuil** (K24), the *port public* de **Languevoisin** is established on the left. Then comes Écluse 15 (K29) dropping the waterway to the level of the Canal de la Somme beyond the prosperous farming villages of **Rouy-le-Grand** and **Rouy-le-Petit** (K30, no shopping although there are such facilities in the nearby small town of **Voyennes**, a short distance down the Canal de la Somme). From here to **Biaches** (K50), beyond **Péronne** (K47), the route is described under Canal de la Somme (Chapter 9). In order, from junction to junction, through distances on the Canal du Nord are as follows: Béthencourt-sur-Somme (K31); **Pargny** (K34); Écluse 14, **Epénancourt** (K35); **St-Christ Briost** (K39); **Eterpigny** (K42); Écluse 13, **Péronne** (K46).

As it climbs away from the Somme valley, the Canal du Nord ascends a series of locks: 12, **Cléry-sur-Somme** (K52); 11, **Feuillaucourt** (K53); 10, **Allaines** (K56); and Écluses 9 (K57) and 8 (K58), **Moislains**, a convenient shopping stop with a public quay. Another reason for halting here is that the scenery in this area is rather dull and a break ashore may be welcome.

Now on the second summit level, the next point of interest, north of **Manancourt** and **Equancourt**, is the beginning of the impressively large **Ruyaulcourt** tunnel (K66) at the end of a deep cutting (see the beginning of this chapter and consult the *Carte Guide*). Beyond, are isolated locks in the open and windswept cornfields: Écluses 7 (K78) and 6 (K80), **Graincourt-lès-Havrincourt**, and Écluse 5, **Mœuvres** (K81). Within walking distance are basic food shops, otherwise, a larger range of facilities and restaurant are to be found in **Inchy-en-Artois** (K84), approached from a bridge in the middle

of the pound between Écluses 4 and 3, **Sains-lès-Marquion**. This is a small town of rusty brick courtyards and massive grain barns.

A noticeable softening of the countryside brings with it more attractive villages including **Marquion** (K88), with public mooring north of Écluse 2, through the bridge on the right bank (garage, restaurant and shopping). The next bridge serves **Sauchy-Cauchy** (K90). The last of the Canal du Nord locks is Écluse 1, **Palluel** (K94). To the west is a pleasant area of lakes along the course of the River Sensée. On the left bank (K94.7) is a junction with a short, private waterway, the **Canal des Malderez**, now partly reserved for angling. Note, close to the Palluel-Arleux road, remains of a very small lock with single gates at each end. A village a little upstream bears the suggestive name of **L'Écluse**. At the junction with the Canal de la Sensée, **Arleux** (K95) is a quay with water point and fuel pump (see Chapter 1). Turn left into the series of waterways collectively known as La Liaison au Grand Gabarit, leading to Calais and Dunkerque, or right for the River Escaut, Valenciennes and the Belgian border.

9 Canal de la Somme

Carte Guide: *Picardie*

From a junction with the Canal de St-Quentin at St-Simon to the English Channel at St-Valéry-sur-Somme, 156.5km with 25 locks. Some 20.5km of the route from near Voyennes to near Péronne is enlarged and shared by the Canal du Nord. The lower section is known as the Canal Maritime d'Abbeville à St-Valéry.

Though virtually inseparable from associations with the appalling slaughter of the Battle of the Somme which claimed about 1.2 million dead or wounded during the summer and autumn of 1916, the River Somme is a remarkably pleasant waterway, at times quite equalling the very best of French navigations in its bucolic charm. That its attractions have rarely been described in print is only partly accounted for by the fact that Calais offers a slightly easier entry to France from the Thames Estuary and the SE coast of England. Given safe conditions at sea, I consider the Somme has considerably more to offer than the Calais route and I personally rate it above entering the tidal Seine at Le Havre. Only in recent years have hire cruisers been available on the Somme: currently at bases in Amiens and Cappy. As a result, it is fast gaining a well deserved reputation as a pleasure boating route of great merit.

Rising in Picardy near Fonsommes, 245km from the sea, the waterway consists of a lateral canal between St-Simon and Bray-sur-Somme and thereafter mostly follows the natural bed of the river to the coast. Throughout much of the course there are numerous lakes alongside: these were formed from flooded peat workings and closely recall the origin of the Norfolk and Suffolk Broads in England. Peat was still dug and burned as a domestic fuel in Amiens early in the 20th century. Teeming with fish, exceptionally noisy frogs and carpets of water lilies, these popular-shaded pools have become one of France's leading angling areas. The shooting of swans was outlawed as a local sport around the beginning of the 18th century. But many other forms of wildlife are keenly persecuted with Gallic fervour and quite tiny towns and villages frequently support emporia filled with sophisticated apparatus to trap creatures that swim, fly or run along the ground.

As with many other *péniche*-sized navigations, commercial traffic has dwindled away almost to nothing since the prosperous days of the 1960s and 1970s. It did not help that there was never any effective seaport for shipping on the coast at St-Valéry. Some, but by no means all, bridges and locks have been mechanised. Except for a 09.30h start on Sundays, keepers work to regular times with a 30 minute break, 12.30h–13.00h. Short conducted boat tours are made of the fascinating Amiens *Hortillonnages*, a complex of small waterways intersecting the city's market gardens: the craft used are traditional open barques. One outstandingly good book that is a 'must' when exploring this waterway is Arthur Taylor's *Spring on the Somme* (Constable, London, 1995). In part it is a travelogue, telling the story of a gentle journey by rowing boat. But it is also an invaluable guide book, recording the rich history of the river.

Brief history. There is published evidence of the Somme being navigable for small craft upstream to St-Quentin in the Middle Ages, but construction of a waterway with locks was not mooted until 1725. Following a survey by M Laurent in 1768–9, plans were agreed the next year and work on the upper end started almost immediately. Early excellent progress saw the navigation in service between St-Simon and Bray (a distance of 54km) by 1772. Numerous problems and delays, however, prevented the through route becoming available to barge traffic until 1843. The sandbank-strewn estuary at St-Valéry was (and remains to this day) a perennial site of difficult navigation. The Maritime Canal of 1835, between Abbeville and the coast at St-Valéry, considerably reduced the distance for ships across the treacherous bay of the Somme: it

greatly improved matters but did not completely solve them. It remains an interesting exercise for strangers to the area to cross the bay between St-Valéry and the open sea successfully.

The Somme was intended for the transport of salt, grain, wood, coal and wine, but never became very busy. In the 19th century barges known as *gribannes* worked the length downstream of Amiens, later assisted by a few steam-powered craft.

Since 1991, the Canal de la Somme from Écluse 7, Sormon (near the junction with the Canal du Nord) and the sea has been controlled by the local authority, rather than the national body, the VNF. No boat licence is currently demanded.

Our journey starts in the marshy valley of the Somme at **St-Simon**. Having risen to the NE of St-Quentin, the river has already served as a feeder for the Canal de St-Quentin for a considerable distance, but it will still be a long while before it becomes navigable in its own right. St-Simon lock, No 1, is virtually at the triangular junction with the Canal de St-Quentin, with Écluse 2 in **Ham** (K6.6), a town best known for having one of the biggest sugar silos in Europe, with a capacity of 26,000 tonnes. Until destruction by the Germans in 1917, there was a massive fortress built between the 13th and 15th centuries, with walls 11m thick. Intended as a place for holding political prisoners, its most notable captive was Louis-Napoléon Bonaparte. After six years he was able to escape to safety in England in 1846. The church of Notre-Dame is a splendid 12th and 13th century abbey, well restored. In a pleasant town centre, all facilities will be found. One splendid feature of Ham is the public Parc Délicourt, intersected by streams crossed by rustic bridges and bordering on the Somme. Once a private garden, it is now a well planted delight. Écluse 3, Ham inférieure, leads to open country with great fields of wheat, potatoes and beet reaching to the horizon. Patches of woodland provide shelter for numerous wild deer and rabbits.

Le Domaine des Iles at **Offoy** (Écluse 4, K12.4) is a combination of water park and leisure centre, with fishing punts and pedalos, riding and a miniature train arranged round a series of lakes. Limited shopping. At the next bridge (K14.8), **Buny** (right bank) and **Voyennes** (left bank) offer several shops. Near **Rouy-le-Petit** (K16.4) the Canal du Nord enters on the left; from here to Péronne the same route is common to each waterway and the improved Canal de la Somme is technically known as the Canal du Nord, 2nd Section. Prosperous farming villages follow in succession, but facilities are fairly sparse. Apart from a public mooring there is little to delay the boater at **Béthencourt-sur-**

Somme (K18.5) but it *must* be worth mentioning that 3km NE lies the stunningly-named village of **Y**, whose entry sign surely makes a unique photograph. Further canalside villages with basic shopping and restaurant possibilities include **Epénancourt** (K22.1) with Écluse 5. A useful restaurant, La Clé des Champs, together with several shops will be found in **St-Christ Briost** (K25.7) at the head of a chain of lakes along the course of the Somme. A fascinating survival is one of the area's two remaining fish smokeries, at the *Bar du Vivier*. Many varieties of freshwater fish are kept in tanks. The 'tradition' of smoking fish here seems to have been introduced to the present proprietor's grandfather by non-militant Germans during World War I.

Écluse 6 (K32.9) appears on the southern outskirts of **Péronne**, an ancient fortified city built at the confluence of the Rivers Somme and Cologne which suffered almost total destruction during 1916 and 1917. Relics do survive from the onslaught, including an early 17th century gateway, the Porte de Bretagne; a 13th century *château* (open to the public Sundays pm); and a Renaissance *Hôtel de Ville*. Fish-filled ponds are a famed centre for eels, eaten smoked or as *pâté*, and there are canal-intersected vegetable gardens known as *hardines*, similar to those in Amiens and St-Omer. They are now cultivated by amateur, rather than professional, growers as was once the case. Behind the *Château de Péronne* is an extraordinary permanent exhibition/museum, *L'Historial de la Grand Guerre*. A visit is obligatory to begin to understand the impact of World War I on this valley. Modern the city certainly is, but it does offer the pleasure boater many services. Commercial traffic gathers at a freight port and a wash-free basin has been expertly converted into a marina where long-term moorings are available. Within 100m are restaurant and garage. It is worth noting that the two large Péronne and Cléry locks both *empty* into the pound that divides them; should they each be drained simultaneously, the equivalent of a tidal wave is created with a rapid rise in water level of as much as 0.5m. At K36.7 the Canal du Nord branches off on its journey to the Canal de la Sensée and the River Scarpe, and the Somme resumes a fairly sleepy existence, rarely disturbed by the passage of commercial traffic although pleasure craft have much increased in recent years thanks partly to hire boat bases at Cappy and Amiens.

We are now approaching the start of a long and quite exciting passage through peat bogs and lakes that can justifiably boast the title 'Fishing Capital of France'. Many of the towns have developed as holiday centres with little weekend homes at the waterside and an assortment of restaurants such as is rarely encountered along inland waterways. Écluse 7, Sormont (K39.1),

within reach of **Cléry-sur-Somme**, is followed by an A1 *autoroute* crossing, and then at **Feuillères** an automated swing bridge (K41.3) close to which are restaurant, garage and good moorings. Nearby, on the course of the natural river, a number of eel traps can be found: metal grills combined with sluice gates. Chalk cliffs begin to dominate the valley on the left, providing views down onto the old course of the Somme, now a complicated pattern of reedy pools teeming with wildlife. Frogs are so numerous (and vocal) that their croaking can cause a sleepless night unless moorings are selected with great care! Écluses 8 (K43.6) and 9 in **Frise** are mechanised, as are a number of the other locks (but by no means all!). Aptly named **Éclusier Vaux** (K46.9) turns out to have no lock at all: merely a manned bascule bridge with shopping and restaurant. 2km N up the road towards **Maricourt** is the **Belvédère de Vaux**, a notable viewpoint from which to look down on the patchwork of willow-fringed ponds.

Cappy (K50.2) at the next road bridge and a little before Écluse 10 has a good range of shops and has really started to flourish in recent years thanks to the establishment of the leading hire cruiser base in the area. *L'Escale de Cappy* restaurant, in a onetime barge horse stable, is famed for its traditional Picardy cuisine: dishes such as *La Marmite de la Batelière* (Boatwoman's Casserole, containing locally caught crayfish, pike, eel, carp and zander). Cappy is served by a charming little steam and diesel-hauled 60cm narrow gauge railway, the **Froissy-Cappy-Dompierre**, with 7km of track. Designed as a World War I military line, it carried up to 1,500 tonnes of munitions a day in 1916. After the Great War, it served a vital rôle in the huge rebuilding programme of the district. After that it was used for many years as a mineral transporter and from 1971 it was restored as a passenger-carrying tourist attraction passing through delightful surroundings along the side of the canal. Thirty locomotives and over 100 items of rolling stock are housed in a museum building by the waterway at **Froissy** (K52.9) which is also the boarding point for the trains. One steeply inclined part of the track is arranged as a switch-back, enabling the sudden change in levels to be overcome within limited space, similar to the systems to be found in the Andes and Himalayas. It operates on Sundays, May–September with additional days July and August. For timetables, tel 03 22 44 55 40. From Froissy to the coast, the navigation mainly occupies the natural river bed, canal cuts largely being reserved for lock approaches.

Extensive urban facilities are to be found in the small town of **Bray-sur-Somme** (K54.1), served by a navigable branch off the main line (draft limited to 1.0m). **Etineham** (K57.1) similarly had a branch, but it is now closed. Next comes Écluse 12, **Méricourt-sur-Somme** (K58.6). Caravans and chalets are concealed in the waterside undergrowth where the little River Somme chuckles along close to the canal adding to the charms of this outstandingly lovely navigation. Most of the villages now encountered remain pleasingly rural with huge ancient hay barns and sufficient shops to keep pleasure boaters stocked with food. In **Chipilly** (K62.3, facing its twin waterside village of Cerisy), is the small *Oasis* restaurant, while the *Auberge de l'Écluse* and the *Auberge de Trois Vallées* provide meals of good value in **Sailly-Laurette** (K65.2) near Écluse 13. A plaque records the rebuilding of this lock in October 1918 by British soldiers of an Inland Waterways section of the Royal Engineers. There is also a small monument to the English war poet Wilfred Owen: he was evacuated from a field dressing station near here by canal boat in May 1917 and recalled the event in his celebrated poem 'Hospital Barge':

Budging the sluggard ripples of the Somme,
A barge round old Cerisy slewed.
Softly her engines down the current screwed,
And chuckled softly with contented hum,
Till fairy tinklings struck their croonings dumb.
The waters rumpling at the stern subdued;
The lock gate took her bulging amplitude;
Gently from out the gurgling lock she swum.

Between the Somme and the River Ancre at Écluse 14, **Corbie** (K74.4) is a sizeable town (all facilities), once famous for its Benedictine abbey, founded in the mid-7th century by St-Bathilde, Queen of Clovis II. Little remains of the establishment apart from a massive stone gatehouse and a great church that seems to dwarf the little town. Another notable building is the *Hôtel de Ville*, an elaborate *château*-like fantasy in pink brick and stone and a series of carved horses' heads over the doorways on the original stable block. It all started life as a private residence in the 1860s and became public offices in the 1920s. There are several restaurants. War graves proliferate throughout the area, for there was very heavy fighting here during World War I; 11,000 Australians who died between 1916 and 1918 are remembered by a National Memorial 3km south of the waterway on the road connecting **Fouilloy** and **Villers-Bretonneux**. The celebrated German 'Red Baron' von Richthoven, who had brought down no fewer than eighty allied aircraft, met his fatal end over Corbie on April 21 1918.

Locks 15, **Daours** (K79.7), and 16, **Lamotte-Brébière** (K84.3), lead to **Camon** (K90.1), a suburb with a pleasure boat yard. Soon afterwards **Amiens**

(K93.3) is reached, capital of Picardy and long associated with the English from the days when Edward VI signed a peace treaty with France's Henri II (1550). Although there was widespread destruction in both world wars, the outstanding Gothic cathedral survived intact: during World War I, it was claimed that the Pope persuaded the Kaiser to intervene and prevent it being shelled. A comprehensive rebuilding scheme for the city resulted in much 1950s concrete architecture, varying from the uninspired to the unpleasant. In complete contrast, the former working class district of **St-Leu**, intersected by a series of small water courses, has in the 1990s undergone a complete regeneration programme. Much of the area is now given over to a university where new structures stand side by side with carefully restored old ones. Much 'instant' character has been created. The best moorings for visiting craft are at the Port d'Amont, a central quayside where the navigation channel makes a sharp turn to the right by the city rowing club. Be careful not to tie on sections allocated to passenger craft. Shops, restaurants and the cathedral are within a short distance.

Amiens is famous for its *Hortillonnages*, 300 hectares of fertile plots known as *aires*, intersected by (a claimed) 55km of small canals (*rieux*) that resulted from medieval peat workings. Today, only a few of these market gardens are worked commercially. The great majority are used as delightful leisure plots, many having small summertime chalets. Traditional flat-bottomed punts (*cornets*), dressed with tar and featuring upturned bows, once

Distance marker in Amiens.

This magnificent early 20th century postcard shows no fewer than five horses pulling a truck laden with stone blocks that have been unloaded from the péniche *at an Amiens quay.*

brought produce to a market in the city centre. Now, several have been motorised to provide tourists with root-level views of cabbages and onions: several embarkation points with associated restaurants will be found just off the main waterway. It is possible, however, that you will see rather more from an investigation on foot.

Throughout the length and breadth of France, rivers and lakes are lined with wooden fishing punts, and although plastic versions may also be seen, the timber-built variety remain common. But it is surprisingly rare to encounter such craft being built: one of these normally secretive yards can be found in Amiens, where heaps of newly sawn wood are formed into elegant little vessels. Speciality foods to search for include *tuiles au chocolat*, almond biscuits shaped like curved 'tiles'; *ficelles Picardes*, pancakes filled with cream, ham, cheese or mushrooms; *pâté de canard en croûte*, duck pâté in a pastry case; and macaroons.

There are many fascinating aspects to Amiens. From the 13th century, it was an important centre of woad production, the crushed leaves as a blue dye for local cloth. In April and October there are annual *réderies*, street fairs and flea markets. Early September every year sees the *Weekend au Bord de l'Eau*, an excuse to have some watery fun, with concerts and fireworks, events on the river such as jousting contests and record breaking attempts to create the biggest macaroon in the

world. Then we cannot ignore the writer Jules Verne who spent his last 35 years in the city and was an enthusiastic local politician. His former house in the rue Charles Dubois is the *Centre du Documentation Jules Verne*, both a museum and a celebration of a hugely popular public figure. Although few readers of this book are likely to be boating in Amiens in the depths of winter, it is worth mentioning that the city stages the biggest Christmas market in the north of France around the *Hôtel de Ville* (from late November). This is the place for all manner of culinary delights and much more.

Past Écluse 17 (K94), open country is soon reached again, with a string of peat lakes, called *Chés Intailles* in the Picardy dialect. If anything, the valley becomes even more beautiful than upstream of Amiens. Écluse 18, **Montiéres** (K97.7), is followed by Écluse 19 in **Ailly-sur-Somme** (K102.5): this latter chamber is one of several on the canal built almost in the form of a two-rise, the lower part having sloping turf sides and intended to be used as a kind of flood lock or perhaps to pass unusually deep-draft craft. Ailly's church is an unusual modernistic structure, its roof looking like a ship's sail. We pass further small lakes and the most interesting little town of **Picquigny** appears on the left (K108), rising from the river front around a thickly wooded hill. The Hundred Years War ended here when Louis IX signed a treaty with Edward IV of England in

1475. In order to prevent any possibility of a murderous attack such as had taken place in Montereau some 56 years earlier (see Chapter 13), the monarchs approached each other on the Ile de la Trève in the centre of the river separated by iron bars! High above the town and commanding a fine view of the Somme are the remains of a once massive fortified *château* with a pair of gateways and a magnificent Renaissance kitchen with vaulted ceiling. It is possible to see a range of tunnels with *graffiti* carved by prisoners of long ago. Cherry trees and wild roses tumble down the grey walls towards the rooftops of houses below. Directly alongside is the collegiate church of St-Martin (13th–15th centuries). A cemetery opposite the *Pavillon Sévigné* contains a number of graves of British World War I soldiers, regimental comrades of the author's father. At the request of his mother, Jack McKnight had attended church in London one Sunday in 1916. While the service was in progress his colleagues in the Middlesex Hussars were suddenly despatched to the Somme: very few were to return. It will thus be appreciated that but for the religious wishes of my grandmother, this book might never have been written! Picquigny has several restaurants and adequate shops. Across the river at **La Chaussée-Tirancourt** are the remains of the largest fortified Gaulish camp in northern France. This 2,000 year old town has been 'improved' as an historical 'theme park', named Samara after the Latin for Somme. The site covers 30 hectares.

NW from Picquigny, **Belloy-sur-Somme** has two *châteaux*, built in the 18th and 19th centuries. In the next reach, the ruins of the 12th century *Abbaye du Gard* may be visited by the public. A long restoration campaign in recent years has enabled a religious house to be established here once more: they welcome visitors who come to stay in *chambres d'hôte*.

Rarely does a waterway present such a rich collection of pleasing villages and small towns. The next, **Hangest-sur-Somme** (K114.5) with shopping, is known for its watercress beds, although the many producers of 60 years ago are now reduced to just one or two. German troops under Rommel crossed the Somme here in 1940. Écluse 21, Labreilloire (K117.5), marks a point where most left bank villages become rather remote from the waterway, with green and lily-filled lakes intervening between the river and the D3 highway. Several features in **Long**, Écluse 22, turf-sided, (K124.8) add to the enjoyment of exploration. While only a small place, it has a spectacular town hall, crowned with an extraordinary 1869 Gothic bell tower recalling the railway station in Abbeville. Nor is the adjacent bar-café what you might expect, for it is a retail centre of expensive and sophisticated angling

equipment with which to capture the giant carp and pike of the vicinity. From 1902 until 1965, Long operated its own little hydro-electric plant; although no longer used full-time, the equipment can be seen in operation during the tourist season. Another big attraction since 1971 is the extensive *brocante* (antiques/junk) market, held annually on the first Sunday of September. Among several shops, one rents out bicycles for tours through the lakeland. Note a fine Louis XV *château* in white stone and pink brick. There is a *halte nautique* 300m upstream of the lock. At **Fontaine-sur-Somme**, across the ponds to the SW, a boat builder sells wooden punts: filled with water to prevent leaks, they can be seen stacked on the edge of the main road.

Even after a moderate summer rainfall, the Somme flows fast through **Pont-Rémy** (K130.6), a village with delightful waterfront, brick and stone church containing mid-16th century stained glass windows, and a 15th century *château* on an island, reconstructed about 1837 in the Gothic troubadour style. Shopping is quite good. Écluse 23, turf-sided (K131.2), is here. **Epagne** (K136) has a jewel of a small *château* and soon afterwards we arrive in **Abbeville** (K141), now an industrial town with dejected outskirts but with considerable charm at its centre. From the 13th–15th centuries it was possessed in turn by the English, Burgundians and the French, but it was not to become a true part of France until the marriage in 1514 of Louis XII to Mary of England. He was 53 and she just 16. It appears that the strain was too much for Louis, for he died the following year of 'consumption'. The British army established a headquarters in the town in World War I and it was very severely damaged in 1940, more than 2,000 houses being bombed with the loss of hundreds of civilians. Waterway banks are well landscaped with moorings amid greenery close to shops and restaurants. Doubtless it is possible to eat well ashore, but I have to admit I once suffered a memorably poor meal is a restaurant that was suspiciously empty, the only customers – as later became evident – being tourists like myself. Abbeville's greatest treasure is not a cathedral or a *château* but the railway station, a wonderful symphony of pink brick and elaborate barge-boarding, dating, astonishingly, only from 1912. It is often called the *Gare des Anglais*, having been much used for British troop movements in the Great War. Note the monument next to a nearby bridge, to a 19-year-old youth who suffered severe torture for failing to salute a procession in 1766! Construction of the great Flamboyant Gothic church of St-Vulfran started in 1488 and was not completed for almost two centuries. Repairing the widespread damage it suffered in 1940 has been a ceaseless activity ever since. As the town is partly built on an island, water-courses are an essential feature. The navigation follows the left channel, terminating at the sloping sided Écluse 24 (K141.7).

After many outstandingly pretty reaches the remainder of the Somme is disappointing, running quite straight and level to the coast. This section, known as the Canal Maritime d'Abbeville à St-Valéry was created about 1835, so avoiding the former hazardous connection with the coast at le Crotoy. Should you decide to moor on this length, remember that the water level may change by as much as 1m. There are several swing/lift bridges, that at **Petit-Port** (K148.2) being alongside a bar/grocer. While these final 15km are lacking in scenic attraction, even if you are not planning to go to sea, it is well worth while pressing on to the ancient little seaport of **St-Valéry-sur-Somme** (K156.5).

Reliable moorings, unfortunately quite a distance from the town centre, are on a pontoon, left bank, before the first of two sluice gates, Écluse Maritime, 25. This and the further gate can either be regarded as a lock chamber several hundred metres long, in which it is not necessary to tie up, or more accurately, a form of that rare structure, the 'staunch', 'flash lock' or *pertuis*. The time taken to make a level, so allowing a boat to leave this section, depends on the state of the tide on the seaward side. The lower gate is normally only worked from 1h before to 1h after high water. There are extensive moorings in the town centre tideway, occupied by sea-going pleasure craft and fishing boats. Although the narrow channel leading out of town and over the ever-shifting sand banks of the Baie de la Somme is buoyed, the tide flows fiercely and appears to drag buoys from their intended positions.

Coming in from the sea, I was once rather ahead of time and rather than wait another half an hour for the tide to make, set off for St-Valéry, travelling faster over the shallows than I might have wished. (In order to maintain steerage, we were moving at a recorded speed of 12 knots, a little rapid when you are gingerly feeling your way up an unknown shallow channel!) My advice is therefore to negotiate the Bay as near to high water as possible, when conditions are likely to be calmest. At low water the channel dries out completely. Slipway, 6-tonne crane and other services are available, with a chandlery by the bascule bridge. Coasters used to navigate the Somme upstream to Abbeville and many picturesque fishing vessels are still to be seen at St-Valéry.

William the Conqueror sailed from here to England in 1066, and Joan of Arc passed through in 1430 before her brief imprisonment at the hands of the English in nearby **Le Crotoy**. St-Valéry is divided into the *Ville Basse*, along the sea front, and the *Ville Haute*, overlooking the coast with remnants of fortifications.

There are steep and winding streets with numerous small hotels. Shellfish and fish are leading local industries. Some restaurants serve *moules* (mussels) prepared in dozens of different ways. Tourism is well established, for there are excellent sandy beaches and dunes all along the coast (the sea retreats a great distance at low tide in the Bay itself). Splendid summertime excursions can be made aboard a little railway serving locations around the bay including **Cayeux-sur-Mer**, St-Valéry, **Noyelles** and Le Crotoy. Opened in 1887, it operates on Sundays. and public holidays, April–September and every day except Mondays in peak season. Steam and diesel locomotives are used over track totalling 27km. Passage of trains over the lock bridge in St-Valéry is accompanied by much hooting, ringing of bells and waving flags as the jolly little outfit momentarily joins road traffic. Some 2,000 hectares of marshes in the NE part of the Bay are a nature reserve where over 300 varieties of migratory birds have been sighted.

10 — Canal de St-Quentin

Carte Guide: *Picardie*
From the River Escaut (Scheldt) at Cambrai to a junction with the Canal latéral à l'Oise at Chauny, 92.5km with 35 duplicated locks. There are tunnels at Bony (5,670m) and Lesdins (1,300m). Branches connect the main line with a short length of navigable River Oise at Chauny, 270m with 1 lock; and from Point Y, near Tergnier with the Canal de la Sambre à l'Oise at La Fère, 3.8km, 0 locks. Additionally, there is a link with the Canal de la Somme near St-Simon.

This is a cracking canal, old and small enough to have masses of historical and engineering details to fascinate every ardent waterways enthusiast. Until opening of the Canal du Nord in 1965, the St-Quentin provided the sole connection between the Channel ports and the River Escaut with Paris and the rest of the French network. Barge traffic has declined very considerably in the last 20–30 years considering that not so long ago this was easily the busiest artificial navigation in the country. Nevertheless, freight craft remain quite active. Rising to a 20.4km summit level, it is provided with duplicated and mechanised locks throughout. One notable feature is a series of iron and glass lock control cabins.

In spite of a widespread belief that this corner of Northern France is both flat and scenically dull, the Canal de St-Quentin is often most attractive, passing through vast plains of rolling cornfields with leafy cuttings along the summit pound. Bankside facilities are generally good. The whole of the summit and its two tunnels are worked on a one-way system. You are advised to seek local information on passage times, which tend to be subject to change.

Brief history The canal is composed of two parts: the King's ministers Colbert and Mazarin had both proposed linking the Rivers Oise and Somme in the 17th century and the resulting Canal Crozat, or Canal de Picardie, was opened between Chauny and St-Simon in 1738. Construction of the remainder, connecting the Seine Basin with the Escaut, was an extended process, having first been designed by an engineer named Devicq in 1727: he died in combat near Prague in 1742. A revised plan was introduced by Laurent de Lyonne, Director-General of Canal Works, and begun in 1768 with the object of passing 1,500 boats a year. There were many objections to the great cost, especially that of boring a single brick-lined tunnel 14km in length at Bony. Building ground to a halt in 1774, pending discovery of a line that would avoid the expensive tunnel. But the urgency of opening up a route to the coast was becoming ever more vital, for the Somme Bay was progressively silting up at St-Valéry. Therefore, in 1781 M de la Fitte de Clavé was charged to dig a navigation from the Oise at Landrecies to the Escaut: this route would have been considerably shorter. Nothing came of this alternative. Wars with England intervened and after endless arguments in favour of different approaches to the problem, Napoléon himself insisted in 1801 that work should begin once more, using the design produced by Devicq 74 years earlier. Greatest effort was devoted to the two tunnels and their approach cuttings. In the longer one at Bony, shafts were cut at 100m intervals and up to 83m deep; after the canal had been in service for a few years only 12 of these remained open to the sky, the others having been sealed up. Osiers were planted to stabilise the cutting sides which reached 35m in height. Generous underground water supplies were tapped in the workings. The Emperor's demand that building should proceed without delay was obviously heeded, for he was able to officiate at the opening of the navigation in April 1810.

The canal was an immediate success, with traffic levels building up to the extent that there was later a need to duplicate locks, deepen the channel, enlarge each tunnel and enhance the water supplies. Improvements in the 20th century involved electric barge traction on rails, installed during World War I, mechanising locks and lighting the most heavily used sections. The latest development is automatic radar operation of the majority of the locks. By 1878 the

waterway had reached saturation point, with up to 110 barges crossing the summit daily. It was therefore decided to duplicate the route by constructing the Canal du Nord, which was not finally completed until 1965 (see Chapter 8). Even though coal traffic from Belgium had started to decline in the early 1950s, the Canal de St-Quentin still had more freight than any other man-made waterway in France, with 8 million tonnes being carried in 1964 alone. In order of importance, these goods comprised construction materials, petroleum products, agricultural produce, minerals and chemicals. In the long term, there is a possibility that the canal may be duplicated yet again by a new 3,000-tonne capacity Seine-Nord Canal. Meanwhile, for pleasure boaters, it offers a more interesting and agreeable route than the Canal du Nord.

Navigation passes from the River Escaut to the canal with no change in levels at **Cambrai** (see Chapter 1). The city is soon left astern. Although the countryside is well populated, it is unexpectedly pleasant. Locks tell of punishingly hard use, with battered timber piers guiding craft into one or other of the duplicated chambers. Locks are moderately frequent on the steep climb to the canal's watershed, beginning with Écluse 1, **Proville** (K2.2), soon to be followed by Écluse 2, Cantigneul (K3.8); Écluse 3, **Novelles** (K4.4); Écluse 4, Talma (K7.3); and Écluse 5, **Marcoing** (K7.8). Shopping and other facilities are not difficult to find, especially in Marcoing. Fierce battles raged throughout the district during the Battle of Cambrai in November 1917, with almost 11,000 German prisoners and 140 large guns being taken by British divisions. But it was not until September of the following year that the Allies gained full control of the area. Beyond Écluse 6, Bracheux (K9.4), a bridge in **Masnièrs** (K10.7) replaces one which collapsed under the weight of a British tank late in 1917 after it had been damaged by German mines. More shopping can be attended to here, or, after Écluse 8, St-Waast (K12.7), in **Crèvcœur-sur-l'Escaut** (K14, Écluse 9). There are further small shops near Écluses 10 and 11.

East of the bridge at Écluse 12 (K17.8, café) lies the 12th century Cistercian Abbaye de Notre-Dame de Vaucelles. Its foundation stone was laid by St Bernard. Magnificent buildings were encircled by 7km of walls. Guided tours are available on the last Sunday of the month, April–October. Between Écluses 12 and 13, an island creates a one-way section at the Pont des Grenouillères; southbound boats should take the right-hand channel. The route is regularly punctuated by locks: Écluse 13, **Bantouzelle** (K20); Écluse 14, **Banteux** (K20.5) and Écluse 15, **Honnecourt** (K23.2) with food shops in each village. Écluses 16, Moulin-Lafosse

A glass-sided lock keeper's cabin at Écluse de St Waast on the Canal de St-Quentin.

(K24.2) and 17, Bosquet (K24.7) complete the ascent to the summit level and the waterway heads into hills, away from the Escaut valley. There is a large basin in **Vendhuille** (K26.6) reserved for cereal barges. All craft must stop before the bridge to await instructions for the tunnel tow. Under no circumstances are craft allowed into the great **Bony** Tunnel until permitted by canal officials. An ever-deepening cutting leads to the northern portal. This point is easily reached by car-bound waterway enthusiasts from a small road running east out of **Le Catelet**.

This is (as far as I am aware) the world's longest operational canal tunnel and one of the very few remaining in France where towage was compulsory until 2004. The story is told that when this mammoth section of underground canal was ready to receive its first barge, all the local boatmen were fearful to enter the vault until it had been proved completely safe. It was therefore decided to grant freedom from tolls in perpetuity to the first vessel to make the passage. It is easy to imagine bargees falling over each other in the rush to gain such a privilege. The winning *péniche*, built of course in timber, is said to have remained in service well in excess of a century, the hull having been completely replaced several times in her extraordinarily long life.

Between 1810 and 1863, gangs of eight men hauled *péniches* through the darkness from the towpath – an operation taking between 12 and 14 hours at an average speed of about 450m per hour! Such slave labour came to an end when a most unusual vessel called *Le* *Rougaillou* was substituted in 1863. (A model can be seen in the Waterways Museum at Conflans-Ste-Honorine.) It comprised a rectangular hull on which an amidships roundabout was propelled by eight horses each standing in its own stall. The circular movement drove gears connected to a submerged chain. After 11 years of use, *Le Rougaillou* and its pit-pony style drive was replaced by a steam-powered chain tug. As might have been expected, this brought about problems with fumes produced by the engine's fire. Finally, electric tugs were introduced. The one that continued in service until recently is a strange and antiquated beast that must already have celebrated its centenary. Two runs in each direction were made each working day. The tow or *rame* was made up, placing laden freight barges at the front, followed by unladen ones. Any pleasure craft came at the back. The procedure was extremely slow, depending on the number of working boats in line: the record is said to have been 74! Everyone was expected to remember the order in which they arrived and so regroup themselves for passage of the locks at the end of the summit level.

Any wait for your turn through the tunnel can agreeably be used by a visit to the canal museum established in the late 1990s aboard one of the vintage tunnel tugs. As this edition was being prepared, it was announced that all tug tows were to be withdrawn during 2004, after which all passages through both tunnels will be self-propelled.

William Moens had a nocturnal adventure while waiting at the southern portal (*Through France and Belgium by River and Canal in the Steam Yacht 'Ytene'*, 1876); at this time, the tug was steam powered and he resolved to jump the queue to avoid its fumes and the smoke of thirty cabin stoves on the barges waiting to pass. 'Suddenly, at about nine o'clock, we heard a great outcry in the tunnel, and men came running along the towing path, asking if we had a pump. We said yes, several, but not moveable; and they explained that one of the barges had struck violently against a stone in the side of the tunnel and had been stove in, and there was great fear lest she should sink in the tunnel itself with the 270 tons of coal with which she was laden. This was a pretty state of things, and we soon thought that our route to Belgium would be barred for weeks and that we might have to retrace our way back again. The tug steamer soon, however, emerged from the arch, and came to a standstill when three or four barges were out of the tunnel. It was the first that was injured, and she was already sunk to within three or four inches of the gunwale.

'Long planks were soon put out to the shore and a crowd of excited Frenchmen assembled, each with a large galvanised iron pump borrowed from the barges behind us. They were all soon at work pumping, and I returned to the *Ytene* to fetch A.... [Mrs Anne Moens] to endeavour to comfort the poor women and children that had been landed with bundles of clothes, &c. as they were afraid that the barge might go down. It was a curious and exciting sight, all those collected together having large lanterns with them; loud and hurried orders being heard from those in charge; the poor women and children, with their cat, huddled together on the bank of the canal, crying and lamenting bitterly as the sinking barge, with all its furniture, was their home and property.

'I ordered my men to go on board and assist at the work, and at last, after great exertions, it was found that the vessel did not sink deeper in the canal, and after some time the pumps, increased in number, began to gain on the water, and the hole was discovered on her starboard bow. There had formerly been a towing path on each side of the tunnel; but it being found that the water space was not wide enough, that on the left hand was cut away, but leaving rough stones and projections; against one of which the unfortunate vessel had struck, being towed at too rapid a pace by the tug. Some planks and nails were obtained, and I contributed some cotton waste, and after some work the leak was stopped. We remained on the scene of action until the women returned to their vessel; their bedding, however, having got quite soaked with the water. After the danger had passed, to cheer themselves, they began to tell fearful stories of accidents on the canal, and of various friends of theirs having been drowned.'

During World War I both tunnels were used by the Germans as defences in the Hindenburg Line, with shafts dug to connect with other fortifications. Virtually impregnable, these underground vaults were fitted with electric lighting and served as stabling, hospitals and command centres. The southern entrance (K34.7) has been made into a tourist attraction with signboards and steps leading down from the N44 road between **Bellicourt** and **Riqueval**. A crumbling stone plaque records the tunnel's completion in 1810. 600m south down the road is a restaurant, with a *Bar du Souterrain* conveniently close. The canal continues south through Riqueval (K36) where a bridge over the cutting was the scene of one of the most remarkable photographs of the Great War. After **Bellenglise** (K38.2) and Le **Haucourt** (K41.1), the Lesdins (or Tronquoy) tunnel appears (K41.9). As it is quite straight and less than one quarter as long, its passage is tame compared with Bony!

Downhill locks start with Écluse 18, Lesdins (K45.2), with further changes in level at Écluse 19,

Pascal (K45.5); Écluse 20, **Omissy** (K46.7, shopping) and Écluse 21, Moulin Brûlé (K48.7). Entry to the city of **St-Quentin** is near Écluse 22 (K50.9) where short and long-term moorings and a wide range of boating services will be found in a large basin to the right (K52.8, about 600m to the town centre). Tales of the First World War destruction might suggest that the rebuilt St-Quentin is an unappealing town, but it has a surprisingly elegant main square surrounded by flourishing shops and restaurants. Notable buildings are the early 16th century Gothic *Hôtel de Ville* (37-bell carillon and magnificent Renaissance chimney piece); the massive basilica whose 9th century crypt is believed to contain the remains of Caius Quintinus, a young Christian nobleman who was martyred in the 4th century and gave his name to the town; and the *Musée Antoine Lécuyer*, mainly devoted to portraits of 18th century celebrities: many are by the celebrated 18th century local painter Maurice-Quentin de la Tour. St-Quentin lies on the (un-navigable) Somme which broadens into a pleasant lake with bathing *plage* near the railway station, but memories of war refuse to disappear. Montmorency's army was soundly beaten by Spanish troops in the Battle of St-Quentin (1557). Further hardships followed a defeat by the Germans in the Franco-Prussian troubles of 1870. And once more the town was in German hands from August 1914 until October 1, 1918: by the time it was retaken by the Allies much had been destroyed and the already ruined basilica was on the point of being blown up. Holes in the stonework show where the demolition charges were to be laid.

A level pound extends as far as Écluse 23, **Fontaine-lès-Clercs** (K58.3), with full shopping and garage beyond the River Somme in **Seraucourt-le-Grand** (K61.1), site of a British war cemetery. Past Écluse 24 (K62.7), **Artemps** (K64.4) offers grass bank moorings by the bridge near a bar and grocer. Now deep in real country, the canal is accompanied by the infant Somme through **Pont-Tugny** (K66.3, *café/tabac*) where a former lock is out of service: take the left channel. The old line is now used as a melancholy dump for disused barges. Shortly before **St-Simon** (see Chapter 9) a tiny island marks the start of the Canal de la Somme, which branches away on the right towards the coast.

Marshland and lakes characterise the waterway through pastoral surroundings with few signs of

British troops on the banks of the waterway at Riqueval, during World War I. Rebuilt, the bridge is recognisable today. Photograph courtesy Imperial War Museum, London.

habitation to **Jussy** (K74.1, most services) with little of note apart from Écluses 26, Jussy (K77); 27 **Mennessis** (K79.6, shopping) and 28, Voyaux (K80.2). **Ternier** (K84.2) and its smaller neighbour **Fargniers** are scruffy iron working centres, the former being a kind of Crewe Junction for the railway network of this part of France. As your boat negotiates Écluses 29–31, Fargniers, there will be opportunities for some of the ship's complement to buy galley supplies, but it is decidedly not an area for unnecessary lingering! At prosaically named **Point Y**, after Écluse 31, you can turn left along the La Fère branch and reach the Canal de la Sambre à l'Oise near **La Fère** (see Chapter 11). This involves 3.8km of level boating. If, on the other hand you are bound for the Oise and the Seine or wish to travel eastwards to the Canal des Ardennes, it is preferable to remain on the main line of the Canal de St-Quentin and work through Écluses 32, Ternier (K85.8); Viry (K88.4); 34, **Senicourt** (K90.8) and 35, **Chauny** (K92.3). Here is the short Chauny branch with a single lock, once providing a link with the Oise; it is no longer in use. Soon after, is the junction with the Canal latéral à l'Oise. For facilities in Chauny, see Chapter 17.

11 ~ Canal de la Sambre à l'Oise

Carte Guide: *Picardie*
From a junction with the La Fère branch of the Canal de St-Quentin at La Fère to a junction with the River Sambre in Landrecies, 67.2km with 38 locks.

Providing a route to Belgium which is continued via the River Sambre, the canal climbs to a summit level and leaves the Oise valley to cross a chalk divide near Oisy before dropping down the valley of the Sambre. This is a country of brick buildings, gravel pits, sometimes scruffy towns and pleasant reaches of water meadows. Some, but not all of the locks are mechanised or arranged in automatic groups. Robert Louis Stevenson canoed this way through flood and rainstorm (*An Inland Voyage*, 1878) but recorded few impressions of the waterway itself: he was more interested in his overnight quarters at small inns, where he and his companion Sir Walter Grindlay Simpson, Bart, were not infrequently taken for pedlars of the roughest kind.

Brief history Proposed in 1749 by an Irishman named Shée (Shea?), who saw the route as being useful for transport of arms from Landrecies, the canal was built as a private enterprise by the *Compagnie du Canal de la*

Sambre à l'Oise. It opened in 1839 and unusually was only taken over by the State as recently as 1949. As it connected the Belgian coal fields in the Mons/Charleroi area with the Seine Basin, coal was a major freight. In the final years of the 19th century mechanical bank traction began to replace horse haulage in the north of France and tractors running on inflated tyres (not rails) provided a service throughout the Sambre à l'Oise until unpowered craft were totally phased out in the late 1960s.

La Fère, where the canal leaves a branch of the Canal de St-Quentin (see Chapter 10), provides useful shopping facilities. It has long been a place of strategic importance, guarding the Oise valley and the approaches to the Ile de France from the fortress *château*, erected in the 15th and 16th centuries. The town fell to the Prussians after a hard-fought battle in 1870 and during World War I was on the Hindenburg Line. Attractions include the *Musée Jeanne d'Aboville*, noted for paintings and archaeology. After passing through Écluse 35, **Travecy** (K2.2), best approach to the town on the left bank, we arrive at a manned swing bridge (K3.5). Then comes Écluse 34, **Vendeuil** (K4.8), with an aqueduct over the River Oise. Vendeuil lies 1.7km west of the next bridge. Among its attractions are a small zoo in the ruins of an 1875 fort and a pleasant water park with swimming and sailing, established close to the canal in former gravel workings. Until this point, surroundings have been slightly industrial: we now enter more agreeable open country.

Midway between Écluses 33, **Brissy** (K8.8) and 32, **Hamégicourt** (K10.3), a bridge leads into **Brissy-Hamégicourt**, a small town surrounded by gravel pits with a range of shops and a church with a curious 'hooded' spire. **Berthenicourt** near Écluse 31 (K12.7) is pleasantly situated by the river. Alongside Écluse 30, **Mézières-sur-Oise** (K14.2), is a restaurant with adequate shops not far away. **Châtillon-sur-Oise** lies west of Écluse 29 (K15.7) with another aqueduct in the pound above. Clues as to one of the canal's freight traffics are given by a large grain silo near Écluse 28, **Sissay** (K17.6), where the charming ruined church was replaced by one with a concrete spire in the 1930s.

While involving a walk of 2km from Écluse 27 (K29.2), **Ribemont** is a sizeable town with a good selection of shops; it was the birthplace of 18th century mathematician and revolutionary Marquis de Condorcet. Much of a hillside has been excavated for cement at **Origny-Ste-Benoite** (K23.3). Here will be found a café by the bridge, overlooking an extensive barge basin. Shops, restaurants and garage are all easily accessible. West of the waterway at Écluse 24 (K26.3) is the

Freight barges at Origny-Ste-Benoite.

charming brick-built village of **Bernot**, a very rural settlement with limited shops. Elsewhere, however, locks are inclined to have a dejected appearance with poorly cultivated gardens. Those shops or cafés that once existed in places like **Hauteville**, Écluse 23 (K28.6), have long been closed down. Nor are there any facilities in **Noyales**, an otherwise superb backwater town of brick houses SW of Écluse 21 (K32.1). Note the

cast iron water pumps in the streets. Another pleasant village is **Vadencourt**, NW of Écluse 19 (K35.6), where groups of poplars line the banks of the flood-prone Oise. Don't miss the fine *château*/farm. There is a fascinating Carpentry Museum. Several houses display exceptionally fine decorative stonework and the 12th century church has an unusually crooked slate spire and intricate carved column heads. There is basic shopping. A swing bridge is followed by Écluse 18, **Grand-Verly** (K37.2). In the next 11km 18 locks indicate the extent to which the canal is climbing to its summit level. We pass through the centre of **Tupigny** (K39.9), perhaps the most pleasant small town on this route, with some shops; a pair of swing bridges enhance excitingly varied architecture, complemented by tubs of flowers. The scenery starts to improve dramatically in hilly country at **Hannappes**, Écluse 12 (K42.2, swing bridge). The Oise has now been left behind and from time to time the Sambre is incorporated into the navigation. Notable features include water mills, 'lumpy' countryside and lock-side flower beds created in old wooden work punts.

Three locks at **Vénérolles** (K43.4) lead to the moderate sized town of **Étreux** (K45.5) at the confluence of the River Noirrieu. Shops and most other facilities are excellent, with a good value restaurant near the *Hôtel de Ville*. A concrete bridge replaces the former swing span. Further basic shops exist in the summit level village of **Oisy** (K51.2) with another brief encounter with the Sambre. Our descent towards Belgium starts at Écluse 1, Bois l'Abbaye (K55.2). Here there is a café/bar and a memorial to British troops of the Sussex Regiment who died while storming the lock in 1918. Quite soon the canal arrives close to the middle of **Catillon-sur-Sambre** (K58.6) whose vast church square is within a short distance of the lift bridge (extensive shopping). **Ors**, by Écluse 2 (K61.5), has little to offer. The canal merges with the canalised Sambre beyond Écluse 3 (K66.9) in the busy market town of **Landrecies**. While visiting the flourishing Saturday morning market, I got into conversation with the lady owner of a large hardware shop and she told me that she owned a most unusual 19th century book describing an Englishman's travels on the waterways of France. Intrigued at the prospect of a hitherto 'unknown' work, I accompanied her to her place of business where she produced with triumph a translation of Robert Louis Stevenson's *An Inland Voyage*. This discovery was almost as disappointing as the canal content of the book itself. Stevenson did not care for Landrecies: in addition to 'simply bedlamite' weather, he found 'it consists almost entirely of fortifications. Within the ramparts, a few blocks of houses, a long row of barracks, and a church, figure, with what countenance they may, as the town. There seems to be no trade; and a shopkeeper from whom I bought a sixpenny flint-and-steel was so much affected that he filled my pockets with spare flints into the bargain.' Exactly a century before, de la Lande, author of the French waterways classic, had commented that the garrison town of Landrecies 'is poor, peopled by retired soldiers, without trade, without manufacture and without commerce'. Matters have since improved.

12 ～ River Sambre

Carte Guide: *Picardie*
From a junction with the Canal de la Sambre à l'Oise at Landrecies to the Belgian border beyond Jeumont. 54.3km with 9 locks. (Navigation continues through Belgium to Charleroi and the Meuse at Namur.)

The Sambre rises near Le Nouvion-en-Thiérache and runs for about 193km before reaching the Meuse. The navigation is often accompanied by some quite delightful country, especially in its upper reaches. Although sometimes suffering from urban development between Maubeuge and the Belgian frontier, where it is still only a moderate-sized river, there is usually something of interest. Several years ago, I navigated upstream when the Sambre was in flood; not only did we have to take care in the vicinity of weirs but we also had to contend with several freight barges descending *backwards*, as they had insufficient headroom to pass under a bridge and the navigation was too narrow for them to turn.

Brief history The waterway was used for the *flottage* of logs from the latter part of the 17th century, and barges are recorded as using the Sambre in 1712 after the army had built a series of 33 locks on the Landrecies-Maubeuge length. These works were not well designed and half a century later the locks were considered to be too few in number to enable boats to carry an economic load. The present structures date from the 19th century. Traditionally, trade mainly served the metallurgical district around Maubeuge with coal from Belgium and return loads of French pit-props.

After **Landrecies** (see Chapter 11), the River Sambre flows past the SE borders of the Forêt de Mormal, soon to find itself in pleasant wooded pastures. Beyond Écluse 1, **Étoquies** (K3), with a lift bridge, we enter the hamlet of **Hachette**, where the *Café des Pecheurs* is a popular weekend resort for anglers by Écluse 2 (K7.7, water point). There's a restaurant beyond the level crossing at Écluse 3, **Sassegnies**, although the village itself, a cluster of appealing rusty-red brick buildings, is best approached from the flat steel bridge (K13).

Berlaimont, mainly hidden from the river by a belt of trees, has a full range of facilities and is easily reached from Écluse 4 (K17.8). Having taken in the waters of the River Sambrette, the stream then swings round two great curves. At the start of the first is **Pont-sur-Sambre** and Écluse 5 (K21.7). The bridge here is the lowest on the navigation, so be wary about air draft when levels are high. This is a most handsome small town, consisting of a long and wide main street where houses display a fascinating variety of architectural styles. At the centre is a tall brick tower, built on a square plan. Seeking overnight lodgings, Robert Louis Stevenson and his canoeing companion, Sir Walter Grindlay Simpson, Bart, were mistaken for pedlars in a Pont-sur-Sambre labourers' alehouse: this was intended as a compliment, judging from the superior class of fare put before them at the communal dining table! The town is now rather more updated and welcoming, with shops and garage to cater for most needs of travelling *plaisanciers*.

Écluse 6, Quartes (K26.2), marks the end of real countryside. Not long after, we reach **Hautmont** and Écluse 7 (K35.4), a positively industrial place where the utility of its shops is in no way matched by its beauty. Such dejected surroundings will reoccur during the remaining journey to Belgium, but to be fair they are interspersed with tracts of former industrialisation, now agreeably veiled by nature. It is perhaps necessary to regard **Maubeuge** (K41.5) in a more kindly light on learning that it was mostly destroyed during air raids in 1940. Much of what we now see is a symphony of 1950s and 1960s concrete in an already outdated 1930s cinema style of architecture. Steel works have replaced onetime

arms manufacture. For 12 days in July there is a beer festival (a concept rather more Belgian than French) with a folklore carnival and procession each Easter Monday. Roger Pilkington was trapped by flood water for a week in Maubeuge and was treated royally when news of his arrival spread through the district (*Small Boat to Luxembourg*, 1967). Earlier in the 20th century, Dr Pilkington's family had operated a French subsidiary of their St Helens-based glassworks in the town, and although long closed down it was remembered with affection by former employees. Fortifications were raised by Vauban and traces remain. Moor near Écluse 8 and a host of shops will be found within shouting distance. In common with other locks on the river, the lock here is situated very close to its weir: entry from below can be exciting when there is a strong flow.

All the adjuncts of industrialised civilisation are present through **Assevent** (K45.3) and **Boussois** (K47.7). Although this is not notably suitable boating country, a number of cruisers will be seen at a *club nautique* upstream of Écluse 9, **Marpent** (K51.8). The frontier town of **Jeumont** (K53.3) offers a convenient quayside mooring with bollards (by a multi-coloured apartment block) and well placed for the shopping centre. The Franco-Belgian border lies a little downstream of the main road bridge.

II · SEINE AND CHAMPAGNE

13 ~ River Seine

Carte Guides: *Seine, Paris-Marcilly; Seine, Paris-Le Havre*
From Marcilly-sur-Seine to the English Channel at Le Havre. 535km with 25 locks. There are two additional locks on the 25km Canal du Havre à Tancarville, which duplicates the lowest portion of the tideway. Travelling downstream, the following junctions are made: with the River Yonne at Montereau; the Canal du Loing at St-Mammès; the River Marne in Paris (Alfortville); the Canal St-Martin (leading to the Canal St-Denis and the Canal de l'Ourcq) in Paris near the Pont d'Austerlitz; the Canal St-Denis at St-Denis (29km below Paris, Ile de la Cité); and the River Oise at Conflans-Ste-Honorine. Between 1851 and 1957, when it was abandoned, navigation was once continued further upstream via a lateral canal between Marcilly and Troyes. (Canal de la Haute-Seine, 44km with 15 locks.)

Not only is the Seine the longest inland navigation in France but it carries easily more commercial freight than any other waterway. A glance at the map immediately reveals the reason for its Latin name *Sequana* – the snake. An obvious and convenient entry to the canal and river network from the English Channel, all long-distance cruises through France are likely to include part of the Seine, while a journey from one end to the other is a fascinating experience.

Personal research suggests that the river can be safely navigated by very small craft between Marcilly and the upstream side of Paris. Below this point, exceptionally busy commercial traffic makes the use of low-powered pleasure boats unwise and many hire boat companies would be unlikely to sanction a passage. Few problems, however, should be encountered by experienced owners of private craft. Numerous regulations apply to the use of pleasure boats and these together with a wealth of other practical information are contained in the *Carte Guides*. They are quite indispensable.

Except on the uppermost reaches where commercial traffic is much reduced, lock keepers aim to pass pleasure craft through in company with other vessels and are entitled to keep them waiting for up to 20 minutes; if no other craft have arrived within that time, you will be worked through alone. For seasonal changes in lock opening times, closures for public holidays and out-of-hours passage through locks (on payment of a substantial fee), consult the *Carte Guides*.

The entire river has excellent navigation markers, although there is sometimes a lack of kilometre posts. Distances are calculated from Marcilly to Ile de la Cité, Paris (K0–K170). They start again from Paris to Le Havre (K0–K365). Night navigation is forbidden for all pleasure craft in the tidal reaches below Rouen. With an adequately powered vessel about four days should be allowed for the passage Paris to Le Havre and three days for Marcilly to Paris: these are, of course, minimum times and the attractions of the Seine are such that many weeks could enjoyably be spent in a thorough exploration. Almost throughout the whole waterway, smaller cruisers may find the wash produced by commercial traffic and passenger boats rather uncomfortable when moored at night. I have known otherwise good sailors to be overcome by seasickness within 15 minutes of lying on the river in Paris. In my view, the only central Paris berth worth consideration is the excellent Bassin de l'Arsenal marina (lowest pound of the Canal St-Martin, near the Place de la Bastille). In certain locations, it is possible to seek protection offered by an island (where commercial vessels take the alternative route), the approach channel of a former lock, or (best of all) off the river altogether in one of the numerous connected gravel workings. This last solution is naturally subject to avoiding pits still being used by barges or where entry is prohibited by notice boards.

Rising in Burgundy, 776km from the sea, the Seine becomes navigable in Champagne and flows through the Ile de France and Normandy before eventually reaching the coast. Often, the surroundings are pleasant rather than spectacular and the appeal of a voyage is derived largely from a wealth of historical towns on the banks, the movement of other boats and the leisure activities of the many people who relax by the side of this great waterway. The finest scenery is found in the 28km between Les Andelys and the Amfreville Locks, where tall chalk cliffs restrict the width of the valley. In this book it is possible to mention only a selection of the attractions. Probably the most useful additional volumes are the Green Michelin Guides *Northern France and the Paris Region*, *Paris* and *Normandy*.

Many would claim that there is no city in Europe to match the beauty of Paris and the highlight of any

Seine cruise must be to arrive by water and moor for as long as you wish, within walking distance of the leading sights. Two decades ago, this was an uncomfortable prospect on account of the almost ceaseless wash from passing traffic. But since 1983 calm berths have been available for visitors in the *Port de Plaisance* de Paris-Arsenal on the Canal St-Martin. This much needed facility is very popular and although not cheap does represent good value compared with the cost of hotels not to mention the lack of security if you were to chance city centre quays on the Seine itself. Advance booking for short stays in the Arsenal Marina is not possible. I have always been assured that space will be found for all applicants on arrival.

Those who come to Paris without a boat have ample opportunity for getting afloat by *bateau-mouche*. One of the most pleasant ways of passing a summer evening is to take a dinner cruise, where exceedingly powerful ship-mounted floodlights illuminate the bankside buildings in defiance of all regulations relating to navigation lights.

The Seine means many different things to different people: river of history, commercial lifeblood of the capital, inspiration to great artists from Turner to Monet and the French Impressionists. But, downstream of Paris it is emphatically not a suitable training ground for the novice boatman.

Brief history Rouen is the fourth largest port in France, handling around 20 million tonnes of freight every year; Paris is the fifth, with about 15 million tonnes. How this has been achieved on a river that was often reduced to 0.23m depth well downstream of the capital as recently as the first half of the 19th century, is a fascinating tale of French tenacity.

About 4,500 years ago, in the Bronze Age, the Seine was used for transport in tiny boats. Rather later, in Gallo-Roman times, it became a somewhat primitive artery of commerce. When the Vikings arrived from northern waters in their longships (*drakkars*) propelled by sail and oar, they found rich pickings as they plundered the abbeys and monasteries which lined the banks. Peace with the invaders was negotiated in the year 911, when Charles the Simple granted Normandy and his daughter in marriage to the Viking King Rollo. This proved to have a decidedly stabilising effect on the Viking, who energetically started Seine training works by building dykes, dredging the channel and draining marshland. Over the centuries that followed, traffic increased as Paris grew in size and importance: firewood was floated down the Yonne from the Morvan to heat the city's houses. Grain arrived from Brie and wine from Burgundy. Passengers made long and sometimes

dangerous journeys by *coche-d'eau*, hauled by men or horses or powered by sail. Freight movement was encouraged by the construction of early canals like the 17th century Briare, linking the Loire valley with that of the Seine. But transport on the river remained a hazardous undertaking and the boats were of very small capacity.

As recently as the 1830s substantial sections of the route downstream of Paris were reduced to a depth of 0.80m for a third of the year. The only lock above Paris, at Nogent, had been built in 1677. Not infrequently between 40 and 60 horses were needed to haul a single barge up a shallow reach. Sailing vessels often required four days to reach Rouen from the sea. Paddle steamers had been successful from their introduction on the Seine in 1825, both on freight hauls and with passengers, but urgent action was need to improve the channel. In 1827 a scheme was suggested that would have largely transferred boats from the Seine to a lateral canal running much of the way between Paris and the coast: its then cost was put at about £6 million, and before work could begin work was shelved in favour of the newly arriving railways.

The Upper Seine was canalised between 1848 and 1899, with 13 locks and five diversions in the Montereau–Marcilly section. A further 44km of totally artificial canal with 15 locks continued navigation up the valley to Troyes: this Canal de la Haute-Seine operated from 1851 until its abandonment in 1957. Today its lock chambers, keeper's cottages and several aqueducts (including the oldest iron aqueduct in France) remain substantially intact. There have been restoration proposals, for the canal could enjoy a bright future for pleasure cruising: it is likely that reopening will take place perhaps in the next one or two decades.

Nine locks were installed on the Middle Seine between Montereau and Argenteuil from 1860 onwards, with improvements in 1912 and again in the 1920s and 1930s. More locks were to be built on the lower reaches, with eight in service between Paris and Rouen by the 1870s, by which time a depth of almost 2m could be relied on for much of the year. The breakthrough which brought sophisticated control to water levels was the invention of a new form of adjustable weir sluice. 1850 saw completion of steam haulage by submerged chain all the way from Le Havre to Montereau. In 1887, the 25km Canal de Tancarville enabled smaller vessels to avoid the most difficult part of the estuary down to Le Havre.

The very serious Seine floods of 1910 prompted more improvements and, although all traffic was halted for a period in World War II, improvement work has continued apace following the restoration of boat movements in 1944. Apart from a few of the uppermost locks, chambers have been mechanised and enlarged to accommodate 3,000 tonne push-tows, new ports have opened or are scheduled; work continues to avoid winding lengths of the river by creating new artificial cuts. The Seine can look with confidence to the future as one of Europe's busiest inland navigations.

Some sources of famous rivers are frankly disappointing: but thanks to the City of Paris which purchased the site in the 19th century, the Seine's origins are suitably grand. In a copse of pines off the N71 and 34km NW of Dijon, a reclining statue of the goddess Sequana has resided in a grotto since 1865. The waters are variously claimed to possess healing or aphrodisiac properties. Numerous Gallo-Roman votive offerings and a magnificent bronze image of Sequana riding in a duck-shaped boat have been discovered here and may be seen in the Dijon Archaeological Museum. Another priceless treasure is the Vase of Vix, a huge decorated bronze urn standing 1.64m high and found in a burial mound near **Châtillon** in 1953. Believed to date from the 6th century BC, it is on show in the local museum.

When Robert Gibbings explored the Seine (*Coming Down the Seine*, 1953) he launched his little rowing boat into floods at **Barberey**, on the outskirts of Troyes. Then, he could just as well have selected the safer but more prosaic **Canal de la Haute-Seine** which connected the city with the Seine at **Marcilly-sur-Seine** (K0). All of the canal has been closed since 1957 (the upper part lost its traffic in the mid-1930s) but as there are quite good restoration prospects it deserves a mention here. A campaigning body exists: *Association pour la Sauvegarde du Canal de Haute-Seine*. After Troyes, the main places served are **Villacerf**, **Méry** and **St-Just**. Craft dimensions were 34m x 5.20m with 1.50m draft and 3.57m air draft. Features include four notable aqueducts and a 2-rise lock at St-Just with guillotine gates. Today, Seine navigation commences where the river receives a tributary larger than itself – the Aube. Marcilly is a truly charming village on the right bank, providing most basic requirements including fuel. As if to emphasise that the Seine acts as a magnet for leisure seekers throughout its long course, there are already camping grounds and a sandy bathing beach. Extensive windings of the river are bypassed by sections of tree-lined canal, starting at Écluse 1, **Conflans** (K3.4), the first of several manually-worked locks whose gate and paddle gear requires considerable effort. Water points are installed at virtually all of the Seine locks. In these early sections there are long stretches of straight canal like that through **Crancey** (K8, limited shopping), **Pont-sur-Seine** (K11, most shops), **Marnay-sur-Seine**

(K14), Écluse 2. We re-join the river below Écluse 3, Bernières, where the chamber has inconveniently sloping sides.

Nogent-sur-Seine (K19.5) is the first sizeable town on the navigable waterway. This is a busy cereal port and final restrictions in the navigation were removed in 2002 to enable 1,000-tonne capacity barges to reach the town. Old half timbered houses contrast with the vast modern flour mills served by *péniches*. There is a rail link with Paris and Troyes: rarely is the Seine far from convenient stations, a useful factor when collecting crew or recovering a car at the end of a boating trip. Designed in a blend of Gothic and Renaissance styles, the 16th century church of St-Laurent is a fine structure in grey stone. An ivy-clad vault is all that remains of the convent of *Le Paraclet* where 12th century lovers Héloïse and Abélard were united in death. Peter Abélard was a brilliant 36-year-old poet and teacher hired by Canon Fulbert of Notre Dame as tutor for his 17-year-old niece Héloïse. Inevitably, they fell in love and secretly married. This action turned out to be ill-advised, for Uncle Fulbert was enraged. Sensing his folly, Abélard placed his wife in the safe-keeping of the Abbess of Argenteuil; but Fulbert was not satisfied and sent a band of men to castrate him. When Abélard died many years later, Héloïse, by then Abbess of Nogent, had his body brought to the town for burial. Twenty-two years afterwards she too died and when her husband's tomb was opened it is said that he rose to embrace Héloïse from whom he had been separated for much of a lifetime. Their remains were reinterred in the Père Lachaise Cemetery in Paris after the Revolution.

Winding reaches below Nogent through open country and poplar plantations are bypassed by a new cut leading directly into a long, wide and rather tedious canal beginning at guard lock **Beaulieu**, No 5 (K23.5). Peaceful moorings exist on both upper and lower sections of the original river, although there is no longer any through route. Écluse 6, **Melz** (K27.2), and 7, **Villiers-sur-Seine** (K31.9) intervene before we join the river again above **Le Port Montain** (K34.4). A slipway is used by owners of high speed ski-ing craft which will be encountered in the *bassin de vitesse*, downstream. It is an extraordinary feature of many French rivers (and of the Seine in particular) that speeds of up to 60kph are permitted in specified reaches! All other users from canoeists to oarsmen upwards are expected to fend for themselves. Food shops and restaurant will be found in **Noyen**, 1km SE of the bridge.

Shortly after Écluse 8, Vezoult (K37.1), comes **Grisy-sur-Seine** (K38, grocer), a village of grey houses with beach and launching ramp suitable for small cruisers. Timber summer houses are dotted about on both sides. Écluse 9, **Jaulnes** (K43), has a weir alongside with no prospect of easy access to the village opposite. In any event, most requirements will be found in **Bray-sur-Seine** (K46), with swimming pool and beach, a tree-shaded riverside walk and good public moorings just above the bridge. St Nicholas, patron saint of working boat people and often to be encountered on French waterways, is represented by a statue in the church. Half-timbered buildings with stucco walls are a foretaste of the Normandy farmhouses of the lower Seine. *Péniches* trade to the prominent flour mills. Navigation continues along the improved course of the original river, Écluses 10, 11 and 12 on the Bray-La Tombe Canal all being disused. We are now entering a region of gravel pits connected with the waterway: those that are no longer worked might provide tranquil moorings, but take care to avoid any with 'No Entry' signs.

From hereabouts, commercial traffic becomes increasingly brisk and the Seine is dedicated wholeheartedly to transport of freight. Écluse La Grand Bosse (K49.2) is one of the new breed of giant lock chambers, electrically worked by a keeper installed in an ultra modern control cabin. It dates from 1979. If working through alone, you will marvel at having your boat penned in such a vast space! Beyond, 8km of concrete-sided channel produces decidedly rough water in a strong wind. There are no possibilities of safe moorings unless you chance slipping into one of several gravel workings. Pusher tugs manoeuvre their sand barges almost without cease. Surroundings improve at the village of **La Tombe** (K57), where further grain silos appear above a bridge. Facilities include basic shopping, slipway and a marina in a former gravel pit on the right.

Another cut begins at K60, leading to **Marolles-sur-Seine** (K61.5), where all traffic uses the right-hand, mechanised chamber of lock 13. Old *péniches* and houseboats line the approaches to the smaller lock where temporary moorings might be found. This is an agreeable little town, providing fuel and shopping; typically good value is the inexpensive *Lion d'Or* restaurant. Expansive sand pits on the right are worth investigating as a potential quiet night's mooring. Ahead, in the distance, tower blocks announce the approach of the major town of **Montereau-faut-Yonne** (K68), entered after the high speed *TGV* railway bridge. To the left is a commercial port serving the city's *zone industrielle* and a little beyond it the remains of a former lock house and wall of the chamber itself. Yet another case of a tributary being more important than the river it joins is the Yonne entering from the left (see Chapter 45). Montereau is very much a barge town;

péniches line the quays, sometimes several abreast, making discovery of pleasure boat moorings a challenge. It is best to waste no time searching on the Seine: instead, turn into the Yonne where 50m of floating pontoons welcome visiting craft. Really rather drab and industrialised, Montereau does not live up to the promise of its historical associations. John the Good, Duke of Burgundy, met the Dauphin, the future Charles VII of France, on the Yonne bridge in 1419; they were to discuss an alliance against the English. But one of Charles' knights suddenly attacked the Duke, killing him in retaliation for the assassination of the Duke of Orléans twelve years earlier. Now, the Duke's son Philip the Fearless took Montereau and signed the Treaty of Troyes, disinheriting the Dauphin and establishing Henry V of England as King of France. Here, also, Napoléon I won practically his last victory over the Allies in February 1814. His bronze statue can be seen on a peninsula between the Seine and Yonne bridges, bearing his statement: 'The bullet that will kill me is yet to be made'. There are launching slips and fuelling facilities used by commercial and pleasure vessels. Facing the junction, on the right, the new town of **Surville** is a typical product of the 1960s, its tower blocks rising 25 storeys.

We have now left the Petite-Seine and will be following the Haute-Seine into Paris. Locks are renumbered from Écluse 1, **Varennes** (K71.5). Banks are mostly well-wooded past gravel workings and several dominant power stations issuing a tangle of pylon lines. Just upstream of one, moorings might be found on the right bank at the former Madelaine Lock (K76.5). **St-Mammès** (K81), at the junction of Canal du Loing, is a famous barge town where dozens of *péniches* can generally be found in the shade of pollarded limes. Moor either at the *Base Nautique* (left bank, K79.6, opposite the village of **La Celle**) or more centrally on the Loing near a disused lock. Otherwise, there is free mooring (limit 48 hours) at an *halte nautique* by the junction of the two rivers. Fuelling points and a selection of village shops are here joined by exciting establishments stocking working boat requirements – everything from tar to rope and powerful brass horns. Where suitable for pleasure craft, items bought in such places are usually much better value than when purchased through yacht chandlers. There is a quayside market on Sunday mornings. St-Mammès (the 's' is silent) is the best (and only convenient) point from which to visit the superb medieval town of **Moret-sur-Loing** and it is well worth boating almost 2km up the Loing to moor below the first lock: from here, Moret is an easy walk. Also while here, an excursion by public transport might be considered to the Palace and Gardens of Fontainebleau (12km), whose forest borders both Seine and Loing. The magnificent structure originated as a royal hunting lodge and was mainly designed under Louis XIV, XV and XVI. English guide books are readily obtained locally, although it would be difficult to better the Green Michelin Guide: *Northern France and the Paris Region*. Louis XV imported gondolas from Venice to convey his packs of hounds over the Seine when hunting: a charming, if eccentric, idea.

Champagne-sur-Seine (K83) is not particularly special, but if a shopping expedition is planned there is a public quay (nearby supermarket), waterside fuelling point and reasonably quiet moorings in the approach to a disused lock on the right bank. Écluse 2 is alongside: a modern device with an upper gate that sinks below water level to admit traffic. Situated on the edge of the Fontainebleau Forest, **Thomery** (K85.5) introduces a pleasingly wooded section of river. There is a quay, adequate shops and dessert grapes in springtime, thanks to the custom of cutting them nearly ripe from the vine in the autumn and placing them in carefully controlled *chambres des raisins* in vases of water where they preserve their freshness until the following April or May. By now sufficiently close to Paris for daily commuters or the convenient use of weekend residences, the Seine is lined with spectacular and fantastic creations in *fin de siècle* Gothic, each cast-iron decorated turret, pinnacle or lavish coursing of patterned brick attempting to outshine those of its neighbours. Trees and lawns exude affluence. Hire cruisers, day launches and rowing boats may be rented in **Valvins** (K89.5), for all the world as if this was Henley-on-Thames and not the busiest waterway in France with commercial traffic surging past almost ceaselessly! (Restaurant, mooring jetties, marina and slipway, left bank, above the bridge.) On the riverside at **Samois-sur-Seine** (K93) an elegant restaurant beckons: as often is the case, there are difficulties in mooring safely and a good site below a small island (keep to the right channel) at a former lock is said to be for short duration only. Shops of most kinds are here and in **Héricy** opposite (slipway). **Chartrettes** (K101) boasts a real *port de plaisance*, right bank above Écluse 3, La Cave. Shopping can be attended to in the very extended town, while a restaurant can be reached by crossing the weir and lock chambers into the village of **Bois-le-Roi**. 10km SW on the edge of the forest, **Barbizon** was a famous gathering place for artists and writers in the 19th century. Millet, Corot, Rousseau and many others are still remembered; some of their houses are open to the public.

More fantasy mansions are scattered over a long distance on the left bank until the approach of the city of **Melun** (K110). Riverbanks here are grassed and tree-covered or lined with a pleasing jumble of houseboats. One deep-water mooring is on the left bank, directly under a road bridge (K109.5). Like Paris, the city grew from beginnings on a river island. There is now some industry, but its origin as a market for the surrounding farmland is not forgotten. Melun eels are celebrated and so is the *Brie de Melun*, a famous soft white cheese, distinguishable by gourmets from the *bries* of Meaux, Coulommiers and Montereau. All commercial traffic takes the channel to the left of the island: pleasure cruisers should as a result discover quiet moorings with sufficient water depth in the right-hand stream. But do avoid setting up camp for the night on the upper part of the island itself: I once did this after a day of unremitting rain in an open boat. Just as I had completed erecting the tent and arranging my bedding within, a stern amplified voice from the trees above my head ordered me to remove myself without delay, adding that the police would be there within minutes if I failed to comply. In the gathering dusk I realised that the 'old fortifications' alongside were the perimeter walls of the city prison and that the disembodied voice belonged to an armed guard in a watchtower. Abandoning a brief attempt at gentle persuasion, I dismantled the soaking tent in fury, getting completely drenched in the process, and made for the noisier roadside bank opposite. That night I would have gladly exchanged my quarters for a centrally heated prison cell!

Once clear of Melun, the Seine again becomes quite countrified, although its villages are now mostly residential suburbs of Paris and much visited by city dwellers at weekends. This is so of **Boissettes** (K114), **Vosves** (K115) and the little town of **Boissise-la-Bertrand** (K116.3) opposite Écluse 4, Vives Eaux. A shop and restaurant are within easy reach if you moor on the right bank, immediately below the weir. Coming to the outskirts of **St-Fargeau-Ponthierry**, another excellent mooring is found at the old lock, left bank (K123). From here to Paris shore facilities become increasingly frequent, with shops, restaurants and fuelling points readily identified from the river or located in the *Carte Guide*.

Vertical stone quays in St-Fargeau (K125) may be used if not occupied by *péniches*. A modern and very select housing development has been created around disused gravel pits, each garden having a lake or river-

Commercial and pleasure craft share the Vives Eaux lock near Melun.

side frontage. Lock numbering is no longer consecutive, some weirs having been removed, so that the next is Écluse 7, **Coudray** (K129.5), with a boat club on the right bank, upstream. Ahead, tower blocks confirm the considerable expansion of Greater Paris in recent decades. Pleasure craft can expect a welcome at Port-Saintry (K131.2), with fuel, good overnight moorings and a convenient restaurant.

Onwards from here the sights and sounds of the metropolis crowd in on each bank: mills, factories, power stations, and increasing barge traffic combine to create a vibrant impression of urban life. Undeniably, deserted rural waterways are delightful, but being surrounded by ceaseless activity can make a pleasant change, especially when you feel slightly remote from it aboard your own boat. **Corbeil-Essonnes** (K134) is the grain store of Paris: moorings on a landing stage (left bank, K133.4). Slipway and further moorings will be found just upstream of the bridge at **Evry-Petit-Bourg** (K137.7), with duplicated Écluse 8, Evry (K138.9). Greenery on the right bank is the expanse of the Forest of Sénart, popular with Parisians for walks and picnics. Romantic School painter Ferdinand Victor Eugène Delacroix (1798–1863) lived on the edge of the forest at **Champrosay** (K141.5), as did writer Alphonse Daudet (1840–97), whose stories included the canal barge tale *La Belle-Nivernaise*. Among useful pleasure boat moorings are the *Port aux Cerises* at **Draveil** (K146) and the *Port Premier Paris Sud* (K148). Rather wasted countryside lingers on around **Vigneux-sur-Seine** (K148.5) but increasingly, gravel extraction and industry seem to be more profitable than raising cattle or growing wheat. After Écluse 9, **Ablon** (K150), a halt can be made at the nautical centre, left bank (slipway, fuel and shopping). **Orly Airport** lies to the NW: if you can tolerate the noise, the *port de plaisance* (K154.6) at **Villeneuve St-Georges** provides fuel, water, crane and restaurant. Alongside a water ski club is *La Guinguette* restaurant. As I was cruising past one evening, the chef beckoned from a window and within seconds was moving boats to create a mooring. Instantly, we decided to dine there and stay the night: food, company and atmosphere were excellent. Another opportunity for coming alongside is at the GDF Harbour (K158.6) in **Choisy-le-Roi**. Power stations and railway tracks lead to the last lock before Paris, Écluse 10, Port à l'Anglais (K161). Much of the city's household refuse is burned in a massive incinerator at **Ivry-sur-Seine** (K163), the heat produced being used for central heating, an admirable example of energy conservation.

The Seine is shortly joined on the right by the River Marne (K163.4, see Chapter 15) and soon thereafter a long vista opens through numerous bridges to the heart of **Paris**. Few of the Seine crossings lack interest. One of the most unusual is the Pont de Bercy (K167), a stone road bridge of 1863–4 onto which a *Métro* viaduct was grafted in 1909: the many rounded arches of this double height structure recall the Roman Pont-du-Gard aqueduct in Provence. A mobile fuelling barge is based upstream of the bridge, left bank. It is a rare surviving narrow beam *berrichon*, a steel-hulled motor boat from the Canal de Berry. Make sure that you are served with tax-paid diesel, not the cheaper variety which is for commercial craft and central heating only! Penalties for avoiding tax in this way are savage. My warning, in an earlier edition of this book, about this particular fueller, brought an angry response from one British reader who revealed that he and his pleasure boating friends had been obtaining illegal diesel here for years! Beyond the Pont d'Austerlitz, the only central city moorings which I can recommend lie inside the Canal St-Martin (Port de Paris l'Arsenal, see Chapter 16). Now in sight are the Ile St-Louis and the Ile de la Cité, the original nucleus of Paris. Here, the Cathedral of Notre Dame is so symbolic of the capital that one learns with surprise that it was reduced to ruins during the Revolution; its present state was not achieved until Viollet-le-Duc's restoration between 1844 and 1864, the window glass, lacy spire and gargoyles all dating from this time.

River traffic is routed on one-way systems past the islands and through the nearby bridges. To avoid confrontations with barges or tripping boats it is vital to follow the directions indicated in the *Carte Guide* and note the times when one-way traffic operates. Infringements are dealt with severely by the water police.

To arrive in the centre of Paris by boat is a great thrill – more so if the voyage has been a long one. The Seine is unquestionably the city's chief thoroughfare and many of the leading buildings and monuments lie alongside the 10km stretch between the Pont de Tolbiac (K166) and the Pont de Grenelle (K176/K6.6, distances being renumbered downstream of the Ile St-Louis, K0). There can be no better way of seeing Paris from the deck of your own boat, with a *bateau-mouche* as a fair substitute. The scene changes with the time of day and season of the year. Take an afternoon in high summer, and it can seem as if the whole population is afloat in water buses or relaxing on the quays. By night, the huge restaurant boats bearing banks of floodlights surge backwards and forwards. In winter, the bare branches of plane trees and the greyness of the buildings seen against a grey sky bring a feeling of melancholy: but spring is never far away and there is nothing quite like spring in Paris.

Paris is frequently the subject of a complete book: here, there is space only to hint at a selection of personal

A barge family on the River Seine in Paris. This delightful painting by Dupuy dates from 1904.

highlights likely to interest the waterway enthusiast. Once you have seen all you can from the water, arm yourself with a copy of the Michelin Green Guide *Paris* (in English), and start to explore on foot. Along the waterside quays, past groups of converted *péniches* and other houseboats – living afloat is widespread; over the bridges of which there are more than 30 in the central area alone; down the banks of the Canal St-Martin with its charming iron footbridges and locks (see Chapter 16); looking at antique, flower and animals markets; browsing in second-hand book shops or the open-air stalls of the *bouquinistes* by the river (especially near Notre Dame). Of all the many museums and galleries, it would be hard to better the superb *Musée d'Orsay* established in a wonderful *belle époque* railway station as a showcase for 19th century paintings, sculpture and decorative arts. For bird's eye views, visit the terrace outside the Sacré Cœur at Montmartre or ascend to the third level gallery of the Eiffel Tower, once the world's tallest structure. Incidentally, the *Jules Verne* restaurant on the second level provides not only spectacular views but also – unlike many restaurants in high places – serves equally exciting food.

Off-beat visits must include the Père-Lachaise Cemetery, NE of the river, containing the tombs of celebrities as diverse as Abélard and Héloïse, Edith Piaf, Oscar Wilde, Chopin, Proust and Molière. With a vast choice of eating places in the city, none I know of has a décor more amazing and splendid than the superb *fin de siècle* 'Le Train Bleu' at the Gare de Lyon. It is highly recommended if you enjoy good food in an astonishingly lavish interior and quite unlike what you might expect of dining at a railway station!

The river water is decidedly unfit for swimming. By way of compensation, the city authorities have in recent years created a mid-summer *plage* by temporary closure of Seine-side roads and the importation of sand and palm trees. The idea grew from the phenomenon where the Quai des Tuileries attracts sun-worshippers whose costumes can graphically be described in French as *le minimum*. Often, these attractive wearers of thongs are outnumbered by the throngs of *voyeurs* looking down from the street above. Paris has a justified reputation for vibrant night life and for sheer lavish spectacle it would be difficult to beat the magnificently dressed (or undressed?) Lido Cabaret in the *Champs-Elysées*: we took two eleven-year-olds who were totally accepted, even if the show does not conform to the Anglo-Saxon notion of 'family entertainment'. Advance booking for the dinner/dancing/show is recommended. The newly-found freedom of modern Paris is such that when dusk falls on the riverside quays, lovers are no longer content to merely hold hands.

In a city of surprises, it nevertheless comes as a shock to discover an English book shop (Shakespeare & Co) in an elegant building near Notre Dame where the proprietor introduced himself as the illegitimate grandson of the American poet Walt Whitman (1819–92). *Free* accommodation is offered to any *bona fide* author who presents himself – patronage of literature indeed!

No brief description of Paris would be complete without mentioning the splendid underground railway network – *Le Métro*. Bright, clean and efficient with trains that glide on rubber wheels, nowhere is more than 500m from a station. Be sure to pass through the Louvre where the platforms are adorned with reproductions from the vast collection of artworks above. On producing a passport, tourists may purchase special tickets, first class, for periods of 2, 4, or 7 days. Apply at larger stations.

Oldest of the Parisian bridges, perversely, is the Pont-Neuf (K1.2), crossing the tail of the Ile de la Cité; it was opened by Henry IV in 1607 and was then unique in that it carried no buildings. Probably the most elegant and elaborate is the Pont Alexandre III (K3.5), a flamboyant structure completed in 1900. It is impossible here not to recall the words of the romantic song 'Under the Bridges of Paris': ashore, most likely, you will now find piles of refuse and 'dossers', which is a pity. Everlasting gratitude must be expressed that a mid-1960s' scheme to replace the waterside quays by fast motor roads was largely discarded. The marshy fringes of the Seine were first embanked during the reign of Henri IV. Americans will note with delight a quarter-scale version of New York's Statue of Liberty at the tail of the Allées des Cygnes island (K6.6). The larger model was presented by France to the USA as a token of friendship in 1886. A Viking longship was discovered here in 1903.

The Seine is reluctant to leave Paris, making one huge loop after another as it winds through the western suburbs, with the Bois de Boulogne appearing to starboard at K8 only to be sighted again at K16. These 900 hectares of former royal hunting forest were given to the people by Napoléon III and modelled on London's Hyde Park. **Versailles** and its great palace of Louis XIV lies about 12km SW. This extraordinary *château* is one of the largest anywhere and is claimed to have over 2,000 windows, 1,250 fireplaces, 67 staircases

and 700 rooms: everyone should make at least one visit. Surroundings are heavily built up past **Boulogne-Billancourt** (K10, fuel), **St-Cloud** (K14.5) and **Suresnes** (K16.5), with Écluse de Suresnes (K17) at the head of the Ile de Puteaux. Motor cruisers of under 10hp will find sheltered waters safe from the wash of passing traffic reached from the downstream end of the island. All larger craft are banned. This is a suitable moment to mention one of the little-known secrets of the Seine, downstream of Paris. Close study of the *Carte Guide* will reveal numerous extensive secondary arms running parallel with the main navigation channel. Although generally not as deep as the more obvious route, they are fully navigable and for cruisers and small pleasure barges provide a more intimate view of life on the river. For here lurk numerous often static houseboats that have been converted from vessels as diverse as vintage motor yachts, submarines and all kinds of ex-freight barges. Some of these homes owe more to the skill and ingenuity of the interior designer than to the naval architect. There are picture windows where huge sheets of glass inserted in a hull are subjected to the constant lapping of water. The more affluent conversions even have on-deck swimming pools with which I have no particular problem. Roof gardens featuring real grass lawns, trees and flower beds are rather different: I cringe when I contemplate consequential deterioration of steel or timber decks...out of sight, out of mind. By no means is everything bad, however, and little wooden walkways connect boats with delightfully flowery onshore gardens. These are the homes of individualists, sometimes eccentric, always fascinating. Unless you are in a hurry, you will really enjoy a diversion through these hidden backwaters. Unfortunately, I seem not to have noted which channels are the most rewarding. So try those between K9–11; K17–18 (entry only possible from downstream); K20–22; K65–67; and K78–80. Should you discover any I have not listed, I would really like to hear of them.

Management of the Seine navigation has left a fascinating array of disused lock chambers up backwaters and duplicated channels that are sometimes reserved for one-way traffic. A long summer is probably not long enough to explore everywhere. All is clearly explained in the *Carte Guide*.

Over 40,000 pet dogs, cats and horses are buried in the world's first animal cemetery on the Ile des Ravageurs (K223.5) at **Clichy**; opened in 1899, it contains the grave of a St Bernard named Barry who saved 41 lives in the Alps. He was sadly killed by the 41st who mistook his snow-covered shape for a bear and attacked him with an ice-axe: Barry staggered off to alert rescuers and expired. Film star Rin-Tin-Tin is also to be found here. A little downstream is the *Port de Plaisance Van Gogh* (moorings, water point).

Ile St-Denis, an island more than 7km long, extends downstream of **St-Ouen** (K25.5). The left-hand channel past **Villeneuve-la-Garenne** (K29) is available throughout for upstream-bound craft, but includes a central section closed to downhillers. Many barge repair yards will be interest to students of commercial transport: *péniches* and other vessels are to be seen hauled out of the water, under construction or being converted into houseboats or floating restaurants. Possibilities for robust mechanical aid to pleasure craft exist. Taking the alternative right-hand channel, you pass **St-Denis** (K27). Legend claims that after his decapitation in Montmartre in the 3rd century, Denis walked on, head in hands, until he collapsed at this spot. During the late 5th century St Geneviève, patron saint of Paris, had a church built on the site. This was later replaced by the present 12th century Gothic basilica. During 12 centuries most French monarchs from Dagobert (629–39) onwards were buried here, although the corpses were disposed of during the Revolution.

On the right bank, K28.8, the Canal St-Denis enters the Seine, offering the prospect of a return to Paris by a different route: it joins the Canal St-Martin and the Canal de l'Ourcq (see Chapter 16). Still in urban surroundings, with extensive commercial basins at the **Port de Genneviliers** (K35), the river divides again (K40.2) below **Bezons** and there is a choice of routes for a little over 8km, separated by an island first known as Chatou, then du Chiard and finally de la Chaussée. The left branch is closed in times of flood and passes through **Nanterre** (K42), known for its miraculous well, *charcuterie* (cold meat production) and madeleine cakes. This is followed in turn by **Rueil-Malmaison** (K45), with Empress Josephine's favourite residence where she died in 1814. It is now a Napoléonic museum. **Bourgival** (K47.5) was a haunt of Impressionist painters Monet, Sisley, Degas and Renoir: many of their best works feature boats and the river. There are pleasure boat moorings above Bourgival Locks (K48.5), below which the Seine unites again. The other, right-hand section, Bras de Rivière Neuve, flows past **Carrières-sur-Seine** (K43) to a lock at **Chatou** (K44.5).

Three sides of the great forest of **St-Germain** are encircled by the waterway. Many kings of France and England are associated with the magnificent *château*, easily reached from the Pont de Pecq (K52) if a suitable mooring can be located. Downstream traffic must pass to the right of the small Ile Corbière (K52.5), leaving the other channel for up-going boats. Numerous pleasure craft occupy an arm called La Petite Rivière on the left (K58.3), below the **Maisons-Lafitte** railway

bridge. Flocks of seagulls cluster round a massive sewage treatment works opposite **La Frette-sur-Seine** (K63), a sure sign that the Paris conurbation is at last astern. Moorings at the *Halte de Plaisance*.

'Home' to inland boat people from all parts of Northern France, **Conflans-Ste-Honorine** (K70) takes its name in part from its situation at the junction with the River Oise (see Chapter 17) and secondly as the final resting place of the relics of a 3rd century martyr. Huge numbers of *péniches* can always be seen here, moored up to five abreast along the quays of each river. Some will be awaiting new cargoes; these days, an unfortunately large number have given up the struggle to remain in trade but continue as family residences. It is an animated scene, with lines of washing and all the ceaseless painting and polishing that seems to fill every idle moment of a boatman's life. A white hulled barge, *Je Sers*, has been converted into a chapel, catering for the needs of the working boat families. It also appears to attract large numbers of vagrants. On the weekend of the last Sunday of June, dozens of barges decorated from end to end with flags and paper flowers congregate here for the *Pardon National de la Batellerie*, a form of *péniche* rally established in 1960. The hilly little town joins in with enthusiasm, attractions including a large fair, fireworks and *son et lumière*. On a terrace high above the Seine, the *Château du Prieuré* houses the National Waterways Museum (details appear under 'Waterways Museums'). On the opposite side of the river, the shady verges of the N184 through the Forest of St-Germain were, until a decade ago, a notorious haunt of extremely blatant 'ladies of easy virtue'. The presence of numbers of police cars resulted, however, from the tendency of distracted drivers to swerve off the carriageways! Then, rather than attempt to impose a direct prohibition on the 'trade', the authorities introduced a rigorously enforced parking ban causing an immediate end to the practice!

Below the wide junction with the Oise (K72.2), the navigation divides: normally you must follow the left channel through the Écluse d'Andrésy (K72.7). However, the alternative route is used when this lock is under repair, the Écluse de **Carrières-sous-Poissy** (K76) operating instead. In either event, all the facilities of **Andrésy** (shops, restaurants, water, refuse disposal, electricity) may be reached by running for 1km down the right arm with quayside moorings at K73. Fully rural once more, with willows along its banks, the Seine flows to **Poissy** (K78), site of a large Talbot car works. By entering a backwater on the left bank you may escape from the effects of passing traffic. A pleasure boat yard, *Plaisance Nautic*, lies at the far end, K80.1. On the right bank of the main river, K81.1, the *Nauti-*

Méchanique marina provides moorings, slipway and other services in a protected basin. Waterside houses with trees and lawns recall the Upper Thames. Pass either side of the Ile de **Médan** (K81.8; NB upstream traffic is not allowed in the Bras des Mottes). In this little town Émile Zola wrote his most important books between 1879 and 1902. Médan Plage is an agreeable inland swimming and boating resort with beach and pool on the island and reached by ferry from the left bank. It was here that I was once amused to see a notice board that informed, enigmatically, *Naturisme Tolérée avec Sexe Cachée* (it should not have been translated too literally!). Clients may moor to the jetty of the *Moulin Rouge* restaurant or alongside quays on the mainland. **Triel-sur-Seine** (K85.2), right bank, has a 13–16th century church. Many gravel pits now line the left shore, resulting in frequent push-tows of barges.

Through traffic remains in the main channel past **Vaux-sur-Seine** (K89.5), but pleasure craft may prefer to explore the navigable arm on the right, behind the island. Shore facilities are numerous in **Les Mureaux** (K93.5) with various mooring possibilities, or, sheltered by Belle Ile along an arm, right bank at **Meulan** (K93). The island fortress which once controlled the fortunes of freight craft passing up and down the Seine was taken by the English and liberated by du Guesclin in 1364. If you stay in the left channel, you will notice a disused lock at K95. The other route, down the Bras de **Mézy**, provides an opportunity for shopping in **Juziers** (K98.3). Products of the massive Renault car works at **Flins** (K97–98) used to be conveyed upstream to another factory at Billancourt or down river for export via Le Havre docks. Specially built double-decker transport barges were used, each holding several hundred vehicles. Sadly, this thoroughly civilised method of transportation has been suspended.

Rouen-bound craft leave the Ile de Rangiport (K101) on the left, the other channel being reserved for vessels working upriver. Beyond, numerous power lines are seen spreading from the generating station at **Porcheville** (K105), to which coal supplies are carried by water. Providing a mooring can be located, all shops are to be found in the town (K103.6). River width increases very considerably by the commercial port (K106.8) upstream of **Mantes-la-Jolie** (K108.5), situated to the left of the Ile de Limay and Ile l'Aumône. Best moorings in the area are on the right bank at a quay below the Pont de **Limay** (K109.4): this is close to most shops. Alternatively, continue to a yacht harbour opposite the junction of the two islands (K109.9). Here, mooring, water and electricity are free for a 48 hours stay. Mantes is the more important and attractive of these two towns, easily reached from the right bank by

bridges. Ownership of it was demanded by William the Conqueror in 1087. Philip I of France refused and went so far as to make insulting remarks about William's famous bloated stomach. This was too much for William and he reduced the place to smoking ruins. Sadly for him, in his moment of triumph he fell from his horse, dying from stomach wounds six weeks later. Despite being heavily bombed in World War II, Mantes' greatest treasure is the massive 12–13th century cathedral of Notre Dame; it stands close to the river and bears comparison with its better known namesake in Paris.

Onwards from here, the river is wide and most attractive. Patches of white chalk cliff protrude from woodland, a characteristic of the Seine for much of the journey to Rouen. **Rosny-sur-Seine**, left bank (K117) is noted for the *Château de Sully*, built during the early 17th century. It is open to the public on afternoons, late July to late August. The town makes a pretty picture from the water and has useful shops. A fuel point (K119) is just upstream of **Rolleboise**, where the river swings to the NE and south again in a great loop. Until the advent of the railway a passenger boat service, using *galiotes* made regular runs upstream to Poissy. Drawn by four horses, the vessels carried 90 people. Three chambers are built side by side at the Écluse de Méricourt (K120.7). A large marina, the *Port de l'Ilon*, offers a wide range of pleasure boat services: the entrance is on the right bank just above the upper approach to the locks. During a cruise between Paris and the estuary, I lay above Méricourt for the night, following the first pusher-tug/barge combination down river at dawn. For the next two hours, the September fog was so dense that we caught only occasional glimpses of the banks for the next 20km. Navigating by radar and expert local knowledge, the working craft ahead rarely slackened speed as it surged into the swirling whiteness: grimly we followed his tail, sometimes losing sight of him altogether. In spite of having radar ourselves, it was not an experience I hope to repeat!

Keeping right around the island of **St-Martin-la-Garenne** (K125), the next town of interest is **La Roche Guyon** (K133). In the shadow of chalk cliffs, a 16–18th century *château* is the property of the La Rochfoucault family, whose ancestor François compiled his pithy *Maxims* here in 1665: a typical example: 'Our virtues are mostly our vices in disguise.' Towards the end of World War II, German Field Marshal Rommel set up a command post in the castle. Take care if mooring, for there is little depth. Similarly, choose any stopping point judiciously in **Bonnières-sur-Seine** (K139.8); all the best places lie in the channel to the right of the island. But, shops apart, there are few attractions, the town's main claim to fame being the Singer sewing

Traffic on the lower river, after the early 19th century painting by J M W Turner.

machine factory. Some protection from the wash of passing vessels is afforded by the approach channels to the former Écluse de Port-**Villez** (K144.9): there are many worse places to spend the night. Increasingly as they work towards the sea, owners of small boats will realise that convenient moorings are few and far between, resulting in a high level of anxiety as dusk approaches with nothing better than rock-strewn walls in prospect. Planning is vital.

As if to celebrate entry into the province of Normandy, several typical half-timbered houses will be seen near **Vernon** (K150), a town with much of interest and well worth making a halt. Even more so because of the charming moorings by the remains of a 12th century bridge on the right-hand **Vernonnet** bank, just below the modern Pont de Vernon. A pontoon of the sailing club is reserved for visitors (free of charge), with showers ashore by the *Château des Tourelles*. Vernon was founded in the 9th century by Rollo the Dane, first Duke of Normandy. The usual eating and shopping facilities are waiting for you ashore. This is the most practical point to leave your boat safely for a visit to the village of **Givernay**, 4km upstream on the north bank. Here, Claude Monet (1840–1926), a leader of the French Impressionists, created his beautiful garden with Japanese bridge and water lily ponds. He lived

here from 1883 until his death. The Monet house and grounds are open throughout the summer, little changed since the great painter's time. The lilies are at their best in June and July.

Chalk cliffs with dense woodland lead to Écluse de **Notre Dame de la Garenne** (K161.1) with no fewer than four chambers and a massive weir. At K171, tail of the Ile de la Tour, a mooring quay is situated on the outskirts of **Bouafles**. Shortly thereafter the Seine's finest spectacle comes into view – the ruins of *Château Gaillard*, 'the Gallant Castle', perched on rocks above **Les Andelys** (K173.4). It was erected in the late 12th century by Richard Cœur de Lion to prevent the King of France passing down the Seine to Rouen. After a long siege, it fell to the French in 1204, Bayeux and Rouen following soon after. England withdrew from Normandy, but failed to recognise the fact until the end of the Hundred Years War in 1453. Nicholas Poussin the painter (1594–1665) was born here. Most boaters will want to linger in this lovely area and it is worth trying to enter the small marina (draft 1m) shortly below the Pont de **Port Morin** and almost in the shadow of the *château* itself. Superb river views from the cliffs. While there is little of individual note as the Seine continues past villages and islands, these last reaches of non-tidal water are certainly the most attractive on the whole river, flanked by the white cliffs with fine houses in brick and half-timbering. Frequently, all this recalls the Upper Thames, but here the scale is larger and pleasure craft are mainly replaced by a ceaseless stream of commercial vessels. It is obligatory to keep left (ie take the opposite to normal side) passing the Ile du Château (K174).

A small basin on the right at **Val St-Martin** (K175.5) is occupied by the *Club Paris-Normandie*, with moorings and a useful range of services. Further moorings are at **Bernières-sur-Seine** (K179.5) and along a Camping Club quay, left bank, draft only 1m, K180.3. Just upstream of the Ile des Grand Bacs, left bank, K183.9, is the entrance to a huge lake where there are peaceful moorings at a *port de plaisance*. In the next 10km past **St Pierre-du-Vauvray**, **Andé**, **Porte Joie**, and **Port Pincé**, all suitable stopping places appear to be private. However, if you enter the right-hand of three channels (the Bras de Connelles, K194.3, draft 1.8m) it is possible to overnight close to *Le Moulin de Connelles* restaurant. We are now approaching the start of the tideway, so it is worth taking care to select a suitable mooring upstream of the final lock from which you will leave at a time which gives you greatest benefit from the current. One such possible quay is on the right bank opposite Ile de la Motelle (K199.3); otherwise, there is a village quay (restaurant), left bank at **Poses** (K201). This is a favoured retirement place for boat families: not to be missed is the Waterways Museum (*Musée de la Batellerie*) on board *péniche Midway II* (see under 'Waterway Museums' at the beginning of this book).

The last lock, Écluse d'Amfreville (K202), offers the chance of making fast in the upstream approach, but stay well clear of barge traffic. Now, tides must be allowed for; their effect is increasingly felt as Rouen comes closer. Here, the rise and fall is generally little more than 1m. Although still far from the sea, the Seine is no longer a typical inland waterway; tide tables must be studied before making the passage, bearing in mind that safe moorings are rare. Often there is no alternative to anchoring. Pleasure craft venturing into these waters will be adequately powered sea-going vessels, able to cope with strong streams and in the charge of people conversant with shipping practice. Night navigation by pleasure craft is forbidden. It is not a place for beginners. Much useful navigational information will be gleaned from the *Carte Guide*.

Steep cliffs above the locks are known as La Côte des Deux Amants, 'the Hillside of the Two Lovers'. Here, legend says, a young squire named Edmond saved Calixte, his childhood friend and daughter of the Comte Rulph, from certain death by a wild boar. The irascible Comte asked the young man what reward he wished: 'The hand of your daughter', he replied. Considering Edmond too lowly, Comte Rulph set him the task of climbing the hillside with Calixte on his back. If he so much as paused for breath, he would be unworthy of the prize. A great crowd gathered to witness the attempt. Either Edmond was in poor shape or his beloved was a big girl, for at the very moment he reached the summit he fell dead on the ground! Horrified, Calixte picked up the corpse (yes, she was a big girl) and the two plunged down the precipice in a tight embrace. Next day, they were buried in a single tomb: he in the clothes of a knight, she in a bridal gown. Shades of Abélard and Héloïse.

In the 19th century there was a lock at **Pont de l'Arche** (K208); long disused, there is no possibility of stopping. Once, this had been the site of the bridge nearest the sea. Beaches of sand and shingle with willow trees look best when the river is brimful at high water. The Seine increases in width after a junction with the River Eure near **Elbeuf**, with a splendid quayside mooring, left bank, between the two bridges (K219.1). Remember to adjust the boat's lines if staying for any length of time. Excellent shops are within 300m, together with fine old half-timbered buildings and the church of St-Étienne, with 16th century stained glass. There is a *port de plaisance* in a side arm, right bank, **St Aubin les Elbeuf** (K217.7): access is possible for 2h either side of local high water for craft drawing 2m. Wooded cliffs accompany the river as it winds in a series of tight loops, especially fine around **Orival** (K221.5). One of the few really reliable and convenient moorings on the entire tideway will be found in the great city and port of **Rouen** (K241). Municipal pontoons that remain afloat at all times have been established on the very central Ile Lacroix (K241.6), reached by taking the right-hand channel and passing under a railway viaduct and the Pont Mathilde. Under constant supervision, this stopping place is reasonably quiet, is supplied with water, showers and electricity and best of all is totally without tidal problems, which will endear Rouen to all true inland boaters! For fuelling points and chandleries, see the *Carte Guide*.

Several further bridges intervene before seaward-bound sailing boats may raise their masts. Make enquiries for the use of a crane in the Bassin St-Gervais (right bank, K245.1). Although badly damaged during bombing raids in World War II, Rouen has been extensively restored: this applies particularly to over 700 half-timbered buildings in the old quarter along the right bank of the Seine. The English are not likely to forget the fate of Joan of Arc (c.1412–1431), burned at the stake in the Place du Vieux Marché. She was not

J M W Turner's early 19th century view of Rouen.

canonised until 1920 and is now patron saint of France. Much of the atmosphere of the city is best absorbed by walking down the bustling pedestrianised Rue du Gros-Horloge and into the market area by the exciting modern church of Joan of Arc, whose curving slate roof recalls the hull of an upturned ship; magnificent 16th century stained glass creates a successful blend between old and new. The huge cathedral of Notre Dame was started in the 12th century and is among the finest examples of the French Gothic style. Its cast iron spire was a 19th century addition. Writers Pierre Corneille (1606–84) and Gustave Flaubert (1821–80) were born in the city and both are commemorated by museums. There is a maritime/fluvial museum with a good range of exhibits from the world of inland waterways (for further details, see under 'Waterways Museums'). And for more information on the many sights of Rouen, consult the Michelin Green Guide *Normandy*.

Rouen to the coast at Le Havre and Honfleur is 114km. Depending on the speed capabilities of the boat and the times of tides, the run is possible in a single day, although it will probably be necessary to lie at anchor for several hours at some stage to avoid punching against the stream, which can flow very strongly – up to 6 knots near Tancarville. Bankside moorings, with certain qualified exceptions, do not exist between Rouen and Tancarville. Because of the near-impossibility of going ashore, these reaches will be described in less detail. The Seine's tidal bore, *Le Mascaret*, is a shadow of its former self thanks to training works in the estuary and it presents no danger.

First-rate buoyage and navigation beacons are installed onwards from Rouen. Remember that only commercial vessels are allowed to travel during the hours of darkness. Pleasure craft that find themselves accidentally under way at night will be pounced upon by patrol launches; even in daylight, your progress is constantly monitored by radar. These measures are for the protection of many ocean-going ships from all parts of the world: they proceed upriver on the tide as far as Rouen in the charge of pilots and frequently have little clearance under their keels. So stay well clear!

It takes a considerable time to travel beyond Rouen's dockland, where ships from such diverse places as Scotland, Casablanca and Singapore are seen exchanging cargoes with swarms of dwarfed *péniches*. Now that there are only two more (high level) bridges, small car ferries will be encountered: without them, waterside villages would be totally isolated from their neighbours on the opposite bank. Further chalk cliffs and wooded scenery provide a pleasant prospect with sandy beaches and weed-covered rocks at low water. A curiosity at K260 is apparatus for detecting (and subsequently warning of) fog and the tidal bore. Upstream of here is a speed limit of 14kph; from this point to the sea it is increased to 28kph. **Duclair** (K278), with its riverside promenade, seems to be a pleasant town but there are no available moorings for private pleasure craft. Even at slack low tide, the echo-sounder measures more than 9m depth in the channel. Provided you are able to see over the banks, there is generally a lovely vista of little half-timbered farmhouses and apple orchards, especially in the reaches above **Jumièges** (K296).

The Belgian writer and mystic Maurice Maeterlinck (1862–1949), author of *The Blue Bird*, lived in the Abbey of **St-Wandrille** (K308). These ruins of a 7th century foundation must have made an unusual setting for performances of Shakespeare and Maeterlinck's own works: rather than change scenery, he moved actors and audience from one location to another and was fond of gliding through the cloisters on roller skates. The Abbey has been occupied by a religious order since 1931. Beyond the high-level Brotonne suspension bridge, note a monument (K308.7) in the form of a concrete aeroplane, erected in memory of a group of aviators lost in the Arctic in 1929. **Caudebec** (K309.5) was formerly a well known place for watching (or being engulfed by) the *Mascaret*. Henri IV described the 15–16th century Gothic church of Notre Dame as 'the most beautiful chapel in my kingdom'. Anchoring near the right bank is possible – with normal precautions – even better is a tripping boat pontoon where it should be possible to find a space. A brief stay would allow for a visit to shops or restaurants

of which *La Marine* on the river bank has a good reputation. Buoys off **Villequier** (K313.3) could provide a chance of stopping, perhaps making an expedition by dinghy to this pleasant little town. A museum recalls a tragedy when Victor Hugo's newly married 19-year-old daughter Léopoldine and her husband Charles were drowned in 1843, after their little sailing boat was overturned by the *Mascaret*. **Aizier** (K323) is considered to be the upstream limit of salt water. Anchoring is satisfactory inside the ship mooring buoys at **Quilleboeuf-sur-Seine** (K331.9).

Growing ever wider, the Seine is now fast-flowing and laden with mud; as the tide drains out huge sand banks appear on the shores. Ahead is the impressive **Tancarville** Bridge (K338.2), with a span of 1,400m and a height above high water of 48m; it was opened in 1959. Immediately, it started to transform the local economy, connecting lands south of the river with the conurbation of Le Havre. Pleasure craft may moor between projecting dolphins and a quayside near **Les Alluvions** (K337.9), on the right bank just upriver of the bridge. The 25km **Canal de Tancarville** was opened between here and the Havre docks in 1887. Entry to the Tancarville locks is from 4hr before to 3¼hr after HW at Le Havre. For full details of the waterway, opening arrangements for the bridges and the operation of locks at the seaward end, consult the *Carte Guide*. Rendered partially obsolete by the increased dimensions of ships, the canal is chiefly of use to pleasure craft if conditions in the estuary are rough. Being tideless, this route will add several hours to a journey. There is a boatyard with limited moorings just beyond the old lock (*Port des Torpilleurs*).

To all intents and purposes, the remainder of the Seine is a seaway and hardly within the scope of this book. On the north shore, **Le Havre** is the second largest port in France, with first-rate marina facilities for

The great Tancarville road bridge.

pleasure craft (see the *Carte Guide*). One final location does merit mention: this is the enchanting little port of **Honfleur**, without question one of the most appealing towns in the whole of France. Situated on the south shore of the Seine estuary, it is approached via a short channel that dries out at low water. If necessary, a jetty at the entrance by a prominent radar control tower is a convenient place to wait for the tide to make sufficiently to negotiate the lock (available 1hr either side of HW). In the 16th century French discoverers set sail from here for the new lands of Canada, numerous settlers following in their wake. Marine trade has long since crossed the estuary to Le Havre, leaving the little town to brightly painted fishing boats, tourists, artists and yachtsmen. At the centre is the Vieux Bassin, filled with pleasure craft and lined on three sides by tall houses, partly faced with slates, the windows decorated with colourful sun blinds. *La Lieutenance*, former house of the town's Governor, stands at the basin entrance. St-Catherine's church was built entirely in timber by shipwrights. Within walking distance along the Côte de Grâce towards fashionable **Deauville** are various pleasant beaches on the Channel coast.

14   Canal Latéral à la Marne

Carte Guide: *La Marne*
From Vitry-le-François, junction with the Canal de la Marne à la Saône and the Canal de la Marne au Rhin to a junction with the River Marne at Dizy, near Épernay; 66.7km with 15 locks. A connection is made with the Canal de l'Aisne à la Marne at Condé-sur-Marne.

This is an unexceptional waterway, closely following the unnavigable course of the Marne but featuring long and straight sections with limited interest. It passes through a mainly rural chalky region giving rise to dust-producing cement works. The canal remains as a route for *péniches* from the barge town of Vitry-le-François to the Paris area, via the Marne. The major industry at the NW end is the world-famous champagne trade, based on Épernay. All locks are automatic.

Designed to offer a more reliable navigation than that provided by the Upper Marne, the canal was completed in 1845. 148km of the Marne from St-Dizier to Dizy became redundant soon afterwards. As well as making possible freight transport of agricultural goods in its densely populated valley, the canal was widely used for carrying coal, coke and building materials.

Most boating facilities, including water, fuel and commercial craft engineers, are to be found in the large town of **Vitry-le-François** (see Chapter 27). However, in recent years several important barge yards here have closed, following serious reduction in the numbers of active freight craft. 2km of the former canal line through Vitry was replaced by a by-pass cut in the 1960s. What remains of the old route is a mooring for retired barges and their owners. Beyond an aqueduct spanning the River Saulx upstream of its confluence with the Marne and on the outskirts of the city is Écluse 1 (K2.3). Écluse 2, l'Ermite (K3.7), is a charming area although all boaters will lament the closure of a canal café, chandlery and fuelling depot that remained active into the 1990s. Note on the left an arm which used to link with the river via one lock. Now the Marne here is a wild and fast-flowing stream, littered with fallen trees: that it was once navigable seems scarcely possible. On the right bank, between a road bridge and Écluse 3 (K4.8), **Couvrot** offers basic food shops. Ahead, the large cement works of the *Société des Ciments Français* dominates the landscape, casting a thin layer of white dust over buildings and canalside shrubs. This situation affects the waterway for a considerable distance, through **Soulanges**, Écluse 4 (K9.2), where there is a small port (*halte nautique*) and a little grey stone church with slated spire. Basic shopping and a restaurant are in **La Chaussée-sur-Marne** (K14.2).

Another substantial cement works is passed in **Omey** (K16.5). The next town, **Pogny** (K17.9, a good quay if not occupied by barges), is convenient for the limited shopping. This is followed by an utterly straight and rather dull run past **Vésigneul-sur-Marne** (K20.4), **St-Germain-la-Ville**, Écluse 7 (shops and restaurant, K21.8) and **Sarry**, Écluse 8 (baker and restaurant, K27). Suburban development intervenes at the approach to **Châlons-en-Champagne** (K32). Pass to the left of a wooded island shortly before Écluse 9; the alternative channel, surrounded by delightful parkland, has been badly silted for many years. Some basic maintenance would create an excellent *port de plaisance*. Central quayside moorings are found at the upstream end of the lock. This was the Gallo-Roman town of *Catalaunum* and was the scene of a fierce battle against Attila the Hun in the 5th century. Early in World War I the Germans held Châlons briefly, before launching into the Battle of the Marne. All the attractions of the city centre will be found close to the canal. As capital of the Marne *Département* there are many fine municipal buildings, with a modern and stylish quarter near the massive Gothic cathedral of St-Étienne. In recent years a number of ancient half-timbered houses have been expertly restored, their structure revealed by stripping off stucco cladding. Two small rivers, the Nau and the

Mau, wind through the centre with lavish municipal planting schemes. The 12th century church of Notre-Dame-en-Vaux is noted for its fine stained glass and a 56-bell carillon. As might be expected, shopping is of a high quality. Industries include brewing and champagne production.

Shortly before **St-Martin-sur-le-Pré** (K34.8), an aqueduct carries the canal over a feeder bringing water supplies from the Marne and the two run in close company almost to Condé-sur-Marne. The waterway continues very straight through **Recy** (K37), Écluse 10; **Juvigny** (K39.3); **Vraux** and Écluse 11 (grocer, K44.3); and **Aigny** (K46.4) with a mixture of waterside woodlands and large, open, flat fields of chalky soil. At K48.4 a junction on the right marks the start of the Canal de l'Aisne à la Marne (Chapter 21) with food, restaurants and fuel in the nearby town of **Condé-sur-Marne**. A short distance into the other canal a towpath towing engine is preserved as a feature of the lockside. Pontoon moorings for pleasure craft with water and electricity.

With the River Marne right alongside, the true champagne country is entered at **Tours-sur-Marne** (Écluse 12, K53), the self-styled 'Cross-roads of Champagne' where the advertising signs of sparkling wine producers vie with each other. This is a charming little town, all shops being within a short distance of the lock. Soon the first vineyards are visible at the approach to **Bisseuil** (K55.4, swing bridge), spreading far over the hillsides.

After Écluse 13 (K58.1), the waterway widens through **Mareuil-sur-Ay** (K59.4), a convenient shopping stop with a garage on the far side of town (K60). There are fine pontoon moorings with water, showers and electricity. An 18th century *château* has long been associated with champagne production. Some years ago when calling at the champagne house of Marc Hébrart to replenish the ship's supplies, we found the *vendage* reaching a crescendo. With scarcely a glance in our direction and assuming that we were the latest intake of temporary labour, a young man commanded that we should stack over a hundred heavy plastic crates in which grapes had recently arrived for pressing. This task completed, everyone (us included) was invited to take a break for a meal at a long trestle table. This seemed to be an appropriate moment to inform the management that we had actually come to collect a not insubstantial order. Several cases were duly delivered to our boat not long afterwards with profuse apologies. 3km north lies **Avenay-Val-d'Or**, well worth a visit to see the ornate church of St-Trésain with its grand organ dating from the 16th century. **Ay**, just before Écluse 14 (K62.6), is another leading town of wine *maisons*, grapes having been cultivated here in Roman times. Its wines were highly prized by François I, Henry VIII of England and Henri IV. There is a wide range of shops. All the atmosphere of pre-World War II horseboats in this very location is admirably portrayed in Georges Simenon's 1931 novel *Le Charretier de la 'Providence'*, published in English as *Maigret Meets a Milord*. Simenon spent several years exploring the waterways of France and the Low Countries, and canals appear a number of times as settings for his Maigret books. Fuel can be obtained from a garage on the left bank at the N51 road bridge at **Dizy** (K64.7), with limited shopping in the village. **Épernay** offers a full range of requirements, its centre being about 3km south of the canal (see Chapter 15). A more convenient approach by water would be to work through the canal's last lock, Écluse 15 (K66.6), join the River Marne and run upstream for 5km to moor in the *port de plaisance* at the head of navigation.

15 ~ River Marne

Carte Guide: *La Marne*
From a junction with the Canal Latéral à la Marne at Dizy, near Épernay to the River Seine at Alfortville, a little upstream of central Paris. The official length of 178.4km has been slightly shortened by improvements, but the former kilometre posts continue in use. There are 18 locks with tunnels on canal sections at Chalifert (290m) and St-Maur (600m). A former inclined plane connection (the *transbordeur*) with the Canal de l'Ourcq near Meaux has long been disused, but there is a possibility that some new form of link may be built in the future, so opening up an exciting pleasure cruising circuit comprising parts of the Marne, Seine, Canal St-Martin and Canal de l'Ourcq (see Chapter 16). There are several navigable 'branches' on portions of the natural Marne which are bypassed by canal sections used by through traffic.

Mention of the River Marne produces two immediate mental images: the production of champagne, mainly in the upper reaches around Épernay, and the engagements of World War I – the Battle of the Marne late in 1914 and the Victory of the Allies from July to November 1918. Many towns and villages were severely damaged and most bridges blown up; there are numerous monuments and memorials. But the Great War does not impose an oppressive atmosphere on the river such as that which is felt on the Meuse in the area of Verdun. This is a gentle and peaceful waterway, flowing past woods and reed-fringed islands with

Pleasure boat moorings in the middle of Meaux.

numerous punt-ensconced fishermen. Much of the course features great loops as the Marne makes its way through hard limestone: navigational improvements have considerably reduced the original length with a series of bypass channels. Scenery is finest between Château-Thierry and Meaux, although it is all very pleasant until a different kind of interest intervenes with the approach of the Parisian suburbs. As with the Upper Seine, the people of Paris flock to the Marne for relaxation, the most fortunate among them living in enviable riverside houses.

Commercial traffic is brisk, especially in the lower reaches and the locks increase in size from the *péniche* chambers near Épernay to structures 125m in length. Locking arrangements are presently in a state of transition. All the large, downstream chambers are mechanised, while some of the uppermost locks are still manually worked but there are plans for automation, dispensing in some cases with keepers.

Brief history While long used for navigation purposes, the Marne was described as 'both slow and dangerous' in the late 17th century, with barges being wrecked 'every day'. Throughout the 18th century a succession of individuals and companies sought to build improved navigation works in return for toll receipts for periods

ranging from 30 to 60 years. But it was not until implementation of a government scheme that the river was finally canalised between 1838 and 1865 with 18 weirs, 20 locks, two tunnels and four branches. Thus was created the navigation that essentially still exists. In the 1840s and 1850s, lengths of completely new lateral canal from the present Marne head of navigation to St-Dizier, enabled 148km of the uppermost section of the river to be abandoned. 20th century improvements include a new weir at Meaux (1939), the replacement of the St-Maur lock with other works (1933), and the deepening of the Marne towards its junction with the Seine.

At the top of the waterway 5km duplicate the course of the Canal Latéral à la Marne between the **Dizy** junction (see Chapter 14) and **Épernay** and this length is normally known as the Épernay Branch; distances quoted do not therefore include this section. Even if making a through passage along the river and canal, it is well worth undertaking this detour for there is plenty of interest in the town, with excellent shopping and mooring facilities. Jetties will be found at a very welcoming *port de plaisance* on the south bank beyond the bridge. Various wars have stripped the town of many of its architectural treasures, but fascinating visits can be made to the cellars of several *maisons* of this leading centre of champagne production. Several are to be found in the Avenue de Champagne dubbed by Winston Churchill 'the most drinkable street in the world'. Moët et Chandon at No 18 offers 45 minute tours including part of a 28km system of underground chambers. Mercier, No 75, invites visitors to travel through galleries on an electric train and see exhibitions devoted to cooperage and grape pressing. The former Perrier *château* is now a Museum of Champagne Production and Prehistory. All around, the countryside is devoted to the cultivation of vines – 24,500 hectares with annual production in the region of 186 million bottles of which about 54 million are exported (half of this comes to Britain). Both black and white grapes are grown, the traditional *grande marque* champagne being blended from 33% white and 66% black.

An unusual navigational characteristic of some of the uppermost Marne locks is that in times of flood, weirs will be partially dismantled, allowing boats to pass downhill through the gap rather than use the lock chamber. With little advance warning and considerable misgivings, I have performed this trick with an 11-tonne motor cruiser. Until it was safely all over, I was unsure if the distant figure standing on the upper end of the lock encouraging me to steer for the raging torrent was a *bone fide* keeper or the village idiot; as the boat gathered speed there was little time to consider the matter.

Dropping down river past a vista of vineyards, mooring in **Cumières** (K1.5) is difficult as the river here and elsewhere tends to be very shallow at the edges. An artificial cut leads right, to the Écluse de Cumières (K3). This and the following two locks feature sloping-sided chambers and pleasure craft are advised to make fast to a pontoon which falls as the lock empties. **Damery** (K5.4) is a charming small town alongside a road bridge and benefiting scenically from a backdrop of vineyards. All shops are a short distance from the quay, right bank, above the bridge. A wooded reach leads to Damery lock cut, with Écluse 2 at the far end (K8.2). The next pound contains two possible ports of call: **Reuil** (K11.8, baker) with moorings beneath the bridge and the slightly industrialised **Port-à-Binson** (K14.8), a town of grain silos with a commercial harbour and pleasure boat jetties (small craft only) on the left, downstream of the bridge. Shopping and eating are good with an official swimming 'beach' at a campsite on the upstream, left, side of an island. **Châtillon-sur-Marne**, 2km north, occupies a 148m hilltop rising from the vineyards and in medieval times was an important stronghold. A giant statue of Urban II, Pope from 1088–99, was erected in 1887 to acknowledge his original name of Eudes de Châtillon. He instigated the first Crusade to Palestine.

Écluse 3, Vandières (K17.7), is built on a short cut (take the right fork to avoid entering the weir stream). At the confluence with the little River Sémoigne (K22.3) be careful of silting on the right bank. Moor near the next bridge, Pont de Try, for a visit to **Verneuil**, 1km north (good shopping). Here there is a lovely 12–13th century church. Beyond, the **Tardenois Plateau** saw fierce action during the Second Battle of the Marne. **Vincelles** (K24.3), right bank, has few facilities and is anyway best avoided for there is a line of rocks alongside, where the river bends. For shopping, continue a short distance to **Dormans** (K26.3), with a mooring quay, right bank, by a public swimming pool/ camp site. Comprehensive supplies with restaurants are to be found, and an official swimming 'beach' is situated on the right bank about 250m upstream of the bridge. All told, this is a very pleasant little town, excellent for an overnight stop if you do not object to the sound of frequent trains. In the religious wars of the 16th century between the Catholics and Henri III, during the Battle of Dormans the Catholic leader the Duc de Guise was wounded, resulting in his nickname *Le Balafré* ('Scarface'). The Chapelle de la Reconnaissance in the grounds of a *château* commemorates both Battles of the Marne. The popular sport of wind-surfing is practised in former gravel pits by the waterway beyond **Trélou-sur-Marne** (K28.5, pontoon mooring). Soon afterwards, Écluse 4, **Courcelles** (K30.5), appears ahead, followed by a succession of small villages on each bank, none of which offer much in the way of facilities. One of the prettiest is **Marcilly** (K35.2), a place of rough stone houses set against a backdrop of vineyards.

Looking upriver from **Jaulgonne** (K37.3), you will be rewarded with a magnificent view of the champagne fields. By using the quay upstream of the bridge a good range of shops will be found nearby. There is also a restaurant with its own mooring. Be sure to stay in the centre of the channel where the River Surmelin enters on the left (K39.5) as the Marne is silted on each side. **Mont-St-Pierre** (K41.5), right bank, offers a choice of two mooring places downstream of the bridge with basic shopping. Downhill traffic passes to the right of a broad island just above Écluse 5 (K42.5), where there is a quay close to the Château-Thierry district navigation office. Further villages lying well back from the river are followed by **Brasles** (K48.2), a slightly industrialised suburb of **Château-Thierry** (K50.4). The town takes its name from Thierry IV, the 8th century Merovingian king. Rather better known is the author of fables Jean de La Fontaine (1621–95), born here, the son of the Director of Waters and Forests. The house of his birth is now a museum devoted to La Fontaine relics and his statue stands near a bridge crossing the northernmost of two river channels. (This route is set aside for navigation, the Fausse Marne being reserved for angling.) In 1814 Napoléon had an engagement here with the combined Russian and Prussian forces under the command of Blücher. In World War I, British troops under General Haig crossed the river at this point in September 1914 and four years later Château-Thierry was the location of the first American offensive. This event is commemorated by a vast memorial at the top of Hill 204. Little remains of the *château* in a park above the *Hôtel de Ville* in the main square. Vertical quays provide excellent moorings for shops and restaurants. One eating place is on a *péniche* (left bank, K51).

The valley of the Marne becomes ever more delightful, with dense woodlands alternating with vineyards. Écluse 6, **Azy** (K56.2), is followed by a long reach to **Nogent-l'Artaud** (K63.3), where there are moorings near the bridge, all facilities and an old water mill. The church is partly 12th century. Beautiful scenery continues past Écluse 7, **Charly** (K66.6), with mooring and restaurant by the bridge. There is a quay (by a diving board, K70). Fuel supplies are conveniently close to a quayside in the village of Crouttes (K73, right bank), while the next town, **Nanteuil-sur-Marne** (K74.2), has moorings by a restaurant at the bridge and a small selection of shops. **Saâcy-sur-Marne** (K76.1) can be reached from the bridge downstream of Écluse 8, **Méry-sur-Marne**. Without question, this is the finest part of the whole waterway as it flows round a great double loop. A good isolated overnight berth will be found on the left bank about 400m above the railway bridge of Saussoy (K85.5).

Although surroundings remain countrified, towns and villages become progressively less rural as we enter an area within commuting distance of Paris. Écluse 9, **Courtaron** (K87.1), is in a lonely situation on the left bank: keep to the same side to avoid a wide shoal shortly below. The Marne increases in size at the junction with the Petit Morin in **La Ferté-sous-Jouarre** (K90.6). It was here that the finest millstones in all France were once quarried. Nothing remains of the one-time island fortress, the riverbanks now being shaded by pleasant walks. Shopping is good; quayside moorings reach a reasonable depth, left bank, downstream of the second bridge, about 100m above a slipway. Alternatively, craft drawing less than 1.2m can use a pontoon behind a small island upstream of the first bridge (K89.9). The British Expeditionary Forces crossed the Marne near here in 1914 using a floating bridge; its site is marked by rectangular stone pylons. Late in 1928, an impressive memorial was unveiled to record the 3,888 Britons who died during the 1914

battles of the Marne, Aisne, Le Cateau and Mons. 3km south is **Jouarre**, whose 7th century abbey is one of the oldest religious buildings in the country. It is open to the public and Benedictine services are held in French and Gregorian chant.

To state that there is little of interest in the succeeding reaches would be to ignore the fact that surroundings are remarkably pleasant, but features of note are rare. Moorings below the bridge (right bank) in **Ussy-sur-Marne** (K95.2) must be approached with great care on account of shallows with rocks: if you do make it safely, you will be rewarded by a small selection of shops and restaurant. Downstream, pass to the right of the Ile de la Fosse-Tournille (K96), but to the left of the next island beyond the *autoroute* bridge (K97.6). Pleasure boating is much in evidence at the approach to **Changis-sur-Marne** and its twin town **St-Jean-les-Deux-Jumeaux**, either side of a road crossing (K99.4), for there is a yacht club with craning facilities. The best shops will be found in St-Jean. Écluse 10 (K100.7) lies a little beyond. Mooring is permitted above the lock provided you leave space for barges to manoeuvre. Neither **Armentières-en-Brie** (K104.1) or **Tancrou** (K108.3) are likely to detain you; give them a miss and press on instead to the riverside resort of **Mary-sur-Marne** (K110.7). Here, locals make fullest use of waterside features including a restaurant in the 18th century *château*. There are plenty of food shops; pedalos may be hired. Now and for much of the remaining distance to the Seine, gravel extraction is an important activity and sand barges are frequent. A glance at the map will indicate how the Canal de l'Ourcq (see Chapter 16) now strikes up an intimate association with the Marne, having run from its northern terminus of La Ferté-Milon. The two navigations share a similar winding course for many kilometres, but there is currently no physical connection between them.

Seemingly in no hurry to reach the Seine, the Marne twists in one direction and then another round the Montceaux Forest, passing on the way **Iles-les-Meldeuses** and Écluse 11 (K113.1), limited shopping and restaurant, and **Germigny-l'Evêque** (K121.2). Ignore channels that pass through islands on the right immediately before the bridge; it is possible with care to moor beyond on the right (shallows). The village offers restaurant and slipway. A full range of shops will be found in **Varreddes**, a town near the Canal de l'Ourcq, about 2km north. Around the next bend, the Ourcq Navigation swings in close to the Marne (K123). Pass to the left of a long island, with boat moorings and facilities at its lower end, close to **Poincy** (K125). This could be an excellent overnight mooring, using the sheltered jetties. Modern French waterways history was made at this site when Pierre Zivy (1929–2001) established his Saint Line hire cruiser base in 1958. A great Anglophile, M Zivy had been inspired to begin his business after enjoying inland cruises in England. He subsequently moved his craft to Baye on the Canal du Nivernais, but like other pioneers had withdrawn from the industry a little before it had turned into today's popular and profitable operation. That many French waterways, long since deserted by freight traffic, remain available to pleasure boaters is all part of Pierre Zivy's legacy. We owe him a huge debt.

Trilport (K127) has shops, fuel, restaurants and adequate moorings just below the bridge on the left bank: but be warned – the narrow channel past a small island just beyond is obstructed by rocks and navigation marks must be followed exactly. Sadly, few signs now remain of a long-disused twin tank inclined plane connection between the Marne and the Canal de l'Ourcq on the right bank at K129, but until recent years, the site was denoted *Transbordeur* on certain waterways charts. Industrial development has engulfed the approach basin. On the opposite bank is the keeper's house of the vanished Basses-Fermes lock.

Meaux (K133.5), 'capital' of Brie, spreads around a horseshoe bend of the river. It is a city with a long and rich past, memorable features being the cathedral of St-Étienne and a charming nearby *jardin* designed by landscape gardener André Le Nôtre (1613–1700). The natural river suffers from an overdose of concrete, all through traffic being diverted through automated Écluse 12 and into 12km of bypass channel, the **Canal de Meaux à Chalifert**. An ancient 450m artificial cut in the centre of Meaux was originally constructed in the 13th century: this **Canal Cornillon** has a single lock dating from 1660. The line declined after the opening of the Chalifert Canal in 1846. Since 1995, the lock has been restored as a heritage monument, complete with wooden gates. It allows pleasure craft to make a circuit on the Marne via Jablines and Trilbardou. Best moorings for Meaux are on a pontoon in the centre (water and electricity: 48hr limit). Excellent shopping is within a short distance with an excitingly varied food and clothing market several times a week, including Saturdays. In cutting off a great loop of the Marne the canal avoids several attractive villages including **Trilbardou, Charmentray,** and **Précy-sur-Marne**. In **Condé-Ste-Libaire** (K141) the **Grand Morin** river flows under the canal to join the Marne, and is shortly followed by its lateral canal which now serves as a feeder for the main line. This former navigation was created as long ago as 1520, changes in level at the 12 mills en route to Tigeaux being overcome by a rare variety of flash lock. It remained in use by barges until about 1925. The appealing village offers several shops

The Chalifert tunnel on a canalised section of the River Marne near Meaux.

and a restaurant. More extensive supplies can be found on the right bank in **Esbly** (K142.5) with a good quay beyond the bridge (garage and all shops within a short walk). **Coupvray** (K144) was the birthplace of Louis Braille (1809–52), inventor of the blind reading system. A museum has been set up in his parents' house.

Soon after Écluse 13, **Lesches** (K145), the canal passes through the 290m **Chalifert** tunnel, controlled by traffic lights. Écluse 14, Chalifert lies beyond a basin at the far end and immediately before a return to the natural river. Facilities here include a boating centre with slipway and a restaurant. 7km of the bypassed Marne may be navigated from here to **Annet-sur-Marne** and onwards via the river to Meaux (see above). One most enjoyable object of this exercise would be to visit the admirable Leisure Park of **Jablines**, where very extensive gravel workings have been expertly landscaped to provide water space for wind-surfing, dinghy sailing, rambling and swimming from a sandy beach. It is a popular attraction for the people of Paris on hot summer afternoons.

The Touring Club de France has a pleasure boat harbour on the left bank (K150.2), offering most aids to civilised boating such as slipway, water, crane, electricity, restaurant and overnight moorings. With the remainder of the journey becoming more and more urban and considering the impossibility of finding a secure yet inexpensive mooring in Paris, there is much to be said for staying here for a period and visiting the capital by public transport.

From now on, shopping and eating facilities are encountered so often that it is not necessary to list them here. While towns follow each other in quick succession, several of them retain a distinct identity in spite of the influence of ever-expanding Paris. One such is **Lagny** (K151), with quay-side moorings, where old houses and a fountain of great antiquity are among the sights. Écluse 15 (K156) at **Vaires-sur-Marne** marks the start of the **Canal de Chelles** bypass channel, with gravel pits, cement works and normally hectic commercial traffic. This continues through **Gournay-sur-Marne** (left bank, K161) and **Chelles** (right bank), past **Noisy-le-Grand** (left bank, K164) and **Neuilly-sur-Marne** (right bank), with Écluse 16 (K164.8) bringing the navigator back onto the river upstream of **Bry-sur-Marne** ((K166.5). The original Marne navigation remains available for boating for 3km between the upper end of the Chelles Canal and a former lock at **Noisiel**; and for 4km upstream past Noisy-le-Grand. All is now busy suburbs whose attributes can scarcely compete with the romance of fast-approaching waterside Paris.

Midway between **Le Perreux-sur-Marne** and **Nogent-sur-Marne** is a chandler and slipway (K170.1,

opposite Ile aux Loups), while good moorings are to be found in the extensive *port de plaisance* at Nogent (K170.9, right bank). A *Métro* station is about 1km distant, providing rapid transport into Paris. One final change to the original course of the river is encountered at **Joinville-le-Pont** (K173.4), where a huge loop through **Champigny-sur-Marne**, **La Varenne** and **St-Maur-des-Fosses** is avoided by the 600m St-Maur tunnel, controlled by traffic lights and soon followed by the St-Maur lock (K174.6). It is possible to cruise, with care, for quite a distance through Créteil to a commercial port area at **Bonneuil**. As no freight traffic uses the section beyond, watch out for anglers and oarsmen (who consider it to be their exclusive preserve).

After St-Maur, there remains just one more lock, Écluse St-Maurice (K177.2, 48hr mooring 400m above) downstream of **Maisons-Alfort**. The Seine confluence is at **Alfortville** (K178) about 5km above the Ile de la Cité and the heart of Paris (see Chapter 13). The Romans called the Marne *Matrona*, The Good Lady, an apt description of her normally placid nature. Although mostly unremarkable the river provides peaceful and enjoyable cruising.

16 ~ Paris. Canals St-Martin, St-Denis and de l'Ourcq

> **Carte Guide:** *Navicarte 33, Canal de l'Ourcq et les Canaux de Paris*
> **Canal St-Martin** from the River Seine, Quai Henri IV, upstream of the Ile de la Cité, to the Bassin de la Villette (Jaurès Métro station), junction with the Canal de l'Ourcq. 4.5km with 9 locks.
> **Canal St-Denis** from a junction with the Canal de l'Ourcq near the Bassin de la Villette, to the River Seine downstream of Paris at St-Denis. 6.6km with 7 locks.
> **Canal de l'Ourcq** from a junction with the Canal St-Martin at the Bassin de la Villette to Port-Aux-Perches, terminus. 108.1km with 10 locks.

This group of three waterways is controlled by the City of Paris. Most easily described as a single canal, the St-Martin and the St-Denis provide an alternative passage to a 30km loop of the Seine, their combined length being little more than one third of the distance. They offer the possibility of a circular cruise through the capital; this is of very great interest, as it provides little known views of the central and western parts of Paris. At the junction of these two canals, the Canal de l'Ourcq heads eastwards, running parallel with the River Marne for much of its course and sometimes directly alongside it. At Mareuil, the bed of the River Ourcq itself is used and is canalised to the terminus at Port-aux-Perches, NE of La Ferté-Milon. Once clear of its urban Parisian reaches, the Ourcq is a surprisingly beautiful navigation, passing through the woods and villages of the Marne valley. Its banks are maintained with immaculate flair, making it an agreeable setting for towpath walking, cycling, fishing, boating and (where suitably surfaced near Paris) roller blading! Each day, Paris uses upwards of 380,000m³ of raw water for cleansing gutters and sewers and for watering parks and flower beds. More than half is supplied by the Canal de l'Ourcq. Water flow is considerable throughout the navigation. Thus an upstream journey is noticeably slower than one in the reverse direction.

Until 1983 the waterways of Paris were virtually closed to pleasure craft; apart from commercial traffic close to the city, the only vessels to use the upper Ourcq were elongated narrow boats (*flûtes*) engaged on maintenance work. Now, all that has changed, and the canals have been revitalised with a magnificent marina in the Bassin de l'Arsenal (just off the Seine) and a system of mechanised locks on the upper Ourcq where access keys are lent to pleasure boaters to work through unsupervised. Elsewhere, there are keepers to operate locks and mobile bridges.

A small number of hire craft are based on or near these canals; of necessity these must be of reduced beam to be able to pass through locks and bridges on the Ourcq. The lure of the rural Marne valley coupled with a possibility of also reaching the heart of Paris is appealing. For details of hirers consult advertisements in *Fluvial* magazine (see Appendix). Passenger vessels are in service over various sections during the summer season. These include one boat that makes a morning run from the Quai Anatole France (by the Pont Solferino) up the Seine and along the length of the Canal St-Martin to the Bassin de la Villette, with a return cruise in the opposite direction in the afternoons. There is also a 10hr voyage available along the Canal de l'Ourcq from the Bassin de la Villette towards Meaux and return on several days each week.

Dimensions of the canals are such as to admit 38m long *péniches* (or slightly larger vessels on the Canal St-Martin and Canal St-Denis); however, the majority of the Canal de l'Ourcq is equipped with unusually long but narrow locks and is only suitable for boats whose dimensions do not exceed 58.8m length x 3.7m beam x 0.8m draft x 2.4m air draft. A small charge is made for using the St-Martin and St-Denis while passage of the Canal de l'Ourcq is free. Necessary permits and keys are supplied by lock keepers on arrival.

Consideration has been given to construction of a new lock, or perhaps a 13m lift, connecting the Canal de l'Ourcq with the River Marne near Lizy. Preliminary studies were carried out in 1984, when it was generally accepted that such a facility would be very useful, thus creating a cruising circuit via the canal, Marne and Seine.

Brief history Rising in the Fôret de Nesles SW of Soissons, the upper part of the River Ourcq was originally made navigable in the 16th century: it featured an early form of pound lock, believed to have been designed by Leonardo da Vinci. The enterprise was not a great success and was taken over by the Duc d'Orléans in return for tolls in perpetuity. He rebuilt the line between La Ferté-Milon and the Marne near Lizy,

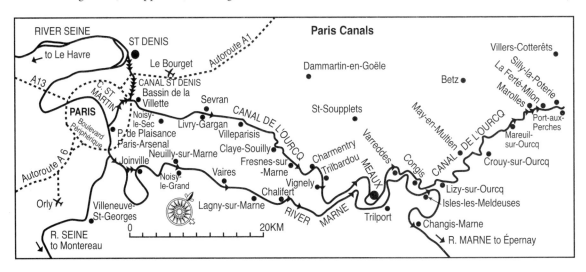

Most favoured pleasure craft mooring in Paris is the Bassin de l'Arsenal. Instantly recognisable in this early 20th century photograph, warehousing on the right has been replaced by lush gardens.

installing 21 locks. It achieved considerable prosperity, conveying great quantities of timber for the fires and stoves of Paris in barges known as *demi-Marnois*. In 1676 Riquet, promotor of the Canal du Midi, proposed an extension of the route which envisaged a canal into the heart of the capital, with water-powered corn mills at each lock in the final descent towards the Seine. Wars intervened and nothing more was to be achieved until the early 19th century.

A decision was made in 1802 to start work on all three canals, the St-Martin and the St-Denis originally being known curiously but quite accurately as the Canal de la Seine à la Seine. At the time of its opening, it was likened to the Regent's Canal in London, where the geographical location in relation to the Thames is very similar. Construction was hardly rapid and although the Bassin de la Villette was completed in 1808, the Canal St-Denis was not finished until 1821, followed the next year by the Canal de l'Ourcq (Paris to Mareuil) and the Canal St-Martin in 1825. Navigation ceased on the Ourcq between Mareuil and the Marne in 1824 and the toll collection rights were removed from the family of the Duc d'Orléans by the City of Paris.

Severe water shortages resulted in long stoppages on the network and pumping stations were subsequently built during the 1860s at Trilbardou and Isles-les-Meldeuses to lift supplies from the Marne into the Canal de l'Ourcq. Also, during this period, part of the Canal St-Martin was roofed over to create a boulevard above, resulting in a long tunnel section known as the Voûte Richard Lenoir. Various other modifications followed such as modernisation of the Canal St-Denis (1884–92), the covering of the St-Martin's Bassin du Temple to create a further tunnel section (1906–07), and the enlargement of the St-Denis (1923) and the

11km of the Canal de l'Ourcq nearest Paris (1925–34). One in each pair of duplicated narrow locks on the Ourcq has recently been widened from 3.2m to 3.7m, enabling a larger number of pleasure boats to use the navigation.

One curiosity was a form of inclined plane railway linking the Ourcq with the Marne near Meaux. This was described in 1936 as a 'roller staircase' and seems to have consisted of a pair of counter-balanced tanks in which merchandise (but not barges) was transferred from one level to the other. Now the site is difficult to penetrate amid the growing sprawl of an industrial estate. In 1890, it was claimed that more than one quarter of all water-based traffic entering Paris emanated from the Ourcq. From a pre-World War II annual tonnage of 905,000, all but the western part of the waterway gradually ceased to carry goods and by the early 1980s its sole function was water supply to Paris. The final chapter in its history came in 1983, when it was designated a leisure waterway with the (then) rare feature of boatman-operated locks. In this rôle it seems assured of a bright future. Cruising facilities throughout are excellent, with liberal supplies of bollards and water points. Distance signboards ensure that you can readily locate your whereabouts.

CANAL ST-MARTIN

One bright morning in early May I journeyed the length of the waterway aboard a public trip boat. I normally find passenger craft rather tame; since that day I have travelled the canal a number of times in my own motor yacht. However, I found that first three hour journey so captivating that I can think of no better way of describing this short navigation than to recount the experience. Having obtained tickets many weeks in advance for my companion and myself, we presented ourselves at the Quai Anatole France by the Chambre des Députés *Métro* station and after a little searching among the moored *péniches* and houseboats discovered the *Eautobus* bobbing gently on the Seine swell. It immediately recalled Mr C J Aubertin's early 20th century craft featured in *A Caravan Afloat*: a rectangular catamaran hull with upright cabin accommodation amidships, forward steering and boxes of red pelargoniums on the bow, which the captain proceeded to water by scooping liquid from the turbid river. In all, there were just six adult passengers, suddenly augmented by an invasion of lively school children who were (thankfully) herded within. We took what we considered to be the best position at the front, next to the helmsman. An attractive girl student was present as guide/hostess, but her unamplified voice did not have the power to deliver a commentary to all on board. She therefore passed the voyage moving between three positions at the extremities of the craft, delivering a well-phrased account of the waterside attractions – in French. Being the only two foreigners, we did not like to insist on the advertised English translation. From time to time, we caught her sneaking a glance at her written notes, keeping roughly one building ahead of the commentary. But, then, it was early in the season.

Opposite the Ile de la Cité we were overtaken, at alarmingly close quarters, by a laden 350-tonne *péniche*. We then pulled into a narrow entrance on the northern embankment just below the Pont d'Austerlitz, where a deep lock could be discerned in the gloom. This is the beginning of the Canal St-Martin. A delay ensued and it appeared that the keeper (able to see us on closed circuit TV) was not ready for our scheduled arrival. The guide clambered ashore and soon afterwards the gates of Écluse 9, La Bastille, opened to receive us. Beyond, is a large pool, now converted into the most extensive marina in Paris: the *Port de Plaisance Paris-Arsenal*. (VHF Channel 9.) Inaugurated by the City Mayor in 1983, it comprises more than 160 berths of which some are always available for visitors (advance bookings are not taken: the management aims to accommodate all arrivals). Other berths are occupied by private pleasure craft and residential vessels up to 25m in length. Visiting craft charges vary according to the time of year, and while not cheap, compare very favourably with most other methods of obtaining a bed in central Paris. There is a reduction for the first night. Safe from the troublesome wash of the Seine, within walking distance of most tourist destinations and, vitally, secure with 24hr guard dog patrols, this is easily the best option for boaters. Annual charges are levied on residential craft

Approaching the radar-activated Pont de Crimée at the head of the Bassin de la Villette, Canal St-Martin.

with the possibility of negotiating leases up to 30 years. Among facilities are a Harbourmaster's office and remote control point for working Écluse 9, toilet block with showers, telephone, waterside planted areas, a children's play enclosure, restaurant and lifting arrangements for boats up to 6 tonnes.

At the far end of the basin (K0.9) is the Place de la Bastille and its July Column surmounted by the figure of Liberty. For many years the canal has been enclosed from this point in a series of shallow tunnels, the Voûtes de la Bastille, Richard Lenoir and du Temple, totalling 2,019m. Boulevards are planted with trees and shrubs overhead. While there is no artificial illumination, the vault is dimly lit by shafts from above and the ghostly columns of light produce a highly charged and eerie atmosphere. The children confined to the cabin of the *Eautobus* fell strangely quiet, while the captain repeatedly tried to persuade me to photograph reflections of bushes and lamp standards – a reminder of the normal world outside. Twin towpaths increase the generous proportions of this tunnel, which has a marked bend beyond its halfway point. Comprehensive cleaning operations are carried out every other year: during a recent stoppage, the tunnel had produced a bath, four sewing machines, several bicycles, a machine gun, assorted revolvers and the remains of a cow, complete with horns and a tail. The Canal St-Martin has long been a popular film location and the passengers exchanged knowing looks when informed that Vigo's *L'Atalante* and Carné's *Hôtel du Nord* were shot here.

Once clear of the tunnel, the waterway takes centre stage surrounded by the streets and buildings of an old Paris that looks just like its film set self, with images familiar from such classic favourites as *Le Ballon Rouge*. Characteristic features are planes and horse chestnuts, several iron footbridges, the swing bridge de la rue Dieu, and three sets of two-rise locks invariably thronged with bystanders when a boat passes through. The first of these is Écluses 7/8, du Temple (K2.8), which lead to the Bassin des Marais.

Commercial wharves receive sand and gravel by barge from the Seine, but most other goods now arrive by road. Écluses 5/6, des Recollets (K3.3), and 3/4, des Morts (K3.9), are close to the Gare de l'Est. Then follows the Bassin du Combat, named after an infamous cockpit. One more tunnel remains to be negotiated, the 103m Voûte Lafayette: there is no towpath and horseboats were once hauled through by an endless tow-rope system, of which vestiges can still be seen. Then comes the final staircase, Écluses 1/2, de la Villette (K4.5), and the junction with the Canal de l'Ourcq's Bassin de la Villette. As we disembarked, several

péniches were waiting to descend to the Seine, evidence that these urban canals still carried respectable quantities of freight. We bade farewell to the *Eautobus* and her friendly crew and made out way to the nearby Jaurès *Métro* station to return quickly, but more prosaically, to central Paris.

CANAL ST-DENIS

Although lacking the scenic interest of the St-Martin, this route (in common with almost all urban waterways) is certainly worth exploring, especially as part of a circumnavigation of Paris. Much of the canal, however, is quite straight and being lined with wharves it takes on the appearance of an extended dock. Commercial traffic is generally heavy and mainly comprises astonishingly overladen sand and gravel barges. As locks are mechanised and duplicated, side by side, no great delays should be experienced. Good shopping facilities are always close at hand. After it leaves the *Gare Circulaire* at the Canal de l'Ourcq junction, the St-Denis immediately plunges into a deep lock, Écluse 1, Pont de Flandre, with a railway station of the same name beyond. Alongside is the splendid museum of science and technology, established in 1985 in a 1960s structure that was originally designed as a central abattoir. The site is dominated by a massive silver dome of the Géode cinema, which has a 1000 sq metre screen. Écluse 2, Quatre Chemins (K1.3); Écluse 3, Pont Tournant (K2.2) and Écluse 4, des Vertus (K3.2) all lie within the suburb of **Aubervilliers**. Just after Écluse 5, Porte de Paris (K4.6, convenient supermarket) is the railway station of **St-Denis**, a town of great historical note and now absorbed into Greater Paris (see Chapter 13). Écluse 6, de la Gare (K5.7), and Écluse 7, de la Briche (K6.5), are shortly followed by a junction with the River Seine.

CANAL DE L'OURCQ

Extending for 700m with a 70m width, the **Bassin de la Villette** acts as a raw water reservoir for Paris. Entered from the west by the Canal St-Martin, it is well served by shops, restaurants and other urban facilities, with a *Métro* station, Jaurès. During the late 1980s, extensive improvements were made to provide pleasure craft moorings and bases for hire cruisers and passenger craft. One of the leading open spaces of the capital, it is dominated by an 18th century former tax office – the Rotunda, designed by visionary architect Nicolas Ledoux. At the far end, the canal passes beneath a remarkable iron lift bridge, de la rue Crimée (K0.8), dating from 1885. Surmounted by heavy winding wheels, the deck rises horizontally by hydraulic pressure when a boat pauses for several seconds by a sensor (as instructed on a notice board). The waterway still carries freight over its first 9.6km, having been widened to Freycinet gauge and rendered suitable for *péniches*. Given a boat of suitably slender dimensions, a return cruise from Paris to the head of navigation can comfortably be made in four days. At K1.4 the Canal St-Denis forks off towards the Seine, and from this point to a crossing of the Boulevard Périphérique (Paris ring road), the Canal de l'Ourcq runs through the Villette Museum Park. After considerable commercial activity at **Port Serrurier**, with grain and gravel wharves, we arrive in the **Pantin** district (K2.9), with a large basin, shops, garages, restaurants and *Métro* station. Very considerable efforts have been made to landscape the canal's surroundings. Virtually throughout, the towpath is admirably surfaced, encouraging use by walkers, joggers, cyclists, sunbathers, anglers and even long-distance roller bladers. All this presents a highly animated scene, illustrating the newly-developed rôle of suburban inland waterways in the Age of Leisure. Curiously, however, pleasure boating has been slow to catch on.

The way ahead lies through a series of built-up districts, liberally provided with railway tracks, always close to essential services. These include **Bobigny** (K4.5, shops, fuel, restaurants and *Métro*), **Romainville** (K5, shops, fuel, restaurants and the 18th century church of St-Germain-l'Auxerrois); **Noisy-le-Sec** (K6.6, shops and fuel); **Bondy**, by a crossing of the A86 *autoroute* (K8, shops, fuel and restaurants); and **Pavillons-sous-Bois** (K9.6), end of the enlarged part of the canal (local shops).

Livry-Gargan, right bank, and **Aulnay-sous-Bois**, left bank K11.2), both feature normal suburban facilities with further shops in **Sevran** (K13.5). Here the lock keeper issues cruising permits and appropriate keys to fit the anti-vandal devices on paddle gear at the remaining nine locks. A degree of fluency in French is helpful if you are to understand lock working instructions arranged in cartoon form in the *Guide*. Check to see if your map book has an English translation. If you feel you would benefit from a personal explanation, request one here. Festoons of ivy hang over the parapet of the Pont de la Pouderie (K15.1), brushing the deck of the boat as you pass. The waterway continues quite straight through **Villepinte** (K15.7, shops and fuel 200m from bridge). A curiosity to visit is the dogs' cemetery, on the road towards **Tremblay-les-Gonesse** (K17.2, shops). Next comes **Villeparisis** (K19.3, shops and market, Sunday mornings) and **Mitry-Mory**

K19.6) on the boundary of Greater Paris, with shopping and fuel 300m from a bridge.

Now the Canal de l'Ourcq increasingly becomes most agreeable with a winding course through hilly country and numerous pleasant villages. In **Clay-Souilly** (K27.3) craft with less than 2.2m air draft will be able to slip under a drawbridge without having to open it. Fuel may be obtained within 200m, while there are also shops, water point and a launching ramp. The first boatman-operated lock occurs near **Fresnes** (K32.9, choice of waterside restaurants): like several others, this was constructed with duplicated chambers, only one of which is now available. Although virtually foolproof, these DIY locks are time-consumingly complicated. By inserting the borrowed key (marked 'A') another is released...and so through six operations paddles and gates are worked until a final key, identical to the one you arrived with, is detached for use at the next lock. Sensibly, all keys are attached to plastic floats. It is intended that keys will be replaced by 'smart cards'. An association with the River Marne begins in **Charmentray** (K35.7), a lovely area of thickly wooded banks with a drawbridge. This part of the river, lying well below canal level, is bypassed by the Canal de Meaux à Chalifert (see Chapter 15). **Trilbardou** (K39) is situated between the Canal de l'Ourcq and the Marne, a pretty little village with lime tree-shaded square, basic shopping, an antique dealer and restaurant. This is the site of a pumping station which lifts water into the canal by means of a hydraulic wheel installed in 1864. A turbine was added in 1920. Visits are possible by making advance arrangements with *La Section des Dérivations et Canaux*, 6 quai de la Seine, 75019, Paris, tel 01 44 89 14 14.

Another lock, Écluse de **Vignely** (K40.2), lies a short distance west of the village where there are shops and a restaurant. Shopping and a café can be reached **Isles-les-Villenoy**, beyond the next bridge (K42.8). Both the Marne and its navigation canal converge on the Canal de l'Ourcq near **Mareuil-les-Meaux** (no access possible) with several shops and a garage about 500m west of a bridge at **Villenoy** (K46). Further on, the Écluse de Villenoy has a dry dock, used for maintenance of the *flûtes de l'Ourcq* workboats. Staff here were unusually anxious to provide us with a conducted tour. One *flûte* was being restored as a museum exhibit. Slipway. The route now describes a broad curve around **Meaux** (K48, see Chapter 15): the best approach is from the twin basins each side of a bridge, very close to the centre of the old city. A full range of facilities is at hand. This is the end of the passenger boat run from Paris.

The next lock, Écluse **St-Lazare** (K54.7), is followed by the remains of the inclined plane railway (*transbordeur*) connection with the Marne (K57.4) with a gradual return to pleasant countryside. **Trilport**, reached down the N3 road from a bridge at K58.5, lies beyond the Marne, while **Poincy** (K60.7) is situated between the two waterways. Each is briefly described in Chapter 15. The canal winds through woodland to a lock near **Varreddes** (K64.7); the surroundings are immaculate with cast iron decorated lamp standards. Shops, restaurants and fuel (500m). Tantalisingly close, the Marne again approaches the canal beyond **Maladrerie** (K66.5) and once more (after the village of **Congis** K70.9, with grocer, restaurants and fuel) near **Iles-les-Meldeuses** (K73). A second pumping station, equipped with a huge Girard hydraulic wheel, installed in 1867, delivers water to the canal at a rate of 420 litres per second. Visits on application to the Authority (address above). The town itself is about 2km SE across the Marne and has adequate shopping and restaurants.

Of several possible locations for a lock or lift connection between canal and river, the confluence of the River Ourcq and Marne (K74.7) appears the most likely. One plan envisages a tank in which boats remain afloat while being trundled down a slope to the lower level, or *vice-versa*. Should a device in this form be chosen, it will be a world first. When built, the cruising potential of each navigation will be greatly enhanced, although a massive financial outlay will be needed to overcome the 13m difference in levels. For a time, the Ourcq runs alongside the canal before eventually becoming absorbed into the navigation at Mareuil. This is a little known valley that boasts several enchanting small towns such as **Lizy-sur-Ourcq** (K76.4, shops, restaurants, fuel and rail station). The 15th century church should be visited to see its ancient stained glass. The waterway played a decisive part in the Battle of the Ourcq in the opening weeks of World War I. Fierce fighting raged from August 24 to September 13 and the Germans made many early gains until the night of September 7, when a fleet of 600 Paris taxis carried 6,000 fresh troops from the capital; the eventual outcome was an Allied victory and the advance on Paris was stopped. **Ocquerre**, east of the canal at K79, is notable for a beautiful Renaissance farmhouse on the road towards Lizy. These upper reaches of the navigation (from east of Meaux to the terminus) must rank as among the most beautiful stretches of canal in the whole of France.

May-en-Multien, NW of the canal at Marnoue-la-Poterie (K83.4), offers a broad view over the Ourcq valley from the 15th century church tower: this served as an invaluable lookout point in World War I. There are shops, a restaurant and garage. Close to the Pont de la Ferme de Gesvres is the moated site of a feudal fortress erected by Louis d'Orléans and much

remodelled in the 18th century as the Château des Ducs de Gesvres. Only fragments of the building now remain. **Crouy-sur-Ourcq** lies beyond the river from a basin at K89, and is a useful source of shops with restaurant, garage and rail station. Nearby, you can discover the remains of the 14th century Château de Houssoy, with four-sided keep tower, all now rather decayed and incorporated into farm buildings. Shops and restaurant are to be found in **Varinfroy** (K90.4) with further shops and cafés at **Neufchelles** (K93).

At K94, a right-angled junction marks the start of the 1.2km long **Canal de Clignon**, a fully navigable waterway which appears to have escaped mention in most modern reference books. Maximum dimensions are 2.9m headroom and 0.8m draft. Boats up to 18m can turn round at the terminus, a very worthwhile objective with the Ancienne Commanderie de Moisy – a superb collection of fortified buildings, derelict church and impressive gatehouse with spiral staircase. We were especially excited to be able to penetrate this branch as its existence was totally unexpected!

We finally join the canalised River Ourcq in **Mareuil-sur-Ourcq** (K96.6) with a slipway in the port, shops, restaurant, garage and rail station. The beautiful 13th century church of St-Martin commands a wide view of the valley. Écluse de Mareuil (K97.2) is the first of four with larger chambers, 62m long x 5.2m wide. The next two are Écluse Queue d'Ham (K99.7) and Écluse de Marolles (K102.4, no facilities). These enlarged upper locks have sloping sides of either grass or concrete which would be difficult to negotiate in a small boat had not the authorities installed ingenious mooring 'rafts' which ride up and down on wheels. About 4km NW in **Autheuil-en-Valois**, a mid 12th century priory church in the Romanesque style has degenerated into a barn.

Perhaps the canal's most interesting town with considerable historical associations is **La Ferté-Milon** (K104.1), site of the uppermost lock. Almost at the head of the waterway, it has sufficient shops, cafés and refuelling points to ensure that there is no sense of anticlimax on reaching the end of the line. Originally standing as one in a chain of medieval fortresses, it features the ruins of an important *château*, started in 1393 by Louis, Duc d'Orléans, who assumed the throne and took Queen Isabeau as his mistress when his brother Charles VI was declared insane. Once guarded by 24 towers and four gateways (of which just two of each remain) the great *château* still retains elements of its grandeur. Even though building work was never completed, Louis being assassinated on the orders of the Duc de Bourgogne in 1407 (for the sequel, see Chapter 13), the structure was able to hold out for four years during the Wars of Religion until it was taken by Henry IV in 1588 and its ramparts demolished. The town was birthplace of poet Jean Racine in 1639. Another architectural feature of La Ferté-Milon is the 12th century church of Notre Dame, largely reconstructed in the 16th century by Catherine de Medici. Much of the exquisite original stained glass was destroyed in bombardments during 1918. One museum is devoted to Racine, while another contains a collection of agricultural machinery.

Deep countryside past **Silly-la-Poterie** characterises the uppermost 4km of the Canal de l'Ourcq, with portions of artificial cut bypassing three natural river loops. Navigation continues to a terminus in the hamlet of **Port-aux-Perches** (K108.1).

17 ~ Canal Latéral à l'Oise and River Oise

Carte Guide: *Picardie*

The Canal Latéral à l'Oise runs from a junction with the Canal de St-Quentin at Chauny to the canalised River Oise at Janville, 33.8km with 4 locks. Connections are made with the Canal de l'Oise à l'Aisne at Abbécourt and the Canal du Nord at Pont l'Evêque. The River Oise continues the line from Janville to join the River Seine at Conflans-Ste-Honorine, 104.3km with 7 locks. A junction is made with the River Aisne at Choisy-au-Bac, near Compiègne.

A most important freight route between the Seine and the Channel Ports and the Low Countries, the River Oise and its lateral canal also have an obvious significance for pleasure craft. Commercial traffic can be hectic. Convoys up to 180m long x 11.4m wide can navigate the river between Janville and the Seine; 91m long x 5.6m wide, Janville to Pont l'Evêque; and from Pont l'Evêque to Chauny the locks admit standard 38.5m *péniches* only. This waterway freight has resulted in plenty of industrial development, although the Oise still features some pleasant reaches. The lateral canal is wide and tends to be somewhat dull. River locks are duplicated, side by side; as entry channels sometimes divide well before the chambers are reached, binoculars are useful to ascertain from light signals which route to take. Otherwise, call the keeper on VHF.

It would be difficult to imagine a better advertisement for the benefits of barge transport than the Oise; but it does underline a requirement for locks on the grand scale. All this is far removed from the 25-tonne capacity narrow boat canals of the English Midlands which I mistakenly (with many other enthusiastic protagonists) promoted for freight use in embarrassingly recent times! This is a 'blue flag' waterway, where commercial vessels are suddenly liable to display a blue board with flashing white light to indicate that they are taking the 'wrong' side of the channel.

The Oise rises in the Belgian Ardennes, close to the French border, and flows in a deep valley carved through chalk and fed by springs from fissures. Its gentle slope demands few locks. Apart from the main public holidays, locks remain open all day, through the year. Night passage of locks at Boran, Isle-Adam and Pontoise is available to pleasure craft on payment of a substantial fee. Conditions relating to this facility are contained in the *Carte Guide*.

Rather because of *where* it goes rather than taking the traveller through outstandingly attractive surroundings, the Oise has often featured in English language cruise accounts. Robert Louis Stevenson (*An Inland Voyage*, 1878), in spite of driving rain, subsequent boredom and finally being arrested on suspicion of spying, declared himself 'the happiest animal in France' while canoeing down the river below Compiègne. William Moens (*Through France and Belgium by River and Canal in the Steam Yacht 'Ytene'*, 1876) found that the 'river is much like the Upper Thames with its willows, poplars and rushes' but generally was more interested in monuments and buildings. E P Warren and C F M Cleverly (*The Wanderings of the 'Beetle'*, 1885) scarcely allude to the Oise itself, finding greater interest in their shore encounters when seeking nightly accommodation. And in his *Small Boat to Luxembourg* (1967) Roger Pilkington takes advantage of flood conditions to miss out the locks and shoot a series of weirs, whose tackle had been raised well clear of the water. An estimated 2–2½ days' run was accomplished in 6 hours, leaving little time to comment on the passing scenery at all! Thus, the Oise has earned an unjustified reputation for anonymity, at least with waterway writers.

And yet, it has to be admitted that this is no dreamy or idyllic stream: just a heavily worked waterway with a number of pleasant ports of call. It could be helpful to remember that the northernmost corner of the French network features various lengths which are infinitely more dreary!

Brief history As a major tributary of the Seine, the Oise has been navigable for many centuries: accounts tell of Norman raids in *drakkars* to ransack bankside villages. Powers were obtained by the Duc de Guise to extend the waterway upstream of Noyon to La Fère in 1662. The exceptionally winding and difficult course of the

Seine resulted in a scheme being launched in 1724 to construct a canal from Paris to the Oise at Méry. Known as the Canal de Bourbon, this would have enabled barges to travel between the two rivers in a single day. Six years later, the project was abandoned; the only portion of the line to be completed was the short Canal St-Denis (Canal de la Seine à la Seine).

With the opening of the Canal de St-Quentin in 1810 and creation of a direct route between the Oise and the Escaut, traffic increased substantially. A shortening of the journey was achieved by laying out a lateral canal to bypass loops on the upper section of the Oise: the Canal Latéral à l'Oise, on which work began in 1821. Electric haulage by tractors on rails was introduced during World War I. Since World War II locks have been enlarged, and in some cases re-sited, enabling the Oise and part of its lateral canal to accept large barges from either the Seine or the Canal du Nord.

Starting at a junction with the Canal de St-Quentin in **Chauny**, the Canal Latéral à l'Oise is well served by a down-market shopping district in this manufacturing area. Diesel fuel and water are available from a barge chandler on the left bank just below the second bridge. There is an excellent *port de plaisance* offering long and short-term moorings, hire cruisers, repairs and use of a small crane. **Abbécourt** (K3), at a junction with the Canal de l'Oise à l'Aisne, is a pleasant little former barge village where the remains of old wooden freight craft can be seen rotting in the reeds. The lockside boatmen's bar/grocer closed down long ago. The countryside is fairly attractive down to the first of the mechanised and duplicated locks (Écluse 1, St-Hubert, K9). Water point with butcher in the adjacent village of **Appily**.

Carving a straight line past the very wriggling Oise, the canal is served by a restaurant near a road bridge at **Le Jonquoy** (K15.4) and arrives at Écluse 2, **Sempigny** (K18, water point), with shopping and eating facilities in **Pont l'Evêque**. The Rousseau-Debacker barge repair works with slipway is located in an arm between the locks and the junction with the Canal du Nord which provides access to the Canal de la Somme and waterways of the North.

Several villages are of little interest to the pleasure boater until **Ribecourt-Dreslincourt** (K27), whose shops are within walking distance of a pair of road bridges. Écluse 3, Bellerive (K28.1), is passed a little upstream of **Béthancourt**. There are numerous facilities in the next pound, through **Thourotte** (K32) and **Longueil-Annel** (K33): they range from shops, restaurants and water point to a choice of barge repair yards and a bankside fuelling depot, on the left before Écluse 4, Janville. This

area, and Longueil especially so, is very attractive: the canal is lined by houses, many of which are obviously owned by former barge people. Now the navigation passes an island (downhill traffic takes the right channel) and from here onwards we are on the canalised Oise, with a reach of about 2km in use by boats from the junction up to the village of **Le Plessis-Brion**.

Augmented by the waters of the River Aisne (left bank, K38), the Oise increases in size on its approach to **Compiègne**. The Aisne and its lateral canal provide a route via Soissons and the Canal des Ardennes to the Meuse. Even if your intended destination is the Seine, it is well worth turning up the Aisne for 5km and through one mechanised lock to moor at **Le Francport**, within 1km of one of the most historic sites of the 20th century. This is the *Clairière de l'Armistice* (Armistice Clearing), deep in the heart of the Compiègne Forest. Railway lines were laid here during World War I to enable massive guns to be brought under cover of the trees. By November 1918 Germany was facing defeat and representatives of the two sides came to this secret rendezvous to discuss terms of surrender. It may well be that the punitive reparations demanded of the enemy by Marshal Foch were in part responsible for World War II, but after four years of slaughter France was not feeling generous. So ended the Great War, and the *Wagon-Lits* dining car where the document was signed was later brought back to its forest lair for permanent exhibition in the landscaped clearing. With more than a sense of history, Hitler performed a reverse ceremony in the same coach in 1940, before it was moved in triumph to Berlin, where it was later destroyed in Allied raids. The Compiègne site was restored at the end of World War II and an identical carriage found, to be equipped in just the same manner as that used by Foch as his mobile office. In spite of frequent swarms of tiny school children far too young to comprehend what they have been brought to see, and a thriving souvenir shop, the monument with effigy of Foch and dead imperial eagle, symbolic of the vanquished Germany, is all strangely moving. If preferred, the *Clairière* may be reached by walking or taking a taxi the 6km from Compiègne.

The city stands on the banks of the Oise about 2km downstream of the Aisne. Ample moorings exist on quays among working *péniches*, but a small *port de plaisance* close to the centre below a railway bridge appears, in my experience, not to welcome visiting boats. It is an impressive town, surprisingly intact considering the wartime punishment it received: the late 18th century bridge was destroyed in 1914, rebuilt in 1926, demolished again in 1940 and re-erected in 1949! Its great treasure is the royal palace, built by Louis

XV and Louis XVI shortly before the Revolution on the site of a 14th century *château*. Third in national importance to Versailles and Fontainebleau, it was improved by Napoléon and enjoyed a glittering if brief period under Napoléon III and his Empress Eugénie in the years that led up to the German invasion of 1870. House parties known as the *Séries de Compiègne* were attended by all the leading personalities of literature, music, art and science. One was expected to arrive complete with personal servant and there are tales of less wealthy guests prevailing on their friends to act as *valets*. But these were far from stuffy occasions and those present remarked on the informal atmosphere and efforts of their Imperial Highnesses to make their guests feel completely at ease. Open to the public throughout the year (except Tuesdays and holidays), the palace contains sumptuous furnishings and a road vehicle museum whose exhibits date from the mid-18th century. There are two statues of Jeanne d'Arc: one by the bridge and another in the square at the magnificent Gothic *Hôtel de Ville*, erected by Louis XII at the start of the 16th century. Alongside, the fascinating *Musée de la Figurine Historique* contains no fewer than 85,000 model soldiers dressed in uniforms through the centuries. Many agreeable walks or cycle rides can be taken in the forest, a district of hills and lakes with villages and leafy prospects. Stylish shops, numerous convenient restaurants, a main line rail station within a stone's throw of the river and tripping boats (details from the local tourist office) combine to make Compiègne the highlight of the Oise. Fuel is obtainable from a tanker barge with chandlery a little upstream of Écluse 1, **Venette** (K41), where the left chamber, above a weir, is the one generally in use except during flood conditions.

But for the intrusion of a railway line, the rural reach that follows would be utterly peaceful, with little to delay the boatman apart from a hire craft base offering various services and brasserie at **Jaux** (K46) and a restaurant by the suspension bridge of **La Croix-St-Ouen** (K49). After passing through Écluse 2, **Verberie** (K54, on the right of the lock island), we arrive at the small town of that name with quay moorings upstream of the bridge, on the left bank or (with permission) at the nearby water-ski club. Shopping is quite good on each side of the river and there is the impressive Château d'Aramont. A rather featureless reach leads under the A1 *autoroute* (K58.2) and on to Écluse 3, Sarron, close to the old lock on a disused loop of the river (K65, water point). Now follows **Pont St-Maxence** (K67.2), a once industrial town producing paper, pottery and metalwork. Today, it is quite a pretty little place with a pleasant waterfront

and a 14th century abbey. The best place to stop is on a quay, left bank, below the bridge, with shops and fuel stations nearby. Here I discovered a purveyor of *brocante* (a term that can imply anything from junk to antiques) who not only objected to examination of his stock but was charging laughably inflated prices. Patches of riverside industry alternate with open country through **Villers-St-Paul** and **Verneuil-en-Halatte** (K75) where there is a slipway by the bridge and food shops in the village (800m).

In spite of first impressions of heavy industry in the twin foundry towns of **Nogent-sur-Oise** and Creil (K79), where overnight stopping is said to be ill-advised, there are several interesting features to be reached from quay moorings above and below the bridge spanning an island. St-Medard's church (13–16th centuries), the Gallé-Juillet Museum with a collection of furniture and *faïence* and the 12th century church of Nogent are all worth visiting. There are streets of old houses, remains of fortifications and quite good shops and restaurants. Water is available on the quay (opposite the long island, right bank). Écluse 4, Creil, is also on the right (K81), the alternative channel and former lock being disused.

Now come considerable tracts of heavy industry, railway sidings and a huge power station with four prominent chimneys. The area improves by the elegant suspension bridge at **St-Leu-d'Esserent** (K86): note the waterside restaurant with mooring about 1km upstream. All facilities are close at hand as is the impressively huge church, built of local stone in the 12th century. Troglodyte houses are to be found in the vicinity. 5.5km SE is the *château* and forest of **Chantilly**, one of the country's leading racecourses and a great centre for breeding horses. It is easy to mistake the magnificent stables at Chantilly for the *château*! (I know: I once did!) Set amid lakes and formal gardens, the palace occupies the site of a Middle Ages fortress and the present structure was planned between the 16th and 18th centuries. 9km further to the east is **Senlis**, whose history began under the Romans and is well worth an excursion: attractions include the cathedral, *Musée de la Vénerie* (devoted to hunting relics) and a *château* of the Merovingian and Carolingian kings, in ruins since the Revolution.

Gravel pits on the right bank lead to the *Pavillon St-Hubert* restaurant in the left bank hamlet of **Toutevoie** (K88); there are convenient quay moorings. Next follows the small town of **Précy-sur-Oise** (K90) with suspension bridge and suitable points to tie up either on the quay under the bridge (shallow water: approach carefully) or on grassy banks. Shops, garage and restaurants are within a few hundred metres. **Boran-**

sur-Oise (K94) is a noted riverside resort, beloved by speed boat enthusiasts. Below the bridge is an extensive swimming pool/*plage*, while yacht club jetties can perhaps be used by visiting craft. After some rather bleak parts of the river, this little market town is really attractive: moreover, plenty of shops, restaurants and fuel station could result in a productive halt. 4.5km SE, the Abbey of **Royaumont** is open to the public every day in summer except Tuesdays. Founded by St-Louis in the 13th century, it was sold into private ownership in 1791. Below Écluse 5, Boran (K95, water point), the channel divides, the left arm following the river's original course behind a large island to **Noisy-sur-Oise** (K99). Provided they adhere to the 5kph limit, pleasure boats may take this course to discover a *base nautique* and pontoons 600m from the heart of the pleasing stone-built village topped by an exquisite church commanding a wide view of the valley.

On each side of a road bridge, **Persan** is a slightly industrialised satellite of **Beaumont-sur-Oise** (K103). Pleasure boat mooring on the right, below the bridge, is convenient for good shopping and eating (there is even a Chinese restaurant). Atop old ramparts is a terrace looking down to the river and relics of a feudal *château*, demolished in the early 16th century. More gravel workings and a power station give way to wooded scenery past **Champagne-sur-Oise** (K106.2, poor moorings and almost too far away to be of interest). One-way traffic indicators send boats round each side of the Ile de Champagne and ahead are seen the twin lock chambers of Écluse 6, **L'Isle d'Adam**, a resort popular with Parisians (K109, water point). To come ashore, pass *between* a pair of islands by the bridge (K110) connecting **Parmain** with L'Isle d'Adam and moor to a splendid floating pontoon on the left (water, electricity and refuse disposal), directly outside a restaurant. The town centre, with all shops, is about 300m away. Known as *Novigentum* in Roman times, L'Isle d'Adam stands on the borders of Ile de France and the Valois. It was invaded by the Normans in the early 9th century and chosen in 825 as the site of a fortified castle, on the Ile du Prieure, by Louis the Pious. This was destroyed 61 years later and rebuilt by Robert the Pious in 1014. Nearby forests covering almost 1,700 hectares were landscaped by Le Nôtre. Honoré de Balzac (1799–1850) wrote: 'L'Isle d'Adam is now paradise on Earth': it remains a delightful place with 14th century church and *Hôtel de Ville* of 1866 in the Renaissance style. The two swimming pools and riverside 'beach' are claimed to the largest inland *plage* in France. The complex was officially opened in 1949 by champion swimmer Johnny Weissmuller ('Tarzan', 1904–84).

Restaurant, garage, baker and slipway are found near a road and railway bridge at **Butry-sur-Oise** (K113). Downstream, the long village of **Auvers-sur-Oise** (K116) is scarcely visible from the river, being concealed by trees and a railway line. Mooring is possible near the slipway before reaching the head of the Ile de Vaux. (Shops, garages, restaurants and rail station.) Passage through the bridges of **Méry-Auvers** and **Chaponval** (K119) is potentially dangerous if pushed barge convoys are approaching: a one-way traffic system is in force in times of flood. Consult diagrams in the *Carte Guide*. Auvers is associated with an important group of 19th century artists attracted here by the quality of the light of the waters of the Oise; among them were Daubigny, Corot, Cézanne, Pissarro, Gauguin and Daumier. Vincent Van Gogh (1853–90), while receiving treatment for his mental problems, shot himself and died in a room at the *Café Ravoux* (now known as *à Van Gogh*); both he and his grief-stricken brother Théo are buried in the cemetery and there is a monument in the Parc Van Gogh.

The river runs past sandy beaches to the ancient city of **Pontoise** (K123), site of a 10th century fortress and to which the *Parlement* was exiled in 1652, 1720 and 1753. Remains of fortification walls and narrow streets recall some of its historic past close to useful mooring quays (by the town bridge, alongside a swimming pool). All facilities are easily reached from here. Pontoise has expanded rapidly in recent years and has a huge new town, **Cergy-Ville-Nouvelle**, in a bend of the river below Écluse 7 (K124, water point). As the Oise begins to curve towards the west, upstream of a rail bridge (K126) there is a *base nautique*, offering moorings, diesel fuel and craneage with restaurant.

We now travel round a giant loop past **Cergy** (K129). Extensive gravel workings have been landscaped as a magnificent water park (no direct access from the river: approach by road from the Pont de Cergy) which features waterside walks, riding, sailing, wind surfing and swimming in a huge 'natural' sand-bordered pool. A combined housing/restaurant/mooring development with 103 boat spaces has been created at **Cergy-Pontoise**. This *Port Cergy Marina* is an example of the very best in modern waterside design. Most boating facilities, including overnight stopping and wintering, are offered. In the remaining distance to the Seine, **Neuville-sur-Oise** (K134) provides useful shops with a full range of excellent facilities in the junction town and leading barge port of **Conflans-Ste-Honorine** (K138). Waterside fuel, water points and slipways are all located here although moorings may be difficult to find, amid a veritable mass of working and retired freight vessels (see Chapter 13).

18 ～ River Aisne and Canal Latéral à l'Aisne

Carte Guide: *Picardie*

The River Aisne is navigable from its junction with the River Oise at Choisy-au-Bac, near Compiègne to a junction with the Canal Latéral à l'Aisne at Condé-sur-Aisne, 57km with 7 locks. The Canal Latéral à l'Aisne continues the line eastwards to a junction with the Canal des Ardennes near Vieux-lès-Asfeld, 51.3km with 8 locks. Connections are made with the Canal de l'Oise à l'Aisne at Bourg-et-Comin and with the Canal de l'Aisne à la Marne at Berry-au-Bac.

The Aisne and its continuation eastwards via the lateral canal forms an important link between the Rivers Oise and Meuse, and consequently provides a connection between Paris and Belgium. With few locks, it offers relaxing boating past woods and meadows, much of the freight traffic encountered being generated by gravel pits. Locks on the river section (46m x 7.95m) are rather larger than those of Freycinet proportions on the lateral canal; all are mechanised, with keepers in attendance.

By 1680 the Aisne was fit for boats between the Oise and Pontavert, about 34km beyond the point where the lateral canal now takes over. For more than a century, a scheme was current to create a canal link from Pontavert to the River Bar and so join up with the Meuse: in 1778 this plan was known as the Canal de Champagne. But when the Canal Latéral à l'Aisne became a reality in 1841 it comprised a longer length of artificial channel than once envisaged, much of the higher Aisne being abandoned by craft except for the floating of timber (*flottage*), an activity practised until the 1930s. The eastern portion of the route, via the Canal des Ardennes, had been finished in 1833 and also consisted almost entirely of a man-made cut. Great quantities of German and Belgian coal were once carried by barge to Paris. But in more recent years commodities have included timber, sugar and beet. In 2003, this route was used by an average of 15 *péniches* each day, while pleasure craft numbers are rising every year.

Flowing into the Oise a short distance upstream of Compiègne, the Aisne is agreeably rural, for it forms the northern boundary of the great Forest of Compiègne for a considerable distance. On arriving in **Choisy-au-Bac** (K2.5) the best moorings are to a quay (left bank, below the bridge). Heavy road traffic does not entirely spoil the town's countrified aspect and shops, restaurants and garages are within close range. A short canal cut leads through Écluse 15, Carandeau (K3.3, water point) to the hamlet of **Le Francport** (K5.5) and the *Auberge de l'Armistice*. Taking care to avoid an underwater shelf beneath the bridge, moor to the right bank to visit the atmosphere-laden *Clairière de l'Armistice*, scene of the German surrender in 1918. It is a walk of about 1km, down a leafy road (see Chapter 17). Still on the edges of the Forest of Compiègne, **Rethondes** (K9) is a pleasing village of stone houses with gardens tumbling down to the water's edge. It has a restaurant, with mooring possibilities above or below the bridge on the right bank.

Écluse 14, Hérant (K10.4, water point) is followed by a pair of slightly industrial towns: **Breuil** on the right bank, facing **Berneuil-sur-Aisne** on the left. Both provide a range of facilities and can be reached from the **La Motte** bridge (K14.6). One curious architectural feature of the region is a pattern of stepped gable ends seen on many of the stone buildings, especially in **Attichy** (K17.7), after Écluse 13, **Couloisy** (water point). You may tie up to grassy banks near the bowstring bridge and walk several hundred metres to the shops. Well worth exploring is **Vic-sur-Aisne** (K22.7), approached either from below Écluse 12 (water point) and across a pedestrian bridge spanning the weir stream, or from the road bridge (moor above, on the left). Near the *Hôtel de Ville* is a very fine moated *donjon/château*, with convenient shopping and restaurants. From the river and dominated by massive concrete grain silos, Vic does not appear as the very attractive town it is. Moving upriver in wooded surroundings, the next place of note is **Port Fontenoy** (K27.8) with a useful landing stage outside the *Auberge au Bord de l'Eau*. Fontenoy itself, about 2km east, can only be reached from here, although it lies but a short distance from Écluse 11 (K29.8). **Pommiers** (K35.4) is surrounded by gravel workings: shopping is minimal. That presents no problem, as it is not far to the city of **Soissons** (K41.7), beyond Écluse 10, **Vauxrot** (K40.2, shopping). Soissons derives little aesthetic benefit from its situation on the river, for it is sometimes imprisoned in a canal-like concrete channel. It must be admitted that the city lacks any obvious beauty, having suffered the misfortunes of war all too frequently. Its history goes back to the days of Belgian Gaul and it was here that Clovis beat the Roman army in AD 486. Its greatest treasure is the 13th century cathedral of St-Gervais and St-Protais in the Gothic style with fragments of an 11th century abbey nearby, mostly demolished in 1805. Within the cathedral Rubens painted the *Adoration* for the monks in gratitude for the care he received while lying ill. A legend concerns the celebrated Vase of

Château and Hôtel de Ville *at Vic-sur-Aisne.*

Soissons, one of a number of items plundered by the Franks from the Church. Newly converted to Christianity, the young Clovis sought to recover this treasure and return it to the rightful owner. Such actions did not meet with wholehearted approval from certain of Clovis' warrior followers, one of whom expressed his disgust by smashing the vase with his sword. Annoyed as he was, Clovis awaited a suitable opportunity to redress the balance. Some years later, he came upon the same warrior in Paris during an inspection of troops, and with a mighty stroke of his sword cut the man virtually in two, remarking: 'I do to you what you did to the Vase of Soissons!' The tale is known to every French school child. Or should be…

Some years ago, an Inspector of Education was making a tour of Soissons: he singled out a boy sitting at the front of his class and asked him: 'Who broke the Vase of Soissons?' The child looked slightly frightened and replied: 'It wasn't me, Monsieur!' At which the class teacher anxiously declared: 'Pierre is an honest pupil. If he says he did not break the vase, you may be sure he is telling the truth!' Horrified at this ignorance of history, the Inspector sent a full report on the affair to the Minister: soon, a substantial file had accumulated. Then, there was an election and a change of Government. A new Minister was appointed and he was determined to bring the Soissons case to a speedy conclusion. 'Does it really matter who broke this vase?'

he questioned. 'I'll pay for a replacement out of my own pocket, and that will be an end to the matter!'

Pleasure boats may moor midway between the upper end of the Écluse 10 lock cut and the Pont du Mail, with easy access to the main shopping street and to restaurants – including one on a converted *péniche*. It is likely that the quays will be busy with working boats. On the eastern outskirts, Écluse 9, **Villeneuve St-Germain** (K44.2, water point), bypasses the Aisne as it flows through **Crouy**. This backwater is used by the local motorboat club, which has a slipway immediately downstream of the lock.

In the final upper reaches of the Aisne, **Venizel** (K49.3, shopping) is alone among several little towns that are likely to be useful to the passing pleasure boat. After **Condé-sur-Aisne** (K56.4), the navigation divides: the left branch is all that remains navigable of the canalised Aisne that once enabled barges to reach Pontavert. It can be followed for 2km to **Vailly-sur-Aisne** (K56.4). But there is little object in so doing, for the Canal Latéral à l'Aisne, entered on the right, passes through a two-rise lock Écluses 7/8, **Celles-sur-Aisne**, (K57.2), and runs almost as close to Vailly-sur-Aisne (K60.5). Although marked '*Bar, Restaurant, Épicerie*', a building near the locks is not obviously any of those: one lunch time I watched a series of suited businessmen arrive, ring a doorbell for admittance, and retire within. It appeared that normal passing custom was not being sought. Perhaps more in-depth research was required, but to date the opportunity has not presented itself! Right of the bridge at Vailly is a petrol station (no diesel) with bar/restaurant, while a short walk over the river bridge introduces civilisation in the form of a large supermarket.

In many ways, it is rather a relief to have left the river with its shortage of safe moorings and to enter a canal that involves itself intimately with towns and villages instead of keeping facilities at a safe distance from the prospect of flooding. For a spell, the canal is, however, as wide as many rivers and even boasts an official swimming pool. I have seen the crews of moored *péniches* happily cooling off here, as a steel barge can be an oppressive home in a heat wave. As the waterway enters a long straight at Écluse 6, **St-Audebert** (K61.6, water point), a bakery may be visited in the bankside hamlet of **Presles-et-Boves** (K63.1). **Cys-la-Commune** (K63.8) is a deeply rural hamlet by Écluse 5, with an odd little asymmetric church in a farmyard. Signs that the canal has outlived a railway at **Pont d'Arcy** (K67.9) are evident from a disused station. Écluse 4, la Cendrière (K69.8), is immediately followed by a left-hand junction with the Canal de l'Oise à l'Aisne and all facilities in **Bourg-et-Comin** (see Chapter 20).

The canal now enters a tract of gravel pits and swamps in the Aisne valley that is wild and by no means unattractive. Just after the second bridge from the junction, **Villiers-en-Prayères** (K69.1) is approached from the water across an extraordinary gravel square surrounded by great barns. Two succeeding villages offer various services: **Maizy** (K75.7), baker, grocer and restaurant – moor well beyond the bridge to a quay, right: a series of open-fronted half-timbered barns face the canal, and **Pontavert** (K83.7), all shops and restaurant, beyond the bridge spanning the once navigable Aisne. Écluse 3, **Berry-au-Bac** (K89.9, water point), stands at the junction with the Canal de l'Aisne à la Marne. It was once a real boatman's town, but with the decline in commercial traffic has changed in recent years. There are good moorings, fuelling facilities and shopping for food. Perhaps the legendary canal shop supplying all needs from fresh fruit and vegetables to rope, oil, fishing tackle, paint and rubber boots...a shop in a similar tradition to those still to be found in remote corners of Ireland and additionally operating as a licensed bar...perhaps the shop of Berry-au-Bac remains in business. But I fear not. One month these canal survivals appear to flourish, then the next month they have closed down for ever. Some years ago, I received such surly service here that I concluded that pleasure boat custom was not welcomed. For all that, I would be very sorry to find that this institution had vanished. There are two eating out possibilities: to the right of the N44 road bridge, *La Cote 108* restaurant, which I have found to be grossly overpriced and unwilling to serve our large boating party; and the *Restaurant de la Mairie*, which, being the complete opposite, is to be wholeheartedly recommended. There are several useful food shops.

Some mysterious variety of chemical works contaminates the towpath at the exit from Berry-au-Bac, followed by a wilderness of swamps and trees to **Condé-sur-Suippe** (K94.5) and Écluse 2, water point. The village has a restaurant and a weird open-work concrete church spire. Away to the left, the Aisne has become a very pleasant stream and attracts many caravans, campers and anglers. Silos and sugar works give a purposeful air to the small town of **Guignicourt** (K95.4), whose comprehensive shopping centre (with garage) lies immediately north of the river. Next comes the agricultural village of **Pignicourt** (K101.1), providing the *Auberge de l'Étang* restaurant and a water point at Écluse 1. 400m towards the Aisne are shops, restaurant and garage in **Neufchâtel-sur-Aisne** (K103). Neither **Brienne-sur-Aisne** or **Evergnicourt** are easily approached from the waterway and the final reach suffers from heavily overgrown banks making mooring difficult. The Canal Latéral à l'Aisne merges with the Canal des Ardennes at the next lock, Écluse de Vieux-lès-Asfeld (K108.3). For a continuation of the route towards the Meuse, see the Canal des Ardennes (next chapter).

19 ～ Canal des Ardennes

Carte Guide: *Champagne Ardenne*

From Vieux-lès-Asfeld, junction with the Canal Latéral à l'Aisne to a junction with the River Meuse (Canal de l'Est [Branche Nord]) at Pont-à-Bar, 88km with 44 locks. There is one tunnel, St-Aignan, 196m. A branch connects the main line at Semuy with Vouziers (terminus), 12.5km with 4 locks.

As part of a direct link between the Oise and the Meuse, the Canal des Ardennes is a continuation of the River Aisne and Canal Latéral à l'Aisne with no visible difference from one to the other. Something of a misnomer, it does not in fact pass through the Ardennes although it points in that general direction. From Vieux-lès-Asfeld it climbs up the Aisne valley, in effect a lateral canal to the river which follows the Vouziers branch from Semuy. No fewer than 27 locks in 9km then lift the waterway to its Le Chesne summit level and soon afterwards the route strikes up an acquaintance with the River Bar which is never far away until the Meuse. Pleasantly unremarkable at the western end to Attigny, the canal is thereafter remote and of great beauty, ending with rolling cornfields and forests towards Pont-à-Bar. Official km marks run from Vouziers to Vieux-lès-Asfeld and from Pont-à-Bar to Semuy. For simplicity, distances quoted below are continuous from one end of the main line to the other.

Traffic is moderately heavy: perhaps up to 15 barges daily. Locks operate to normal hours with a half-hour midday break. The 27-chamber flight and seven locks nearest the Meuse are automated. Time and again waterways writers have commented on the very Englishness of the Canal des Ardennes, a conclusion with which it would be difficult to find fault.

Brief history There was a plan in the latter part of the 17th century to connect the Aisne and the Meuse, in part using the River Bar; but nothing was to be achieved until work began on the line in 1823, completion coming ten years later. One key to water supplies was creation of the Étangs de Bairon reservoir, whose 5 million m³ capacity was sufficient to maintain levels in

the Le Chesne summit except in the driest of summers. Each of the seven locks nearest the Meuse were equipped between World Wars I and II with pumping stations and, as a result, the waterway is almost always able to cope with *péniches* loading 250 tonnes. Its original depth of 1.3m was subsequently increased to 1.8m, and it is generally regarded by commercial users as a quicker and more convenient route than the Canal de la Marne au Rhin.

In the 1960s, proposals were made to enlarge and improve the Canal des Ardennes, replacing the 27-lock flight with an inclined plane lift overcoming the 75m change in levels in a single operation. The resulting new summit level would have been 30km long and a new St-Aignan tunnel was to have been followed by one deep lock falling to the same level as the Meuse. This idea appears to have been abandoned.

The Canal Latéral à l'Aisne undergoes a metamorphosis into the Canal des Ardennes at a bridge by Écluse 14, **Vieux-lès-Asfeld** (K0, restaurant). The village itself is a pleasant little place, reached from the following bridge, next to a grain silo. **Asfeld** (K2.9) lies to the right of the next bridge and is notable for a remarkable late 17th century Baroque church of pinkish brick. The main part of the building is circular with a series of interconnected walkways and galleries; a brick colonnade, forming an extended porch, provides a link with the tower. This most unusual structure can be seen to good advantage across a large grassy square, with terraces of little houses in matching brick. The town is at the heart of a flourishing agricultural region and is well served by shops, restaurants and fuel stations. Écluse 13, Asfeld (K4.6), is succeeded by a rural length leading to the English-sounding **Balham**, and **Blanzy-la-Sablonaise** (K9.5) with limited shops and restaurant.

Never far from the River Aisne, the waterway continues to Écluse 12, **Pargny** (K12.5). A timber yard and silos by a bridge mark the approach, via a pair of river bridges, to the useful small town of **Château-Porcien**; this makes an excellent shopping stop and has a notable *Hôtel de Ville* standing at the base of a chalk cliff. Pleasing wooded scenery now accompanies the route through **Nanteuil-sur-Aisne**, Écluse 11 (K20.2), and Écluse 10, **Acy-Romance** (K22.3). Soon comes the important town of **Rethel** (K24.4), north of the Aisne and the only opportunity for really comprehensive shopping on the entire waterway. A centrally placed mooring quay, left bank, is equipped with water point and refuse bins. There are remnants of a 10th century *château* and the imposing 13/16th century church of St-Nicolas, comprising two naves, side by side. The earlier one was for the use of Benedictine monks, while that built later was intended for people of the parish. Photographs show how extensive was the destruction in 1940, with windows wrecked and the lofty vaulted roof completely smashed. But apart from the modern design of the replacement glass, it is difficult to detect where the damage occurred. In the two world wars 85 per cent of Rethel was reduced to rubble and rebuilding has been to an unusually high standard. The river crossing has always been of strategic importance: a plaque on the town bridge records invasions in 1411, 1543, 1650, 1814, 1870, 1914 and 1940.

Écluse 9, **Biermes** (K27.5), is followed by the expanding but still predominantly rural village of **Thugny-Trugny** (K30.3, Écluse 8). The road to **Roux** leads from the lock to a very tranquil tree-bordered reach of the Aisne whose deep and chalky waters are tempting for a swim on a hot summer's day. **Seuil**, near Écluse 7 (K33.9), offers a bar/restaurant and baker. After Écluse 6, **Givry** (K40.8), we soon arrive at **Attigny** (K43.1, quay moorings), a small town that assumes considerable importance, being the last possible food-buying stop before Le Chesne, 28 locks and a good day's boating ahead. Note the late 19th century bandstand and a restaurant close to the bridge. For fuel, collected in cans, cross the river into **Feubourg du Moulin**.

Beyond Écluse 5, Attigny, the canal becomes increasingly beautiful. Beyond **Rilly-sur-Aisne** (K47.9) is a broad basin with an unusual arrangement of two locks side by side. On the left, Écluse 27 continues the through route towards the Meuse and lowers craft into a short navigable reach of the Aisne. The right-hand lock, Écluse 4, provides access to the **Vouziers Branch** fed by the now very twisted Aisne. A single lock cottage served both routes and has a good example of a tiny window providing the keeper with a view of approaching traffic. Boats wishing to navigate the branch may do so during normal hours except on Sundays, when advance permission must be obtained by phone. For details, consult the *Carte Guide*. The Branch is countrified, remote and experiences little traffic. There are no facilities until the terminus. Locks are encountered at **Voncq** (K4 from the junction), **Vrizy** (K7.3), and just before the head of navigation at **Vouziers** (K11.6). Moorings in the town (K12.5) are adequate; there are ample shops and restaurants. The 16th century church of St-Maurille has an intricately carved triple portal. Vouziers developed into a leading commercial centre when in 1516 François I awarded it the charter for a fair.

Heavy concentrations of locks are moderately rare in France, as the waterways have mainly been engineered to avoid long flights. The eastern ascent to the summit of the Canal des Ardennes is a memorable

exception, with all 26 in the series now remotely controlled by radar beams and bars that are physically activated as craft enter or leave the chambers. Manned control points are established at Écluse 26, Semuy (K49.5) and Écluse 1, Le Chesne (K57.9). Needless to add, this is hilly country, providing splendid views over fields and woods. Once launched into such an automatic flight, I have doubts about the advisability of stopping for anything unless you are caught out by the power being turned off at night. To be frank, there is little reason for stopping (unless eating or taking a rest are high on your priorities). Should you decide to moor up, only do so after making prior arrangements with keepers at Écluse 26 or 1 or by telephoning them with your intentions. In this way, the locks can be remotely set in your favour once you are ready to resume your journey. Whether the bridge in **Montgon**, below Écluse 14 (K54.9), is slightly lower than most, I am not certain: but I well remember some worrying moments for an unladen *péniche* as it scraped through with barely the clearance of a matchbox – and that was with wheel house dismantled! Respite arrives at Écluse 1, water point, shortly before the highly convenient summit level town of **Le Chesne** (K59.6). Moorings on the right in a small basin by the Pont X; shops, restaurants and garage are within a stone's throw. In hot weather a pleasant excursion might be made from here to the canal's reservoir, **Le Lac de Bairon**, a magnificent sheet of water 3km north with fishing, bird-watching, sailing, wind-surfing and swimming with diving pool and sandy beach.

Now dropping down the valley of the River Bar, we meet the first descending lock, Écluse 1, near **Sauville** (K67.4). Already, the scenery is not unlike that of the Meuse, with meadows and patches of woodland. Within a short walk of Écluse 2, **La Cassine** (K71.1), where there is a massive concrete blockhouse from World War II, the village has an appealing little church beyond a *château*. After a sharp bend to the right, moor near a bridge to visit a splendid village of stone houses and imposing church: this is **Vendresse**, where farm buildings are huddled together for protection from invaders. Shops, garage and restaurant (about 2.5km). Écluse 3, **Malmy** (K75.9), marks the beginning of dense woodland, the likely haunt of *sangliers* (wild boar). As the River Bar encircles a further tract of forest, the canal dives into **St-Aignan Tunnel**, 196m long (K81.7). It operates on a one-way basis and boats must take care not to enter unless the route is clear. Écluses 4 and 5 are situated immediately afterwards, divided by a blind right-angled turn.

Arguably the prettiest village on the waterway is **Hannogne-St-Martin** (K85) whose brown stone

Tight fit for an empty péniche *at one of the Montgon locks.*

church was remodelled in the 18th century with a dome covered in slates shaped like fish scales. We have now moved from a region of tiles to the slate-land of the Meuse valley, although more recent buildings do not always respect such local traditions. There is a baker. Fully in keeping with inland waterways' conventions, the junction village of **Pont-à-Bar** (K87.1) is tiny, having nothing of interest to the general public except a bar alongside Écluse 6. Here, note the open air skittles enclosure, with chute for the return of balls. The heart of every boater will be gladdened at the sight of a comprehensive range of boat facilities, including waterside diesel pump, commercial dock, water point and a chandler who adds such necessities as *Carte Guides* to his stocks of bottled gas, rope and other *péniche* requisites. Our journey ends at Écluse 7 (K88), connecting the canal with the Meuse between Sedan and Charleville-Mézières.

20 ∾ Canal de l'Oise à l'Aisne

Carte Guide: *Picardie*

From a junction with the Canal Latéral à l'Aisne at Bourg-et-Comin to a junction with the Canal Latéral à l'Oise at Abbécourt, 47.8km with 13 locks. Much of the summit level is within the Braye Tunnel, 2,365m.

Remarkably similar to the nearby Canal de l'Aisne à la Marne in terms of age, length, purpose and layout, the Canal de l'Oise à l'Aisne likewise climbs to a summit level on its journey between two rivers and crosses the watershed via a substantial tunnel. With regard to the scenery, the Oise à l'Aisne is infinitely more beautiful, passing through deeply rural countryside throughout and hardly touching a village, let alone a town. At its best in early summer when the banks are ablaze with wild flowers, it may well qualify as the most endearing waterway in northern France.

A glance at the map indicates that the canal is a useful connecting link. Commercial traffic remains moderately heavy. All the locks are mechanised, Nos 10–13 working as an automatic set in conjunction with passage of Braye Tunnel.

In canal building terms, this one is modern, having been opened in 1890. It suffered serious damage during World War I and was not returned to service until complete reconstruction was finished in 1931. Up to 1914, annual freight had included 2 million tonnes of coal alone, so the subsequent necessary detour of 55km during the long closure was regarded seriously. Water

supplies were improved as part of the rebuilding programme. Until horse drawn barges were phased out in the 1960s, there was electric bank traction and an electrically driven towing device suspended from the tunnel roof.

We enter the Canal de l'Oise à l'Aisne at a junction with the Canal Latéral à l'Aisne, soon to cross a small aqueduct (uphill craft have priority) over the River Aisne at the approach to the village of **Bourg-et-Comin** (K0.3, supermarket). A long straight leads to the first of four locks on the ascent to the summit level, Écluse 13, **Verneuil** (K2.9). All work as an automated series: for operating instructions, consult the *Carte Guide*. Surroundings are hilly with cornfields – on a summer's day the epitome of everything you seek in waterway travel. By Écluse 12, **Moussey-Soupir** (K3.8) is a useful grocer/bar. Two further locks lead to a deep cutting and the impressive Tête Aisne portal of **Braye-en-Laonnois** tunnel (K7.1), illuminated inside and out. Entry is controlled by lights, with a waiting time of up to 1hr. Totally rebuilt in concrete in recent years, the tunnel mouth is equipped with a large extractor fan. A lane to the right provides an approach into Braye village, a lost little farming settlement in a hollow with a succession of cast-iron street pumps (no shops). Beyond the tunnel's far end, known as Tête Oise, the first bridge leads, right, into a charming small town called **Chevregny** (about 3km). The compelling reason to pay a visit is the small Departmental Museum of Elementary Education, set up in a former school. Exhibits mainly date from the early 1900s and provide a fascinating insight into that regimented system of learning processes where endless repetition was once intended to produce proficiency. Two examples of pedagogical propaganda that caught my eye were line after line of childish copperplate proclaiming '*L'Ivrogne boit le sang de ses enfants*' (The drunkard drinks his children's blood) – presumably part of a 'project' on alcoholism; and '*Je ris. Je sais lire. Je suis content!*' (I laugh. I can read. I am happy!) There are also three tramway cars and a hand-operated local fire engine. The museum opens Sundays only.

If waiting overnight for the tunnel on a southbound journey, consider a stop at Écluse 9, **Pargny-Filain** (K12.7) – but do warn the keeper of your intentions, otherwise the traffic control sequences for the tunnel and locks 10–13 may be reduced to a state of confusion. In addition to bar, grocer, baker, restaurant and water point, the Lac de Monampteuil reservoir adjacent to the waterway has been admirably adapted for various forms of water sports with swimming from a *plage*.

Écluse 9 is the first of the descending locks. The

In spite of its 2,365m length, lighting and ventilation systems greatly assist the navigator at Braye-en-Laonnois Tunnel.

majority have water points. On arrival at a quay with grain silo by Écluse 8, **Chavignon** (K14.1), a bar will be found on the left of the busy N2 road crossing, with a garage about 1km to the right. A similar distance in the opposite direction brings you to Chavignon village (baker and restaurant), which can also be reached (3km) from Écluse 7, **Chaillevois** (K16.7). Now comes a long, shaded pound through the Forêt de Pinon to Écluse 6, **Pinon** (K21.7). Stop by the first *road* bridge afterwards to visit the good shopping centre of **Anizy-le-Château** (K22.3) with a garage nearby in the Pinon direction. Further dense woodland with a great feeling of remoteness lines the canal past Écluse 5, **Vauxaillon** (K25.7), and Écluse 4, **Leuilly** (K30.6). Note the restaurant and garage by the D1 road crossing between the waterway and the hamlet of **Béthancourt** (K31.8). An Oise tributary, the Ailette, is never far away to the right for the remainder of the journey.

Écluse 3, **Crécy-au-Mont** (K33.5), is the closest approach to **Coucy-le-Château**, about 3km north, a splendidly defended town within a ring of 28 towers until it was disastrously bombarded in 1917. But enough remains of the *château* to make a visit worthwhile (open throughout the year except Tuesdays). There is an interesting local history museum in the Porte de Soissons. Another tourist attraction is the exceptionally beautiful small stone church in **Pont St-Mard**, 1.2km south of the bridge before Écluse 2, Guny (36.4). **Guny** itself, left of the canal, has several basic shops.

The final pound runs through the **Arblincourt** woods and past **Bichancourt** (K45.7), close to which is a poignant reminder of the troubled recent past. Six poplars surround a memorial stone in the windswept cornfields with an inscription recalling the secret parachute drops made possible by *Résistance* worker Ernest Pruvost and the people of Marizelle-Bichancourt in the summer of 1943. An aqueduct carrying the canal over the Oise is followed by a basin, the final lock, Écluse 1, **Abbécourt** (K47.6), and the Canal Latéral à l'Oise junction (see Chapter 17).

21 ～ Canal de l'Aisne à la Marne

Carte Guide: *Champagne Ardenne*
From a junction with the Canal Latéral à la Marne at Condé-sur-Marne to a junction with the Canal Latéral à l'Aisne at Berry-au-Bac, 58.1km with 24 locks. There is one tunnel at Billy-le-Grand, 2,302m long.

Climbing up to the Billy-le-Grand summit level from the Marne valley and dropping northwards to the valley of the Aisne, this waterway is a useful connection via the city of Reims. Banks are of concrete virtually throughout and although largely rural and pleasant, it can scarcely be described as a beautiful navigation. The most appealing part is the southern ascent, through rolling terrain with horizon-reaching views. It is quite heavily used by *péniches* (especially between Reims and the Aisne) and consequently all locks are mechanised with the majority grouped in automatic radar-controlled series. A half-hour closure for lunch takes place at 12.00–13.00h, depending on traffic. Because of water leakages it is forbidden to moor in the section from Écluse 24, Condé-sur-Marne, to Écluse 17, Vaudemange, when the canal is closed on public holidays: 3½hr must be reserved for negotiating this flight to avoid being 'trapped'.

Opened to traffic in 1866, the canal soon became very busy. After World War I electric bank traction speeded up freight movement and water transport played an important part in revitalising the seriously damaged industries of Reims. Among goods now carried are sand and potash for the Reims glassworks and supplies for the numerous bankside sugar refineries. There are important commercial docks in Reims. Most recent modernisation increased the flow of boats through the locks and the Billy tunnel. Now, in an average day, there might be up to ten barges.

Although equipped with all basic facilities, water point and garage, **Condé-sur-Marne** is rather a featureless town. Here, the first of eight locks in an automatic sequence introduces an agreeable climb through remote woods and cornfields towards the summit level. Most road bridges are of utilitarian steel girders. **Isse** at Écluse 22 (K3.5) is devoid of shops, as is **Vaudemanges** some distance west of Écluse 17 (K6.6). A shallow cutting leads to the portal of **Billy-le-Grand** tunnel (K9.3) which operates on a one-way system controlled by lights. A keeper is installed in a modern concrete cabin over the mouth of the vault: his life would seem to be an enviable existence, watching craft movements on closed-circuit television and exercising

his angling skills in the periods between telephone calls. Further lights and an internal telephone system are installed at the far end.

After the tunnel, we share a valley with the River Vesle as far as Reims; this stream eventually joins the Aisne above Soissons. To the right of the second bridge, the village of **Sept-Saulx** (K14.8) is one of the numerous places in the vicinity where champagne is produced. In addition to a barge port (water point), there are good shopping facilities and the *Cheval Blanc Hôtel/Restaurant* with mini-golf and tennis. Still on the summit pound, **Courmelois** (K17.5, right bank) is soon followed by the first of the descending locks, Écluse 16, **Wez** (K18.5), with **Beaumont-sur-Vesle** (K19.7) at Écluse 15. Within 200m of the large basin are plenty of shops, a restaurant and a garage. After Écluse 14, l'Espérence (K22.5, large war cemetery), **Sillery** (K24.1) offers good shops and a garage, with fuel and moorings available at a pleasure boat yard. Beyond Écluse 13, to the right of the canal by the N44 highway, the Fort de la Pompelle is on view as a museum of World War I relics. Constructed in 1880, it safeguarded one approach to Reims and played a decisive part in the two Allied victories on the Marne. It is open throughout the year.

Outer suburbs of Reims make their presence felt after **Taissy** (grocer and baker with a restaurant near the bridge of **St-Léonard**, K28.6). From the waterway, the city is no beauty, as it is virtually bisected by the roaring A4 *autoroute* and other high speed roads as well as being encircled by industrial sprawl. A series of three automated locks (Écluse 12, Huon, water; 11, Château d'Eau; and 10, Fléchambault, water) lead to municipal pleasure craft moorings near the centre (water, electricity). The vicinity is unpleasantly noisy for all but a short stay; as it is open to the street, overnight security is non-existent. I once paid a substantial sum to leave my boat here for ten days and returned to discover that it had acted in that time as home for a petty thief. Consequently, I shall always regard the Reims moorings with distaste. However, if you can overcome any unfavourable initial impressions, Reims is a city of great interest, even though 80 per cent was destroyed in World War I. Founded by a Gaulish tribe, it became the provincial capital *Durocortorum* under the Romans. The cathedral of Notre Dame, begun in the 13th century, is among the finest churches in Western Europe. Extensive restoration was needed after the 1914–18 bombardments. Other attractions include a selection of museums, beautifully landscaped city centre and several champagne houses, each with cellars extending as far as 18km. Full details of visits can be supplied by the *Syndicat d'Initiative*. Needless to add, shopping and eating facilities are comprehensive.

Although central quays are often busy with empty barges, cargoes are handled in a big basin, the Port Colbert (K37.7) to the NW. Boat diesel is available here.

All shopping facilities, including a vast supermarket, will be found either side of the bridge in **La Neuvillette** (K40.5). The final run to the Canal Latéral à l'Aisne is a little dull, the most notable feature being shops and restaurants at **Loivre** (K48.7). A huge military cemetery is a prominent feature of the otherwise pleasant countryside around the last five locks (automatic sequence) leading to **Berry-au-Bac** junction (K58.1). This lively canal settlement provides a variety of services for boaters (see Chapter 18).

A freight péniche *emerges from the 2,302m Billy-le-Grand tunnel.*

III · FRANCHE COMTÉ, ALSACE, LORRAINE AND THE ARDENNES

22 — Canal de l'Est (Branche Sud)

Carte Guide: *La Meuse et le Canal de l'Est*
From a junction with the canalised River Moselle at Messein, near Neuves-Maisons to a junction with the River Saône at Corre. 121.5km with 93 locks. Junctions are made at Méréville with the Nancy Branch leading to the Canal de la Marne au Rhin at Laneuveville-devant-Nancy (10.2km with 18 locks); and at Golbey with the Épinal Branch, which runs to a terminus in Épinal (3.4km, lockfree).

Sometimes treated as a continuation of the River Meuse and the Canal de l'Est (Branche Nord), and otherwise known as the Canal des Vosges, this waterway has in fact always connected with its northern section by a shared length of the Canal de la Marne au Rhin between Troussey and Toul (see Chapter 27). 25.3km of the Branche Sud's course from Toul to Messein were originally laid out using the River Moselle. But following the canalisation of the Moselle to Grade IV standards, completed in 1978, the old Branche Sud works have been replaced and navigation now follows the Moselle Waterway (see Chapter 29).

Rather heavily locked, the Branche Sud climbs up the Moselle valley to a summit level near Épinal, 360m above sea level. It then seeks out the River Coney which remains close by until the Saône is reached at Corre. Almost from end to end the canal passes through thickly wooded surroundings of considerable beauty. Several peculiarities of this route should be noted: owners of deep-drafted craft or large vessels such as converted barges will find that there are somewhat shallow sections with a stony bottom and sides. In places, two substantial boats may have difficulty in passing. In recent years, locks have been closed to all traffic on Sundays, giving keepers one day of rest followed by a Monday of traffic jams! Such local oddities make little sense now that in summer pleasure boats by far outnumber freight craft. It would be wise to check the current position as such a silly rule cannot be expected to remain indefinitely. A speed limit of 6kph (8kph for pleasure craft under 20 tonnes) is strictly enforced throughout the canal with travelling times between the locks carefully noted and compared by telephone. Transgressors will be savagely fined. Mobile keepers are employed for passage of most locks between Charmes and Corre. Advance instructions are issued before arrival in this section and pleasure boats are grouped together where possible. Elsewhere, a proportion of the keepers are former boat people. Many of the locks have water points and refuse disposal facilities. Repeatedly, you will notice small open barges with upswept bows: these are ice-breakers, a reminder that conditions can become very cold in winter.

With few exceptions, French inland waterways seldom provide opportunities for short circular cruises. However, an agreeable circuit, demanding perhaps two days of boating, may be tackled by navigating the Nancy Branch, a part of the Canal de la Marne au Rhin and the uppermost reaches of the River Moselle.

Brief history The Roman general Lucius Vetus is said to have made tentative plans to link the Moselle with the Saône along a line similar to that occupied by the present waterway. It is difficult to understand how this might have been achieved at a period many centuries before invention of the pound lock. Towards the end of the Middle Ages the Moselle was certainly used by horse-drawn barges in the Épinal area, and it appears that some form of connection existed between there and the Rhine. During the latter part of the 18th century, a M de la Galaizière made attempts to join the Moselle and the Saône, with the support of the ex-Polish King Stanislas of Nancy. But it was the loss of 'German' Lorraine to the Prussians after the French defeat of 1871 that acted as an incentive for building the Branche Sud, so avoiding a passage through hostile territory. Works commenced in 1874 and were finished by 1882. By 1936 annual freight tonnages were not far short of 3 million; this had been reduced to about 400,000 tonnes in the mid-1960s. Towing of unpowered barges by rubber-tyred bank tractors ceased in the early 1960s.

About this time, a plan was proposed for a new 1,350-tonne capacity barge canal to replace the Branche Sud (see Chapter 29) but this plan seems unlikely to come to anything. If ever carried out this will follow the same route between Neuves-Maisons and Charmes and then diverge to the west through

Mirecourt before reaching the Saône at Corre. The present course of the Branche Sud will then be taken out of service, except for the portion from Charmes to Épinal, remaining as a *péniche*-sized arm. In recent years, the French authorities seem to have rather lost their appetite for new waterway construction. It is now quite difficult to envisage this plan coming to fruition.

After the massive new basin of the Moselle Waterway and its **Neuves-Maisons** steel works at Messein – basic shopping, restaurant and garage with waterside diesel (see Chapter 29) – the surviving section of the Branche Sud begins at Écluse 47. Just after Écluse 46, **Mereville**, the **Nancy Branch** (for boats wishing to reach the Canal de la Marne au Rhin) enters on the left, with a flight of five locks leading up to a 2.7km summit level, the *Bief de Partage du Mauvais Lieu*, a narrow and rock-lined cutting. Surroundings are moderately rural but rather scruffy, with many of the lock cottages now deserted. Descending locks 1–10 are arranged in a flight 1.9km long. Écluse 11 is situated on its own, followed in due course by the last pair of very deep chambers at the Canal de la Marne au Rhin junction in **Laneuveville-devant-Nancy** (see Chapter 27). In recent times, this Branch had become decayed and was actually closed for several years. In 2003 extensive restoration works were begun at the 18 locks and advanced signalling systems installed.

Southwards, the continuation of the main line of the Branch Sud is past the village of **Richardménil** (K3.5), with the gardens of small houses backing onto the water. There are free overnight moorings (electricity, water and a facility until now almost unheard of in France – a chemical WC emptying point). Always close at hand between here and Épinal, the shallow course of the Moselle is a profitable source of gravel, with cranes excavating its bed. Plastic storks in lock gardens are a reminder that Alsace lies to the east: for there, the bird is prized as a symbol of good fortune and fertility. The N57 highway is close to the canal for a long distance: while its intrusion may be regretted, it does encourage useful facilities including restaurants and garages. Quietest overnight moorings are often to be found close to locks, where the road briefly swings away from the waterway. Écluses 45 and 44 are encountered at **Flavigny-sur-Moselle** (K5.7), with a good range of shops and restaurants on the far side of the river. I once worked through Écluse 43 (K7.9) while the keeper was attacking a wasps' nest with an aerosol of poison and the air was thick with angry insects. As soon as was humanly possible, we launched into the impressive 125m aqueduct which carries the canal over the Moselle, and an unladen *péniche* hovered at the far end.

Shortly before the next bridge is a café/restaurant, left bank; it is very popular with truck drivers, a sure sign of value and quality in France.

All the while, the canal is becoming more and more pleasant, with dense shade in the Forêt de Benney at the approach to Écluse 42 (K13.2). Be prepared for the possibility of a curious floating bridge on oil drums (hoot for it to be pulled aside) at **Neuviller-sur-Moselle** (K18), near Écluse 40. In addition to a church with a witch hat spire, a 19th century *château* rises from a lovely complex of ancient fortified farm buildings. If you moor by Écluse 39 (K20.9), all facilities will be found in Bayon, about 2km east beyond the river. Alternatively, there is food shopping and a restaurant close to the next lock, Écluse 38 in **Roville-devant-Bayon** (K22). Rocky castle remains appear at Écluse 36, **Bainville-aux-Miroirs** (K25.2, garage); on the river is a charming little bathing *plage* with a sandy bottom. Tall wooded cliffs characterise the next pound to Écluse 35, **Gripport** (K27.7), which has food shopping. Water point at Écluse 34.

Locks 34–31 lead to **Charmes** (K35.7). Drinking water will be found about 500m downstream of Écluse 31, with a wide selection of shops and several restaurants. Deep water quayside moorings are near the bridge. At first sight Charmes seems to benefit from a singularly inappropriate name: you cannot but help regarding it in a more favourable light on learning that in the 14th century it was overcome by plague and famine; in the 15th it was effectively burned to the ground by Charles the Bold and most of the inhabitants killed; similar misfortunes occurred in the 17th century; and finally during World Wars I and II. All was bravely rebuilt between 1947 and 1952. Poor unlucky Charmes! The most notable building is a modern *Hôtel de Ville* with roof of multi-coloured Burgundian glazed tiles.

Soon follows the village of **Vincey** (K38.5, food shopping and restaurant). Worth visiting are the 17th century chapel and an old spinning mill. Across the Moselle in **Portieux** is a glass factory with retail shop. On approaching the sharp bend above Écluse 28, Portieux, it is wise to warn any approaching traffic with a prolonged blast on the horn. A small aqueduct only 6m wide immediately follows Écluse 26, l'Avière (K43.5). To the left lies **Châtel-sur-Moselle**, a small town of red tiled and slated roofs, while **Nomexy** is rather closer on the right with a good mooring just before Écluse 24, **La Héronnière** (K46.3), suitable for a shopping expedition. Écluse 22, **Igney** (K48.9), has basic food shopping in the village.

Thaon-les-Vosges (K51.4) can be reached from either Écluse 20 or 19; it is slightly industrial and offers

Aqueduct over the Moselle near Flavigny.

most shops (800m), with a garage and bankside diesel by the road at Écluse 19. Locks are becoming more frequent at the approach to the summit, especially after No 15, Côte Olie (K57.3, drinking water and motel/restaurant). Here the **Épinal Branch** forks off on the left, soon to cross the Moselle via a substantial aqueduct. Between here and the city of Épinal is a level run of 3.3km by the side of the river, terminating in a rather drab basin quite close to the centre. As this is the only large settlement between Nancy and Chalon-sur-Saône, the detour can be recommended. On Maundy Thursday an old tradition, the *Fête des Champs-Golots*, marks the end of winter. Gutters of the Rue de Général Leclerc and adjoining streets are filled with water along which children pull illuminated toy boats. The surroun-

ding woods are ablaze with thousands of wild daffodils. Among the more interesting buildings is the basilica of St-Maurice, parts of which date from the 11th century. Many fascinating hours could be spent in the *Musée Départemental des Vosges et Musée International de l'Imagerie*, situated on the head of an island in the river a short distance upstream of the navigation limit. Displays range from an outstanding collection of paintings from all parts of Europe to local history and folklore. In France, publication of colourful story books in strip cartoon form has long been established (for adults as well as children): many of these are designed and printed in Épinal.

Back on the main line, 14 closely spaced locks in slightly squalid scenery lift the canal to its summit at **Bois l'Abbé** (K60.5). They are collectively known as the Montée de Golbey and each is separated by a short but broad pound, designed to conserve water supplies. If working astern of another craft it is best to stay at least one lock away to avoid problems resulting from temporary lowering of levels. My motor yacht was once stranded on a mud bank and was only released when two dozen locals were persuaded to haul on a 100m line that I rowed ashore in the dinghy. Even the most ardent canal devotee is likely to welcome the respite of 10.9km along the winding summit level to the north of the large Bouzey canal reservoir. After the small villages of **Les Forges** (K63.3) and **Sanchey** (K65.3), we arrive at a most agreeable little place called **Chaumousey** (K67.8), lying well below the level of the embanked waterway. Five small tunnels for pedestrians and vehicles pass under the canal at intervals, and provided other traffic can see you from a reasonable distance, there are good towpath moorings close to the church (its over-zealous clock strikes each hour twice). Facilities have declined in recent years (in common with many French small towns) and perhaps remaining shops and the restaurant will have vanished by the time this appears in print. Another mooring possibility is at the far (western) end of a basin (beware silting elsewhere) on the side of Chaumousey nearer the descent towards the Saône. The southern section of the summit enters a cutting lined with stone blocks and with little space for two *péniches* to pass.

Between here and the Saône is an almost endless chain of locks, never more than 4km apart and often much closer. These are generally operated by mobile keepers driving or motor-biking ahead of the boat: fortunately, the towpath is in excellent condition. Arrangements for 'booking' a passage change from time to time. A schedule of current regulations is supplied to each boat about one day's travelling time from the locks in question. No additional payment is demanded although I have always thought it a kindness to make a present of a couple of bottles of wine or to invite the keeper to share your lunch, while in summer cold drinks from time to time are always welcomed! Earning on an hourly basis, these peripatetic lock staff can expect to accumulate a better weekly wage than workers based at a single location; those in the latter category earn the same money for passing three boats daily as they would for twenty. We once spent a day with such a mobile keeper, a delightful young man named Étienne. After enduring our far-from-fluent French for several hours, he came out with the astounding news that we spoke his language better than he did! One great disadvantage of this system is that there is almost no opportunity to stop the boat for more than a few minutes: any required shopping must be undertaken by a spare crew member released from locking duties and sent off on foot or by bicycle. If for

any reason you must halt, you will not unreasonably be requested to wait there until the following day's convoy.

These 13 locks drop the canal from Écluse 1, **Trusey** (K71.3, some shops and a garage in the nearby little town of **Girancourt**), to **Thiélouze** (K79), Nos 5–11 being known as the *Descente du Void de Girancourt*. Impressive farm buildings at Écluse 5, Void de Girancourt, are based on the outer walls of an old *château*. Surroundings are really lovely near **Méloménil** (K80.8, restaurant). During the height of the pleasure boating season many of the locks from No 14 to the Saône may be manned by students, who are well compensated for their agreeable task in the sunshine. Such an arrangement enables regular keepers to take a holiday and overcomes the delays that would otherwise occur where more than one lock is normally in the charge of a single employee. There is a butcher's shop near Écluse 18, **Uzemain** (K82.8), with several shops and a restaurant a fair walk away in **Charmois l'Orgueilleux**. An association is struck up with the little River Coney near Écluse 20; this is a delightful stream of twinkling weirs and mill houses among the trees. It will stay with us all the way to the Saône. Pretty lock cottages punctuate the journey through pine woods and on to a swing bridge by a factory in **La Grande Fosse** (K87.3) between Écluse 23 (restaurant *Au Saut de la Truite*) and 24. From here, a bicycle pilgrimage might be staged to visit the source of the Saône at **Vioménil** 9km NW along the D44 and D40 through **Thunimont**, **Harsault** and **La Haye**. Close by is the *Caveau des Fées*, rising place of a Moselle tributary, the Madon. Thus, water runs in one direction to the North Sea and in the other to the Mediterranean.

Moving onwards through Écluses 25–28, we arrive at No 29, **Port de Bains** (K93.7). A locally renowned beauty spot, it has a restaurant, *hôtel*, group of holiday apartments and water point. For shopping, it is necessary to travel 4km east to the small spa town of **Bains-les-Bains**, known in Roman times and very fashionable since the 19th century. The waters range from 31° to 53°C and are used in the treatment of heart ailments and circulation problems. Further locks, among them the delightfully-named Écluse 31, Manufacture de Bains (K95.4), lead to a stone-lined cutting with blind corners shortly before **Fontenoy-le-Château** (K99.9). Over the last 20 years, this small place has not decayed like some other canal villages: it has blossomed thanks to the growth of pleasure boating. Now there is a Crown Blue Line hire cruiser base, a *port de plaisance* with a range of facilities, a passenger boat service, restaurant and water point. This fascinating and ancient settlement makes an excellent overnight halt. It was an important fortified town between the 13th and

A laden freight péniche *on the summit level near Chaumousey.*

17th centuries, but declined after an attack by French and Swedish troops in 1635. Easily the biggest event since then was the coming of the canal in the 1870s. You can scramble up a low cliff by the towpath to arrive among vegetable gardens with a bird's eye view of the waterway as it passes through Écluse 35 on its way through the town centre in a narrow cutting. The Coney and other streams trickle past old water mills, one with an ancient round tower. Former shops are scattered around, rather than being gathered in a single place. Unfortunately, most, if not all, have now closed down. Some have the appearance of shutting their doors for the last time at some point prior to World War I. I remember discovering, in the 1970s, René Pérochon's canalside bakery. He would apologise for having no fresh bread until 9.00am on account of his wood-fired ovens being a little slow. He quickly assured me that his loaves were vastly superior to any modern substitute; he then motioned me to follow him through to the back of the building where stacks of logs were piled alongside an object like a giant-sized cast iron kitchen range. Latest information is that this remarkable relic sadly operates no more. Madame Pérochon told me that until recent times 'the biggest man in the world lived here, selling postcards. He weighed more than 300kg'. On checking the accuracy of this claim with Norris McWhirter of the *Guinness Book of Records*, I was told that they generally bothered to list only people well in excess of 300kg. The giant of Fontenoy was not among them. In the main street is a notable Museum of Embroidery, and above rooftop level the very fragmented remains of a *château*, now partly used as a graveyard.

The remaining portion of the journey is through first-rate scenery, rocky cliffs rising from the Coney with numerous watermills and weirs. Beyond Écluse 37, Gros-Moulin, the splendid **Château de Freland** hides behind monumental railings and alongside is a disused swing bridge. Take care at an extremely sharp bend in the canal between Écluses 36 and 37. Food shops and a restaurant are within easy reach in **Selles** (K110.8), access to this Burgundian red-tiled village being from the swing bridge (see also Chapter 47), while a pleasant woodland mooring will be found at Écluse 42, **Village de Selles** (K112.7). Now nearing the Saône, the woods that have accompanied the canal for most of its course finally give way to open meadows supporting a rich flora, with carpets of autumn crocus (*Crocus nudiflorus*) in early September. 3km NW of the bridge at **La Basse Vaivre** (K114.3) in **Passavant-la-Rochere**, the glass-blowing works is reputedly the oldest in France (open to the public most summer afternoons, but make local enquiries before setting off).

Demangevelle (K117.8, several shops and restaurant), near Écluse 44, is remarkable for its rows of ugly barrack-like dwellings, erected shortly before World War I as accommodation for cotton workers. After

Écluse 45, **Vougécourt** (K120), the grey stone spire of **Corre** church will be seen ahead. Moor either side of the bridge to reach a variety of shops and garage in this pretty, flower-filled little town. Pleasure boaters are unusually well catered for, with a hire boat base in the town (facilities include fuel); and a substantial marina recently created from a green field site a short distance up the Saône close to its junction with the canal: boats lifted up to 15m and 18 tonnes. About 200m from the canal, the *Restaurant du Centre* is the hub of Corre's social life. Not only does it offer diners first-rate value, but in the garden at the rear a covered skittle alley has kept the younger members of our party amused late into the evening. Extensive Roman remains were discovered during the 19th century, among them a magnificent white marble Venus, beautifully preserved. Objections to her nudity resulted in the statue being broken into a number of fragments: the abdomen was converted into a holy water stoop which can still be seen in the church porch. Other, less precious antiquities were removed to a museum in Besançon. One final lock is situated just upstream of the confluence of the Saône and the Coney (see Chapter 47).

23 ~ River Meuse (Canal de l'Est – Branche Nord)

> **Carte Guide:** *La Meuse et le Canal de l'Est*
> From a junction with the Canal de la Marne au Rhin at Troussey to the Franco-Belgian border at Givet, 272.4km with 59 locks. A junction is made with the Canal des Ardennes at Pont-à-Bar, west of Sedan. There are four tunnels: Ham 565m, Revin 224m, Verdun 45m and Kœur 50m.

It is a marvel of French bureaucracy that one of the country's most attractive river navigations should officially be known as the Canal de l'Est (Branche Nord). Yet, except in its uppermost reaches, where the waterway is mainly a lateral canal, it mostly uses the course of the River Meuse itself. From its source on the plateau of Langres near Bourbonne-les-Bains, the Meuse makes a 950km journey through France, Belgium and the Netherlands before entering the North Sea as the Maas. In the French Ardennes the river offers some of the finest forest boating to be found in the whole of Europe. Unlike the holiday resorts which characterise its banks in the fashionable southern part of Belgium, the French Meuse is little known to tourists and although it is well

equipped with facilities in a succession of towns and villages, pleasure boating is far from well developed. There are few hire cruisers compared with other regions: this situation would, of course, be quite different if the Meuse enjoyed the Mediterranean climate of the Canal du Midi. It has to be admitted that the weather in the Ardennes is decidedly changeable. In my experience, it is best to visit the region in anticipation of frequent rain: any heat waves encountered can then be regarded as an unexpected bonus!

An inevitable consequence of rain (which repeatedly features in numerous published Meuse cruising accounts) is springtime flooding, although this is probably no more likely than on many French rivers. High water levels have been recorded since ancient times but never with such interesting results as in March 1408 when thawing snows inundated much of the Meuse valley, demolishing buildings and wrecking bridges. In appearing before a gathering of stricken farmers, the Devil claimed that he had been responsible for the chaos; he would, however, remove the flood water, repair all the damage and go so far as to guarantee a total freedom from flooding for the next century. All that he required in return was the souls of any children born before the end of Mass and the beginning of Vespers on the Feast of the Annunciation. When news of the bargain spread there were some who were dismayed, no least those families expecting an increase in their numbers. Eventually, an ingenious solution was devised: on the date in question, Mass celebrated throughout the region would be extended to last until it was time for Vespers! Thus, the children born on March 25, 1408 were saved from the clutches of Satan; and, although effectively outwitted, he seems to have stood by the agreement, for no further really serious flooding was to engulf the Meuse until 1510.

Through the Netherlands and Belgium the Meuse is of large proportions, locks conforming at least to Class IV dimensions up to the French border. The French length, however, is effectively to Freycinet *péniches* standards only, even though Écluses 20–58 are both longer and wider than the 38.5m x 5.1m locks between Troussey and Verdun.

It is impossible to travel the Meuse without constantly being reminded of repeated wartime slaughter, culminating in the dreadful Verdun bloodbath of World War I. This border country has been fought over for centuries, towns fortified by Vauban including Givet, Charleville-Mézières, Stenay, Sedan and Verdun. Charleville-Mézières alone was bombarded in 1815, 1870, 1914, 1918, 1940, and 1944, while smaller places were quite literally reduced to total oblivion. Around Verdun, there are no trees that pre-date the 1914–18 holocaust. Vast cemeteries are an essential ingredient of the landscape. Time has healed the scars and peace has returned to the valley, but an inevitable sombre quality lingers.

In places, slate and iron industries have long been established, but rarely do they detract from the beauties of this gem among French river navigations.

Food specialities include various freshwater fish, *jambon cru* (raw ham), *pâté de sanglier* (wild boar), *pâté de grives* (thrush pâté, sometimes in a pastry case), *quenelles be brochet* (mousse of pike), *dragées de Verdun* (sugared almonds) and *madeleines de Commercy* (shell-shaped sponge cakes).

Brief history In ancient times the Meuse formed part of a freight and passenger route through the Ardennes: by resorting to an overland portage near the source at

Langres, communication was possible via the Saône and Rhône with the Mediterranean. One frequent 8th century traveller by this method was St Hubert. But it was not until the demands of the iron industries around Nancy became considerable during the 19th century that a proper canalisation scheme was put in hand. Present locks mostly date from 1875–80. By 1964 the border port of Givet was the 16th busiest in France, with the French Meuse carrying an annual 3.5 million tonnes of goods. From 1908 a steam tripping vessel, the *Givet-Touriste*, ran a regular summer service on the northern reaches, freight traffic then consisting of horse-drawn *péniches* and smaller flat-bottomed barges. One improvement of recent times has been the installation of automatic equipment at locks in the Sedan-Revin section.

After its junction with the Canal de la Marne au Rhin near the village of Troussey (see Chapter 27), the Canal de l'Est (Branche Nord) descends through a series of four locks to the hamlet of **Sorcy-Gare** (K2). Water

The infant River Meuse near the canal at Sorcy.

Hay-making by the River Meuse in Troussey.

point, Écluse 1, **Troussey**. Nearby, the small and reed-fringed River Meuse winds through meadow land and briefly joins the navigation for the first time down-stream of Écluse 5, **Euville** (K6.1, restaurant and water). Typical of many villages that will be passed, this is an intensely rural settlement with a most elegant classical fountain. Not long afterwards a mobile weir, right, marks the junction with a canal cut leading into **Commercy** (K10.2), a pleasing town with foundries, narrow hilly streets, various weir streams and an impressive square entered via gateways. All supplies can be obtained within easy reach of the public quay by the main bridge. Its chief claim to fame is as home of *madeleines*, light sponge cakes which when dipped in tea produced the celebrated flood of memories recounted by Marcel Proust in *A la Recherche du Temps Perdu*. The delicacies are reputed to have been first served in 1755 to ex-Polish King Stanislas, Duke of Lorraine, who was responsible for the 18th century splendours of Nancy. In England, our version is known as a 'fairy cake' and is not generally considered to be in any way special! Commercy boasts a vast early 18th century *château*, now used as municipal offices, police station and post office.

From time to time the navigation channel follows the true course of the river, but for the majority of the distance downstream to Stenay we shall be travelling along a lateral canal. A succession of villages, all of which are well worth exploring, is now encountered: **Lerouville** (K16.4, shops, restaurant, sloping-sided guard lock); **Vadonville**, by Écluse 7 (K17.5); and **Sampigny** (K20.3, shops and garage). It was here that St Lucy lived with a hermit after travelling from her native England. In order to avoid a broad loop of the Meuse, the waterway passes through the 50m **Kœur** tunnel (K22.8) where, for the first time, tree-covered cliffs provide a hint of dramatic scenery yet to come. Écluses 8 (water point) and 9 lead to the village of **Bislée** (K26.2) and a glorious reach of river upstream of **St-Mihiel** and Écluse 10 (K30.8). Limestone rocks are a picturesque background to this medium sized town; all facilities with moorings by the boat club. A Benedictine abbey was founded here in the 8th century and during the 16th century it became the centre of a brilliant school of religious art led by the sculptor Ligier Richier. Examples of his work are to be found in the churches of St Michel (*The Swooning Virgin*) and St Étienne (*The

Placing of Jesus in the Tomb). During the St-Mihiel Sailient of 1914–18, the town was a German bridgehead and French forces were unable to bring reinforcements and supplies via the river. Some 2,500 local inhabitants were held prisoners in their own town for nearly 50 months.

We now leave the river for a long canal section, passing **Maizey** (K36.4) and Écluse 11, **Rouvrois-sur-Meuse** (K38.3), with the possibility of mooring near Écluse 12 (water) in **Lacroix-sur-Meuse** (K41.2, shops, restaurant and garage). In addition to a fine grey stone church with slender slated spire, this village boasts an amazing fountain erected in 1836 in celebration of the arrival of a pure water supply. Latin inscriptions adorn a massive arch with human figures and a pair of giant fish. Later wording shows how it was adapted as a village memorial to those who fell in World Wars I and II.

Troyon near Écluse 13 (K46.6) has several shops and a restaurant, while its neighbour **Ambly-sur-Meuse**, Écluse 14 (K49.5), has little beyond a military cemetery, having lost its shops among which was what the lock keeper once described to me as 'the best baker on the River Meuse'. **Génicourt-sur-Meuse** should be visited for its remarkable 16th century church with fine stained glass and wood carvings attributed to Ligier Richier. **Dieue** (K57.7), reached from Écluse 15, is a pretty village of stone houses. There is a restaurant and a small supermarket on the lockside. First impressions of **Dugny-sur-Meuse**, beyond the river shortly before a crossing of the A4 *autoroute*, are that it is a dirty little quarry town with a military cemetery, but it does possess a rather splendid 12th century Romanesque church.

The large town of **Verdun** is entered after negotiating a 45m tunnel through defensive walls, immediately before Écluse 19 (K68). Free floating moorings for visiting pleasure craft (water and electricity, etc) were completely renewed in 2001. Everything about the city pales into insignificance on learning that no fewer than 800,000 men lost their lives here in the most terrible battle of World War I. In spite of savage bombardment, the 12th century cathedral of Notre Dame remains, as does the extensive Citadel, built during the 1890s to become the strongest fortress in the whole of Europe. The public are admitted to view a maze of underground galleries and brick-lined dormitories where French troops would rest before returning to the battlefield. It was from here, in 1920, that the Unknown Soldier buried in the Arc de Triumph in Paris was selected. The town hall has a War Museum devoted to the city's rôle in the 1914–18 massacre; there are reminders of nine villages that were totally destroyed and never rebuilt. One of these was the unfortunate **Fleury**. In the surrounding countryside pine forests have disguised some of the scars of the tortured landscape. If the imagination should need any prompting, numerous forts, cemeteries and other reminders may be visited. Perhaps the most telling sites are the Trench of the Bayonets, where troops were found buried while still fighting, and the vast Ossuary of Douaumont, burial place for 100,000 unidentified soldiers. Detailed information is contained in the Green Michelin Guide *Alsace Lorraine Champagne* (in English), or in an English language leaflet available from the Verdun Tourist Office, on the right of the navigation opposite the Porte Chaussée. World War I has become a major tourist resource in the city and while the subject may well lend itself to picture postcards and similar souvenirs, chocolate shells containing a small detonator seem tasteless in the extreme.

Verdun displays considerable style in its 19th century buildings, all carefully restored so that it is now almost impossible to imagine their once ruinous state. Shopping and eating ashore are available in great variety close to the central quays, while a tripping vessel enables the car tourist to get afloat. At the height of the season, it makes four short journeys each day, working through the nearby lock and tunnel and returning to the city centre. Fuel can be bought from a garage downstream of the Porte Chaussée.

Downstream of the city is unpleasantly smelly, so it is advised to press on past the twin towns of **Thierville-sur-Meuse** and **Belleville-sur-Meuse** (K70.5) to the village of **Bras-sur-Meuse** at Écluse 20 (K76.2) where there is a water point. **Charny-sur-Meuse**, on the side of the river, is notable for its exceedingly run-down railway station which would require little adaptation to render it ideal for a film set in the early 20th century. The canal winds considerably in close company with the Meuse as they pass through a shallow dish-shaped valley and on to **Champ**, at Écluse 21 (K84), and its associated village of **Neuville**. Old tractors and wagons clutter the muddy streets, where most buildings are either barns or farmhouses. A sign near Écluse 22 (K88) proclaims '*Ici était Samogneux*'. **Samogneux** existed until 1916 when it was blown to pieces, leaving not a single building.

Beyond Écluse 23 at **Brabant-sur-Meuse** (K91.1) we join the Meuse once more and shortly arrive at the most inconvenient lock on the whole river: No 24, Consenvoye (K93.4), a sloping-sided chamber. **Sivry-sur-Meuse** (K98.2), situated next to a long canal section, is as rural a village as you might find almost anywhere in France. It has moorings in a fine basin, basic shops and a restaurant. **Vilosne**, a flowery village on the river after Écluse 25 (K99.8), has an alarmingly large number of names on its World War I memorial and it would seem that virtually all the young men were killed. Old shells up to 2m high adorn the doorways of cottages in the little farming settlement of **Liny-devant-Dun**, by Écluse 26 (K106.7). At a respectful distance from the centre is a German World War I cemetery, still carefully tended but almost 90 years on rarely visited by the families of those that lie there. Willows, weirs and intent fishermen typify these reaches.

The river winds through flat meadows to arrive in **Dun-sur-Meuse**, Écluse 28 (K110.1, *halte nautique* moorings, upper end of the weir stream). Most shops and several restaurants will be found in the long main street. The oldest quarter and church are clustered on a cliff, high above the water. Shops for fishing and hunting equipment point to the popularity of *la chasse*, although the casual visitor is more likely to encounter stuffed wild cats or boar than the live article! Ironwork of the town's Meuse bridge feature a 'stars and stripes' design, with a plaque recording: 'The Veterans of the Fifth Division of the American Expeditionary Forces have erected this railing to commemorate the crossing of the Meuse River and the establishment of a bridge-head on its eastern bank by their Division during the World War'. Near the church, the ruins of a building destroyed in World War I are all that remains of the house of Étienne IX, who reigned as Pope for a mere eight months in 1057–8. Downstream, former gravel workings have been landscaped into a pleasing example of water space with a small beach and fishing facilities. If you moor on the river between **Milly-sur-Bradon** and the stop lock at **Sassey-sur-Meuse** (K114.1), a 3km walk or cycle ride to the west will bring you to the important 11th century church at **Mont-devant-Sassey**; during the 17th century wars it was transformed into a fortress.

Further water parks based on gravel pits are followed by the rural town of **Mouzay**, Écluse 30 (K120.3, shops). Navigation once more passes into the Meuse to arrive at Écluse 31, **Stenay** (K123.6), with moorings in a small port reached from the lower end of the weir stream. Although local industries include paper making and iron production, this is a lovely old town, fortified by Vauban under Louis XIV. It was held by the Germans throughout much of World War I, and from the *château* the German Crown Prince directed the attack on Verdun for 18 months. All shops, restaurants and fuel are close at hand. Part of the 16th century citadel is now the European Beer Museum.

Once more in the form of a poplar-lined canal, the navigation runs through **Martincourt** (K128.5) before returning to the river after Écluse 32, **Inor** (130.2), an isolated village of massive stone barns and basic shops. Onwards from here, most of the journey is along the

Meuse itself, by now a sizeable river with impressive weirs, mill houses and reed beds.

Pouilly-sur-Meuse, Écluse 33 (K134.5), is a particularly charming village even though it offers little in the way of facilities. All the time the scenery is becoming more spectacular, and there is every incentive to linger in the coming length that extends to the Belgian border. Écluse 34, **l'Alma** (K141.6), is succeeded by a delightful reach leading to the ancient town of **Mouzon** (K149.3). *Port de plaisance* with good range of facilities in a side channel upstream of the lock. Shopping and restaurants. This remarkable place dates back to Gaulish times, was a Roman market and was not absorbed into France until 1379, during the reign of Charles V. Several Spanish houses recall an Iberian siege in 1650. Alone among remaining fortifications is a four-storey gateway, the Porte de Bourgogne (local archaeology and history museum). There is also a Museum of Felt, a local industry with applications from carpets to clothing and floor coverings. The church of Notre Dame began life as a late 12th century Benedictine abbey. Although it is now a very small town, it is easy to appreciate its former greatness.

We now run downriver through beautiful surroundings past **Autrecourt**, **Villers-devant-Mouzon** (K152.7),

The goddess of the Meuse pressed into service to advertise locally brewed beer. An enamel sign, produced in 1905.

and **Remilly-Aillicourt** (basic shops, restaurant). Écluse 36, Remilly (K159.6), is one of a series of radar-controlled automatic locks between here and Revin. See the *Carte Guide* for operating instructions. The weir stream is navigable for several hundred metres from the downstream end to a mooring with restaurant, beyond the **Bazeilles** bridge. A little further up this stream is the confluence of the **River Chiers**: in 1921 this was listed as navigable for 35km via **Douzy**, **Brévilly** and **Carignan** to a terminus at **La Ferté-sur-Chiers**. Its very twisting course was lock-free and used mainly by small fishing craft and a few gravel barges. It would appear still to offer adventurous exploration at least for small, shallow draft vessels. **Bazeilles**, best approached from the bridge upstream of Lock 36, offers limited shopping. A former café, known as *La Maison de la Dernière Cartouche* (The House of the Last Cartridge), is a curious little museum, containing 5,000 objects from the Sedan battlefields of 1870.

Sedan lies on both sides of a short cut leading to Écluse 37 (K165.4), central control point for the automatic locks. Best overnight moorings are at the *halte nautique* by a campsite (pontoons, water, electricity, slipway): this is situated in a side channel approached from the upper end of the lock cut. All facilities will be found in the town. The name Sedan is synonymous with the capitulation of the French under Napoléon III to the Prussians, resulting in the proclamation of the Third Republic, the Siege of Paris and the loss of Alsace-Lorraine. A huge fortress, started in the 13th century and much enlarged in the 15th, glowers over the town with 30m-high ramparts. Within is the Palace of the Princes of Sedan and a fascinating museum. From the 16–18th centuries, the city was a leading centre of quality cloth manufacture. Resulting prosperity is reflected in fine 17th century houses in the Rue du Ménil. Fortunately, they escaped destruction during a series of bombardments. An enjoyable visit can be made to the Botanical Garden near the river to the south of the *château-fort*.

Villette and Écluse 38 (K169.1) are on a cut which avoids a loop of the river and are followed by the useful shopping stop of **Donchery**, Écluse 39 (K172.8). On the river's left bank is the **Pont-à-Bar** junction with the Canal des Ardennes (K176.1, see Chapter 19). A diversion through the first two locks brings you to a boat yard and chandlery offering various facilities including gas, fuel and repairs. Basic shopping is possible at **Dom-le-Menil**, Écluse 40 (K177.5); or alternatively in **Nouvion-sur-Meuse**, where the railed enclosure of a former swimming pool 1,000m upstream of the road bridge or a quay above the bridge are mooring possibilities. The very pleasant curving river reaches now lead to Écluse 41, **Roméry** (K188.1).

Charleville-Mézières (K192.7) is a pair of quite distinct towns that taken together form the largest urban area on the French Meuse. They spread around two great bends of the river each of which is bypassed by canal cuts with Écluses 42 and 43. Mézières is the older place, with fortifications and ramparts; Charles IX married Elizabeth of Austria in the church of Notre-Dame d'Espérance in 1570. The outstanding attraction is without doubt Charleville's vast *Place Ducale* (Square) enclosed by 17th century buildings with covered arcades at street level. It bears comparison with the *Place des Vosges* in Paris. One most unfortunate decision, taken in 1843, was the replacement of the Ducal Palace by the present *Hôtel de Ville*, but at least the chosen style of the new building blends well with the yellow stone and pink brick façades of the earlier structures. Until a thorough cleaning and restoration in 1982, many of the frontages bore faded but elegant examples of painted 19th century sign-writing. A flourishing market including *brocante* is held in the square and among bargains to be discovered are again-fashionable decorative wood-burning iron stoves cast in this part of the Ardennes.

Charleville was founded as a 'new town' in the 17th century by Charles de Gonzague, Duke of Nevers, Rethel, Montferrat and Mantua, and his statue graces the Place Ducale. He set up factories making carpets, glass, marble and printing, but none were as successful as the nail-making operation he founded which in time expanded into arms manufacture and now specialises in mechanical engineering. In spite of such industrial origins, the town is a bright and cheerful place with an thriving pedestrianised shopping street. Since 2002 there has been an excellent purpose-built pleasure craft mooring for 88 craft at the lower end of a weir stream (coming downstream, turn left up the original river, rather than enter Écluse 43, Montcy). Alongside, the former Mont Olympe swimming pool has been replaced by a magnificent new leisure pool which features two 'slides' of which the larger is 9m high and 87m long. Opposite, on an island, is the *Vieux Moulin* (old water mill) a monumental four-storey structure which houses a museum devoted to local poet Arthur Rimbaud (1854–91). Since 1941, the city has been staging puppet shows with such success that the World Festival of Marionette Theatres is now held here at three-yearly intervals.

Now begins one of the finest portions of river landscape in Europe. Thickly wooded hills close in, the almost impenetrable foliage serving as cover for wild boar. Though long associated with iron-working, **Nouzonville** (right bank, K199.8) is a pleasant little town with moorings on a quay by the bridge close to all

The Place Ducale, Charleville.

facilities, including a heated swimming pool. Small terraced fields with sheep and orchards cascade down to **Joigny** and Écluse 44 (K202.2, basic shopping and restaurant). Good moorings are on the left bank above the lock, or (rather closer to the town) downstream of the bridge, again on the left. An acute bend leads past **Braux** (K207.3) to Écluse 45, **Levrézy** (K208.6, Metal-working Museum). **Château-Regnault** (K209.4) has a public jetty with water and electricity on the right, upstream side of the bridge and provides all shopping and eating facilities. The town was once part of a tiny principality. Its castle was destroyed by Louis XIV. A little downriver on the right, cliffs are known as the *Quatre Fils Aymon*, their forms said to represent the legendary horse Bayard and the Four Sons of Aymon who incurred the displeasure of Charlemagne and who were pursued to their mountain hideout above the Meuse by the Emperor's men. On the opposite bank are the lofty *Roche aux Sept Villages* and the *Roche de Roma*: their summits provide spectacular views of the Meuse meanders.

Until the 1920s, the extremely tortuous River Semoy (entering the Meuse, right bank at **Laval-Dieu**) was considered navigable for small freight craft for 18km to **Les Hautes-Rivières**, on the Belgian border. Its valley provides attractive walks through woods of chestnut and fir. Magnificently situated at the corner of a tight bend, **Monthermé** (K213.9) lies beneath towering wooded slopes formed by the *Longe Roche* spur. Brightly painted houses cluster along the water's edge with a good range of shops and restaurants. As there are convenient moorings, this delightful little town makes an ideal centre for a prolonged stay with exploration on foot of the waterside forests of both Meuse and Semoy. Monthermé is within walking distance of several rocky peaks including the *Roche à Sept Heures* and the *Roc de la Tour*. The church of St-Léger in the Old Town was built between the 12th and 15th centuries and is fortified.

Sliding past immense forests, the navigation channel passes to the right of an exceptionally long and narrow lock island at the approach to Écluse 46, **Deville** (K218.2). In the 1970s this was the home of a donkey named Tonerre: he helped boats pass through by hauling on their lines! Deville village on the left bank is useful for basic shopping. One of the finest moorings on the entire Meuse is beyond Écluse 47, la Commune (K222.4), at the village of **Laifour**, restaurant. Sheer-sided cliffs are densely clothed with a variety of trees, ranging from dark-leafed pines and yews to the light green of limes. The valley reverberates with the whine of power saws (all these trees are not being grown because they look pretty).

A considerable distance of the left bank up to and beyond Écluse 48 (K227) is known as *Les Dames de Meuse*: nowhere are the cliffs more impressive or dramatic. This time, the legend concerns Hodieme, Berthe and Iges, the promiscuous wives of three knights, turned into stone for their infidelity. There must be worse fates than to be immortalised as the centrepiece of

such a splendid view! After Écluse 49 (K231.7) a loop of almost 360° is bypassed by a short cut with the 224m **Revin** tunnel (one-way) immediately followed by Écluse 50 (K233.3). There are official pleasure craft moorings upstream of Lock 50 in the loop of the Meuse, left bank, beyond the second bridge. The town's old quarter is not without interest and meets all shopping and eating requirements. A wonderful river panorama of Revin, the *Dames de Meuse* and the *Vallée de Misère* can be obtained by walking to the 400m summit of *Mont Malgré Tout*. Those in search of an idyllic rural mooring will find a stone quay on the left bank at the camping site in the *Bois de Fumay*, several hundred metres upstream of Écluse 52 (K239.4). **Fumay** (K240.2) is a brooding little slate quarry town, with useful shops and restaurants, very close to the Belgian border where a narrow strip of

France extends north along the river. A *port de plaisance* has been created midway between the town bridge and Écluse 53, Vanne-Alcorps (K246.7). Cowering beneath a magnificent craggy hillside, the small town of **Haybes** appears on the right bank by a road bridge. All around here is admirable walking country, objectives including viewpoints at **La Platale** and the *Roc de Fépin*, north of Écluse 54 (K250).

Vireux-Molhain and **Vireux-Wallerand** (K257.4), either side of a road bridge below Écluse 55, introduce a brief element of industry with their ironworks. Moor on the left bank well above Vireux bridge (but do not attempt to continue down this side of the island and through the bridge arch). Alternatively, there is a section of quay adjacent to the navigation channel, immediately upstream of the bridge. Useful shops and restaurants will be found. The next town downriver, beyond Écluse 56 (K259.3), is **Aubrives**, surrounded by rich green meadows with lumber yards. A little further to the west will be found the ruins of a frontier *château* at **Hierges**, constructed between the 11th and 16th centuries. One final loop of the river is avoided by a cut at **Ham-sur-Meuse**, where Écluse 57 (K264) is succeeded by an iron drawbridge and then the 565m Ham tunnel, cutting under a hill at the neck of the Meuse peninsula.

Our journey along the French Meuse ends at **Givet** (K268.4), a place of considerable interest for a border town, with the massive Fortress of Charlemont, ruined

Givet, close to the border with Belgium.

and overgrown. Originally planned by Charles V and updated by Vauban, it was heavily bombarded during World War I. Pleasure craft may moor to a quay, left, immediately before the road bridge or otherwise on pontoons below the bridge, right (water, electricity, showers, washing machines, etc). Industrial activities, notably metalworking and textiles, are served by an extensive river port alongside a cut leading to the final French lock, Écluse 59, Les Quatre Cheminées (K271.9). 4km east are the Grottes de Nichet, open to the public May–September and comprising 12 chambers well encrusted in the approved manner of underground caverns.

Until the effective ending of frontier controls with introduction of European Community legislation, the French Customs post at Givet was a notorious problem for pleasure boatmen who were all regarded as potential smugglers. Now, most such concerns can be forgotten, even though there remain positive signs that you have passed from France into Belgium. Within metres of the border the (Belgian) *Léonard* Chandlery supplies diesel fuel markedly cheaper than that available in France; and forgetting that it was ever French, the Meuse discards its air of secrecy and assumes a rôle of well-organised gaiety with lavish waterside mansions, flag-decked hotels, tripping launches and much increased activity. All craft venturing onto Belgian waters must fly a *drapeau de navigation*, available from local boat shops, on the bows. This is intended to indicate to lock keepers and other vessels that your boat is under way even if temporally moored up. The flag consists of a red square with about 50% of its centre comprising a white square.

24 ∾ Canal du Rhône au Rhin

Carte Guides: *Doubs et Canal du Rhône au Rhin* (Vagnon) [Saône-Rhine only]; *Canal du Rhône au Rhin* (Navicarte) [Saône-Rhine only]; *Naviguer en Alsace* (Fluvio Carte) [Includes Colmar Branch and the Rhinau-Strasbourg section of the Canal du Rhône au Rhin].

From a junction with the River Saône at St-Symphorien-sur-Saône to a junction with the Grand Canal d'Alsace at Niffer, 236km with 114 locks and 2 tunnels. An additional part of the original line between Ile Napoléon (Mulhouse) and Friesenheim/Neunkirch (totalling 61km) was taken out of service when duplicated by the canalised Rhine [Grand Canal d'Alsace]. One short portion remains available, so maintaining a connection between the Grand Canal d'Alsace at Neuf-Brisach and the Canal du Rhône au

Rhin's Colmar Branch. Neuf-Brisach to Colmar is 23km with 3 locks. Work is currently in hand to reinstate the abandoned waterway between Neuf-Brisach and Neunkirch (see below). A further isolated section of the canal remains in service as a link between the Grand Canal d'Alsace at Rhinau/Friesenheim with Strasbourg, junction with the River Ill and the docks (with communication to the River Rhine and Canal de la Marne au Rhin), 35.8km with 14 locks. Other branches are: on the River Doubs at Besançon, 3km, 1 lock; the Belfort Branch, from the main line at Allenjoie to 4km short of the original terminus in Belfort, 9.9km with 5 locks; and to the Nouveau Bassin in Mulhouse, 1.9km. A portion of the former Huningue Branch (originally extending almost to Basle, but now duplicated by the Grand Canal d'Alsace), remains navigable between the current main line and the town of Kembs, 1km, 0 locks.

From the early 1960s until 1997, this outstandingly scenic navigation was due to be rebuilt for large international barges, providing an important heavy tonnage link between the Rhine and the Saône (and via the Rhône to the Mediterranean). Had the scheme been carried out, it would have provided a 1,350-tonne capacity link from the North Sea to Southern France (the capacity is currently 350 tonnes). Sadly for devotees of inland water transport a vociferous 'green' lobby achieved a defeat for the plan on environmental grounds; another consideration, of course, was the very high construction cost.

Climbing from the Saône up the Doubs Valley, the waterway traverses the rugged Franche-Comté or Jura region, which remained quite independent of France until the 17th century. Almost throughout its association with the Doubs the surroundings are spectacular, with great wooded cliffs and progressively bluer folds of hills receding towards the Swiss/German border. The two leading towns, Dole and Besançon, enjoy dramatic settings. A summit is reached near Montreux-Château, after which the waterway falls sharply through many locks towards Mulhouse, with decidedly Swiss and German influences to be found in architecture and language as the route passes into Alsace. The main line terminates at a junction with the canalised Rhine – the Grand Canal d'Alsace – on the border with Germany only a little downstream of Switzerland. While still (just) remaining in France, boats must use part of the canalised Rhine before entering (at Rhinau) a detached portion of the Canal du Rhône au Rhin leading to the heart of Strasbourg. Boating on these 71km with ceaseless wash created by a succession of inland ships is not for the faint-hearted pleasure boater; the option is not normally available to hire craft. 27km and 11 locks of the abandoned waterway between Rhinau and the Colmar Branch; and a further 6km with 4 locks between Kunheim and Neuf-Brisach is now being completely restored with a likely completion date around 2006. It is unfortunate that an existing *autoroute* near Mulhouse prevents restoration of that part of the line, meaning that even after 2006 it will continue to be necessary to use part of the Grand Canal d'Alsace to travel between Mulhouse and Strasbourg or *vice-versa*. But at least hire craft and others unsuited to the canalised Rhine will be able to add to their itineraries a cruise from Strasbourg to the attractive cities of Colmar and Neuf-Brisach.

Commercial traffic on the confusingly-named Canal du Rhône au Rhin is now very light, only increasing significantly on the short length between Mulhouse and the Rhine. For many years while it seemed likely that the whole route would be enlarged, maintenance and replacement of navigation markers was neglected. Some improvements have lately been carried out, but it is vital to know that the River Doubs section has always been a slightly 'difficult' navigation, requiring greater vigilance than many French rivers. It is necessary to follow the chart with great care as otherwise grounding on rock will be the inevitable result. Even in wide reaches of the river the dredged navigation can be surprisingly narrow, so pay great attention to marker buoys. As a general rule it helps to remember that this waterway was created for horse drawn barges: the channel almost always stays close to the towpath. Unless directed otherwise, that is the safe place to be. Anticipate the sometimes concealed entrances to lock cuts; lack of attention could easily be followed by heading for open and unprotected weirs. I have once descended the Doubs when, although locks remained in service, it was seriously affected by floods. It was a worrying experience that I would not wish to repeat. But for the comforting knowledge that the keepers were telephoning ahead to have the next locks ready to receive us, we would not have attempted the journey. Having to hover in midstream above a raging weir with normal bankside moorings under water would not have been pleasant! After all these warnings, it is only fair for me to admit that during many passages through this route, I have suffered only one (quite gentle) grounding. And it would be quite wrong to lose sight of the fact that this must rank as one of the most gloriously beautiful inland waterways in Europe.

While some of the locks are operated by resident keepers, elsewhere mobile staff will work ahead of a boat through a whole series. Additionally, some radar-controlled chambers are activated by a portable 'zapper' lent to each vessel. While sections of the route are intensely rural, shopping, restaurant and boating facilities are generally adequate and can be regarded as a huge improvement since the mid-19th century account of the journey of three Englishmen taking a rowing boat from Paris to the Rhine (*Our Cruise in the Undine*, by Edmund Harvey, 1854). This is one of the earliest published accounts of a Continental boating expedition and it records the very primitive communal sleeping arrangements then provided in waterside inns along the Canal du Rhône au Rhin, with five-course meals (wine included) available for 7p.

Brief history In Roman times freight is known to have ascended the Rhône and Saône from the Mediterranean and thence been taken via the Doubs to Montbéliard, where it was portaged overland to the Upper Rhine. Without the aid of locks these ancient craft must have been of extremely shallow draft. A properly engineered waterway was first proposed by de la Chiche in 1774, but no progress was made until the scheme was taken up by Bertrand and construction started in 1784. It halted in 1802 and began again under the Restoration with engineer Joseph Liard in charge. By this time it was known as the Canal Napoléon. Stopping again at the fall of the Empire, the waterway was eventually completed (under the name of Canal Monsieur) between 1821 and 1833. Alsace was annexed by Germany in 1871, resulting in more than 50km of the line between Montreux-Château and the Rhine and the 100km continuation from Mulhouse to Strasbourg being removed from French control until the end of World War I. In spite of this, the 93km St-Symphorien-Deluz portion was enlarged to Freycinet gauge by 1882; the Germans had similarly upgraded the Mulhouse-Strasbourg length by 1892. But it was not until 1921 that the Deluz-Mulhouse section was improved, allowing the 38.50m *péniche Maréchal-Joffre* to travel from one end of the Rhône au Rhin to the other.

The next major development was the enlargement, by 1961, of the Canal de Huningue between the Grand Canal d'Alsace and Mulhouse for 85m x 12m Rhine barges. At the same time the original canal from Mulhouse to Friesenheim/Neunkirch was closed to traffic, as it had been duplicated by the Grand Canal d'Alsace (Rhine). Parts of the abandoned line are now being restored (see above).

Following completion of the Rhône and Saône to Class IV standards by the early 1980s, the Canal du Rhône au Rhin became the only sub-standard portion of a 1,350-tonne route via the Rhine between the North Sea and the Mediterranean. A scheme to correct this situation was projected in 1961 and agreed in 1965. In its modified form, it would have comprised 24 large locks able to accommodate 183m convoys comprising two barges and a pusher tug. The minimum channel width was to be 55m with a 4.5m depth. Total construction cost in 1979 was estimated at £900 million. As explained earlier, none of this is now likely to materialise. As a commercial freight route, the Canal du Rhône au Rhin will continue to wither thanks to the demands of local environmentalists. In compensation, the magnificent scenery of the Doubs valley will remain unchanged.

Important canal junctions are quite often non-places. So it is with the grandly named **St-Symphorien-sur-Saône**. You could quite easily cruise past the entrance lock of the Canal du Rhône au Rhin without realising that this is the beginning of a vital route to Germany and Switzerland. Marked by a large three-storey keeper's house, the canal joins the Saône some distance upstream of St-Symphorien itself. All facilities are to be found in the major boating centre of St-Jean-de-Losne, 4.3km downstream (see Chapter 48). Entry to Écluse 75, Saône can be difficult when the river is in flood. First encounter with the lock gear reveals highly efficient paddle levers which instantly release a solid mass of water into the chamber, with wheels mounted on tripods to work the gates. Between here and the River Doubs at Dole, navigation is via an artificial canal. Surroundings are pleasant but unremarkable, through woodland carpeted with cowslips in springtime. The Bourgogne Marine boat yard at Écluse 74, La Perrière, specialises in conversion, repair, sale and moorings for cruising barges: a selection of characterful vessels can always be seen here. At Écluse 73, La Tuilerie (K1.1), a stone mill was still grinding flour by water power until recent years. Locks 73–70 are electric. In **Abergement-la-Ronce** (K6.8) will be found restaurant, grocer and a baker famous for the quality of his bread. Overhead cranes and the brief intrusion of industry discourage lingering near **Tavaux-Cité** (K10.4) with its Solvay chemical works.

First meeting with the beautiful River Doubs is at Écluse 68, La Prise d'Eau (K17) downstream of **Dole**, a real gem of a town (K18.5). There are good central moorings with boat facilities and a hire cruiser base. This area provides a magnificent view of the Notre-Dame basilica rising above tiers of brown-tiled houses. Once the independent capital of Franche-Comté, it experienced a troubled but often glorious past and was not officially absorbed into France until 1678. Dole is best remembered as the birthplace of Louis Pasteur (1822–95), father of immunology. His childhood home in the Rue des Tanneurs is a museum with collections associated with the famous man as well as his father's

leather tanning business. Next door is the *Musée Pasteur*, devoted to his scientific achievements. The town is a charming jumble of historic buildings with excellent shops and places to eat.

East of Dole, the canal passes through Écluse 66, Charles-Quint (K19.4) and along a pound shaded by great plane trees, recalling the Canal du Midi. **Brevans** (K21.2) is a waterside village with a veritable jumble of rooftops set at all kinds of angles. This canal section ends after a guard lock at **Rochefort-sur-Nenon** (K25.8) where an ascent (by road) offers a rewarding view down to the Doubs and a fortified mill. There is a good pontoon on the river by a group of trees: water, electricity, slipway, several shops and restaurant. Onwards from here great care must be taken to follow the chart, so avoiding rocks and weirs. *If you are directed to remain 5m from the right bank, it means exactly that!*

Audelange lies on a short canal between Écluse 64 (K27.6) and the guard lock, 64 *bis*, which is followed by another reach. This alternating pattern of canal and river is typical of much of the Doubs. **Orchamps** (K33.6) is on a canal by guard lock 63N; avoid mooring in the narrow section of cut. Keeping near the left (towpath) bank on the following river reach, enter a short rock-lined cutting with restaurant and bascule bridge near Écluse 62, Moulin des Malades (K37.6). Beyond, the canal, while occupying part of the river bed, is at the highest level of a three-tiered arrangement of channels. After Écluse 61 (K38.6), normally operated by the keeper of the previous lock, we arrive at the canalside village of **Ranchot** (K39.4, mooring stages, shop and restaurant). After this, the already attractive waterway becomes increasingly beautiful: long lines of hills stretch into the distance and numerous heron and kingfisher can be seen.

Weaving from river to lock cut, this lovely navigation passes few villages of much importance, although some basic shops will be found in **Dampierre** near Écluse 60 (K40.7) and **Fraisans**, between canal and river by guard lock 60 *bis* (K42.3). Although 1,500m from Écluse 59, **St-Vit** (K45.6), the town provides a full range of services and there are useful pontoon moorings for visitors. Stop at **Osselle** (K53.4) for a visit to the *Grottes d'Osselle*, about 4km by road. This system of caves extends for about 8km and has been visited since the early 16th century. The network includes an underground river, spanned by an 18th century bridge. A long loop of the Doubs is bypassed by the 185m **Thoraise** tunnel (K59.5, *halte nautique*), partly excavated from living rock. The far portal shelters a statue of the Virgin, a wise precaution in view of the 90° corner that follows: hoot vigorously! The bend is so sharp that horse boats had to be poled round, imitating

Cruising on the River Doubs downstream of fortified Besançon.

a railway locomotive on a turntable. Now follows a very fine reach past rocky cliffs rising to a great height and topped by the ruined tower of the **Château de Montferrand**. Caution is required when leaving the river to pass into the two-rise Écluses 54/55, Rancenay (K63.1), especially if a strong current is flowing. **Avanne-Aveney** (K66.1) lie beyond a 411m one-way section of canal; they are two villages linked by a river bridge. Full range of shops and restaurant.

From here to **Besançon** we follow the natural course of the Doubs, Écluse 53, Gouille (K68.3) and Écluse 52, Velotte (K70), having boulder-strewn weirs directly alongside. Midway between the two is a floating chandlery and boat yard, right bank, with a fuel station just upstream of No 52 Besançon's fortifications and citadel provide an impressive approach to the city, capital of Franche-Comté. Walls and turrets snake along the skyline, with tree-covered cliffs rising from the water. After you have negotiated the mechanised

Écluse 51, Tarragnoz (K73.5), central moorings lie directly ahead, right bank. Immediately alongside, Écluse 50 is half concealed in the entrance to the 394m Tunnel de la Citadelle, which takes the navigation underneath the city. Exciting though this is, a more scenic and interesting route is to stay on the river loop (*La Boucle du Doubs*) as it nearly describes a circle around Besançon: this 4km line has only been reopened to boats (drawing up to 1.3m) in recent years. There are several moorings en route, including by the Pont Battant (K2); the Port République (K2.8, water point); and the Port St-Paul (K2.9, water and electricity), immediately before the loop's single DIY lock, Écluse St-Paul.

Originally established in Gallo-Roman times, Besançon has a long and rich history, sometimes as the centre of an independent province, sometimes under Spanish rule. Its most notable feature is the hilltop *Citadelle*, fortified by Vauban in the 17th century. Reached on foot from the waterway at Écluse 50 by way of many steps or a steep road, it now contains a series of museums devoted to local history, the *Citadelle*'s history, natural history and the Resistance and Nazi atrocities of World War II; there is also a small zoo and an aquarium. Many visitors, however, are happy to make the ascent merely to enjoy the spectacular view down to the Doubs valley. The city has long been associated with clock-making and has a remarkable 19th century astronomical clock in the cathedral bell tower. Here, in 1884, was produced the world's first artificial silk ('rayon'). Born in Besançon were the writer Victor Hugo (1802–85) and the cinematography pioneers Auguste Lumière (1862–1954) and his brother Louis (1864–1948). A small sight-seeing street train provides a relaxing introduction to Besançon, while waterways enthusiasts without their own boats can travel river and canal aboard the tripping vessel *Vauban*. Craft following the loop eventually rejoin the main navigation by the upstream tunnel portal, with a view ahead of very dramatic wooded cliffs. Downhill craft should ask the keeper of electrically-operated Écluse 49, La Malâte (K76.3), to telephone Écluse 50 and have the tunnel lighting turned on, if they have selected that route.

Chalèze (K82.7) marks the end of a particularly fine river section. After Écluse 48 (with the *Restaurant Coursaget* offering regional specialities), a canal cut extends to the guard lock at Roche-Les-Beaupré (K85.2), with a good mooring before the narrow bridge, convenient for shopping and a restaurant. Most facilities (including a railway station) are to be found in Novillars (K87.8), shortly followed by a two-arched bridge connecting Vaire-le-Petit (restaurant) with Vaire-Arcier (K88.1). There is little advance warning of arrival at a two-rise staircase lock, Écluse 46/47, Deluz (K90.4), providing access to a charming little town with good shops on a canal cut. A halt is recommended to enjoy a magnificent selection of summer flowers planted in a wide variety of antique artefacts such as farm carts, vintage prams and seed-sowing machines. As soon as we have rejoined the river, we can appreciate one of the most dramatic sections of the navigable Doubs with towering cliffs. These extend past Écluse 45, Aigremont (K94.7), to Laissey (K96.5) whose lock is obstructed along one side by concrete beams (supporting an industrial building), necessitating either an agile or a very short keeper. Several shops and a restaurant in the village.

For a time there is an absence of artificial cuts, locks being placed close to river barrages. One especially lovely reach is above Écluse 43, Douvot (K99), with an island (mooring pontoon, restaurant), willows and cliffs extending to Écluse 42 at Ougney-Douvot (K101.4). Scenery remains consistently fine past Fourbanne Écluse 41 (K103.6), and Esnans, where there is a 17–18th century *château*. Écluse 40, Baumerousse (K107.1)

marks the beginning of a canal section serving the substantial town of Baume-les-Dames (K109.6), reached from a bridge beyond guard lock 40 and on the left bank of the Doubs. All shops lie within a moderate walking distance, while essential services are close at hand: water point almost opposite the navigation authority yard, a huge and extremely comprehensive supermarket near the river bank, and a garage on the nearer outskirts of the town centre. The greatest point of interest for boating enthusiasts is that here on the river, the world's first experimental steamboat was tested in 1776, many years before such craft were generally introduced. With virtually no precedent to guide him and only using the services of a local blacksmith, the Marquis Claude-François-Dorothée de Jouffroy d'Abbans constructed his extraordinary vessel. It was 30m long with a beam of 1.95m; a Watt steam engine drove elementary paddles. The boat made a series of successful journeys between Besançon and Montbéliard, but thereafter little seems to be known about its fate and it was left to later engineers to perfect marine steam propulsion. The Marquis died in 1832 and in 1884 a monument was erected to his memory. Now rather worn and decayed, this stone memorial stands by the Doubs, a splendid collection of nautical devices surmounted by a funnel and paddle wheels.

Monument at Baume-les-Dames to the Marquis de Jouffroy d'Abbans, inventor of the world's first steam boat.

Rejoining the river, a sharp turn to the left is made at the confluence with the unnavigable River Cusancin, soon followed by an equally sudden bend to the right into Écluse 39, Lonot (K111.7), at the beginning of a short cut. Care is necessary to follow the channel closely from Écluse 37, Grand-Crucifix (K116.1), to Écluse 34, the keeper here also being responsible for Écluse 33, Branne (K123.2), beyond the village of Roche-les-Clerval. For the first time in quite a long distance all services are within close range at the pleasing twin towns of La Vesselotte and Clerval (K126.6), either side of a road bridge. Each features brownish red roof tiles, with a church in Clerval containing relics of St Herminfroy, a 16th century *pietà* and a tower topped with a structure like a harebell, characteristic of the region. With a choice of several restaurants, this is an obvious overnight halt. There are convenient pontoon moorings, for which a charge is made.

Pompierre-sur-Doubs (K130.5) lies left of Écluse 31, alongside a length of artificial channel. There are no shops, but clusters of flowers, a pretty church and a café by the railway station are all reasons to make a visit. The next lock, No 30, Plaine de Pompierre (K132.1) lies in a flat and marshy region, very unlike most of the Doubs valley. As the waterway finally leaves the Doubs at the entrance to a cut at Écluse 27, Papeteries (K139.7), its surroundings are as beautiful as ever, but from here onwards its only function is as a feeder to the lateral canal before eventually swinging away to the south and through a series of magnificent gorges towards its source near Mouthe. As its name suggests, L'Isle-sur-le-Doubs, left of the canal at Écluse 26 (K140.8), is partly surrounded by water. Pretty houses and shops rise from the banks of backwaters, with ornate balconies and small overhanging rooms whose purpose is evident from the basic plumbing. Busy shops and restaurants are near a square with bandstand. As the canal is narrow, moorings must be chosen with care: the best place is on the left, opposite the rail station, before reaching the bridge and Écluse 26. Headroom here is as tight as anywhere on the whole navigation; if necessary the lock keeper (who also operates No 27) will arrange for water levels to be dropped slightly.

Locks now increase in frequency as the canal climbs to its summit level, closely followed by the Doubs as far as Voujeaucourt. Several of the villages offer basic resources and are most attractive: a typical example is Colombier-Châtelot by Écluse 23 (K147.5), a place bright with flowers, streams once serving water mills, stone houses and huge barns. St-Maurice-Échelotte near Écluse 22 (K149.9) is one of many little towns on the route with a railway station and hotel. Some years ago

the lock keeper told me that he used his pack of assorted hounds for hunting wild boar, catching more than two dozen each year. Water is available at Écluse 21, Colombier-Fontaine (K151.8), with a full range of shops and garage near the lift bridge. Moorings on a vertical quay just before Écluse 18, Dampierre (K157.4), are convenient for restaurant and baker. After passing through a guard lock, Écluse 18 *bis* (K159.1), the Doubs is crossed on the level at a four-way junction, potentially dangerous when water levels are high. I was once taking the first boat in two weeks down the Doubs after a period serious flooding. At this point the stream slammed us violently to one side before use of all available engine power allowed us to gain the safety of the artificial channel beyond. Uphill craft should keep to the right (following the towpath) and will soon be out of harm's way at Écluse 17, Voujeaucourt (K159.9). Tie up above the lock for the shops, garage and restaurants.

A further lift bridge after Écluse 16, Courcelles (K162.1), marks the start of the Montbéliard conurbation, home of a Peugeot car factory (visits possible). Its hilltop was a Roman stronghold. In the Middle Ages, the city was an independent county until becoming a German principality. Later it was a Protestant refuge for French Huguenots, not becoming absorbed into France until 1793. The main historical attraction is an impressive *château*, partly constructed in the 15th century. Although noisy, there are excellent moorings in a basin before Écluse 14 (K164.8), with water, electricity and slipway. In recent years, several hundred buildings in the centre have been decorated in various pastel colours, much as they would have appeared under the former German rule.

Improvement works completed about 1913 resulted in certain locks becoming disused and the numbering of those now in service reveals that three of the original chambers have been dispensed with. Écluse 12, Exincourt (K168.2), is a *Bureau de Contrôle*, where arrangements must be made for keepers to travel with craft during the descent between Montreaux and Mulhouse. Several km of totally new waterway with a deep mechanised lock were opened in 1987: this was intended to form part of the planned modern navigation (now discarded). It also permitted a huge expansion of the Peugeot works. Landscaping included planting 700 semi-mature trees, conveyed from a nursery near Lyon aboard two *péniches*. After Écluse 10, Marivées (K171.3), the canal makes a 90° turn to the left, passes through Écluse 9, Allenjoie, and then crosses the River Allen via an aqueduct. A large basin at the far end marks the start of the 14.9km branch to Belfort. Originally designed as the Canal de Montbéliard à la Haute Saône, it was intended to form a link with the

Saône at Conflandey but it was never finished – nor is it likely to be. Construction began in 1882 and suffered various interruptions, so that opening was not achieved until 1923. A portion of the route west of Belfort was additionally dug with tunnels of 650m and 1330m, but these 10km were never flooded. Since the early 1990s, when the three locks nearest Belfort were infilled, total length of the branch has been reduced to 9.9km with just five locks. Craft wishing to explore its pleasantly shaded reaches should first obtain updated local information from the Service de Navigation, Port Fluvial, BP207, 25200 Montbéliard, tel 03 81 81 18 55. Normally, there should be no difficulty in negotiating the first two locks to **Châtenois-les-Forges**, a town with all facilities including boatyard.

On the main line, Swiss or German influences in architecture, place names and language itself increase during the final climb to the summit. Navigational instructions appear in German alongside the French and Alsatian German is widely spoken in the villages – sometimes, it would appear, in preference to French. Écluse 8, Fontenelles (K174.1), is followed by a pleasant reach of the River Allen at its confluence with the Bourbeuse: avoid getting too close to a weir if there is floodwater. The ascent is completed at Écluse 3, **Montreux-Château** (K185.5), a useful little town with water point and most kinds of shopping.

A deep summit level runs past **Montreux-Jeune** and **Montreux-Vieux** (offering limited facilities) before starting the descent at Écluse 2, **Valdieu**, towards Mulhouse and the Rhine. Passage through this section will have been booked the previous day at Écluse 12 (for Rhine-bound craft) or at Écluse 41, Mulhouse (for boats heading towards the Saône). These special arrangements are necessary to benefit from teams of mobile keepers who travel from one lock to the next by car. Boats will be grouped together where possible, although single working is practised when traffic is light. Efficient though the arrangement is, it allows no opportunity for mooring throughout the day's locking, except during the keepers' lunch break. However, any spare crew members can decide to take off on their own for sight-seeing or shopping, catching up with the boat farther down the canal. Scenery is mostly of a high quality, with broad open fields of cattle or maize, huge half-timbered brick barns and massive stacks of logs – the winter's domestic fuel supply.

Écluses 3–13, from Valdieu to **Retzwiller** (K193.3, some shops and restaurant), are arranged in a dramatic flight with curious keepers' 'lobbies' on the locksides, crowned with heavy red-tiled roofs. **Dannemarie** near Écluse 16 (K195.1) has all services and moorings with facilities, while another equally useful town is **Illfurth**

by guard lock 32 (K208.4). Rather than halt by Écluse 38, to patronise the shops of **Brunstatt** (K216.3), it is preferable to continue through Écluse 39 (K217.4) and so benefit from the resources of the city of **Mulhouse**.

A large and bustling place, noted for its industry and university, Mulhouse is not obviously very attractive, but at least its services are highly convenient for the canal traveller. Moorings are easily found along the tree-lined banks, although the best and most secure place, with pontoons and water supply is the *Vieux Bassin*, opposite the railway station. An indication that you have temporarily left rural France for the 'amenities' of a large city is provided by numerous 'ladies of the night' seeking custom from car drivers in the waterside boulevards as dusk falls. In addition to shopping and restaurants, Mulhouse has an elaborate 16th century *Hôtel de Ville* with a painted façade; a superb collection of steam locomotives and other relics in the French Railways Museum, 2km north of the centre (off the Ave de Colmar); museums of wallpaper (in Rixheim, 6km towards Basle), printed fabrics and electrical energy.

Two quite outstanding attractions should on no account be missed: they are both unique in Europe. First, the Schlumpf Car Collection (192 Ave de Colmar) is a remarkable display of over 500 road vehicles from earliest times to the present, displayed under cover along 2km of walkways illuminated by a forest of cast iron lamp standards. The priceless exhibits include a number of Bugattis (among them one of only six Bugatti Royales ever built). I am not especially a car enthusiast yet I consider this to be one of the most thrilling museums I have ever visited. The extraordinary story of how this hoard was seized from its rightful owners and opened to public view in 1982, is, however, not at all a happy one. Secondly, about 12km north of Mulhouse at Ungersheim, the Alsatian Open Air Museum (*Ecomusée*) has re-erected over 50 traditional rural buildings on a 25 hectare site. Mostly of timber-frame construction, each has been restored complete with appropriate farm animals, vineyard huts, barns, dovecotes and most remarkable of all, a 12–13th century fortified dwelling tower, discovered during demolition of shops in Mulhouse in 1983. Operated with obvious enthusiasm and mainly run by volunteers, the *Ecomusée* has an admirable traditional restaurant and extensive shop containing Alsatian gifts. In several hours here, you can learn more of bygone Alsace than would be gleaned from weeks of touring through the region! It is almost certainly the leading non-waterway excursion recommended in this book.

For two centuries Mulhouse was a free city, belonged to Switzerland from 1515 until 1648, next became an independent republic until absorbed into

A 12–13th century fortified tower is among more than 50 traditional Alsatian buildings at an Ecomusée *north of Mulhouse.*

France in 1798, and finally came under German control between 1871 and 1918 and again between 1940 and 1944. Not surprisingly, people of the area still regard themselves as Alsatian rather than French.

After the *Vieux Bassin*, a 140m tunnel takes the navigation under a square by the main railway station, with garages on the reach that follows or more convenient fuelling services just beyond Écluse 41 (K220.4), where there is a water point.

Ile Napoléon (K223.1) marks the start of a broad-gauge enlarged section of concrete lined channel, capable of taking 85m Rhine barges. At the junction of the abandoned portion of Canal du Rhône au Rhin towards Strasbourg is a commercial boatyard with slipways and heavy lifting equipment. To access the next section of the waterway, all craft must use the Grand Canal d'Alsace (canalised River Rhine, see Chapter 25). This is reached via the modern Kembs-Niffer Branch, 13km of lock-free navigation passing through pine forests. The connection with the canalised Rhine is made through one of a pair of duplicated locks. The older one boasts an ultra-modern concrete control building designed by Le Corbusier. The newer, larger lock was added in 1995. Temporary/overnight moorings for pleasure craft are good, with the usual facilities. When joining the Grand Canal d'Alsace, turn

right for Basle and for the upper navigation limit of the Rhine at Rheinfelden on the Swiss/German border; and left for Strasbourg and the French/German border, the connection with the Colmar Branch and the Rhinau access to the northern portion of the Canal du Rhône au Rhin leading into Strasbourg.

Remaining on the upper level, it is possible to explore a remaining fragment of the former Canal de Huningue which formerly provided a connection with the Swiss city of Basle. This is navigable for 1km to the small town of Kembs, a pleasant little place with good moorings.

DETACHED SECTION OF THE CANAL DU RHÔNE AU RHIN, NEUF-BRISACH TO STRASBOURG

Entry is possible (1) from the Grand Canal d'Alsace at K226.5, downstream of Vogelgrün Locks. NB this only connects with the Colmar Branch until restoration works are completed c 2006. (2) from the Grand Canal d'Alsace at K256, Rhinau. (3) from the Canal de la Marne au Rhin in Strasbourg. When reopened throughout, this length will total 65.6km with 28 locks. Distances in the following description are measured from Neuf-Brisach.

Southern terminus of the restored navigation will be Neuf-Brisach, a stronghold built in the late 17th century as a defence against Brisach on the opposite shore of the Rhine. Vauban's huge octagonal fortress survived bombardments during the Franco-Prussian and Second World Wars. The fortification walls are 2.4km long. A pleasure craft mooring is to be created 500m from the centre. Écluses 59, Biesheim (K3), 60 (K4.5), 61 (K4.8) and 62 Kunheim (K6.2) lead to the Neuf-Brisach Link Canal. Turn right to join the Grand Canal d'Alsace, 6.4km distant with 1 lock at the Rhine end. There is a pontoon suitable for a shopping stop in Kunheim.

After Écluse 63, there is a junction, left (K10.5), with the 13.3km Colmar Branch, which makes a most enjoyable diversion, with much to see in Colmar, where the terminus basin has been admirably remodelled as a pleasure craft marina. The branch was opened to traffic in 1864. For the first 11km it runs very straight and level, scarcely touching the villages of Muntzenheim (restaurant), Wickerschwihr and Bischwihr. Although these waters have lately become quite popular with privately-owned German pleasure craft, they are generally fairly deserted with few signs of life apart from water fowl and anglers. After climbing through

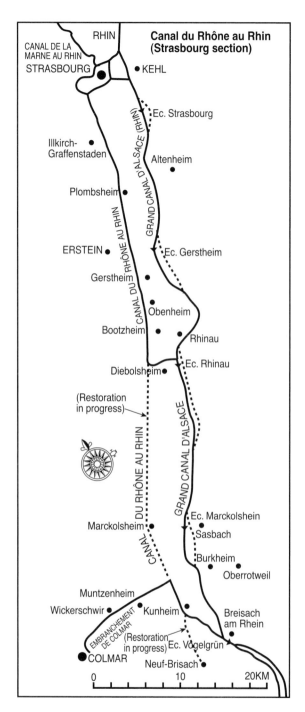

the Écluse d'Ill, the navigation crosses the River Ill and enters a canalised portion of the River Lauch. We pass under the A35 *autoroute* and arrive at the outskirts of **Colmar**. Possible moorings on the right. The former commercial port at the terminus has been transformed into a fine marina with more than 50 berths, some of them reserved for visitors. Facilities include showers and a laundry. One feature is an ancient blue-painted crane that was considered worth retaining whereas it might otherwise have vanished under a less intelligent municipal scheme. In spite of these moorings being moderately expensive and quite a long walk from the city centre, it is well worth boating as far as this, for Colmar is a city of great historical interest and beauty: see the Green Michelin Guide *Alsace Lorraine Champagne*. One of the great medieval cities of France, it was fortunately saved from serious damage during World War II. Narrow streets at the centre are filled with a wealth of carved wooden houses of which the finest are the *Maison Pfister* and the *Maison des Têtes*. As the capital of Alsace, Colmar's food is distinctly Germanic, many varieties of sausage taking pride of place. Local wines are celebrated with a fair in the middle of August and a *Fête de la Choucroute* in the autumn. Buildings that might have been imported from a film set line the banks of the Lauch in the *Petite Venise* quarter. Two world famous paintings must on no account be missed: Martin Schonhauer's 15th century *Virgin and the Rosebush* in the church of St-Martin; and Mathias Grünewald's Issenheim altarpiece from the early 16th century. Comprising scenes from the New Testament it is the great prize of a superb collection in the *Musée d'Unterlinden*, housed in a 13th century monastery.

We now return to the main line at K10.5, to continue the journey towards Strasbourg: from here to K34, junction with the Rhinau/Friesenheim Link Canal, is not likely to be in service until c 2006. The waterway is never far from the Rhine and runs in a completely straight line through pleasant but not very exciting rural surroundings. There are locks at **Artzenheim** (No 64, K11.4); No 65 (K13.5); and No 66 (K15.2). The small town of **Marckolsheim** (K15.3, shops and restaurant) has a basin where a *port de plaisance* is planned. From 1919 until 1965, from the Ardennes to the French frontier on the Rhine, a series of defence works constituted the Maginot Line. Marckolsheim has its own memorial and Rhineside Maginot Line Museum. Here can be seen a Soviet gun, a Sherman tank and a casement containing a display on the battle fought here in June 1940. Écluses 67–74 occur at 2–3km intervals as the canal passes a succession of small villages: **Artolsheim** (K20.8); **Schwobsheim** (K24.7); **Sundhouse** (K26.7, *port de plaisance* projected); and **Bindernheim** (K30.2).

Shortly before guard lock No 75 (K34.9) we reach the section of navigation that escaped abandonment. All locks are automated. Turn right at the junction (K34) to enter the 3.8km **Rhinau-Friesenheim Link Canal** which terminates with a *péniche*-sized lock fitted with sideways-sliding gates: this connects with the canalised Rhine 1km downhill of the Écluses de Rhinau. Restaurant in **Rhinau** village. The main line continues to Écluse 76, **Boofzheim** (K37.3). Here, the Crown Blue Line hire cruiser company has a relay base with moorings and other facilities. A restaurant is nearby. If you have come off the canalised Rhine, the friendly intimacy of the waterway is a pleasure to savour. Commercial use is light and bankside facilities are sparse, with little beyond the occasional café. However, the area annually becomes increasingly popular with pleasure boaters. **Obenheim** (K39.8) provides moorings, right, just before Écluse 77. There is a restaurant in the village, 1km, and another near the **Gerstheim** bridge (K42.8). At 3km distance from the sugar refinery bridge (K45.3), **Erstein** may be too far for a shopping trip; but if you negotiate Écluse 79 (K46.3) you will arrive at a level crossing of the River Ill with Flood Lock 80 (K47). 2km of the river are navigable to and beyond a useful mooring quay in the town. Hire boat base and moorings with restaurant at **Krafft** (K47.3).

Between Écluses 81 (K50.4) and 82, a little boatman's chapel stands in isolation in a meadow: *Notre Dame du Chêne* (visits possible). **Plobsheim** (K52.6, restaurant) and **Illkirch-Graffenstaden** (K60.1) both offer shopping possibilities, although you may prefer to wait for all the city centre possibilities offered by Strasbourg. Near the edge of **Strasbourg** the navigation passes through a memorable avenue of plane trees. Be sure to fill water tanks at Écluse 85 (K63.6, lift bridge), especially if planning to stay in the River Ill area of the city.

Soon (K64.1), the Ill enters on the left. By turning right, you will arrive at Écluse 86 with boatyards, converted barges and the *Bassin d'Austerlitz*, an extension of the large dock area of Strasbourg. An old electric towing 'mule' has been preserved near the lock. This is the most direct route to the canalised Rhine at Écluse Sud, or to the Canal de la Marne au Rhin and the Rhine at Écluses Nord. To reach the heart of the city and to enjoy the delights of one of the finest urban moorings in Europe, keep straight on via the Ill, a little known but quite enchanting navigation that passes close to the cathedral and makes a junction with the Marne au Rhin. This route is shallow (maximum draft below *La Petite France* is said to be only 0.7m), there is reduced clearance under several bridges and characteristically aggressive tripping vessels may claim that

private craft have no right to be there. Small boats should not be put off! Larger cruisers must, however, reach the city centre via the docks. For details and a description of Strasbourg, see Chapter 26.

25 ∼ River Rhine and Grand Canal d'Alsace

Carte Guide: *Le Rhin et La Moselle* (Éditions de la Navigation du Rhin). Or *Rhein-Handbuch 1 – Basel–Koblenz* (DSV Verlag, text in German). Or *Fluvio Carte 1, Naviguer en Alsace* (Rheinfelden–Strasbourg, including Grand Canal, Strasbourg Section of Canal du Rhône au Rhin and River Ill).

Part of the upper reaches of the navigable Rhine lie along the border between France and Germany and consequently find a legitimate place in this book. From the French/Swiss frontier at Huningue to Lauterbourg, where the river starts to flow entirely within Germany, 183.5km with 10 locks. Junctions are made with the Canal du Rhône au Rhin at Kembs-Niffer (K185.5); the Rhône au Rhin's Colmar section via the Neuf-Brisach Link (K226.3); the Strasbourg section of the Canal du Rhône au Rhin at Rhinau (K258); the Strasbourg Docks at Écluse Sud (K291); and the Canal de la Marne au Rhin in Strasbourg, Écluses Nord (K295.5).

Navigating the upper Rhine is rather like eating tripe: interesting for the first few mouthfuls and exceedingly monotonous thereafter. A century and a half of far-reaching works have changed the ambience of the river beyond all recognition. Frequently, the surroundings alternate from an arid wasteland of gravel pits to nearly endless lengths of concrete-lined channel. Interest is, of course, provided by frequent encounters with large-scale commercial traffic and the engineering grandeur of the massive locks. But apart from a limited number of pleasure craft harbours, there is little possibility of mooring in safety, and even lying at lock approaches should only be contemplated provided you are instantly ready to move if several thousand tonnes of cargo vessel appears and seems to want to tie up exactly where you are lying.

It must be stated that the Rhine is not a suitable waterway for timid pleasure boaters. Decades of management has greatly reduced its flow: nevertheless, moderate currents can be expected in the vicinity of the hydro-electric power stations and on remaining sections of natural river. Having travelled (downstream) on the

French Rhine in a hired cruiser of no more than average power (with special permission) I found that it presented no great dangers or difficulties (unlike the treacherous German reaches in the Gorge below Bingen). For preference, smaller craft might be well advised to time their journeys to avoid being on the waterway overnight. The 106km passage from Kembs-Niffer to Strasbourg can be accomplished in a displacement cruiser during a single long day. Otherwise, there are opportunities to escape to the quiet waters of the Canal du Rhône au Rhin as well as to various German yacht harbours on the east shore.

Curious effects of wash from commercial traffic will be experienced: sometimes a severe buffeting arrives as much as five minutes after a vessel has passed, the waves bouncing off concrete hundreds of metres away. Pleasure craft are generally ignored by the lock keepers, so allow all commercial traffic to enter a lock first and then quickly take up a position at the back of the chamber. Filling or emptying reaches a vertical rate of about 3m per minute, but floating bollards sliding up and down in cavities in the walls avoid any need to adjust lines. Pleasure craft have to make fast, bow and stern, to a single bollard, as they are positioned at the widely spaced intervals that suit big barges.

Passenger ships offering a considerable degree of luxury operate throughout the Rhine from the Netherlands to Switzerland. Some are truly gigantic, able to cater for 1,200 clients; halts at main towns and cities allow for some sight-seeing ashore. A journey encompassing the whole river takes four days downstream or five days up. Day trips are also possible from Basle and Strasbourg. Local enquiries will provide the necessary details.

Brief history In use as a navigation for more than 2,000 years, the Rhine is Europe's greatest inland waterway, carrying vastly greater volumes of freight than any other route. It flows from Switzerland's Lake Constance (the Bodensee) and first receives traffic at Rheinfelden, 145km from the source. A long-standing plan advocates modification of these uppermost reaches, making them suitable for boats. Nothing is likely to come of the scheme in the immediate future. Passing near the Black Forest, with two locks in Switzerland, the Rhine enters the French territory of Alsace at Huningue, the right bank of the river being in German Baden. Total distance to the North Sea beyond Rotterdam is 1,030km from Constance.

The upper waters above Strasbourg, once 3–4km wide with hundreds of islands, were navigated in ancient times by rafts or light craft hauled by men or horses. Initial measures to improve the channel were started in 1818 by the engineer Gottfried Tulla, who built a series of dams to convert the wide, shallow river into a deep, fully navigable one. This was not completed until 1876, the course being shortened by no less than 82km. Steam tugs had clawed their way to Switzerland since the early 19th century. As 'improvements' progressed the Rhine ran ever faster and more powerfully, causing severe scouring. Former ports found themselves stranded far from the new waterway, while the scrub land and 'desert' that was created was regarded as an ecological catastrophe.

After the return of Alsace to France under the Treaty of Versailles in 1919, it was decided to build the Grand Canal d'Alsace as a lateral canal. First consideration was creation of a series of hydro-electric power stations with associated navigation locks, each capable of passing six 1,500-tonne barges. Work commenced in 1928, with French architect Le Corbusier contributing design schemes for the barrages. Installations at Kembs (1932), Ottmarsheim (1952), Fessenheim (1956) and Vogelgrün (1959) were all built on a canal quite independent of the river. It was only then appreciated that consequential reduced river levels were producing disastrous effects, so the remaining four locks were sited on shorter lengths of channel, allowing water to return to the Rhine at regular intervals. The later locks are Marckolsheim (1961), Rhinau (1964), Gerstheim (1967) and Strasbourg (1970). Together, the eight power stations can produce 7,000 million kW hr of electricity a year, roughly equivalent to the consumption of Greater Paris.

This was intended to be the end of Rhine engineering, but it was found that severe scouring below Strasbourg Lock still threatened to leave nearby ports stranded. There was no alternative but to build another lock at Gambsheim (1974), and still one more, in German territory, at Iffezheim (1976). Earlier problems were repeated and consideration has been given to constructing yet more locks further down river. Constriction of the river's course has posed a very serious threat from flash floods, which might one day create monumental inundations in the German cities of Karlsruhe and Mannheim. It is therefore likely that a new series of dams will have to be built throughout the upper Rhine, encouraging floodwater to overtop the banks progressively and in a controlled fashion: the habits of the river will thus revert to the situation that prevailed in the early 19th century, before man began to interfere.

Falling 140m in its French length, the Rhine is used by rather more than 30,000 barges annually; about 25% of all Swiss freight arrives by water, principally timber, coal, chemicals, grain and oil. In Alsace, 65km² of canalside land has been earmarked for industrial development as a result of the excellent transport facilities, and already levels of chemical pollution are massive: 90% of the Rhineside woodlands were destroyed as a direct consequence of changes to the river during the 20th century. France has achieved a waterway larger than both the Suez and Panama Canals, but at huge cost, financial and environmental.

Distances in the following description follow the normal convention of measuring from Lake Constance (Bodensee). **Huningue** (K168.5), a suburb of the flourishing city and port of Basle, marks the upstream limit of the French Rhine. The right bank of the river is Swiss, becoming German at K170.

Boats wishing to travel to the river's highest navigable point at the Swiss/German border town of **Rheinfelden** (K150), should note that the only practical mooring for visitors to Basle is in the Kleinhüningen harbour (K170) at the downstream approach to the city. You can expect a very thorough investigation at the Swiss customs post here. Even in summer, the current is fierce through the city and particularly under the bridges. We managed quite well with our 8 knots cruising capacity. Two Swiss locks, **Birsfelden** (K163) and **Augst** (K156), take the navigator to the charming town of Rheinfelden. Here, the water flows very fast; motorised craft should not attempt to proceed through the town bridge. A possible mooring is to the uppermost series of piles, west bank *inside* a small island just below the bridge, by arrangement with the *Café Graff*.

Below Basle, the fast current does not deter oarsmen and canoeists, who seem quite relaxed about taking their chances with heavy freight traffic, passenger vessels and private cruisers. Car ferries link one shore with the other. Industrial development, especially on the German bank, with large waterside houses in France, provides plenty of interest. Until about 1961, the **Canal de Huningue Branch** of the Canal du Rhône au Rhin offered an alternative route from here to Kembs. Its course remains largely intact, with drawbridges by several of the disused locks.

Entry to the upper end of the Grand Canal and the Bief de Kembs is at K174. Generally, banks are higher than the surrounding countryside, which consists of a wilderness of willow trees and melancholy swamps. Nothing can be seen of various quite pleasant villages such as **Rosenau** (K178), where a military tank has been preserved as a war memorial to events in this much disputed land. Anyway, shore attractions must be ignored, for mooring is rarely practicable. The first of the duplicated locks is **Kembs** (K179); each has a fall of around 15m and working is accompanied by an unearthly screeching as the floating bollards slide up and down. A left turn at K185.5 marks the start of the main line of the Canal du Rhône au Rhin. Beyond, a nature reserve has been established in desolate land at Ile du Rhin, soon followed by an expanding industrial zone and the Port of Mulhouse-Ottmarsheim, downstream of **Ottmarsheim** Locks (K194).

Commercial traffic apart, there really is very little of interest to **Fessenheim** Locks (K210.5), site of a nuclear

The twin chambers of Marckolsheim Lock, completed in 1961.

power station. **Vogelgrün** Locks (K224.5), where the hydro-electric works are open to the public, mark the point where the Rhine is rejoined and escape is possible from the Grand Canal d'Alsace. At K226.5 is the entry, left bank to the **Colmar Branch** section of the Canal du Rhône au Rhin (see Chapter 24). A very useful recent addition on the French shore at **Breisach** is a floating pontoon mooring for pleasure craft. Alternatively, cross to the German shore and head upstream to find the Breisach yacht harbour with fuelling facilities and water point (K226). Close by is an agreeable town to explore.

Each section of the Grand Canal now alternates with a length of river navigation, whose width reaches 1km. The journey continues down the canalised Rhine between K226 and K234.5 where a left fork leads to **Marckolsheim** Locks (K240). Scenery finally improves, several appealing towns on the German bank having half-timbered houses and vineyards. Once more, the navigation divides at K249, the left channel connecting with **Rhinau** Locks (K256) with possible moorings at a yacht club near the entrance to the Strasbourg section of the radar-operated Canal du Rhône au Rhin (see Chapter 24). We found that in the long hours of mid-summer daylight (but depending on waiting time at the locks) it is possible to tackle the Kembs–Strasbourg run non-stop via the Grand Canal. However, if in doubt, make advance plans to avoid being on the Rhine overnight. Anyway, unless you are in a great hurry, the older and far more pleasant 'back door' route to Strasbourg via the Canal du Rhône au Rhin is preferable. Any initial enjoyment provided by the Grand Canal is possibly wearing a little thin by now! The next fork downstream is at K268.5, upper end of the **Gerstheim** Locks section (K272). Shortly afterwards a vast compensation basin appears on the left: reserved for sailing dinghies, it cannot be entered from the navigation.

Pleasure boat moorings may be available at a yacht club on the German side, above the great Strasbourg barrage (K283.7). A further (French) club lies inside No 4 Dock of the Strasbourg complex, below **Strasbourg** Locks (K287). The city offers various mooring possibilities near the Écluse Sud exit from the Rhine (K291) or on the German side of the river by the Strasbourg–Kehl road and railway bridges (K293.8, fuelling point). For further information on Strasbourg, see Chapter 26.

The final section of French/German Rhine, Strasbourg to the border with Germany at Lauterbourg, comprises the river's natural course with locks at **Gambsheim** (K309) and **Iffezheim** (K333.7). Yacht harbours have been created upstream of Gambsheim Locks (K308, German); near **Offendorf** (K313.6, French, where there is a barge life museum aboard the *péniche Cabro*); at Greffern (K321.2, German); and below Iffezheim Locks (K335.4, French). Finally, the commercial harbour at **Lauterbourg** (K349.2) may have space for a pleasure boat in need of overnight shelter. I stopped there once, provided alcoholic entertainment for a boatful of off duty French Customs officers (they disappeared with European unification) and enjoyed a walk round the French border town with its entrance gateway in red brick and stone. It has to be admitted that, scenically, all of the French Rhine is disappointing and in no way approaches the grandeur of the Gorges between Bingen and Koblenz.

26 ∼ River Ill and Strasbourg

Carte Guides: *Fluvio Carte 1, Naviguer en Alsace* (includes the whole of the Ill from Strasbourg to Ostwald, as well as other Strasbourg waterways). *Canaux de la Marne au Rhin et Houillères de la Sarre* (only shows Strasbourg section of the Ill).

From a junction with the Canal de la Marne au Rhin by the Palais de l'Europe, Strasbourg to Ostwald, terminus. 9.9km with 2 locks. Junctions are made in the Petite France district of Strasbourg with the 2km Canal des Faux Remparts, which is available only to official trip boats; and with the Strasbourg–Neuf-Brisach section of the Canal du Rhône au Rhin near the canal's Écluse 85. There was a connection with the canalised River Bruche, 3.6km from the upper terminus of the Ill, but this is now abandoned.

When navigating the Canal du Rhône au Rhin towards the city of **Strasbourg**, most craft will negotiate the canal's Écluse 85 and then turn right for the *Bassin d'Austerlitz*, the Strasbourg Docks, connections with the Rhine and the beginning of the Canal de la Marne au Rhin. However, for shallow draft boats (the official depth is stated to be only 0.7m) and with a height above water not exceeding 2.75m, there is a delightful excursion available on the River Ill, through the famous *Petite France* district, eventually emerging onto the Canal de la Marne au Rhin by the European Parliament building. Even though many boats will be unable to use the central section, it seems more logical to describe it from the lowest reaches to its head of navigation, rather than start in the middle and work up and down stream.

Now the largest port on the Upper Rhine and the fifth biggest in France, Strasbourg attracts international freight and is served by an extensive network of docks off the river. The original Celtic settlement was *Argentoratum*, but by the 6th century AD it had become

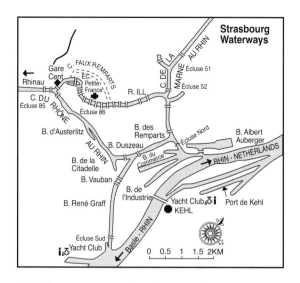

Strasbourg Waterways

Stratisburgum as even then it was an important cross-roads. Throughout the centuries, various rulers have arrived and been deposed, the most recent domination being by the Germans for 47 years until 1918 and again during World War II. Germanic influences remain a powerful force. While Strasbourg is one of the finest cities of France, it has to be admitted (in a sweeping generalisation) that people serving in shops and restaurants often lack the caring charm so noticeable in other parts of the country. It seems almost as if, safe in the knowledge that the city has been capital of Europe since 1949 and boasts so many splendid buildings, sufficient tourists will come regardless! The Old Town is listed as a World Heritage Site. It is hopeless to attempt to list all the sites of interest here. Supreme is the great Gothic 11–15th century cathedral. The spire, recalling a multi-tiered wedding cake, soars to 142m; among the treasures are many superb stained glass windows and an astronomical clock of 1838 which trundles into fascinating action with moving figures at 12.30h each day (curiously showing a time half an hour later than normal).

The boatless visitor can get afloat in tripping craft that operate from a quay on the Ill near the cathedral. Itineraries include the Ill, *La Petite France* and the docks and last from 1½ to 3hr.

Craft of generous dimensions will have no difficulty in navigating the Ill for the first 2.1km from its junction with the Canal de la Marne au Rhin. Here, the massive 1977-built *Palais de l'Europe* stands on the left of the river while on the opposite bank is a great curving edifice designed by British architect Richard Rogers – the European Court of Human Rights. The river banks are pleasantly landscaped with affluent private houses mixed with commercial premises. The current can flow quite strongly. A right-hand junction (K2.1), where a fountain rises from the waterway marks one end of the **Canal des Faux Remparts**, a 2km navigation with 1 lock that is exclusively reserved for trip boats. On the left of the Ill, the *Quai des Pêcheurs* used to be a favourite visitors' mooring, being reasonably secure and wonderfully central. Annoyingly, in recent years all spaces have been allocated to static barge restaurants, whose owners can be alarmingly disagreeable if you ask permission to moor alongside. For reliable, if less convenient, over-night stopping places try one of the boatyards/marinas in the *Bassin d'Austerlitz* area, to the south.

Private craft drawing less than 0.7m are permitted to use the Ill as it passes through the superb *Petite France* area of ancient half-timbered buildings: but they are allowed to do so in a downstream direction *only*. This is to lessen interference with trip boats which always travel upstream. These restrictions do tend to make the private boater feel unwelcome: I was initiated into the canal world under a British régime in the late 1950s where we enthusiasts believed strongly in insisting on our rights of navigation. So, if you have a suitable boat, I strongly recommend you to try it. But you will have to approach Écluse A and *La Petite France* from the upstream direction: coming past the junction of the Ill and the Canal du Rhône au Rhin, continue along the Ill. Soon the channel splits into several arms. Ignore the first watercourses, right, which are mill streams passing under the *Ponts Couverts*. Instead, follow the next opening (K3.9) and pass under an arch in the *Barrage Vauban*. (A further channel leads to the upper end of the Canal des Faux Remparts, reserved for passenger craft.)

You will shortly arrive in **La Petite France** (K3.6), a beautifully preserved district of 16th century gabled timber buildings, once housing tanners, fishermen and millers. It gained its name as a place of safety for Huguenots escaping from religious persecution. Several buildings, such as the Tanners' House of 1572, former seat of the Tanners' Corporation, have become restaurants, specialising in Alsatian wines, beer and food. At one time the giant plane tree here could be climbed via a wooden stairway; drinks would be served to customers high among the branches. Other notable nearby buildings are the lock keeper's half-timbered residence and, about 500m down river, the Old Customs House, dating from 1345 and one of the oldest structures in the city. Several attics are quite open to the wind and were used for drying skins during tanning. The traditional bird of Alsace is the stork: efforts are made to encourage pairs to nest on roof-tops, an increasingly rare event; when chicks are successfully hatched, they are accorded front page newspaper coverage! Quays and buildings are floodlit by night.

The La Petite France *district of Strasbourg.*

This was once a thriving port area, with barges carrying all manner of freight. The Ill was also put to a more sinister use, criminals being plunged in cages into the heavily polluted water in order to extract a confession. Murderers were not so fortunate: they were merely cast into the stream in weighted sacks. Perhaps Strasbourg's darkest time was in the mid-14th century when 16,000 citizens were killed in an earthquake, followed in turn by a raging plague. Somehow, the Jewish community was blamed for these misfortunes: their property was seized and no fewer than 1,884 men and women and 900 children were stripped and set alight in a huge fire. Over half the children and a selection of the more attractive women were rescued by a group of appalled citizens. Hysterical acts of penitence followed, the population indulging in an orgy of mass flagellation.

Best moorings are to a stone quay on the right, a little before a swing bridge operated by the keeper of Écluse A around the next bend. Alternatively, he may allow you to lie between bridge and lock, where you

will immediately become a tourist attraction for hoards of visitors to this, the most appealing area of the city. I found it difficult to believe my luck when permitted to moor here over night. But that was in the 1980s. There are now many more private pleasure boats and urban canal officials are no longer universally helpful.

More than 5km of the lock-free River Ill awaits exploration upstream of the Canal du Rhône au Rhin junction. Throughout, the journey is through leafy suburbs. On the left at **Kœnigshoffen** (K6.3), the disused **Canal de la Bruche** once ran for 20km with 11 locks to **Molsheim**. It was built in the late 17th century chiefly to transport building material for the fortification of Strasbourg. The last commercial loads passed through in 1939 and abandonment followed in 1957. The gateless lock chambers remain, the channel has stayed in water and the towpath is popular with walkers, cyclists and, on special occasions, horse riders. The Ill's head of navigation is at a former wharf at **Nachtweid** (K9.9) on the edge of **Ostwald**.

Most pleasure craft travelling between the Canal du Rhône au Rhin and the Canal de la Marne au Rhin or the River Rhine itself, will take the route south of Strasbourg city centre. Technically, between the Ill junction and the *Bassin Dusuzeau* of the port of Strasbourg this is part of the northern branch of the Rhône au Rhin. The *Bassin de l'Hôpital* (K64.6) provides good moorings and facilities at the Strasbourg Yacht Club: a walk of about 900m brings you to the city centre. After the canal's Écluse 86, it is only a short distance to the *Bassin d'Austerlitz* and access to various dockland basins. There are several yacht clubs and the marina, chandlery and boatyard of *Koejac Bateaux* (moorings, fuel, repairs, etc). In recent years, this has become my chosen Strasbourg stopping point.

27 ~ Canal de la Marne au Rhin

Carte Guide: *Canaux de la Marne au Rhin et Houillères de la Sarre*
From Strasbourg, junction with the River Rhine to Vitry-le-François, junction with the Canal de la Marne à la Saône and the Canal Latéral à la Marne. Originally 313km, one section of 23.4km between Frouard and Toul has been closed, a through route being provided instead by the canalised River Moselle. There are 152 locks (not including those on the Moselle), an inclined plane boat lift at St-Louis-Arzviller and four tunnels: Arzviller (2,306m), Niderviller (475m), Foug (866m) and Mauvages (4,877m). A branch leaves the main line between the Mauvages Tunnel and Demange-aux-Eaux and terminates at Houdelaincourt, 3.2km. There are additional connections with the River Ill in Strasbourg; the Canal des Houillères de la Sarre near Gondrexange; the Nancy Branch of the Canal de l'Est at Laneuveville-devant-Nancy; the River Moselle at Frouard and at Toul; and the Canal de l'Est (Branche Nord) at Sorcy.

Given one day to convert a person to the delights of French canal cruising, I would choose to take them along the 20km of Canal de la Marne au Rhin from Saverne to Niderviller in NW Alsace. We would climb through radar-controlled locks into the steep-sided and thickly wooded valley of the Zorn to Lutzelbourg; marvel at this charming little town in the Vosges; journey onwards to where the St-Louis-Arzviller inclined plane lifts our boat up a cliff face; voyage through the pine trees; and finally dive underground through two tunnels towards the more gentle countryside of Lorraine. It is a 20km microcosm of all that I find irresistible about French waterways.

While this section is the highlight of the waterway, almost from one end to the other it is packed with interest, well supplied with waterside restaurants and shopping facilities and still retains a little commercial traffic to satisfy the true canal enthusiast. Post-war modernisation ensures a good standard of maintenance and the majority of locks (except for some at the western end) are mechanised, many being radar-controlled. Surprisingly slow to be discovered by the pleasure boating industry, the canal now has a number of hire bases: indeed, the portion near to Strasbourg has become one of the most popular holiday boating areas in France. The automatic locks are negotiated quite easily, with instructions in French, English and German available on entry to the navigation. In some areas, boat crews are issued with a portable electronic 'zapper' which activates paddles and gates. Bank traction, once a great feature of the canal, lasted through the Foug tunnel until 1980.

Starting in Strasbourg, the route leaves the Rhine and climbs to the valley of the Zorn. It crosses four watersheds, passing through the valleys of the Sarre, Sânon, Meurthe, Moselle, Ornain and Saulx, but avoids direct contact with any of these rivers. Apart from a brief association with heavy industry near Nancy, the course is intensely rural virtually throughout with delightful villages and small towns among the most interesting of NE France.

Brief history Built between 1838 and 1853, the object of the Canal de la Marne au Rhin was to connect Paris and the north with Alsace, the Rhine and Germany. Considerable obstacles had to be overcome in hilly terrain, hence the many locks and several tunnels. In places, construction was facilitated by its exact contemporary, the Paris–Strasbourg railway. Water supplies were assured by reservoirs, notably at Gondrexange and Stock, augmented by pumping in dry seasons. Early in the life of the waterway, Alsace and Lorraine fell to the German Empire, the eastern part of the canal passing from French control. As a result, plans were rapidly implemented to create an alternative new line towards the Saône – the Canal de l'Est (Branche Sud) from near Nancy.

It was designed with locks to accommodate 35m x 5m *flûtes* with 1.6m draft and subsequently enlarged to the 38.5m Freycinet standard. Traffic flourished and a period of considerable prosperity followed the return of the lost portion at the end of World War I. During the late 1950s barge use had practically reached saturation point, many of the craft being wooden *bilanders*, lumbering box-like 300-tonne capacity vessels, mainly hauled by the towpath tractors of the *Compagnie Général de Traction sur les Voies Navigables*. As early as 1925 financial inducements were offered to operators of *automoteurs* of finer lines and greater speed, there being as many as 7,000 *bilanders* in use throughout France. Yet the last of them were to linger on until the 1960s, forcing all other boats down to their tedious pace. With the end of towpath traction they were made to disappear overnight. Coupled with important improvements to the waterway itself, the Marne au Rhin was able to achieve a new level of speed and efficiency.

The 1960s saw the replacement of 17 locks in the Zorn valley by the St-Louis-Arzviller inclined plane and the substitution of 6 further locks by a single deep one at Réchicourt. On the 151km Nancy–Strasbourg section, the number of lock-kilometres was reduced from 236 to 216 and the barge journey time improved from about 94 hours to 53. Most recent improvements include lock mechanisation and the suppression of the Frouard–Toul length by taking advantage of the newly canalised Moselle between these points. Thus, of *péniche* waterways, the Marne au Rhin had become one of the potentially most efficient and up-to-date in the country. Most unfortunately, since the early 1980s, commercial traffic has declined sharply: you can now expect to meet just one or two barges a day. On the other hand, parts of the waterway are so busy with pleasure craft in summer that it is difficult to imagine freight traffic ever being able to return to its levels of the 1970s.

Entry to the waterway from the Rhine is through the Écluses Nord, situated in the NE part of **Strasbourg** by its docks complex. Adjoining waterways of the city are described in Chapter 26. The first of the canal's mechanised locks, mostly equipped with radar sensors since about 1979, is Écluse 51 (K1.7). The pleasant village of **Souffelweyersheim**, with facilities, lies immediately after Écluse 50 (K6.1), where there are admirable moorings, water, slipway and electricity. (If a small town considers it worthwhile to encourage boating visitors in this way, why is it that many large cities are incapable of providing overnight moorings?) There is much to be said for stopping here and using the good public transport into Strasbourg. The bridge (K9.1) following the A34 *autoroute* crossing is close to a large supermarket, while the **Vendenheim** railway bridge (K10.8) is near to restaurants, shopping and a garage. Locks 46–42 and a further set from 41–37 are operated in an automatic sequence, passage through one preparing the next chamber. Mooring up midway is probably ill-advised.

There are many shopping and eating possibilities between here and Saverne. **Waltenheim** (K22.1), with food shops and the *Restaurant de l'Ancre*, offers a first encounter with the River Zorn, whose steep-sided valley contributes greatly to the attractions of the route. Mooring and water point above Écluse 44.

Hochfelden (K27), to the right of the D25 road bridge, is a modern town. Lines of distant hills ahead indicate the proximity of the Vosges, with a progressively steeper ascent for the waterway. Useful shopping in **Dettwiller** (K35), with further possibilities and a restaurant at Écluse 36, **Steinbourg** (K39.3).

Churches with sharply pointed spires dominate each village. When using Écluse 34 (K40.8) pay attention to the notice warning of strong currents: tie up securely. A patch of industry in **Monswiller** (K42) is notable for one factory advertising its products in the form of a giant wheelbarrow; the same motif is repeated in its decorative boundary fence. Soon, we turn sharply into a large basin and arrive in **Saverne** (K44), a magnificent Alsatian town of half-timbered houses, some carved and painted. If possible, do try to allow for a stay here, if only for a few hours. It is a rose-growing region and an important touring centre with many signposted walks into the surrounding hills. The basin is home to a hire cruiser company and offers facilities for visiting boats although available space is at a premium during peak holiday weeks. From the moorings, you can enjoy a view of the vast Neo-classic summer palace of Cardinal Louis de Rohan. It is rather an overpowering structure of local red sandstone now somewhat half-heartedly used for various municipal purposes and a museum (archaeology and fine art). Saverne has several good restaurants and flourishing shops in a pedestrianised main street. Regional souvenir hunters are guaranteed satisfaction. It is also the last easily approached town with a comprehensive range of services for a long distance. Local industries include cut glass and the creation of exquisite Alsatian scenes in marquetry. We placed an order at the *atelier* of M Straub for a framed view of our motor yacht, leaving him with a photograph from which to work. Some weeks later, the finished product was despatched to England: a remarkably accurate representation with an authentic backdrop. There is a sharp turn at the end of the basin, followed by an unusually deep lock, Écluse 30/31, the result of combining two conventional chambers in 1880 and utilising the principle of the underground side-pond, whereby one third of water consumed on downhill workings is saved for use on the following uphill passage. Rise and fall is 5.43m.

Now begins one of my favourite stretches of canal in Europe: it is worth taking slowly, stopping where practicable (but locks operate in a linked sequence) and reserving time for walks in the nearby forests. Almost every crag in the surrounding hills is crowned with a ruined castle. One was reputed to be a finishing school for witches long ago (*École des Sorcières*). Another is the **Château de Haut-Bar**, overlooking the canal and about

5km from the centre of Saverne. The castle ruins contain a most acceptable restaurant, decorated in a traditional local style with wall paintings and typical Alsatian furnishings. It is well worth an expedition on foot or by bus to visit this famous viewpoint, with broad views over the Alsatian Plain and the Zorn Valley. In clear weather, the cathedral spire of Strasbourg is visible.

Lumber yards and the whine of power saws are an essential ingredient of the district, with tree trunks arriving by lorry from the nearby forests. This really is an area to discover at a leisurely pace, for its great beauty encourages lingering. Nowhere is this more so than at **Lutzelbourg** (K54), a real gem of a town grouped about Écluse 22, close to which is a dry-dock. Road, canal, railway and River Zorn are all squashed into the narrow valley, with bright green woods and tiny fields providing a backdrop to slate-roofed buildings in pinkish sandstone. A church spire peeps shyly over the top of an extraordinary butcher's shop with stone sphinxes and a Dutch gable overlooking the water. Sadly, this had closed for business by 1989. In the *Hôtel des Vosges* we discovered an old established restaurant that can hardly have changed since the 1920s. It took little effort to imagine a jolly Dornford Yates party climbing from their touring Bentley to occupy a table in the large dining room. Among the delicacies on offer were blue trout from the Zorn. There is a hire cruiser company here, so take the opportunity to replenish fuel and water supplies.

Four more locks ending with Écluse 18 (K57) bring a glimpse of the **St-Louis-Arzviller** inclined plane boat lift, a concrete track up a tree-clad cliff face, opened in 1969. This marvel of waterway engineering replaced Écluses 1–17. After considering various existing types of lifts, water slopes and longitudinal lifts (similar to that at Ronquières in Belgium), an international competition was held and a transverse lift was eventually selected as being most suitable for this particular site. It is a single water-filled caisson or tank, able to accommodate a *péniche* or several pleasure craft, fitted with 32 flanged wheels running on a pair of rail tracks. It travels up or down a 108.65m path angled at a 41% slope. Electrically operated guillotine gates seal the ends of the tank, which weighs 850 tonnes when filled with water. Two sets of 14-wire cables run from the tank, over a pair of winch drums in the building at the top and back to two counterweights on either side of the central spine. Travelling at a maximum speed of 0.6m per second, each boat takes about 25 minutes for transfer from one level to the other, compared with $8\frac{1}{2}$h for working through the former locks. During a 13h working day, no fewer than 39 craft passages can be achieved. The design allowed for installation of a second caisson running side by side with the existing tank, but this has not yet been required. Should it ever be added, daily capacity would increase to 78 tankfuls. Arzviller was regarded as a small-scale prototype for 1,350-tonne routes once projected between the Rhône and the Rhine. It was completed in a little under 5 years at a then cost of about £7.5 million. 1,209m of new approach channel was excavated at the lower end with 3,308m of new canal dug from the cliff face at the top. Riding on the plane is a thrilling experience, the journey being exceptionally smooth with splendid views over the forests of the Zorn Valley. Passage is free for all VNF licensed boats, while land-based tourists must pay an entry fee for the upper complex, with a guided tour, souvenir shop and café and the option of excursions aboard a trip boat. This runs daily from spring to autumn. On the bank at the top, a St-Jean-de-Losne-registered *péniche* is preserved ashore as a graphic indication of the size of barge able to use the structure. A small canal museum is contained within, where specialist waterways books may be purchased. Tourist excursions around the site are available aboard a little road-based 'train'.

The series of old locks is now closed to traffic: they remain as an awe-inspiring spectacle, each with a keeper's cottage alongside and generally still inhabited. It is all well worth exploring on foot or by bicycle. The best approach is to moor at the top end, but do inform the nearby tunnel keeper of your intentions so that he can schedule your passage. Derelict waterways are usually sad places, but there is little hint of *tristesse* here as few boaters would wish to return to doing the hard day's work once demanded. Although the canal bed is virtually dry, lock gear remains substantially intact together with portions of narrow-gauge railway, once used for hauling barges. At one point the track crosses a pound elevated on a structure of steel girders. Note the former locomotive shed near the top of the flight with several engines slowly rusting on their tracks.

Shortly after the junction with the line leading to the old Écluse 1 (K61) the control house containing an array of switches governing traffic signals, closed-circuit television, ventilation fans and sodium lighting for the Arzviller and Niderviller Tunnels (2,306m and 475m long) will be seen. Each is still equipped with towpath and rail tracks on which the electric 'mules' once operated. The bores are separated by an 802m open section where craft can pass. Lights warn of any oncoming boats, both tunnels being one-way.

Twenty six-km of summit level between **Niderviller** and the next lock at Réchicourt offers a remarkable contrast to the restricted valley of the Zorn. The canal winds through rolling hills and pasture land less dramatic but

Pleasure cruisers in the Arzviller inclined plane boat lift. Valley of the River Zorn, near Strasbourg.

nonetheless very pleasant. The large *Bassin d'Altmuhle* (K66, moorings, shower, slipway, water, electricity) is a possible stopping point for Niderviller. Rather closer is another basin (lacking facilities) three bridges further on (K67.5). Within a short walk there are two restaurants, several food shops and the famous Niderviller *Faïencerie* (earthenware factory) founded in 1735. Customers are encouraged to tour the extensive showrooms and place orders which might range from a luxury hand-painted dinner service for twelve (expensive) to a set of mass-produced tea cups and saucers for everyday use. 6km NW, the substantial town of **Sarrebourg** on the River Sarre has a fortified *château*, a regional museum (includes 14th century ceramics and Gallo-Roman remains) and a World War I cemetery containing about 13,000 graves. Reputedly the largest stained glass window in Europe, by Marc Chagall, can be seen in the Chapelle des Cordeliers.

Villages with exceedingly un-French names include **Schneckenbusch** (K69.5) and **Hesse** (K72.3), the latter with a wide section where Crown Blue Line opened a cruiser base in 1985. At the time we were very unsure if it was wise to encourage hire craft on a waterway so busy with freight craft. Now, the waterway is thronged with hire boats and the commercial traffic has declined nearly to extinction. Arrangements can usually be made for maintenance, repairs and long term care of private craft. Good local food shopping in the attractive partly fortified village. The River Sarre is crossed via a 45m aqueduct (de Laforge). Now comes a tree-lined cutting with stone banks, near **Imling** (basic shops), with a further embanked section providing glimpses of distant towns at the approach to **Xouaxange** (K76.8, restaurant). This village is a hilltop cluster of buildings in reddish-brown stone with slate roofs. Several places in the area announce their presence by signs on the canal bridges – a good idea that might usefully be copied elsewhere.

Héming (K80), with prominent cement works, is a useful little town (some shops and restaurant) followed shortly by **Gondrexange** (K82.4, shopping, taxi, restaurant) where a guard lock is fitted to cope with the possibility of any burst on the embankment which divides the waterway from its vital water supplies at the adjacent Étang de Gondrexange reservoir. This lake is well used as a recognised holiday area with windsurfing, sailing, caravans and camping. A lonely junction, right, marks the start of the Canal des Houillères de la Sarre (Sarre Coalfields Canal). In spite of the off-putting name, it is a delightful route leading to the Sarre Navigation which connects with the German Moselle (see Chapter 28).

Engineering features of the Marne au Rhin are notable as the canal begins to fall away from its eastern summit. Considerable changes carried out in the 1960s have replaced six locks with a single deep one at **Réchicourt-le-Château** (K90.5), now known as Écluse 1. First, you pass through the level chamber of the old top lock and ahead the former line of the canal will be seen branching to the right. Instead, take the left fork to arrive at the new structure, whose rise and fall is a massive 16m. It empties by raising the guillotine gate at the lower end, an impressively rapid procedure akin to pulling out a highly efficient bath plug. I once came through here accompanied by a hire cruiser, seemingly crewed by just two men. When the lock was nearly empty, nine further crew members emerged from the cabin, all holding wind instruments; they took up positions on deck and treated us to a brief brass band concert. They were a musical ensemble from Switzerland and were taking every opportunity to test the acoustics of unusually cavernous lock chambers and canal tunnels!

A keeper is on hand to offer advice and instructions. Very necessary floating bollards are a great help. Beyond, the waterway now passes through the centre of the Étang de Réchicourt reservoir – a novel experience – with re-entry to the canal alongside the old Écluse 6, where the stone wall has been partially removed. A combination of wind and water flow can produce a strong current here. Following locks are radar-controlled, the first being No 7 (K93.2). Note the long-closed *Épicerie-Café-Dépôt-du-Pain* whose faded sign probably dates from the early 20th century.

Not far to the right of Écluse 8 (K94.4, basin) is **Bataville**, an 'industrial new town' which has a factory shoe shop, supermarket and restaurant. **Moussey**, left of Écluse 9 (K96), has food shopping. Facilities in a collection of waterside villages now encountered are sparse but most necessities are available, especially if a scout can be sent ahead by bicycle while the boat negotiates locks. **Port-Ste-Marie** (K97.6), a tiny hamlet near Écluse 10, boasts a garage (useful for boat fuel) owned by the proprietor of the *Auberge du Port*, an eating house whose fortunes seemed doomed as commercial traffic declined only to pick up again when pleasure boating became increasingly popular. Here, the little River Sânon strikes up a close relationship with the canal that is to last all the way to Dombasle and the River Meurthe.

Lagarde (K103.2), near Écluse 12, is well worth a visit, being intensely rural with exceptionally friendly villagers serving in the baker, grocer and restaurant. A hire boat base has brought unimagined prosperity to this isolated backwater. (Fuel, gas, water, slipway, etc.) Reeds, corn, sheep and tracts of dark forest characterise the reaches past **Xures** (K107.1) with a section of canal up to 200m wide west of **Parroy** (K111.4). A former butcher/grocer by Écluse 16 (K114.6) is now a bar/restaurant. If you have time, go ashore at **Bauzemont** (K117.9), near Écluse 17; few supplies are on offer, with the exception of milk and eggs at a farm, but the grouping of houses, massive barns, haystacks, tractors and wagons in the main street is most picturesque. **Einville** (K121.9) is one of those small towns that seem to have seen better days. The few shops appear to open at irregular hours, if at all. But there is a taxi service, garage by the bridge and an hôtel/restaurant at the far end, before a useful mooring basin. Steaming pans are evidence of salt production. Écluse 18 (K122.6, restaurant), like others in the area, has an elegant cast iron name plate. Limited shopping in **Crévic** (K129.6), shortly before Écluse 20.

After Écluse 22 (K133.5) begins a rare but extremely interesting area around the chemical works of **Dombasle-sur-Meurthe** (K134.6). Massive factories line the waterway, with numerous bridges and gantries connecting one bank with the other. This is the Belgian Solvay soda enterprise; its products are used in glass, aluminium and plastics. Not very many years ago up to two dozen Solvay *péniches* in their smart livery would be encountered, loading and unloading. The fleet numbered nearly 100 craft. The complex is best viewed from the isolation of a boat, rather than stopping to make use of the shore facilities. However, there are useful moorings (*port de plaisance*, restaurant) after the bridge that follows Lock 22. Several locks were duplicated, side by side, to cater for the now vanished Solvay traffic. These start with Écluse 23 (K135.7, mooring, restaurant). Should you pass through one chamber while the other is occupied by a barge, you will experience the curious effect of simultaneous vertical and lateral movement.

Virtually without a break, Dombasle merges into **St-Nicolas-de-Port** (K136.6). This little town on the banks of the Meurthe was the chief industrial centre of Lorraine during the Middle Ages. Its towering Gothic basilica, built between 1494 and 1530, attracted many pilgrims and from an earlier church Joan of Arc set off on her celebrated mission. Long ago, before construction of the canal, shallow draft barges would make their way from the Moselle and up the **Meurthe** to St-Nicolas, an appropriate destination for craft whose owners venerate the saint as their special patron. As recently as 1921, 127km of the river was still available for *flottage* (transport of log rafts, up to 100m in length), although only the 12km upstream of the Moselle junction was then navigated by conventional boats. The brief incursion into an industrial landscape, recalling something of England's Black Country, ends as suddenly as it began. Although odd patches of factory development are scattered in the fields around **St-Phlin** (K140.6), there is a stretch of comparative countryside before the start of further urbanisation at the outskirts of Nancy. An aqueduct carries the canal over the Meurthe a little before duplicated Écluses 24 with a similar pair of locks in **Laneuveville-devant-Nancy** (K144, water point). This little town is exactly the kind of place that you would be unlikely to visit except by boat – always an endearing feature of canals. It offers useful shopping and a congenial atmosphere in the *Restaurant de la Marine*. Here is a left-hand junction with the heavily-locked **Nancy Branch** of the Canal de l'Est, the quickest route to the Saône. (See Chapter 22. It is currently undergoing major restoration works; seek latest information.)

The Canal de la Marne au Rhin now follows the valley of the Meurthe through one more pair of duplicated locks – Écluses 26 at **Jarville** (K146.5) – before entering the conurbation around the great city

of **Nancy** (K149.2). It is an important manufacturing region, leading industries including salt and ironworks. Until recent times, canal transport played a vital rôle in distribution of goods with three extensive loading basins near the centre. Of these, the *Bassin Ste-Catherine* (K149.4) is reserved for freight craft. Pleasure boats are catered for at the *Bassin St-Georges* (K149.2) and the *Port de Malzéville* (K150.7, dry dock); of these, *Ste-Catherine* offers the most comprehensive marina services. Nancy is much more than an industrial complex. It has many large and stylish shops and several outstanding restaurants including the luxury *Le Capucin Gourmand* (31 rue Gambetta). In its Place Stanislas, Nancy has perhaps the finest square in France, a magnificent group of 18th century classical buildings with superb wrought iron gateways, gilded lanterns and a huge fountain with an astonishing gilded screen. These features were introduced by ex-King Stanislas of Poland, who was granted the Dukedom of independent Lorraine by his son-in-law Louis XV on the understanding that it would pass to the French crown on Stanislas' death. The former ducal palace houses the Lorraine Historical Museum. Nancy's greatest and most rewarding claim to fame is that it was here that *Art Nouveau* architecture and design flourished to a unique degree at the turn of the 19th and 20th centuries. Numerous glorious *Nouveau* buildings can be seen. The city tourist office offers a brochure detailing various walking tours. Totally unmissable is the *Musée de l'École de Nancy* in a suitably opulent Art Nouveau villa (38 rue du Sergent Blandon). The period interiors are filled with an explosion of artefacts from glass to ceramics, bookbinding to posters, furniture to fabrics.

On reaching **Frouard** (K158, shopping), an extensive inland port, through navigation is achieved via a lock on a short branch and entering the canalised River Moselle, some distance upstream of Metz. This section of the Class IV waterway was opened to traffic in 1972 and the subsequent extension of the river navigation up to Toul and Neuves Maisons was gradually achieved in the years that followed. The canal has been closed to traffic as far as Toul, its course being duplicated by the Moselle (see Chapter 29). Much of the former line has been filled in, an impressive 187m aqueduct over the Moselle at **Liverdun** demolished (little more than a decade after it had been enlarged) and the adjacent charming port and approach to the 388m Liverdun Tunnel reduced to an overgrown wasteland. Thus 23km of the canal are now replaced by the Moselle. As an aid to planning travelling times, this distance is counted in the figures quoted here.

We leave the Moselle at K369.2, shortly before **Toul**, turn right into a new linking branch and pass through the boatman-operated automatic Écluse 27 *bis* and back into the Marne au Rhin at the Port of Toul. (If bound for the Canal de l'Est [Branche Sud] and the River Saône, it is necessary to remain on the Moselle until K394.) To complicate the situation still further, about 20km of the Canal de l'Est's through route shares a course with the Marne au Rhin up to Sorcy (K204.4). The intricate and confusing layout is explained in the *Carte Guide*.

Toul occupies the pre-historic bed of the Moselle and has long been a frontier city. Massive stone fortifications originally designed by Vauban are pierced by the waterway as it runs through the city's moat towards the Port de France, a convenient mooring between Écluses 26 and 25 within easy reach of shopping and a garage. Water, fuel, and electricity. Note the preserved barge towing locomotive. Larger craft may find mooring easier at the Connoisseur hire cruiser base, nearer the Moselle junction. The city was heavily bombarded in 1940 and 1944 and many old buildings were destroyed. Fortunately, the 13–16th century cathedral of St-Étienne was spared and much restoration work carried out on it during the 1980s. Sadly, the violent Millennium Storms blew the roof off and it is closed for prolonged rebuilding. Electric locks 24–14, the last with chambers duplicated side by side, lift the canal through pleasant suburbs to **Foug** (K190.9). All facilities lie to the right, the other side of a railway. Ahead, a one-way cutting runs up to the 866m Foug Tunnel which is illuminated and controlled by lights. Until 1980 boats

Inside the 866m Foug Tunnel.

were hauled through by electric mules. Now craft proceed under their own power. Vessels approaching from the west end at **Lay-St-Rémy** (K192.8) may be required to wait in a newly constructed basin until the way ahead is clear; information on traffic movements is available from a keeper.

North of the waterway, the Lorraine Regional Park acknowledges tracts of fine countryside that extend to the canal as it winds along a 19km level close to willow-fringed water meadows by the infant River Meuse. The course alternates from grassy cutting to broad corn-fields and clumps of woodland. Almost all the villages have great charm: **Pagny-sur-Meuse** (K196.6) has mooring pontoon with water, basic shopping and a restaurant while **Troussey** (K200.6) by the reedbeds of the river, is a noted angling centre. A prominent lime works stands by the junction with the Canal de l'Est (Branche Nord) at **Sorcy-St-Martin** (K201.4), the route for the canalised Meuse, Belgium and the Netherlands (see Chapter 23). Modernisation resulted in the old stone Troussey Aqueduct being replaced by a concrete version (K202.3). There are magnificent views in this green and wooded valley. Heading SW, the canal skirts the splendidly run-down little town of **Void** (K208.7), a place of agricultural equipment suppliers and with a massive cast-iron hand-operated street side water pump and a bridge over the fast-flowing rock-strewn course of the delightful little River Meuse. Grain silos are served by *péniches* and on the canal bank an obelisk erected in 1969 commemorates Nicolas Joseph Cugnot (1725–1804), to whom is attributed the invention of the automobile. A plaque illustrates the steam-driven vehicle for which he was responsible. There is shopping and a waterside office of Voies Navigables de France. Several km south, the small town of **Vaucouleurs** is worth a visit: there are fragments of a medieval castle and not far from here Jeanne d'Arc (1412–31) was born and set in motion her crusade to rid France of English domination.

Locks 12–1 raise the waterway to another of its summit levels. They are controlled by lights and pleasure craft must be quite sure to hold back the metal bars when entering and leaving the chambers for 10 seconds (as is unavoidable by barges for which this switching system was devised); otherwise the mechanism will not function. When this apparatus was installed in 1979, one manually-operated paddle was left at each end of the locks for use in the event of power cuts. The scenery here is superb: rolling pastures as the hills gradually close in ahead. The lovely village of **Sauvoy** by Écluse 7 (K214.4) deserves investigation.

Some delay is likely at the one-way **Mauvages** Tunnel (K220.3), perhaps providing an opportunity to

On the climb through locks at Sauvoy towards the Mauvages Tunnel.

walk from a bridge into the single-street village of Mauvages where the occupants of grey stone farmhouses once drew water supplies from elaborate cast-iron pumps decorated with curious faces. Narrow-gauge towpath locomotives stand disused in a cutting leading to the 4,877m tunnel, and portal plaques record the original construction in 1841–6 with rebuilding in 1911–14 and 1919–22. Present regulations still state that all craft must join a convoy behind a venerable electric chain tug, dating from 1912. Similar in design to the tunnel tugs of the Bourgogne and St-Quentin canals, this dinosaur heaves its *rame* (convoy) at the speed of an *escargot*, each tow consisting of up to ten barges with pleasure craft positioned at the back. Making up the tow is a noisy and exciting operation, but once engines have been silenced and boats move off into the darkness (there is lighting at intervals), the passage is surprisingly quiet and relaxing. Adequate fenders are recommended. As the tug moves through the vault, it trips switches, automatically lighting the approaching length and turning it off astern. Two convoys pass in each direction, every working day. Timings are posted at nearby locks. In recent years, reduced commercial traffic and a realisation that dangerous fumes will not be created by a single boat, have resulted in the once obligatory tug being used less frequently. Several years ago, I passed through astern of the tug (but not attached to it!) and propelled by my own engines. More recently, no tug was used at all: a

waterways' employee rode his motor bike along the tunnel towpath, stopping to turn lights on and off, while I steered through at normal cruising speed. On both these occasions, the statutory towage charge was still demanded.

At the far end a 3.2km branch on the left leads to a terminal basin in the small town of **Houdelaincourt**, with the *Auberge du Pere Fours* restaurant, a garage and several shops. At nearby **Gondrecourt-le-Château** there is a *Musée du Cheval*, devoted to the part once played by horses in transport and agriculture.

The remainder of the journey is quite heavily locked, as a long descent begins through hilly and broken countryside, starting at Écluse 1, Tombois (K228, shops, restaurant and *halte nautique* with facilities). At the time of writing, all locks between No 12, Void and Bar-le-Duc, are operated by a portable 'zapper'.

Never is there a shortage of beautiful villages all close at hand in this delightful rural scenery: **St-Joire** (K234.2), **Tréveray** (K237, some shops, garage, water), **St-Amand-sur-Ornain** (K240) and **Naix-aux-Forges** (K242.2, supermarket). Here, wooded cliffs of chalk rise from the water, remaining through **Menaucourt** (K244.7) and **Givrauval** (K247.4) to the historic market town of **Ligny-en-Barrois** (K249, pontoon moorings with useful services, slipway and garage, below Écluse 22). All supplies are at hand and there are elaborate decorated gateways at the town's main road entries. An enjoyable visit can be made to the *Musée de la Tour de Luxembourg*. Further shops, restaurant and garage are near Écluse 25, Velaines (K252.9), while there is a supermarket on the nearby main road below Écluse 27 (K258) near **Tannois**.

By this point, locks have become the chief pre-occupation: there are no fewer than 70 in the 87km between Mauvages and Vitry-le-François! Most remaining manually-worked chambers are fitted with an ingenious overhead connecting device enabling both bottom gates to be opened by operating winding gear on only one side of the chamber – a considerable saving of time and energy for the keepers. Do make time for a brief glance at **Longeville** (K261.1, supermarket) whose houses are clustered in all manner of angles. For the first time since Toul, we soon arrive at a substantial town, **Bar-le-Duc** (K265.5). Although now a flourishing manufacturing centre, with products ranging from textiles to clock-making, woodwork and engineering, Bar was virtually an independent country from the mid-10th century and in 1354 its counts took the title of dukes. Towards the later 15th century it was absorbed into Lorraine and became fully French in 1776. The sizeable River Ornain is a feature of the town with numerous fine 15th century buildings. In World War I it provided the only viable route to besieged Verdun, 58km to the north: this road remains un-numbered, being known simply as the *Voie Sacré*. The Marne au Rhin passes quite close to the centre with a pair of bascule bridges; moorings here are somewhat noisy, alongside the railway station. In fact, from the water there are few hints that this is both an historic and an attractive town. The most convenient shopping is at a supermarket (with garage) on the left a little before Écluse 38, Marbot.

Note the three-arch aqueduct – one of a large number on this section – by Écluse 40, Chantereines (K268). In the rather urbanised village of **Fains-les-Sources** (K269.7), there is a supermarket not far from Écluse 42. A very convenient eating place is halfway down the pound 42/3. In its final reaches, the canal is pleasant but unremarkable. The next place of any size is **Revigny-sur-Ornain** (K280.7, shopping), followed by the slightly industrialised **Sermaize-les-Bains** (K288, shops, restaurant near the lock), with a disused dry-dock and barge-building works. Now we are in the valley of the River Saulx, buildings are generally of red brick rather than the previous stone. Between locks 63 and 64, **Pargny-sur-Saulx** (K293.4), there are good moorings with facilities and shops.

We cross an aqueduct by Écluse 65, **Etrépy** (K296), a small place notable for its traditional *cheminées* (fireplaces) factory, stone drinking fountain and *lavoir* (public wash-house). The canal then passes vast expanses of unfenced fields. Among features in this length are the shallow and winding course of the willow-fringed Saulx and a huge classical style *château* in grey stone near **Bignicourt** (K298.2). Lights control traffic on a tight bend above Écluse 68, **Brusson** (K306).

The last 14km of the waterway comprise two very straight sections, rural but rather lacking in features (water point at Écluse 70, St-Étienne, K309.7), leading to **Vitry-le-François** (K313), an important barge town at the junction with the Canal de la Marne à la Saône (Chapter 49) and the Canal latéral à la Marne (Chapter 14). Many *péniches*, including a sadly high proportion withdrawn from trade, lie at moorings around a short branch that ends by a disused dry dock. A recently flourishing barge chandlery and fuel point has been replaced by a housing estate. The best pleasure craft moorings are to be found a short distance into the Marne à la Saône (electricity, water, showers, slipway, etc). Vitry, capital of the Perthois, was established by François I in the mid-16th century as a fortified replacement for the medieval settlement of **Vitry-en-Perthois** which was destroyed in 1544 by the forces of Charles V. The centre lies quite close to the Marne à la Saône and although not a place of any great beauty, with much municipal housing and a sizeable Turkish population, it is worth visiting the main square, the *Place d'Armes*, dominated by a 17–18th century church. In the middle, a terracotta fountain of 1842 features the goddess of the River Marne, a paddle firmly grasped in one hand: graphic evidence that we have reached a very different region from the Rhineland where this journey began.

28 Canal des Houillères de la Sarre and River Sarre

Carte Guide: *Canaux de la Marne au Rhin et Houillères de la Sarre*
From a junction with the Canal de la Marne au Rhin near Gondrexange to the canalised River Sarre at Sarreguemines, 63.4km with 27 locks; 9.3km of navigable River Sarre with 3 locks runs from Sarreguemines to the German frontier beyond Grosbliederstroff.

Translated as the Sarre Coalfields Canal, this waterway suffers undeservedly from its gloomy title, with scarcely a hint of mining activity throughout the French portion. It drops steadily from the Marne au Rhin past a succession of lakes in the Lorraine Regional Park. Beyond Sarrable the navigation is along the River Sarre, an important stream comprising the Sarre Rouge and the Sarre Blanche which both rise near the French town of Donon. After Sarreguemines the line is officially known as the Canalised Sarre, and only on reaching the frontier with German Saarland is there any evidence of coal production.

Together with the Rhine and the Moselle, the Sarre (Saar in German) offers a water route from France to Germany. Following canalising of the Sarre all the way to the German Moselle near Trier (completed in 2000: see below), a really interesting circular cruise became a reality. This comprises the Houillères de la Sarre, the French and German Sarre Navigation, the German and French Moselle and the Canal de la Marne au Rhin. Since opening of the Sarre throughout, meaning that the Canal des Houillères is no longer a cul-de-sac, its pleasure boat traffic has increased steadily.

Brief history There is evidence of commercial traffic in small boats on the River Sarre during the Middle Ages, but the waterway that now exists dates from the 19th century. First projected by Napoléon I, the canal was not finally constructed until 1862–6, just before the Franco-Prussian War of 1870 and the loss of Lorraine to Germany. Before any such problems had arisen, the French and Germans had agreed to co-operate in making the Sarre navigable from Sarreguemines to Luisenthal (25km with 6 locks), later extended a further 14km with 3 locks to Ensdorf, still a considerable distance from the German Moselle. For more than a century a German fleet of barges based on the Saar had to make a long French detour via the Canal des Houillères, the Marne au Rhin and the Rhine before reaching the main part of the German network. The French Sarre and its canal handled 1.2 million tonnes of freight, mainly coal, in 1936. Freight traffic on the line is now insignificant.

The Germans published a plan for the canalisation of the lower Saar to link with the Moselle near Trier in 1930. Nothing materialised until 1969 was it ambitiously proposed to construct a completely new 130km waterway, the Saar–Pfalz-Rhine Canal, direct from the Saar to the Rhine. This was to have had three inclined planes, an 18m-deep lock and three long aqueducts. Estimated to cost £250 million in 1970, the idea was discarded. Three years later creation of a new navigation along the German Saar that would be suitable for large Rhine barges and push-tows was agreed. This included building six locks 190m in length with extensive excavation works to lessen the effect of exceptionally tight bends. The new route was completed upstream of the Moselle by 1989, except for a short section near the Franco–German border. The breakthrough came in time for the boating season of 2000.

The Canal des Houillères de la Sarre branches off the Marne au Rhin at a lonely junction near the Étang de Gondrexange (see Chapter 27) and skirts a thickly wooded area near **Houillons** (K1.9) on the borders of the Lorraine Regional Park. At the time of writing, it is necessary to book mobile lock keepers before 16.00h the previous day. This can be done by telephoning various offices, some of which can receive VHF calls on Channel 18 (see the *Carte Guide*). But with increasing use of the waterway, it is likely that locks will soon be available for use on arrival, as is normal elsewhere. Mooring basin with water and electricity at a guard lock (K2.3). The waterway runs along the east shore of the extensive Étang de Stock (K5.5), a very attractive lake serving as a canal reservoir and heavily used for leisure activities. In an inlet on the west bank, the appealing village of **Rhodes** has a waterside church and a main street devoted to agricultural matters: it is filled with herds of cattle, hay carts and stacks of winter fuel in the form of logs. Écluses 2–12 form a flight spread over 6.4km between **Albeschaux** and **Angviller-les-Bisping** (K17.4). We are now in the 4,500 hectare Forest of Fénétrange, noted for roe deer and wild boar. The canal passes through part of the Grand Étang de Mittersheim and arrives at Écluse 13 in **Mittersheim** village (K20). The 220 hectare lake serves as a reservoir, maintained by the navigation authority and is admirably adapted for sailing, small motor cruisers and bathing. A vast congregation of summer chalets and caravans takes advantage of the delightful location. There is a hire boat base in Mittersheim, with moorings, waterside diesel, shopping and restaurants. A left fork between Écluses 13 and 14 is the start of the disused **Canal des Salines**. This was planned in 1806 as part of a scheme for a waterway between the Sarre at Sarrable and Dieuze, 17km SW of Mittersheim. Only 4km of what became regarded as this 'branch' was completed to **Loudrefing**. It was closed in 1939, following subsidence caused by brine pumping.

7km east of Mittersheim, along the rural D38, and thoroughly meriting discovery by bicycle, lies **Fénétrange**, on the banks of the Sarre. Established as a fortified medieval border town, it is entered via a well-preserved gateway, *La Porte de France*, featuring an *oubliette* complete with skeleton. There is a castle and a tourism office housed off an extraordinary curved stone courtyard. Several quite elaborate restaurants indicate the town's popularity with visitors. Here, German (or at least the 'Alsatian' version) appears to be spoken almost as much as French: the frontier is only about 36km to the north.

There is a large restaurant alongside Écluse 15 (K22.6) and another near Écluse 16. Good moorings between locks 17 and 18 near **Harskirchen** (K33). Also boatyard services, shopping and restaurants. The River

Sarre closely approaches the canal at **Sarralbe** (K41.1) and remains never far away until it eventually forms a navigation in its own right at Sarrguemines. Sarralbe is a thriving little town and the first place of any size on the canal. It is worth going ashore to see the 18th century gateway and a working watermill. The A34 Metz–Strasbourg *autoroute* spans the waterway outside **Herbitzheim** (K44.9, some shops and restaurants). Écluses 22–26 are situated on a winding section with a good choice of restaurants at regular intervals. Villages include **Wittring** (K52), a pleasing settlement of somewhat upright houses clustered around the church, and **Remelfing** (K61.1, shopping and restaurant).

The final canal lock, No 27 (K63.4, moorings, water and fuel), introduces the beginning of the Sarre Navigation and the substantial town of **Sarreguemines**. It is famous for its pottery, founded in 1790; more than 3,000 workers were employed in the early 20th century. Production is now mainly concerned with floor tiles, but in earlier times Sarreguemines was associated with its beautiful *faïence*. Note the pair of preserved *faïence* kilns behind the *Hôtel de Ville*. An even more striking building, on the right bank of the river above the main bridge, is the *Casino de Faïences*, an early 20th century structure decorated with coloured tiles and murals. It operates now as an Alsatian restaurant. Just downstream is a really amazing gateway in the form of a turreted gazebo with elaborate stone embellishments and all that was state-of-the-art architectural taste when it was erected in 1880. Nearby are good pontoon moorings within a short distance of a thriving shopping centre.

Three locks take the river into Germany, through **Welferding** (K66.4), where the right bank is German and the left French. Only at the twin towns of **Grossbliederstroff** and **Kleinblittersdorf** (K71.6) is there at last any evidence of the mining that gives the canal its name, for here overhead cables carry an endless procession of coal buckets. Once across the frontier, spoil tips and power stations are a feature of the **Saarbrücken/Völkingen** conurbation. By then, the river has become the Saar and it offers some spectacular scenery during the memorable voyage downstream to the Moselle (*Mosel*) and the vineyards of Trier.

29 ~ River Moselle

Carte Guides: *Lorraine Ouest Moselle No.13* (Vagnon). *Alsace Lorraine* (Editions du Breil). The section Neuves-Maisons to Frouard appears in **Carte Guides** *Canaux de la Marne au Rhin* and *La Meuse et le Canal de l'Est* From a junction with the Canal de l'Est (Branche Sud) at Neuves-Maisons to the border with Luxembourg and Germany at Apach. 152.2km with 16 locks. (The German Mosel then continues to join the Rhine at Koblenz.) Where new cuts have been excavated, certain of the former river reaches remain in use by pleasure craft and are noted in the following text. There are extensive dock systems at Thionville, Richemont and Metz, with two branches: the Embranchement d'Hagondange, from K283 to the Port d'Hagondange, 1.5km; and a line serving the Port de Nancy–Frouard, from K346.6, 2km with 1 lock. Additional connections are made with the Canal de la Marne au Rhin (West Section) at Toul, K369.3; and the Canal de la Marne au Rhin (East Section) off the Nancy–Frouard Branch, near K346.6. Parts of the original Canal de l'Est (Branche Sud) and Canal de la Marne au Rhin have been replaced by the course of the newly canalised Moselle which now provides through routes in each case (see Chapters 22 and 27 respectively).

Since World War II the Moselle has been totally reshaped to provide a Class IV navigation suitable for 1,500-tonne barges and 3,000-tonne push-tows all the way from Neuves-Maisons to the Rhine at Koblenz. Previously only its central portion was used by *péniches*, although the length from Neuves-Maisons to Toul formed part of the lateral Canal de l'Est (Branche Sud). The far-reaching works that have been carried out are one of the great success stories of modern French waterways, although it must be admitted that commercial traffic levels are disappointingly low.

Pleasure craft should experience little difficulty in sharing the route with large barges provided they adhere to the regulations and apply customary common sense. At various points yacht harbours have been established and not infrequently there are side arms or sections of the old river for an escape to wash-free overnight moorings. Barges tend to move between dawn and dusk, even during the long daylight hours of midsummer.

Rarely does the scenery approach the celebrated grandeur of the German Mosel. Rising in the Vosges near Bussan, the Moselle first becomes navigable at Neuves-Maisons, noted for its steelworks. The downstream run to Frouard, near Nancy, is extremely pleasant with hilly tree-covered banks. Industry intervenes here and returns again between Metz and Thionville, with steel production predominating. As the Moselle nears Germany the first vineyards appear on the banks and thereafter its course remains spectacular all the way to the Rhine.

It can be important to realise that between 1871 and 1918 the river from Arnaville (upstream of Metz) to the present frontier lay within German Lorraine. This occupation, while detested by the French inhabitants, has left lasting reminders of Prussian influence in architecture, language and food. Passenger vessels operate at Metz and from Thionville to the German border.

Brief history Freight rafts were in use on the Moselle during Roman times, and according to Tacitus, there was a scheme to link the river with the Saône thus providing a navigation all the way from the Rhine at Koblenz to the Mediterranean. But this dream was not to materialise (at least over that particular course) until the mid-20th century. Initial attempts to render the Moselle fit for barges were made in the 17th century by Vauban; but by the late 18th century the river was reported to be useless for regular trading. A start was made at Chedeaux in 1816 to deepen the channel and ill-fated trials carried out with a passenger steamer, *Ville de Metz*, in 1839. Lack of water depth and problems with the Prussians killed the project. Two years later, four steam-driven paddle wheel *inexplosibles* went into service from Nancy to Metz and Metz to Trier. They had been built on the lower Loire at Nantes and were navigated all of 2,011km to the Moselle via the Loire, Seine, Oise, Meuse, Belgium, the Netherlands and the Rhine. Floods and droughts eventually put paid to this scheme; railways were being opened and within seven years the vessels were sold for use on the Rhine.

Renewed efforts to tame the river began in 1867 with a programme of lock and weir construction from Frouard to Metz. The Franco-Prussian War intervened and the section remaining in France (downstream to Pont-à-Mousson) was opened by 1876. Prussian railway interests obstructed further progress and traffic from French Lorraine was forced to reach the Rhine (at Strasbourg) via the heavily locked and longer Canal de la Marne au Rhin.

With the 1918 peace and the return of German-occupied Lorraine to France, thoughts again turned to Moselle improvements and from 1929, 30km with four locks was canalised between Metz and Thionville. Known as the Canal de Mines de Fer de la Moselle (CAMIFEMO), it was finished in 1932. Meanwhile, Hitler's Third Reich had begun to canalise the German

Mosel: work continued until 1944 and the first lock at Koblenz was completed in 1947.

Subsequent history of the river is a prime example of the benefits of European co-operation. A *Societé Internationale de la Moselle* was established between France, Luxembourg and Germany in 1956 with the object of creating a Class IV waterway. The Thionville–Koblenz section was inaugurated in 1964; an extension upstream to Metz followed in 1970; the new inland port of Frouard was ready by 1972; and the final stage, Frouard-Neuves-Maisons was ready for traffic in 1978, that final part alone having cost nearly £40 million. Soon, more than 12 million tonnes of freight was passing up the Mosel at Koblenz each year. About 9 million tonnes of this was destined for France. And now that the waterway existed, it could begin to attract new traffics and industries in addition to those for which it was initially designed. Although German waterway traffic has continued to grow year by year with navigations being upgraded or completely new routes being constructed, similar enthusiasms started to wane in France during the 1990s. As a result, it seems unlikely that the mid-1960s scheme to link the upper Moselle to the Saône at Corre will now materialise. This imaginative proposal envisaged a 52km summit level served at each end by inclined plane barge lifts 42m and 68m high.

In the description that follows, distances quoted coincide with the kilometre posts which are measured from the Rhine at Koblenz.

Waterways enthusiasts – especially devotees of commercial traffic – will regard the start of the Moselle Navigation at **Messein** (K394) with pleasure but other travellers may consider the area rather dreadful. Pretty it isn't. As the *péniche*-sized Canal de l'Est (Branche Sud) passes through its Écluse 47 (see Chapter 22) it is instantly transformed into a route for Eurobarges at a big concrete-sided basin. Ahead, alongside a broad reach of new canal, are the steelworks of **Neuves-Maisons**, with an even larger basin at the far end shortly before the first of the massive locks. Flood marks show how the Moselle, a little distance to the left, has at times put the whole complex under more than a metre of water. Note a concrete wall rising from a road by the side of the lock: it is recognisable as part of the chamber of a demolished Canal de l'Est lock. The town is frankly rather dreary, with rows of squalid foundry workers' houses; nevertheless, we found the shopping to be most comprehensive even if we did begin to regret having piled the bicycles with laden cartons which then had to be pushed 800m in sweltering heat back to the boat! There is the promise of charming countryside soon to come. 5km of artificial canal leads past the suggestively-named **Sexey-aux-Forges** (K388), a hilly little town set above the river and the decaying remains of the Canal de l'Est. Now that we have joined the natural river in rural surroundings, **Maron** (K387.2) provides some shore facilities if a suitable mooring can be found near the D92 road bridge. **Nancy** lies about 12km NE on the far side of the Forêt de Haye.

The following reach to the fortified village and citadel of **Villey-le-Sec** (K380.6) is extremely pleasant. Pleasure boat harbours are planned for basins off the right bank at K381 and K380.5, above and below an electric cable crossing. If you wish to explore Villey, moorings might be possible with care on the portion of river that leads to a weir (right bank). The Écluse de Villey-le-Sec lies on a short canal to the left. **Pierre-la-Treiche** (K376.1) is followed by **Chaudeney-sur-Moselle** (K374) where a quite modern concrete road bridge was demolished to allow for the passage of large barges. Pleasure craft are permitted to work through an old *péniche*-sized lock at **Toul** (K371) alongside the modern large-gauge Moselle chamber. The fortified city is a short distance away (see Chapter 27). Several hundred metres downstream of the Pont de Toul, a left turn provides access to an automatic lock (worked by the boat's crew) on a short branch. This leads to the western part of the Canal de la Marne au Rhin in the direction of Vitry-le-François (Chapter 27). There are good moorings on the canal at the *Port de France* between Écluses 25 and 26.

At intervals on the left bank of the Moselle will be seen bridges and lock houses of a closed portion of the Canal de la Marne au Rhin, withdrawn from service when the Moselle was opened to traffic. Much of the old line has been filled in, a curious and rather sad situation for a navigation that so recently carried heavy quantities of freight. From K373 to K361 the waterway is contained in an artificial channel, somewhat isolated from small towns such as **Gondreville** (K365.4) and Fontenoy-sur-Moselle, where there is a lock (K364). After **Villey-St-Étienne** (K361), junction with the natural river, it is possible to turn upstream and cruise safely for almost 5km to a weir beyond Gondreville. On the way you will pass Fontenoy once more where a substantial number of small cruisers lie on moorings by a slipway and petrol point.

Aingeray Lock is situated on a short canal at K356. An agreeable wooded reach now extends to a broad loop at **Liverdun** (K352), site of a demolished Marne au Rhin two-way aqueduct and disused tunnel which pierces the tree-covered hill on which the town is built. The area is ambitiously known as 'Little Switzerland in Lorraine', and has sign-posted waterside cycle paths.

One road entry is through a 16th century gateway. Houses are clustered in layers amid the greenery of a cliff, and the once charming canal basin is now a bleak wasteland overlooked by a former boatmen's café where a faded sign advertises stabling for barge horses (see also Chapter 27). A basin upstream of the first of two rail bridges is equipped with a mooring pontoon (shopping and restaurant).

Industry begins to close in as the valley narrows at the approach to **Frouard** Lock (K348), followed without a break by **Pompey** (K347), a place of ironworks. There are moorings with water point on the left near a *café*: this is a useful shopping stop. After a railway bridge is an important junction: right leads to the *Port de Nancy-Frouard*, a sizeable commercial harbour reached through the Écluse de Frouard-Clévant. Pleasure boats should aim for the smaller *Freycinet* chamber on the right which provides access to a large basin with an arm at the top that links with the eastern part of the Canal de la Marne au Rhin, direction Strasbourg. Even if travelling further down the Moselle, it could be worth making a detour along here in order to visit **Nancy** by water (see Chapter 27). Otherwise public transport or taxi would serve the same purpose: the distance is only about 8km.

Take the left fork at Pompey junction to continue down river, with the Moselle's once-navigable tributary, the Meurthe, reaching its confluence near K345. Although it is close to the A31 Nancy-Metz *autoroute*, the next section of river is pleasant, especially below the Écluse de **Custines** (K343.6) and on to **Belleville** (K341.5). Here a weir across the river marks the start of the short Belleville cut, the Moselle being rejoined at K339.5. Remains of the old *péniche*-sized waterway include a disused but intact lock and canal near K338, with a further length leading out of the new Blénod-Liégeot Dérivation at K334.9 and running as far as **Pont-à-Mousson** (K327.5). This well known foundry town boasts one of the finest waterfronts on the entire Moselle. Moorings will be found either on a vertical quay near the bridge or alongside meadows. Constant bombardments in World War I and again in 1944 resulted in serious damage to this gateway to German Lorraine. An encounter between the American forces under General Patton and the Nazis is recalled by a large fountain decorated with lamp standards, presented to the town by the United States. It dominates the remarkable Place Duroc, an almost triangular 'square' surrounded by 16th century stone buildings with arcades at street level and quite equal to the rather similar centre of Louhans, on the River Seille in Burgundy. The *Maison des Sept Péchés Capitaux* illustrates the Seven Deadly Sins in carvings, while another fine structure is the delightfully named *Château d'Amour*. East of the river is the *Butte de Mousson*, a hill surmounted by the ruins of a feudal castle built by the Dukes of Bar. Walk to the top for a magnificent view over the surrounding countryside. Pleasure craft are welcomed at a harbour downstream of the town, on pontoons under a bridge (K326.8).

Navigation from K325.7 to the Écluse at **Pagny-sur-Moselle** (K318) is by means of a canal, with the village of **Vandières** (K321.6) en route. Between K314 and K316 is a very pleasant wooded and hilly reach of original river. The years of the Prussian occupation up to 1918 are remembered in **Arnaville** (K315) by the *Rue des Anciennes Douanes*, where there was once a frontier customs post. Various pleasure boat facilities are available at the *Port Fluvial de* **Corny-sur-Moselle** (K311). Remains of a Roman aqueduct which spanned the river will be seen between **Jouy-aux-Arches** and **Ars-sur-Moselle** (K307): 18m high and about 4m wide, it was built in the 1st century AD to bring water supplies from Gorze to Metz. By the Middle Ages, it was widely believed to have been constructed with the help of the Devil! Now comes the Écluse d'Ars. At K302.3 (left bank) is the Metz Yacht Club (fuel, chandlery, with supermarket – selling bottled gas – 600m distant). To reach a very agreeable mooring in the heart of **Metz**, take the channel at K298.5 just upstream of the *porte de garde* at Wadrineau; follow the river on the far side, pass beneath the A31 *autoroute* bridge and emerge in a broad pool by the Esplanade and near the Allée Victor Hugo. Many cruisers are moored here on floating stages. If you continue to a quay (right) a little upstream of the Protestant Temple, you can try to tie up (as I have done), although this is not an official site. In 1986, 11km of the 1930s Moselle Navigation, with two locks, which had been closed for over 20 years, was brought back into use for pleasure boats. This duplicates the route of the main waterway between Jouy-aux-Arches (K306) and the centre of Metz. Conditions for its use seem to change regularly: the latest enquiry suggests that the Écluses Citadelle and Esplanade are available only during weekends in July and August.

Metz is a French Army garrison city founded 2,000 years ago. A 13th century *château-fort*, the *Deutches Thor* or *Porte des Allemands*, straddles the little River Seille. In later years fortifications were designed by Vauban and these same structures helped the Germans hold out against General Eisenhower for more than two months in 1944. There was dreadful slaughter in this vicinity during the Franco-Prussian War and a great gloom and sadness settled on Metz after 1871, many of the French inhabitants moving away. The vast Gothic cathedral of St-Étienne is among the finest churches in

the country with magnificent stained glass from the 13–20th centuries. By climbing to the top of the *Tour de Mutte* a splendid view is obtained. A famous bell cast in 1605 has been rung on momentous occasions such as the German defeat at the end of World War II. The long *Pont des Morts de Metz* is a bridge spanning two arms of the Moselle. Building and maintenance costs were obtained for 500 years from the 13th century by means of a law that required every man dying within the See of Metz to leave his best suit of clothes to be sold for the benefit of a special fund. The church of St-Pierre-aux-Nonnains is the oldest basilica in France, once attached to a 7th century abbey. When the railways arrived, tracks were laid over the site of a huge Roman amphitheatre – an appalling act of vandalism. Shopping facilities are excellent with a large classical market hall. Éric Humbert's butchers/delicatessen (8 rue du Grand-Cerf) is an award-winning establishment, noted for its lavish displays of food. A fascinating reference to one-time domestic washing arrangements in Metz is provided by an American, George Waring, whose book *The Bride of the Rhine – Two hundred Miles in a Mosel Row-Boat*, was published in 1878. He learned that it was possible for residents to order a hot bath to be brought to their homes: a wagon would arrive at the front door bearing two portable tubs, a barrel of water and a stove and boiler to heat it. On payment of 1.20 francs, servants would carry the necessary equipment indoors while the neighbours would be supplied with the fullest details of the frequency of one's personal cleansing!

Beyond Metz, navigation is along the course of the river, through the Écluses de Metz (K297) and past the entrance to the *Nouveau Port de Metz* (K294), an area that increasingly attracts industry. The river broadens into a delightful elongated lake (K290–K288) bordered by large houses and much used by dinghy sailors. At the far end, you turn off into a long section of canal with a pair of locks at **Talange** (K283.6) followed immediately by a branch serving the Port d'**Hagondange**. After the Écluses de l'Orne at Richemont (K277.7) we rejoin the river with yacht clubs at K277.6 and K275.6. Another length of canal begins at K273.2 with connections to extensive railway sidings in the *Port Public de Thionville-Illange*.

Thionville is entered after locks (K269.9) and is seen to good advantage from the waterway. The city marks the end of a succession of steelworks, power stations and refineries, and, although containing its fair share of industry, is not without considerable interest. It was

Moorings in the centre of Metz.

once the centre of Lorraine iron and steel manufacture, but no iron ore mining now remains. Over the centuries, the town has frequently changed hands. The Merovingians built a castle which was adopted by Charlemagne in the 8th century. By the 13th century, the Counts of Luxembourg had raised a huge fortified *château* which in subsequent years was held in turn by the Burgundians, Habsburgs and the Spanish. Finally, the city was granted to France in 1659 and the ubiquitous Vauban surrounded it with fortifications. While under the Germans from 1870 to 1918, Thionville was provided with additional defensive works and many impressive buildings reflecting the Prussian taste in architecture. Recent years have seen the creation of a pedestrianised shopping centre. Facilities including moorings, fuel, gas and chandler will be found in the pleasure boat harbour upstream of the lock, while downstream are floating stages convenient for town centre shopping.

Pleasant scenery now follows the valley of the Moselle past the villages of **Ham** (K262) and **Basse-**

Ham (K260) a little before a short cut leading to the Écluse de **Kœnigsmacker** (K258.2), with overgrown gravel workings now popular with anglers. **Malling** (K254) is on the river bank and dominated by the spire of its Gothic church. **Rettel** (K249) has possible moorings on a wall (check depth) and the first terraced vineyards for which the lower Mosel is so famous will be seen here. Apple orchards and plantations of walnuts are a feature of **Contz-les-Bains** (K247) as the valley narrows through wooded hills. Until the late 19th century, a curious and ancient rite was performed here each midsummer, when bonfires were lit on the Stromberg Hill, above the vines. A great wooden wheel, bound with straw, was rolled ablaze towards the river, guided by young men clutching flaming torches. If the wheel ran beyond a particular well, the nearby town of Sierck had to present Contz with a barrel of white wine; but when it stopped short, Contz would provide Sierck

Vineyards near the frontier with Germany.

with a large wicker basket of cherries. Should the wheel travel as far as the river, where the flames were extinguished, a notable vintage could be expected in the autumn.

Sharp bends demand that commercial traffic slows to a tickover as barges line up for the next reach, leading past a yacht club (K246.3) into the delightful little town of **Sierck-les-Bains** (K245.5). Like other border settlements it has suffered a stormy history, and was sacked by the Swedes in the Thirty Years War, with further serious damage towards the end of World War II. Vines cover the slopes on the opposite shore and a busy little railway divides the main part of the town from its waterfront. Useful shopping with a choice of restaurants are an encouragement to moor up, the best site being a small concrete jetty directly alongside the K246 marker post or rather further out of town in the *port de plaisance*, just downstream of a camping site. Do not attempt to lie on walls elsewhere: these are obstructed by underwater rocks. Sierck is dominated by the ruins of a very extensive *château-fort*, extending along the skyline. Its intact outer walls look down onto the roofs of houses and provide a splendid viewpoint for watching craft moving along the Moselle. Built in the 11th century on the foundations of a Gallo-Roman fort, it successfully held out against the British Duke of Marlborough in 1705, was demolished after the Treaty of Utrecht a few years later and was rebuilt in its present form in 1773. Many roofed portions remain, with vaulted tunnels and stairways leading to circular rooms: it all provides scope for a fascinating tour of discovery. Seen from the riverbank at night, the *château* is pure magic, the lower parts illuminated by orange lights with the upper towers in white. It floats above a dark band of rock and trees, with street lamps twinkling in the water far below. Barges move through the gloom, their engines chuffing relentlessly, proving that their skippers have intimate knowledge of every metre of the waterway, for only the bridge arches are lit after dusk.

One last lock remains in France, at **Apach** (K242.5), a village of railway sidings and former customs posts at the frontier with Germany and Luxembourg. Craft are now able to pass down river unchallenged – one positive benefit of the European Community.

IV · BRITTANY AND THE LOIRE COUNTRY

The Brittany and River Loire waterways systems form an extensive inter-linked network but are not connected with the main body of French inland waterways. All are maintained and operated by regional or local bodies rather than by Voies Navigables de France.

30 ~ River Rance

Carte Guide: *Bretagne*
From the Atlantic coast at Dinard and St-Malo to the Marine Lock at Le Châtelier, near Dinan, junction with the Canal d'Ille et Rance: 22.6km with 2 locks.

The Rance in its lower reaches occupies a flooded valley, with steep wooded banks and numerous inlets. For experienced sailors this is most attractive water, but it should be regarded more as a tidal estuary than an inland waterway. An 800m barrage incorporating a tidal power station also provides a road link between **Dinard** and **St-Malo**. Exceptionally high tides make the site very suitable. A 65m-long lock on the Dinard side of the barrage operates at all times when there is a depth of at least 4m above and below. Full details of the operation are contained in the *Carte Guide*. Depending on the requirements of the generating station, there can be a strong flow in the impounded estuary upstream, with water levels falling by as much as 1m in 10 minutes. Having calculated the tide times, it is advisable to pass through the Rance without delay and reach real inland water beyond the second lock, **Le Châtelier**. The most favourable time to leave the barrage is about 3hr before high water, thus having the advantage of the flood tide over the mud banks at **Mordreuc**, near the upper end of the tideway. Le Châtelier Lock operates day and night when tidal levels are suitable.

Yachtsmen accustomed to the ways of the sea will take these problems in their stride (their real fears only usually begin on entry to shallow still-water canals, with bridges and waterway bottoms threatening the ship from more than one direction!). But inland boating enthusiasts, and especially those in hire cruisers, will stay well clear of the tidal Rance. Instead, you can embark on a passenger vessel which completes the journey from St-Malo and Dinard to Dinan or *vice versa* in about 2½hr (May–September). It is possible to leave your cruiser in Dinan, travel down the estuary, enjoy a day at the seaside in either of the two resorts and return by water in the evening. Dinard is a fashionable watering place, not unlike Torquay, developed since the middle of the 19th century and long popular with the British. By contrast, St-Malo is an ancient fortified port, fully restored after the destruction of World War II, and now a busy sailing centre for more than 800 craft in two huge basins.

31 ~ Canal d'Ille et Rance

Carte Guide: *Bretagne*
From the estuary of the River Rance at Le Châtelier Lock, near Dinan, to Rennes, junction with the River Vilaine: 84.8km with 47 locks.

A very verdant waterway through lush pastures and little changed since the days – now long gone – of commercial traffic, the Canal d'Ille et Rance is quite well maintained. Some locks – unusually for France – retain wooden balance beams to open gates. All are operated by keepers. The towpath is generally suitable for cycling or walking. The most notable engineering feature is a flight of 11 locks at Hédé, normal enough for the habitual canal user but regarded with a degree of horror by the crews of the many small sailing craft using this route between the English Channel and the Bay of Biscay. A large proportion of private craft appear to be owned by Channel Islanders. The canal is rural throughout and one of the most attractive lengths is the section nearest Dinan, along the valley of the Rance. Seldom in France are the lock gardens so magnificently filled with flowers as on the Ille et Rance.

Brief history By 1539 the River Vilaine was navigable from the Bay of Biscay to the Brittany capital, Rennes. It was one of Europe's first waterways to be equipped with pound locks. An obvious further move was to cut a canal from there to connect with the Rance and so open a trade route to the Channel coast. Plans were eventually drawn up in 1736, but progress was dreadfully slow: by the time of the Revolution in 1789 little had been achieved. According to various printed sources, the Canal d'Ille et Rance was eventually inaugurated in 1838, 1839 or 1842. It was considered only of secondary importance at the time of the Freycinet Act of 1879 and like other Brittany canals was never enlarged. Lacking a reliable connection with the rest of the French network, any great upturn in trade seemed unlikely. At the beginning of the 20th century freight craft in service included Rance *chalands*, *gabareaux de Rennes* and *pénettes de Redon*. Most were built of timber and remained horse drawn; some were rigged as sailing barges for estuary work. Some motorised barges were introduced in the late 1920s, mostly working near Rennes. Cargo vessels appear to have lingered on until the early 1960s. For a time thereafter, before the growth in pleasure cruising, there was a strong possibility that this and other Brittany canals might be closed down. Exploitation of the leisure use of the navigation was carried out by the Committee for Promoting Tourism on Breton Canals. Maps and guides were published, signboards erected at town and village moorings advertising the facilities, and advice given to prospective hire cruiser companies. As a result, waterways of this area are now among the best managed in the country from a pleasure boating viewpoint.

An electrically operated lock at **Le Châtelier** is effectively the upstream limit of the maritime River Rance (see Chapter 30). It is said that high tides can still, on occasion, flow over the weir and affect levels as far as the second canal lock, Pont-Perrin, No 46. Moorings here tend to be somewhat congested with private craft and hire cruisers (water and electricity). There is a slipway and restaurant. Wooded cliffs fringe a broad pool, up to 450m wide. Stakes and buoys mark the navigation channel, which only begins to narrow at the approach to the often congested but delightful tourist town that is **Dinan** (K7). We are still very much in the world of the yachtsman and there are extensive jetty moorings along the right bank, packed with sailing craft and cruisers; any attempt to tie up on the deserted quays opposite will result in an encounter with an agitated harbourmaster. Considerable fees are demanded (water, fuel, showers, slipway, winter storage, mast-lowering crane, etc), but the attractions of the town are such that inland boaters must become resigned to paying for facilities that are frequently free elsewhere in France. Charming old buildings line each side of the port, together with a large modern hotel, several restaurants and some basic food shops. Diesel engined passenger craft operate a service to Dinard and St-

Malo, replacing the steamers that worked over the route towards the end of the 19th century.

The old town of Dinan stands high above the river, surrounded by ramparts and fortifications. It can claim to be one of the best preserved medieval towns in France. A great local hero is Bertrand du Guesclin, a peasant warrior who defended the fortress against the English in the 14th century. Steep cobbled streets lined with half-timbered houses (many of them 15th century) lead the visitor from the river up into the town centre. There are many craft centres, souvenir shops, bars and small restaurants. One of the finest buildings is the 15th century Governor's House in the Rue du Petit-Fort. Visits should be made to the 14th century *château* with its 34m Coëtquen Tower and the slightly later Clock Tower in the Rue de l'Horloge. Splendid views down to the river are obtained from the English Gardens, overlooking a massive stone viaduct carrying the N176 across the deep valley. Shopping is varied and good. Do visit the retail fish market, a curious structure of concrete colonnades.

Above the bridge the waterway immediately narrows and follows a winding course through dense woodland. The well-surfaced towpath provides an agreeable walk to Écluse 47, **Léhon** (K9), downstream of the partly ruined priory of St-Magloire with 12th century church (vaulted roof and tombs) and 17th century cloisters. Moor at a small landing stage above the little stone bridge. Open air swimming pool. The possibility of floods has resulted in the prohibition of overnight mooring between Léhon and Écluse 43, La Roche; as there is little danger in summer, the rule appears not to be enforced.

Past a *château* with slated towers among the trees, Écluse 46, Pont-Perrin (K11), is approached via a channel on the right (if in doubt, always follow the towpath). Where the river is regained, at a junction above, is a huge stone quarry with buttercup-filled water meadows, white poplars and alders. One of the most delightful locks on the whole canal is No 45, **Boutron** (K14), on a short artificial cut. Immediately alongside the chamber, which is spanned by an iron swing bridge, is a stone water mill with intact wheel; the keeper's house built into a cliff on the right is approached up a double flight of steps, an indication of the likelihood of flooding. Derelict ivy-clad farm buildings rise from the towpath, above. Several of the locks in this area have gates operated by a capstan arrangement. Elsewhere, wooden balance beams are used, although these have sometimes been sawn off and a more modern winding device installed. The Rance finally leaves the navigation at Écluse 43, La Roche (K18). Floods are not the only difficulty to have blighted

A lockside mill near Dinan.

the canal in the past, for a plaque on the lock cottage at **Évran** (K19) records a drought that resulted in total closure from June 1921 to February 1922. Almost all the Brittany waterways were similarly interrupted by the Great Drought of 1976 (when my hire cruiser holiday was transformed into a seaside vacation, using the boat only for overnight accommodation) and again towards the end of 1989. The small town is dominated by a large church with spire. Convenient shopping; moorings are on a towpath quay with water point above the lock. The 17th century *Château de Beaumanoir*, 1.5km north, is open to the public.

Repeatedly one is surprised in France that superb little historic buildings can sink into complete dereliction. It is said that having been in the same family for many generations, the owners would rather see them crumble than sell them off. Opposite Écluse 41, des Islots (K23), a turreted stone building bearing the date 1641 stands empty and unloved. It cries out to be restored, but with a flourishing farmhouse directly alongside it is presumably surplus to requirements. **Trévérien** (K24) has a canalside church with square tower and spire, a wharf with water point and shopping facilities. Écluse 40 and 39 are followed by a pound into **St-Domineuc** (K28), a rather ugly little town strung out along the busy N137, with shops, restaurant and garage. Pleasant countryside with woodland and cornfields

Left: *Sunset at Honfleur harbour, estuary of the River Seine.*

Below: *Boating on the Canal de Somme at Dreuil-lès-Amiens*

Left: *Moorings on the Canal de l'Ourcq at Villeparisis, outskirts of Greater Paris.*

Right: *In the city of Metz, off the Moselle navigation.*

Below: *Laden péniches on the River Meuse at Givet, on the border with Belgium.*

Right: *Brittany seafood lunch on the River Vilaine.*

Below: *Working through a lock in the Hédé flight, Canal d'Ille et Rance.*

Left: *Lockside building on the Canal de Briare near Rogny.*

Below: *Canal Latéral à la Loire. The world's longest navigation aqueduct at Briare.*

Left: *Late summer colour at a lock cottage on the Canal du Centre near Chalon-sur-Saône.*

Right: *Canal du Nivernais. In the deep summit level cutting near Baye.*

Below: *River Yonne. The Auxerre waterfront.*

Left: *Life-sized angling figures on the Canal de Bourgogne at Vandenesse-en-Auxois.*

Right: *River Saône, Lyon. St Jean's Cathedral and the Basilica of Notre-Dame-de-Fourvière.*

Below: *Canal de Bourgogne. Summer morning mist on the southern descent from the summit level.*

Opposite: *Canal de la Marne à la Saône. A laden péniche runs south near Chaumont.*

Left: *An occasional hazard of boating in February: on the River Saône at Tournus.*

Below: *River Sèvre-Niortaise. In the Marais Poitevin at Coulon.*

Left: *Petit Rhône. Swimming from a 'desert island' at K293.*

Below: *Côtes du Rhône wine country at Tournon.*

Right: *River Rhône. The famous Pont d'Avignon.*

Below: *A particularly fine 'lavoir' (public wash-house) near the Canal Latéral à la Garonne at Valence d'Agen.*

Left: *Canal du Midi. Cruising boats share a typical curved-sided lock chamber, Lalande, near Carcassonne.*

Right: *River Lot. A lock beneath one of the arches of the 14th century Pont Valentré at Cahors.*

Below: *In the Camargue. Flamingoes by the Canal du Rhône à Sète near Frontignan.*

Above: *On the River Baïse at Nérac.*

Left: *Étang de Thau. Sunrise at Marseillan harbour.*

accompanies the canal past locks 38 to 34 before we reach **Tinténiac** (K38), the leading town between Dinan and Rennes, and grouped about a massive 19th century church. Good moorings with facilities, shopping and restaurants. Several *châteaux* in the neighbourhood are worth an excursion. The nearest, **Montmuran**, is 5km via the road to Les Iffs. Its oldest parts date from the 12–14th century, and Bertrand du Guesclin was knighted here after his encounter with the English. Other possibilities are **Combourg**, 13km NE, 11–15th century and owned in the 18th century by the Count of Châteaubriand, father of the celebrated writer François-René de Châteaubriand; and **Caradeuc**, in a fine park, 10km along the D20 to Bécherel.

Open county leads past Écluse 32, La Moucherie (K40), to the beginning of the 11-lock **Hédé** flight through woodland to the summit level. Most keepers are responsible for two locks each, and assuming slight delays for other boats or chambers not being made ready in advance of your arrival, the series should be negotiated in a little under 2hr. With grassy banks and thick foliage, the Hédé Locks are among the most pleasantly situated of any in Brittany. To visit the town, moor in a basin immediately north of Écluse 28, La Madeleine (K43) – but inform a keeper of your intentions. Alternatively, continue with the boat to the top lock, moor and return by bicycle to the bridge just below Écluse 25, Parfraire. Hédé is about 2km, partly up a steep hill past a crowded cemetery. At the outskirts note the big 19th century Gothic *château* with exceptionally slender towers. The quiet little town has a broad square in front of a Romanesque church where the clock strikes the hours twice, so as to make quite certain that everyone has heard. Continue down a lane containing the *Théâtre de Poche* (Pocket Theatre) to arrive at the impressive ivy-clad ruins of an 11th century feudal *château* on the edge of a precipice with distant views over the plain below. Within are two tarmac sports pitches and a pile of World War I shell cases that have been removed from the memorial. There are a number of shops and restaurants. Back at Écluse 28, the keeper's house contains a small canal museum devoted to archive photographs, documents and models illustrating the history of inland waterways in Brittany.

Deep in a shaded cutting, the 7km summit level is supplied by two reservoirs: the *Bassin de Bazouges* and the *Bassin de Partage des Eaux* at **La Plousière** (K50). By La Plousière bridge is a stone quay and café/bar. Water supplies are augmented by a 50m circular basin above Lock 20, **Villemorin** (K51), whose duplicated upper gates face in each direction for conservation of water in the event of an accident. Here, the descent to the River Vilaine begins down the valley of the little River Ille.

Some of the locks are worked by keepers responsible for two, and they will race off by motorbike down the towpath in an attempt to have the next chamber ready in advance of your arrival. Above Écluse 17, Lengager (K53), is a good stone quay with mooring bollards. Follow the D12 eastwards for 1.5km to the centre of **Montreuil-sur-Ille** (shops and station). There is a water point at Écluse 16, de Haute-Roche (K54). I once arrived at Écluse 15, Ille (K55), to discover an amazing machine in use near the top gates. Looking not unlike a wood-fired traction engine, this turned out to be a travelling cider still with shining copper and brass pipework. Its proud owner informed me that he lived in St Médard-sur-Ille and was licensed to operate throughout 20 parishes in the district. Farmers would bring barrels of the previous year's cider which, after distillation, flowed in a steady stream from a tap in the form of a throat-burning *eau de vie*. Although it was yet early morning, I hesitantly accepted the jolly operator's invitation to sample some. Further practitioners of this traditional craft were later encountered on the Vilaine and the Sèvre-Niortaise.

After **St-Médard-sur-Ille** (K58), conveniently close to Écluse 13 for shops, restaurant and garage, the waterway passes through a narrow cutting crossed by three bridges of the Rennes–St-Malo railway with its little red and cream three-coach trains. Honeysuckle, dog roses, hazel, alder and sweet chestnut create a confused tangle on the banks: sometimes it seems as if there is barely room to pass another boat. Through Écluse 12, Bouessay, and on to the 11th lock, **St-Germain-sur-Ille** (K61), there is a small water authority yard where winter moorings are possible. Here is the workshop where wooden lock gates are still constructed. Moor just below, left bank, for drinking water. Climb a steep hill into St-Germain for most shops. In the post office, a marble plaque sadly records (in translation): 'Here Armandine Mallet, postmistress, was killed by the Germans at the age of 45. August 1, 1944.' Shortly afterwards, this part of France was liberated.

It is appropriate to mention that all canal locks have been equipped with safety ladders and ropes slung along the chamber walls at both full and empty levels, a practice that is found elsewhere but is not yet universal. Écluse 8 at **Chevaigné** (K66.8) has a water point and several village shops. Between **Betton** (K72) and Rennes the River Ille wanders in and out of the canal, much of its original course being indistinguishable from the navigation. Betton has a quay, right bank below the bridge, with a good view of the hilltop church beyond a modernistic civic centre, incorporating *Mairie* and post office. Shopping is good here or alternatively on the opposite side of the canal in **La Levée**, where the banks are situated. One recommended restaurant is *La Levée* a short distance left of the bridge. A hire boat base supplies fuel.

As it approaches Rennes, the Canal d'Ille et Rance remains pleasantly rural past Écluses 6, 5 and 4. Even the landscaped housing estates of **St-Gregoire** (K80) are not without interest, with traditional building designs and individual gardens *au style anglais*. (Shops, restaurants and water point.) Further suburbs and then factories follow the waterway to Écluse 2, St-Martin (K84), a mechanised structure with a sinking radial gate at the top end. Écluse 1, Mail (K84.8), works on the same principle and it is essential to wait for a green light before navigating past the submerged gate. City centre moorings, with water point, are immediately uphill of Lock 1, where seats and shrubbery are a magnet for inebriates. The lock keeper's house is the other side of the bridge, overlooking the Vilaine. Pass through the dark bridge-hole to finally leave the canal and join Brittany's chief river navigation.

Rennes, the region's leading city, is an important administrative and industrial centre. Much of the medieval town was destroyed in a great fire which burned 1,000 houses in 1720. Fortunately, many ancient buildings do remain and a long pedestrianised street of shops makes sight-seeing a pleasure. This leads from close to the canal to the magnificent *Palais de Justice*, the former Houses of Parliament. Domestic shopping for the galley can be attended to in excellent covered and open-air markets (especially notable for crabs, lobsters, fresh fruit and vegetables, flowers...); alternatively, try the comprehensive food department of a large store facing the river in the Quai Châteaubriand. Notable features of Rennes include the Thabor Garden, the Museum of Breton Life and the Breton Motor Museum (about 3km NE of the centre).

32 ⌁ River Vilaine

> **Carte Guide:** *Bretagne*
> From shortly upstream of the Rennes junction with the Canal d'Ille et Rance to the Bay of Biscay at Tréhiguier: 137km with 14 locks. Junctions are made with the Canal de Nantes à Brest (Northern Section) at Redon and (Southern Section) at Rieux.

This is a long river of variable scenic quality. The navigation's finest reaches are past wooded cliffs upstream of Port-de-Roche, where many locks are accompanied by old stone water mills and extensive weirs. Flat and somewhat featureless meadow land characterises long stretches of the middle river, above and below Redon. Then, from Foleux down to the final lock at the Arzal barrage, beginning of the tideway, the wooded rocky banks recall the estuary of the Dart in Devon or even the lochs of the Caledonian Canal. No fewer than 42km between Redon and Arzal are lock-free (79km from Arzal to Mâlon, if the Redon barrage is in its raised position), enabling rapid progress to be made by craft running between the Channel and Atlantic coasts. This is excellent sailing water for small cruisers and dinghies, now greatly changed in character since construction of the Arzal barrier has excluded the tide.

The Vilaine suffers from a reputation for shallowness and many yachtsmen tell stories of being grounded. But those who experience trouble tend to be the owners of deep keel sailing boats. Provided your draft is within 1.60m and you pay due attention to navigation marks, no problems should result. Often, the channel in the upper river lies close to the towpath, in spite of the apparent width of the waterway. It will, of course, take many years before the Great Drought of 1976 is quite forgotten. By late summer the waterways system of Brittany was all but drained and even shallow-draft motor cruisers were unable to make progress over shallows upstream of Guipry.

Winter floods can be ferocious with lock sites completely awash. Perhaps this is the origin of the river's name – literally, 'nasty' or 'unpleasant'. Or maybe the one-time shallows and difficult tidal reaches should take the blame.

Brittany is famous for its seafood, *crêpes* and cider, and the Vilaine is a good area to try local specialities. Outstanding dishes to sample in restaurants include *civelles nantaises* (deep-fried baby eels), *boguette* (traditional fish soup), *boudin aux pruneaux* (savoury pudding or sausage with prunes), *rillettes de lapin* (preserved rabbit pâté), and *maingaux* (cream cheese or whipped cream, served with fruit).

Brief history The Vilaine was the first river of France to be rendered navigable by using 'pound' locks (two closely spaced sets of gates to impound a section of river) as opposed to 'flash' locks or navigation weirs. Craft were able to ascend from the sea to Rennes by 1542, and further improvements were carried out over the next 40 years. Traffic increased with the opening of various canal links to other parts of the region in the earlier part of the 19th century. It is recorded that 3,787 barge journeys were made on the Vilaine in 1886, representing a total freight tonnage of 172,500. Returns for 1936 show only a slight decrease to 163,000 tonnes, mostly in horse drawn craft but with some motor barges. Shallows and rocks reduced the size of loads and all traffic on the river was subject to tides that then flowed beyond Redon to the first lock at Mâlon.

Working boats lingered on. Almost the last were a pair of sand barges running between the Loire and Redon until the long drought of 1976 forced them out of business. In 1980 there were still several sand and gravel boats working through three locks between Blossac and Rennes.

Of recent changes, the most dramatic was the construction of a barrage and lock near the sea at Arzal, in 1968–9. This resulted in an expanse of impounded water between there are Redon, which had previously been tidal. Rocks were cleared from the channel around Mâlon in 1964 and many facilities for pleasure craft have since been created, following transfer of most financial responsibility for the waterway from central to local government. Now that it is devoted entirely to tourism, the Vilaine has become an important contributor to Brittany's economy.

Originally, the Vilaine's head of navigation was at **Cesson**, 6km and 2 locks upstream of its junction with the Canal d'Ille et Rance in **Rennes**. These upper reaches had been little used by boats for many years and in an astonishingly inept act of town planning 300m of the waterway in the city was encased in a low headroom tunnel in 1963. The Boulevard car park thus created was not exactly a visual improvement. For a brief description of Rennes, see Chapter 31. Downstream of the city the river surroundings are rather urbanised with factories, electricity pylons, tower blocks and a prominent communications mast. After passing through Écluse 2, du Comte (K1.8, swing bridge), the waterway dives under a new concrete bridge and after a further group of factories emerges in countryside that constitutes some of the loveliest cruising water in Brittany. Locks 3, 4 and 5 were mechanised in the 1970s to speed passage of gravel barges then operating in this area. After passing through Écluse 3, Apigné (K5.5), a slipway will be found up a backwater, reached from the lower end of the poplar-shaded cut (turn upstream, on the right). Use the quay downstream of the **Chancors** road bridge (K9.3) to eat at a nearby restaurant. A powered bascule bridge spans Écluse 4, Cicé (K11). It is possible to moor upstream of Écluse 5, Mons (K14.3), and visit the small town of **Bruz** (2km distant, all shopping facilities).

Gravel workings line the right bank and past a small group of islands (keep to the left bank) to Écluse 6, **Le Pont Réan** (K17.8), where the skeletal remains of two wooden freight barges can be seen upstream of the chamber. Take care to avoid marked shallows between the lock and a fine old eight-arched stone bridge: the navigation arch is the third from the left bank (when descending). Visiting boats should find space on the quay (some facilities, including water). Here is useful shopping and a pleasant waterside restaurant.

Easily the most spectacular section of the Vilaine begins at a railway viaduct upstream of **Le Boël** (K21). Towering cliffs of slate, well covered with undergrowth, tumble down to the water. The area has been designated the *Parc Naturel de Boël* and an easy climb via paths presents you with a superb view of the open weir with a wonderful old water mill at its centre, the wall facing upstream acutely pointed as a cutwater designed to deflect floods. This is a popular summer weekend destination for the inhabitants of Rennes. Although it is some years since I have eaten there, I would like to recommend what I remember as one of the Vilaine's best restaurants: this is *Le Vieux Moulin de Boël*, a creeper-clad building on the lockside, shaded by a huge horse chestnut tree. It is small, pleasingly decorated and rather expensive (booking is recommended). If the *carré d'agneau* I selected can still be regarded as typical, the presentation of food can only be described as astonishing! It arrived on a vast silver salver, liberally decorated with marguerites, sprigs of fir tree and fennel. The channel stays near the right, towpath, bank and past some tiny rocky islands followed by a bridge at **Laillé** (K23.7), close to the *Château de Bagatz* and other late 19th century mansions. A restaurant, *Au Fil de l'Eau*, stands on the towpath.

The next lock, No 8, **La Bouëxière** (K26.8), has a stone mill house of four storeys dated 1885 and well restored, and another restaurant, *Le Moulin de Bouëxière*, will be found towards the end of the lock cut. **Glanret** (K28.5) is a small village with bridge, followed by an exquisite mooring above a weir at the hamlet of **La Courbe** (K30.2). Flower-decked houses overlook a grassy square and there is a small restaurant. The little town of **Bourg-des-Comptes** is not far away to the left (shops and restaurants). During normal summer water levels, safe swimming is possible in a lovely natural 'pool' above the weir, reached by crossing a narrow planked walkway. Yet another of the late 19th century converted water mills is close to Écluse 9, Gailieu. With spacious living accommodation over four storeys, a high level balcony and conservatory and wonderful river views all round, this magnificent property was offered for sale in 2004 for just 330,000 Euros (£230,000).

The river now winds past a series of *châteaux* to Écluse 10, Molière (K38.8), with yet another restored mill on an island. Pedalos and rowing boats can be hired at a riverbank resort shaded by poplars at the bridge of **Pléchâtel** (K35.3, restaurant with shopping in the nearby town). Cliffs in the steep-sided valley extend down river to **St-Malo-de-Phily** (K39.9), where facilities include shopping and a restaurant with mooring pontoon. A much extended mill house, now a factory, lies on the weir stream by Écluse 11, Macaire (K40.5): keep a watch for approaching craft in the narrow high-walled lock cut below.

Excavations in the 1970s off the river, left, produced a marina complex upstream of **Messac** (K47), some pontoons being reserved for Crown Blue Line's hire fleet, while others are for visitors or private craft. A wide range of boating facilities can be found here, including repairs, fuel, crane, slipway and water. The site constitutes one of Brittany's leading inland boatyards. Services in the twin towns of Messac and Guipry are most conveniently reached by stopping at a stone quay below Écluse 12, **Guipry** (K48, slipway), where a main road bridge is situated. Both this lock and No 13 have been automated. Until the 17th century this was an important river town owing to the salt trade, using barges working upriver from the coast. Collection of salt taxes developed into today's department of Customs. Shopping is good and includes a supermarket several hundred yards from the lock towards Guipry town centre. Cross to the Messac side for the railway station and the pleasant *Hôtel de la Gare* restaurant. Near the lock is the tiny chapel of Notre Dame de Bon-Port, built in 1644 as a thanks offering by the Lord of Tréguilly whose valuable stores of sea salt were threatened by an unusually high flood. The fête of Notre Dame de Bon-Port is held on the last-but-one Sunday in July.

Various markers and signboards inform boatmen that although the river is wide below Guipry, the deep-water channel lies close to the right, towpath, bank: elsewhere, there are rocky shallows. Ignoring the flood gate at Redon, Écluse 13, **Mâlon** (K52), is the last change in level before reaching the tideway at Arzal, 79km downstream. Dense woodland cloaks both banks at the *Bois de Bœuvres* and the *Bois de Baron* with a spectacular seven-arched railway viaduct and tunnel (K56.7), **Corbiniéres**. Rocky cliffs are well covered with pines, sweet chestnuts and oaks with cascades of blackberries towards the end of summer. Little fishing punts and hundreds of rickety wooden platforms point to the popularity of angling. Upstream of the bridge at **Port-de-Roche** (K62.2), note a beautiful mellow old manor house with extensive outbuildings. Cast iron plaques on the lattice-girder bridge of 1868 bear the initials of Louis Napoléon Bonaparte and his Empress Eugénie. A startling example of the way in which earlier beliefs were Christianised is provided by the legend that 28 ancient menhirs (*Cromlech des Demoiselles*) are the

bodies of a group of young girls, changed by God into stones for dancing one Sunday morning instead of attending Mass! They can be found south of the station at **Langon**, 3km from Port-de-Roche via the D56.

Scenery remains attractive as far as **Beslé** (K69.2), a pleasant little town upstream of a bridge with moorings on a stone quay. The restaurant of the *Hôtel du Port* overlooks the water, while a short walk over the level crossing and up a hill brings you to shops and a garage. Moorings are less convenient at **Brain-sur-Vilaine** (K71.6), whose quay is fairly derelict. Meals are available at the *Auberge des Moulins Neufs*. Deserted and flat countryside with tumble-down farm buildings and numerous fishing punts bearing names like *Mon Repos* and *La Disette* (*The Shortage*) accompanies the river until the outskirts of **Redon** (K89.2), cross-roads of the Brittany waterways. The Canal de Nantes à Brest joins the Vilaine at right angles near the town centre with entrance locks on each side of the river. Neither are now in regular use: if you wish to travel towards Nantes, continue for 7km downstream to another canal entrance at Écluse de Bellions. There are good moorings on the Vilaine, just past the junction. This involves passing beneath the central guillotine of *Le Grand Vannage*, a prominent barrage with three sluices which marked the start of the Vilaine tideway until construction of the Arzal barrage at the mouth of the estuary. Except in times of flood, there is a free passage.

A railway bridge over the navigation at Corbiniéres.

Should the barrier be closed, it will be necessary to turn sharp right, into the first lock of the Canal de Nantes à Brest, Écluse de l'Oust; straight on is the route for Josselin and Pontivy, while a left turn into the Écluse du Grand Bassin provides access to the extensive *port de plaisance*, with facilities ranging from moorings to cruiser hire, water, fuel, slipway and crane. This is the best place to lie while visiting the town. An exit to the Vilaine will be seen at the far end of the basin.

Redon dates from the 9th century and is a bustling place that relies heavily on water-based tourism at its navigational cross-roads. There are ship-wrights' houses with cast-iron balconies from the 17th and 18th centuries and the former abbey church of St-Sauveur with an important Romanesque 12th century tower. The lively open-air market is bisected by a railway. As recently as the early 20th century, all traders bound for the market would be stopped by the *Agents d'Octrois*, officials who levied a tax on all produce from a basket of apples to a cartload of pigs. Well worth a visit is the local waterways museum (*Musée de la Batellerie de l'Ouest*).

Now that the strong tidal flow has been banished from the Vilaine, the reach between Redon and the sea is an ever-widening stretch of water with a succession of small 'drowned' creeks. Surroundings are unremarkable at first, past a modern concrete bridge at **Cran** (K101.9, mooring, slipway, restaurant) with opening span for large craft and sailing vessels (motor cruisers can pass beneath). From here onwards, the pine-covered rocky shores recall the lochs of the Scottish Highlands and among the boats you can expect to meet are occasional coasters, passenger tripping launches and many large sea-going yachts. Gradually, the world of the inland waterways is superseded by a more marine atmosphere. Numerous craft are gathered on buoys at **Foleux** (K114.9, with various facilities and a restaurant).

The first intimation of **La Roche-Bernard** (K122) is a magnificent 376m-long bridge spanning the Vilaine at a height of 50m. The large numbers of sailing cruisers in the new marina on the river and the original harbour up the St-Antoine Creek whose entrance is guarded by a massive rock, emphasise that boating traditions here are more maritime than fluvial. This was an important ship-building town in the 17th century. It witnessed the launch in 1634 of the *Couronne*, the first three-decked man-of-war to be built in France. Now pleasure boating is the town's *raison d'être*, with facilities including fuel, water, showers and repairs. Dozens of delightful stone buildings of great antiquity will be found alongside the port and up steep passages leading through the Old Quarter into the town centre. Boating enthusiasts have 'discovered' La Roche-Bernard since the mid-1970s, so it is a bustling and thriving place in summer. There are

The former tidal estuary at La Roche-Bernard.

numerous restaurants and Breton *crêperies*. A wide variety of livestock can be inspected in the regular street market, together with excellent dairy produce and locally made clogs. A visit should be made to the *Musée de la Vilaine*, opened in 1986 in celebration of the area's maritime past.

Just 9km of non-tidal water remains down river to the barrage of **Arzal** (K131), where a full range of boating facilities and moorings caters more for the deep-water sailor than the river man. If moorings are congested on the right shore, it is worth trying the jetties of a hire cruiser base, opposite. Access to the sea via the last 6km of river is through a lock spanned by a lifting road bridge. Boats may pass through every day, on the hour, between 07.00 and 20.00 provided it is daylight. Developments include a restaurant, shopping centre, tripping boat office, boatyards and sales offices, fuel, water, cranes and slipways. It must be admitted that the area is modern, bleak and dominated by concrete. Inland boaters will prefer the more agreeable upper reaches of the Vilaine.

Enquiries in La Roche-Bernard will produce details of bus services for excursions to the coast and several towns of great interest. However, there is so much to attract the tourist that it is worth reserving several days for a tour by car. Among the highlights are the following (with distances measured from La Roche-Bernard): the beach at **Plage de la Mine d'Or** (13km) near **Pénistin**; plenty of other sandy beaches are found all along the coast and one popular with naturists is **Pen Bron** (35km), south of **La Turballe**; to the NW the city of **Vannes** (39km) has ramparts, beautiful moat gardens and fashionable shops on the shores of the Golfe du Morbihan: this could be combined with a visit to the unique Ménac Lines of no fewer than 1,009 ancient standing stones at **Carnac** (68km), a place of huge fascination, especially in early morning or late evening, when deserted. Although there are no obvious opportunities for getting afloat, a 57km road circuit can be made through the **Grande Brière** (18km), an atmospheric region of marshes, peat bogs and pastures, long ago the delta of both Vilaine and Loire. Covering 7,700 hectares, it is intersected by many tiny canals on which the locals use flat-bottomed craft called *blins* for the transport of thatching reeds, bog oak and hay. It is a great wild fowling and fishing centre, now designated a regional park and so preserved from development. In contrast to the dark Celts of much of Brittany, the people of the Grande Brière are often fair-haired and are said to be the descendants of ship-wrecked Saxon pirates; they are very insular and much inter-married. A suggested road tour of the area can be found in the Michelin Green Guide *Brittany*.

33 ∼ Canal de Nantes à Brest

Carte Guide: *Bretagne*. Alternatively, *Bretagne et Loire Atlantique* (Vagnon), which additionally includes coverage of the detached Branche Finistèrienne.

From a junction with the River Loire and the Sèvre Nantaise at Nantes to Pontivy, junction with the Canal du Blavet. The through route of the Canal de Nantes à Brest is currently interrupted here. 207km with 107 locks. Junctions are made with the Upper River Erdre near Nort-sur-Erdre; the River Vilaine at Écluse des Bellions, near Redon; and the River Aff near Écluse 19, upstream of Redon. It is hoped that at some time in the future the line between Pontivy and the Bay of Brest will again become navigable throughout. The following sections of the Branche Finistèrienne are presently available to boats: Guerlédan Dam to La Pitié, 25.6km, 10 locks; Goariva (Écluse 192) to Landévennec (Bay of Brest) 110.3km, 46 locks, although work may still be in progress in the Goariva area. Local enquiry is advised.

This long waterway offers as much variety as any navigation in France. Almost always, the scenery through the Breton interior is very beautiful, taking the boater to places rarely visited by the tourist. Combining sections of canalised river with artificial cuts, it is very heavily locked at times, but for those in no great hurry it offers a fascinating passage between the South Breton coast and (via the River Blavet, see Chapter 34) the west coast at Lorient. After leaving Nantes, the course is first through the broad lakes of the River Erdre; then follows a canal and the River Isac to the Vilaine at Redon; from here to Rohan the waterway largely consists of the River Oust; the journey continues by canal with numerous locks to Pontivy, junction with the Blavet. A long portion of the Nantes à Brest is out of service after Pontivy until navigation is resumed beyond the Guerlédan Dam. After 27km, there is a further break (see above) until we join the navigable courses of first the River Hyères and then the River Aulne.

The Canal de Nantes à Brest has not seen freight traffic for many years. Pleasure craft annually grow in numbers, especially hire cruisers on the Redon-Josselin section, although nowhere does it become really crowded. The Finistère portion is almost completely deserted. The beautiful lakes of the Erdre are much frequented by small cruisers and sailing craft, with luxury passenger vessels providing a service from Nantes that is only equalled in France by the *bateaux-mouches* of Paris. Some of these craft are ultra-modern and boast splendid restaurants for public trips and private functions. Unusually, some operate a restricted winter service with central heating. Keepers are employed on locks throughout the eastern part of the waterway (excepting a series of locks between Nantes and Redon), while boat crews must work the Finistère length unaided.

Brief history Some of the river sections – notably the Erdre – have been navigable for many centuries. Among famous visitors who travelled by boat were the Queen of Navarre in 1437, René Descartes in 1617, Madame de Sévigné in 1680 and the Duchess of Berry in 1828. But it was not until Napoléon's time that serious consideration was given to a barge route between Nantes and Brest to ensure carriage of freight, safe from the threat of the British fleet off the Atlantic coast. Work began at Port Launay near Châteaulin in 1811. But Napoléon was soon to meet his Waterloo and the period of unrest and financial stringency that followed was not favourable to expensive public works. Construction recommenced in 1822 with the establishment of a Canal Company of Brittany. By 1836, 385km of waterway with 238 locks providing a change in levels of 555m was opened from coast to coast. Improvements, including deepening the channel, continued until 1875. While Napoléon never saw his concept completed, his nephew, Napoléon III declared open a sea lock on the Aulne at Guilly-Glas, below Châteaulin, during his Breton tour of 1858. Financially, the new route was not a great success and freight receipts were disappointing. From less than 10,000 tonnes of goods in 1860, traffic gradually increased to 40,000 tonnes. One unfortunate mistake of the early 1860s was the construction of a fleet of 62 iron barges, each with a capacity of 140 tonnes: but the water depth dictated that they could only carry 70–80 tonnes. Leading traffics were Welsh coal and Spanish iron ore.

By 1870 freight tonnage had fallen back to its 1850 level. Horses replaced bow-hauliers and the journey time between Châteaulin and Redon was cut from 25 to 15 days. For a brief Golden Age between 1890 and 1914 the canal carried around 35,000 tonnes annually. An important commodity was fertiliser which transformed agriculture along the banks. World War I growth of road transport and the opening of the Carhaix-Châteaulin-Camaret railway in 1911 all contributed to a slump in barge traffic. Finally, a hydro-electric scheme and barrage at Guerlédan, finished in 1928, divided the waterway into two separate halves. There was early talk of building a barge lift around the obstacle, but this was never carried out. Most of the barge operators elected to stay on the eastern section, always the more prosperous part. The last barge passed through Châteaulin Lock in 1942 and elsewhere lingered on until the 1976 drought forced the remaining Nantes-Redon gravel craft into retirement. Now the working boats are just a memory: some had highly evocative names such as *Berceau-du-Marin* (*Boatman's Cradle*), *Brise-des-Nuits* (*Night Breeze*) and *Fleur-du-Mai* (*Mayflower*).

From the mid-1960s, the main section has gradually been improved for tourism although draft in some canal reaches is reduced from 1.40m to 1.10m. Meanwhile, the western part of the navigation along the Hyères and the Aulne fell into disuse after World War II and was officially closed in 1957. At a time when there was very little inland boating activity in France, the length in the *Département* of Finistère was transferred to local authority care in 1966. 73km with 33 locks was reopened in 1975 and a further 8km with 11 locks brought back into use between Kergoat and Goariva in 1983. Sadly, all this was very little used and serious flooding in 1994–5 resulted in widespread damage and closure. Some work has been carried out to improve the situation since then (seek local information to ascertain the latest situation). The only realistic long term answer must be to construct some form of boat lift to overcome the obstruction caused by the Guerlédan Dam. Only then will there be any point in restoring the currently disused Pontivy–Guerlédan length. All this will eventually happen, but it is not possible to estimate when that might be.

At its junction with the tidal waters of the River Loire very close to the centre of **Nantes**, the Canal de Nantes à Brest enters Écluse 1, St-Félix, electrically operated. Craft can pass between tideway and canal 3hr before Nantes HW until 3hr afterwards, subject to times when keepers are on duty (see the *Carte Guide*). Nantes is a city of many attractions; in 2004, for the second year in succession, it was voted 'the most liveable city in France', ahead of Dijon and Strasbourg; Paris came a poor 15th. For further details, see Chapter 35. From 1929 onwards, parts of the waterway near the cathedral were roofed over, so creating the 800m St-Félix Tunnel; at the far end, moorings in the Bassin Ceineray (K1.4) are conveniently close to the city centre. Not far beyond (left) is a hire cruiser base (K2) in the *Port de l'Erdre*. Most boating facilities, including long-term moorings and fuel, are available here.

Most of this River Erdre section of the waterway, between Nantes and the second lock at Quiheix, is exceptionally wide, giving the impression of a series of beautiful lakes. This arrangement is said to result from a dam constructed in the 6th century by St-Félix, Bishop of Nantes, who was anxious to 'drown' unhealthy marshland upstream of the city. It ranks as one of the most beautiful rivers in the whole of France, with more than a dozen outstanding *châteaux* visible from the water. Tripping boats from the *Port de l'Erdre* (Quai de Versailles). Large numbers of powered and sailing boats point to the great popularity of the Erdre with the Nantaises. Cruising, wildfowling, coarse fishing, board sailing and water ski-ing are all practised in an area that can be likened to the Norfolk Broads.

Bankside moorings are sometimes few and far between: if in doubt about water depths, it is safer to drop the anchor and go ashore by dinghy. The first time that the British Army used inland water transport in France during World War I was when a depot for sick horses was established at a *château* at **La-Chapelle-sur-Erdre** (K9, quay and hire boat base). The problem of conveying fodder from supply ships in the Loire was solved by using canal barges and unloading them at a wooden wharf in the *château* grounds. There is a waterside restaurant and shops. The next place of interest is **Sucé** (K15.1), at a narrows by a road bridge. Sandy beaches, quay, boatyards with cruisers for hire, shops and restaurants are all here in this friendly little town. Above the bridge, the navigation broadens once more into the huge **Lac de Mazerolles**, 5km long with a width up to 500m. Its banks are fringed with willows and the sandy bottom is ideal for swimming. Trailed boats can be launched from the end of a lane leading from the D69 in the middle of the west shore (K18): if you have only a few hours to spare, it would be difficult to imagine anywhere more pleasant for an afternoon's boating. As the lake narrows, Écluse 2, Quiheix (K21.7), will be seen on the left: this is the route for Redon and points beyond. A very pleasant diversion can, however, be made by staying on the Erdre for a further 6km to the terminus in **Nort-sur-Erdre**. En route, is a boat repair yard, situated up an arm on the right. The head of navigation features a small port with visitors' moorings, showers, restaurants and shopping. The adventurous can continue still further by dinghy, up a winding stream fringed with alders.

For some years, a number of the locks between Quiheix and the Vilaine have been adapted for working by boat crews unassisted. Modifications include reduction of paddles to one per set of gates, with sliding locking bars preventing gates from being opened while paddles are raised. The system, which is fairly fool-proof, is rather slower than normal. Most of the locks have water points, but otherwise there are few facilities as you climb through Nos 3–7, spread out over 6km. We have now reached the summit level, with a descent towards Redon beginning at Écluse 8. By the N137 bridge, **Glanet** (K38.3), a halt can be made for restaurant or garage. Useful moorings have been established near the village of **La Chevallerais** (K42.3, restaurant). Dense forest surrounds the town of **Blain** (K50.2), beyond Écluses 8–11. Moor on pontoons below the imposing *château*. There is an excellent restaurant and range of shops; also water point, showers and slipway. Most of the waterway's course is now along the canalised River Isac, a very winding stream. Parts are especially lovely, particularly the loop that passes the mid-17th century *Château de Carheil-en-Plessé* in its wooded 200 hectare park (K69). Moorings are available on both banks by the Pont St-Clair, with all facilities (including a public swimming pool) in **Guenrouet** (K72.8). The church has some exquisite stained glass, erected 1944–51, with background colours mainly in tones of deep blue. Shortly before the canal leaves the Isac, there is a sandy river beach at **Le Cougou** (K79) with the *Château de Bogdelin* on the edge of the Forest of St-Gildas. This stretch of waterway is very peaceful, offering 23km of lock-free cruising.

At the second bridge after the river junction, **Pont-Miny** (K83.3), it is about 3km by road into **Fégréac**, once a Gallo-Roman settlement. Old houses and a 15th century Calvary – an ecclesiastical speciality of Brittany – are among the attractions. There are also shops. Soon after, a junction is made with the Vilaine at Écluse 17, des Bellions, with the small town of **Rieux** on the far bank of the river. All craft must take this route, as 6km of the Canal de Nantes à Brest is now closed to traffic, although northwards access remains possible to the village of **St-Nicolas-de-Redon**. Therefore, if bound either for Redon and the Canal de Nantes à Brest to the NW or for the waterway to Rennes, proceed up the Vilaine for 7km. The canal's through route is reached by forking left into **Redon**'s *Grand Bassin*, working through a lock at the far end with bascule bridge and then turning left. (For information on the town see Chapter 32.) This diversion from the original course adds little in distance and presents an identical number of locks.

The River Oust provides a navigation route for the canal most of the way between Redon and Rohan: however, the first 7km out Redon are via an artificial channel. If wished, about 10km of the Oust can be navigated between the Vilaine (downstream of Redon) and a barrage, running parallel with the Canal de Nantes à Brest; but there is no link between the two at the upper end. We leave Redon by means of a rock-lined cut and the Oust is joined above a weir (K101.7). This is without doubt the finest portion of the river, with a width of between 200m and 300m and pine-covered cliffs rising to 45m. There are plenty of pleasant moorings and enough space to sail a dinghy. In summer, a woodland café/bar operates a thriving business selling the ubiquitous *crêpes* (pancakes in variety, savoury and sweet) that are a firmly established part of Breton cuisine. Local activities include canoeing and rock climbing. The navigation channel lies near the left, towpath, bank and bears away into a section of canal cut at Écluse 19, La Maclais (K105.3) alongside **L'Ile aux Pies** (Magpie Island).

Before following the through route, it is thoroughly recommended to make the fascinating short diversion up the mysterious **River Aff** for 9km to the little town of La Gacilly. Continue straight ahead into a wide pool edged with reeds and water crowfoot. Almost immediately the atmosphere undergoes a complete change: there are fishing boat stakes projecting from the marked channel and a sense of utter desertion. If you wish to visit the village of **Glénac**, carry on to a substantial wooden landing stage to discover basic shops and a restaurant. To enter the Aff itself, turn right into the middle of a vast reed bed up to 1km wide. Very much like one of the least frequented of the Norfolk Broads, this is an extraordinary marshland and a potentially alarming place for suffering an engine breakdown, as there is little possibility of locating solid land to get ashore. In spite of the assurances of the chart, you feel that you must have taken a wrong turning. After a road bridge near **Sourdéac** the river narrows between high banks overhung by oak trees whose branches brush the deck. But for stone bank protection at a second bridge, it is difficult to believe that commercial traffic ever penetrated this *African Queen* waterway, let alone as recently as 1965. Boulder strewn cliffs and pines finally lead to a modern three-arched bridge with weir and elaborate municipal wash-house in 1930s concrete, decorated with geraniums. To the left is a small quay, where a British day boat hirer operates. This is the head of navigation at **La Gacilly**.

In the hilly streets of old stone houses are shops, restaurants and a garage. The town is something of a craftsmen's colony, with workers in iron, glass, pottery, leather and semi-precious stones (fine tables and lamps in onyx). A stone mason sculpts granite into fire surrounds, plaques and sundials; he will proudly inform you that he has carried out restoration on Nantes cathedral. Much older relics are to be found in the shape of a dolmen, the *Tablette de Cournon*, and a 5m-high *menhir*, the *Roche Piquée*, in a sweet chestnut grove. It takes about 70 minutes to return by boat to the Oust and to the more prosaic straight canal which leads via a set of flood gates, Écluse de Limure (K109.8), back to the river with drifts of water lilies. Moor by the Pont d'Oust (K112.5, restaurant and water point) for **Peillac** (all facilities within 2km).

After Écluse 21, Le Guesclin (K116.6), a bridge of eight square arches appears, with two restaurants and basic shops in the waterside village of **St-Martin-sur-Oust** (K117.9). 9km SW by the D777 lies the famous *ville fleurie* of **Rochefort-en-Terre**, surely one of Brittany's most delightful towns, built overlooking the little River Gueuzon. The main square contains a wonderful collection of 16–17th century granite buildings. For an old-fashioned provincial French restaurant it would be difficult to better the *Hostellerie Lion d'Or*, where I was once served my first ever mouth-watering *Ile Flottante*: caramelised poached egg white with almonds, floating in a sea of vanilla custard. Beyond Écluse 22, Rieux, **St-Congard** appears on the left bank by a bridge (K123.7, several shops). In the early 1980s, I discovered here a mobile wood-fired distillery: according to a brass plaque, it was built by Charles Coyac of Nantes in 1927.

Malestroit (K132.2) is an important small town with a lively atmosphere. Dating back to 987 and originally fortified, it is situated by an island with many Gothic and Renaissance houses. The church of St-Gilles was built in the 12th and 16th centuries. Half-timbered buildings are decorated with humorous painted carvings including those of a man in a night-gown

beating his wife, a hare with Breton bagpipes (*biniou*) and a pig spinning. A local produce market is held on Thursdays. The *Maison d'Eau*, in a timber-clad building by the waterway, is an exhibition centre devoted to the ecology and good management of rivers: emphasis is more angling than navigation. Shopping is good and there are a number of restaurants. The best moorings are on the left, immediately before the first of three bridges (water point). Flash floods in summer can cause sudden rises in water level on the Oust along with a strong current, in contrast to upper parts of the canal which sometimes run rather short of water. Virtually all the locks are now mechanised and many of them resemble small farms with cattle sheds, rabbits, chickens and goats; although there are vegetable gardens few keepers seem to bother to sell produce, ice cream, wine or postcards to passing boaters as happens on some more heavily used routes. Lock cottages are in traditional Breton style, often single storey with dormer windows in the roof and granite door and window surrounds.

Écluse 25 is situated on the edge of Malestroit. The waterway continues up a straight cut lined with poplars and acacias. This is a lovely area in early summer: the meadows are ablaze with buttercups while yellow iris fringes the banks. The river is rejoined after Écluse 27, Lanée (K135.4, stop lock normally open at each end), and winds past farmhouses to **Le Roc St-André** (K141). The eleven-arch bridge with a cross at the centre was built in 1760 and carries the N166 road between Ploërmel and Vannes. Use the sole navigation arch, third from the left. High on a cliff alongside, the church has an ornate open spire; there is also a grotto and altar by the towpath. Excellent menus, with a choice of seafood, will be found at the *Val de l'Oust* restaurant; shops are conveniently close to the mooring (water point). In the reach that follows, the towers of the *Château du Crévy* appear among trees on the right (mooring stage). This has been a castle site since the 3rd century, although the present fine building is 14th century and later. It houses a splendid Costume Museum with examples of fashion from the 18th century to the present.

Derelict-seeming houses will be found in **Montertelot** (K143.7), with an elegant waterside church, moorings and a slipway at Écluse 29. Dense woods and hills lead up to Écluse 31, **Guillac**, and if you want to visit the sizeable town of **Ploërmel**, 7km distant, moor at the preceding bridge (K147.9). It was once the seat of the Dukes of Brittany, contains a number of fascinating old buildings and has a lakeside arboretum planted with no fewer than 220 different species of hydrangeas (flowering season, May–October). A little to the east is the extensive **Forêt de Paimpont**, none other than the ancient Forest of Brocéliande where, according to the Arthurian legend, Merlin the Wizard was beguiled by the sensuous Lady Vyvyan. Writing in 1927, yachtsman Capt Leslie Richardson (*Brittany and the Loire*) comments on this place: 'Wolves, boars and deer, woodmen and charcoal burners were the only inhabitants of the great forests. Today one may still meet with all of them, though the wolves are almost if not quite extinct… *Wolf Hunting in Lower Brittany* is unfortunately out of print in English, though a capital French translation can be obtained in Paris.'

Écluses 32–34 intervene in a nearly deserted landscape filled with summer flowers – dog roses, yellow broom, red campion and foxgloves – until we arrive at the architectural *pièce de résistance* of the Canal de Nantes à Brest, the magnificent *Château de* **Josselin** (K157.5). Posters or brochure photographs of Josselin's trio of massive towers rising sheer from the river have persuaded many cruiser hirers to choose the Brittany waterways: the reality of the castle is in no way a disappointment. Home of the Rohan family since the 14th century, it was seized by François II, Duke of Brittany, in 1488 and dismantled. His daughter, Anne of Brittany, on becoming Queen of France, compensated the Rohans and in rebuilding the *château*, Jean II de Rohan showed his gratitude by decorating the structure with ornamented letter As. The Rohan motto *Roi ne puis, Prince ne daigne, Rohan suis* (I cannot be King, I scorn to be Prince, I am a Rohan) illustrates their proud outlook. In 1629 Henri de Rohan, leader of the Huguenots, suffered partial demolition of the castle; five of its nine towers were destroyed by Richelieu. Boastfully, the Cardinal cried: 'Monsieur le Duc, I have just sent a ball into your ninepins!' 200 years later, Josselin fell into ruins but was restored in the early 20th century. There is a fine view from the terrace down onto the river and the lock, but, while open to the public, the interior is less fascinating than might be expected, especially if you have difficulty in understanding the learned remarks of the French guide.

During the Middle Ages, eating meat was strictly forbidden in Lent, much to the delight of the Josselin fishmongers. However, their greatly enhanced earnings were subject to a special tax, and on Low Sunday those who would not pay were forced to remove all clothing but their shirts and jump into the river, to the ribald jeers of the townsfolk. A basilica, *Notre Dame du Rancier* (Our Lady of the Bramblebush), dates from the 11th century and commemorates the finding of a statue of the Virgin by a peasant in about AD 800. He carried it home only to repeatedly discover it had reappeared in the fields, where a church was subsequently erected. An important *pardon* (a Christianised form of the Druid

ritual, consisting of prayer and fasting) is held there on the second Sunday of September. A legend tells of Our Lady, disguised as a beggar, seeking alms of washer-women on the banks of the Oust. When they refused to provide offerings, they and their descendants were condemned to bark like dogs. As would be expected of a town that sees numerous tourists, there are plenty of restaurants and useful shops. Note a series of charming gazebos in the gardens of waterside houses. The former lock cottage is now a *gîte*: at the back are railed enclosures catering for pony-trekkers. Boaters can use a long pontoon mooring (right bank) virtually under the *château* walls. Several hundred metres upstream, left, is a launching slipway.

Locks now increase in frequency as the waterway climbs into the hills. At one stage there are no fewer than 55 in 22km – unusual, but certainly not unique. Compare them with 24 locks in 7.6km (Baye area of the Canal du Nivernais); 55 in 38km (northern climb to the Pouilly summit, Canal de Bourgogne); 38 in 27km (near Mulhouse, Canal du Rhône au Rhin); 35 in 11km (Devizes, Kennet & Avon Canal); 58 in 48km (Worcester & Birmingham Canal); and 74 in 32km (Huddersfield Narrow Canal).

There is a restaurant and moorings by Écluse 38 Rouvray (K161.4) and 39, Bocneuf (K163.1). There are shops in Les Forges, 3km NE of Écluse 43, Cadoret. At **Penhouët** (K175.4) a bar/*crêperie* lies 100m west of Écluse 48. Close to Écluse 50, **Timadeuc** (K178.4), Trappist monks founded an abbey in 1841. The monastic buildings are closed to the public, although a slide show with commentary is available at the gate-house. Sung Mass with Gregorian chant can be heard from Easter to mid-September at 11.15h (10.45h on Sundays and holidays).

The last opportunity for shopping in a real town before the 'thick' of the locks begins is at **Rohan** (K181.5), a pleasantly uncommercialised place with a large mooring basin, hire boat base and various facilities including boat fuel. The town takes its name from a 12th century *château* built on the *Roc'Han* by Alain de Porhoët. One of the most famous of French families, the Rohans, originated here.

In wild country with very few facilities, the canal now embarks on one of the greatest concentrations of locks in France. These are obviously well worth tackling if it is your intention to continue down the beautiful River Blavet from Pontivy. Traffic is currently light and water depth onwards from Rohan may be reduced to as little as 0.8m. The 55 locks from Écluse 53, St-Samson (K182.2) to Écluse 107, Ponteau, in Pontivy (K205.5) represent an extremely full day's work. But done in a day they can be, if you are determined!

Once you have begun this arduous task, there will be little opportunity to halt for sight-seeing: indeed it is preferable to press on, as your arrival will always be anticipated by the lock keepers. Unless you appear keen, you cannot expect their full interest and co-operation. A final parting with the River Oust comes between Écluses 54, Le Guer, and 55, Coëtprat (K185.8). The 5km summit pound, 129.59m above sea level, is reached near **St-Gonnery** (K191.3). Descent starts at Écluse 79, Kéroret (K196.3, restaurant) and some crew members may wish to leave the boat to go shopping in **St-Gérand**, a walk or cycle ride of just under 4km if you rejoin the boat at a bridge below Écluse 87 (K197.3). Locks 88–97 (K200.8) are arranged in a flight; the final 11 are more widely spaced. If craft and personnel are still intact, you will arrive in **Pontivy** (K205.9) in a state of near exhaustion, but hopefully glowing with a real sense of achievement! One plan that considerably speeds up the operation is to send a crew member ahead, down the towpath, by bicycle (or even motor bike) to alert the next keeper and help to prepare the lock.

Pontivy lies at the junction with the canalised River Blavet (see Chapter 34) and provides moorings, water point, slipway, good shopping and restaurants. This meeting of the waters is dominated by a brooding *château*, with ramparts, 20m-high walls and moat. Erected by the seemingly insatiable castle builder Jean II de Rohan in the 1480s, it later attracted the attention of Napoléon who created a military centre here as part of his trans-Brittany canal plan. The town was known as Napoléonville for a time. Bustling shopping streets are within 200m of the waterfront, with a selection of 15th and 16th century houses in the Rue de Pont, Rue du Fil and Place de Martray. Passing through, Capt. Leslie Richardson (*Brittany and the Loire*, 1927) noted with pleasure: 'The *Ouest Éclair* came out with a most flattering account of *Sylvabelle II* and her crew. This is a capital little paper produced in Rennes.' Not everything in Pontivy was, however, to his liking: 'Our departure was hastened by the arrival of a boatload of drunken coal-heavers, who jumped overboard, dived off the bridge in their clothes, and carried out other manoeuvres.'

At the time of writing, plans to reinstate the 20km of Canal de Nantes à Brest and its 12 locks between Pontivy and the **Guerlédan Dam** have not been scheduled. The dejected and semi-derelict navigation is likely to be rehabilitated in spite of the objections of local anglers. Some form of boat lift to overcome the considerable change in levels at Guerlédan will be an essential part of the work. Waterway enthusiasts quite rightly resent the present break in what should be an important through route, but it must be admitted that the Guerlédan Lake is a beautiful expanse of water about 10km long with thickly wooded banks. It is well used for dinghy sailing and its attractions include passenger boats and sandy 'beaches'.

BRANCHE FINISTÈRIENNE

Until this currently isolated section of the Canal de Nantes à Brest is fully restored and reunited with the rest of the inter-connected Brittany network by constructing some form of boat lift at the Guerlédan dam, it will, sadly, continue to be of limited interest and use to inland boating enthusiasts. Distances quoted here are from Nantes. Its uppermost reaches (about 8km with 17 locks) disappeared under water with creation of Guerlédan Lake in the 1920s. 26km with 10 locks (Nos 137–146), and including a part of the lake, are navigable to **La Pitié** (K252.4).

Thereafter, there is another long break in the line until the canal crosses the border at Goariva into the *Département* of Finistère (26k with 44 locks). From this point to the coast was restored to navigation in the 1980s only to suffer serious flood damage during the winter of 1994/5. Repairs were not undertaken with any great sense of urgency. At the time of writing, the waterway is navigable from Écluse 213, Rosily (K305.3), on the canalised River Aulne. This leaves 26km and 22 locks to be reinstated to take the canal from the sea to Goariva again. Local advice should be sought on what progress has been made.

Boaters are expected to work their own locks. A windlass (handle) can be hired from the navigation office at 1 Rue du Stade, Châteauneuf-du-Faou. This upper part of the route with lush woodlands and very few boats is a magical waterway. The canal leaves the River Hyères and joins the River Aulne at **Pont-Triffen** (K298, shop); within 2km at **Landeleau** there is fuel, a restaurant and further shops. Several locks intervene with a rocky slate scree cascading into the river 1km before Écluse 217, Boudrac'h. To the south lies **St-Goazac**, on the edge of the Montagnes Noires. Such lost and isolated villages have changed little since Mrs Lewis Chase came through here by rowing boat (*A Vagabond Voyage through Brittany*, 1915): 'Small children clung to their mothers' skirts when meeting us on the road, bigger ones, less afraid, jeered at us and one old woman crossed herself. We were apparently agents of the devil because we came from the outside world'. At this time country folk and Breton lock keepers regularly wore their traditional costume.

Several broad loops eventually lead to the quay at **Châteauneuf-du-Faou** (K317), a charming little place with waterside auberge *Le Chaland* and ancient ivy festooned bridge. There are moorings, a small boatyard and slipway. The centre of the town is well above the river. In the early 1980s of special interest in the main square was the *Bar-Musée*, a café filled with antique Breton furniture and presided over by an elderly lady adorned with Breton *coiffe* and dress. Framed press photographs indicated that she was something of a celebrity. A *pardon* is held on the penultimate Sunday of August. Châteauneuf is perhaps the most appealing part of the Aulne Valley and is noted for its salmon and pike fishing. Most of the locks are equipped with special salmon weirs, enabling the fish to run upstream to their spawning grounds.

While many locks retain their original keepers' cottages, they all appear to have been sold into private ownership and many are elaborately extended as weekend retreats. Some lock sites are remote and the towpath is maintained in excellent condition from end to end, allowing riparian owners car access. Further expense has been lavished on buoys to mark the approach of the open weirs, a feature often lacking elsewhere. Small restaurants will be found at **Pont-Pol-ty-Glas** (K324) and **Ty-men** bridge (K331.5). Throughout, the river banks are thickly wooded and there is never any hint of

Port-Launay near the start of the Atlantic coast tideway.

commercial development. When you reach **Pont Coblant** (K338, most shops, restaurant, hire craft, fuel and water) is it worth a 6km trip by taxi or bicycle into **Pleyben**. Its parish close is full of treasures, including the largest Calvary in the whole of Brittany (16–17th centuries), two belfries, one of them a magnificent Renaissance tower, and a 15th century ossuary. The church interior is a remarkable display of painted baroque.

As the Aulne approaches the sizeable town of **Châteaulin** (K360), it describes a series of six giant loops, increasing the straight-line distance several times. Making the most of its riverside situation, the town has tree-shaded quays with a colourful market. One old legend tells of the Duke's park being surrounded by a high wall 30km long and built in a single night by the Devil in return for his soul. Between February and July anglers arrive from far and wide for the celebrated salmon: the fish features on the town's coat of arms and somewhat irreverently the locals are known as *Pen Eog* (Breton for salmon heads). There is a hire cruiser base on the quay. After Écluse 236, Châteaulin, with a massive viaduct, the river enters a maritime world at **Port-Launay** (K364), whose onetime commercial quays now offer moorings for substantial sea-going pleasure craft. Supermarket, garage and restaurants are all nearby. Although upstream of the sea lock, this reach is sometimes affected by high tides. One final lock, **Guily-Glas** (K366), provides access to the tideway: its 40m x 10m chamber is considerably bigger than those up river. The keeper will be pleased to provide information on the 27km of estuary that extends from here to the sea at **Landévennec** (K391). It is an outstandingly beautiful run past pine-clad rocky hills and under a great suspension bridge, the Pont de Térénez.

34 ~ Canal du Blavet

> **Carte Guide:** *Bretagne*
> From Pontivy, junction with the Canal de Nantes à Brest, to a junction with the Blavet Maritime below Hennebont, 59.8km with 28 locks.

Why the Blavet should officially be described as a canal is a mystery, as in all respects it is a normal navigable river. Forming the western part of a through route from central Brittany to the Atlantic coast, it is an exceptionally attractive waterway, quite well maintained and passing through heavily wooded countryside. Very serious flooding in 1996 and again in 2000–1 damaged locks and weirs: each time reinstatement was a prolonged process. This was presumably because traffic levels are slight compared with the most popular French waterways. During a cruise down the Blavet you are likely to get closer to the true heart of Brittany than on any other route. Most of the locks retain their keepers; those without are operated by the guardian of the adjacent lock. Abiding memories will be of rural isolation and lively weirs.

Brief history Conceived by Napoléon as a military necessity for the shipment of goods free from the coastal interference of the British (and especially in order to create a supply line to the fortress town of Pontivy), the Blavet was not finally opened to traffic until 1825. Further information is oddly elusive. For the next century, a certain level of success was achieved, among leading cargoes during the 1930s being pit props from the Armorican uplands of Brittany for export to Wales with return loads of coal for the steel works at Lochrist, near Hennebont. Barges were pulled by horses or tractors and made 2,709 individual journeys in 1936, with a total tonnage of 163,000. After World War II, freight movements declined rapidly, what remained being carried in motor barges. By 1966 all the working boats had gone.

From its **Pontivy** junction with the Canal de Nantes à Brest (see Chapter 33), the route is briefly slightly industrial, but by the time Écluse 2, Lestitut (K2.4), is reached, wooded and hilly banks, so characteristic of the Blavet, are there to enjoy. Throughout the non-tidal section the navigation channel lies near the left, towpath, side; elsewhere, rocky shallows may cause grounding. For the uppermost 34km a railway closely follows the river, but is rarely intrusive. Écluse 5, Divit (K9.6), epitomises the very best qualities of a rural French river: a lock cottage with customary small farm, tumbling weir comprising semi-circular waterfalls and footway, and clusters of mature trees. Where fields are under cultivation they appear extremely fertile. Occasional glimpses of stone farmhouses are often the only sign of civilisation. From Écluse 7, Kerbecher (K13.9), a steep hill leads through woodland for about 3km to the amazingly ornate and impressive Chapelle **St-Nicodème**, a 16th century Gothic church with superb carved stone details. Repeatedly in Brittany you are reminded that there are almost too many ecclesiastical monuments of the very highest quality for many of them to be maintained much beyond a level that verges on dereliction. So it is with St-Nicodème, situated by a cluster of farm buildings. Ask for the key at the house alongside if you wish to see the interior or climb the massive tower. It is generally deserted except during its *pardon*, held on the first Sunday of August. An alternative, closer, approach from the river is up a track that leads from the towpath some distance upstream of Écluse 8, Guern (K15.8).

There are so few waterside villages that most boaters will wish to stop at **St-Nicolas-des-Eaux** (K17.8), a settlement of thatched houses in a deep valley by two loops of river that each turn almost completely back on themselves. There is shopping, good food at the *Hôtel de la Vallée*, moorings and a water point. High above the navigation on the D1 road to **Castennac**, you will discover a lookout point with a superb view down onto the Blavet. This is close to the pre-Roman Celtic *Site de Castennac*, with an ancient burial chamber (now within a small caravan site!). Reminders of former beliefs are never far beneath the surface of Christianised monuments in Brittany. On the Montagne de Castennac is a holy well where a stone image of Isis dates from Roman times. The goddess gradually became known as *Notre Dame de la Couarde* (Couarde being a local sorceress) and the idol was said to cure the sick of various complaints. When, in 1661, the Jesuits had the statue cast into the Blavet in an attempt to stamp out non-Christian practices, the villagers were irate and blamed the following winter's floods on this foolish action. Accordingly, they dredged the stone from the riverbed, only to have it thrown back once more by Count Claude de Lannion. There was little surprise among the local population when the Count was unseated from his horse and remained unconscious for 24 hours. There persists a strong belief along the Blavet valley in the equivalent of Ireland's 'little people'. Most powerful are the *poulpicans* (fairies' husbands) who like to dance round dolmens or menhirs. They will exact savage penalties from wanton young girls, wickedly embrace maidens who stay too long at fairs, ring bells to mislead shepherdesses or goat-herds, and issue dreadful cries on dark winter nights. Within living memory, mothers would leave a jar of honey outside at night to deter the *poulpicans* from removing babies from their cots and substituting fairy children. Beliefs like these seem almost possible when you moor up in the woods by the curious little chapel of **St-Gildas** on the right bank below the railway bridge that follows Écluse 10, La Couarde (K19.6). Built like a stone barn into the base of a bare rocky cliff, this was once a holy place of the Druids. Gildas appears to have travelled widely throughout the Celtic world of Cornwall, Wales, Ireland and Scotland. He arrived in Brittany in about AD 540 and is said to have preached Christianity to the people from a rough pulpit, now contained within the chapel.

The surrounding countryside is notable for astonishingly rustic farming villages, little changed in many

St-Gildas chapel on the riverbank below Écluse 10.

centuries. A typical example to visit is **Bieuzy**, about 2km from the river to the right of Écluse 11, Camblen (K21.1). After an uphill walk you will enter a jumble of old stone houses, each with a decorated stone well and cattle looking out of barns in the main street. There is very basic shopping, a restaurant and a fuel station (there are few easily accessible garages on the upper Blavet). At a similar distance from the navigation at Écluse 13, Boterneau (K25), the village of **St-Rivalain** has a restaurant, baker and grocer. Several of the Blavet weirs drive small hydro-electric power stations, dating from the 1930s: an admirable way of using 'free' energy, provided, of course, navigation is not obstructed. These include locks 16, 17 and 23, all demonstrating that even rivers with a gentle gradient can be utilised in this way. Moor on the bank immediately upstream of Écluse 16, **St-Adrien** (K30.9) to explore the village of great charm and tranquillity (bar, grocer and baker). A rare small boatyard with water and electricity will be found in a basin at **Pont-Augan**, just above Écluse 18, St-Barbe (K36.4, some shops and restaurant). Downstream of the bridge and a junction with the River Evel, avoid the remains of a bridge support in the middle of the waterway. Up to Écluse 19, Minazen (K39.4), weirs and lock chambers have been immediately alongside each other, but here there is a real lock island, with short canal.

In the pound between Écluses 20 and 21 the restaurant *Au Vallée Vert* by the D102 bridge, Pont Neuf (K46.5, quay), would be convenient for an overnight stop. Further delightful scenery with several more locks leads to the slightly industrialised little town of **Lochrist** (K54.6). This is the last chance for shopping or a visit to a *crêperie* before the tideway at Écluse 28, Polhuern (K57.3). There is little except the lock to mark the transition from a peaceful waterway to the upper reaches of an estuary that virtually dries out at low water, to reveal a rock-strewn channel. Inland craft would perhaps be advised to travel no farther. However, if bound for the coast, boats should aim to leave the lock about 1hr after HW and moor to a pontoon immediately above the first of two bridges in **Hennebont** (K59.8) until there is sufficient headroom to pass beneath. Travelling in the opposite direction, leave the coast at **Lorient** 2hr after low water, so having sufficient depth to clear the shoals while still being able to get under the bridges. Hennebont is an interesting fortified town, dating from the 11th century. It was under siege in 1341, during the War of Succession and was relieved when the English fleet sailed up the Blavet. There is a well-equipped *port de plaisance*, with nearby shops and restaurants. The onetime important iron and steel industry of this region is celebrated at the open-air *Écomusée Industriel de Inzinzac-Lochrist* and the *Musée des Métallurgistes des Forges d'Hennebont*. 13km nearer the sea at the river mouth, the modern town of Lorient provides safe pleasure boat moorings in the *Bassin à Flot*, whose tidal lock operates from $1\frac{1}{2}$hr before HW until 1hr afterwards. In all, there are three marinas as well as the submarine pens of World War II. Most boating facilities are available including slipway and cranes. The appropriate marine chart is 120 544 9, published by Éditions Grafocarte.

35 — River Loire

Carte Guide: *Les Pays de Loire*

From Nantes, junction with the Loire Maritime to Bouchemaine, junction with the River Maine (for the Rivers Mayenne, Oudon and Sarthe): 83km with 0 locks. Although most official publications and the *Carte Guides* do not consider the Loire to be navigable upstream of Bouchemaine, it is regularly used by small craft for a considerable distance beyond this point; indeed, there is a form of buoyed channel at least as far as Saumur. The river from Nantes to the coast at St-Nazaire (52.5km) is really a seaway, accepts shipping drawing about 9m at all states of the tide, and is beyond the scope of this book. Junctions are made with the River Erdre section of the Canal de Nantes à Brest and the Sèvre Nantaise (leading to the Petite Maine), both in Nantes. One short isolated length of the River Loire, 1.2km, links the Canal Latéral à la Loire with the Canal du Nivernais at Decize (see Chapter 41). Another small section of the Loire can be used at Roanne (access from the Canal de Roanne à Digoin, see Chapter 42).

The Loire is the fourth longest river in Western Europe and the longest in France, extending about 1,000km from its source in the Massif Central, a mere 160km north of the Mediterranean and 48km from the Rhône at Valence. But it chooses to flow northwards through gorges towards Nevers and Orléans and then west past Tours, Angers and Nantes to the Atlantic. Once navigable for 825km and officially described thus in highly optimistic terms as recently as 1936, the waterway is a shadow of its former self. Now, no fewer than 685km are virtually abandoned by commercial traffic with the exception of very local and limited use by gravel barges. What does remain is lock-free, tidal and slightly difficult, a narrow channel wandering between vast expanses of shingle and sand. In spite of a reputation of being lined with great *châteaux*, these are generally to be found only in the middle reaches which are not available to anything much larger than a portable vessel. Determined canoeists *might* contrive to journey downstream from Orléans, making portages over obstructions during low summer water levels or taking a severe risk at times of spring flooding. The scenic attractions from a small boat are rather limited as the wasteland of willows and sand banks soon becomes monotonous; the majority of towns and villages sensibly lie well back behind high flood walls.

Both J L Molloy (*Our Autumn Holiday on French Rivers*, 1874) and C S Forester (*The Voyage of the Annie Marble*, 1929) brought little boats down the stream from Orléans to Nantes and wrote glowing accounts. Forester considered it 'the loveliest river in Europe' and was so enraptured with the final length that he abandoned all attempts to make notes and shamefully dismisses this part in a single page! Molloy was equally impressed by 'the noblest of French rivers'. While there are few navigational problems for pleasure boats down river of Bouchemaine, I find the surroundings often far from exciting. The channel is clearly marked with buoys and no difficulty should be had in picking a way through the various branches provided you carefully follow the *Carte Guide*. Facilities, and especially safe moorings, are adequate but not extensive. For many, therefore, the Loire will be seen as a useful approach from the coast to a network of much more pleasing

J M W Turner's 19th century view of Tours.

river navigations controlled by locks and allowing access to such towns as Segré, Laval and Le Mans. The various tributaries are well served by hire cruiser firms but the whole area is generally remote and under-used. It is perhaps the region of France where inland navigation most seems like a genuine voyage of discovery.

There are numerous ramps for launching small trailed craft from the tops of stone flood banks. When using larger boats care should always be taken when approaching former commercial quays, some of which now rise from rock-strewn shallows. If in doubt, stay in deep water, lower the anchor and come ashore by dinghy. Drinking water and other boating supplies are not plentiful, so top up as the opportunity arises. Where it is cultivated, the flood plain of the lower Loire is very fertile, producing cheap but most acceptable wines. Nearer the coast a famous example is Muscadet, a fresh, dry white that normally accompanies seafood. Further upstream, you will discover the Coteaux d'Ancenis, an area of white, rosé and red. Among food specialities are several notable varieties of duck and pork near Nantes; elsewhere, try *brême farcie* (stuffed bream), *alose à l'oseille* or *beurre blanc* (shad flavoured with sorrel or a butter sauce, shallots and Muscadet), *tanche au four* (baked tench), *quenelle de brochet* (pike dumpling), *fritures* (freshwater 'whitebait'), *andouilles* (tripe sausages), *chevreuil* (venison) and all kinds of game.

Brief history The story of freight and passenger transport along the Loire is utterly absorbing, as it was one of the great highways of France for well over 2,000 years until its collapse with the introduction of the railways during the 19th century. Better documented than most river navigations in the country, it was used by the Romans upstream to Roanne (*Rodumna*). Even earlier, the Phoenicians and the Greeks had regularly taken goods up the Rhône to Lyon, where a great market was established. From there, it was a fairly short overland journey with packhorses to reach the Loire and so gain access to the Atlantic coast. Much later, there are records of the city of Tours being besieged by the Vikings, who had arrived in longships.

River traffic reached its height in the 17–19th centuries, although a toll system was widely used in medieval times. Various payments were exacted by feudal landlords such as the Count of Nevers, Duke of Bourbonnais, Count of Gien, Count of Touraine and the Duke of Brittany. Additional charges on freight transport were levied as 'town tolls' (at such places as Gien, Tours, Decize and La Charité). Then there were 'church tolls' and 'special tolls' on the carriage of pilgrims, Jews and corpses. Exemptions applied to the clergy, merchants bound for fairs and arms makers. Collection points were set up where boats could most easily be boarded, for example when passing through the arches of bridges.

For very many years attempts were made to keep open a navigable channel with wooden embankments and dredging. During the 17th century, Colbert undertook a programme of stone training walls and quays from Roanne to Nantes which certainly helped to make the river more reliable. Navigation was none the less frequently interrupted through flood and drought, and as late as 1860 the Loire between Orléans and Tours was passable for only 129 days by craft drawing as little as 0.5m and for 149 days in the section Briare to Orléans. As boatmen were normally paid by the journey rather than the time taken, there was every incentive to travel on floods, with wrecks being predictably frequent. In 1707, Loire floods were said to have drowned 50,000 people; during their height, the water rose more than 3m in two hours at Orléans!

Many different types of craft were used, with timber hulls universal until the early 19th century. Until about 1760 the most common vessels were *chalands* (sometimes called *sapines*), 25–30m long on a beam of 3–4m. *Toues* were of similar construction but smaller; both drew under 0.5m. Later versions were *sentines* or *vergées*, the latter equipped with a mast and sails. All were built with pine planking on oak frames. *Cabanes* and *coches d'eau* (water coaches) capable of loading 50 tonnes were rowed. Typical passenger time tables for the 316km, Orléans to Nantes, allowed eight days for the trip and upwards of 14 days for the reverse direction against the stream. The most affluent travellers would have their coaches placed on board the boat for a modicum of home comforts. The celebrated diarist Madame de Sévigné made such journeys on the Loire in 1675 and 1680. Rather later, the English writer Arthur Young travelled on the river, recording his impressions of the passenger boats between Orléans and Nantes in *Journeys in France*. Aboard one, he had six fellow travellers who each paid a golden Louis for the privilege of sleeping on the ground at night during the voyage. They feasted off lampreys, salmon and shad and were regaled with fine wines which abounded throughout the valley. Where craft were not rowed or sailed they were hauled by horses (sometimes up to their necks in water) or oxen, a form of traction that survived on several navigations including the Rivers Adour and Dordogne until the 1930s. Bow-hauling by teams of men was also practised.

A further variety of vessel was the *Roannaise*, a big barge of pine with oak sheathing built for one-way down-river trips from Roanne. On arrival, they were dismantled and the timber sold, certain fittings being retained for future use. The master boatmen were a hardy race and an important section of the community in every river port. During cold weather they sustained themselves with mulled wine, well sweetened and taken with slices of toast. One traditional boatman's dish was

matelote, a fish stew which modern travellers may like to prepare, perhaps adapting the recipe to suit the galley of a pleasure cruiser. Take a large copper cauldron and hang it over an open wood fire on a tripod of tree branches. Slice an assortment of fish such as eel, tench, pike and barbel, removing the heads, and cover with red wine, adding plenty of salt, pepper and garlic. Cook for 15–20 minutes. Then mix a liberal quantity of butter with a little flour and some of the hot wine; add this to the fish and boil briefly. The wine should have a high alcohol content, enabling the stew to be flambéed for a few moments. The matelote is now ready to be served.

While the boat people's patron, at least from the time of the Troubadours, was St-Nicolas, on the Loire he had competition from St Arigle, a Bishop of Nevers. His final wish was that his body should be placed on a boat and left to the mercy of the river current. Great was the surprise of the spectators when the vessel began to travel upstream, eventually coming to rest at Decize, after a 32km journey against the flow.

Sometimes owning several craft, the Loire mariners were a proud band of men, wearing loose pantaloons and a blouse or smock of canvas or blue serge, fixed at the waist with a silver pin. A bright red scarf (known as a *tabac*, for it was a useful in which to keep pipe tobacco), wide-brimmed black hat and wooden shoes of poplar or willow completed the outfit. Relics of the life are preserved in an excellent small museum, the *Musée de la Marine de la Loire* at Châteauneuf between Orléans and Gien. Displays are devoted to photographs, paintings, documents, boat models, clothing, cabin furniture and barge equipment.

Steam-driven craft appeared on the Loire shortly after the beginning of the 19th century and for the first time it was possible to work upstream with a degree of reliability. These vessels were almost exclusively used for passengers, with scheduled services operating between Nantes and Orléans by 1829. Six years later, lighter faster boats were introduced, known as *hirondelles* (swallows). But there were several dramatic and costly accidents caused by over-taxed boilers, notably an 1837 disaster between Angers and Nantes. The publicity resulted in a rapid decline in passenger numbers and so a new type of boat, the *inexplosible*, appeared in 1838–9, gradually spreading throughout the Loire and its tributary the Allier. Speeds of 10kph upstream and 16–18kph downstream were achieved. At this time, freight steamers or *remorquers* appeared, carrying 15,000 tonnes in 1843. Foreign imports such as leather, salted fish, Spanish oranges, English metals and Welsh steam coal arrived in Nantes by coaster while a whole range of commodities came downstream from the French interior. Many of the barges acted as floating

Barge haulier using breast harness, 1897.

shops, selling produce at towns en route. 1843 was a peak year for passenger traffic: the upper Loire carried 37,440 passengers and the lower river 69,504.

The boom was not to last for long. After the mid-1840s passenger traffic started to move to the newly constructed railways and the four regular steamboat lines were eventually forced out of business in spite of their smaller charges. Canals serving the river's higher reaches (the Loire Latéral, Berry and Orléans) kept their freight, but, with the exception of rafts of pine logs until 1895, trade on the Loire died above Bouchmaine.

There remained some advocates of river transport and in 1900 the *Société de la Loire Navigable* proposed building a fully usable waterway between Nantes and Briare: 24km was actually completed from Angers to Montjean. However, traffic upstream of Nantes declined still further, dropping to a mere 12,000 tonnes annually by 1923. Thereafter, any works were restricted to making training walls and dredging in the Nantes–Angers length. What had once been the greatest inland waterway in France was now virtually dead. From time to time grandiose schemes have been proposed that might have given the Loire a transport status commensurate with

the Seine or the Rhône. One of the more recent, in 1962, envisaged making the Loire fully navigable to near Tours, junction with the River Cher. A new waterway would then pass through the valleys of the Cher and Yèvre to Bourges, then along the line of the disused Canal du Berry to Beffes, and finally join up with the Canal Latéral à la Loire to gain access to the Saône at Chalon via the Canal du Centre. Although Général de Gaulle was said to support the idea, new construction of such Freycinet dimension navigations for freight is now unthinkable.

Little needs to be said of the broad estuary of the Loire from where it leaves the Atlantic at the port of **St-Nazaire** to run for 52.5km to Nantes. The lower portion is in every sense a seaway, accessible to large ships and covered by Service Hydrographique chart 5456. St-Nazaire was a harbour as far back as Roman times and achieved importance under the Duke of Brittany. In 1850, the population was a mere 4,000; since that time the port has expanded greatly as a ship building centre and harbour for Nantes, itself inaccessible to modern ocean-going vessels. No difficulty should be experienced in working upriver on a rising tide, keeping to the marked deep-water channel. En route, anchorages can be used at the entrances to the now disused Canal Maritime (south shore) in **Paimbœuf** and **La Martinière**.

Surroundings vary from salt flats on the coast to commercial wharves and oil refineries, with muddy banks and willows growing just above high water mark. If mooring in St-Nazaire, several lovely southern Brittany seaside beaches are within quite easy reach, notably a craggy cove with fine sand at **Chémoulin**, between St-Marc and Ste-Marguerite, about 9km SW of the city centre.

More than most French rivers, the Loire is subject to considerable fluctuations in height. Under normal conditions, the tide above Nantes only flows to Ancenis. It is strongly advised to follow the *Carte Guide* regarding the depths that can be expected in the river at any given time. Built at the confluence of the Loire, Erdre and Sèvre Nantaise, **Nantes** is a thriving modern city with considerable evidence of its one-time greatness as capital of Brittany. It lost its independence under the Dukes of Brittany in 1491 when Anne de Bretagne, daughter of Duke François II, was married to King Charles VIII. A quarter of a century before, the huge *Château des Ducs*, whose towering walls are the city's showpiece, had been begun. Now open to the public, the most interesting sections are a Maritime Museum, with some exhibits relating to Loire navigation, and displays of traditional Breton folk art and furniture. Visitors should also see the Gothic cathedral of St-Pierre-et-St-Paul, started in 1434 and not finished until the late 19th century. Long one of the leading ports of France, Nantes was eclipsed for a time in the 19th century by St-Nazaire; it suffered dreadful destruction during World War II. More recently, improvements to the river channel brought about a resurgence in trade. Until the 1930s, it was the main French importer of Welsh steam coal, while rather earlier slave ships (*negriers*) called here from Africa before sailing to the West Indies and America. In the troubled times of 1793, prisoners (mostly royalists) crowded the gaols and the revolutionary Carrier solved the problem with a drastic solution: 4,000 men, women and children were herded into river barges which were then flooded with water or completely scuttled. The victims became known as the *Noyades*. Within months Carrier was tried, found guilty and guillotined.

Once celebrated for its shipyards and biscuit factory, Nantes has had to reinvent itself in recent years. Various administrative operations have been relocated here from Paris. The west coast has suddenly become more 'chic' than the South of France (or so claim the Nantes publicists). The city expanded to half a million inhabitants during the 1990s and in 2004 was voted the country's 'most liveable urban area'.

Various pleasure craft facilities on the River Loire in Nantes will be noted in the *Carte Guide*, including mooring pontoons downstream of the Pont Anne de Bretagne (lower end of the *Bras de la Madeleine*). However, in many ways it is preferable to lock out of the river and into the Canal de Nantes à Brest, on the left bank of the *Bras de la Madeleine*, just upstream of the Pont Aristide-Briand. Moorings will be found beyond the 800m St-Félix Tunnel (see Chapter 33).

Nantes spills onto a large island – Ile Beaulieu – both river channels being navigable. If you take the right-hand course (*Bras de Pirmil*), you will pass a junction, right, just beyond the first railway bridge; this is the entrance to the **River Sèvre Nantaise**, open to boats for 21.5km. When making this detour along the attractive but seldom frequented waterway, it is best to leave the Loire about 1hr before HW. The half-tide sluice here is open for 1hr either side of HW (look out for sign boards). 45 minutes should bring you to the river's only real lock at **Vertou** (K6.7, good shopping). It functions every day except public holidays. Upstream, the scenery becomes delightful as the river slides past the Muscadet vineyards; official draft is reduced to 1.20m. Several *châteaux* are situated close to the water: de la Frémoire, de Rochefort at **La Haie Fouassière**, and du Briel. At K9.2, **Portillon**, the **Petite Maine** enters on the right and can be navigated for 6km past **Château-thébaud** to the present head of navigation at the disused Écluse Pont **Caffineau**. Draft on the Petite Maine is 0.90m.

As we leave Nantes to head up the Loire, the great river soon assumes its characteristic form: a wide expanse of sand banks, substantial islands and willow-overhung backwaters. Boats larger than dinghies are strongly advised to keep within the buoyed channel. During hot summer weather, this can be a wonderful setting for idle cruising: stopping to swim or make barbecues from driftwood fires on deserted sandy beaches. Admittedly, there are long stretches with few facilities of any kind. Where stopping points are suggested here this must not be taken to imply that proper bankside moorings exist, unless specifically stated. Shortly upstream of the first bridge after Nantes is a quay accessible only near HW in **Bellevue** (K6 above Nantes, restaurant). Soon after, the channel divides (K8): take the right fork and pass upriver to a bridge connecting **Le Haut Village** (K10.5, right bank, pontoon and restaurant) with **Thouaré-sur-Loire** (all shopping). Dramatic tree-covered rocks rise high from the river on the left for a long distance.

There is a village restaurant in **La Chebuette** (K12.5, right bank). A good range of boating facilities and nearby shops will be found in the Port de **La Pierre Percée** (K15, right bank). Close to the bridge of **Mauves-sur-Loire** (K16.5, left bank) are moorings for shops and restaurants. A further pontoon is on the left bank near **Vandel** (K21.5) together with one of many launching ramps. Really good Loire pleasure boat harbours are few and far between and one of the best is near the mouth of the little River Hâvre at **Oudon** (K25, left bank. It is quite a relief to leave the Loire briefly for a hint of civilisation and the small *port de plaisance* features pontoon moorings, slipway and a garage 200m uphill to the left. Moreover, there are two restaurants overlooking the water with several shops in the village. The tower of a medieval keep (open in midsummer) rises alongside the port, its rooftop providing broad views up the valley.

We are now on the edge of Anjou, a great wine-producing region: one of the most popular varieties is *rosé*. **Champtoceaux** (K26.8, right bank), however, specialises in white. There are convenient moorings shortly upriver in the Port de La Patache (K27.3). Seated on a great rock, Champtoceaux features a *belvédère* (lookout point) near the church. 7km SE at **St-Sauveur-de-Landemont** is a luxury hotel and restaurant in the ancient *Château de la Colaissière*, well worth a visit if you are ready to be spoiled. The next place of note is **Ancenis** (K34, left bank), with pontoon mooring, water point, shops and restaurants. Its 500m-long suspension bridge dominates the river. On the borders of Brittany and Anjou, the town has an impressive 16th century *château* which is now a school (visits possible, after-noons during school summer holidays). Much of the charm of this place lies in its hilly streets of old houses, ranged in tiers above the Loire. It was originally a busy port and centre of sail-making. Leading activities now are the pig market, Muscadet wine and the *rosé* Gamay. Among the important *caves* is that of Bossard (retail sales) in **St-Géréon**, 3km NW. Plenty of shops, restaurants and other facilities are close to the bridge where there is also a small slipway and a monument to members of the *Résistance* who fell in the defence of 1944. Tidal flow is scarcely a consideration above this point.

Buoys in the long reach that follows are changed according to the scours created as the channel alters; there is little worthy of comment in these 11km until we reach the hamlet of **Marillais** (K45) at a confluence with the small River Evre. There are few signs that here Charlemagne had built what is variously described as a great church or a royal palace in the 9th century. Legend tells that he arrived at a lake then by the river and struck a rock thrice with his gold and silver sword decorated with diamonds: the rock shattered and he flung his sword towards the water, saying 'Where this sword falls shall be erected the church of Notre Dame!' The resulting edifice was a structure of great magnifi-

cence, progressively enriched by succeeding Carolingian monarchs. Its 45kg bell of solid gold was hauled from the Loire by fishermen in the 11th century. In later years the building was repeatedly plundered and little remains today.

Upstream, **St-Florent-le-Vieil** (K47) stands on the right bank at a bridge crossing with visitors' mooring. It occupies a most attractive situation on a rocky outcrop, crowned by an early 18th century church in the classical style. The town features in an exquisite series of 61 steel engravings, *The Seine and the Loire*, produced from paintings made by English artist J M W Turner and first published in 1833–5. In his *Our Autumn Holiday on French Rivers* (1874), J L Molloy describes St-Florent as 'the loveliest spot we had yet seen either on Seine or Loire'. The travellers spent several days there and recorded its historical associations with 'the beginning and the end of the great Vendéan insurrection. In 1793, the inhabitants of La Vendée rose to a man against the Revolution, and declared themselves for the King, the priests and the nobles. It commenced in this little village on the 10th of March, and the first movement had for its chiefs two men of the people – Cathelineau, a *voiturier*, and Stofflet, a gamekeeper. Then came Rochejacquelein and Bonchamps-Charette, Marigny, and the rest. For a time they had a vein of brilliant success. They took Thouars in May, Saumur in June, and followed up by driving the garrison out of Angers.

'But the same month they went down to Nantes – were defeated, and lost Cathelineau. Thenceforth everything went against them. They had neither science nor organisation, and what guns they possessed they had taken in battle. The army of Mayence, under Kleber, followed them, and in October routed them mortally. They fled in confusion, and at night eighty thousand people, soldiers, old men, women and children, found themselves once more at St-Florent, with no alternative but to abandon La Vendée and cross the Loire. There were 4,000 Republican prisoners shut up in the church, and the Vendéans, to avenge their disaster at Cholet, were pointing their cannon upon it when Bonchamps, who was mortally wounded, begged for their lives with his dying breath.'

In the church is the tomb of Bonchamps, the work of the great sculptor David d'Angers. Today, St-Florent is a popular riverside resort with plenty of shops of several restaurants. The next town, **Le-Fresne-sur-Loire** (K55, left bank), provides a floating mooring (shops and restaurants). Alternatively, continue a short distance to **Ingrandes** (K56), where there is a pleasure craft quay. This is a long, grey town overlooking vast sand banks crossed by an exceptionally wide 19th century multi-span bridge, with nearby slipway.

Shopping is conveniently close and the *Hôtel du Lion d'Or* is greatly recommended, both for its appetising seafood and its reasonable prices. Two or three hundred years ago there were notorious battles between Customs officers and salt smugglers, but it is now difficult to visualise the onetime extensive port. Further memories of vanished industrial activity are provided by realisation that in the 19th century extensive coal pits were here and downstream to **Montrelais**, some of the seams reaching under the Loire itself.

Following the now well-established pattern of most facilities and potential moorings being located near bridge crossings, little of note intervenes until the right bank town of **Montjean-sur-Loire** (K60.3). Here, the most impressive features are a six-arched suspension bridge, massive stone-built quays with iron mooring rings and vast quantities of granite setts and training walls: all evidence of the disused infrastructure of the commercial waterway. Craft should stem the (sometimes) strong flow and pass through the second bridge arch from the right. There are moorings on the quay immediately below the bridge, but as often is the case on the Loire, approach carefully. Facilities include a slipway, garage (300m uphill) and most types of shop with a choice of restaurants. 3km NW of the bridge are the ruins of the *château* of **Champtocé-sur-Loire**, whose one-time owner Gilles de Rais (1404–40) was believed to have been the inspiration for Charles Perrault's infamous Bluebeard. Devotees of the macabre may care to visit the setting for his magic rites which demanded a regular supply of children's blood. Forty skeletons were discovered here and twice that number again at Bluebeard's other residence, the *Château de Machecoul*.

The Loire now divides, the navigable part being to the right of a large island, the Grande Ile de Chalonnes. Exploration of a tree-hung backwater, right, K63, is worthwhile to reach a pretty hamlet, **La Maison Blanche** – a cluster of peaceful stone cottages, fishing punts, car ferry and the hilly hinterland expanses of vineyards. **Chalonnes-sur-Loire** (K69) stands on the right bank by a series of bridges that cross no fewer than four Loire channels, close to a junction with the River Layon. This used to be navigable for 60km to the town of Thouarcé. The church, founded in the 6th century by St-Maurille, Bishop of Angers, was once so popular that open-air services were the only way of accommodating the crowds; a balcony encircles the bell tower as a form of pulpit. Flax for sailcloth was once an important crop of the area. Today, its place has been taken by tobacco. Numerous pleasure cruisers will be found here, for there are good moorings to a gently sloping quay just above the suspension bridge. Slipway, water point at the camping site, garage, boat mechanic,

shops and restaurants combine to make this a welcoming town if you arrive by water. Across the river, 7km north at **St-Georges-sur-Loire**, is the superb moated *Château de Serrant* from the 16–18th centuries. After 1749 it was home to several generations of a noble Irish family named Walsh who had supported the Stuart cause by conveying Bonnie Prince Charles to Moidart. The interior of the building contains magnificent furnishings. Guided tours, April–mid-November: details, tel 02 41 72 14 80.

Towards the upstream limit of the Ile de Chalonnes is an intensely rural little village called **Le Tête de l'Ile** (K70). Cows and chickens spill into a narrow waterside lane by stone farm buildings with clusters of climbing roses and Madonna lilies. Here operates one of the professional Loire fishermen, whose signboard advertises 'bulk and small supplies'. Unusually noisy frogs croak in the surrounding marshland. Several streams unite downstream of a railway bridge and 3km further, left bank, is the small town of **La Poissonnière** (K74.6) where there is an official mooring, slipway, water at the camp site, most food shops and a garage. The narrow streets make a pleasant shore excursion.

It is possible to pass either side of the large Ile de Béhuard: the left channel has a sloping quay mooring above the bridge. The alternative, right-hand route, provides access to a pontoon mooring, left, above the road bridge near **Les Lombardières** (K78.3). A restaurant is down the road. **Savennières**, 2km north, may be visited for a moderate selection of shops and two celebrated vineyards producing dry white wines: *Coulée de Serrant* and *Roche aux Moines*. Perhaps the most appealing village on the entire navigable Loire is **Béhuard** (K79), an extraordinary island settlement of buildings rising from rocky outcrops. (Use the mooring mentioned above.) From the 5th century there was a chapel the speciality of which was saying of prayers for those in peril on the Loire. The present 15th century church, with one wall of living rock, was built by Louis XI as a thanks offering following his escape from a near-drowning. There is also an unusual chapel consisting of an altar backed by a stained glass window and otherwise open to the sky. Facilities include several restaurants and a food store. Quite small boats should be able to moor (approach carefully) on the delightful sandy beach from which the village is approached via an avenue of willows and ash trees.

Two final stopping places are available before the upper navigation limit of the waterway: on the left bank at **Chantourteau** (K82), where fishing punts will be found on the ends of dykes (limited shopping) and to a pontoon on the left, just inside the mouth of the River Maine (K83.5). Upstream of this junction, the

Loire is not officially said to be navigable. That does not prevent local use by small cruisers, sports boats and fishing punts for a long distance up to and beyond **Saumur**. A passenger vessel regularly operates here and there is a converted barge restaurant which presumably arrived by water. A degree of local knowledge would seem to be well advised.

36 ～ Rivers Maine and Mayenne

Carte Guide: *Les Pays de Loire*
From a junction with the River Loire at Bouchemaine to Mayenne, 133.7km with 46 locks. Junctions are made with the River Sarthe upstream of Angers and with the River Oudon above Grez-Neuville.

This truly exquisite river rises in the Orne *Département* in Southern Normandy. The navigable portion winds through a steep-sided valley, often remote from towns or even main roads. Locks are all fairly small at 31m x 5.2m (the lowest eight are slighter longer). Lately restored locks above Laval are worked by boat crews; others have keepers. Lasting memories will be of timeless rural villages, numerous water mills, many of which are converted into splendid houses, and secretive reaches past shady meadows. Technically, the lowest 11km, from the confluence with the Sarthe at Angers to the Loire, are known as the River Maine; everything upstream of that point is called the Mayenne. Both lengths are invariably treated as a single navigation.

Brief history One authority writes of the Mayenne as being used by barges as early as 1492, but it is unlikely that much trade was possible until after the inhabitants of Laval had petitioned the King in 1536 to render the route suitable for large craft. This achieved, there were interminable disputes relating to freight taxes. During the mid-17th century Cardinal Mazarin undertook to extend the waterway from Laval to Mayenne. Locks then in use were time and water consuming navigation weirs or flash locks (*portes marinières*) of which 22 existed in the 36km between Château-Gontier and Laval by about 1724.

The present appearance of the river results from the canalisation programme of 1859–64, most of the new locks being designed with weirs directly alongside. Already railway competition had arrived, but a steady traffic in chalk, stone, wood, coal, grain, fruit and vegetables built up, using 130-capacity barges. In 1899, there were 1,244 movements through Écluse 34,

Château-Gontier, alone, and steam-driven passenger craft operated in the summer. By 1936 annual tonnage carried was 218,000 and the leading cargo was slate from the great quarries near Angers. Thereafter traffic died away and locks began to decay in the middle and upper reaches. By the time pleasure cruising, especially in hire craft, was starting to become established in the early 1980s, the navigation was derelict above Laval. The uppermost 26km with 17 locks were reinstated 1986–90. Later still, an additional lock and barrage were constructed downstream of Angers to cure the long-standing nuisance of shallow water in these 'uncontrolled' reaches, a problem that had been particularly bad in hot dry summers.

Coming in from the Loire, we enter a broad reach of the River Maine, soon to arrive at **Bouchemaine** (K1.3, left bank) where there are several moorings, including the pontoons of a boat club (visitors welcome). Shopping and restaurants are nearby. Wide flood meadows accompany the river up to the city of **Angers** (K9). Shortly before the Pont d'Atlantique, a new lock – Écluse du Seuil en Maine – and weir were built in 1992 to ensure that a reasonable summer water depth is available in the reach that follows. During the winter (November–April) boats may pass through the weir. At other times, they must work through the automated lock which is operated by the boat's crew. Long ago, there were strong connections between Angers and England, resulting first from the marriage in 1129 of Geoffroi, son of the Comte d'Anjou, to Matilda, granddaughter of William the Conqueror. Geoffroi's habit of wearing a sprig of broom (*Planta genista*) gave rise to the name Plantagenet. The son of this union married Eleanor of Aquitaine in 1152 and soon afterwards was proclaimed Henry II of England. Angers is now a large town, noisy with motor traffic and overlooking a busy water front. Sometimes known as 'Black Angers' on account of the roof slates produced in an 800-year old quarry at Trélazé, 8km east, and responsible for more than half the slates mined in France, the city is dominated by 17 round towers of a huge *château* erected by St-Louis in the early 13th century. Among its treasures is a collection of tapestries, including the famous 14th century Apocalypse Tapestry 168m in length. Converted *péniches* and cruisers in the *Cale de la Savatte* opposite the *château* indicate the best place for visitors to lie, but take care to avoid the tripping boat berth. Otherwise, try the *Quai du Bon-Pasteur*.

Upstream of Angers, we enter a region of flat marshes, liable to flooding. Immediately beyond a railway bridge is the confluence with the River Sarthe (see Chapter 38). We turn left for the Mayenne, passing the west side of the huge **Ile St-Aubin** which can only be reached from the 'mainland' by ferry. A further junction (K14.8) at the NW corner of the island is with a channel known as La Vieille Maine, offering an alternative approach from the Mayenne to the Sarthe at Écouflant. The first village on these somewhat bleak lowest reaches of the river is **Cantenay-Epinard** (K15.5), a pleasing settlement with range of small shops, restaurant, garage and mooring with water point. Once above the next lock, Écluse 45, **Montreuil-Belfroy** (K18.1), the river assumes its beautiful character. Take advantage of the water hose at the lock. 1km of uphill walking from here brings you to the town centre (all services and restaurant). A quay on the left above a road bridge at **Juigné-Béné** (K20.6) is convenient for restaurant and garage. 5.5km NW lies a magnificent *château* at **Plessis-Macé**, begun in the 11th century and enlarged in the 15th. Guided tours are available at various times: details, tel 02 41 32 67 93.

On the right side of a bend in the river, grandly named **Port-Albert** (K23.3) consists of a pair of cottages fronting a grassy meadow with mooring rings. Several shops, restaurant and garage are 1.5km NE at **Feneu**. When the Roman legions set up a camp in this area in the winter of 57–56 BC they discovered a riverside tribe and their temple dedicated to various Celtic gods. Écluse 44, **Sautré** (K24.3, water, slipway), is situated in woodland, alongside a broad weir and mill. Another charming mill house has been converted into a private residence at Écluse 43, **La Roussière** (K26.4), with splendid cruising above and below. There is a *château* among the trees just before the lock.

Bankside moorings at the site of a disused ferry enable a visit to be made to **Pruillé** (K27.4, slipway), an ancient village high above the waterway (left bank) where several shops and a restaurant are only 400m distant. **Grez-Neuville** (K30.8) spreads over both banks by a road bridge below Écluse 42, unusual in that it is equipped with pneumatic transmission. Nearby is a lovely collection of mainly 17–18th century houses in grey stone with a 12th century church, lily-filled backwaters and mill. Water and slipway at the *Anjou Navigation* hire cruiser base, meals in *Le Cheval Blanc* restaurant situated in a classical stone building. Quayside moorings above the bridge. There are basic food shops with petrol available at a garage in **Crieul** 1.5km SW. The lock cut is shortly followed by a junction with the River Oudon along which a diversion can profitably be made for 2km to **Le Lion d'Angers** for all facilities including a quay with drinking water (see Chapter 37).

Montreuil-sur-Maine (K36.8) is a small hilly village near Écluse 41, grass bank moorings close to a noisy church clock that strikes the quarters but mercifully

stays silent after 21.00hr, and convenient pontoons downstream of the lock whose right wall is flanked by a substantial water mill erected in 1858. Avoiding the broad curve of a weir, Écluse 40, **La Roche Chambellay** (K40.1, slipway), is entered on the left bank. Not far beyond, the bridge of **Chambellay** comes into sight (K41.6, moorings, shops and restaurant). Children will welcome a fluvial swimming pool, right bank by the football field, where there is also a water point. As a reminder that an idyllic calm has not always prevailed, there is a crucifix near a cross-roads east of the Mayenne erected 'In memory of the Liberation of Chambellay and Chenillé-Changé, 8 August 1944'.

Isolated from **Chenillé-Changé** (K43.1), Écluse 39 is on the left bank. The attractive brown stone village is one of the most pleasant on the entire river: perhaps this impression is partly due to the crenellated mill still being used to grind flour (visits possible). The mainly 19th century building is remarkably similar to those on Southern Ireland's Barrow Navigation. Jetties cater for visitors and while there are no shops, the *Table du Meunier* restaurant is recommended, especially for its fresh river fish. *Maine Anjou Rivières* have a hire cruiser base here. Showing no signs of decreasing in width, the river continues past tree-covered slopes to **La Jaille-Yvon** (K45.7), perched high above the water. Moorings

A corn mill on the waterway at Chenillé-Changé.

and slipway are situated close to several shops. Yet another massive water mill looms up at Écluse 38. During the 19th century river views from the hilltops attracted the wealthy to construct *châteaux* throughout the valley. One of these stands on the right bank at **Le Port-Joulain** (K47.6). Now comes the small town of **Daon** (K49.9), a busy inland resort with water ski-ing, slipway, vertical stone quays each side of the road bridge, a camping site, *France Mayenne Fluviale* hire cruisers, garage and restaurants. There is a swimming beach with water slope, pedalos and other small boats to rent. Among numerous *châteaux* in the vicinity, the most outstanding is the 16th century *Manoir de l'Escoublère*, whose ancient turrets are surrounded by a moat. The owner may grant you permission to walk round the exterior. From Daon, take the road towards St-Michel-de-Feins and turn left down a long avenue (about 3km).

Beautiful river reaches extend both sides of Écluse 37, **Fourmousson** (K51.6) and on to **Ménil** (K55.9), a useful overnight halt with ferry with basic shopping, restaurants and visits to the *Château de Magnanne* (open Tuesdays July and August). Écluse 36 is on the left by a pair of wide weirs with well restored mill house. On the outskirts of Château-Gontier will be found a slipway, mooring pontoon and water point in **Azé** (K61.3, right bank) 300m downstream of a railway bridge. (Nearby shopping.) At the heart of the *Chouan* country, home of the Royalists during the Vendéen War of 1793, **Château-Gontier** (K63.2) was once a leading river port. It holds one of the France's biggest cattle markets on Thursdays with up to 5,000 calves for sale. Facilities are comprehensive with quayside moorings and water point beyond the older of two road bridges. Details of local attractions can be obtained from the tourist office housed in a *péniche*. Should you be seeking a more rural overnight stop, continue to Écluse 33, **Mirvault** (K65.3), with old and new mills in contrasting styles each side of the weir and a pleasant restaurant.

Take care to avoid water skiers in the following stretch leading to Écluse 32, **La Roche de Maine** (K67.9). Having negotiated Écluse 31, Neuville (K71.5, moorings and restaurant), note the impressive *Château de la Rongère* on the left bank, upstream of Écluse 30 (K74.3). There are now few towns and villages near the river, so it may be necessary to moor below the Pont de la Valette (K75.2) and walk almost 2km uphill into **Houssay** (food shops, garage and restaurant). Curving past wooded slopes, the Mayenne climbs through Écluses 29, **La Fosse** (K80.5); 28, **La Bénâtre** (K82.5, water, restaurant); 27, **Briassé** (K83.9) and 26, Persigand (K88.7) to finally arrive at a bridge in **Port-Rhingeard** (K89.8) where there is a mooring pontoon on the right

at the foot of a vertical weir alongside Écluse 25 (most of the Mayenne weirs are sloping). Close by is the Trappist Abbey of Port du Salut, founded in the 13th century. The monks made and marketed famous Port Salut cheese here until they sold their licence to a commercial company in 1959; it operates a factory nearby. Visits may be made to the abbey.

Now close to Laval, the river maintains its secret quality through Écluse 24, **Bonne** (K91.4), with good moorings and slipway in the old village of **St-Pierre-le-Potier** (K94.4). Écluse 23, **Cumont** (K95), provides access to the outskirts of the city of **Laval** (K99) with Écluse 22 in **Avesnières** (K97.8) and No 21 opposite the ramparts of the severe 11th century *château*. Built by the Counts of Laval, but seized at the time of the Revolution, the *Nouveau Château* has been extended to act as Law Courts. Visits are possible to the interior of the vast *Vieux Château* (details, tel 02 43 53 39 89). In the Old Town are many beautiful 16th century houses with overhanging upper storeys. Waterways enthusiasts will be fascinated by a pair of well-restored *bateaux-lavoirs* (laundry barges), once a feature of many large French towns but now very rare. One houses a Nautical Club and tripping boat office, while the other, *St-Julien*, is a museum – almost certainly the only one of its type in the country. It is very much worth a visit. These vessels are believed to have first arrived in Laval about 1850 and within 20 years there were no fewer than 25 of them. By 1925, numbers had fallen to 13, with just 5 remaining in 1960. Several designs were to be seen, mostly built on hulls in Angers. *St-Julien* dates from 1904, features two decks, accommodation for the proprietor and his family, and a series of coal-fired boilers to heat cauldrons of river water. Professional washerwomen would collect laundry from private houses, wheel it to the boat in barrows and work up to 12 hours a day in reasonably unpleasant conditions. Artefacts preserved include old photographs and an archaic electrically-driven spin drier of massive proportions. In spite of the advent of domestic washing machines, *St-Julien* remained in service until 1970 and was presented to Laval by its owner the following year. On the day of my first visit a decade later, an enthusiastic student provided me with a guided tour accompanied by frequent interruptions from her grandmother, a retired *lavandière*.

Laval makes excellent use of the waterway, providing central moorings at several locations, slipways, hire craft, passenger vessels and small day boats. Numerous shops are within a close distance of the river.

The uppermost reaches of the river, restored in recent years, are frequently punctuated by boat crew-worked locks. There are few shopping or other facilities and the waterway will often appear to be almost deserted.

Laval.

Villages are mostly little more than a cluster of houses. Twenty locks intervene in the 30km to the head of navigation at Mayenne. Small electricity generators were installed at many of the weirs in this section during the 1950s. Working on a siphon principle, they are efficient and (better still!) do not interfere with navigation as has sometimes been the case elsewhere in France.

Almost the only shopping stop en route is at **St-Jean-sur-Mayenne** (K107.4), where there is a mooring quay (take care to avoid stones). In addition to restaurant facilities here, it is also possible to eat out at establishments downstream of Écluse 16, l'Ame (K109.8); at *La Guinguette*, by Écluse 14, **La Fourmondière** inférieure (K113.6); and in **Montgiroux**, close to Écluse 7, Bas Humbers (K119.4, food shop). The keeper at Écluse 10, **La Nourrière** (K116.4), is well known for staging a local history exhibition every summer, while his colleague at Écluse 3, **Grenoux** (K126.2), sells traditional country food products including loaves baked in his garden bread oven.

The river terminates with a flourish in **Mayenne** (K133.3), long a place of strategic importance which suffered widespread destruction during World War II. Its feudal fortress/*château*, dating from the 11th century, remains largely intact. There are convenient central moorings for visiting craft, passenger vessels and environmentally friendly electric launches for hire. Navigation should not be attempted upstream of the Pont MacRacken as the river rapidly becomes shallow.

37 ~ River Oudon

Carte Guide: *Les Pays de Loire*
From a junction with the River Mayenne above Grez-Neuville to Segré, the terminus, 18km with 3 locks.

What the Oudon lacks in length is more than compensated for by scenery with excellent facilities in its two leading towns, Le-Lion-d'Angers and Segré. Surroundings are similar to those on the nearby Mayenne (see Chapter 36).

Brief history Painstaking research has failed to provide much information about the origins of this little navigation. Seemingly it is too insignificant to feature in any of the standard reference works. It would appear likely that its development followed similar lines to the neighbouring River Mayenne, with the few locks constructed in the mid-19th century. A publication of 1888 comments that all haulage of barges was then by men on the towpath, neither steam tugs or horses being used. As recently as 1968 the Segré head of navigation was visited by no fewer than 416 commercial craft, carrying a total of 15,449 tonnes of freight. The Oudon is now the preserve of pleasure boats alone. During very dry summers, there is a tendency for the water levels to become uncomfortably low.

Beginning at a confluence with the Mayenne upstream of Grez-Neuville, the Oudon passes through gentle pastoral scenery and shortly arrives in **Le-Lion-d'Angers** (K2) where landscaped moorings and water point are immediately above the bridge on the left. The town is best known for its horse stud (*Haras National de l'Isle Briand*) in 160 hectares between the two rivers. Visits are possible by advance arrangement (tel 02 41 95 82 46). A Romanesque church begun in the 11th century contains a series of ancient and faded murals discovered during restoration work in 1852. Facilities of interest to the boater include numerous shops, a slipway and garage near the bridge. Markets are held Friday mornings. While eating ashore is one of the frequent delights of cruising in France, there are two possible pitfalls: Sundays are traditionally an occasion for families to dine out, meaning that booking is advised, something that is frequently not an option when boating. In order to recover from hectic Sundays, many of the smaller establishments close on Mondays. Consequently, the itinerant waterways explorer may be faced with two days of self catering. The impressive-seeming *Hôtel des Voyageurs* opposite the moorings in Le-Lion-d'Angers bears a cluster of enamel plate recommendations, including one from the Automobile Association. Monday or not, I judged them to be open for business, made a gesture towards respectability by recovering socks and trousers from the nose of my inflatable dinghy and, after a moment's consideration, decided that I stood a good chance of being admitted to the restaurant without a tie. Appetite sharpened, I discovered that the only fare advertised was 'Workman's Dinner' at a bargain price 'Wine Included'. Main dining room closed, I entered the bar, approached a formidable but efficient Madame and requested a table: the place was half-filled with blue-denimed lorry drivers. She eyed me briefly and bluntly declared 'It's Monday. We're closed!' 'But the Workman's Dinner', I protested, realising that perhaps the socks had been a mistake. She studied me once more and decided that I might *just* qualify. Five minutes later when I was well into my 'inclusive' carafe of red wine, she loudly declared to the assembled company that more expensive meals were unexpectedly available after all, but not the 'Gourmet's Menu' at the top of the range. In the event, I consumed the equivalent of a 'Luxury Workman's Dinner' for which the bill was trifling, wine, coffee and service *compris*. It was the best French meal I had enjoyed for many days. On leaving, I stole a glimpse into the proper Tuesday–Sunday 'posh' restaurant and decided, on balance, that an evening in the company of truck drivers had been both educational and more interesting.

With a gentle breeze rustling the trees, the upstream run is sheer magic, with scarcely a house in sight until arrival at Écluse 3, **Himbeaudière** (K8). 2.5km NE across the fields is a fine old stone mansion, *Le Logis de Coudray*, run as a cultural centre with concerts and exhibitions. Signs of civilisation are few and far between: if the need is great, it may be necessary to make an overland foray from the Port aux Anglais bridge (K9.2) 2km west to **Andigné**, passing an isolated *crêperie* en route. The hilltop village provides no more than a tiny store and a garage.

Écluse 2 is located at the lower end of a short cut in **La Chapelle-sur-Oudon** (K14.2, water). Here is a fine converted mill and a broad pool. 150m up a hilly lane from the upper end of the cut brings you to the heart of the village, a sleepy little place with much atmosphere and a delightful church with typical 'harebell' spire. An incongruous feature of the burial ground is the grave of a local count, protected by a metal-frame greenhouse! 3km NW lies the classical 18th century *Château de la Lorie* (open to visitors 1 July–15 September).

The journey up this little river ends with a fittingly small climax in **Segré** (K18), capital of the Segréen, an area of wooded farmland. Shortly below a junction with the River Verzée, the local boating club has excellent pontoon moorings for several dozen smallish cruisers with bar/clubhouse, slipway, 4-tonne crane and water point: a perfect example of the kind of facilities that should be found at the head of every navigation. The town spreads on both sides of the deepening valley of the Oudon, with waterside walks, a domed church (like a small-scale version of the *Sacré Cœur* in Paris) and a wide choice of shops and restaurants. Road and rail transport provides communication with such places as Angers, Nantes and Sablé, making for easy car recovery if cruising one-way with a trailed boat. Upstream, the Oudon is canoeable for a further 16km to **Châtelais**. 7km NE of Segré is the *Domaine de la Petite Couère*, an open-air museum in 80 hectares of parkland. There are collections of vintage cars and tractors, various animals (both farm and exotic) and a reconstructed small village illustrating the rural way of life as it was in the early years of the 20th century.

38 ～ River Sarthe

Carte Guide: *Les Pays de Loire*
From a junction with the River Maine/Mayenne above Angers to Le Mans, terminus. 131.6km with 20 locks.

The Sarthe rises on the south side of the *Forêt d'Ecouves* upstream of Alençon. In many ways it closely resembles its neighbour, the Mayenne, meandering through woodland and meadow in the district known as the *Angevin Maine*. Famed for cereals and vegetables with extensive orchards towards Angers, the riverscape is gently pastoral, its greatest interest being supplied by the many small bankside towns. Most of the 30m x 5.2m locks have associated water mills and long weirs, generally protected with buoys at the upper level. (The four locks nearest to the Mayenne have chambers 33m x 5.15m.) The peaceful valley encouraged building of numerous *châteaux* and large country houses.

Brief history Earliest navigation development of the Sarthe took place in the 14th century and there was a sizeable fleet of *gabarres* working in the 17th century, when a flourishing barge-building works operated at Juvardeil. Later, conditions deteriorated so much that demands were made to *restore* the waterway in 1744 and again in 1751. A tributary, the Huisne, was rendered suitable to float timber from the *Fôret de Bonnetable* to Le Mans in 1750. By 1778 barges were able to work through 3.7m wide flash locks upstream as far as

Malicorne-sur-Sarthe, 40km below Le Mans. At this time, there was a plan to extend the barge route up to Alençon, dig a length of canal from there to the headwaters of the River Orne and so create a communication between Brittany and the Normandy coast via Caen. The present locks and associated sections of canal were constructed in the middle of the 19th century.

Rapid decline of commercial traffic resulted in some of the uppermost locks falling into disrepair after World War II, but with the introduction of small numbers of hire craft in the late 1970s and early 1980s the whole line is now well maintained up to Le Mans.

Sarthe and Maine converge at the southern tip of the great Ile St-Aubin a short distance up the Maine from Angers. Almost immediately we are into the Sarthe, there is a hazard in the form of a low ferry cable that must wearily be wound below water level before a boat can safely pass. Until 1992, these lowest 18km were lock-free like the Loire and prone to shallows during a dry summer. This problem was mainly solved by building a barrage and lock near Angers (see Chapter 36); nevertheless, these reaches remain somewhat bleak until we reach the village of **Écouflant** (K4.6), opposite a junction with the Vieille Maine (which provides an alternative route into the Mayenne). Here you can moor at a pontoon for shopping and restaurants or visit the 12th century *Abbaye du Perray*. 2km away is a commendable leisure park, *Les Sablières*, created from worked out gravel pits. Very popular with people from a wide area, it provides sandy beaches, pine trees, and pleasant waterside walks. The Loir River enters the Sarthe on the right (K9.7). **Le Loir** is quite independent of its larger neighbour, La Loire, and rises west of Chartres. It was once navigable for 117km to **Le Port-Gautier** and was equipped with 34 flash locks (*pertuis*). All was claimed to be functioning in 1921; now, the river has effectively returned to nature. On the Sarthe, cherry, apple and pear orchards abound. **Briollay** (K11.7) on the right bank is the Celtic *Briara-Ledus*. There is a mooring: approach slowly, as it tends to be shallow. Water point, garage, shops and restaurants, one of which ambitiously sets out to be both *crêperie* and *brocante*.

After passing the right-bank village of **Verigné** (K16.2, restaurant), continue for about 1km and moor with care on the left bank downstream of the rocky remains of a former weir. From here, you can walk or cycle 4km along small lanes to visit the outstanding *château* at **Le Plessis-Bourré**, approached via a causeway bridge over its broad moat. This exquisite white building with slate roof was erected in the 15th century by Jean Bourré (1424–1506), Financial Secretary to Louis XI. For details of opening times, tel 02 41 32 06 01.

After Écluse 20, **Cheffes** (K18.3), river scenery greatly improves. Although smaller boats can approach the town on its downstream side, where scores of fishing punts lie in an island backwater, it is preferable to work through the lock and moor to a pontoon (water point and electricity). Shops and restaurants are within easy reach near the church. The luxury 3-star *Hôtel du Château de Teildras* boasts an excellent reputation: the splendid building is open to clients only. A slightly adventurous diversion, that is perhaps better conducted by dinghy rather than a large cruiser, can be undertaken where the river divides (K21.6). The right-hand channel, *Bras du Moulin d'Ivray*, introduces a fascinating area of small canals, sand banks and abundant wildlife.

Juvardeil (K25.8) extends along the left bank, with two possible mooring points. Shops and garage near the 14th century church. It was here that the royalist leader Bonchamps was born (see Chapter 35). **Châteauneuf-sur-Sarthe** (K28.3) has almost everything you could wish for in a riverside town: welcoming pontoons below the bridge where you can tie up; several stylish restaurants, ample shops within a few steps; and the *Maine Anjou Rivière* hire cruiser base offering all normal boating services. A kind of waterways museum is contained in the *Maison de la Rivière*: this shows how the Sarthe operated in the days of flash locks. There are also models of freight and passenger vessels. For opening times, tel 02 41 33 91 64. In the reach that follows, take care to avoid the submerged remains of an old weir about halfway to **Brissarthe** (K34.3), and another on the right just below the town. Moorings with bollards are by a grassy square downstream of an island. Many of the buildings are fine examples of Anjou architecture. The town has adequate shops and restaurants. In 886 Robert le Fort, sent by Carolingian King Charles the Bald to fight the Normans, was killed in front of the church. Once through Écluse 18, **Villechien** (K38.2, water point), an almost straight reach leads to **Morannes** (K41.1, all facilities, market: Thurday mornings). Moorings downstream of the bridge. Rowing boats and fishing punts may be hired and a passenger vessel operates. For those wishing to stay in the area (perhaps while exploring the river by day boat or car) inexpensive self-catering apartments can be rented in a *gîte rural*, established in the impressive waterside *Château des Roches*, 2km towards Précigné. **Chemiré-sur-Sarthe**, left of the bridge, has a fine 19th century *château* and a range of shops, but is considerably further from the river than Morannes.

Écluse 17, **Pendu** (K44.4, water point), is on a short cut to the left of an island with mill house. This is followed in due course by **Pincé**, on the right bank

downstream of Écluse 16, **Beffes** (K50.3). It is a delightfully sleepy hamlet where vegetable gardens extend to the water's edge and there is a restaurant and slipway. Sites of former weirs (both on the right) will be seen at islands near **La Cognière** (K55.5) and **La Bouverie** (K57.1), before reaching the important town of **Sablé-sur-Sarthe** at Écluse 15 (K58.5). As its name suggests, this was once a sand barge port. There are good moorings close to a network of narrow streets full of shops and restaurants. Little shortbread-style butter biscuits, known as *sablés* are a local speciality. Hire cruisers (*Anjou Navigation*) and passenger craft; a morning market is held Mondays and Fridays. On the left bank, a huge 18th century *château* was constructed by Colbert de Torcy, nephew of Colbert, the Minister of Louis XIV. It is now used by the National Library. The Sarthe is an important feature of the town, with waterside flower beds and attractive walks. Nearby, black marble veined with white was once quarried to be used in such buildings as Versailles. Beyond the bridge, the River Erve flows in from the NW.

Écluse 14 (K61.6) and its lock cut introduce **Solesmes** and the towering granite mass of the Benedictine abbey of St-Pierre. Founded in the early 11th century, most of the buildings were erected at the end of the 19th century in a Romanesque-Gothic style. You do not need to be a Roman Catholic or even particularly religious to appreciate Solesmes' celebration of the Latin Mass, sung in Gregorian chant. Although there are suitable moorings on each side of the river, shopping is fairly basic both here or on the facing shore in **Le Port de Juigné**. In common with most sites of Catholic pilgrimage, there is a first-rate hotel, the *Grand*. After days of the simple river life, it can be good for morale to be pampered. For a very reasonable charge, I dined here magnificently (two half bottles of wine included) on hors d'oeuvre; wild salmon in thin slices with vinaigrette sauce and salad, served with toast; wood pigeon in pastry with truffles and mushrooms; green salad, local cheeses and fresh strawberries. This was a pilgrim's feast indeed!

Near Écluse 13 (K63) is the little harbour of **Juigné-sur-Sarthe**, a place of 16–17th century houses and a good view of the abbey in Solesmes. The rough stone tower of its Romanesque church looks like part of a medieval fort. Good shopping facilities. Quiet reaches lead to Écluse 12, **Courtigné** (K68.6), and on past **Avoise** (K71.1, basic shops) with a 15th century manor house *La Perrine de Cry* and moorings to a quay on the upstream side. Restaurant and garage. **Parcé-sur-Sarthe** (K73.6) is a medieval hilltop village with many 16–17th century stone buildings: possibly the most pleasing spot on the entire waterway. Best access is through

Écluse 11, up to the head of the lock island and back a little way down the weir stream to a quay with bollards. A swimming enclosure is sited just downstream of the weir itself. All shops, garage and restaurant. Not far beyond is Écluse 10, by the *Moulin d'Ignères* (K76.6), followed by a long lock-free section (restaurant in the right-bank hamlet of **Dureil**, K79.6) running into the sizeable town of **Malicorne-sur-Sarthe** (K85). Splendid moorings have been created on a quay by the mill: these are reached by negotiating Écluse 9 and turning downstream from the upper end of the lock cut, through the bridge and stopping immediately before a weir. Otherwise, tie up on the bank just below the weir. A lovely 17th century moated *château*, frequently visited by diarist Mme de Sévigné, is very pleasing. Shops, restaurants and several *faïence* potters' workshops encourage lingering here.

Moving upstream and past the *Château de Rivesarthe*, Écluse 8, **Noyen** (K90.6, water point), is followed by a long cut with a substantial railway viaduct spanning the river beyond. Moor alongside the town, left bank, where there is a quay and slipway 200–300m from shops and restaurants. Houses, mill, weir and gardens together create a delightful picture. The next village upriver is **Fercé-sur-Sarthe** (K99.1), at a bridge crossing past Écluse 7 (water point). This is a peaceful little place rising above waterside trees and has a handful of shops and a restaurant. Turning to the east, the river now heads for Écluse 6 and **La-Suze-sur-Sarthe** (K105.1), with bollard moorings, shops on each bank, garage and several restaurants. Cruisers are available from here by *Rives de France*. Thursday is market day. The 15th century *château* was built on the site of a 12th century fort. Small craft can be launched at a ramp below the bridge in **Roëzé-sur-Sarthe** (K108.6); moorings on a grassy bank 75m from the church square (shops and restaurants). Écluse 5, Roëzé (K109.6), marks the beginning of a long cut bypassing the town of **Guécélard**; protected by a guard lock at its upper end, the navigation is reunited with the river at **Fillé** (K115.3), a village that is both charming and convenient, having fuel, shopping and restaurant facilities.

A further tree-shaded lock cut begins at Écluse 4, **Spay** (117.5). Stop by the lower bridge for a grocer and restaurant in **Prélandon**. Alternatively, walk over the same bridge, cross the unnavigable river and within 1km will be found a variety of shops, restaurant and garage in Spay. Rather than establish a headquarters in nearby Le Mans, the *Club Nautique Maine-Marine* has created a welcoming boating centre just beyond the Spay lock cut at **Le Noyer**, an easy taxi journey from the city. Visitors are offered the use of the club house, moorings, water and electricity points, slipway and 6-tonne crane. Not far upstream, the outer suburbs of Le Mans increasingly become evident and the river gradually starts to lose the rural freshness so characteristic of earlier reaches. After an island, **Arnage** (K121) will be seen on the right bank: a useful halt for shops, restaurants and fuel station. Between Écluse 3, Chahoué (K125.5), and Écluse 2, La Raterie (K126.6), each built with a short lock cut, Gallo-Roman remains from a local archaeological site will be found in an exhibition in the town hall of **Allonnes**, reached from a road bridge.

K128.6 is the confluence of the **River Huisne** which, from the 18th century, was *flottable* (used for transport of logs) over a distance of 25km with ten 'passes' in the weirs. First impressions of **Le Mans** (K130.7) are not entirely favourable, for the river is overlooked on each side by tall blocks of modern apartment buildings. Nevertheless, there are central moorings on rather high stone quays, very convenient for food shopping. The city dates back to 4th century Roman times. It was the birthplace of Henry II of England; today, it is better known for its associations with motor cars, the Bollée's 12-seater road steamer of 1873 having reached speeds in excess of 40kph. Since 1923 the Le Mans 24-Hour Race has attracted motor sports enthusiasts from many countries. Renault established a factory here in 1936 and there is a Motor Museum with 115 exhibits. Substantial portions of the medieval town remain within the massive ramparts of Gallo-Roman fortification walls, rising sheer from the Sarthe. Detailed information on ancient houses, a selection of museums and the magnificent Gothic cathedral of St-Julien will be found in the Michelin Green Guide *Châteaux of the Loire*. Restaurant specialities to try include Loire Valley *rillettes* (diced pork, preserved in jars); *chapons* (capons cooked with cider); and *poulardes dodues* (roast chicken). The Sarthe is navigable for about 2km beyond Écluse 1. There are central moorings for visiting boats by the Pont de Fer and upstream of the (footbridge) Passerelle St-Jean (K131.6).

V · BURGUNDY AND BOURBONNAIS

39 ~ Canal du Loing

> **Carte Guide:** *Les Canaux du Centre*
> From a junction with the River Seine at St-Mammès to a junction with the Canal de Briare at Buges, near Montargis. 49.4km with 19 locks (including 1 flood lock that is normally left open).

The Canal du Loing forms part of the Bourbonnais route between the Seine and the Saône and is a really pleasant and interesting waterway in its own right. Apart from two sections where the course of the River Loing is put to use, the navigation is a lateral canal along the river valley with a total fall of about 37m. Popular with motor yachts in transit between Northern France and the Mediterranean, the Canal du Loing still retains a few commercial craft although *péniches* are far fewer than 20 or 30 years ago. Almost from end to end surroundings are of woodland with a succession of pretty villages, convenient for shopping and eating ashore. The Loing has a reputation for teeming with coarse fish: anglers will be seen in large numbers on the canal, and seated in small black or dark green punts in the secretive and shaded pools of the river. It is always appropriate to read of the experiences of other waterway travellers: two contrasting accounts are C S Forester's delightful *The Voyage of the Annie Marble* (1929) recording a journey by motorised camping dinghy along the Seine, Loing, Canal d'Orléans (now gradually being restored) and Loire; and *Isabel and the Sea* by George Millar (1949, reprinted 1983), which recounts the progress of an auxiliary ketch from the Channel to the Mediterranean via the Bourbonnais route.

Brief history Construction of the Canal de Briare, completed in 1642, provided a water route between the valleys of the Loire and the Seine. But dry summers or contrary winds on the Loire between Briare and Orléans prompted Louis XIV's brother the Duke of Orléans to create an alternative and more reliable canal link from Orléans to the Briare near Montargis. Building of this, the Canal d'Orléans, started in 1682 and the 78km line with 28 locks was finished 10 years later. Now attention was turned to that part of the Loire–Seine route which used the River Loing from

Montargis to the Seine. Hampered by 26 inconvenient and time-wasting flash locks (navigation weirs), it sometimes suffered from serious flooding. At other times, boatmen were forced to bargain with numerous mill owners to 'buy' water supplies and so be able to pass the obstacles. Not infrequently, it would take 5–6 weeks to negotiate this section instead of 2–3 days. At the end of a downstream journey towards Paris barge proprietors were known to have sold off their craft at rock-bottom prices rather than face the delays and difficulties of re-ascending the Loing. Inspired by the success of his first canal and anxious to better its trading prospects, the Duke of Orléans sought letters patent to build a Loing lateral canal. Engineered by the Régemortes (father and son), it was begun in 1720 and finished remarkably quickly by 1723. Many of the locks had sloping earth-sided chambers and at two places (near Nemours and approaching the Seine junction) the original bed of the Loing was used, these lengths being known as *râcles*. Consignments bound for Paris included large quantities of firewood and timber. The Canal du Loing obviously prospered for 3,815 loaded barges passed through in 1752 alone. In the early days Paris was connected with Montargis and Briare by a passenger-carrying *coche d'eau* service, taking precedence over freight vessels and achieving a Briare–Paris journey time of 5 days, the equal of which would remain quite a feat 250 years later.

The Canal du Loing, together with the Canal d'Orléans, was purchased by the State in 1860 and extensive modernisation was put in hand over the following 30 years, enlarging lock capacity and improving the channel. Water supplies were improved in 1912 when an electric pumping station went into service at Fay-aux-Loges. 5km of new canal, running alongside the Loire, had, by 1921 taken the waterway into the heart of Orléans: previously it had been necessary to rely on the unreliable river navigation at this point. By 1936, the Loing and Briare Canals together carried an annual 1,524,000 tonnes with 9,675 barge journeys. George Millar found that conditions had deteriorated badly immediately after World War II, poor depth and heavy weeding impeding the few motorised barges. Most traffic then consisted of horse or tractor-hauled wooden vessels, including the painfully slow, small capacity *berrichons*.

Canal boat stabling on board a berrichon. *Early 20th century.*

Today, the great majority of craft are intent on pleasure and many towns and villages have enthusiastically provided convenient overnight moorings. Too many motor yachts rush through these 'Bourbonnais' canals on their impatient voyages to or from the Mediterranean. These owners are making a huge mistake, for there is much of interest in the towns and villages en route. Everyone is recommended to slow down and enjoy the experience!

There could scarcely be a greater contrast between the wide and busy waters of the Seine – where there is still a great deal of commercial barge activity – and the intimate Loing at **St-Mammès**, which is well supplied with shops, restaurants and boating requirements including water, fuel and a barge repair yard (see also Chapter 13). The old Écluse 20, just inside the entrance, has been redundant since River Seine levels were changed. It could be a useful mooring. After an impressive railway viaduct, most tourists or travellers (but probably excluding the high-speed boat delivery crews) will want to find a mooring, for there is a real treat in store, a positive highlight of the journey:

Moret-sur-Loing (K1.7, all urban facilities). I have several times tied up on the towpath immediately below Écluse 19: this is not ideal, but there really seems to be no obvious alternative. The superb town of Moret, for which I would want to reserve at least half a day, stands a few minutes' walk from the canal, on the far side of the beautiful River Loing. It was fortified with gateways and has many royal connections going back to the time of Louis VII (1137–80). Its bridge is one of the most ancient in Ile de France. Old buildings stand in a ravishing waterside setting with willows. Saturday evenings, June 20–September 5, are devoted to a summer festival, with *son et lumière* on the banks of the Loing recalling the town's history over 900 years. The Paris-born Impressionist painter Alfred Sisley (1839–99), totally unrecognised during his lifetime, lived and worked here for many years; his former studio is at 19 Rue Montmartre. The river is (locally!) claimed to be better supplied with fish than any other watercourse in France. Many of these creatures find their way onto the tables of Moret restaurants, together with a wide variety of edible fungi, as much appreciated here as they are neglected in England. In a timber building near the church of Notre Dame you can buy a caramelised barley-sugar speciality, once made by nuns: it is known as *sucre d'orge*. Passenger boats provide excursions on the Loing from the *Vieux Pont*. Moret is a convenient departure point from which to make a trip (by public transport or taxi) to the Palace of Fontainebleau (see Chapter 13).

Skirting the SE fringes of the Fontainebleau Forest, the Canal du Loing soon reaches the village of **Bourgogne** (K2.5). Beyond Écluse 18 is *La Grange Batelière*, a thatched cottage inspired by buildings in the Vendée. It was built in 1926 by Michel, son of the Prime Minister Georges Clemenceau (1841–1929) who led France towards the end of World War I. It is now a museum dedicated to the memory of the great statesman. Moving on, we pass old gravel workings landscaped with poplars. **Écuelles** (K4.2), left bank before Écluse 17, has several shops and a restaurant while there are similar facilities in Épisy (K8.4), near Écluse 16. A full range of shops is to be found in **Montigny-sur-Loing** within 2km of the canal at the road bridge beyond Écluse 15, Berville (K10.7). This, and the village of **Grez-sur-Loing** (approached from the bridge after Écluse 14, Bordes), are both pretty riverside settlements. The English composer Frederick Delius (1862–1934) lived in Grez. Surprisingly, for a waterway that not very many years ago was hectic with barge traffic, locks on this section were never mechanised or converted to automatic operation. Note the keeper's little lobbies (huts) with heavy tiled roofs and a wood-burning stove for winter warmth.

Montcourt-Fromonville (K14.5), a straggling village on the left, has a grocer and restaurant and is followed by guard lock 13, Fromonville (K16.8), leading into a broad section of the River Loing, a tempting place for a swim on a hot day. Left of the junction, is the Restaurant *Au Chaland qui Passe* (presumably a reference to Jean Vigo's 1934 classic barge film of the same name). The peace and greenery is momentarily shattered by a high-level bridge carrying the A6 *autoroute* over the river. Take care at the blind right-angled junction just before the next bridge, with Écluse 12, Buttes (K19.3, water point), concealed on the right. Alternatively, remain on the river for 400m to arrive at official moorings with water, electricity and refuse disposal. Situated in park land reasonably close to the centre of **Nemours**, this is a good place for shops and restaurants. Other diversions include a 12th century castle, the 12th century church of St John the Baptist erected to house relics of the saint brought back from the Second Crusade, and a park containing an array of curiously formed rocks, the *Rochers Gréau*.

In 1979, I experienced one of my strangest ever canalside French meals in the family-run *Auberge au Fil de l'Eau* by Écluse 11, **Chaintréuville** (K22). We had moored nearby for the night and as we approached the building a flock of white ornamental doves scattered. The main door was obstructed by two cockatoos and a mynah bird perched on top of their cages. As we took our places at the table, a woolly half-blind dog of uncertain breed, a small alsatian and a whippet grouped themselves expectantly. A shoal of tropical fish swam in a tank the length of the substantial bar. During the meal, doves would fly in through the open window in search of crumbs. Furnishings were equally bizarre: well-worn easy chairs and sofas with Far Eastern antiques, paintings and ecclesiastical items that might once have graced the village church. When he had finished his work in the kitchen, the *patron*, in a grubby once white apron, came to drink with us, all the time giving kisses to the cockatoo that perched on his shoulder. In spite of somewhat lax standards of hygiene, the food was both palatable and inexpensive and, judging by the clientele of anglers and the lock keeper, visitors from the outside world were probably rare. Twenty years were to pass before I had another opportunity to eat at the *Auberge*. To my dismay, I found that it had long before ceased trading.

The canal winds on under avenues of planes, with the Loing flowing through woodland close by on the right. Shopping is good in **Bagneaux-sur-Loing** near Écluse 10 (K23.7) and almost sophisticated in the small town of **Souppes-sur-Loing** (access from the third bridge after Écluse 9, Beaumoulin K28.2). A little aqueduct spans the water lily-filled River Fusain beyond Écluse 7, **Néronville**. Beyond the next bridge, very pleasant woodland moorings have been created, with bollards. Although we are not yet far enough south to find extensive vineyards, patches of grapes will be seen in private gardens. This is a remarkably pleasant stretch of waterway, where long worked-out quarries have been colonised by wild hops; from time to time, there are glimpses of attractive houses together with several old water mills.

Nargis (K39.1) is approached along a magnificent avenue of planes, some of them growing at curious angles. The little town has most shops and a restaurant near Écluse 5 and its church is surmounted by a bulbous slated spire like an upturned tulip. Beyond the river, to the left, the Forest of Montargis introduces a deeply rural character to the waterway, most evident between Écluse 3, Montabon (K43.5, restaurant on the towpath), and Écluse 2, des Vallées (K44.3). Years ago, I complimented the keeper on his lovely lock house with speckled brown roof standing against a backdrop of trees, as he cut me a supply of spring lettuce from his productive garden. He agreed wholeheartedly, adding that after spending 30 years there he was convinced that there was no finer place on earth.

A barge hauliers' encampment on the Canal du Loing at St-Mammès, 1897.

Lights control a passage through a narrow concrete-lined section by the bridge in **Cépoy** (K48.3, all normal shore facilities). Until creation of the Canal du Loing, this length of waterway formed one end of the Canal d'Orléans with a junction lock (long ago disused) into the River Loing. The present Canal du Loing's Écluse de Cépoy began life as the very first lock to be constructed on the Canal d'Orléans. You can read the date MDCLXXX on the stonework. With plenty of patience and an interest in canal history it is quite possible to discover evidence of other navigation structures that became redundant in the first quarter of the 18th century! Still standing is the keeper's cottage of the long demolished Écluse de Montigny. Elsewhere are traces of the River Loing's rudimentary flash locks. No fewer than three impressive mansions (described locally as *châteaux*) still exist in or near Cépoy. They date from the 17th century and were used by important waterways officials including the Director General and the Chief Accountant of the Canal d'Orléans and the River Loing.

The modern-day Canal du Loing ends at a junction with the Canal de Briare at Écluse 36, Buges (K49.4). Close by is a marble monument to the unfortunates who were transported to labour camps by the Nazis, the

first part of their journey being by canal barge. Below the lock, the partly disused **Canal d'Orléans** enters on the right. 79km long with 28 locks, rising to a summit at **Le Gué-des-Cens** and then falling towards a junction with the Loire, it was abandoned as recently as 1954, the locks never having been enlarged to Freycinet standards for *péniches*. When last fully in use, maximum craft dimensions were: length: 30.18m; beam: 5m; draft: 1.3m; air draft: 3.35m. By the time all barge traffic had forsaken the Upper Loire in the 19th century, the Canal d'Orléans found itself only serving sparsely populated rural communities and the city of Orléans itself. Principal places en route include **St-Maurice-sur-Fassard, Chailly-en-Gauhais, Fay-aux-Loges** and **Combleux**. C S Forester had little to find its favour when he passed through in 1928, describing it as 'utterly filthy and swarming with mosquitoes'. His impressions were doubtless soured by breaking a propeller near Lorris and having to wait impatiently for a replacement to be brought out from England. In 1936, a mere 439 animal-hauled barge journeys were made. Apart from several hundred infilled metres in Orléans, the canal and its locks remained remarkably intact, with upper lock gates generally replaced by concrete weirs.

Complete restoration began in the latter 1980s, with establishment of a *Syndicat mixte de gestion du Canal d'Orléans*, based in Fay-aux-Loges. Compared with similar schemes elsewhere in France, progress has been slow. At the time of writing, two lengths have been returned to a navigable state: 14km with 4 locks between the Canal du Loing junction and the Écluse Marchais-Clair; and 19km with 3 locks from Fay-aux-Loges to the end of the waterway in Orléans. So far, the only permitted craft are trip-boats, although it is anticipated that the remainder of the canal will be reopened in due course and the whole line made available to the boating public. Local enquiries should be made to establish the latest situation.

There is an active canal society, *Les Amis du Canal d'Orléans*, which has the 1930-built steel *berrichon* barge *Le Sauve*, fitted out as a mobile waterways museum and exhibition centre. The vessel is normally based at Donnery, near Orléans. Details, tel 02 38 59 29 29.

40 ～ Canal de Briare

Carte Guide: *Les Canaux du Centre*
From a junction with the Canal du Loing at Buges, near Montargis, to a disused lock that used to connect with the River Loire in Briare. 56.8km with 35 locks. A junction is made with the Canal Latéral à la Loire at Belleau, near Briare.

An agreeable and well established waterway, now more than 350 years old and consequently very much a part of the towns and villages along its course. Shore facilities are quite numerous. The Canal de Briare climbs from Montargis to a summit level between Dammarie-sur-Loing and Rogny and then falls towards the River Loire. Up to the 1970s, it remained exceptionally busy with commercial traffic when, during working hours, every lock could either be guaranteed to contain a barge, have one about to enter or had just seen one leave. Small amounts of freight traffic still remain. Numerous relics of the original 17th century navigation works are of particular interest to canal enthusiasts.

Brief history Planned as the first watershed canal in Europe, the Briare was conceived by Henry IV and the Duc de Sully in 1604. Its object was to provide communication between the valleys of the Loire and the Seine. Taking Italian and Belgian experience as a model, the engineer Hughes Cosnier started work on the line in 1605, using up to 6,000 men. Navvies' wages were paid in the form of tokens, exchanged in establishments set up by the proprietors on the work sites. Each coin carried the wording *Via Ligeris in Sequanam* (the Way from the Loire to the Seine). Those for meat were

marked *Necessitas supplementu*; for drink, *Recreatio laboris*; and for bread, *Laboris fulcimentum*. Changes of policy on the King's assassination in 1610 resulted in building coming to a halt when 35 of the locks were substantially complete. This brought financial ruin to those who had backed the scheme. Nothing more happened until 1638, when Jacques Guyon and Guillaume Bouteroue were granted permission by Cardinal Richlieu to recommence works. All was ready to receive traffic by 1642. Although supplied from carefully designed reservoirs the canal at first suffered from water shortages, reducing the draft of the barges to 2–3 *pieds* (about 0.6–0.9m), though this was no worse than often allowed by the depth of the adjoining River Loire. Locks were built at 24 sites: examples of double, triple, quadruple and at Rogny septuple staircases resulted in a total of 41 chambers. Craft were able to negotiate each chamber in about 6 minutes.

As late as 1778 all hauling was done by men, generally two to each boat or log raft. Typical cargoes included wines from the Mâcon, Beaujolais, Charollais, Sancerre and Languedoc regions; firewood, timber, coal and iron; *faïence* from Nevers and fruit from the Auvergne. Most was destined for the Paris area and attracted heavy tolls. By the mid-18th century more than 500 wine barges were in regular use. Disadvantages of this route were canal stoppages and Loire water shortages which often brought closures of 2–3 months each year. Great improvements to the canal's fortunes followed completion of the Canal Latéral à la Loire in 1838: now the fickle Loire could largely be ignored. Together with the Canal d'Orléans, the Briare was purchased by the State in 1860 and locks enlarged to *péniche* standards by 1893, all the multiple chambers being replaced by single locks on new sites. At Briare a steam (later electric) pumping station arrived in 1895 and the Bourdon reservoir was added in 1904.

While in recent years freight traffic has experienced a dramatic decline, pleasure craft have increased hugely and the facilities provided for them by town and village authorities are generally excellent. As a part of the Bourbonnais chain of waterways, the Briare sees much use by private motor yachts and cruisers as of the several possible canal routes between the Seine and the Saône it is generally agreed to be the quickest while allowing for slightly more generous air draft.

From its junction with the Canal du Loing just north of Écluse 36, **Buges**, the Briare follows the valley of the Loing as far as Rogny. The union of the two waterways is an agreeable place, with a substantial lock house and the Canal d'Orléans entering on the right (see Chapter 39). It is a short distance through Écluse 35, Langlée (K1.8), to **Montargis** (K4), capital of the Gâtinais area. Before reaching the town, there is a quay with bollards on the right which is very convenient for a supermarket. Écluse 34 is automatic. Several picturesque side canals branch off the navigation in a plane tree-shaded reach below Écluse 33, de la Marolle, giving the town its slightly fanciful title *Venise Briarde*. Not available to craft larger than punts, these streams are lined with ancient houses where the water laps at the backdoors. Many have *lavoirs* (washing places). A charming municipal notion is to anchor dinghies planted with petunias and other flowers at strategic points. In the town centre the canal is crossed by a steel footbridge. Close to the waterway is a large 19th century stone monument with Latin inscription marking the former northern terminus of the Canal de Briare. Note also the iron Cross of St Nicholas (the boat people's patron) on the bridge of that name. It bears the date 1826. There is a busy open-air market and a wide choice of eating places. In the days of Louis XIII, the chef of the Duc de Plessis-Praslin invented a recipe for a confection made from roasted almonds covered with knobbly sugar. They became known as *praslines* or *pralines* and first went on sale in a shop opposite the church de la Madeleine. We once spent the night at the *Grand Hôtel de la Poste* while returning home to England after a hire cruiser holiday. Suitably impressed at our arrival in an elderly (but much admired) Bentley, the proprietor showed us to his best table, where a brass plaque recorded the visit of no less a personage than 'The Prince of French Gastronomes'! In this challenging situation we had no choice but to order from the most expensive and lavish menu. It was disappointing to discover some years later that this old fashioned establishment had been modernised out of all recognition following its acquisition by an hotel chain. There is a water point at Lock 33, together with a *Bureau de Contrôle*. The unusually deep chamber was a two-rise lock until completely rebuilt towards the end of the 19th century. Visitors' moorings, with facilities, soon appear on the right.

Écluse 32, La Tuilerie (K8.7), has a nearby restaurant. The lock chamber, in spite of extensive rebuilding in 1830 and again around 1890, still displays elements dating back to the original structure of the 1640s. In several places there are reminders of horse-drawn barge traffic, which only finally disappeared at the end of the 1960s. These take the form of a wheel and pulley arrangement, designed to pass towlines under bridges that lack a towpath. The keeper of Écluse 31, Sablonnière (K10.7), is the proud owner of a collection of 1920s and 30s road vehicles (mostly Citroën and Renault): some are beautifully restored. Others might easily keep him occupied for a lifetime. Locks 30–27 are mechanised.

Until recently, there was an ingenious device in the pound between Nos 28 and 27 where a curve obstructs vision to the next lock. Black or red panels were displayed, remotely changed by wires, a simple form of traffic signal. On the right of the modern locks little but a keeper's cottage remains of the old five **Chesnoy** locks of which three were a staircase. **Montcresson** (K16.5) provides good shopping and a restaurant. Remnants of an ancient amphitheatre can be seen on the right shortly before **Montbuoy** (K22.4, shops, restaurant and *halte nautique*). The Roman relics came to light during excavation of the canal in the 17th century. Even today, when the channel is drained for maintenance it is possible to see artefacts including sections of mosaic. Écluse 26, here, is unusually deep: nearby are signs of further old chambers. Steel bascule bridges will be encountered at various locks. The first is at Écluse 25, Lépinoy (K24.7). Their purpose at first appears somewhat obscure until you learn that they were installed to enable the towing masts of horse-boats to pass through in an upright position. Many French locks feature gravel where you might expect to see lawns; and nowhere more so than on the Bourbonnais route. Sometimes, it is painstakingly raked into intricate patterns, so beware walking across it.

Châtillon-Coligny (K27.8) was already old when the canal arrived in its centre. During the summer you may visit the exterior of a 12th century *château*, reconstructed in the 16th century by Admiral Gaspard de Coligny and much damaged at the time of the Revolution. In early September, reputedly at 7-year intervals, the little town holds a great fair 'in honour of agriculture': buildings are lavishly adorned with festoons of crêpe paper flowers and sheaves of corn. Car and tractor salesmen demonstrate their wares and an illuminated marquee dance hall throbs far into the night. Shops and restaurants are conveniently close to the *port de plaisance*. Disused portions of the former navigation include one length crossed by an iron swing bridge.

Several regularly-spaced locks lead to **Dammarie-sur-Loing** (K33.4) where there are a few shops and garage. Well worth seeing is the impressive four-chambered lock staircase alongside Écluse 21, Moulin Brûlé (K32.3). Built by Cosnier in the early 17th century, the locks were enlarged in the 1830s and then made redundant in the 1890s. They were improved by a restoration programme in the early 2000s. The circular stone building is an old limekiln.

Six electrically-operated locks at **Rogny-les-Sept-Écluses** (K38.1) are separated by short pounds. This was not always so, for here is one of the great achievements of French waterways engineering: the famous seven-rise staircase, preserved as an ancient monument

The seven-lock staircase at Rogny, which dates from the mid-17th century. Since the late 19th century, it has been replaced by individual chambers, but is preserved as an ancient monument.

and floodlit by night. Major renovation was completed early in the 21st century. Providing a change in levels of 34m, they were taken out of service in 1887, having seen 245 years of use. In 1894 plans were drawn up to replace the old staircase by a single chamber with a massive rise and fall of 20.4m, filling and emptying relying on a series of side-ponds. Many deeper lock chambers have since been constructed elsewhere but not with a beam of just 5m. Had the idea progressed to reality, this Great Lock of Rogny would have been like boating in a very deep well! Six conventional chambers were constructed instead. There is a pleasure boat port with good facilities, left, along part of the River Loing, together with hire cruisers and good shopping and restaurants at the bottom of the locks. A 4.6km summit level follows the locks, constructed rather deeper than normal in order to conserve water supplies. There are no fewer than 15 reservoirs in the vicinity with a capacity of 18 million m³. The descent towards the Loire begins at Écluse 12, Gazonne (K44.3), where there is a good example of a towline pulley system under the bridge. Further disused locks and keepers' cottages are found by Nos 10, 9 and 5. Shopping and fuel from a garage can be obtained near to quayside moorings in **Ouzouer-sur-Trézée** (K48.5), where

caravans and tents make good use of a summertime camp site by the river. Note near Écluse 6, Courenvaux (K50.8), the roof of a small house at the same level as the canal's towpath: this results from the building having stood alongside the old waterway which here was considerably lower than its replacement. At a V-junction (K53.6) the route divides. The left channel is the start of the 1896 extension of the Canal Latéral à la Loire, leading to the celebrated Briare Aqueduct (see Chapter 41). The branch on the right is the final section of the Canal de **Briare** (Canal 'Henry IV') leading directly into the town of Briare and originally connecting with the River Loire until the aqueduct was completed. Long closed to boats, this length with three electrified locks 30.4m x 5.2m was reopened to navigation in 1988 so that the town could benefit from the boom in pleasure boating. Officially maximum draft is said to be 1.2m, but I have had no problems at all with 1.3m. There is a well-planned *port de plaisance*. Worth visiting are the huge and splendid 19th century church decorated with Briare enamel mosaics, which are themselves the subject of a nearby museum; also the local history museum where exhibits include items of inland waterways interest. Should you not wish to divert with your boat down the final three locks, the main street of Briare is within easy walking distance of moorings in the 'New Port' of the Canal Latéral à la Loire at the approach to the aqueduct.

41 Canal Latéral à la Loire

Carte Guide: *Les Canaux du Centre*

From a junction with the Canal de Briare at Bellau, near Briare, to a junction with the Canal du Centre at Digoin, 196.1km with 37 locks. Connections are made (via the Decize Branch and the River Loire) with the Canal du Nivernais; and with the Canal de Roanne à Digoin at Chassenard, near Digoin. There are several short branches once providing links with the Loire: these remain navigable except that in some cases the final lock into the river no longer functions. (1) Châtillon Branch, from the main line to the Loire near Briare, 4.3km with 3 locks. (2) St-Thibault Branch, from St-Satur to the Loire at St-Thibault, 0.7km. (3) Givry-Fourchambault Branch, from the main line to the Loire at Givry, 2.4km, 2 locks. (4) Nevers Branch, from the main line to a terminus near Nevers, 2.8km, 2 locks. (5) Decize Branch, from the main line to a navigable length of the Loire and thence to the Canal du Nivernais, 0.5km, 2 locks. (6) Dompierre Branch, from Abbaye de Sept-Fons to a terminal basin at Dompierre-sur-Besbre, 2.4km.

Yachtsmen passing non-stop through the waterway sometimes complain that it lacks interest. This view is only justified in part, for if you bother to explore nearby towns and navigate the short branches you will discover many fascinating places. There are several features guaranteed to make a real waterways enthusiast quite excited (several large aqueducts, former links with two narrow beam canals, and a magnificent and intact circular lock). A perennial difficulty is that the waterway's name suggests a non-stop prospect of wonderful Loire *châteaux*. These, however, are mainly to be found much further downstream, beyond Orléans. From one end of the canal to the other the Loire is rarely far away, but it really is rather a dull river of great shingle banks and willow trees, navigable by small craft only on a very localised basis. The Canal Latéral à la Loire boasts three important aqueducts, the Briare being quite outstanding, and there are few locks in proportion to its length. It passes through a leading wine production region around Sancerre. Travelling from north to south, the waterway climbs throughout, the descent to the Saône beginning much later as the Canal du Centre heads SE.

An early 20th century view of the splendid Briare Aqueduct which carries the canal across the Loire.

Brief history By 1790 and completion of the Canal du Centre the Bourbonnais route from Seine to Saône was substantially in its present form except for a length of navigable Loire between Briare and Digoin. Beset with problems arising from winter floods and summer droughts, widespread dredging works and introduction of steam haulage failed to produce a reliability similar to that offered by the canals. Accordingly, the Canal de Grande Jonction (or Canal Latéral à la Loire) was constructed between 1827 and 1838, traffic largely ceasing on these reaches of the Loire after that date. Aqueducts were designed to carry the navigation over the River Allier at Le Guétin and the River Loire in Digoin. Perhaps surprisingly, a similar method of spanning the Loire at Briare was not adopted, mainly because of the river's extreme width. Instead, the new canal was excavated along the river bank upstream of Briare and locked into the river to make a crossing on the level near Châtillon-sur-Loire. This procedure brought obvious disadvantages.

This deficiency was to be rectified towards the end of the 19th century when the whole of the Bourbonnais route was extensively rebuilt with larger capacity locks. Some 13.5km of new canal was built from Belleau to L'Étang and a steel-trough aqueduct erected over the river upstream of Briare. At 662.69m, the Briare Aqueduct remains almost certainly the longest such structure in the world. It was opened to navigation in September 1896 and the whole of the new line went into service in October of the following year.

We leave the Canal de Briare at its junction with the 'old route' down to the Loire and shortly the Canal Latéral à la Loire arrives at a basin a little before the great **Briare Aqueduct** (K2.9). Here are moorings (various facilities including water, electricity and fuel) and an embarkation point for passenger craft. Over the years I have several times eaten at the *Le Pont-Canal* restaurant which overlooks the aqueduct's northern approach. Always good, on the most recent occasion it excelled itself for quality and choice of food as well as value. Opposite, on the other side of the canal, a very different attraction is the jumbled yard of a *brocante* merchant, where I once bought a delightfully ornate wood-burning *Petit Godin* stove for one-tenth of its market value. A pumping station was restored as an exhibition hall for the centenary of the aqueduct in 1996. The great aqueduct is most impressive, particularly when illuminated by dozens of original electric lamp standards. Carried on a series of 15 masonry supports at 40m intervals, the ironwork was constructed by the *Société des Établissements Eiffel* (of Tower fame). The twin towpaths are sufficiently wide to accommodate small cars, while it is not unknown for *péniche* skippers to walk alongside, leaving the barge to steer itself. Architectural detail, in an early *Art Nouveau* style, is very fine, especially on the entrance columns, bearing the arms of Nevers, Roanne, Montargis and Paris, together with the names of many towns that can be reached from here by water. One arch was blown up by the French *Résistance* in 1940 and repaired. Four years

Detail at the entrance to the Briare Aqueduct of 1896.

later, a flying bomb tore a hole in the trough. Pairs of stop gates enable the structure to be drained for maintenance via eight sluices. Fairly obviously, the crossing is one-way, priority being given to the boat that gets there first!

The canal now continues to **Châtillon-sur-Loire** (K8.6), a useful shopping and restaurant halt, complete with *port de plaisance*. Note the bathing *plage* ('beach') on the river. Soon, what was the line of the canal until the 1896 aqueduct improvements is seen on the left, at a lower level. The navigational crossing of the Loire was near here; dumb barges relied on the services of a steam tug. Another long section of canal on the river's far bank, linked with the waterway in Briare. The part now alongside us was reopened to navigation in 1998, with historically correct timber gates installed at the original Écluse 40, La Folie, on our left and again at Écluse 39, where old and new lines unite at **L'Étang** (K13.5). Craft drawing no more than 1m can travel on this section as far as the fine Mantelot Basin in Châtillon. A contact telephone number allowing arrangements to be made is signposted at the junction. Basic shops, a flourishing market and a restaurant are in **Beaulieu** (K15.5, good mooring). Now comes a stretch with widely-spaced locks at **Maimbray** (K17.8, restaurant and tiny shop); Écluse

37, **Belleville** (K20.6), where there is good shopping, several restaurants and pleasant overnight moorings; **Sury-près-Léré** (K23.2, garage, baker, restaurant); **Léré**, (K24.8) an attractive, once fortified, village with all basic shops a good *halte nautique*, and a recommended restaurant, *Le Lion d'Or*; Écluse 36, **Houards** (K26.6, grocer); and Écluse 35, Peseau (K30.5). Moor at the bridge in **Les Fouchards** (K32.1) to walk 2.5km to **Cosne-sur-Loire** on the far side of the river. This former river port was a leading centre for casting cannon and anchors until the factory was closed in 1872, its fortunes reduced by the extinction of the Loire barge traffic. There are all urban attractions and a Museum of Loire Navigation. A short distance from the canal in the other direction brings you to a magnificent private *château*.

The next length includes the village of **Bussy** (K32.9) where you can visit a silkworm farm (*Le Jardin de Tisserand*). After Écluse 34, **Bannay** (K34.4), there is *La Buissonnière* restaurant. We are now approaching what is quite possibly the most worthwhile part of the whole canal, where you might well consider spending several days. I once encountered a hire cruiser party who had started at Marseilles-lès-Aubigny and who were more than content to have travelled a mere 34km through 7 locks in order to pass most of their holiday moored up here, by the three towns of Sancerre, St-Thibault and St-Satur. **St-Satur** (K40.6), opposite a junction with a short branch that leads to the Loire, at first appears a little dull and grubby, but it improves on further inspection, with narrow streets of stone houses. There are several shops and restaurants. Situated at a height on a hilltop west of the waterway, **Sancerre** thrives on its famous dry white wine made from Sauvignon grapes, with red and *rosé* from the Pinot Noir. Views of the immense vineyards are obtained from the *Promenade de la Porte César* on the ascent to this town of shady alleys. During the 16th century, the *château* was a Protestant Huguenot fortress: nothing remains but the 14th century *Tour des Fiefs* whose rooftop provides a superb panorama of the Loire Valley. A notable product from nearby **Chavignol** is small round goat cheeses bearing the curious name of *crottins* or 'goat droppings'. Best moorings in the area (but not very suitable for larger craft such as barge conversions) are down the short branch canal and just before the lock which once connected with the Loire. Fuel, water and dry-dock at a boatyard. This is the village of **St-Thibault**, once a river barge port, with a charming row of stone cottages overlooking a sandy river *plage* and swimming area roped off from the sometimes rapid flow of the former navigation. St-Roch (alternative to St Nicolas), patron of local bargemen, is recalled in the name of the church. His feast day is celebrated with a watery carnival on 16 August. His was the name given to a famous floating restaurant based on the steel-sheathed hulls of two rare *berrichon* boats (see Chapter 44) that was moored here on the Loire for many years until it was condemned in 1998 for failing to comply with the latest European electrical regulations. Its owner was so furious with this excess of officialdom that he destroyed the boats before they could be secured for the preservation they so merited. The last river barge worked to here in 1903; now the only sizeable river craft (excepting sand dredgers) is a tripping vessel operating during summer weekends. There is a choice of restaurants in St-Thibault and St-Satur: some offer freshwater fish specialities, such as *Matelote d'Anguille* (eel stewed in wine). Shops in each village with a supermarket by the main line, 700m after the branch.

Ménétréol (K43.1) is a friendly canalside settlement with moorings, limited shopping, two restaurants and, at the time of my last visit, an English-run tea room, just like you might find in Cheltenham. Lying a little away from the canal at the second bridge after Écluse 33 is **Ste-Bouize** (K47.5). It has apparently lost its shops in recent years but still retains a restaurant. As elsewhere on the rural canals of France, wild flowers are abundant together with numerous lizards (some bright green examples are surprisingly big), butterflies and jumping beetles. Scenic interest is somewhat lacking past Écluses 32, **La Grange** (K50) and 31, La Prée (K55). Many of the lock gardens display flowers planted in wheelbarrows, milk churns, defunct dinghies or, when desperate, plastic or concrete containers obtained at garden centres. Around here, adapted wine barrels or old wine presses serve the same purpose. Food shops, restaurant and water point are available at **Herry**, Écluse 30 (K58, wharf with bollards). Unless in a great hurry, you will want to stop in the basin at **La Chapelle Montlinard** (K63.1, boatyard, dry dock – rather shallow, small restaurant) and travel by foot, bike or taxi to **La Charité-sur-Loire**, about 2.5km distant, across the river. This is a UNESCO World Heritage Site and a delightful old town with a 16th century stone bridge of many arches. A great Benedictine priory, of which parts remain, was built in the 11th century; the generosity of the monks gave the place its present name. While held by the Burgundians in 1429, La Charité was unsuccessfully placed under siege by Joan of Arc: this lack of divine aid was a material factor in determining her eventual fate. Useful shops and restaurants enhance a visit to the town.

Villages that not so long ago offered a range of attractions now lack even the most basic shops, although this trend can be reversed and a waterside restaurant suddenly appear. So…expect little of **Argenvières**, Écluse 28 (K67), although you may still find shops in **Beffes**, Écluse 27 (K71.7). Here is a restaurant where the locals prefer to eat. It is situated directly on the waterside near a cement works (K73.6) and was just the sort of establishment most liked by the boat people when they worked through here in large numbers until the 1980s. Named *Au Papillon Rose* it has a deep mooring right outside and a tiny terrace with tables overlooking the canal. It offers no choice of menu and represents good value in a non-*cordon bleu* way. Now follows the once important canal port of **Marseilles-lès-Aubigny** (K74.5), with Écluses 26 and 25 at its centre close to the island-filled River Loire. While there are several food shops, including an excellent butcher, there were no immediately obvious restaurants when I last looked. A little before Écluse 26 is the *L'Équerre* boatyard with a comprehensive range of facilities and services, including dry dock. This was once the junction with the romantic and extensive narrow beam system that was the **Canal de Berry** until its lamented closure in 1955. So efficiently has virtually every trace of the waterway been removed at this point, that it is difficult to believe that the junction was on the right, between the upper lock and the extensive pontoons of the *port de plaisance*. Elsewhere parts of this exciting network are slowly coming back to life. Complete restoration will undoubtedly be achieved one day (see Chapter 44). 8km down the old line towards **Fontblisse** you can find an intact lock with single gates at **Patinges**. Meanwhile, a not very appropriate pastiche of a Berry bascule bridge stands at the centre of a traffic roundabout in Marseilles-lès-Aubigny.

British couple Anita and Richard Watson have a quay on the right at **Les Poids de Fer** (K76) where boats will be looked after for short or long periods and various other services performed. **Cours-les-Barres** (K80.1) has invested in an excellent *halte nautique* with shower/WC block. There is an assortment of friendly shops and a restaurant. Soon follows the 2.4km **Givry-Fourchambault** Branch (K81.5) with Écluse 24 *bis* at the junction and Écluse 24*ter* making a connection with the Loire at the far end, in **Givry**. Twenty-four hours advance notice to navigate this length should be given to the canal authority's St-Satur office.

An agreeable wooded section around Écluse 24, Laubray (K84.1), leads up to a junction (straight ahead, K88.5) with the 3km **Lorrains Branch**, now closed to navigation and used solely as a feeder from the River Allier which flows into the Loire nearby. Until the earlier part of the 20th century boats could use a remarkable circular lock to gain access to the Allier, a lock-free waterway 247km in length. It is well worth investigating (on foot or by bike) the complexities of the Écluse de Lorrains, a beautiful stone structure 32m in diameter, where three sets of gates provided links with the river on two levels, above and below a weir. The ensemble is overlooked by a very fine and large canal engineer's house.

Back on the main line, bear left for the two-rise lock **Le Guétin** staircase (Écluses 21/22, K89.7), followed immediately by a splendid 18-arch aqueduct, 343m long, spanning the Allier. Especially for commercial traffic, this arrangement is a notorious bottleneck, for in the case of a southbound *péniche* the narrow cross-section of the trough prevents refilling the locks until the vessel has completed its river crossing. There is a small shop and two restaurants, the area being something of a tourist magnet, with a pleasant walk down the river to its confluence with the Loire.

From **Plagny** (K97.5, good mooring with shops) the city of **Nevers** can be seen in the distance. Well worth a detour down the 2.9km branch with two mechanised locks. A final lock into the Loire has been obliterated by a multi-tiered municipal swimming pool complex. Good moorings in a large basin, above. Nevers, reached by walking across the river bridge, is the capital of the Nivernais and has a long history. The Duchy of Nevers passed to the Gonzaga family from Mantua in 1565; this explains the strong Italian influence in the Ducal

A laden péniche *in the two-rise locks at Le Guétin.*

Palace. A famous *faïence* industry was introduced from Italy at the same time. The hand-painted enamelled earthenware is widely sold and makes pretty souvenirs. Tours of the oldest pottery, *Bout-du-Monde*, are conducted at 14.50h every Wednesday from the firm's shop near the *Porte-du-Croux*, a magnificent 14th century gateway. The uncorrupted body of Ste-Bernadette of Lourdes (1844–79) can be seen in a glass casket in the chapel of the Convent of St-Gildard, Boulevard Victor-Hugo. She died here and was canonised in 1933. Various objects associated with the saint are preserved in the Convent's museum; these include the chair in which she died, her umbrella and items of hand-knitted underwear (which somehow is not what you expect to find in such a sanctified collection). Many other Nevers buildings deserve a visit, especially the great cathedral of St-Cyr and Ste-Julitte, a huge structure combining architectural styles from the 10th to 16th centuries.

The canal's main line continues through pleasant farming country and takes the boater past a succession of little villages: **Chevenon** (K106.7) – 14th century *château* (private) and some shops; Écluse 20, **Jaugenay** (K110.4); **Uxeloup** (K114.3) with Écluse 19 and the 13th century fortress of *Château de Rosemont* (private) about 2km away in the direction of **Luthenay**. In **Fleury-sur-Loire**, Écluse 18 (K119.4), will be found a good restaurant. **Avril-sur-Loire** (K123.3) has a quay very handy for an *Ecomusée*.

An important junction occurs at **St-Maurice** (K131.7, water point) with the two-lock Decize Branch leading through a former gravel barge basin into the Loire. Crown Blue Line hire cruiser base, with nearby supermarket. By navigating 1.75km down the Loire (follow the chart carefully to avoid shallows) the entrance to the beautiful Canal du Nivernais is reached at **St-Léger-des-Vignes** (see Chapter 46). Until the demise of horse drawn traffic a chain tug hauled dumb craft between the two canals and as recently as the mid-1970s a fee was demanded of all motorised vessels for this unrequired and (by then) unavailable service! Another casualty of the 70s was a pair of donkeys used for pulling sand barges on the river. They were trained to walk in a circle round a lockside bollard, thus halting the boat unaided. In addition to the two canals and the Loire, the Vieille Loire and the River Aron all meet here, with **Decize** mainly situated on an island between the two Loire branches. Most conveniently visited by mooring near the river bridge, it is an agreeable hilly little town with a wide variety of shops, several good restaurants and some gigantic plane trees in the Promenade des Halles. Should you wish your boat to remain on the Canal Latéral à la Loire, you can walk about 2km into Decize from the N478 bridge west of the junction.

Unremarkable country takes the canal through **Les Feuillats** (K135.7, with popular restaurant). Several shops, restaurant and garage lie 1km from the waterway in **Gannay-sur-Loire** (K147.4), Écluse 12, Vanneaux, with Connoisseur hire cruisers (electricity, water, slipway, fuel). Note the remains of an ancient tree, protected by a shingled roof. 900m beyond Écluse 10, Rozière (K154.7), is a useful garage, with most services in **Garnat-sur-Engièvre** (K159.7). **Beaulon**, close to Écluse 8 (K162.5), similarly has a range of shops with *crêperie*, a distinctly odd 19th century church in red brick and pebble-dash and the *Musée Rural de la Sologne Bourbonnais*. Although the Trappist *Abbaye de Sept-Fons* (K170.1) is closed to the public, a slide show on the 18th century building is presented on Sundays and holidays in the afternoon. This is situated near the beginning of a short branch line leading to **Dompierre-sur-Besbre**, with *Locoboat Plaisance* hire base at the terminal basin. A good range of shops and restaurants in the town, with public showers and a swimming pool (about 5 mins' walk). There are lovely old hilly streets and alleys lined with stone houses. A (now derelict) hotel was once occupied by Napoléon I on his return from the Battle of the Nile.

The main line crosses the River Besbre via a four-arched aqueduct at Écluse 6 (K171). **Diou** (K174.7) has several food stores, service station and restaurants, with similar facilities in the charming little town of **Pierrefitte-sur-Loire** (K180.9) which has a splendid 19th century *château*. Here you will find the moorings of Alain and Geneviève Fievet who have operated a barge-based pottery on the French canals since 1980. Their products are most attractive and reasonably priced. Better still, one of their boats, now used as a showroom, is a rare steel-hulled narrow beam *berrichon*. Well worth a visit. **Coulanges** (K185.8) lies beyond Écluse 3, Oddes, and has a *halte nautique*, some shops and restaurant. There are moorings at **Molinet** (K192), shops and a restaurant (about 600m). On the right bank (K194) a T-junction marks the beginning of the Canal de Roanne à Digoin (see Chapter 42).

With memories of vineyards reaching to the horizon around Sancerre, fields ablaze with the brilliant yellow flowers of rape seed in early summer and the broad, deserted reaches of the great River Loire, this efficient and well-engineered canal is now nearing its end. One burst of magnificence remains: the eleven-arched **Digoin** Aqueduct (K195.2) whose 241.57m trough provides a last view of the river that has been our close companion for so long. The town flourishes on a trade of ceramics and *faïence*. Ahead is the Canal du Centre, last link in the chain of waterways between the Seine and the Saône.

42 ~ Canal de Roanne à Digoin

> **Carte Guide:** *Canaux des Centre*
>
> From a junction with the Canal Latéral à la Loire near Digoin to a connection with a short length of the River Loire in Roanne, 55.6km with 10 locks.

Not very many years ago this waterway had become virtually deserted by commercial traffic and was awaiting discovery as a pleasure boating route. Serious consideration was given to its abandonment in 1971. Best regarded as a continuation of the Canal Latéral à la Loire, the navigation climbs up the Loire valley to Roanne, where a junction provides a link with a short section of the river. Its windings along the contours provide tranquil cruising of a kind now virtually undreamed of in England and rarely encountered in France. Although it lacks any outstanding features, it is a remarkably rewarding route to travel with an all-important goal at the terminus: the substantial town of Roanne. Disregarding halts, a one-way trip will take a little over nine hours.

Brief history Designed for barges loading between 100 and 150 tonnes, the canal was built by the Franco-Suisse Co and opened to traffic in 1838. In its original form there were 13 locks, reduced to the present 10 during major improvement works (1895–1903) which made the line available to 38m *péniches*. A notable feature was railway sidings extending out into the large Roanne basin, allowing interchange of goods from barges. 549,000 tonnes of freight were carried in 1936, 300,000 tonnes in 1962 and a mere 19,500 in 1976. By that time barges rarely exceeded two or three each week. Most of the traffic was to steel, cotton and textile mills in Roanne, with coal and other cargoes coming in from the nearby Canal du Centre.

In 1982, after some years of doubt about its future, an association was formed under the presidency of the mayor of Roanne to seek the canal's preservation and development. This received the support of the Loire, Loiret, Saône and Allier *Départementales* authorities. A greater success than once would have been thought possible has followed, with regular traffic generated by hire cruisers, and several congregations of pleasure craft throughout the waterway. Most important of these is the very popular and extensive *port de plaisance* in Roanne, which is widely agreed to offer excellent value among those in search of long term or residential moorings.

After its junction near Digoin (see Chapter 41), the waterway rises through Écluses 10–8. Water point at No 10. The keeper for all three is based at No 9, Beugnets. No 8, **Chassenard** (K3.6), has a daunting rise and fall of 6m. This dates from the 19/20th century rebuilding programme and reduction in the number of chambers. There are a grocer and restaurant in the village. Now follows a 25.7km level past **Bonant** (K13.1) and **Avrilly** (K15.2) to Écluse 7, **Bourg-le-Comte** (K19, small shops and restaurant). Lock 7, at 7.2m rise and fall, is the third deepest Freycinet-sized chamber in the country (after Réchicourt on the Marne au Rhin and Crissey, near Chalon-sur-Saône). Frequently the Loire is within easy reach, as for example in the village of **Chambilly** (K22.5) with a good range of shops including one that sells draught wine (*en vrac*) and a restaurant. The keeper for locks 4–6 can be found at Écluse 5, Montgrailloux. 2.5km across the river lies the medium-sized town of **Marcigny** with a pottery museum in a 15th century tower, many fine half-timbered buildings and a wide range of eating places.

The next pound of 18.2km serves **Artaix** (K26.5, preceded by moorings), **Melay-sur-Loire** (K29.5, some shops) and the former Loire port of **Iguerande** (K34.4), useful for a full range of urban amenities (1.5km) and reached from a bridge by the isolated restaurant *À la Belle Marinière*. Shortly before Écluse 3 is the little town of **Briennon** (K40.9): after Roanne, this is the canal's most useful port of call. Extensive landscaping by the *port de plaisance* assures visitors that Briennon enjoys its canal frontage status. The moorings provide a hire boat base with fuel, repairs and slipway. Shopping and a restaurant with another by the river on the road to nearby **Pouilly-sous-Charlieu**, about 3km east (all shops).

Oudan (K53.5) has a large basin on the right (badly silted at the time of writing). What might appear to be a high-sided metal bridge over the canal is in fact a late 19th century aqueduct. Known as the Pont Pisserot, this carries the diverted River Oudan. Soon afterwards comes the final lock providing access to the vast 800m x 80m **Roanne** basin (K55.6). Visitors' moorings are mainly at the far end, with other areas retained for passenger craft and long-stay boats. A lock allows craft to enter the river, which is navigable for only 1,000m. Although the Loire was once considered to be a transport route for a further 102km *upstream* of Roanne to La Noirie (and *flottable* for another 57km even beyond there), virtually no freight was carried on these upper reaches within a few years of the opening of the Canals Latéral à la Loire and the Roanne à Digoin. It does seem extraordinary that this once great river navigation should have shrunk in less than two centuries from 882km to a mere 138km. Roanne's long history as a port, first on the Loire and later on the canal, assured its place as a successful industrial centre. A wide range of products are made of which the best known is textiles and clothing. The *Musée Joseph-Déchelette* contains a wide assortment of collections with large displays of locally-made *faïence*. The modern desire to show industrial relics to their best advantage is evident in the *Écomusée du Roannais*, established in a former towelling factory. Waterways enthusiasts will wish to visit a small riverside chapel, dedicated in 1630 by the barge community to their patron saint, St Nicolas. What is reputedly one of the best restaurants in France will be found at the *Hôtel des Frères Troisgros*, awarded three rosettes by *Michelin*, meriting the comment: 'Superb food, faultless service, elegant surroundings…One will pay accordingly.' (Place de la Gare, booking essential.)

43 ～ Canal du Centre

Carte Guide: *Canaux des Centre*
From a junction with the Canal Latéral à la Loire at Digoin to the River Saône at Chalon-sur-Saône, 112,1km with 61 locks.

For much of its life the Canal du Centre derived a substantial proportion of commercial traffic from the coal mines at Montceau-les-Mines. Most evidence of mining disappeared in the final decades of the 20th century. Only rarely does the waterway present an industrial face and the abiding impression gained is of a very winding, thickly wooded canal, parts of which are exceptionally beautiful. From Digoin, it runs NE along the valley of the Bourbince, climbing to a summit level at Montchanin. Then comes a rapid descent down the valley of the Dheune, before turning SE towards the Saône. All locks on the southern side of the descent are automated and numbered 1-M onwards from the summit, the M-suffix denoting '*Méditeranée*'. Similarly, those in the opposite direction start with 1-O, the O standing for '*Océan*'. Situated throughout in Burgundy, local restaurant cuisine often reaches high standards. One unusual feature of the canal is that its towpath serves as a public road almost from end to end. Although this arrangement inevitably creates a degree of intrusion from road vehicles, it can be of great use if sending crew ahead by bicycle or motorbike to help set the next lock. The dangers of the system to the barge horses which remained until the late 1960s will be obvious.

Brief history Originally known as the 'Canal du Charollais', this communication was first suggested during the 16th century, under François I, with a detailed plan by Adam de Craponne in the time of Henry II. But no positive action was taken until the Chief Engineer of Burgundy, Emiland-Marie Gauthey, obtained building powers in 1783. His scheme relied on selecting a route which climbed the chain of hills dividing the valleys of the Loire and the Saône with the provision of adequate water supplies at the summit. The first stone was laid by the Prince de Condé in 1784. In spite of the intervention of the Revolution, the works were completed by 1794. Eighty individual locks were built to climb 77.64m from the Loire, followed by a 130.9m descent to the Saône. No fewer than 20 reservoirs provided water at the summit. Exceptional floods on the Loire in 1790 totally wrecked a new port in Digoin and put back completion by many months.

The canal brought new life to the Charollais district and within 20 years of its opening many new villages were thriving along its banks. Writing in 1822, Huerne de Pommeuse looked forward to completion of the Canal Latéral à la Loire, commenting that this development would triple the toll income of the Canal du Centre (*Des Canaux Navigables*). In 1867–69 a feeder to the River Arroux near Digoin was made navigable for narrow *berrichon*-sized barges, and between 1880 and 1900 the whole line was enlarged to Freycinet standards by rebuilding all the locks (which were reduced in number from 81 to 65). Wooden lock gates were replaced by metal ones. During 1936 some 1,622,000 tonnes was carried in 9,825 barge journeys and Montceau-les-Mines became one of 10 inland ports in France to handle over 1 million tonnes, most of it in coal.

At the end of the 1950s about 5km of canal with three locks through the centre of Chalon was replaced by a new cut to the Saône upstream of the town with a single 10.76m lock. Mechanisation of many locks has been carried out, including all of those on the Saône side of the summit, with photo-electric cells detecting boat arrivals. Pleasure craft should remember that the lock sensors were designed for slow-moving *péniches* and stand a better chance of functioning if they are approached slowly.

Digoin, at the junction with the Canal Latéral à la Loire, provides a useful range of shops and restaurants, public moorings with normal facilities including dry dock and a boat yard that can undertake repairs (see also Chapter 41). Until the 1838 completion of the Canal Latéral à la Loire and the Digoin Aqueduct, the Canal du Centre terminated at a basin with a lock providing a link into the River Loire. From 1838–1955 (when it was in-filled), this section was a branch line with three 30m-long locks. I particularly like the early 20th century post office with elaborate clock tower. One fascinating aspect of French canals is that lock equipment was frequently designed specially for a specific waterway: here, gates that remain manually operated are fitted with a heavy bar and chain mechanism at ground level, worked by massive cast iron wheels that are generally painted pea-soup green.

A fixed iron bascule bridge marks the start of a 14km feeder bringing water supplies from the **River Arroux** (K2.5). It was made navigable in 1869, to provide waterway communication between the Schneider ironworks down the arm at Gueugnon and the same company's site on the Canal de Berry at Montluçon. As Schneider already had a fleet of narrow beam *berrichons* it was not considered necessary to widen the line to accept barges of 5m in beam. Instead, the two locks built were 30.7m long x 2.7m wide. Unusually, some 20 passing places were created along the abnormally narrow channel. One notable feature is an iron aqueduct, taking the canal over the River Bourbince. This branch line remained in use by boats until the start of World War II, when trucks took over from the *berrichons*.

Écluses 26–24 intervene before **Paray-le-Monial** (K12.8) whose magnificent triple-towered Romanesque basilica was built by St-Hughes, Bishop of Cluny in 1090–1109. During the late 17th century Marguerite-Marie Alacoque, a nun, witnessed a succession of visions of Christ with his heart exposed, but it was not until the 19th century that the devotion of the Sacred Heart made Paray-le-Monial a town of international pilgrimage. Sister Marguerite-Marie was canonised in 1920 and hotels cater for an influx of religious tourists. There is no shortage of shops stocked with ecclesiastical objects, some of which are quite tasteful. The waterfront of the River Bourbince is memorable. Central (but often roadside) canal moorings are available over a long distance. There is a very convenient supermarket on the northern outskirts.

Alongside the canal at Écluse 19, **Digoine** (K26), is the popular and flower-covered *Auberge de Digoine*, with a huge range of menus. A little further on, note an elegant 18th century *château* (not open to the public) on the site of ancient fortifications. Basic facilities and restaurant are to be found in the small town of **Palinges** (K29.2, diesel). On the bank beyond Écluse 17, **Le Montet** (K31.6), is a waterside bar. All basic shops and several restaurants in **Génelard** (K32.6), with houses grouped around a wide basin (moorings) overlooked by *Le Chaland* café/bar. In this area, there are many rusting road signs '*Attention au Halage*' warning drivers of the long-departed boat horses. Another pretty village

is **Ciry-le-Noble** (K38.6), with several shops and a waterside garage. It is immediately obvious that Écluse 13, **Azy** (K40.3), is in the charge of a former boatman, connections with the *batellerie* including a steel dinghy filled with flowers, flags and clusters of plastic blooms. Just before Écluse 11, Vernois, (K46.5), is the *Pont de Vernes* restaurant. Passing by one lunch time and seeing a dozen lorries parked outside, we made an instant decision to eat ashore, in spite of our onboard meal being nearly prepared. The truck drivers were right: tasty food, keenly priced, a good atmosphere and ample wine included (which worryingly was being consumed by the majority of clients!). Onwards from here, locks are automated. Really delightful hilly pasture land with a wealth of pleasing farm buildings begins to give way to the urbanisation of **Montceau-les-Mines** (K50.2), a town dominated by a power station, occasional glimpses of pit-head winding gear, railway sidings and an impressive coal washing plant served by a huge basin which I was privileged to visit in the company of a canal enthusiast friend who also happened to be a world expert in coal washing techniques. The once intensive industrial activity of this town (which so well illustrated the advantages of freight transport by water) has now all but vanished. Montceau has reinvented itself as a surprisingly pleasant town, its main square lined with plane trees near a canal basin, partly infilled to provide car parking. Both the swing bridge and an exceptionally robust steel bascule bridge have been adapted to open automatically for canal traffic. Immediately beyond is a large, well equipped *port de plaisance*, enabling boaters to take advantage of the most comprehensive shopping stop on the whole canal.

This location was well remembered by that ever-resourceful European boating enthusiast the late Lord Harvington. His large and glorious motor yacht *Melita* was trapped here by an emergency stoppage in the mid-1970s. With an important *rendezvous* elsewhere to collect British Parliamentary guests and no time to seek an alternative route, he secured the services of a crane and low-loader to take his vessel round the obstruction. The crane collapsed and his Lordship became embroiled in a complicated lawsuit; but to his eternal satisfaction he was able to keep the appointment with his friends.

To the north, the industrial **Creusot Basin** used to thrive on coal, steel works, brick fields and potteries. In the middle of the 19th century a navigable branch line, with 1,267m tunnel, served the area via Torcy. A chain of mechanised locks extends from **Blanzy** (K54.9), an attractive place with shops, good moorings and the *Restaurant-Hôtel du Centre*, one of a number of most convenient eating places close to the waterway. As it climbs towards the summit the canal is extremely pleasant and rural. There is a good value *Routiers* restaurant by Écluse 2, Bronots (K60.8), while in a basin beyond Écluse 1, Océan (K62), are moorings with a range of facilities, fuel and hire cruisers. We are now 301m above sea level. The 4km summit level lies in a deep tree-shaded cutting near the iron-working and tile-making town of **Montchanin** (all services, with supermarket within about 500m). With numerous locks coming up, this pound is an obvious overnight stop, but it is best to stay away from the noisy TGV railway bridge a little before the first downhill lock. A much more pleasant mooring can be found well back, alongside a reservoir, one of a series that hold water supplies of 17 million m³.

Locks are renumbered from Écluse 1, Méditerranée (K66), with the first group of four still known as **Les Sept Écluses**, a situation that was changed more than a century ago. A number of the present chambers have a rise and fall greater than 5m and are helpfully equipped with floating bollards. Various small shops, garages and bar/restaurants are scattered throughout this section, all easily identified from a boat. Multi-coloured Burgundian roof tiles of local manufacture decorate houses in the village of **Écuisses** (K68.4). Between Écluses 5 and 6 is a Waterways Museum, featuring the original lock 9 and the 1950-built *péniche Armançon* that finished its freight-carrying life in 1990. The compact living accommodation can be seen, while in the hold are exhibited boat models, historic photographs and artefacts that include barge horse tackle. The Museum's opening times appear to be rather variable: enquire at Écluse 1. The canal now runs in company with the River Dheune past **St-Julien-sur-Dheune** (K69.8, moorings) where there is a recommended lakeside restaurant about 1km from Écluse 9. Here you can find remnants of an old lock chamber. The reaches between locks 8 and 14 are exceedingly pleasant through rolling scenery and poplar trees. Given unlimited time, the opportunities for eating ashore are numerous – there are restaurants at Écluse 8, in the pound 9–10, and at locks 14, 15 and 17, **St-Bérain-sur-Dheune**, K77.3. Good shopping in **St-Léger-sur-Dheune**, with moorings, fuel, repairs, dry dock and hire cruiser base. The bridge reduces headroom to about 3.42m compared with 3.50m elsewhere. Surroundings become more populated, with baker and restaurant at **Dennevy** (K63.8) and a restaurant in **St-Gilles** (K85.9). After Écluse 23 a welcome 11km pound commences with some shops and restaurant 1km away in the pretty village of **Cheilly-les-Marange** (K88.1).

We are now on the southern edge of the famous vineyards of the Côte d'Or with the town of **Santenay** (K89.6) within walking distance of a *halte nautique* on the left. Plenty of opportunities for buying locally-produced wines: almost everyone in the district seems to have connections with the industry. Next comes **Chagny** (K94.9), a slightly gloomy industrial town that provides useful facilities and generally turns out to be rather better than might be supposed from first impressions. It is approached by a concrete aqueduct (dating from about 1970) over a railway. Remains of the former stone aqueduct, basin and canal approaches can be seen. There is a hire boat company and a sizeable basin offering moorings. Surprisingly for this location, in the Place d'Armes, is the renowned, excellent and therefore very expensive *Lameloise* restaurant, an establishment that boasts three *Michelin* rosettes.

Twelve more locks in the final 15.9km to the Saône are generally without facilities as the canal drops downhill on the edges of the Forest of Chagny. Remains of long-disused locks and lengths of old canal can be seen, all resulting from the extensive rebuild carried out late in the 19th century. One good example is between locks 28 and 29. Note the charcoal kiln in a timber yard at the approach to **Le Gauchard**, by Écluse 32 (K103), where there is a choice of two restaurants. The Canal du Centre then passes beneath the A6 *autoroute* and skirts **Chalon-sur-Saône** (see Chapter 48). Pleasure craft are not permitted to enter the truncated remnants of the former canal into the town centre (St-Gobain Branch). On the left, three bridges before the final lock, is a very convenient supermarket with adequate moorings. Écluse 35, **Crissey**, a cavernous chamber with a drop of 10.76m, lowers boats to river level just upstream of the commercial *port fluvial* with extensive barge building/ repair yards. Moorings and all requirements for cruisers are to be found at a marina on the Saône, opposite the town. Larger pleasure craft such as converted barges should be able to find somewhere suitable to lie on the central quay sides.

44 · River Cher and Canal de Berry

Carte Guide: *Pays de la Loire et Le Cher Navigable*

The Cher is navigable at present from the Écluse de Larçay (about 21km upstream of its confluence with the Loire) to Noyers-sur-Cher, junction with a restored portion of the Canal de Berry: 54.4km with 14 locks. Maximum permitted draft is currently 0.8m, although there is normally at least 1.2m depth over lock sills.

A reopened section of the Canal de Berry extends from a junction with the Cher at Noyers-sur-Cher to Selles-sur-Cher: 12.1km with 6 locks. All locks except Noyers are narrow beam, 28.65m x 2.7m. Draft is restricted to 0.8m.

For the time being isolated from the main waterways network, these navigations have been restored from complete dereliction, following establishment of a consortium of local councils established for that purpose in 1985. British-built narrow boats are offered for hire. The available length is sufficient for a leisurely week's exploration, out and back. The rural surroundings are extremely pleasant, while passage through the arches of the magnificent *Château de Chenonceau* is an experience unique in France. Apart from those at each end of the Chenonceau reach, Cher locks are electrified and like several bascule bridges on the Canal de Berry are activated by magnetic cards. These may be purchased for periods ranging upwards from one day, from: Syndicat du Cher Canalisé, Route du Blanc, 41110 St-Aignan, tel 02 54 75 20 96.

To date, access has been limited to official hire craft. Private boats trailed to these waters are likely to be welcomed in the near future when further repair work has been completed. The entire navigation was closed throughout 2003 to enable all the old-style and inconvenient needle weirs to be replaced. Until then, reopening of the waterway after winter floods had to wait until river flow had reached a level where it was safe to reassemble the structures. It is hoped at some time in the future to restore a currently derelict lock at Larçay and construct further new locks, so connecting the Cher's 21km downstream section with the Loire via Tours. Updated information should be sought before planning journeys on the river.

The part of the Canal de Berry so far restored is a tantalising fragment of what must eventually be reinstated as one of the most delightful and romantic canals in Europe. Although only capable of use by craft of similar dimensions to English narrow boats, the waterway certainly has a bright future once restored to the fullest extent and reconnected to the main network at Marseilles-lès-Aubigny on the Canal Latéral à la Loire. To achieve this large and expensive project will obviously take time.

Brief history Once *flottable* by rafts of timber in its upper reaches from the Moulin d'Enchaume to Vierzon (131km), this unlocked part of the Cher was abandoned by commerce after duplication by the Canal de Berry in 1834. A further 70km of Cher with flash locks between Vierzon and Noyers was described in 1888 as 'rarely used' by light drafted barges. 62km with 18 locks, from Noyers to Tours, canalised from 1840–50, was navigated by 65-tonne capacity sailing barges known as *gabares* until the early part of the 20th century. The route was abandoned in 1933.

The Canal de Berry was built as an extensive Y-shaped system, connecting the Canal Latéral à la Loire with the Cher at Noyers. An additional section ran southwards along the valley of the Upper Cher from St-Amand to a terminus at Montluçon. The network totalled 261km with 96 narrow beam locks, 2.7m wide. Constructed 1822–40, the Berry was used by special barges, known as *berrichons*. They were hauled variously by donkeys, mules or the boat people themselves. Most were built in timber with a central stable and very compact living accommodation at the stern. Maximum capacity was about 80 tonnes. In later years, some motorised versions were produced in iron. A handful still exist, converted into houseboats, for pleasure use or as museum exhibits. One especially attractive example works as a fuelling barge in Paris. A leading traffic was cast iron from the Montluçon forges, with coal, pit props, cement, lime, building sand, wines and spirits, slates and tiles.

Enlargement to the Freycinet standard in the 1880s was considered too costly in terms of likely benefits. In spite of growing railway competition and problems with water supplies that necessitated decreasing available draft, the Canal de Berry achieved its best-ever traffic figures in 1905. By 1936, tonnages had slumped to less than 400,000, representing about 5,000 boat journeys. Then followed a further decline, resulting in total abandonment in 1955.

While several km from the Marseilles-lès-Aubigny junction have been completely infilled, the great majority of the Canal de Berry remains intact, although former swing bridges are fixed and lock gates frequently replaced by weirs. Some local clearance and restoration has taken place in recent years and most of the system remains in water. Considerable sums of money have been spent by the Société des Amis du Canal de Berry on restoration of a 17km length with two locks and an aqueduct between St-Amand and Ainey-le-Vieil, while a small canal museum at Reugny near Montluçon exhibits two *berrichons*, various artefacts, documents and photographs. It is open at weekends, July–September, or for parties by arrangement with René Chambareau, an English-speaking enthusiast for all European waterways: Les Vignauds, 18 Rue des Godignons, 03190 Reugny. Among some fine engineering features is the 96m-long Tranchasse aqueduct, near St-Amand. Situated partly in a deeply rural region, bordering the mysterious lakeland wilderness of the Sologne, setting of Alain Fournier's compelling novel *Le Grand Meaulnes*, this is one waterway that definitely deserves to be restored.

RIVER CHER

Navigation currently begins above **Larçay** lock (K0). These lower reaches, while pleasant enough, are rather too close to the large city of Tours to compete with the bucolic charm of the Cher further upstream. The high speed TGV railway (Atlantique) crosses on a bridge (K1.2). **Véretz** (K2.8) with a road bridge offers shopping opportunities. Écluse de Roujoux (K5) is followed by the village of **Azay-sur-Cher** (K6.6). Écluse de **Nitray** (K10.1) is soon succeeded by a bridge (K11.1) from which the small town of **St-Martin-le-Beau** makes a useful halt (about 1.8km). After **Vallet** lock (K14.1), all facilities are available in **Bléré** (K17.7, lock), a pleasant market town with ancient buildings in the main square. Écluse de **Civray** (K21.8) and Écluse de **Chisseaux** (K25.5) have both been rebuilt as 19th century replicas, with wooden gates and balance beams and manually-worked paddles, in recognition of the environmental importance of the intervening pound. A mobile keeper supervises passage through each. One curious stipulation of the restoration scheme was that up to a maximum four boats at a time would be allowed to enter this section, where no mooring is permitted, on the grounds that larger numbers of pleasure craft would detract from the delights of the celebrated **Château de Chenonceau** (K23.9), which spans the river. (It might be regarded as mischievous to question the visual impact of the thousands of trippers who arrive by car and coach every day throughout the summer season and descend on the *château* in swarms.)

Of all French *châteaux*, Chenonceau is perhaps the most memorable, being built bridge-like on six stone arches across the full width of the Cher. The great white and slate-roofed edifice dates from the early 16th century. On the death of its owners it was appropriated by François I, in settlement of debts. Henry II presented it to his mistress, Diane de Poitiers, in 1547 and subsequently it passed to Catherine de Medici. During this period, it became the setting for lavish parties, where arriving guests were welcomed by mermaids emerging from moats alongside the approach avenue while groups of nymphs would appear in the undergrowth. Naval battles were re-enacted on the river, with grand fireworks displays. Restored in the 19th century, it is now the property of the Menier family, and open to the public throughout the year. Among the leading attractions is the Great Gallery, 60m (197ft) long over the river; the formal parkland; the extensive kitchen gardens, filled with flowers as well as vegetables and fruit; and shops both at the *château* and in the nearby small town, where souvenirs include red and white Chenonceau wine.

Chissaux is a riverside resort (most facilities), with moorings and water point, left, upstream of the lock. A charming manor house occupies the site of a fortified mill on an island. Once through the Écluse de **Chissay-en-Touraine** (K28.6), it is possible to moor at Le Port and cross a bridge into the little town (most facilities, including supermarket) where the 15/16th century *château* is flanked by a series of round towers.

After working through a lock (K32.3, *gîte*), it is well worth halting by a trip boat landing stage (left bank, water and electricity) to explore the delightful and busy little town of **Montrichard** (all facilities including several good restaurants). Sites include a dominating medieval castle keep (visits), houses with half-timbered façades and the Caves Monmousseau, 15km of wine cellars housed in former quarries. There are guided tours of the wine-making museum with tasting throughout the summer. Take care to follow the correct channel past several islands above and below Écluse de **Vallagon** (K35.2). Further locks, Vineuil (K37.7) and **Mazelles** (K41.5, *gîte*), are situated in prosperous farming country, renowned for goat cheese production, mushrooms cultivated in caves, asparagus, fruit and vegetables.

A quay, left, downstream of the bridge, is convenient for investigation of the impressive Roman remains (each side of the Cher) at **Thésée** (K42.8), shops and restaurants. Troglodyte dwellings in tufa chalk cliffs. Midway between Écluses **Talufiau** (K45.1) and de la Méchinière (K48.4), there is a useful overnight quay mooring at a campsite, opposite the wine-producing village of **Mareuil-sur-Cher** (access difficult).

St-Aignan (K51.9) is a pretty little town of pale grey stone buildings, rising above the waterway. The lock is built into an arch of the road bridge. Good moorings (water and electricity), upstream, right. There are adequate shops and restaurants, but mostly you will remember how the vast *château*, partly inhabited, partly ruined, towers over everything. Not far beyond, the unnavigable Cher continues, right, while a channel leads through massive steel flood gates to a large basin at the beginning of the Canal de Berry at **Noyers-sur-Cher** (K54.4). Here are extensive floating pontoons in a small port that is base for the charter narrow boats. The whole area is pleasingly landscaped. A wide beam lock enables craft to rise to the level of the canal proper.

CANAL DE BERRY

This is an operational fragment that is more than enough to whet the appetite for the eventual restoration of a fascinating miniature canal network. The reopened length features narrow-beam locks and

Hauling a berrichon *barge on the Canal de Berry. Early 20th century.*

several automated bascule bridges. Starting close to the unnavigable River Cher at **Noyers-sur-Cher**, lock 1 (K0, slipway, shops and restaurants), and after further locks, Hémonnière (K1.6), the delightfully-named Trompe-Souris (Trick-the-Mouse, K2.4) and des Roches (K3.4), the canal emerges into a 7.1km pound, spanned by lifting bridges at **Les Martinières**, **La Rue**, **Trévety** and **Châtillon-sur-Cher** (shopping and restaurants).

A fine stone aqueduct carries the canal over the River Sauldre, shortly before reaching Val de Sauldre lock (K10.5). What is currently the final lock, de **La Thizardière** (K11.3), is soon followed by Le Port de **Selles** (K11.9) with moorings and a turning basin at the present head of navigation. The way ahead is now blocked by a level roadway where originally there had been a bridge. Selles-sur-Cher should be visited for its abbey church of St-Eusice (local history/folklore museum in the cloisters) and the *château*, part 13th century fortress, part Renaissance mansion.

45 ~ River Yonne

> **Carte Guide:** *Yonne or Bourgogne Voies Navigables Tome 1*
> From a junction with the River Seine at Montereau-faut-Yonne to a junction with the Canal du Nivernais at Auxerre, 108km with 26 locks. There is a connection with the Canal de Bourgogne at Laroche Migennes.

Navigation on this splendid river with its succession of wide, sparkling weirs, is far more extensive than is suggested by the data above, for it continues to quite a distance upstream of Auxerre, at which point it has metamorphosed into the Canal du Nivernais. Its chief problems are a number of locks with awkwardly sloping sides and a tendency to flood in the spring. Scenery is consistently good with several towns of outstanding interest and a mass of pleasing villages. As on so many of French waterways today, commercial traffic has become very modest, especially in the upper reaches, except perhaps during late summer and autumn when barges are loaded with grain. Some of the large locks are mechanised. Those that remain manually worked generally feature heavy but highly efficient gate paddles where a lever is moved through 180°.

Brief history Canal promoter the Duc d'Orléans commented in 1740 that there was no river more risky to navigation than the Yonne, cluttered with rocks and suffering for much of the time from a depth of only 30cm. By the late 18th century the section from Auxerre to Montereau was obstructed by 13 sluices built mainly for milling purposes rather than as an aid to traffic. Freight, chiefly log rafts from the Morvan, could manage downstream journeys only with great difficulty. Conventional barges were able to take just one third of their designed load, the contents of three boats being transferred into a single identical craft when they arrived at the Seine.

Frequent early attempts to improve the navigation resulted in the works being washed away in floods and it was only when the Canal du Nivernais and Canal de Bourgogne were fully operational that a rectification of the Yonne was considered imperative. Canalisation started in 1840 when a series of artificial cuts was dug and huge locks built, often with one or both sides of the chamber of sloping stone blocks. Further improvements were carried out late in the 19th century following the Freycinet scheme for nationwide waterway enlargement. Few changes were made in the 20th century, except where alarmingly decayed structures were rebuilt or substantially repaired after World War II. Commercial traffic (only 104,000 tonnes in 1936) has slumped to very light levels except in the reaches nearest the Seine. Pleasure craft, however, increase in numbers every year with much improved facilities for hire cruisers and private motor yachts. In common with many French rivers, the Yonne is prone to flooding in spring and great care is advised when approaching locks situated directly alongside weirs.

Barge activity on the Seine and around its Yonne junction in **Montereau** (K0) can result in most otherwise suitable mooring places being occupied. The best prospect is 50m of pontoons reserved for pleasure craft, convenient for the town's many shops. The Saturday morning street market is very popular. Otherwise, there is not much to interest boating visitors. (See also Chapter 13.) Soon comes an introduction to the river's far from conventional design of locks: **Cannes**, Écluse 17 (K3.3), where each slippery side has a pronounced slope. Twin-screw craft are the most vulnerable, especially when descending. Techniques are to lie alongside a *péniche*, with permission and where space permits; to hold station under power in the centre of the chamber and have crew members hold the boat away from the walls with shafts (not all keepers will permit this); or to lie close to the short vertical section near top or bottom gates, taking care to avoid being lowered onto the sill. One would expect all locks to have been built to a similar design; instead, they vary considerably in length and width. The walls range from both vertical, to one sloping and the other vertical, or sloping on both sides. Restaurant by the lock, with several shops in the nearby village. Initial reaches of the Yonne are a little dull, past gravel workings and large open meadows.

Écluse 16, La Brosse (K7.3), has two sloping sides, as has Écluse 15, **Barbey** (K11.8). If you can select a suitable mooring on the left bank downstream of the road bridge, **Misy-sur-Yonne** (K13.6) is a useful and delightfully situated village halt with basic shops and restaurants including the gastronomic (and expensive) *La Gaule*. Up to now locks have been located directly alongside their foaming weirs, with potentially hazardous approaches when the river is in flood (a not infrequent situation). Écluse 14, **Port-Renard** (K16.2), marks the entry to the first portion of artificial channel, bypassing several loops. Known as the *Dérivation de Courlon*, it has another lock in the middle: Écluse 13, **Vinneuf** (K17.8, both sides sloping). Deep-drafted craft should keep strictly to the centre of the channel when returning to the original river after a guard lock at **Courlon-sur-Yonne** (K20.9). A bridge dated 1868 pin-

A kilometre stone by one of the locks.

points the year when this cut was excavated. The village has a pleasant atmosphere: restaurant and basic shopping. Scenery has by now started to improve greatly.

A long reach runs past groups of islands and the hamlet of **Serbonnes** (K25.9) to Écluse 12, Champfleury (K27.8). The original historic bridge at **Pont-sur-Yonne** (K29.6), of which an Avignon-like portion remains, was demolished in 1952 to facilitate the passage of barges. Old photographs show that its central navigation arch did not exactly constitute a hazard: such action does look very much like official vandalism. There is good shopping and a variety of restaurants. Waterside houses are clustered around an attractive 13th century church. Moorings with bollards are to be found on the right bank downstream of the new bridge, while on the opposite shore is a garage. The popularity of the riverside is evident from a huge caravan park although local pleasure boating – fishing punts and hired pedalos apart – is still surprisingly limited. Further locks intervene: **Villeperrot**, 11 (K33.5, sloping sides) – just upstream is a speciality fish restaurant with landing stage; and **St-Martin**, 10 (K38.4, water point). Boat repairs, moorings, etc, at Evans Marine, by the next bridge.

The broadening of the river by a large island (follow the left channel, the other side has a 1.5m draft limit) marks the approach to **Sens** (K41.2), an ancient city named after a Gallic tribe, the Senons. Modern industrial expansion, waterside grain silos and traffic-filled streets should not be allowed to detract from the many historic sights. Most important is the great Gothic cathedral of St-Étienne, started in the 12th century; among its treasures are vestments of Thomas à Becket of Canterbury. The roof is partly covered with coloured tiles. Architectural delights of another age are to be found in the 19th century cast-iron market hall (near the cathedral), while the *Musée Municipal* contains a very fine collection of Gallo-Roman antiquities and other objects, among them the hat worn by Napoléon at Waterloo. Good moorings will be found on a vertical quay a little downstream of the bridge and not far from the main shopping centre. There is also a small *port de plaisance* with a range of services at the upstream end of the island. Some 20 restaurants in all price brackets are within walking distance of the river. Wooded hills enhance the landscape as we leave the city at Écluse 9, St-Bond (K41.7), sloping sides. Then comes Écluse 8, sloping sides, **Rosoy** (K47.4). Beyond, a small village, upstream, left bank, has moorings for a shop and pair of restaurants. A café/restaurant (lunch only) is all remaining of once more extensive facilities in **Étigny** (K51) set back from the river near a concrete road bridge. **Véron**, left bank, lies about 1km from Étigny bridge and offers a range of basic shops. Écluse 7 (K51.9, sloping sides) shortly appears upstream.

Typically, **Villeneuve-sur-Yonne** (K57.9) is now anything but new. It was created in the 12th century by Louis VII, husband of Eleanor of Aquitaine. Entry by road is through one of two magnificent gateways, the *Porte de Sens* and the *Porte de Joigny*. Further remains of fortifications include a red brick tower at the water's edge, with moorings alongside; otherwise, tie up at a quay below the bridge or by arrangement with a hire cruiser base (water point). Quiet, now that it is by-passed by the N6, Villeneuve is a charming little town of red-roofed buildings, compact and with convenient shops and eating establishments. Anyone who was a schoolboy in the late 1950s/60s cannot fail to select the quayside *Auberge La Lucarne aux Chouettes* (lit. 'The Dormer Window of the Owls', although I am informed that it is best translated as just 'Owls' Nest'). In the early 1990s, this small hotel/restaurant was created and remains closely supervised by film star Leslie Caron (*Gigi, Daddy Long Legs, An American in Paris*). It has an excellent reputation for interesting décor, delicious food and reasonable prices. Locals would probably prefer to forget the mad Dr Petiot, of 56 Rue Carnot, elected Mayor of Villeneuve in 1927 and guillotined on May 25 1946 for mass murder: there were 24 known victims. Moving quickly upstream once more, we pass through Écluse 5, **Armeau** (K63, sloping sides), where

basic shops, restaurant and garage can be found, left bank. A bridge connects **Villevallier** (K66.1) with **St-Julien-du-Sault**. The former has limited shopping, restaurant and garage, while St-Julien has a full range of facilities about 2km from the waterway. Legend tells of St-Julien's horse making a remarkable leap here to escape his enemies. Fine stained glass windows in the 13th century church with a magnificent view onto the river and up to the next lock, Écluse 4, Villevallier (K67.6). This is perhaps the loveliest part of the navigable Yonne. Moor near **Villecien** (K71.6, left bank) where there is a restaurant; alternatively, continue a short distance to the start of the *Dérivation de Joigny* and select a suitable stopping place at Écluse 3, **St-Aubin** (K72.6, sloping sides); the village has a grocer and restaurant. 1.5km SW lies **Cézy**, a charming small town providing several shops and restaurant.

Reaching a cutting depth of 20m in places, the acacia-lined canal rejoins the Yonne by the Épizy guard lock (K75.3), with a navigation authority dry-dock on the right bank. Ahead lies the lovely town of **Joigny** (K76.6) whose medieval street pattern and numerous 15–16th century timber-framed houses arranged around small squares, passages and courtyards are a delight to explore. Rising sharply from the river bank, the heart of Joigny is reached via a pedestrianised shopping street where quality goods range from practical supplies for the galley to appealing souvenirs. St-Jean's church crowns a sea of brown-tiled roofs. Quays provide central moorings, with all normal services and fuelling available at the *Locoboat Plaisance* hire cruiser base, opposite. There is a riverside market every Wednesday and Saturday morning. Garden vegetables were available from the keeper at Écluse 2, Pêchoir (K79.3), during my last visit. In the following reach two small islands mark the site of a former lock and weir with keeper's house. Launching small craft is possible at a slipway near the hamlet of **St-Cydroine**, on the left bank a little downstream of Écluse 1, Épineau (K83.1).

Laroche-St-Cydroine (K84.2) signals the start of the Canal de Bourgogne (see Chapter 47). Depending on their overall dimensions, Saône-bound craft have a choice of turning off here or carrying on to Auxerre, the equally attractive Canal du Nivernais, the Canal Latéral à la Loire and finally the Canal du Centre. Shopping in **Migennes** can be achieved by staying on the Yonne and mooring near the Pont de Laroche railway bridge, rather than turning into the Bourgogne. But if you need fuel, you will have to work through the first Bourgogne lock to reach the Connoisseur hire base. There are several restaurants in the vicinity. Englishman Jo Parfitt operates a boatyard here on the river, specialising in repairs and converted barges.

Numbering of Yonne locks now changes, presumably because the nine uppermost ones were in service first as a link between the Bourgogne and the Nivernais. Thus, Écluse 9, La Gravière (K86.8), appears on the right bank shortly before a confluence with the River Armençon, along whose valley the nearest section of the Bourgogne was dug. Next feature is a road bridge connecting the villages of **Bonnard** (K90.1, restaurant) and **Bassou** (several shops and small restaurant). Soon, the River Serain enters on the left with Écluse 8, Bassou (K90.9), directly ahead. One side is vertical, the other slopes. Keep to the left bank to enter the Gurgy Canal at Écluse 7, Raveuse (K92.6). Much of the canal near Écluse 6, Néron (K94.1), is bordered by security fencing and watch-towers belonging to a military training centre. Eating ashore is possible at an isolated restaurant on the right, a little beyond the next bridge. 4km SW lies **Appoigny**, a small town on the original river with all facilities but probably too far to be of use except in an emergency. The long canal cut ends at a guard lock in **Gurgy** (K97.9), an expanding village that is both useful and attractive. Slipway, quite good shopping and a restaurant. The very tumbledown church incongruously has a small fire station attached to one end.

Fine countryside leads to a bridge of the A6 Paris–Lyon *autoroute* (K99.1), with Écluse 5 (K100.4) on the outskirts of **Montéteau**. All traffic follows a channel on the left of the river, past an island above the lock and up to a bow-girder bridge. Shopping and a garage within close range. Also two restaurants of which *Le Lido* has moorings alongside. Three further locks, Écluse 4, Boisseaux (K102.1), Écluse 3, Dumonts (K103.7) and Écluse 2, l'Ile Brûlée (K105.5), bring the navigator to the edge of the beautiful city of **Auxerre** (locally pronounced 'Ossaire') and junction with the Canal du Nivernais (K108). After the final lock, Écluse de la Chainette (water point), the flying buttresses of St-Étienne's Gothic cathedral come into view with a superb waterfront of elegant buildings lining lower ground on the right bank of the Yonne. Extensive deep moorings can be found here, along the Quai de la Marine, or on the left shore in the *port de plaisance*. Facilities include water, electricity, showers, diesel fuel and a slipway. Details from the port office. There are also hire craft and a tourist office. Auxerre was the first major French city I arrived at by water, during an autumn cruise in 1968. Since then, it has become firmly established as one of the country's most pleasant ports of call and every keen inland navigator will eventually moor here and admire the memorable view. Recent years have seen much progress in revealing and restoring scores of wonderful timber-framed buildings. The city centre is reached via a series of sharply rising streets leading to pedestrian shopping areas where an outstanding feature is the 15th century tower embellished with a richly decorated 17th century clock. Little remains of fortification walls begun in the 12th century and replaced in the 18th and 19th by tree-lined *boulevards*. Auxerre's position close to the A6 *autoroute* makes it an ideal overnight stop for British car travellers heading for the south. One hotel that provided my party with a regular welcome over many years is the *Normandie* in the Boulevard Vauban; there is a restaurant almost next door. Statues of St Nicolas are not infrequent by French waterways, for he is the boat people's patron: none is finer than the painted stone effigy on the wall of a building in a small square upstream of the Pont Jean Moreau.

Auxerre is as good a place as any to sample Burgundian cuisine and the products of the nearby Chablis vineyards. Among a wide choice of restaurants one of the best (although expensive) is *Le Maxime* on the Quai de la Marine. The area's specialities include chocolate *escargots* and real ones cooked in wine *matelotes* (freshwater fish stews), crayfish in wine, and (originally from Joigny) saddle of veal.

St Nicolas, patron saint of the barge people, on a quayside building at Auxerre.

46 ~ Canal du Nivernais

Carte Guide: *Bourgogne Tome 1*
From a junction with the River Yonne at Auxerre to a junction with the Loire at St-Léger-des-Vignes, providing a connection with the Canal Latéral à la Loire at Decize: 174.1km with 110 locks (4 are stop locks) and 3 tunnels. A 3.9km branch with 2 locks links the main line near Écluse 70, St-Aignan, with Vermenton.

One of the loveliest canals in the whole of France, the waterway climbs to a watershed between the Loire and the Yonne, passing through a thickly wooded area of the Morvan. Quite heavily locked and with a central section admitting craft smaller than normal Freycinet navigations, it is now unused by commercial traffic but has seen a dramatic increase in pleasure boat use since the mid-1970s. There are few large towns but numerous delightful villages, thus sustaining an interest that is difficult to match elsewhere. North of the summit level at Baye its course lies in the valley of the Yonne, the river serving as a navigation channel for most of the 60km between Auxerre and Clamecy. Having crossed the divide, it descends to the Loire down the valley of the Aron.

While not the quickest of the four routes between Paris and the Seine, the Nivernais is certainly the most charming. The French network features rather few circular routes which can be travelled within a reasonably short time: but that comprising the Yonne, Nivernais, Latéral à la Loire, Briare, Loing and a short length of the Seine can be tackled in an energetic fortnight (but three weeks would be preferable), requiring about 116 cruising hours. Because my first French boating trip followed this course, starting and finishing on the Nivernais in the autumnal mists of 1968, I have a special affection for the area. By the early 1990s, some alarm was being expressed at low levels of maintenance, for the waterway is under local rather than national control. However, in 1999, I navigated the whole waterway with a boat drawing 1.3m and seldom touched the bottom even in the allegedly shallowest sections south of the summit level.

A Nivernais tradition was to plant the banks with varieties of fruit and nut tree, the crop helping to defray running expenses, with produce from seven trees each side of the locks belonging to the keepers. Lock gate and paddle gear is of extraordinary variety: wooden balance beams in one place with iron rods elsewhere; paddles that must be wound up to be closed! It is claimed that the tireless efforts of the *Résistance* during World War II to sabotage equipment and so frustrate movement of goods was in part responsible for this curious mixture. In recent years many young people have been taken on as lock keepers, attracted by the rural life and delights of a pretty house and garden. Almost without exception they are friendly and helpful, often augmenting their slender earnings by selling vegetables, eggs and other produce. Students are widely used to help out at times of peak use.

With the Nivernais situated in western Burgundy, a certain amount of gastronomy is to be expected. Specialities of the Morvan include *cul de veau à la Clamecyçoise* (cold chump end of veal with vegetables); *jambon à la Morvandelle* (ham braised in wine and served with cream sauce); *potée Morvandelle* (a thick meat and vegetable soup); *fricassée Morvandelle* (stew of liver, ox tripe and blood); *galettes* (open pastry tarts, both sweet and savoury), and *macarons*.

Brief history The idea of connecting the Loire and Yonne across the Nivernais was first proposed in 1708 when it was suggested that the Canal de Cosne should follow the valleys of the Nohain and the Druyes, with a junction at Surgy near Coulanges-sur-Yonne. There was prolonged opposition from the Duc d'Orléans, proprietor of the Canal du Loing, and the scheme eventually foundered. Jean de Gert's early 17th century plan under Louis XIII had envisaged a link up the valley of the Aron from the Loire at Decize to the Beuvron and thence to the Yonne at Clamecy. In modified form, this was the line chosen by Mannassier on which construction started in 1785. From the start it was considered inferior to the Bourbonnais route via the Briare and Loing on account of the very winding and shallow navigation of the Yonne, the large number of locks and the cost and inconvenience of the tunnels and cuttings at La Collancelle summit. The canal was built over an exceptionally long period, not being open throughout until 1842.

A mainstay of the freight carried was pit-props to the coalfields of the North, together with timber and firewood for Paris. *Flottage*, a system of floating logs from the Morvan forests down various streams and into the Yonne where they were assembled into giant rafts, had been practised since the 16th century. This traffic continued after completion of the Nivernais but had to be declared illegal in 1881 on account of the disruption it created. Thereafter, all timber was required to be carried aboard barges. The last free-floating logs (as opposed to those formed into rafts) nevertheless were to leave Clamecy as late as 1927. 58km of the central part of the canal between Sardy and Cercy-la-Tour remained with locks 30m long instead of the general Freycinet 38.5m standard. By 1936 there were only 1,932 barge journeys with a total of 208,000 tonnes. Fewer than 50 craft of all types a year made a passage in the early 1950s and the threat of closure was very real. It was difficult to justify keeping paid keepers at every lock, in contact with each other by an antiquated internal telephone system that was to survive for a further decade.

At this period, uneconomic French waterways were regularly abandoned with scant public discussion. One key factor in saving this ravishing navigation for posterity was Roger Pilkington's voyage in his motor yacht *Commodore*, which is so beautifully described in *Small Boat Through France* (1964). But the decisive event that determined the canal's future was brought about by waterways enthusiast Pierre-Paul Zivy, an Anglophile who had cruised rivers and canals in England and established the first inland hire cruiser fleet in France on the Marne. Having obtained assurances that neglected maintenance would be tackled by the authorities, he set up his Saint-Line cruiser base at the Baye summit level in 1964 and campaigned for the threatened section to be transferred to the local *Département*. This act was astonishingly courageous and foresighted. It would be another five years before the country's second such boat operation appeared on the Canal du Midi. There are now many holiday boat firms and hotel barges using the Nivernais, not forgetting private craft. The canal has become one of the most popular routes in the network and any notion of it being closed is quite unthinkable.

In Britain, many waterways were saved from closure or restored from dereliction by enthusiastic volunteer societies. Strangely, France has generally failed to adopt such an approach with the notable exception of the *Amis du Canal du Nivernais* (tel 03 86 53 83 10). Boat rallies and other events are staged with the object of safeguarding the waterway's future.

Once you can tear yourself away from the delights of **Auxerre** (see Chapter 45), association with the River Yonne is by no means finished, as the Canal du Nivernais uses its course for many more km. The navigation undergoes its name-change above the Pont Paul-Bert and soon enters its first lock, Écluse 81, Batardeau (K0.4). Rudimentary weirs built of clusters of 'needles' were designed to be dismantled for the passage of timber rafts and release of flood water. **Augy** (K5.5) lies to the left of a lock cut (Écluse 79), but access to the limited shops is not easy. Fishing punts, summer houses by the water and a concrete bridge of lattice construction are features of the pleasant village of **Vaux** (K6.2), a waterside resort beyond Écluse 78,

with useful food shopping, moorings and an unusually good restaurant (*À la Petite Auberge*).

Écluses 77, Toussac (K7.9), and Bélombre, 76, are linked by a long mole, dividing the navigation from the natural river. On the left bank **Champs-sur-Yonne** (K9.1) has a wide selection of shops and two restaurants, with moorings above the lock. From the Middle Ages onwards, the wines of the Auxerre region were widely appreciated. During the 19th century, the vines were all but wiped out by phylloxera; restocking with disease-free stock from the USA recovered the situation. The champagne-type *Crémant de Bourgogne* can be purchased at cellars in **Bailly** (K10.6), beyond Écluse 75. It is also a good point from which to visit the ancient wine-making town of **St-Bris-le-Vineux**, 5km. Here a great network of medieval cellars extends under the town (visits possible). Red, white and *rosé* wines are produced. Half-timbered and stone buildings, many of them centuries old, date from when this was an important fortified market centre. **Vincelles** (K13.5, shopping, fuel and mooring) and **Vincelottes** (recommended restaurant – *Auberge des Tilleuls*) face each other across the river between Écluses 74 and 73. The latter has a splendid 13th century cellar where wine was once loaded into barges for the journey to Paris. Another delightful Burgundian wine village is **Irancy**, 4.5km NE, surrounded by vines and fruit trees (shops, no restaurant).

Rocky ridges cultivated with vineyards rise to the left of the valley. Note on this side the disused lock on a short branch originally providing a navigable connection between canal and the Yonne. See also the remains of some derelict wooden barges. Next is **Cravant** (K18.4, shops and garage), with a basin. This was the site of a battle between the victorious Anglo-Burgundian forces and the King of France in 1423. The following lock, Écluse 71, du Maunoir (K19.7), stands by a lovely old house in stone with a red tiled roof. 3.9km of branch canal leads via two locks to Vermenton. This makes a very agreeable diversion, especially as the keeper of the first lock, La Noue, is French waterways writer, historian and illustrator Charles Berg. Regular readers of *Fluvial* magazine will know that he is a fund of information as well as having a penchant for populating his line drawings with scantily-clad nymphets. **Accolay** is pleasantly situated where the canal comes close to the River Cure. Moorings are readily found and there are useful shops and two restaurants. Beyond is Accolay lock which is soon followed by a flood gate leading to the large terminal basin on the outskirts of **Vermenton**. This broad reach is actually an impounded section of the Cure. Moorings can become crowded, as this is also home to the hire firm, Burgundy Cruisers. The medium-sized town is rather special with good shops and restaurants, many delightful buildings and a really pleasant *Parc Municipal des Iles*, with streams, bridges and waterfalls. Vermenton was an ancient settlement on the Roman route between Rome and Boulogne. Wines of the locality are remembered in the old saying with its built-in pun on the town's name: '*Chablis, Cravant, St-Bris, Irancy Vermenton vous font la trogne rouge et non pas vert menton*', or '…Vermenton may give you a red and boozy face, but they won't leave you with a green chin'.

As we continue up the main line, almost every village in the green and peaceful river landscape is worth exploration and most have at least basic shops. Sometimes care is required to locate lock cut entrances which are not always well indicated: there are several opportunities for taking a wrong turning into unnavigable weir streams. **Mailly-la-Ville** (K28.7) provides shops and a water point. This is a convenient place from which to travel 8km east to the valley of the River Cure, a fast-flowing stream once used for the *flottage* of timber and now favoured by canoeists. A system of underground caverns, *La Grand Grotte d'Arcy-sur-Cure*, contains a subterranean lake and fantastic geological formations. Visits throughout the summer. The canal describes a huge horseshoe bend beneath the heights of **Mailly-le-Château** (K32.4). Near the bridge in the lower town is a restaurant, while a steep ascent by road or an even steeper climb up a rocky path with steps leads to a terrace by the 19th century *château* with a superb view down to the bosky valley of the Yonne (some shopping). Upstream lies the most impressive section of the entire river: the cliffs of **Le Saussois** above guard lock 59b (K36.2). Formed from hard chalk, they reach a height of 50m and are a popular

At the towering cliffs of Le Saussois, the waterway uses the course of the River Yonne.

training area for mountaineers. A track provides a less energetic method of reaching the top. Moorings are in demand on the river directly below where there is a bar/restaurant. I prefer to anchor off the opposite bank getting the benefit of the best possible view in this dramatic setting. The village of **Merry-sur-Yonne** can be approached via the bridge at Écluse 59b.

The first indication of **Châtel-Censoir** (K41.5) is its small country railway station. Elegant stone houses are clustered on a hill by the fascinating church of St-Potentian, parts of which date from the 11th century. Pontoon moorings. There is a surprisingly good choice of shops and restaurants and a range of services at a boatyard. By now, the majority of the navigation channel is composed of artificial cut, although the Yonne continues to act as a feeder for a long distance. Earlier open reaches come to an end at **Lucy-sur-Yonne** (K48, small restaurant) notable for the 15th century *Château de Faulin*, which has effectively become little more than an unusually splendid farmhouse. At Écluse 55, Lucy, we once spotted a sign *'Defence à ramasser les escargots'* ('collecting snails is forbidden'); not withstanding, several shifty characters with plastic bags were busily beating the undergrowth with sticks in search of these prized constituents of Burgundian cuisine. Doubtless the haul was destined for a local restaurant.

From **Coulanges-sur-Yonne** (K51.3), where garage and a selection of shops and restaurants are within about 15 minutes walk of the basin, it is around 20km to **Vézelay**, an historic hilltop town in the Cure valley. Ste-Madeleine's great basilica is all that remains of a monastic foundation of the 9th century. Allowed to decay after the Revolution, it was restored by the ever-busy Viollet-le-Duc between 1840 and 1859. Near Coulangnes are the remains of Gallo-Roman baths at **Fouilles des Fontaines Salées**, with traces of a rather earlier Mesolithic camp dating from 10,000–3,000BC, where 19 wooden dug-out boats have been discovered.

Further chalk cliffs are passed beyond **Surgy** (K53, some shops and two restaurants), soon followed by guard lock 51, Basseville, leading to a level crossing of the Yonne, with a weir on the right. Such an arrangement can become navigationally dangerous when there is flood water. Ahead, craft must immediately pass out of the river into Écluse 50 (K55.6, small restaurant), a manoeuvre where horse-drawn barges required help from winches when there was a strong river flow. At the approach to the sizeable town of **Clamecy** (K59.7), 1.5km of canal together with locks 48 and 47b has been abandoned. Instead, all craft now turn into a pleasantly wooded reach of the Yonne. There are normally adequate moorings, even though Clamecy is a popular port of call, being the only substantial town on the

canal between Auxerre and Decize. All facilities are available, with a water point by Écluse 47, Les Jeux. Two restaurants I can particularly recommend are *La Boule d'Or* (its dining room was once the nave of the original church of *Notre Dame de Bethléem*) and the *Hostellerie de la Poste*. Narrow and hilly streets are lined with ancient buildings. For five centuries the exiled Bishops of Bethlehem lived here. A bronze statue by the river commemorates Jean Rouvet, who founded the local *flottage* industry in 1549. Logs from the Morvan forests were floated down streams and rivers to be assembled into rafts up to 72m long for transport via the Yonne and the Seine to Paris. Clamecy was the leading centre of this activity, which reached its peak early in the 19th century when an annual 70,000 tonnes of timber took about nine days to reach the capital. The traffic continued until 1927. When the river was filled with logs from bank to bank freight barges were seriously delayed. The history and lore of *flottage* is fully recorded in several publications on sale in the town and a fascinating collection of associated relics and ephemera is preserved in a museum in the former Hôtel de Bellegard. At the centre of the *Pont de Bethléem* a stone image of a *flotteur* with *picot* (hooked shaft for dragging logs) is another reminder of this activity. Timber trades continue to flourish in the district and it is still possible to encounter charcoal burners in woodland glades.

Onwards from here, the narrowing River Yonne adopts a subservient rôle as feeder to the canal with several disused locks indicating one-time connections between the two. Upstream of Clamecy the Canal du Nivernais is bordered by a cliff covered with huge beech trees. **Chevroches** (K64.2), a hilltop village rising above the woods between Écluses 45, **Armes** (basic shops), and 44, Chantenot, is followed by lines of old fruit trees laden with mistletoe. There are plans to construct an extensive new pleasure port at Chevroches with moorings, restaurant, boutique and harbour master's office. Anticipated opening date was spring 2005. Meanwhile, beware very variable water levels in the Chevroches pound, where the canal bed suffers from chronic leaks. Moored boats may become grounded overnight. This is unfortunate in view of the recently constructed quay which otherwise offers a pretty halt. The first in a series of bascule or swing bridges over the next 23km is just outside **Villiers-sur-Yonne** (K69.5); this example is generally left open; others are either the responsibility of the nearest lock keeper or alternatively are worked by boaters. For shops and restaurants you have to travel 2.5km NE to **Dorney**. Nearby is a Merovingian burial place where tools, jewels and arms are on show. The bridge before Écluse 40 (K72) carries a road into **Brèves**, a peaceful village on the banks of the Yonne. Lovers of French *brocante* should stop at **Anois** (K73.9) where an old chapel is packed to the rafters with an assortment junk among which there *might* just be a few treasures. The village also has a small grocers.

Tannay, 2km west and uphill of a two-rise lock (Nos 39/38, K76), is a good shopping centre with supermarket providing an opportunity for sampling local white wines. At **Tannay Gare/Cuzy** (K78.3) Crown Blue Line has a hire boat base with modern, elegant buildings (moorings and most services). Further lift bridges follow, the first of which stands by a delightful old house with circular tower. Lying beyond the Yonne, **Monceaux-le-Comte** (K83.5) is a lovely village with a few shops. Two more bascule bridges are encountered at the farming settlement of Dirol (K84.7), a place of vegetable gardens, walnut trees and stone buildings with brown speckled roofs.

Close to Écluse 31, Gravier (K89.5), is **Marigny-sur-Yonne**: no shops. A drawbridge guards the approach to a wide basin with moorings at **Chitry-les-Mines** (K92.3). Silver and lead were exploited here centuries ago. English marine engineer Ted Johnson runs Marine Diesel, will repair all makes of engine and specialises in British Leylands. His experience of French waterways dates back to the very beginnings of hire craft in 1959 when he was involved with the formation of Pierre Zivy's Saint Line. There are no shops here, but, by appointment, visits may be made to the impressive 4-towered 18th century *château*, owned by a noble French family. It was a centre of *Résistance* activity during World War II. At the top of the two-rise Écluses 26/25, Eugny (94.3), the N77 road leads 3km to **Corbigny**. This once fortified town is well known for its cattle market and is a leading shopping centre for this part of the Morvan. The narrow La Chaise one-way section of canal runs to Écluse 24, Yonne.

Locks sharply increase in frequency as the waterway climbs through delightful woodland to its summit: Nos 22–1 occur within the space of 6km, an obvious situation for sending at least one person ahead on foot or by bike to help prepare the flight. The long wooden building with a veranda by Écluse 22, Surpaillis (K97.5), housed German refugees in the First World War and French refugees in the Second. Avoid mooring near the noisy and dusty neighbourhood of Écluse 21, Picampoix: it is dominated by a porphyry rock crushing works. Not surprisingly, the lock cottage is untenanted. Features of this length include a lovely 15th century *château* in **Marcilly** beyond the river from the road bridge between Écluses 22 and 21; and a hire boat base near Écluse 16 (K100.5, water point) with bar/grocer/restaurant in nearby **Sardy-les-Épiry**.

These Sardy locks are quite delightful. I always regard working through such a flight as an enjoyable experience if taken at a reasonable speed, making the best use of the boat's crew. It is an opportunity for walking or riding up the towpath; chatting to other boaters and practising your French on the generally patient lock keepers. Working such a concentration of locks should be regarded as a pleasurable achievement, not an activity to be dreaded! When reaching Écluse 4, Roche (K103.3), at the hamlet of **Port-Brûlé**, pause to remember the great Pierre-Paul Zivy (1929–2001) who owned this delightful lock cottage during his final years. His silver portrait bust, with him holding a Saint Line cruiser, stands on a rock plinth in the garden, overlooking the ravishing canal which he saved from certain closure.

On reaching the summit level, be sure to tell the keeper whether you intend to moor here or wish to pass directly through the three tunnels to the first downhill lock at Baye (K108.2). Most of this length is subject to one-way working, controlled by lights. Water supplies for the northern descent towards the Yonne are brought from a reservoir to the east: the **Lac de Pannesière-Chaumard**, with more than 20km of feeder channel and an impressive aqueduct over the Yonne at **Montreuillon**. It is uncertain if the authorities would approve, but I know of one enthusiast who came downstream on the *rigole* in a dinghy only a little narrower than the channel at speeds of between 2 and 6kph. The miniature waterway is equipped with tunnels and many small aqueducts and passes through exciting rocky terrain.

The summit of the Canal du Nivernais combines magic with atmosphere. It vividly recalls Thomas Telford's deep and rocky cuttings on the Shropshire Union Canal in England. Of the two, the Nivernais is probably the more impressive. A magnificent motorised and unique Nivernais ex-freight barge named *Aster* frequents these waters with loads of passengers. She was one of a group of four wooden boats built in 1950 and was briefly horse drawn. Soon, an engine was added, driving a propeller attached to the huge rudder. *Aster* remained in trade until 1974. Many of her timbers were extensively renewed at a cost of about £200,000 in 1998. Seeing her navigate the summit emphasises just how narrow is this wonder of canal engineering. In addition to her massive tiller-worked rudder at the stern, the helmsman controls ropes laid the length of the deck to a bow rudder. Trees and trailing creepers have colonised the rocky banks, Amazonian fashion, and there are waterfalls. The canal burrows underground via three tunnels near the village of **La Collancelle**: Breuilles (212m), Mouas (268m) and

La Collancelle (758m). At several points, the passage is so restricted that barges approaching the maximum dimensions of the locks can get through only with difficulty. At the far end you enter a broad pool with a hire cruiser base, providing slipway, water, fuel and electricity. Ahead, the extensive **Étang de Baye**, covering 100 hectares, is connected to the canal via a guard lock, although much of the lake is reserved for sailing and fishing. Northwards, the **Étang de Vaux** (198 hectares) brings water supplies to the southern part of the navigation. Attractive moorings are to be found all along a stone dyke that divides the Baye lake from the canal. Restaurant and water point close to Écluse 1, Baye, start of the descent towards the Loire.

There are two locks at the village of **Bazolles** (K110.5, basic shopping), followed by a cluster in **Chavance** (K115.6). These comprise a three-rise staircase (Écluses 4/5/6, basic restaurant), a large basin and then the two-rise staircase (Écluses 7/8). It is customary to fill the chambers without closing the intermediate gates, causing impressive turbulence. The same applies at the two-rise **Marré** (Écluses 7/8, K117, restaurant and pool). Once, when working through here, I helped the keeper remove the bloated corpse of a large fish from the lock chamber. 'Can you eat that fish, monsieur?' I asked him. Horror-struck, he replied that the fish had been dead for weeks! 'Non, monsieur', I explained. 'Can you eat that variety of fish?' He gave me a withering look and then added gravely: 'In France, we eat *all* fish!' On another occasion, a friend found himself in identical circumstances. Indicating a rotting fish (and purely in the interest of polite conversation), he observed to the keeper: 'La pollution, monsieur?' 'Non, monsieur', came the answer. 'C'est un poisson!'

Several locks intervene before **Châtillon-en-Bazois** (K123), an atmospheric little town (shops, including a convenient supermarket and restaurants). There are towpath moorings, left, opposite the towers of the 13/15/17th century *château*, illuminated at night. Vestiges of ancient stonework suggest that the canal occupies the site of its moat. Beyond, is a right-angled turn with a complete lack of visibility: extreme caution is necessary, coupled with use of the horn. Locks 14 and 15 stand at each end of a long basin (hire cruisers and facilities), all overlooked by a different elevation of the same *château* encountered earlier. In closely following the course of the River Aron, the canal winds very considerably for the next 15km. Take care to keep close to the towpath and so avoid shallows in a river section above guard lock Cœuillon (K125). The bridge at Pont (K126.6) provides access to the village of **Alluy** (1.5km, a few shops and restaurant). Alternatively, try the unusual shop/restaurant in **Biches**, reached from a

bridge (K132.2, *relais de plaisance*) in the middle of the pound between Écluses 18, **Meulot**, and 19, Villard. Close to Écluse 21, **Fleury** (K136), is a restaurant, campsite and a delightful feature in the form of a natural swimming pool, using an impounded length of the clear waters of the Aron. It has convenient moorings right alongside, where we once spent an idyllic midsummer afternoon cooling off. It was popular that day with locals, but there was ample space for everyone. Unlike many rivery swimming places, it is neither muddy or weedy. A real bonus in hot weather.

After Écluse 24, the Aron is entered once more. Just before guard lock 25, **Pann. eçot** (K144.5), turn left by a small island for a well-equipped and attractive *port de plaisance* with various facilities at the adjoining camp site. In spite of warnings to the contrary, I have had no difficulty in this basin with a 1.3m draft. Additional berthing space is available on the downstream side of the lock (water point). Pann.eçot makes a really tranquil overnight halt, although the village only offers a dark little bar which also acts as a *depôt de pain*. A full range of shops will be found in **Moulins-Engilbert**, 5km NE, where there are remains of a *château* built by the Comtes de Nevers. An excursion well worth taking is to travel 4km NE, either from the Pont des Hâtes de Scia (K148.1) or Écluse 27, **Moulin d'Isenay** (K150.5). You will arrive in the little town of **Vandenesse** (basic shopping) and discover a really huge *château* with many towers dating from 1475. The next place of interest is **Cercy-la-Tour** (K158.2, shops and restaurants), a charming town rising above a navigable length of river on which a 'beach' has been established. Pontoon moorings with water, electricity and slipway with nearby camp site. A large church square provides a view down to the navigation. Little remains of onetime fortifications, but it is claimed that an underground passage rises from the river to the *Café de la Tour* (currently closed), built as an hotel in 1786 and now mostly divided into apartments. Here we were once served coffee in cups decorated with lurid fruit designs, sufficiently unusual to merit comment. 'We have had them these last thirty years', replied Madame, adding with barely a hint of menace: 'and not a single one has ever been broken!' A white statue of the Madonna, considerably larger than life-size, is lit up by night. The Rivers Alène and Canne now add their waters to that of the Aron. The *Hôtel Val d'Aron* is recommended for sophisticated cuisine and its swimming pool. Cercy provides the best railway service on this part of the Nivernais, with connections to Nevers, Paris and Dijon.

Several interesting features are passed as the canal nears its end: a pair of old towers by the towpath at **Le Chantelier** (K163.6); the village of **Verneuil** (12th century church with wall paintings and 15th century private *château*) lies 2km NW of a bridge at K164.2; and a small aqueduct over the River Andarge above Écluse 32, de Roche (K165.9). **Champvert** (K170.5), beyond Écluse 33, perfectly epitomises the idyllic scenery in this agreeable valley. It has a church with a twisted spire, an assortment of shops and bars and a garage. The Port de la Copine (K171.1), right bank, was recently a boatyard and may well become one again. Surroundings become slightly urban at the outskirts of **St-Léger-des-Vignes**, where a useful stop can be made below Écluse 34, Vauzelles (K172.2, garage and supermarket on the left). Dry dock and quayside moorings above Écluse 35, Loire. St-Léger (K174) extends along the right bank above a junction with a short navigable section of the Loire. Good shopping, water and fuel are available nearby. Due north, the curiously-named town of **La Machine** (suggesting all kinds of possibilities) is disappointingly nothing more exciting than a former coal mining district. As we arrive at the river, note the ancient tug *Ampère*, preserved ashore as an historic artefact. It once hauled horse boats along the Loire, where that river serves as the link between the Nivernais and the Canal Latéral à la Loire. For details of this passage past **Decize** (all facilities), see Chapter 41.

47 Canal de Bourgogne

Carte Guide: *Voies Navigables de Bourgogne*
From Laroche-Mignennes, junction with the River Yonne, to St-Jean-de-Losne, junction with the River Saône. 242km with 189 locks. A 3,350m summit level tunnel at Pouilly-en-Auxois is worked one-way under the control of keepers.

Of four available canal routes between the Seine and the Mediterranean, the Bourgogne is the shortest. However, as it is more heavily locked than the Bourbonnais line via the Canal de Briare, it does not provide the quickest journey. But, for scenery, historical interest, gastronomy and all that is best in French waterway cruising, the Bourgogne is difficult to better. The 50km in the Ouche valley from the summit to Dijon is quite outstanding.

Perhaps because this canal comprises an almost unrelenting series of locks it has not developed into as popular a cruising route as some other navigations. Taken at a gentle pace, locks are enjoyable and a boating holiday need not be judged a success merely because a great distance has been travelled. Ideally, at least three weeks should be allocated to an end-to-end passage of

the Bourgogne. But it has to be admitted that there are certain yachtsmen and boat delivery crews who have raced from the Channel to the Mediterranean in that time!

Running SE from the Yonne, the canal follows the windings of the River Armançon towards the Pouilly-en-Auxois summit level, flanked by the Langres Plateau to the east and the Morvan Regional Park to the SW. After the watershed, the navigation seeks out the valley of the River Ouche (adding a considerable distance in the process) and beyond Dijon carves out a straight and less interesting course towards the Saône.

At the heartland of France, one immediately obvious feature is the excellence of Burgundian food and wine. There are numerous regional specialities, ranging from delicious varieties of Dijon mustard, blended with herbs and spices, to *jambon persillé* (cold ham in a white wine jelly, pressed with parsley); fungus in profusion, such as *girolle* (chanterelle), *mousseron* (the St George's mushroom) and *cèpe* (boletus); many types of cheese, made from both cow and goat milk; Dijon gingerbread and *cassis* liqueur; and classic dishes like *boeuf bourguignon* (beef in red wine with mushrooms and onions). Nowhere are the *escargots* hunted and devoured with greater fervour and it is a common sight to encounter drab figures beating the undergrowth with sticks after a rainfall. And in Burgundy it is scarcely necessary to draw attention to the range of local wines.

A small proportion of the locks work electrically, but the great majority are operated manually, by keepers. One exception is a handful on the Saône side of the descent from the Pouilly summit. These are the responsibility of pleasure craft crews who are given instructions (in French or English) at the preceding locks. Craft longer than 20m must be accompanied by staff at these DIY locks. Elsewhere, most paddle gear is very efficient; one variety of 'ground' sluice has indicator dials marked 'O' and 'F' (*ouvert* or *fermé*). The normal gate-opening mechanism is an iron scissor-like device, a cranked version of the balance beams widespread on English canals. For reasons that are not satisfactorily explained, all locks are left empty after use, with bottom gates opened; while such a practice is of help to uphill craft, quite the reverse is so when you are descending. The waterway is closed to all pleasure craft from mid-November until late March; also on various public holidays when navigation is, however, possible on payment of a special and substantial locking fee. Detailed explanations and opening times appear in the *Carte Guide*.

Lock numbers on the northern side of the summit level bear the suffix 'Y' (for Yonne); those on the southern side, 'S' (for Saône).

The use of canal towpaths as long-distance traffic-free cycle-ways is a good idea, provided cyclists do not interfere with the enjoyment of habitual waterway users. *Côte d'Or Tourism* publishes a comprehensive free guide to cycling the Bourgogne between Tonnerre and Dijon, with details of hotels, shops, camp sites, bike repairs, etc. Available from: tel 03 80 63 69 49.

Brief history First contemplated in the early 16th century under François I, and seriously considered by the Midi's celebrated engineer Riquet in 1676, the Canal de Bourgogne was eventually started in 1775, at almost exactly the same time as the Canal du Centre and the Canal du Nivernais. Three gangs totalling 600 navvies were put to work on the northern section between Laroche and Tonnerre. Eight years later the Burgundy States was granted permission to commence the Dijon-Saône section. Progress was slow, much hampered by the Revolution and its accompanying turmoil. It is claimed that English prisoners of the Napoleonic Wars were employed in the construction of the great Pouilly Tunnel: sealed inside the workings, food was lowered to them via shafts with the promise of release when the task was completed. Few are said to have survived and the corpses of many were buried behind the stone lining. By 1808 the first barges reached Dijon from the Saône. Little more was achieved until 1822 when a scheme to attract private capital was launched with the aim of connecting the finished portions. Late in 1832 a barge left Paris, navigated the tunnel and arrived in Dijon on January 3 1833: the canal was finally an operational through route. Further necessary work involved construction of five reservoirs near the summit, ensuring adequate water supplies in all but the driest of summers.

Railway competition now presented a threat, with much of the route duplicated in 1851 by a new line running between Paris and Lyon. Waterborne traffic immediately declined. Something of the atmosphere of these times is contained in two published cruising accounts written by Englishmen travelling through the Canal de Bourgogne by rowing boat in 1854. Edmund Harvey in *Our Cruise in the Undine* comments: 'In towing barges, &c., along the canal, horses are seldom, if ever, used. The method generally adopted is this: when (as is frequently the case) they are one family travelling with the barge, the mother on one side of the canal and son on the other, with a rope each, haul the barge along, necessarily at a very slow pace (say a mile and a half an hour), while the father stays on board, smokes his pipe, and steers the barge.' And when nearing Tonnerre: 'We here learnt that the Emperor was to pass along this canal in a few days, and the good people supposed that we

were the engineers appointed to conduct his small steamer for him. Some opined that ours was the boat in which he was to travel; while others said it was only the convoy.' Beginning his 1854 voyage in Dijon, Robert Mansfield (*The Log of the Water Lily*) had to contend with a raging cholera epidemic in Burgundy: 'The three principal directions given by the French physicians in the printed notices about the cholera were, that everybody should avoid fruit, and never expose himself to night air, and check on the first début of colic: consequently we ate all the ripe fruit we could get, always slept with our windows open, and therefore never had occasion to observe the third rule.'

Mechanical bank haulage was introduced to the Bourgogne in 1873, such a practice then being quite novel in France. It lasted until 1968 on the reaches nearest the Saône where dumb craft regularly carried sand and gravel to Dijon. In 1936, 4,447 barge journeys were recorded, with 797,000 tonnes of freight. All boats were said to have then been hauled by tractors or horses. Horse-drawn traffic continued to navigate the whole waterway until after World War II. Gradual decline in commercial carrying very nearby resulted in parts of the canal being converted into an *autoroute* near Dijon during the 1960s. By the 1970s, the majority of traffic was by motorised *péniche* with small numbers regularly passing over the summit. Now working boats have completely deserted the waterway, except for the rare occasion when an unladen vessel is taken through in order to avoid a stoppage elsewhere.

Pleasure boating has become firmly established with hire and private craft as well as a number of hotel barges. Nevertheless, traffic levels on the Bourgogne are well below other routes such as the Nivernais and the Midi. The exceptionally dry summer of 2003 resulted in low water levels and finally total closure for a long period. Already, there had been disquiet at the main-tenance backlog which had forced most of the deep-drafted hotel barges to move elsewhere. Early in 2004, it was announced that EU and French Government funding amounting to 25 million Euros had been allo-cated to the canal. The waterway is expected to be fully rectified with a more reliable water supply by 2006. Meanwhile, it remains completely navigable for pleasure craft of average draft.

The Canal de Bourgogne begins a little inauspiciously, leaving the River Yonne at the twin towns of **Laroche** and **Migennes**, a bustling railway junction with few attractions other than the broad basin of the waterway, entered via an unusually deep lock. Here is a hire cruiser base with water and diesel fuel, a dry dock and full range of shops and eating places. Locks are more or less constant throughout the canal, increasing in frequency on each side of the summit. After the second lock, Écluse 113Y (K1.7), the canal runs quite straight through the hamlet of **Esnon** (K7.9) to **Brienon** (K9.2), a not unattractive little town with useful shops (supermarket) and a fine 18th century *lavoir* (wash-house) with oval basin. Market on Tuesdays and Fridays. The pound below Écluse 110Y (K15.1) is crossed by a TGV railway.

Excellent moorings with comprehensive boat facilities are established in the *port de plaisance* following Écluse 108Y (K18.8), where the delightful River Armançon flows under an aqueduct at **St-Florentin**. There is a lively weir far below the heights of the town, which is topped by an outstanding 14-17th century church with 24 superb 16th century stained glass windows. Here, I once attended a slightly curious secular brass band concert: somehow, the 'popular' selection of music played seemed at odds with such a venerable ecclesiastical building. More bizarrely, in mid-performance, I noticed with horror that a huge crucifix propped against a pillar was slowly falling. I shouted a warning to the musicians who scuttled from its path before it fell to the floor with a resounding crash. Once heavily fortified, St-Florentin contains a wealth of ancient stone buildings and is a tourist magnet with quality shopping and restaurants. The camping site enjoys a riverside location beyond the basin with safe swimming for children just two minutes from the canal. Well known cheeses, St-Florentin and Soumaintrain, are made locally, and a bloodless bullfight is staged each year on 1 July. A delightful

Gothic fountain ornamented with bronze gryphons is a 1979 replica of the 1512 original demolished in 1859! Market days are Monday and Saturday.

The next place of note is the former double lock of **Germigny** (bottom chamber alone in use, fall 5.14m), Nos 106/7Y (K21.8). Small scale shopping and restaurant. **Percey** (K27.5), midway between Écluses 104Y and 103Y, has several shops and a restaurant. The area provides some classic Burgundian countryside. Then comes **Flogny/La Chapelle**, Écluse 100Y (K30.9), with several shops and restaurants. Market on Tuesdays. Restaurant and a garage are close to a bridge in **Tronchoy** (K37.9), a collection of jumbled waterside stone buildings with a butcher reached from the next lock, Écluse 98Y, **Cheney** (K39.1). A further pleasant village is **Dannemoine** by Écluse 97Y (K40.3, water point). Basic shop and restaurant.

We shortly arrive in the sizeable town of **Tonnerre** (K44.2). The basin, between Écluses 96Y and 95Y, is home to the Canal Concept hire fleet (some facilities available). Situated where the Armançon divides into several channels, Tonnerre is the Roman *Tornodorum*. 2000 years ago its chief source of drinking water was the *Fosse Dionne* (Divine Ditch), now a pool containing greenish-blue spring water. The huddled collection of ancient houses is absolutely typical of Burgundy, each capped either by a rusty-red roof of tiles or the thin layers of stone known as *laves*, a speciality of the

St-Florentin.

district. *Notre-Dame des Fontenilles* is a hospital founded in 1293 by Marguerite de Bourgogne, sister-in-law of St-Louis. The great 80m-long ward with carved wooden ceiling and the chapel containing a 15th century *pietà* are open to the public. One peculiar – indeed notorious – inhabitant of Tonnerre is still remembered: Charles Geneviève Louis Auguste César Andrée Timothée Déon de Beaumont (1728–1810) who spent a long life alternating between male and female – and with brilliant success. Among his/her exploits was a journey to Russia as a lady secret agent, followed by a period in London as (male) secretary to the French Ambassador. He/she was created Chevalier d'Eon by Marie Antoinette, spent part of his/her declining years in England and died near Tonnerre, well known as a woman of huge appetite. D'Eon had been a source of curiosity for very many years and it was only after the corpse was examined that he was conclusively declared a man. The word 'eonism' will be found in comprehensive English dictionaries.

The long ascent continues up the Armançon valley to **Tanlay** (K52.2) between Écluses 90Y and 81Y. There is a small *port de plaisance* with shops and restaurants. Surroundings are particularly fine, with rolling hills, creamy Charollais cattle and poplars festooned with mistletoe. Of all Burgundian *châteaux* that at Tanlay is generally acknowledged as the finest. In fact, there are two buildings, the *petit* and the *grand*, the larger approached via a bridge over a moat. Mainly 16th century, it has remained in the ownership of one family since 1704. Visits from April to November.

The canal continues to wind along the course of the Armançon where several little villages probably still have the odd shop or restaurant (although it is difficult to keep track of changes in rural France). They include **St-Vinnemer** (K56.4) by Écluse 88Y; **Argentenay**, near Écluse 87Y (K59.6); and **Ancy-le-Libre**, Écluse 86Y (K61.4). Being rather larger, **Lézinnes** provides most services including water, restaurant and garage near Écluse 85Y. Écluse 84Y, Batilley, is the first of a group converted to automatic working in the 1980s.

A useful halt for shopping or restaurants can be made by the bridge connecting **Cusy** with **Ancy-le-Franc** (K73.7) shortly before Écluse 80Y, water point. Ancy has a magnificent Renaissance *château* – a great square structure in grey stone with massive towers at each corner and a suitably grand front door. The interior decoration is rich beyond description and is quite unlike the rather austere outside elevations. Notables who stayed here include Henri IV, Louis XIII, Louis XIV and Mme de Sévigné. There are guided tours throughout the summer. **Chassignelles**, near Écluse 79Y (K75.4), has some basic shopping with a restaurant

in the hilly street of grey stone with a fuller range of facilities in the pleasant town of Ravières (K82.6), midway between Écluses 76Y and 75Y. An age-old conflict between spiritual and bodily needs is summed up by a sign dating from 1701 in the church. It states that 'a solemn Mass with Benediction is held each evening for three days before Ash Wednesday in atonement for the excesses of the pre-Lenten Carnival'. Water may be taken on at **Cry** (K87.2, bar but no shops). Scenery continues to be very pleasant.

All canal enthusiasts will enjoy a visit to an extraordinary industrial site, **La Grand Forge** (K94.5), whose complete restoration was carried out in the 1980s. The Great Forge was created by Buffon (see below) in 1768. Water was harnessed to work hydraulic powered bellows for a furnace and hammers which transformed cast iron into pure iron. In keeping with other examples of 18th century industrial architecture, the buildings and their details are delightful. A balcony was designed so that visitors could view the casting process down below. Open to the public, summer afternoons (not Tuesdays). There are several small restaurants close to the canal: at **Buffon** (K95.5); **St-Rémy** (highly recommended) and **Blaisy** (K98.7) before Écluse 67Y; and by Écluse 66Y, Fontenay (K100.6).

Montbard (K101.7) is a small industrial town whose prosperity was due to the Comte de Buffon (1707–88), a leading iron master. He established himself on the site of a fortress built by the Dukes of Bourgogne (only two towers now remain) and there compiled his important *Histoire Naturelle*, published volume by volume during a 40-year period. His park and workroom are on public view. Canal travellers will perhaps show equal interest in the large covered market from which provender can be carried back to the boat. Not only is shopping very convenient from the upper basin (K102.5) but this is the last opportunity for visiting comprehensive stores until arriving at Pouilly-en-Auxois 53km and a lot of locks further on. At the lower basin (K101.7) is a hire cruiser base with a range of facilities for all pleasure craft.

Soon follows a feature of the Canal de Bourgogne which is regarded with dread by many coast-bound yachtsmen, and genuine interest (or even enjoyment) by those travelling the waterway for its own sake: a chain of no fewer than 56 locks in the 30km that remain to the Pouilly summit. Arranged in two groups with a 10km break, their negotiation tends to take precedence over every other activity. Further, once launched into this exercise, mobile keepers are understandably not enthusiastic if you decide to moor up for a couple of hours and then expect them to accompany you again. It pays to have at least one member of the crew working ahead by bicycle. A good place to lie for the night in contemplation of the next day's task is **Venarey-les-Laumes** (K115.6), between Écluses 56Y and 55Y. There is an agreeable pleasure craft harbour (hire craft) with water point and adequate shopping (supermarket, 1km near **Les Laumes** rail station). Should you wish to further postpone the fateful time when the real work begins, stop near the bridge (K116.3) in the pound Écluses 55Y/54Y and travel 4km east to **Alise-Sainte-Reine**, site of the fortress of Alesia where Caesar besieged Vercingetorix in 52BC and Gaul finally fell to the Roman Empire. During the 1860s, excavations discovered many relics that are now displayed in two museums. The hillside is crowned by a massive bronze statue of the Gallic hero, visible from a long distance.

And so, eventually, to the locks, some of which, fortunately, are electrically operated. They occur in a succession of flights: Mussey (53Y, 52Y); Pouillenay (51Y–37Y); Chassey (36Y–31Y); Marigny (30Y–18Y) and Charigny (17Y, 16Y). Then follow three widely spaced ones, Braux to Pont-Royal, succeeded by a 10km pound. A final 12 chambers lift boats to the watershed. Set in magnificent gently rolling cornfields, amid terrain well known to all A6 *autoroute* travellers, they offer the distinct possibility of overnight stranding far from village amenities. So travel prepared! There are water points at Écluses 48/9Y, 45Y and 27Y. If circumstances allow, moor up in **Pouillenay**, Écluse 46Y (K119.6, basic shopping) and take a taxi 10km west to **Semur-en-Auxois**, a perfect example of a small medieval Burgundian city. Set in a hollow of the Armançon valley, the town is guarded by four circular 14th century towers that rise from a mound of pink granite. You cannot help being slightly fearful of the several structural cracks that run from top to bottom. One of them, the *Tour de l'Orle d'Or*, houses a small museum, quite fascinating for its amateur dreadfulness. Elsewhere are ancient stone gateways, precipitous views onto riverside vegetable gardens and restrained tourist development. Notre-Dame de Semur is possibly the most beautiful Gothic church in Burgundy.

Back on the canal, we plunge into the thick of the locks. By **Marigny-le-Cahouet** at Écluse 26Y (K125.8), another pause may be called for. It has very basic shopping. Within walking distance, *La Ferme de la Cure* is a highly recommended restaurant where clients share the same large table. The building has been owned by one family since the 16th century. Check locally that it still operates, as it is several years since I ate there at reasonable cost. A plaque at Écluse 23Y records the cottage as the birthplace of one Bernard Roy, who overcame his humble origins to become Governor

General of Tunisia. The *Auberge du Chaudron* restaurant in **Villeneuve-sous-Charigny** is within walking distance of Écluse 16Y (K129.9): the proprietors can generally provide transport to return clients to their boat. Grandly-named **Pont-Royal** just before Écluse 13Y (K137.5) has little to offer except a friendly bar and a broad quayside. 1,130m of narrow cutting at Creusot is followed by a bridge providing access to **St-Thibault** (K140), whose 13th century church was erected to shelter St Theobald's remains. Having learned of the richly decorated Gothic doorway and columbarium suspended over the high altar, worked by a series of chains and pulleys for displaying the Blessed Sacrament, I persuaded half the ship's crew to venture across the dew-laden meadows to attend Mass one August Sunday morning. From previous close association with such matters, I calculated that a service would begin at 08.00h. To our consternation the great building was locked. As we retired to the nearby *boulangerie* for freshly-baked breakfast *croissants*, we learned that M le Curé was absent. 'Why, even the good Lord must take his summer holiday', exclaimed Madame. Thus thwarted, we returned crestfallen to the boat, where the heathen members of the family were still in bed. As in other French villages, the grocer and restaurant of St-Thibault are similarly threatened by August closure during the *congé annuel*.

The A6 *autoroute* veers close to the canal at Écluse 12Y, **Gissey-le-Viel** (K147.9), a steady roar of traffic making the next 7km slightly disagreeable. But doubtless, when the waterway was dug close to a lovely old fortified *château-ferme* on the right bank at **Éguilly** (K149.4), the intrusion was considered barely tolerable. Now this noble building is subjected to the thunder of motorway wheels, for the six-lane highway passes a few metres from the walls and completely isolates the *château* from its village. For some years after the *autoroute* arrived, it stood forlorn and deserted. An astonishing plan to use it as a 'medieval service station' (!) proved abortive and in 1983 it was bought by Françoise and Roger Aubry who have since carried out the huge restoration task virtually single handed. On request, an English-speaking tour can be arranged. It is suggested that visitors make a suitably generous donation towards the cost of works which have received no form of Government grant. This huge and glorious 13th–17th century *château* is undoubtedly one of the canal's highlights, not least for its admirable recent recovery.

Once through the remaining locks, we arrive in a sizeable basin, the port of **Pouilly-en-Auxois** (K154.7) where there is a full range of facilities for passing boaters, including a dry dock, although no hire firms at the time of writing. The small and flourishing town is 1.6km distant and while is it lies on the canal (literally), many travellers afloat will see nothing of it for they will be underground in the great Pouilly Tunnel. There are shops and restaurants aplenty, including a supermarket midway between the port and the town square. The whole of the summit level (from Écluse 1Y to Écluse 1S) is worked one-way, with permits to proceed issued to boats by keepers at each end. Headroom in the 3,350m tunnel is rather less than normal: 3.1m at the centre, reducing to 2.2m at the sides. If in doubt, it is safer to obtain precise details from the authorities in advance of arrival, supplying an exact drawing, with measurements, of your boat. Years ago, the problem of unladen *péniches* being unable to pass beneath the vault was solved by a simple but elegant method. A rudimentary vessel known as the *bac* (ferry) was fitted with sluices like lock paddles. The barge was floated on board and, by changing water levels, a 0.6m reduction in air draft was achieved. Commercial craft were drawn through by an electric chain tug, taking power from a perilously close overhead live wire. Now, all craft proceed under their own power. Boats, including converted barges, may take advantage of a supply of log fenders fitted with lines to ensure that their superstructures cannot make contact with the roof if the helmsman steers too close to the tunnel walls.

Tunnel safely tackled (K159.4), you can now relish the pleasures of one of the finest portions of navigable inland waterway in the whole of France. From here down the valley of the River Ouche to Dijon is a succession of delights. After emerging from the stone-lined tunnel cutting, the canal arrives in the large **Escommes** basin (K160.4, moorings and dry dock). Although there are no amenities in this intensely rural place, a supermarket and restaurant are to be found in **Créancey**, 2km north. A flight of closely-spaced locks lowers the canal from its summit. Nos 1S–13S are a DIY electrified series for use by pleasure craft up to 20m. Larger vessels must be accompanied by canal staff. Instructions are issued in French and English. Cunning safety devices are installed to ensure correct operation. Feeders from several reservoirs bring water supplies to the navigable channel in this area.

Another mooring basin appears after Écluse 8S, **Vandenesse-en-Auxois** (K163.1), a pretty little village with tiny shop and restaurant. Ahead, on the left is the first view of the most romantic and fascinating village on the entire canal: **Châteauneuf-en-Auxois**, occupying a prominent hilltop a little under 2km east of a bridge in the middle of the pound between Écluses 10S (K169.3) and 11S, **La Rèpe**. A little like a miniature version of Carcassonne on the Canal du Midi, but devoid of commercialism and hoards of tourists, Châteauneuf is an amazingly intact and original 12th century survival comprising a gaunt turreted castle begun by Guy de Chaudenay and further extended and fortified throughout the following 300 years. Now belonging to the State, there are guided tours throughout the year (details, tel 03 80 49 21 89). Views from the heights, across the glinting ribbon of the canal to the far-off woodlands of the Morvan, are among the finest in Burgundy. *Château* apart, the village within its encircling walls is fascinating, containing a variety of elegant houses built for rich Dijon merchants in the 14–17th centuries. Commercialism is restrained with little more than an antique store and craft shops. Any visit will be enhanced by a meal at the *Hostellerie du Château* in the shadow of the feudal castle. I enjoyed a truly gastronomic experience when I dined there, my meal including a *vol-au-vent* filled with salmon and frogs' legs; slices of duck in *cassis* with black currents and lightly cooked fresh vegetables; peaches in white wine; and a selection of prime local cheeses. Presentation of the food and the pleasant atmosphere of the establishment, which is also a small hotel, made this perhaps the best value I have ever encountered in France. Although an uphill walk from the waterway (a taxi is always a possibility) lunch or dinner in Châteauneuf would be a highlight of any cruise (tel 03 80 49 22 00).

As you travel southwards down the canal, there are repeated views of Châteauneuf beyond the towpath poplars, although the A6 *autoroute* is uncomfortably close from Écluse 12S, Revin (K165.1), to Pont-d'Ouche: if possible, overnight mooring is best avoided in this reach, well known to motorists roaring along between Paris and Lyon. Each change in level is punctuated by delightful little lock cottages whose continued working existence was threatened by proposed destruction of the waterway in the late 1960s. **Crugey** at Écluse 16S (K169.2) has a very popular fixed-price restaurant and soon afterwards facilities begin to proliferate as we approach the very beautiful section within easy driving distance of Dijon. Écluse 17S, Rempart, is by a quarry on a very sharp bend. Écluse 18S, Roche aux Fées (K171.4), is in a thickly wooded area with high cliffs. In keeping close company with the River Ouche, the navigation, having run SE since Pouilly, swings sharply to the NE at **Pont-d'Ouche** (K172.6). Here in the large basin is a hire cruiser base with associated facilities, an English-run restaurant and a low two-arched aqueduct. The A6 sweeps across the valley on a great concrete viaduct. Good progress is being made to restore an extremely early narrow gauge railway between Pont d'Ouche and **Bligny-sur-Ouche**, 9km south. Conceived as a connection between Épinac and the canal, it was opened in 1837 with oxen and

The 12th century fortified town of Châteauneuf-en-Auxois.

horses pulling trucks on level sections, stationary engines being used for the inclines. It was gradually replaced by larger railways and road traffic, although portions remained in use for freight and Sunday fishermen until total closure in 1968. Ten years later, the first 3km was reopened from Bligny to **Oucherotte**. Steam-hauled passenger trains operate weekends, 1 May–1 October, with diesel runs on weekdays. One locomotive, *La Burgonde*, dates from 1910 and saw service during World War I.

There now follows a succession of riverside villages scattered along the steep-sided valley, each with a backdrop of dense forest. **Veuvey-sur-Ouche** (K175.7) midway between Écluses 22S and 23S has a camping site on the canal banks and an attractive pointed spire church. **La Forge**, Écluse 25S (K179.1, tiny supermarket, baker) with **La Bussière-sur-Ouche** on the opposite, left, side below Écluse 26S (K179.6). Visits can

be made to a restored 13th century Cistercian abbey, now a centre for retreats. The buildings and gardens are quite delightful with a specially notable stone dovecote and topiary. **St-Victor-sur-Ouche**, after Écluse 29S (K182.5), consists of a jumble of well restored stone cottages by a disused railway station with café/restaurant. A really worthwhile excursion from here is the **Château de Marigny**, a walk of about 2.5km via Auvillard. This 11th century structure was partially demolished in the 1700s. Much overgrown, the remains have been made accessible by a local preservation society. To be seen are ramparts, a chapel and a dovecote. It is all very romantic in a Gothic kind of way.

The special character of this length of canal owes much to rows of poplars planted on each bank, to the fine Burgundian architecture and to the hillyness of the terrain. Most canal bridges lead to much older crossings of the Ouche as in **Gissey-sur-Ouche** (K186.5), after Écluse 32S, where there are restaurants, a small supermarket and day boats for hire. Descending rapidly down the valley, we shortly arrive at **Ste-Marie-sur-**

Ouche, Écluse 36S (K190.5), a picture postcard village set around an ancient stone bridge. One of the best seasons for a cruise through this Dijonnaise countryside is autumn, when the trees become a blaze of red and yellow. Now never very far away from the busy Dijon *autoroute* spur, the canal nevertheless retains a tranquil identity of its own with restaurants and baker in Pont de Pany, Écluse 38S (K193.5). All basic shops, restaurant and garage will be found in **Fleurey-sur-Ouche** (K196.7) between Écluses 41S and 42S.

Shopping and eating ashore are similarly possible in **Velars-sur-Ouche**, Écluse 45S (K201.7). 6km south, the 600m high **Mont Afrique** provides outstanding views to nearby Dijon and the plains of the Saône far beyond: it is said that in the clearest weather it is possible to see Mont Blanc. A series of lock cottages and their gardens are among the most pleasing to be found anywhere, but gradually real countryside turns into suburbs as Dijon approaches. Note the little tourist railway on the canal's left bank from Écluses 46S–48S. **Plombières-les-Dijon**, not far from Écluse 50S (K207) is an excellent stopping place with all shops, garage and restaurants. With public transport links into Dijon, there is much to be said for mooring here rather than using the rather expensive facilities offered by the city. Children might enjoy an outing to the splendid leisure lake extending from Écluse 51S to 52S. The best approach from the canal is to walk through a small railway arch. This 'lido' was formed by damming the Ouche; it takes on the appearance of a Mediterranean beach during hot summer days. Activities include swimming, windsurfing and dinghy sailing.

Locks 52S–54S lead to the centre of **Dijon** (K212.2) where a smart landscaped basin with most facilities is reserved for pleasure craft. This facility dates only from the early 1980s and is about 1,200m from the main shopping area. Unfortunately charges for a single night's mooring are very considerable and you may wonder at the long line of deserted bollards where free mooring is forbidden in favour of anglers! For a time in the 14–15th centuries Dijon was capital of Burgundy which then extended as far north as Flanders and across to Switzerland and the Rhine. Parliament building and Ducal Palace, the 13th century cathedral of St-Bénigne, museums devoted to fine art, sculpture, Burgundian life and folklore: the choice of attractions is extensive. Some roofs are covered with riotous patterns of brightly coloured glazed tiles, a widespread form of decoration in this part of France. No stay would be complete without a visit to an old established mustard merchant, whose shop is filled with antique *faïence* jars. Replicas can be bought containing many varieties of the condiment. The recipe for the most popular type

dates from the 4th century AD. 300 quarts were consumed during a feast laid on by the Duke of Burgundy for Philip de Valois in 1336. Although a modern and expanding city, Dijon retains much from its brilliant past and many pleasant hours could be spent in exploring the maze of narrow streets around the *Quartier Ancien*.

As you leave the city on its southern side, there is every opportunity to appreciate Dijon's commercial and industrial expansion of recent decades. Gone are the earlier windings of the Ouche valley: the waterway strikes out across a great plain in an utterly straight line for the remaining 30km to the Saône. It is not exciting boating. One saving grace is the succession of charming and original lock houses, little stone bungalows, each with an ornate circular attic window overlooking the chamber. After **Longvic** (K216.7, comprehensive shopping) and its bank of airport lights, we enter open country once more. Villages within easy reach are mostly farming settlements whose buildings are grouped tightly together for protection from the marauders of long ago. **Thorey-en-Plaine**, Écluse 67S (K226.3), has a restaurant, while **Longecourt-en-Plaine**, Écluse 69S (K228.2), offers several shops and boasts a beautiful private *château* almost on the canal bank.

Écluse 71S, **Aisery** (K231.8), is notable for a big sugar processing works. There are several shops in the village 1.6km distant. **Echigey**, a similar walk to the east has a restaurant. Two supermarkets and a recommended restaurant make **Brazey-en-Plaine** an attractive prospect. 300m west of the bridge that follows Écluse 74S (K236.9). Those in search of an ecclesiastical excursion can take a taxi for 12km to the **Abbey de Citaux**, established in 1098 as the first Cistercian house. Only fragmented ruins remain of the original buildings, but members of St Bernard's order set up a new community here in the 19th century. 14km west of Citaux is **Nuits-St-Georges** at the heart of the world-famous Burgundian vineyards.

The Canal de Bourgogne finally joins the Saône at **St-Jean-de-Losne** (K242), a town long devoted to commercial waterway traffic and since the 1980s the pleasure boating centre of France. Every possible need can be satisfied here from brokerage of cruisers and converted barges, to dry dock, fuelling, repairs, moorings and chandlery. While there are moorings and other facilities on the final pound of the canal, it is necessary to work through the last lock into the River Saône and then turn left into the vast *Gare d'Eau* which is the centre of the town's boat activities. For full details, see Chapter 48.

48 ～ River Saône

Carte Guide: *Saône*

From a junction with the Canal de l'Est (Branche Sud) at Corre, to Lyon, junction with the River Rhône: 365.4km and 24 locks and 2 tunnels. Additional junctions are made with the Canal de la Marne à la Saône at Heuilley; the Canal du Rhône au Rhin at St-Symphorien; the Canal de Bourgogne at St-Jean-de-Losne; the Canal du Centre at Chalon-sur-Saône; the River Seille at La Truchère; and the Canal de Pont de Vaux at Fleurville, 3.5km with 1 lock.

The Saône ranks as one of the most important navigable rivers in France for pleasure craft. All or at least a substantial part of its course will be followed by boats cruising between the north and the Mediterranean. Equally, the gentle scenery of Burgundy and the Bourbonnais, at the very heart of the country, is well worth exploration for its own sake. Almost totally rural surroundings with numerous attractive towns and villages have encouraged establishment of a range of hire cruiser bases: facilities for pleasure boats are thus better than in many parts of France.

The uppermost reaches, between Corre and Port-sur-Saône, are often little wider than a standard *péniche* canal, with numerous artificial lock cuts which bypass some of the more twisting sections of the natural river. As far downstream as Auxonne, locks are restricted to the 38.5m length of the Freycinet gauge; but from there to Lyon, far-reaching modernisation has resulted in locks 185m long, enabling 5,000 tonne push-tows to operate. Commercial traffic has become quite light in the upper reaches, although it is rather busier further downstream. Now that the scheme for enlargement of the Canal du Rhône au Rhin has been abandoned any prospect of an increase in freight activity seems unlikely.

The Saône has a very gentle gradient, falling a mere 59m over its total navigable length: consequently, the current is normally slight. Conversely, serious flooding is not infrequent in the winter and craft are then directed over some of the upstream weirs, the adjacent locks being temporarily taken out of service. But during the cruising season the river is normally placid, with unusually clear water. There are many opportunities for swimming from small sandy beaches.

Typical Saône features are long avenues of bankside poplars, broad meadows where white Charollais cattle graze, multi-coloured glazed Burgundian roof tiles and waterside villages in grey stone. Rarely spectacular, the scenery is at times monotonous – rather less so when illuminated by a summer sun that already promises more than a hint of the south.

Although much of the river is within easy reach of the famous Burgundian vineyards, they are rarely in evidence from the water. Excellent local wine is of course readily available; the food is as would be expected of this richly productive part of France. Lyon proudly boasts that it is the world centre of gastronomy and a reputation for first-class cuisine extends far beyond the city limits. In addition to the wines of Chalon, Mâcon and Burgundy, the outstanding dish of the Saône is *pôchouse*, where freshwater fish such as eel, bream and burbot are stewed in white wine with garlic. Verdun-sur-le-Doubs claims credit for the recipe, but it will be found on the menus of restaurants throughout a wide area.

Brief history Together with the Rhône, the Saône has formed a vital transport corridor through France since prehistoric times. It was a major trade route during the centuries of Roman domination, while later there are records stating that the river was navigable downstream of Auxonne at the time of the Crusades. But a lack of weirs and other navigation works resulted in frequent low water levels which hindered traffic until a management plan was adopted in 1837. This determined to provide a minimum water depth of 1.6m, similar to that of the newly completed Canal de Bourgogne. In the upper reaches, from Port-sur-Saône to Verdun-sur-le-Doubs, it was considered possible to manage without locks, improving the depth by dredging and building submerged training walls. This work was mainly carried out between 1842 and 1855. The programme met with limited success and in 1864 legal measures were adopted for the installation of a series of weirs with locks: 15 from Corre to Gray; 9 between Gray and Verdun-sur-le-Doubs; and a further 6 between there and Lyon. The French defeat by the Prussians in 1871 with consequent loss of territory to the east, prompted building of the Canal de l'Est northwards from Corre (completed by 1882). In this form, the Saône became part of an important north–south line of navigation and remained substantially unchanged until the 1970s.

Up to the beginning of the 19th century, barges and boats using the river were of very shallow draft: various regional types evolved, including *savoyardes*, *scysselandes*, *penelles*, *sapines*, *cadoles*, *flûtes* and rafts. Passenger craft (*coches d'eau*) worked with sails and oars or were hauled by men and horses. Great improvements came with the introduction of steam tugs from about 1835, and a tradition was established for the construction of iron-hulled barges in Chalon from 1839. Passenger-carrying paddle steamers first went into service on the Chalon–Lyon section in 1826; there were

17 by 1850 in which year 449,736 people travelled aboard them.

The river supported a wide range of trades of great commercial importance to the region. Floating mills and other types of mobile water-powered factories were common in the early 19th century. Professional fishermen, floating wash houses, and sand and gravel dredgers all derived a living from the Saône. In surprisingly recent times it was suggested that owners of large pleasure craft were well advised to employ a local pilot for the lower reaches of the Saône, where submerged training walls were said to still present a hazard. This is no longer necessary, provided due attention is paid to navigation marks and to the chart.

Pleasure boating came earlier to the Saône than to many other French waterways. A rowing regatta was established in Mâcon in 1873, while steam launches were in use by 1886, according to Philip Hamerton's *The Saône* which records in great detail a summer voyage between Corre and Lyon. Englishman Hamerton hired a donkey-hauled *berrichon* to travel the upper reaches, using his own sailing catamaran downstream of Chalon. He noted that this part of the Saône was 'the best river to sail on in Europe, and probably the world', having a slow current in summer and 'good exposure of the surface of the water to the action of different winds'. Regularly used throughout the 20th century by yachts on passage through France, the river only became popular as a cruising ground in its own right after the establishment of a number of hire craft companies in the 1970s.

The Saône's most recent development was carried out from the mid-1970s, with the building of very sizeable engineering works to upgrade the lower section from Auxonne to Lyon. These measures were completed by the early 1980s and were designed to improve the navigation to international standards as part of a projected North Sea–Mediterranean Waterway. All locks were replaced or eliminated; the huge new concrete chambers measure 185m x 12m with a normal depth over the sill of 4m. This work involved excavating several new lock cuts and the removal of former weirs. Some of the old locks remain intact, their approaches creating useful moorings for commercial and pleasure craft. Stupidly, all this effort was to prove virtually fruitless, as an essential part of the plan has been scrapped on environmental grounds. This was to similarly upgrade the canalised River Doubs from the Saône to the Rhine. Thus, hectic commercial traffic on the Rhine, using large capacity craft, is unable to access the Saône and Rhône. It would appear that there is little prospect of this situation changing.

Meanwhile, the uppermost reaches of the Saône have been little altered since the 19th century improvements, except that some of the locks are now equipped for automatic working, without the need for keepers. Pleasure craft are issued with a leaflet at the final manned locks up or downstream of this series giving instructions on how to activate the gear.

Although the Saône's navigable length has been reduced in recent years to 356km by creation of new artificial cuts, the kilometre posts on the banks continue to take account of many natural bends, since bypassed. The distance from Corre to Lyon might thus appear to be as much as 407km. As an aid to identifying where you are on the river, the old post distances are used in the following description, so following the pattern established by the *Carte Guide*s.

A three-way junction between the unnavigable Saône, the little River Coney and the Canal de l'Est (Branche Sud) marks the start of the waterway on the outskirts of the small town of **Corre**, where there are good boating facilities (see Chapter 22). As the Coney is the larger of the two streams, it would appear to have the greater claim to the name 'Saône'. In former times boats were built on its banks at **Selles** and floated 11km down to Corre on the winter floods. Very light drafted freight barges regularly used this length, working through a number of flash locks. All this activity ceased with the opening of the Canal de l'Est in 1882.

These uppermost sections of the river are moderately wooded in quite hilly surroundings, unlike the wide open meadows so characteristic of much of the downstream Saône. Shortly after K405 is the first of many lengths of artificial cut, leading past the village of **Ormoy** (piled mooring and some basic shopping) to a lock, one of a series converted to automatic operation in 1980. Many of the weir-streams resulting from the 19th century improvements may be explored (with care) in small craft; indeed some of them provide the only practicable access to villages that have long since been bypassed. A guard lock towards the top end of the cut can be closed to prevent flood water passing into the canal.

The second lock is similarly approached by a long cut near the village of **Cendrecourt** (K392), a charming place of grey stone farmhouses, red roofs and basic shopping. The nearest mooring is at the lock, although it would be safer to lie downstream of the D46 road bridge. There are some shops and a restaurant in the pleasant little town of **Jussey**, about 2.3km. At K386 an extremely sinuous part of the river has been avoided by a short length of canal, the **Coupure de la Hang**. This is soon followed, left, by the village of **Montureux-lès-Baulay** (K385.5), a collection of houses strung out along the bank and featuring a charming church with zig-zag patterns of coloured tiles. Access is difficult and there are no facilities. Another lock with short cut follows at K383.

Baulay (K380) has a pontoon mooring near the road bridge and lies within easy walking distance. Here are several shops and (on my last visit) a restaurant. It is a pretty little place, in summer filled with flowers. Cut wood lies in giant stacks as a source of winter fuel. A little upstream on the opposite bank is **Fouchécourt**, situated on a ridge above flood level.

Mooring bollards will be found by the bridge of **Port d'Atelier** (K376). Up the road to the left, the village itself provides some shopping, a garage and a restaurant. Pleasant countryside continues to Conflandey Lock, which has no approach cut: merely a foaming weir alongside the stone chamber. The barrage is constructed of numerous small 'needles', which can be removed to allow surplus water to escape. To do this, the keeper is wound over the torrent in a cradle suspended from a gantry. In times of serious flood, passage of the lock becomes unnecessary and craft merely pass over the weir, rather like boats negotiating the flash locks that remained on the Thames above Oxford until the 1930s. Take care just below the lock, where a stream on the left can produce a strong current across the navigation channel. Below, a large island marks the approach to **Conflandey** (K372): downstream traffic takes the right channel, upstream boats the left. While there are good quayside moorings on the right, opposite the head of the island, shops and restaurants have now all disappeared. Locals rely on the mobile shops that serve villages throughout the region.

That **Port-sur-Saône** (K366) was once a town of some importance is suggested by the availability, from the stationer's, of a substantial book on its history. The single street boasts a good range of shops and restaurants. Port is situated on a canal section where I was once trapped for several days during spring floods. Several times we ate at the *Restaurant de la Pomme d'Or* (across the Saône bridge) and I recommend it wholeheartedly. Good moorings are to be found a little below the bridge by the *Service de la Navigation* offices, where there is a water point. A marina is established opposite, in a basin: services available include hire cruisers, repairs and fuel. This is a specially lovely part of the river, with woods and fields leading to the short cut and lock at **Chemilly** (K360). A wide weir bars the entrance to the stream on which the village is situated, but it can be approached by boat from the lower end, mooring near the impressive towers of a beautifully restored fortified *château*.

Although now bypassed by the through navigation, **Scey-sur-Saône** (K356) is worth a detour, following the natural course of the river from the upstream end of the lock cut. Ski-ing and other water sports are popular

here. A convenient jetty mooring is within 500m of the shops and restaurant, but lies above the weir so should not be approached if there is a strong current. One surprise here is the vast supermarket, concealed behind a narrow frontage. Halfway down the lock channel is the *Restaurant des Deux Ports*, opposite a large basin with hire cruisers and most facilities. The town lies about 1km from here. Not long after Scey lock is the 689m **St-Albin Tunnel** (K353). It is, of course, rather unusual to encounter tunnels on river navigations; this example resulted when a huge loop of the Saône through the village of **Traves** (some shops) was bypassed. An approach by water can be made by navigating the old river course upstream for 5km from the Écluse de Rupt. The tunnel and its approaches are worked on a one-way system extending to the bridges above and below. Craft must wait for traffic lights before proceeding: they are operated by the keeper at Rupt, and downstream craft are required to hoot at the entrance to the tunnel cutting. A loud-speaker system relays the sound to the lock, more than 2km away.

Rupt-sur-Saône (K343) demands a visit. Visible across the fields from the lock, it is dominated by its *château* with a tall round stone tower rising above the treetops. Village tradition claims that the tower once had a roof as tall as itself. Moor by the Pont de Chantes and walk a short distance up the road. At the turn of the 18th and 19th centuries, the *château* was the property of the Comte d'Orsay, who was born in Paris and died here. An elaborate tomb in the churchyard is directly visible from his former home. The higher parts of the village provide good views of the river. This is an exceptionally sleepy place, more so now that its few remaining shops have closed down. The public washing place (*lavoir*) is enhanced by a large 19th century bronze lion. Another quiet village worth walking to is **Ovanches**, situated in the centre of the island formed by the river and the Rupt lock cut; it is approached from the road bridge at the downstream end of the tunnel.

A broad weir marks the beginning of the cut leading to **Chantes** lock (K340). This is followed at K338 by a guard lock (normally open) on a cut near **Cubry-lès-Soing**. The landscape here is open and very appealing. Yet another canal section avoids a broad loop of the river (K333). Craft cannot reach **Soing** by water at this point and it is not permitted to moor in the narrow lock cut. However, if you work through the Écluse de Soing, it is possible to turn left and cruise for 3km up the old river course. There are moorings a little downstream of the bridge, several shops and a restaurant (the grocer delivers orders to boats). At K328, a right-angled bend leads to **Charentenay**, at the upper end of the lock cut. On the natural river, a little downstream of

Approach to the St-Albin Tunnel on the higher reaches of the navigation.

this junction, is a *relais nautique* with pontoon moorings by a camp site (showers, water, slipway) and the *Auberge de Paris* restaurant where steaks are prepared over an open wood fire. A fine wooded reach of canal leads to Ray lock (K324), below which is one of the finest scenes on the entire French waterways system.

After turning right up the natural course of the river, the village of **Ray-sur-Saône** rises from clusters of willow trees. Buildings of creamy stone with brown-tiled roofs are topped by a church, dated 1768, whose tower is crowned with a four-sided bell-shaped structure riotously decorated with glazed tiles in a zig-zag pattern. (A particularly fine early 16th century *Entombment* is within.) Still higher are the crenellated towers, massive walls and park of the *château* of Ray, lately the property of Comte Hubert de Salverte, a descendant of the Duc de Marmier. He began extensive restoration work in 1941. Parts of the structure go back to medieval times. It was reduced to ruins during the Ten Years War (17th century) and rebuilt and extended in the 18th century. The strategic site was a stronghold in Roman times. The *château* is open to the public (Sundays and

The château *at Ray-sur-Saône.*

holidays, pm, Easter–1 October) while its park is open throughout the year. It is claimed that a passageway excavated through rock connects the *château* with the river. Do look out for the impressive *lavoir* with an oval basin and roof. There are moorings near the village centre and limited shopping with restaurants.

A guard lock on a long artificial cut at **Ferrières-lès-Ray**, although normally open at each end, presents problems for deep-laden barges, such as the somewhat under-powered *péniche* I once watched being winched over the sill. Boats drawing up to 1.5m can take the alternative and longer river route, avoiding this canal section altogether. **Recologne** (K319), at the tail of the cut, offers no facilities but is a pleasant little village with flowers and cattle sheds among the houses.

At K315 begins another long and narrow cut with the 643m **Savoyeux Tunnel**. Downstream boats should hoot to alert the keeper at Savoyeux lock and wait for a green light before proceeding. The very extensive basin

of the *Port de Savoyeux*, 1km upstream of the tunnel, was developed as a marina and hire craft base in 1981 (moorings, repairs, water, fuel, slipway, etc). A range of shops and restaurant can be found in the nearby small town of **Seveux**. Pleasant but unremarkable scenery takes the navigation down to **Véreux** lock cut (K298–296) and on to **Prantigny** (K294), where mooring is possible downstream of the bridge on the left bank. Apart from a pleasing cluster of stone barns and houses, there is little reason for exploration ashore. The lock cut at **Rigny** (K289) is unusually treeless. Rigny, 10 minutes' walk from the middle of the cut and over a river bridge, offers limited shopping and a restaurant. Onwards from here, the river opens out and the hilly surrounds of its uppermost reaches are left behind. For the first time a series of black and white buoys (K286) warn of rock in the riverbed: keep well to the right bank. Similar navigation markers will be observed frequently during the journey down to Lyon.

In keeping with its growing proportions, the Saône now meets its first real town – **Gray** (K280). Initial impressions are of considerable industry, for this is an important agricultural centre with grain silos and rail connections. Occupying a hilltop with the church of Notre Dame (prominent onion-shaped tower and begun in the 15th century), it is a first-rate shopping centre. There is a swimming beach, left bank on the upstream outskirts (K284); a hire cruiser base selling fuel; and public moorings, left bank, downstream of the lock and weir. Some care is required when approaching the lock on the right bank because of the adjacent weir. The chamber itself is spanned by the road bridge. We noticed that the lock keeper took his midday meal at a small restaurant to the right of the bridge and accordingly moored up to follow his example. Crowded with workmen, this establishment provided us with a meal of excellent value. There are fine views over the river from the flag-decorated bridge, with formal gardens. A magnificent honey-coloured stone *Hôtel de Ville* in Renaissance style dates from 1568; its roof of coloured glazed tiles is one of the best in Burgundy. The 18th century *château* houses the Baron Martin Museum, whose 20 rooms contain a fine collection of European paintings from the 16–20th centuries. It is interesting to recall that Gray and the lands of Franche Comté were lost by France as recently as 1688: the Saône had long been a natural frontier and Hamerton notes that in 1886 the bargemen continued to refer to the left bank as the *Empire* and the right bank the *Royaume*.

Quite one of the loveliest moorings on the Saône is reached at **Mantoche** (K276), where a 130m quay extends along the river frontage of a real gem of a small *château*, reputedly a former royal hunting lodge. On one occasion, the lady living there accepted an invitation to come aboard our hired cruiser and we were sorry that pressure of time preventing us visiting her exquisite home the next morning (it is not normally open to the public). Another *château* is concealed by dense foliage nearby, with the coloured tiles of a tower just visible among the trees. Narrow lanes lead into the village centre, where there are several shops and a restaurant. The normally placid Saône here seems more like an ornamental lake than a river.

The approach to the upper end of the **Apremont** lock cut (K275), once dangerously close to a weir and presenting a blind corner, was improved by excavating a new channel in 1983. Écluse 17, at the far end, is rather wider than the *péniche*-sized chambers upstream and, like some of the disused locks further down river, was designed to accommodate freight craft side by side. We pass from the Haute-Saône *Département* into the Côte d'Or at K268. Dense woods, the haunt of anglers and summertime caravanners, characterise the 11km reach to the next lock cut at **Heuilley** (K257). At K260.3 a mooring on the left is convenient for the *Auberge du*

Vieux Moulin restaurant: they will organise a taxi if you telephone. Small craft may be launched at a former ferry crossing, opposite on the right. **Heuilley-sur-Saône** lies conveniently close to the canal (moor at the bridge), although the shopping/eating facilities of not many years ago seem to have vanished. The main activity in this area is farming and market gardening: local enquiry should result in the purchase of fresh vegetables. Immediately before the lock is the junction with the Canal de la Marne à la Saône (see Chapter 49).

Large meadows, low banks and grazing cattle now establish a type of scenery that will last for much of the journey to Lyon. **Pontailler** (K251), a pleasant little town with fine architecture in its domestic buildings and large Italianate church, offers convenient moorings with rubbish disposal and water downstream of the bridge on the right bank. The riverside *Restaurant des Marronniers* is agreeably situated and all shops are within easy reach together with a garage and obliging taxi service. For those with a yearning for slight adventure, the town may be circumnavigated by small boat using the course of the Veille Saône. This sometimes narrow waterway, likely to be congested with fishing punts in places, joins the main navigation a little upstream of the road bridge over the Saône. A very convenient *halte nautique*, used in part by a hire cruiser company, offers pontoon moorings and water supplies for boats in transit. Draft beyond this basin may be limited to little more than 1m and a speed of 6kph is imposed. The 2km course of the Vieille Saône passes a public park (mooring possible) before finally returning to the Saône at K249.5. Pontailler was virtually destroyed by Général Mercey in August 1636: a mere 22 people and five houses escaped. It was here that Philip Hamerton was imprisoned by the police aboard his *berrichon* in 1886, his sketching activities having been mistaken for spying (the Franco-Prussian War was still a fresh memory). Negotiations at a high level secured his release. Modern travellers are probably safe from massacre or arrest in Pontailler, through it might be unwise to test the present extent of official complacency by mooring on a forbidden section of bank from K249.5–247. This effectively prevents all approach to the town of **Vonges**. The trees conceal a national gunpowder works: punted fishermen can be noted lying here in considerable numbers (waiting for stunned fish in the event of an explosion?).

And so on to **Lamarche-sur-Saône** (K246), a little town with most facilities and mooring on the far bank, downstream of the bridge. Launching slipway 300m down river (town side). 3km on, the canal cut and lock of **Poncey-lès-Athée** are reached, followed at K234 by the sizeable town of **Auxonne**, former capital of a small state independent of both the Duchy of Burgundy and the Kingdom of France. Sailing, wind surfing and water-skiing are popular here. Very convenient moorings will be found on pontoons just upstream of the bridge, with a nearby slipway. Napoléon I spent a year in the town barracks in 1788, his stay being commemorated by a collection of relics in the Musée Bonaparte (open May–end October). Turreted fortifications remain on the river bank. Generally, the shops are rather old fashioned and offer little to tempt the passing tourist, but several fine timbered buildings remain in the town centre. Trees line the long straight cut leading to Auxonne lock (K230), the last of the 'small' unmodernised chambers of the Saône.

The next place of note is the junction with the Canal du Rhône au Rhin (K219) upstream of the small village of **St-Symphorien**. On the canal are a lock with keeper's house and yard of barge conversion specialists Bourgogne Marine (repairs). See Chapter 24.

St-Jean-de-Losne (K215), not long ago regarded as a leading inland freight port, has, over the last two decades, been developed as the most important pleasure boating centre on the French waterways: some would claim in Europe. The town is ideally situated at a junction with the Canal de Bourgogne, route for Dijon and the River Yonne (see Chapter 45). Through the canal's lock 76S lies an extensive basin with wharves, dry-dock and packed moorings for cruisers and barges

(the latter increasingly being used for pleasure rather than cargo). Alongside, at river level, is a huge grass-banked basin, the *Gare d'Eau*, with two tree-covered islands at the centre. This originated as a safe place for traffic to lie out of reach of Saône floods or where freight tows could be assembled. The longest established business in the basin is that of M Joël Blanquart, a former barge captain, who presides over one group of pleasure boat moorings, with a floating chandlery and offering most services including fuel. Next to arrive was the hire craft base of Crown Blue Line, whose premises are centred around a most ingenious dry-dock adapted from a large barge. Since the 1980s, Charles Gérard's H_2O company has built up a reputation as France's leading broker for all types of inland pleasure craft. Fluent English is spoken. The firm provides extensive long-term moorings, carries out conversions, repairs and modifications, operates a comprehensive chandlery and offers residential moorings at another site (the approach cut to the Saône's obsolete St-Jean-de-Losne lock, K211). The town regularly hosts rallies of commercial barges (the *Grand Pardon des Mariniers*, generally on the second Sunday of June) and similar events for pleasure boats. Numerous other facilities in the town include bankside visitors' moorings (water

A light snow fall at St-Jean-de-Losne.

and electricity) on a central quay above the river bridge; near the tourist office are showers, coin-operated washing and drying machines, a multi-lingual book swap and an internet café; there is a VNF office where waterways licences can be bought; and train tickets can be purchased at the SNCF shop. On the town outskirts is a station providing a rail link to Dijon and the high speed TGV network. In addition to supermarkets, most other shopping facilities are available including a *Maison de la Presse* that carries English papers. Restaurants range from traditional Burgundian to Chinese. Facing the *Mairie* is a small but fascinating waterways museum. It really is remarkable how this sleepy small town has regenerated itself over the last 20 years.

St-Jean was an important river port long before arrival of the Canal de Bourgogne. Little remains of the original fortifications from its glorious history. In 1273 the lords of Franche-Comté attacked with 500 men dressed as women: the townsfolk discovered the deception and killed them all. Then in 1636, when Pontailler was decimated at the start of the Thirty Years War, 80,000 troops of the Holy Roman Empire arrived, including Hungarians, Croatians and Spaniards under the command of Général Gallas. Considering St-Jean to be the gateway to Burgundy and the city of Dijon, he laid siege to it, expecting little resistance from the 400 arms-bearing citizens and 150 soldiers. The town held out for a week and the situation became so desperate that plans were about to be carried out to burn the houses and wreck the river bridge if the walls should be breached. Only just in time, reinforcements arrived from Auxonne. The Imperialists, having lost 800 men, retreated: against huge odds, St-Jean-de-Losne was saved. Ever since it has proudly carried the suffix *La Belle Défence*. A German advance was similarly repulsed in 1870. These brave deeds are commemorated by a stone monument between the bridge and the church.

Recent 'improvements' to 20km of the navigation have reduced the waterway's length by 10km: a straight canal now runs from K208, some distance below the former St-Jean-de-Losne lock. From a scenic viewpoint these developments are a disaster: much of the new channel is steel-piled or concrete lined with high banks making for tedious cruising in a small underpowered boat. Sections of the former through route remain navigable: notably 11km between Seurre and the disused Le Châtelet lock, available from the downstream end only; these possibilities are only likely to be of interest to local boaters.

After the depressing surrounds of the **Seurre** lock cut it is agreeable to emerge on the river once more. H₂0 operates a marina in a basin left of the downstream end of the lock approach channel. There are lines of

horse chestnuts, numerous little fishing punts and a row of brick and stone buildings fronting a quay upstream of the bridge. Good moorings for visiting craft. The town is well worth investigating, both for its shops and the restaurants. One of these, facing the river, offers a number of freshwater specialities, including *fritures* (tiny fried fish), frogs' legs, snails, trout and river crayfish. The huge 17th century building (partly converted into private houses) has at various times been a salt warehouse, a hospital and a bridge toll office. Reputedly, it was visited by Napoléon I. Remains of the demolished weir can be seen on each side of the channel by the infilled cut of Seurre's original lock (K184).

Chazelles (K181.5) lies on the left bank at the border between the Côte d'Or *Département* and Saône et Loire. Several long barns in stone with red roofs overlook the water. There is a restaurant and a sloping quay with mooring rings. **Charnay-lès-Chalon** (K178) has now been bypassed by the new cut and lock of Ecuelles. To approach too closely would bring a boat dangerously near the weir. However, it is worth mooring somewhat upstream and walking along the riverbank to visit one of the Saône's prettier settlements. It was here, during the 19th century, that the mayor so much hated the schoolmaster that he set fire to all but one of the thatched houses, accused the teacher of arson and brought about his transportation. Years later, the mayor made a death-bed confession and his former enemy was pardoned; but he remained so bitter that he rejected any idea of returning home.

Water and telephone are at Ecuelles lock, a large mechanised chamber of few attractions. By contrast, the village of **Écuelles** (K174), right bank, is almost Italian in appearance, intensely rural and worth exploring. Moorings are moderately good on a grassy bank in front of the church. Facilities amount to nothing more than a restaurant.

Now follows a very fine reach, with wooded cliffs on the right, leading to a camping site (left) on the outskirts of **Verdun-sur-le-Doubs**. A 19th century lock remained in service here until 1986. There is now no change in water levels. To reach Verdun, it is necessary to turn into the mouth of the River Doubs, the same river that forms much of the course of the Canal du Rhône au Rhin. This section of the Doubs is navigable, with care, for about 6km past the villages of **Saunières** (restaurant), and **Sermesse** (limited shopping) to the authorised upper limit at **Pontoux**. Keep a careful lookout for gravel barges which may be dredging this length and avoid their mooring hawsers. The trip is mildly adventurous and you are unlikely to meet many other pleasure craft.

Historic Verdun has perhaps a finer waterfront than any town on the Saône: a jumble of irregular stone

A delightful diversion up the Doubs to Verdun.

buildings rising sheer from the river. Excellent shops surround a small square. *Pôchouse*, a freshwater fish stew with wine and onions, is the local speciality. For this and other good value cuisine, try the *Restaurant des Trois Maures*. The *halte nautique*, comprising a series of pontoons, is often congested with craft of the hire fleet based here.

Chauvort (K165) offers a restaurant by a stepped quay near the site of a former suspension bridge. Few ancient bridges remain on the Saône, for it has experienced too many invasions over the centuries. The following reach is wide open, with tiny sandy beaches ideal for swimming on a hot day. Upstream of the Pont de **Gergy** (K159) are several fine country houses, one of which is decorated with a Burgundian tiled roof which somehow avoids looking gaudy in the green surroundings. Near the bridge are useful moorings with a range of facilities. Restaurant, 500m. The village of **Verjux**, a short distance from the river on the left, was home to a poor young laundress in the middle of the 19th century. She travelled to Paris and married a shopkeeper who

soon died, leaving her his business. The shop prospered, becoming a leading store of the capital – *Bon Marché*. Never forgetting her origins, Madame Boucicaut dispensed a sizeable fortune to charity, and in 1886 provided the then considerable sum of £20,000 for construction of a new bridge over the river at Verjux.

Little of note is passed on a long straight reach past **Port d'Allériot** (K150), whose restaurants are of use only to craft of shallow draft. Unless you choose to lie at anchor and go ashore in a dinghy, a procedure that I have sometimes adopted when cruising in a large motor yacht. Otherwise, you could consider using a small jetty at K151. Allériot faces the river square-on, seemingly deriving pleasure from its situation, unlike many other Saône settlements that shrink away from the waterside, doubtless fearing winter floods.

Now follows one of the major cities of the valley: **Chalon-sur-Saône** (K142). Open countryside gradually gives way to houses and just downstream of K145 is the entrance to the Canal du Centre, one of four possible routes to the Seine and the English Channel (see Chapter 43). This is soon followed on the right bank by extensive barge works capable of handling the largest vessels trading on the river. In the 19th and early 20th centuries there was a great shipbuilding enterprise here, Schneider de Chalon. Its production included 81 torpedo boats for various navies between 1889 and 1906, together with destroyers, submarines and various steam tugs and other inland vessels. The problem of transporting large sea-going craft to the Mediterranean via the Saône and Rhône, whose depth was clearly insufficient, was cleverly solved by building a shallow draft ship carrier, the *Porteur*, hauled by a pair of steam tugs.

An important town in pre-Roman times, *Cabillonum* was chosen by Julius Caesar as a food store during the Gallic Wars. Little remains of Roman fortifications or architecture other than several museum relics. In the summers of 1982–3 remains of a 3,000 year old Bronze Age village were discovered in the river, under 5m of water. Working from a specially adapted *péniche* named *Praehistoria*, archaeologists recovered an amazing collection of objects including bronze vases, swords, over 350 ceramic pots and a 15th century boat loaded with pottery artefacts. They are all now preserved at the town's Musée Denon. Under the Romans, the city marked the head of navigation with its own river superintendent (*praefectus navium araricarum*). About the 6th century Chalon was the capital of the Kingdom of Burgundy, extending north–south from Sens to Avignon, and east–west from Lake Geneva to the Loire. Under the Duchy of Burgundy, in the 15–16th centuries, it was a stylish city with fortified bridge, walls and towers. A few timber-framed buildings survive from this period. Although owing everything to its position on the Saône, Chalon has many times suffered from winter floods: as in the early part of 1982 when all communication with Mâcon was severed for several days, with the exception of the A6 *autoroute*. Throughout the following summer, debris caught in the trees remained as evidence of the great height to which the water rose.

Excellent visitors' moorings are in the *port de plaisance* on the Bras de la Génise to the left of the Ile St-Laurent, peaceful yet fairly convenient for the shops and main attractions. Supermarket, 300m. Among the full range of boating services is a floating *gîte*, a jolly little houseboat designed in a maritime style of architecture. Larger pleasure craft such as converted barges will find moorings among commercial vessels on the sloping quays of the main river.

The 15th century *Tour du Doyenné* (Deanery Tower) was removed from its original site near the cathedral and rebuilt on the Ile St-Laurent in 1928 (open for visits). Close by, the hospital of 1528 displays fine carved wood, early stained glass and a collection of *faïence* jars. On the right bank is the main part of the town, where several streets have been pedestrianised. Leading attractions are the cathedral of St-Vincent,

founded in the 5th century and mainly built in the 12th and 15th centuries with 19th century towers; the Musée Denon, an Empire-style former convent whose collections include examples of Gallo-Roman sculpture and the history of Saône navigation (open daily except Tuesdays); and the splendid stone river quay, decorated with flamboyant flower planters: it was built by local engineer Émiland Gauthey who was also responsible for the Canal du Centre and parts of the Canal du Rhône au Rhin. In late February and late June, Chalon stages *foires aux sauvagines* (wildfowl fairs) a tradition dating from medieval times.

Even the briefest halt should allow time to pay homage to Chalon's greatest celebrity, Nicéphore Niépce, the father of photography. Born in 1765 in the rue de l'Oratoire, he managed to preserve a photographic image produced with a *camera obscura* in 1822. Among other of his achievements was the design for an internal combustion engine. His statue, on the quay, was inaugurated in the later part of the 19th century with a day of celebrations that included brass bands, speeches, a banquet and fireworks. 150 years after the world's first photograph, Chalon set up the Musée Nicéphore Niépce in a splendid 18th century building overlooking the river at 28 Quai des Messageries (open daily except Tuesdays). Chalon makes a good centre for visiting Burgundy and the vineyards: the famous wine town of Beaune lies 33km distant.

The New Port of Chalon, in a huge basin south of the town at K137, increases the river's width almost to 1km. There would appear to be ample scope for greater use of its facilities. A hint of the approaching south, in the form of Provençal red pantiles, is noted at **Port d'Ouroux**, a small village by a bridge at K131 (restaurant and pontoon mooring). The little **River Grosne**, right bank, K128.5, is navigable by light craft for a short distance to the village of **Marnay** (shops and restaurants). Long unchanging vistas take the navigator by the former lock at **Gigny** (K123, moorings and restaurant). **Ormes**, left bank (K120.5) is notable for a most attractive small *château* with Burgundian tiled roof, cottage and gazebo. Then comes the giant Ormes lock (K119), completed in 1979. If water levels are high, craft are directed over the weir, a phenomenon I once experienced in mid-June.

One of the most pleasing towns on the entire river is **Tournus** (K112) with good moorings to a quay above the bridge and on pontoons below. All facilities are at hand. The abbey church of St-Philibert shelters the remains of St-Valerian, a 2nd century martyr. This splendid Romanesque church dates mainly from the 11th and 12th centuries, although the crypt is 6th century. Surprisingly, the recorded choral music played for the benefit of pilgrims/tourists actually enhances the experience of a visit, as does the modern abstract stained glass. Tasteful souvenirs available in the town include reproduction stone carvings and basket work. There is an over-priced antique shop in another 11th century church and a collection of antique dealers installed in an equally historic building where the traders have the effrontery to charge a not insubstantial entry fee!

6km below Tournus, the Saône is joined by its sole navigable tributary (discounting the Doubs, which is a locked waterway in its middle reaches only). This is the beautiful River Seille (K106, see Chapter 50). A sloping quay offers moorings outside an isolated restaurant where the road from **St-Oyen** runs down to the waterside (K100.5).

On the left bank by the bridge of **Fleurville** (K97.5, shopping 1.5km) the **Canal de Pont-de-Vaux** runs for 3km to the town of that name. After being disused for many years it was restored in 1993 at a cost of about £1 million and may be used by craft drawing up to 1.3m. Effectively a lateral canal to the River Reyssouze, there are good moorings and urban services at the terminus, together with hire cruisers and a very convenient supermarket. Restaurants exist on each side of the Saône with moorings below the canal's entrance lock.

The Saône navigation continues to the right of the long wooded Ile de Brouard (K96). In clear weather it is possible to see the snow-covered heights of 4,807m Mont Blanc, 160km SE. From here to Mâcon the busy N6 is often close on the right bank and beyond it the A6 *autoroute*. Waterside restaurants are situated at **Asnières** (K90, pontoon and water point), **St-Martin-Belle-Roche** (K89) and near **Vésines**, where there is a pontoon (K87.5). Upstream-bound craft have a fine view of the *château* at **St-Jean-Le-Priche** (K87).

High-rise buildings are the first indication of **Mâcon** (K81), now bypassed by a large new canal, running between K83.5 and K79 and enabling large commercial craft to avoid the city's Pont St-Laurent with its restricted clearance. Smaller vessels and pleasure craft are able to follow the natural course of the waterway through the city centre. At K83, right bank, is the excellent *Port de Plaisance de Mâcon*, with all services including fuel, water, 3,000kg crane, slipway and long-term moorings. Nearby is a supermarket and various fast-food restaurants. The marina, however, lies about 30 minutes' walk from the centre of town. As an overnight stop, the central Quai Lamartine (water point) might be preferable, as it is close to shops and the market: while much of the wall is inclined, there is a vertical section. Its name recalls Alphonse Prat de Lamartine, the poet and politician (1790–1869) who was born here. Although Middle Ages fortifications

have now vanished, the eight-arched Pont St-Laurent dates from the 14th century and was reconstructed in the 19th. Thus, it is a Saône rarity, other ancient bridges having been destroyed in the frequent battles that have raged in this border country. A statue of St-Nicolas, patron saint of barge people as well as of children, occupies a niche between the second and third arches on the right, upstream, side: quite correctly, he is visible only to river travellers. Little more than two octagonal towers remain of St-Vincent's cathedral, mostly destroyed in the French Revolution. The Mâconnais vineyards, extending from Beaujolais in the south to Tournus, may be visited from here, the celebrated villages of **Pouilly** and **Fuissé** being about 8km distant. Mâcon is a sunny town of red pantiles presenting a distinctly southern air. Worth visiting are the *Préfecture* in the French Renaissance style and the *Hôtel-Dieu* with its collection of apothecaries' jars. Opposite the downstream junction with the river and the new bypass channel is the commercial barge port (K79), with a much larger *Nouveau Port*, right bank (K77).

Downstream of the Ile d'Amprun (K75) is a viaduct carrying a line used by the exciting TGV trains. In 1990, one on the French Atlantic route broke the world record with a speed of 479kph (298mph). **Arciat** (K73) is notable for excellent deep wall moorings and on pontoons, right bank, downstream of the bridge. Restaurant, water point and slipway. There is a further quay, left bank, K69. Fuel supplies (at garage), basic shopping and a restaurant are available at **St-Romain-des-Iles** (K66) which lies between the A6 and the Saône: moor at the small marina. **Thoissey** (K63, jetty) is 1km east of the navigation, with several restaurants, comprehensive shopping and a sandy beach by the bridge. Another of the new locks is the Écluse de Dracé (K62, right bank). Be careful of the strong eddy when the chamber is filling. The reach that follows provides good views of the hills to the right, with a *château* on the left bank. Changes in the river levels resulting from rearranged navigation works have produced an effect of a 'drowned valley' in reverse: from here for the next 10–15km the shoreline has the appearance of a tideway at low water. There is ample depth in the channel, but many former quays now rise from sand banks and mooring for all but the smallest boats can be difficult. As the years pass, these lengths of exposed foreshore are gradually becoming covered with vegetation. Typical of the towns with mediocre access is **Belleville** (K55), a sizeable place 1km beyond the A6, providing shops and restaurants. Medium sized cruisers may be able to lie bow-on to a shoal above the bridge; otherwise, subject to its commercial use requirements, investigate using a gravel barge quay.

Below a pair of islands, **Montmerle** (K52) in part occupies a hill, left bank, surmounted by its church and is a good shopping centre. There are several pontoons for visitor use. One of the restaurants is *Guide Michelin* listed. **Port Rivière** (K48.5) has several restaurants, useful provided you can find somewhere to stop. The *Nautic* Boatyard (K43) with fuel, restaurant and other services is perhaps the best mooring for **Beauregard**, less than 1km downstream; here are shops and further eating places. The *Auberge Bressane* offers an elaborate menu and has a terrace overlooking the suspension bridge. A convenient (but rather commercialised) mooring lies downstream, right bank, at the port of **Villefranche-sur-Saône**, (K40.4). The town itself is 2km to the west and is dominated by tower blocks (all facilities). **Jassans Riottier** (K40) on the opposite bank has useful marina moorings with most services nearby. Increasing leisure use of the river is now evident as we come within commuting distance of Lyon. There are numerous camping and caravan sites, small swimming beaches and widespread use of little motor cruisers.

Thickly wooded surroundings past the village of **St-Bernard** (K35) are popular with sunbathers throughout the summer. Many people doubtless come from **Trévoux** (K30.5), the onetime capital of the Principality of Dombes and not incorporated into France until the mid-18th century. Built on a hilly site on the left bank, the town is one of the most attractive on the entire river. There are several sections of quayside where mooring is possible, if not ideal. A sour note is introduced by the activities of small high-speed motorboats that race through the town, creating a wash far more dangerous to little cruisers than that produced by 1,500-tonne freight craft. Frantic gestures to prevent these thoughtless maniacs swamping my inflatable dinghy were of no avail. A serious accident will some time inevitably result and perhaps then the authorities will be pressured into enforcing the speed limits. Such behaviour on most British waterways would bring instant prosecution with heavy fines or even imprisonment. The centre of Trévoux consists of a terrace high above the river, with the church on one side and the late 17th century *Palais du Parlement* (superb painted beams) on another. Italianate turrets and pantiles in the steep and narrow streets are very southern in feeling, especially in the delightfully named and precipitous *Rue Casse-Cou* (Broken Neck Street). A very sharp incline leads to a feudal 10–13th century *château* at the top of the town with walks along the battlements, ruined towers and a magnificent view along the Saône valley and across to the Beaujolais hills. Philip Hamerton described this panorama as 'the fairest landscape on the Saône, perhaps the fairest scene in France', a claim that

is not greatly exaggerated. A market is held on Saturday mornings. Slipway on the east bank, below the bridge.

No longer is the Saône the quiet river of its upper reaches: the closeness of Lyon has brought much development of the valley and this rather enhances the pleasure of cruising, with added sights and people to watch. Note the cluster of converted barges at a former lock on the left (K26). There remain sandy beaches like that in a grove of white poplars at K24. Ahead, are the wooded slopes of **Mont d'Or** (625m), with good moorings, left, at a boatyard (K23.7) offering a full range of services. This is followed by another similarly extensive yard on the right (K22.5) below **St-Germain au Mont d'Or**.

Villevert and **Neuville-sur-Saône** are either side of a bridge (K21) with convenient moorings and good shops and restaurants close by. The Écluse de Couzon (K17) is the final Saône lock downstream of a spectacular reach with wooded cliffs. At this end of the 45km pound that extends all the way from the Écluse de Dracé, water levels have been raised, 'drowning' numerous trees whose dead remains rise direct from the river. In 1983 a steel *péniche* the *Parfair Amour*, was inaugurated as an inland waterways information centre. Raised onto the lockside and planted on piles, it provides an excellent opportunity for appreciating how large these 38m craft really are. The shore side of a floating pontoon at **Rochetaillée** (K16.5) may be used for private craft (the outside is reserved for trip boats). From here it is a short walk to the *château* which houses the Henri-Malartre collection of more than 180 motor cars, public transport vehicles, cycles and motor cycles. River traffic follows a one-way course round each side of the Ile de Roy (K14) as the Saône narrows through a shallow wooded gorge. Several grand houses perched on the slopes were the 19th century residences of Lyon merchants. Among the most famous restaurants in France is that of Paul Bocuse, upstream of a railway bridge at **Collonges** (K12). This allegedly superb, but very expensive establishment, which attracts lunch time custom from as far away as Paris, is served by a landing stage.

One of the most perfectly situated homes on a French river rises from a rocky outcrop at the head of the **Ile Barbe** (Wild Island, K10): 600m long and up to 130m wide, this place was occupied by a leading Lyonnaise abbey for a thousand years, from the 5th century. Eventually the monks became so rich and powerful that they were submerged in turpitude and vice. With disarming honesty, they petitioned the King to be disestablished; the request was passed to Pope Paul III, who duly granted them their wish in 1549. A suspension bridge now connects the lower end of the island to each bank of the mainland. There is a public park, a fine restaurant, the *Auberge de l'Ile*, several houses and the crumbling remnants of the ecclesiastical past.

To arrive by water in any great city is a fascinating experience. **Lyon** (K7 onwards) is no exception for this is the second city of France, the self-proclaimed gastronomic capital of the world, and a place so full of attractions that a week would be long enough to explore just a tiny proportion of them. I came here for my first foreign holiday as a 14-year-old and subsequent visits never fail to recall the adventure of wandering through the streets alone, always a little uncertain that I would safely find my way back to my apartment off the Rue de la République. It would be impossible to describe all the sights, which are more than adequately covered in the Michelin Green Guide *Auvergne Rhône Valley*. Although the population of Greater Lyon exceeds 1,200,000, its historic centre is fairly compact. Important Roman remains include two well-preserved amphitheatres and the remnants of a water supply aqueduct. There are broad quays along the banks of the Saône and the blue-green glacier-fed Rhône. In all, there are no fewer than 23 museums. The famed silk industry, dating from the 16th century, is commemorated in a sumptuous fabric museum. Among other important highlights are the wonderful *Musée des Beaux Arts*, in France second only to the Louvre (paintings, sculpture and antiquities); the *Musée des Arts Décoratifs*; and the *Château Lumière* (a remarkable late 19th century building now devoted to cinematic history). Around 80 antique shops are clustered in the Rue Auguste Comte. A particular favourite of mine is the *Parc de la Tête d'Or* with magnificent flower displays of French carpet bedding and a splendid 19th century glass house. Fashionable stores will be found along the Rue de la République. Contributions of the late 20th century include a sparkling new *Métro* system that serves the splendidly revamped Gare de Parrache rail station: a bus terminal is incorporated into this complex of glass and orange plastic, with escalators and brightly lit shops under cover. Come here to view the record-beating TGV trains. Limited research indicates that the best value in restaurant food is near the station, although *Michelin* lists an array of establishments offering superb fare in this centre of gastronomy.

Navigation through the central part of the city is arranged on a one-way basis in times of flood, at 2½ hr intervals. Consult the indicator boards. Façades of tall Renaissance Italianate buildings by the Pont de l'Homme de la Roche are succeeded by several bridges to the city centre. Currently, the best recommended mooring is at the old *port de plaisance*, a rather scruffy quay with no facilities facing the Gothic cathedral of St-Jean (left bank, between Pont Maréchal-Juin and Pont Bonaparte). As in any large town, the security of a boat cannot be guaranteed and it would be wise to ask the skipper of a nearby vessel to keep an eye open if you plan to be absent only briefly. From the Gare St-Jean, take the funicular railway to the huge 19th century Basilica of Notre-Dame-de-Fourvière: at a considerable height, there are views down over the rooftops to the two rivers. The Roman theatres are close by. For many years it has been disgraceful that a city of the importance and prestige of Lyon has not bothered to provide welcoming and suitable moorings for visiting boaters. Many hundreds of towns and villages through the waterways network have been successful where this city has utterly failed. Past promises have to date resulted in nothing. A current plan (2004) does, however, envisage a full scale *port de plaisance* as part of the far reaching regeneration programme due to be carried out on a huge site at the confluence of the two rivers.

No matter how short your visit, do reserve a little time to wander at will, savouring the sights, the open-air flower and fruit market by the Saône, the clusters of barges, and absorbing the colourful Lyonnaise atmosphere. Many holidaymakers will have seen a little of Lyon from the main north–south *autoroute*, which dives through tunnels and along the Rhône quays: but there is much more to discover in this wonderful place, where tradition claims that there are *three* rivers – the Saône, the Rhône and the wine!

The navigation finally empties into the Rhône below the Pont de la Mulatière. A former lock now provides moorings for pleasure craft: if a long stay is contemplated this could be the place to try. Water and fuel are available at K1.8; alternatively about 1km up the Rhône from the junction.

49 ⌁ Canal de la Marne à la Saône

> **Carte Guide:** *Champagne Ardenne*
> From a junction with the Canal de la Marne au Rhin and the Canal Latéral à la Marne at Vitry-le-François to the River Saône at Heuilley-sur-Saône: 224km and 114 locks. There are two tunnels: Condes (308m) near Chaumont and Balesmes (4,820m) near Langres.

Of four possible routes between Paris and the Mediterranean, the Canal de la Marne à la Saône is the longest; but, having the same number of locks as the

77km shorter Bourbonnais route, it is well worth consideration. And for craft crossing France from Belgium or the Netherlands, it is an obvious first choice.

The northern part of the waterway is, in effect, a lateral canal to the River Marne which it follows closely to a point near the river's source on the Plateau de Langres, 71 locks on from Vitry-le-François. After passing through Balesmes summit level tunnel, the route falls sharply via 43 locks in the valley of the River Vingeanne to join the Saône upstream of Pontailler-sur-Saône. Only one sizeable town lies directly on the canal and a degree of careful planning is required to ensure that adequate food and fuel supplies are in reserve. Drinking water points are infrequent: information supplied by lock staff will be found more reliable than the *Carte Guide*.

Rural almost from end to end, the waterway is a little straight and dull through gravel-bearing land from Vitry-le-François to St-Dizier. Thereafter, the scenery is consistently fine, past wooded cliffs, riverbank water mills and an amazing variety of trees, many of which are planted in avenues on the canal banks. These include Scots pines and larches.

The majority of locks are manually operated, travelling keepers being employed over quite long distances. Paddle and gate-opening gear is heavy but efficient. A substantial quantity of locks on the Saône side of the summit have been automated with a number of swing, bascule and vertical lifting bridges converted to automatic operation with radar beams activated by the passage of craft; instruction leaflets are issued to boats as they enter the section concerned. Canal architecture and engineering is often most interesting, from the lock houses whose date plaques enable the traveller to trace the progress of construction during the latter part of the 19th century to a large number of small aqueducts, frequently situated at the upstream ends of locks. Traffic has long been halted by Sunday closure of locks – a situation that must surely soon be rectified. The one-way working of Balesmes Tunnel could result in a delay of as much as 10 hours; here it is best to arrange a halt where some shore facilities are available. For no very obvious reason, only small numbers of pleasure craft use the waterway, while freight vessels become fewer each year. Although boating facilities have been improved in recent years, there are currently no hire craft based on the waterway.

Brief history Conceived as a continuation of the Canal Latéral à la Marne, opened in 1845, and originally known as the Canal de la Haute Marne, the waterway ran for 73km from Vitry-le-François. Construction was carried out between 1863 and 1879. Soon afterwards,

the far-reaching Freycinet Plan for French waterways development was introduced, resulting in enlargement of the newly built locks to their present *péniche* dimensions and the extension of the line southwards to join the Saône. All was completed by 1907 and the canal was renamed.

Four large reservoirs near the Langres summit (La Liez, La Mouche, Charmes and La Vingeanne) ensure excellent water supplies and closures through drought have been rare. Two exceptions were for 42 days in September/October 1954 and 43 days in November/December 1964. A pumping station was installed at the Charmes reservoir in 1956 for use in exceptionally dry conditions.

Chiefly designed as a linking waterway, with few ports en route, the Canal de la Marne à la Saône mainly carried pit-props, building stone, pig-iron and coal up to World War II, totalling 849,000 tonnes in 1936. By 1963 the figure has increased to 935,000 tonnes. 23km of branch line with eight locks was opened in 1883 to serve the metallurgical district of Wassy-Brousseval, south of St-Dizier. It became a victim of World War II when 2km was infilled by the Germans to enlarge St-Dizier airport. Thus detached from the network, the remainder of the Wassy Branch was rendered useless for freight purposes and was officially abandoned in 1952. Although parts of the canal have vanished without trace, elsewhere sections remain in water and it is possible to find some of the locks and their keepers' cottages.

The once important barge town of **Vitry-le-François** has experienced the collapse of freight traffic in recent years and has been slow to reinvent itself as a pleasure boating port. The best approach to the town is from any point between the second bridge and Écluse 71, Désert (K1.1, water point). Waterside supermarket, right, a short way into the canal. For details of Vitry, see Chapter 27. Lock operating gear – especially at Écluse 71 – is very heavy. Scenery in the early reaches is not particularly inspiring, being through fields of maize with avenues of pines and periodic gravel pits.

Orconte, an expanding village by Écluse 66 (K13.5. moorings) is a useful port of call with picturesque half-timbered buildings recalling those of the Normandy orchards. There are several shops and two restaurants. That nearest the canal once provided us with a very agreeable simple meal of many courses (no choice) at half an hour's notice. Within seconds of taking our booking, Madame was noted scurrying into the butchers to buy supplies. From here, a long straight leads all the way to St-Dizier, with a restaurant on the N4 between Écluses 64 and 63; the village of **Perthes**

(K20.2) at Écluse 63 has basic shops and a garage. Garage and restaurant (also on the N4) are reached from Écluse 61, **Hallignicourt** (K24.1), the most suitable point from which to travel 4km north to **Villiers-en-Lieu**, home of the French Car Museum where 150 vehicles are on show (open most afternoons).

To the south is **St-Dizier** airport, with a *port de plaisance* and boatyard offering various services including fuel at a basin (all that remains of the Wassy Branch) immediately before Écluse 59, La Noue (K29.6). Though now an industrial town based on iron and steel working, St-Dizier was an important 16th century stronghold and in 1544 earned the gratitude of François I when 2,500 citizens repulsed 100,000 soldiers under Charles V. It is the only really convenient town between here and the Saône and the shopping centre 500m right of Écluse 58 is both attractive and comprehensive. Close to the left-hand side of the canal is a main line rail station. There are impressive urban mansions and magnificent public gardens in the Place Winston Churchill. Suburbs lead to a railway swing bridge and a road bascule shortly before Écluse 57, **Marnaval** (K34.1).

Now the scenery steadily becomes much prettier and surroundings remain consistently pleasant all the way to the Saône. This is partly accounted for by the canal clinging to the windings of the River Marne, with regular sightings of stone water mills. Care is necessary at a very acute bend by the railway bridge at Écluse 56, **Guë** (K36.3); a plaque records building of the lock in 1865 and its lengthening in 1880. A good range of shops, all very close, is found in **Chamouilley** (K38.9): moor at the concrete bridge before Écluse 55. An extensive wood-processing yard, once an important user of canal transport, now receives deliveries by road. Here the design of paddle gear changes; from now on, locks are fitted with four massive and highly efficient ground paddles that require few turns to open fully. Thick woods and a twisting channel lead to **Eurville** and Écluse 54 where instructional leaflets are issued to southbound craft; these explain the functioning of radar-controlled opening bridges scattered throughout the next 50km. The chief point to remember is to avoid mooring within 500m of either side: this can result in bridges staying open longer than necessary, to the frustration of motorists. The village, a short distance from the lock, is a charming place with limited shopping.

In addition to the succession of radar bridges, this part of the canal is notable for alder-filled swamps and shady pools by the edge of the Marne, with several small aqueducts. **Bayard** at Écluse 52 (K45.9) offers restaurant and grocer, while grocer and baker will be found in **Gourzon** (K47.2) by a lift bridge some

distance before Écluse 51, **Fontaines-sur-Marne**. Here, only the closeness of the railway breaks the illusion of remoteness. Écluse 50 (K50.6) has a restaurant offering a good choice of reasonably priced meals, with all shopping about 1km east in the small town of **Chevillon**. Three bascule bridges in succession are encountered after Écluse 48, **Curel** (K54.6) where there are several shops and restaurant in the hilly stone-built village. The waterway swings around the base of a wooded cliff at Écluse 47, **Autigny** (K57.1), and after passing through Écluse 46, **Bussy** (K59.3), we arrive at **Thonnance-lès-Joinville** (K61.1) where a restaurant and several shops can be reached from a mooring near the bridge.

Joinville (K62.5, *port de plaisance*), on the right beyond Écluse 45, stands in the shadow of a hill once dominated by a feudal *château*, birthplace of the Ducs de Guise. The site is now occupied by the 16th century *Château du Grand Jardin*, open to the public and containing a fine collection of exotic trees. The Marne flows through the town centre which features waterside walks with displays of flowers. Shopping is good. Barely providing space for two *péniches* to pass each other, a narrow stone-lined cutting takes the canal southwards, past **St-Urbain-sur-Marne** (baker) 1km from Écluse 42 (K67.6). The river water at Écluse 41, **Mussey-sur-Marne** (K70.4), seen from a fine triple-arched aqueduct, is crystal clear. Limited shopping in the village, with restaurant and garage. *Port de plaisance* at **Donjeux** (K72). By now, there is a distinct feel of having ascended into higher terrain, through fields of maize and wheat punctuated by patches of dense woodland. **Rouvroy**, by Écluse 40 (K73.2), sees the Marne flow under the canal once more. Écluse 39, **Gudmont** (K76), is not only noisy from trains crossing a bridge, but a pall of dust from a stone-crushing works hangs everywhere. Rural peace returns, and after a sweeping bend by Écluse 37, **Provenchères** (K81.2), the waterway arrives at the little town of **Froncles** (K82.2, *port de plaisance*) with a quantity of useful shops scattered along the banks of the Marne.

Almost at any time during the summer, the great variety of greens displayed by trees along the Canal de la Marne à la Saône is particularly notable. This is especially so in the reaches that now follow. **Vouécourt**, Écluse 34 (K89.7), provides a grocer; 4km NW lies **Vignory**, situated in a hollow where there is a ruined *château* and a perfect example of a mid-11th century Romanesque church, St-Étienne. The pound between Écluses 33 and 32 features a radar-operated bridge at **Viéville** (K93.2, *port de plaisance*), with a shallow, stone-lined cutting above Écluse 32. All facilities can be found in **Bologne**, beyond the river at Écluse 30 (K97.4), with an aqueduct over the Marne soon afterwards. In a meadow on the river bank, left, shortly before Écluse

29, **Riaucourt** (K101), a stone cross within a fenced enclosure is a memorial to some children drowned here in the 19th century. The tragedy had a considerable impact on the local community which organised a collection to pay for the monument. **Brethenay** (grocer) has the most pleasingly situated lock on the entire canal, No 27 (K104.6). Just below is an old drawbridge, with the river and a ruined mill alongside; high above, on the right, the N67 runs along the edge of a cliff. After a further lock, we reach the exceptionally wide **Condes Tunnel**, 308m long (K105.6); passage of this and the drawbridge beyond an aqueduct on the south side is controlled by the keeper at Écluse 26. Craft travelling northwards pass through a radar beam before they reach the bridge. Numbers displayed at locks between here and the Langres summit do not always correspond with those printed in the *Carte Guide*.

The waterway winds past the east side of the city of **Chaumont**, whose commercial port is seen on the left bank after Écluse 25, **Reclancourt** (K108.9). Good supermarket about 400m. Closest approach to the town is from the bridge in the pound that follows and up a steep and winding road for a little over 2km. This is probably too far for a shopping trip, unless you are prepared to return by taxi. There is a choice of two restaurants close to the canal: one of them sells petrol. Water may be obtained from the visitors' moorings between locks 25 and 24. From its lofty setting on a ridge between the Rivers Marne and Suize, Chaumont was a stronghold of the Counts of Champagne in the 13–14th centuries: fortified ramparts remain from this era. Other features are the Basilica of St-Jean Baptiste, the Square Philippe-Lebon and an outstanding 600m railway viaduct with 50 arches on three levels spanning the Suize valley. Écluse 23, **Choignes** (K111.9) is an alternative approach to Chaumont. Clusters of pines on a rocky cliff overlook a stone-lined canal cutting, with a water mill on the river. By this point lock houses bear the date 1884. There are numerous grassy bank moorings and quite lovely scenery. In this area the cast-iron lock paddles are of a very interesting pattern, with a dial and pointer indicating whether the aperture is open or closed.

Shopping for bread and groceries can be done in **Luzy-sur-Marne**, at Écluse 19 (K120.5). However, if you wait until **Foulain** (K124.3), with excellent moorings by a meadow in the reach between Écluse 17 and 16, you can walk across a railway level crossing and into the flourishing village to find a selection of shops, restaurant and garage, all within 350m of the waterway. The final series of locks to the summit level offers an assortment of limited facilities. The bridge shortly before Écluse 9, **Rolampont** (K139.2, convenient moorings), is close for most kinds of shopping, this village being one

of few on the route which spreads along the canal bank. Upstream of Écluse 8, St-Menge (K140.4) is a bridge carrying the A31 Langres-Toul *autoroute*. Three of the canal's important supply reservoirs are quite close by. At **Humes**, Écluse 5 (K144.4), with its somewhat scruffy commercial port, there are basic shops. A manually worked swing bridge mounted on an 'island' in the centre of the canal is a leading feature of **Jorquenay** (K145.9), while at Écluse 3, Moulin-Rouge (K148.1), will be seen a substantial timber yard, complete with proprietor's ornate 19th century residence and outbuildings which include an extensive wash-house with cistern. Rising in the distance beyond are the ramparts of Langres. A *halte nautique* has been set up at K148.8.

In spite of the 3km (uphill) walk from the canal near Écluse 2, Moulin-Chapeau (K149.8), **Langres** is well worth a journey, both for sight-seeing and for more practical shopping purposes. Although I once narrowly escaped death on this road when flung from the pillion of the ship's motorcycle and into the path of a lorry, subsequent visits confirmed an initial impression that the city has much to offer. Set on a high point overlooking the Langres Plateau and close to the source of the Marne, it was one of three capitals of Gaulish Burgundy. In addition to the cathedral of St-Mammès, every visitor should make a circuit on foot of the

An unusual variety of paddle gear at Écluse 19, Luzy-sur-Marne. The indicator hand shows how widely the sluice is opened.

fortified ramparts punctuated at intervals by towers and gateways. The views are superb. A passenger car on a short length of track has been preserved from a former rack railway that once rumbled along a steep incline below the city walls. Shops are good. At this 'Gateway to Burgundy' one of the most agreeable restaurants is at the *Hôtel d'Europe*.

Updated information on passage times for the one-way **Balesmes Tunnel** (4,820m) can be obtained from the keeper of Écluse 1, Batailles (K152.5). Craft pass through the illuminated vault under their own power. At the far end, a stone-lined cutting leads to the not insignificant village of **Heuilley-Cotton** (K161.6), with moorings at several points including a 'port' on the left before the first of two bridges. Pleasant though this deeply rural settlement is, it sadly suffers from a complete lack of facilities. But it is a safe place to leave a north-bound boat while visiting Langres by taxi if it is necessary to kill time waiting for your turn in the tunnel or if you have been caught by the Sunday lock closure. A rather better Sunday halting point, still within taxi distance of Langres, would be **Villegusien** (K167.7), just uphill of Écluse 9 in a series of closely-spaced deep locks descending towards the Saône. Here are good butchers and bakers and an amazing emporium selling most requirements from summer dresses to infra-red lamps for raising chicks. These and the majority of the remaining locks are automated. Staff from the control centre at Écluse 1 may be relied on to assist if the gear is reluctant to function as it should.

Consistently pretty surroundings accompany the waterway as it follows the valley of the River Vingeanne past the delightful village of **Piépape**, just before Écluse 12 (K169.5). Bankside facilities are very sparse for a while with little of note until **Pouilly-sur-Vingeanne** (K195): 5km west lies **Fontaine-Française** (all urban requirements). Nearby, in 1595 Henri IV with a mere 510 horsemen beat a 15,000-strong army composed of troops from Spain and the *Ligue*. The *château* is open to the public. **St-Seine-sur-Vingeanne**, 2km east of the canal at Écluse 29 (K196.7), is notable for its Burgundian Romanesque church. On the left beyond Écluse 32, **Fontenelle** (K199.5) is an impressive fortified farmhouse, while the *Château des Rosières* 3km NE of Écluse 33, Licey (K201.8), dating from the 15–17th centuries, merits investigation.

The bridge north of Écluse 34, **Dampierre-sur-Vingeanne** (K204.3), is the best point from which to walk or cycle 2km into **Beaumont-sur-Vingeanne** for glimpses of the exterior of a delightful 18th century *château* (not open to the public). It is of quite small proportions and features a fine roof of coloured Burgundian tiles. Both river and canal are crossed by a huge concrete railway viaduct a little before Écluse 38, **Oisilly** (K210.5). Not many years ago, **Renève**, at Écluse 39 (K214.2, *halte nautique*), boasted a full range of shops: now, it is reduced to just a baker and restaurant, startling evidence of the social changes in rural France brought about by car ownership and large supermarkets.

With the Saône junction now quite close, the last point of great interest is the small town of **Talmay**, 3km NE of the bridge (K221.1) in the middle of the pound between Écluses 41 and 42. Here is a notable *château*, guided tours July/August 15.00–18.00h, not Mondays. The oldest portion is a 46m high 13th century keep to which is attached a Classical mid-18th century mansion in cream stone under a roof of coloured glazed tiles. At Écluse 42, **Maxilly-sur-Saône** (K222.7, restaurant and basic shopping), taxis may be hired for a 5km trip into **Pontailler-sur-Saône** (all services, see Chapter 48). One more lock, Écluse 43, Chemin de Fer (K223), intervenes before the approach to the Saône's **Heuilley-sur-Saône** lock cut where the right-angled junction is controlled by traffic lights. Water is available from the Saône lock keeper.

50 ~ River Seille

> **Carte Guide:** *Saône*
> From a junction with the River Saône (K106) near La Truchère, to a terminus at Louhans. 39km and 4 locks.

An enchanting – almost enchanted – waterway, until recently little known and generally ignored by yachtsmen making for the Mediterranean or rushing to home ports in the north. For many years its only traffic was a handful of sand barges, but these had ceased to trade by the late 1970s. Hardly touched by main roads, the Seille winds through a charming landscape of fields and trees, with agreeable grass bank moorings available almost throughout. Now that it is regularly used by hire cruisers, it is no longer possible to describe the Seille as a peaceful backwater. Indeed, without the present levels of traffic it would be foolish to justify the costs of keeping the navigation open. The first lock at La Truchère is manned; the remainder are operated by boaters. Without hurrying, the river can easily be explored from one end to the other in a single long day, although there will always be a temptation to linger much longer.

Brief history It is recorded that rock salt was transported from the Jura to Louhans by wagon and small boats about AD 1000, then transferred to larger craft and moved down the Seille by the monks of Tournus. Return loads of building stone and later coal aided the construction and development of the medieval market town of Louhans. Work on the present locks started in 1777. It seems highly likely that the local bridges, highways and canal engineer Émiland-Marie Gauthey was involved. Lock chambers are 30.4m x 5.17m. Only the lowest one at la Truchère was enlarged to Freycinet dimensions.

For a number of years following ending of freight transport on the river, maintenance was minimal. Silting seriously reduced draft in the lock cuts and urgent remedial work was carried out in 1981 to save the waterway from complete dereliction. Conditions are now very good and, under normal conditions, craft drawing at least 1.3m should experience no difficulties.

The river's entrance from the Saône at K106 is not immediately obvious. Ignore a wide upstream channel (which is a weir outfall), turning instead into a little arm, just before a copse. This leads to La Truchère lock, with landing steps each side of the tail wall. The keeper lives in a cottage alongside an upper chamber marking the site of a former lock. **La Truchère** (K0.5) lies on the left bank, a collection of small houses and narrow winding streets, facing the water. There are two rest-

aurants, including the attractive waterside *Auberge de la Grenouillère*, a passenger vessel and a selection of jolly motorised catamarans for self-drive day hire. A restored water mill stands by the weir. **Pont-Seille** (K3) is a three-arched concrete bridge with small restaurant. Trees and meadows, very reminiscent of the Yorkshire Derwent, lead to **Ratenelle** (K8), with mooring possible by the bridge against a wall on the right. There is limited shopping and a restaurant. An unusually plain church with spire stands near the water's edge. Gallo-Roman relics have been recovered from the river bed.

The five tall, slated turrets of the *Château de Montrepost* among the trees announce the presence of the small town of **Cuisery** (K13). A channel on the right leads to Écluse 2, where the former keeper's cottage is festooned with an ancient and magnificent *glycine* (wisteria). The lock cut leads to a broad reach at the head of a weir stream, just below the N75 bridge carrying the main road between Tournus and Louhans. Beyond is a well-equipped *port de plaisance* on pontoons. The town with selection of shops (market, Tuesday mornings) and several restaurants is one of the celebrated four *Villages du Livre* (Book Villages) of France. There are numerous

A mill at Loisy.

second-hand book shops and an open air book fair on the first Sunday of each month. One fault of the town and an overnight mooring near the bridge is a noise of almost ceaseless lorries and croaking frogs.

Lush meadows, with frequent potential mooring places, accompany the river as it winds towards **Loisy** (K17), with a magnificent stone water mill at the head of the weir stream, left. Access to the village is not easy: small boats can approach the bank in this stream. Otherwise, take the lock cut and cross the lock island from the abutments of a former bridge (this, however, leads over private property). While the lock is normally unmanned, students are employed to assist as peak times. Well above the level of the flood meadows beyond the lock is a sizeable *château* with imposing horse chestnut trees; it commands a fine view of the Seille.

A famous product of this region is *Poulet de Bresse*, free-range chicken, fattened on buckwheat and maize. Bordering the river are several farms rearing these seemingly content creatures. Flocks of several hundred of the white feathered birds will be noted roosting in the lower branches of trees. Even more unlikely are the turkeys in a similar habitat. *Poulets de Bresse*, offered for sale with grave pomp and solemnity and authenticated with metal tags to prove their origin, are astonishingly expensive. Just once, I bought one in the interests of supporting local trade and traditions and had reason to regret my decision: the scrawny fowl was woefully inadequate when it came to satisfying the appetites of three hungry boaters.

Occasional farms and riverside cottages are the only features in a totally rural landscape of trees and meadows as the Seille winds this way and that; mid-summer brings carpets of *fritillaires* (snake's head lilies) and glow-worms in the intense silence of night. It is possible to navigate a long backwater, left, to reach the old port of **Branges** (K35). A hire cruiser centre was established here in 1983. Currently it is a Connoisseur base. It can be difficult to find a free overnight mooring in summer: if you do, shopping is comprehensive, with a *Restaurant du Port* and the *Auberge de l'Écluse* by lock 4 on the through navigation. Distant hills to the east are a reminder that the Swiss border is a mere 80km away.

The first evidence of **Louhans** (K39) is the superb spire and roof of the church of St-Pierre, richly decorated with lozenge patterns in yellow, green, brown and rust-coloured tiles. Packs of wolves that once roamed the area – *loups* – are the reputed origin of the place name. Every waterway terminus benefits from having a worthwhile cruising objective, and this little town makes a fitting end to the journey. Centre of the highly productive farming region known as *Bresse*, it stages an important market (Monday mornings) with regional speciality fairs on the 1st and 3rd Monday of each month. Pontoon moorings near the junction with the River Solnan are convenient for shops and rail station (trains connect with Seurre, St-Jean de Losne and Verdun-sur-le-Doubs). Water point.

Louhans was first recorded in the 5th century. Its leading attraction is the *Grande Rue*, where shop fronts are sheltered by 15–17th century timber and stone arcades, providing coolness in summer and shelter from winter rain. One of its historic monuments is an ancient Baroque hospital (open to the public, every day); within is an outstanding collection of *faïence* apothecaries' jars.

VI · THE ATLANTIC COAST

51 ~ River Sèvre-Niortaise

> **No Carte Guide currently available**
> From Niort to the Atlantic at Charron, 72km with 8 locks. Junctions are made with several marshland waterways of which the most important are: an extensive complex of tiny canals at Coulon totalling a huge distance; the Canal de la Vielle Autise between La Barbée and Courdault, 10km with 1 lock; the Canal de Mignon from Bazoin to Mauzé, 17km with 4 locks; La Jeune Autise from Maillé to a weir at Château Vert, 8km with 1 lock; and the Canal Maritime de Marans au Brault, 6km with 1 lock.

While the Sèvre-Niortaise has no connections with the rest of the French system, it is a significant network in its own right. It is little known outside its immediate region and is almost exclusively used by local craft. The uppermost reaches are really delightful and well worth exploring by trailed boat or inflatable, with the possibility of cruising the 54km between Niort and Marans during one single long summer's day. The amazingly complicated and quite fascinating series of little canals west and south of Coulon, known as *La Venise Verte* (Green Venice) is best entered aboard one of the passenger punts (*barques*) available for hire by the hour with knowledgeable boatman in attendance. If travelling by car, you should consider diverting to the area to enjoy this unique experience. Other trips into the maze of channels (a conservation area known also as the *Marais Poitevin*) operate from the following towns: La Garette, Arçais, St-Hilaire-La-Palud, Le Mazeau and Maillezais.

Farming, architecture and the whole way of life of these waterways is very special. Admittedly the lower reaches across drained marshland are somewhat bleak; but if you appreciate the English Fenlands you will experience a similar compelling fascination here. Most locks have keepers, but it is advised to give a little advance warning of a passage, by first contacting the authority's office in Niort. Although no cruising guide is available, the Direction Départementale de l'Equipement des Deux Sèvres, Subdivision de Niort, Cale du Port, 79000 Niort, publishes a small free map showing the main navigable routes with maximum dimensions. To obtain the fullest enjoyment from a journey, excellent large-scale maps are worth buying: they show every tiny water channel through the marshes on a scale of 1:25,000. The appropriate sheets of this *Carte Topographique* are 1528 Est, 1528 Ouest, 1428 Est and 1428 Ouest, published by the Institut Géographique National, 107 rue La Boétie, 75008 Paris.

Brief history Two thousand years ago, the Atlantic coastline extended to Coulon and Niort was served by the estuary of the Sèvre. A collection of islands was scattered throughout the bay. As the result of silting and drainage works this has become the *Marais Poitevin*, and the sea has retreated more than 40km. From the 11th century five important abbeys created drainage channels, fisheries, dykes and weirs. These canals became silted up through neglect during the Hundred Years War, but a comprehensive new plan to win back land from the marshes was proposed by Henri IV in 1599 and put into effect in the early 17th century by a Dutchman, Humphroy Bradley de Berg op Zom, who was granted the title 'Engineer in Chief of Dykes of the Kingdom'. Today, some 55,000 hectares have been drained: 40,000 nearer the coast are highly productive agricultural land, while the remaining 15,000 are the wetlands of *La Venise Verte*. Nothing was to come of a 1751 plan for a navigable canal from Vivonne on the River Clain downstream of Poitiers to the sea via Niort and Marans. Connecting with the Rivers Vienne and Loire, this would have provided water communication with Paris. The cost was to be defrayed by a lottery. In 1808, Napoléon I ordered modern navigation works to be undertaken on the Sèvre: these were not fully completed for several decades.

Most of the freight craft used were quite small open punt-like barges. An 1882 census identified no fewer than 8,902 in use and even today there are thought to be in excess of 2,000. The first steam vessel arrived on the Sèvre in 1840. Otherwise, long trains of poplar logs were floated to the saw mills. By the early 20th century, the largest barges in use loaded a mere 60 tonnes: many only carried up to 30 tonnes. The waterways continue to be used for transport of agricultural goods and animals, especially in parts of the *Marais* where there is no road access.

Rising at Fonbedoire, the River Sèvre-Niortaise becomes navigable in the city of **Niort**, known by the Romans as

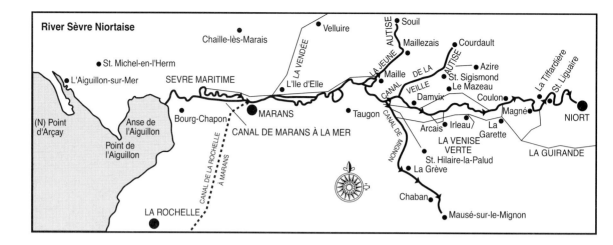

Novum Ritum (New Ford). At the end of the 12th century there was a busy river port with rudimentary barges and rafts used to transport goods to and from the coast. Throughout the Middle Ages a great market and fair was held here, with salt, fish, corn and wool being exported to the Low Countries and Spain. The leading import was furs from Northern Europe and later Canada. An extensive leather industry became established and glove-making continues today. At the time of the Revolution there were 30 fulling mills at work. The city's most notable building is the severe stone-built *Donjon*, a fortified 12–13th century *château* believed to have been started by Henry II of England and completed by Richard the Lion Heart. In its original form there was 700m of encircling wall; a pair of massive crenellated square towers are joined by 15th century additions. Used as a prison under the Bourbons, it now houses a regional folklore museum, the collection including a reconstructed peasant house interior and a number of Niortaise head-dresses or *coiffes*, known as *grisettes*. Rising from the riverbank, it is a most impressive structure and provides good views from the ramparts. Other highlights are the former town hall built in 1535 on a triangular plan and now the *Musée du Pilori*, the *Musée des Beaux Arts* and a number of old buildings in the area of the Rue St-Jean, among which is the 16th century Governor's House, with delicate sculpted decorations. One Françoise d'Aubigné was born in the city: widowed at 25, she secretly married Louis XIV and exerted a considerable influence on the monarch. She is better known as Madame de Maintenon. A marble plaque on the former *Hôtel de la Boule* in the Avenue de Paris records Napoléon I's last stay on French soil, before his exile in 1815.

Niort is noted for a number of culinary specialities, especially angelica, the candied stem of a herb; during the 18th century annual production reached 10 tonnes. It is the basis of *Sève d'Angélique* (a liqueur), used for cake decoration and such desserts as *les Œufs Angélique* and *Soufflé glacé a l'Angélique*, an iced soufflé. When he visited Niort in 1852, Louis Napoléon Bonaparte was presented with an imperial eagle made entirely of angelica. Other regional dishes are *Poulet sauté à la Niortaise* (chicken with fried onion and potatoes), *Jonchée* (a goat's milk cheese) and *Tourteau fromagé* (a delicious goat's milk cheesecake).

The river divides into a series of mill streams during its passage of the city, the uppermost limit for most craft being Le Port, where the navigation office is situated. Shops, restaurants and a slipway for launching. Écluse 1, Comporté (K1), is on the edge of town with cottages and allotment gardens. The upper gates are conventional mitre doors with a guillotine at the bottom. The Sèvre then enters a broad reach past the *base nautique*, with rowing boats, a small number of cruisers and water-skiing. Even in early June, this section tends to be very weedy. Floating duckweed can be a problem throughout the waterway. Low banks provide views of cattle in meadows among numerous white poplars. Elsewhere there are fine houses, suggesting that this is one of the more exclusive residential areas of Niort. Take care to avoid the chains of two pedestrian ferry punts near the village of **St-Liguaire** (K6). Where several little lanes run down to the water, left bank, trailed craft could be launched. As always, when the channel divides keep to the towpath side to pass islands and weir-streams. Summertime chalets bear jokey names like *Mon Rêve* (My Dream) and *Mieux que Rien* (Better than Nothing), just as if this were the Upper Thames.

Navigation markers are well maintained, so there is little excuse in heading for a low three-arched bridge, instead of turning sharply to the left to enter Écluse 2, **La Roussille** (K7). Like the first lock, this has an irregularly-shaped chamber; its top gate is an electrically operated guillotine. The lock cottage is dated 1808 and faces the *Auberge du Roussille*: this group of riverside buildings is most pleasing and judging from the numbers of towpath joggers, strollers and fishermen is a popular retreat on hot summer days. Lock 3, **La Tiffardière** (K8), has conventional gates but a chamber with sloping sides: the only lock on the river without a keeper, it is worked by boat crews, the windlass being concealed in a hedge by the former lock house. About 500m of a branch line (K10.1) can be navigated by small craft to the bridge at **Sevreau**. Beyond a railway bridge the Sèvre becomes quite narrow before arriving in the large village of **Magné** (K11), slipway on the left bank. A double-leafed bascule bridge at Le Grand Port

is flanked by a wood-fired pottery kiln, a Romanesque church and delightful cottages. Everywhere, there are little wooden boats, mostly black and green, or sometimes blue or red. The upper gate of Écluse 4, **Marais-Pin** (K14), is an electrically propelled sinking guillotine, with retracting footbridge over the chamber.

Boat people's houses line the banks of the river through **Coulon** (K16), a place animated by numerous small passenger punts (*barques*) offering excursions into *La Venise Verte*. Holding up to six people, they are propelled with a long pole (*pigouille*) or single paddle (*pelle*). Negotiate with a boatman for tours of an hour or longer through the maze of nearby waterways. A vast

In the heart of the maze of waterways known as La Venise Verte, near Coulon.

grid of navigable channels, all named with signposts, extends north and south of the river: the total length is several hundred km. Some are very shallow and should not be entered by cruisers. In any case there is a powered boat prohibition on certain routes and during weekends and public holidays. The marshland waterways of *Le Marais Poitevin* are classified according to size and ownership. First, are the tiny *fossés*, little larger than flooded field ditches and privately controlled; then the *conches*, between 2m and 6m wide and maintained by the local community; the *canaux*, state-controlled and providing links with many villages including one (K16.6) that runs to **La Garette** and another connecting with **Le Vanneau**; and the *rigoles*, over 6m wide and under the responsibility of the *Syndicat des Marais*. It would be possible to spend a week by punt or canoe, penetrating this beguiling area where white poplars, willows, ash and alder edge tiny fields of intensely green grass. Ash is used for binding the banks and cropping for firewood, and poplar is felled for the sawmills, one important use being match sticks. Life abounds in the clear water and among species that find their way to market and restaurant table are pike, stickleback, zander, minnow, bleak, perch, chub, loach, roach, eel, tench, crayfish and frogs. In the shade of the tree canopies many varieties of wild plant will be found, such as arrowheads, water lilies, water hornwort, floating moss (*azolla*) and duckweed. One fascinating highlight is the *Village des Rouches* (Rush Village) on the banks of the **Canal de la Garette**, near Coulon. This is a re-creation of a typical marshland settlement where *huttiers* (hut dwellers) would have lived until the 1820s. Although local people now inhabit conventional stone or timber houses, many continue to derive a living from the marsh, grazing creamy cattle and goats, fishing and in the winter and wild fowling for duck, plover, snipe and heron. With very limited road access, everything must be conveyed in the small *barques*: animals, tractors, churns of milk and timber. Until quite recent times, wedding and funeral processions were often to be seen on the water. Where fields have been drained, and especially on the former marsh towards the coast, fertile market gardens raise globe artichokes, onions, garlic, melons, courgettes, broad beans and a delicious pulse bean (*mojette*).

Coulon has a slipway, shops, restaurants and an open-air market on Sundays. Greatly recommended is the quayside *Restaurant au Marais*, where local dishes are served; such as *mouclade* (sea mussels in white wine and cream with a dash of curry) and *bouilliture* of stewed baby eels. From here almost to the sea small farmhouses stand on the river banks – long low structures with cattle sheds and barns under a single roof. **La Sotterie** (K19, literally, The Place of Fools) is a tiny village opposite a hamlet named **Le Paradis**, on the edge of *Le Marais de la Princesse*. Here, Écluse 5 is fitted with two pairs of mitre gates. Meals may be obtained at *L'Auberge de l'Écluse*. Everywhere, named side channels branch off into the marshes. **Irleau** lies 1.2km south of the Sèvre at **Le Pont d'Irleau** (K21.2, restaurant) and is served by its own small waterway, the **Rigole de la Garette**. Like its neighbour Le Vanneau, it is a popular local fishing centre.

One of the most charming villages of *Le Marais* is **Arçais**, 1.5km south of the river and approached from the navigation at K25.2 via the **Bief Minet** (suitable only for small craft). An old *château* overlooks the tiny port. 300m before Écluse 6, **Le Bourdettes** (K29), a bar/restaurant stands among a group of cottages, with a lift bridge by the lock itself. **Damvix** (K30), with a tall grey church spire, is a small town with most facilities including moorings, slipway and garage. Pedalos can be hired with access to *La Venise Verte*. By a junction with the **Nouveau Béjou Canal**, take the right fork through **La Barbée** and bear left at a junction with the **Canal de la Vielle Autise** (K32). This waterway may be followed for 9.7km to a basin at the head of navigation in **Courdault**, passing en route the village of **Bernegoue** (K1.3), the **Écluse de St-Arnault** (K2.9) and **St-Sigismond** (K6.4).

Three weirs control water levels at a triple junction at **Bazoin**, Écluse 7 (K34). Another diversion from the through route is possible by turning into the **Canal du Mignon** which runs SE for 17.1km via **La Grève-sur-Mignon**, to a terminus at **Mauzé-sur-le-Mignon**. The locks are Bazoin (K0.1); La Grève (K7.2); Sazay (K11.5) and Chaban (K14.4).

Continuing down the main line, soon after Bazoin lock, *Le Vieux Batelier* restaurant will be seen on an island, with bridge providing access to the shore. Although the scenic interest in these lower, rather treeless reaches is limited to the many little farmhouses, there is widespread boating at weekends.

La Jeune Autise is navigable from **Fosse du Loup** (K37) by turning right and into the town of **Maillé**, returning if wished by an alternative route down the **Contour de Maillé**. Impressive waterside ruins of the 11th century abbey of St-Pierre are at **Maillezais**. A further circular cruise of about 2km is offered by the **Contour des Combrands** and the **Canal de Sablon** (K41). While considerably shorter, the **Canal de Pomère** is uncompromisingly straight (K46) and the original course of the river via the **Contour de Pomère** is much prettier. The landscape is decidedly Dutch in character and many of the waterside buildings could have been imported direct from Friesland.

At the outskirts of **Marans** (K51) fork left; shortly the town appears, with pleasure craft moored on a reach lined with buildings. Shops and other facilities are plentiful. The town is well known for its dairy produce and pottery. The river port has a positive maritime flavour, with shipyards and extensive moorings. Craft of up to 1,500 tonnes can penetrate this far from the sea. Several junctions are now reached: first, with the **Canal de La Rochelle à Marans**, 26km long and no longer available to boats. Ahead, the route divides (K54): the left fork is the start of the **Canal de Marans à la Mer.** It is utterly straight and joins the tideway of the Sèvre below a sea lock at **Brault** (K61). Alternatively, take the right channel at Marans, pass through the Écluse des Enfreneaux, No 8, and follow the tidal windings of the Sèvre Maritime to the coast.

For those in small inland boats, Marans may well be the end of the journey. From here, a regular bus service back to Niort will reunite you with your car (trains also run but are infrequent). Car or bus excursions can be made to the historic port of **La Rochelle**, 25km SW; and one of the most beautiful beaches in the area is on a pine-covered peninsula, **Pointe d'Arçay**, south of **La Faute-sur-Mer**, 43km by road from Marans via the N137, D25 and D746 across drained marshland.

52 ～ River Charente

Carte Guide: *Charente*
From Angoulême to the Atlantic Coast at Rochefort, 147km with 21 locks. Subject to the restrictions mentioned in this chapter, there are connections with two additional lengths of waterway: the River Boutonne, between the Charente at Carillon and St-Jean d'Angely, 31km with 4 locks and an opening tidal barrage; and the Canal de la Charente à la Seudre, from the Charente between Tonnay-Charente and Rochefort (Écluse de Biard) and Beaugeay, 16km with 1 lock.

The Charente is fortunate in that Henri IV (1589–1610) described it as the 'most beautiful river in my kingdom', a testimonial with which it is easy to agree today. Especially in the uppermost reaches, the riverscape is one of wood-fringed meadows, old water mills, stone built hamlets and luxuriant wildlife. While there are several hire cruiser bases, traffic remains insignificant in the 119km of non-tidal water.

Rising near Rochechouart in Limousin, the river flows gently in summer, although the current can be quite fierce early in the season. From Angoulême to Saintes much of the landscape is devoted to vineyards producing grapes for the world-famous Cognac, once exported by river barge.

Apart from the two nearest the sea, all locks are operated, unsupervised, by boats' crews. Such a practice in France results from a long period of dereliction from which the river has not long been rescued. Low-geared paddle equipment is easy to use.

In addition to self-drive hire cruisers, there are opportunities for getting afloat on passenger craft. Private vessels may enter from the sea and there are several launching sites for trailed boats. While a one-way exploration of the non-tidal river could be made in three days, there is ample interest for a week's trip.

Brief history Although commercial traffic long ago vanished from the Charente, the story of many centuries of successful navigation is better recorded than on many French waterways. Starting from limited use of the lowest reaches in Gallo-Roman times, there is evidence of vessels trading to Cognac in the 10th century. By the 12th century, wines of the region were regularly exported by water to England, Denmark and the Low Countries. King Louis IX took steps to improve the waterway in the 13th century and a port was authorised at Angoulême by Philippe the Bold in 1280. Marguerite, grandmother of Francis I, ordered various works to be carried out, but by 1590 local merchants were complaining that the river was in ruins. Under Henri IV conditions became much better, but only at the expense of excessively high tolls. New traffic was generated by the creation of a military port at Rochefort, near the river's mouth, in 1666. Thirty years later came the first of several schemes to provide a navigable link with the Loire and the Vienne, for which three pound locks and no fewer than 70 flash locks (*portes mariniers*) were required on the upper Charente alone, between Angoulême and Civry. Barges were certainly using this section in 1777, albeit with difficulty.

Tolls were virtually abolished in 1737. One scheme that failed to be carried out was suggested in 1760: this would have resulted in a network of waterways from the Charente to the Garonne, via the Dronne. Many of the present locks were provided from 1767 onwards, at last ridding the river of inefficient flash locks that caused endless disputes between boatmen and millers. There were then about 66 barges in service, taking up to two weeks for a round trip between Angoulême and Rochefort.

Several different types of craft were used: the *galiot* was a barge loading about 10 tonnes; the *galion* a small sailing barge; the *allège* loading 30–40 tonnes; and the ubiquitous *gabare*, a sailing barge between 20m and

35m in length with a single 12–15m mast and loading 80–200 tonnes. Cargoes included paper and stone blocks from Angoulême, cannon and munitions from Ruelle, brandy from Jarnac and Cognac; corn, linen and meat. Upstream goods ranged from coal and salt to fish and wood. On the tideway it was not unknown for 30 pairs of oxen or 200–400 men to bow-haul a single vessel. Upriver, 15 or 20 men would suffice, the work also being undertaken by women and oxen. Steam arrived in 1822 in the form of a vessel named *L'Hirondelle*: her machinery was built in Liverpool. By 1840 three return trips weekly were offered by steamer between Saintes and Angoulême, with an annual 40,000 passengers in the 1850s. Four locks were rebuilt and others repaired in 1842. Trade flourished. Then came the railway in 1867. Throughout most of the navigation no immediate effect could be detected as far as freight traffic was concerned. Indeed, 1892 was a record year, with 7,600,000 tonnes carried. Reclassification of the waterways in 1879 had resulted in the Charente being treated as a major navigation. Conversely, on the 27km between Angoulême and the original head of navigation at Montignac, by 1881 it was stated 'all traffic has long since vanished and the old locks have been abandoned'.

As the 20th century advanced, goods progressively moved to rail and road transport. During the Great War, four horses to each *gabare* replaced steam tugs. Thereafter the decline was dramatic. First, the section from Montignac to Cognac was officially closed to traffic (*déclassé*) in 1926. The next 7km to Port du Lys were similarly treated in 1927. In spite of the attempts of riverside traders to reintroduce navigation, the last barge would sail from Jarnac in 1930 and all traffic had deserted the tideway by 1944. Some of the last barges were requisitioned by the Germans in World War II and destroyed in British bombing raids on St-Nazaire.

The Charente appeared to have come to the end of its life as a navigation when it was struck off the official list of waterways in 1957. Attempts were made to put a *péniche* into service in 1967, with only limited success. Passenger traffic was restored in 1969 and has since flourished. During the late 1970s, dredging work and lock repairs reopened the river between the sea and Angoulême and a fleet of British hire cruisers was established at St-Simeux in 1980. The resulting publicity has brought tourists to this lovely waterway and hire craft are now provided by several of the country's leading operators. Management of the Angoulême–Cognac length is in the charge of the Charente *Département*, while responsibility for the lower reaches comes under Charente Maritime. More than two decades have passed since long distance boating came to this beautiful waterway. It still remains relatively deserted.

Although once navigable for a considerable distance above **Angoulême**, the city is now considered to be the upstream point to which normal craft can ascend. Exploration beyond should be possible by dinghy, taking care to avoid any obstructions. 1km further up is a junction with the **River Touvre**, originally used over 7km by barges bringing cannon from the foundry at **Ruelle**. Angoulême is an important industrial and commercial centre, built on a fortified hilltop high above the river. Founded by the Romans and later the capital of the former province of Angoumois, it has been famous since the Middle Ages for paper making. Completely surrounded by ramparts from which there are impressive views of the countryside, it has a first-class pedestrianised shopping centre. St-Pierre's Cathedral dates from the 12th century and features a remarkable sculpted façade. **L'Houmeau** is the name given to the river port area where there are moorings with facilities and a slipway. Gastronomes should consider sampling the regional speciality *Tripes à mode d'Angoulême* (ox tripe and trotters in white wine with tomatoes and garlic). Écluse 1, St-Cybard (K1.1), is downstream of the port.

We soon leave the city behind and the Charente assumes a totally rural character, flowing through a green and peaceful valley. Écluse 2, **Thouérat** (K4.6), is followed by the village of **Fléac** (K6.5), surrounded by vineyards, orchards and walnut plantations. Twisting once more towards Angoulême, Écluse 3, **Basseau** (K7.8), is accompanied by a very good launching ramp. Various facilities are available from the *Charente Croisières* hire base. Lock 4, Fleurac (K10.3), is followed by **Trois-Palis** (K12.8) where there is a church with spire covered with reddish tiles. After Écluse 5, **La Motte** (K13.3), a reach extends all the way to **Sireuil** (K20.3), where the 6th lock is situated. En route, there are moorings possible near the Pont de **La Meure**, with a restaurant and comprehensive shopping in **Nersac**, which lies some distance beyond the railway. Locks 7, **La Liège** (K22), and 8 lead to the very pretty village of **St-Simeux** (K24), with moorings, old water mills and a restaurant.

A sheltered climate and pellucid water make the river ideal for swimming, while there is rarely a shortage of temporary moorings in total peace. Avoiding weirs on the millstream, left, enter a shady cut leading to Écluse 9, Malvy (K24.7), with a pantiled stone cottage. Willows and alders lead past an island (Les Peyronnets) to **Châteauneuf-sur-Charente** (K27.7) with launching ramp shortly before Lock 10, left bank. To operate the gate-opening mechanism, it is necessary to enter the private garden of the former lock cottage. There are excellent moorings on a pontoon near the modern concrete road bridge making it easy to visit this pleasant and useful small town, with convenient shops, restaurants, swimming pool and garage. As there is a railway station on the Angoulême–Cognac line, this could be a useful point from which to recover a car when cruising by trailed boat. Little remains of a stone *château* built to guard what was once the only river crossing between Angoulême and Cognac: it replaced a wooden structure burned down in the 11th century.

Take a right-hand fork (K30.7) and after passing some islands turn sharp left under a single-arched stone bridge and into the approach cut of Écluse 11, **Vibrac** (K33.2). Silting is likely at this junction with the weir stream, so any approach by water to Vibrac village (grocer) is not advised. Instead, walk about 1km from the bridge. Sloping stone walls are a feature of the exceptionally wide lock chamber; there is a section of vertical wall on the downhill, left, side where craft should moor. But be wary of a concrete shelf close to the empty water level: a descending boat could easily become trapped. This curious design dates from the rebuilding programme of 1842. Although there may be occasional unmarked shallows in the river channel, it is not these that produce small whirlpools, but the emergence of subterranean springs.

St-Simon (K35.2) is one of the Charente's most attractive villages: clusters of ancient little stone houses with narrow streets overlook a quay (moorings) with pollarded horse chestnuts. At weekends and on public holidays water-skiers are entitled to use this reach, with a 45kph speed limit – a surprising and potentially dangerous concession but one which is quite normal on French rivers. During the 19th century this was a leading barge-building centre, 1½–2 years being taken to complete each vessel. There is an excellent museum recalling the village's barge building past, *La Maison des Gabariers*. On display are boat models, ancient tools and other artefacts. In the cemetery, a number of bargemen's tomb stones are decorated with devices such as anchors. Pass under the four-arched stone bridge of **Juac** (avoid underwater abutments) and take the left fork to Lock 12 (K36.2) with the ruins of an old keeper's cottage opposite a more recent structure protected by an ugly security fence. Draft at the village quay is only about 0.7m.

A lovely reach of dense woodland, the *Bois Charente*, leads to the cut of Écluse 13, **Saintonge** (K39.2), on the right. The chamber appears to date only from 1913, when considerable works were carried out. Hidden among trees on the left is an earlier sloping-sided lock in ruins with a pretty stone cottage, bearing the date 1837. Follow a woodland path for a view of Saintonge village and its rocky weir. **Bassac** may be reached from the next bridge, Pont de la Vinade, a walk of about

1.5km (range of shops and restaurant). Bassac Abbey, built c AD1000, suffered in the Hundred Years War and again in the Wars of Religion. Disestablished during the Revolution, it has been a house of the Missionary Brothers of St-Theresa of the Infant Jesus since 1947. The public are admitted. A small distillery near the bridge is open to visitors.

Vineyards are much in evidence, growing grapes for the brandy industry; another local product is the aperitif *Pineau des Charentes*, a blend of fresh grape juice and Cognac. **Gondeville** (K43.4) may be approached from below Lock 14; alternatively, with care, down the weir stream from above. The short cut, grandly known as the *Canal de Gondeville*, was dug in 1776–7. Its associated weir, like most others on the river, is in the form of a rocky waterfall, festooned with aquatic plants.

On the outskirts of **Jarnac** (K46), a delightful *château* on the right bank is approached by its own private backwater. Écluse 15 was lengthened to 80m in the early 20th century and is the largest on the navigation. Alongside, pleasing stone houses stand alongside the weir pool, where canoe slalom is a popular sport below the millraces. Jarnac is a busy little town with really good shopping, restaurants and a large open-air swimming pool in the weir stream. Visitors' moorings will be found close to the bridge. Crown Blue Line operate a hire cruiser base. The market square is dominated by the huge *château*-like Courvoisier distillery (visits possible and also to Cognac Bisquit). Note also, the extremely fine 19th century administrative buildings in the style of *châteaux*. On no account should you miss the edible delights on offer in the covered market hall. Founded in Gallo-Roman times, the town is best remembered for a duel between François de Vivonne and Guy Chabot, Count of Jarnac, which took place in 1547 in the presence of Henri II and his court: de Vivonne died of his wounds. Another encounter is recalled by a monument to the Prince de Condé, killed in the 1559 Battle of Jarnac, during the Wars of Religion. Perhaps of greater interest in modern times is the fact that François Mitterand, who became President of France in 1981, was born in Jarnac in 1916.

Now, for the first time, the Charente broadens to the width of a real river. Keep to the right bank, past a newly built weir, to enter Lock 16, **Bourg-Charente** (K50). In the village of grey stone buildings with red pantiles, left bank, are several shops and a restaurant, with moorings and slipway on the left, just below the bridge. Next comes a superb wooded reach of 3km. Opposite an island, stop at the right-bank hamlet of **La Maurie** (K53.6) to walk about 2km to the dolmen of **Gare-Epée**, near the D157 (signposted). Past the *Château de Perron* (left bank), Écluse 17, **St-Brice** (K54.7), is easily seen on the port side. Catherine de Medici, Queen of Henri II, visited the magnificent Renaissance *Château de St-Brice*, a creamy stone building on the river bank with turrets and a slate roof. Well maintained park land features topiary and a larger than life stag hunt in bronze. After the three stone arches of a bridge at **La Trache**, we enter the fringes of **Cognac**. Note, by the bridge at **Châtenay**, an old building marked *Bureau d'Octroi*, a toll house. Skirting the borders of the *Parc François I*, left, the river becomes almost completely rural again. Apart from racing craft from a boat club, the Charente is often completely deserted here, a situation impossible to imagine at a tourist town of similar importance in Britain. Avoiding an open weir, right, there is a waterside restaurant with landing, port side: this is good, if fairly expensive. Entry to Écluse 18, **Cognac** (K61.7), is via a channel on the right.

Boating facilities are unusually good, with a hire cruiser base near the main bridge and a marina offering most services established in a basin on the left. Remains of old fortifications and the 15–16th century castle over-looking the river downstream of the *Pont St-Jacques* have been a distillery since 1795. The Duke of Angoulême was born and raised here: he was destined to be crowned François I and is commemorated by a fine equestrian statue in the town. This was cast in Paris and carried down the Seine and then by sea to Cognac in 1864. When ascending the Charente, exceptionally low water levels left the barge stranded and a great team of oxen was required to pull it clear. Brandy was first produced in large quantities in the early 17th century: the 'burnt' or distilled wine was called *brandewijn* by the Dutch. Huge consignments were carried down river in *gabares* for trans-shipment and export. Many of the leading merchants are British in origin. About 80% of production is exported, notably to Britain and the USA. Some notion of the size of the industry is provided by the startling fact that the 2% of the stored spirit lost to evaporation each year is the equivalent of 20 million

A mill alongside the La Baine lock, near Cognac.

bottles! This is delightfully described as 'the angels' share'. The white wine is distilled twice in copper pot-stills, then aged in oak casks from the Limousin forests. Among the oldest of the firms are Martell, founded by a Jersey family in 1715, and the Irish Hennessy company which started in 1765. Brandies more than 100 years old are blended with new spirit, although some of the most sought-after and expensive types offered by Hennessy are truly Napoleonic, being laid down at the time of Waterloo. Details of visits to the distilleries are available from the local tourist office. The most interesting, perhaps, are Otard, in the former *château*, and Martell which preserves the original premises of 1715. Cognac has good shops, many of them in a long pedestrianised street.

Écluse 19, **Crouin** (K66), was practically destroyed in floods in February 1980. It is the final one to be operated by boats' crews. Beyond here, the Charente undergoes a character change, with rather muddy banks and fallen willows. The slipway of a water-ski club on the right at **Chez Landart** (K71, restaurant) could doubtless be used for launching. The river now describes a broad loop before running past the base of a grassy hill topped by the ruins of an old castle. At **Dompierre-sur-Charente** (K79) are moorings with facilities, a nearby camping site, baker's shop and a small 11th century church with interior vaulting and an unusually good modern stained glass window.

Just before rail and road bridges, the village of **Orlac** (K81.6) advertises a restaurant. Now that we have passed from the jurisdiction of Charente to Charente Maritime, navigation signs start to appear much more often, beginning with an arrow pointing to the cut above Écluse 20, **La Baine** (K85). It is a strange experience now to be under the orders of a lock keeper with overnight and lunch time closures. Sheltered by a giant pair of plane trees, the lock house stands in a green meadow, backing onto a broad pool below a stone water mill.

There are further launching possibilities at the ferry crossing in **Chaniers** (K86). Here are moorings for the range of shops and restaurant a short walk away from the river. The disused ferry ramp at **Port-Hublé** (K90) is available as a slipway. Now coming into the city of **Saintes** (K97), the Charente skirts the base of a wooded cliff with a proliferation of small fishing punts and trim market gardens. Saintes, capital of the former province of Saintonge, was thriving before Caesar's invasion of Gaul in 58 BC. Survivals from the Roman occupation include the impressive Arch of Germanicus, re-erected in 1842 in a waterside garden setting on the river's right bank. More relics can be seen in the nearby archaeological museum. There is much to see in this large and busy city: the cathedral of St-Pierre, the *Abbaye aux*

Dames, and remains of a 1st century arena only a little smaller than that at Nîmes. Extensive quays were constructed towards the end of the 18th century and by 1839 there were no fewer than 31 wind or water mills. Severe floods swamped the lower parts of the town in 1904 and again late in 1982 when even the massive flood wall was unable to save the streets. In 1960 the river was described as being one great lake all the way from Châteauneuf to Saintes. There are several mooring possibilities conveniently close to the centre.

Taking time to recover from the urbanisation of Saintes, the Charente has regained its rural charm by the time we reach the village of **Narcejac** (K103.5), with a fine stone manor house in its miniature walled park. The succession of large country houses, while rarely of the proportions of Loire *châteaux*, does introduce a special interest to the waterway. A little upstream of Narcejac is the tiny Middle Ages hamlet of **Port-Berteau** (right bank) where artist Gustave Courbet set up a studio in 1862. A crossing of the A10 *autoroute* comes shortly before **Taillebourg** (K109), once a small port. Good moorings close to all facilities. Little remains of the feudal *château*, where Louis IX defeated Henry III of England in 1242. 18th century gardens with a terrace offer a broad view over the river. Water meadows with grazing cattle and a widening of the valley are a reminder that the tideway is approaching. Many villages are set well back from possible flooding. **Port d'Envaux** (K112), however, is strung along the left bank, with quay, restaurant, shops, garage and slipway. Tranquil country houses overlooking the water make this one of the Charente's most appealing villages. **Crazannes** (K116) acknowledges an increasing interest in boating with a small *port de plaisance* (fuel, slipway and day boats for hire).

Extensive pleasure craft moorings on pontoons are the first indication of **St-Savinien** (K119). The navigation channel forks to the left for the last lock before the tideway: straight on leads to the centre of town, past the gardens of some delightful houses, many of them once occupied by barge masters. Building of freight craft was a major activity, the last being launched in 1859. There is a good selection of shops and restaurants. On a river with several outstanding small towns, St-Savinien is perhaps the most agreeable. Pleasing details include an ornate 19th century cast-iron water pump surmounted by an urn, by the bridge, and clusters of tiny daisies sprouting from crevices in the river walls. Slightly tidal conditions will be experienced here, even upstream of the attended Écluse 21, although most of the water is held back by a weir.

If this is to be the limit of a cruise, there are trains (rather infrequent) and buses to Saintes, Cognac,

Belle Époque cast iron pump on the waterfront at St-Savinien.

Châteauneuf and Angoulême, facilitating reuniting boat with car and trailer. In the seawards direction, public transport provides links with Rochefort and the coast at **Châtaillon-Plage**, south of La Rochelle, for the attractions of the seaside.

After St-Savinien, the atmosphere of the Charente totally changes. The tideway passes through a marshland world of glutinous mud banks, frequent fishing nets suspended on cranes and typical Saintonge farmhouses with red pantiled roofs. Maritime cargo vessels loading up to 6,000 tonnes regularly navigate 26km of the tideway between the Atlantic Ocean at **Port de Barques** and **Tonnay-Charente**. At **Port-la-Pierre** (K133) is a junction with the **River Boutonne**. Rising at **Chef-Boutonne**, 94km above the confluence, its lower 31km are navigable through **Tonnay-Boutonne** to **St-Jean d'Angely**, with four locks evenly spaced out on its course (Écluses de Bel-Ebat, de l'Houmée, de Voissay and de Bernouet). Though closed

in 1935, a programme of lock restoration had made the route navigable again by the summer of 1984. A basic chart showing lock approaches is available from Direction Départementale de l'Equipement de la Charente-Maritime, BP 125, Bassin No 3, 17301 Rochefort-sur-Mer. The first 500m is subject to Charente tides as far as the Carillon Barrage, through which boats can pass when the levels equalise. This system is far from convenient and does not encourage boaters to use the river. A proper lock is proposed.

Back on the Charente, fishing boats are clustered on mud-berths in **Tonnay-Charente** (K141), with a 204m suspension bridge erected in 1885. Mooring within a short distance of shops and restaurants is possible on the quay, which is, of course, subject to tidal rise and fall. A little below, the 39km **Canal de la Charente à la Seudre**, built about 1812 with five locks, once provided a connection with the coast to the south via **St-Agnant** and the oyster beds at **Marennes**. Small craft with a draft not exceeding 1m and a headroom sufficiently low to pass beneath several former swing bridges (no longer operable), may travel 16km from the Écluse de Biard, junction with the Charente, to the Écluse de **Beaugeay**, provided 48 hours' notice is given to the Biard lock keeper.

In the Place Colbert at **Rochefort** (K147) the final arrival of the river at the coast is celebrated in a massive stone fountain, on top of which classical figures represent the marriage of Charente and Ocean. All boating facilities are in a tide-free basin, the *port de plaisance*, entered via a lock: craft waiting on the river may use a floating pontoon. Fortified towers and walls are a reminder that it was here that Colbert established a sheltered naval base in the mid 17th century to protect the Atlantic coast from the English. From 1690 to 1800 some 300 ships were built. Rochefort ceased to be a military port in 1921. One of its claims to fame is that it is home to the sole surviving French transporter bridge (*transbordeur*), one of just 21 built world wide. Designed by Ferdinand Arnodin (1845–1924), it consists of lofty pylons on each bank of the river, connected by a gantry sufficiently high as to allow masted ships to pass beneath. From this is slung a cradle or gondola carrying vehicles and passengers. This is wound from one side to the other. This *Le Martrou* bridge was inaugurated on July 29 1900 with a day of lavish celebrations. Eventually it became inadequate for modern traffic and was withdrawn from service in 1967. Fortunately, unlike others of its breed, it was not dismantled enabling it to re-emerge restored in 1996 as a fully operational and popular tourist attraction. Downstream, the estuary gradually widens, eventually meeting the Atlantic opposite the **Ile d'Oléron**, second largest island off the French coast after Corsica. A 3,027m bridge has connected it with the mainland at Marennes since 1966. This delightfully unspoiled holiday area has some magnificent sandy beaches, including the vast *Grande Plage* on the SW shore.

53 ∼ River Dordogne

No Carte Guide available
From Bec d'Ambès, junction with the River Gironde (26km downriver of Bordeaux) to St-Pierre d'Eyraud, 118km with no locks. A junction is made with the River Isle at Libourne.

Mention the name Dordogne and you instantly have a mental impression of deep limestone gorges with thickly wooded shores. Rocky pinnacles are capped with ancient *châteaux*. This, however, applies only to the higher reaches of the river, well beyond the limit of navigation for normal craft. Accessible only to canoeists and downstream drifters in inflatables, these idyllic waters for 173km below Argentat are outside the scope of this book. Almost all the section available to large craft is tidal and frankly lacks much interest in the first 34km up to Vayres. In common with many tidal navigations, a journey up the Dordogne is likely to be slightly adventurous rather than relaxing.

Brief history Once clear of the broad expanses near its confluence with the Gironde, the Dordogne was always regarded as the most difficult and dangerous navigation in south west France. Including the uppermost 147km from the junction with the River Rhue near Bort to Meyronne which was once considered only to be *flottable*, the Dordogne was more or less navigable for some 414km. True, the capacity of barges on the upper waterway was often as little as 12 or 15 tonnes. Such craft were built as economically as possible, for they were only able to make a single downstream voyage. Passengers and goods (especially oak for barrels) were transported to Bordeaux, the boats generally being broken up for timber on arrival.

After 1840, several of the most troublesome rapids where the river makes a sharp descent in its middle reaches, were bypassed by the magnificent Canal de Lalinde. This commenced at Tuilières, 12km above Bergerac and ran for 15km before rejoining the river at Mauzac. It featured nine locks, massively constructed in stone, of which six comprised two three-rise staircases at the canal's downstream end. Disused by the 1930s, these monumental works remain substantially intact and decidedly merit a visit. The Dordogne's only other lock was situated a short distance downstream of Bergerac. By 1936, the river was said to be navigable 'under favourable conditions' for 133km to Bergerac, where the draft varied from 1.1m to as little as 0.3m. Nevertheless, in that year 5,502 barge journeys were recorded on the waterway with 255,000 tonnes transported. Traction was exclusively by horses and oxen.

Since the 1930s, navigation conditions have deteriorated on this free-flow waterway. The first 77km from the Gironde to Castillon-la-Bataille is tidal, with floating pontoon moorings at a number of points. In dry seasons, problems may be experienced upstream of Branne (56km from the Gironde) with available draft sometimes reduced to as little as 0.3m.

The lower part of the Dordogne, from the Gironde to Libourne, appears on Maritime Chart 6140, published by the *Service Hydrographique*. These 43km are not difficult to navigate for those with experience of tideways, for there is a buoyed channel and no obstructions other than the nets of lamprey fishermen. Moorings are few and far between: at **Bourg** (K4) there is a slipway and quay and arrangements can be made to moor alongside a ferry which takes workers to the extensive oil refineries on the far shore, more than 1km away. The town is situated on a cliff, reached from the port by flights of steps. There are excellent views over the river from the terrace of the *Château de la Citadelle*, the former residence of the Archbishops of Bordeaux. Upstream, the scenery is dull to **Vayres** (K34), where the grounds of the *château* extend to the river bank: gardens in the style of Louis XIII were laid out as recently as 1938. The river is subject to a tidal bore – the *Mascaret* – sometimes reaching a height of 1.5m. Its effect is greatest at Vayres. Predicted times of the greatest bores are available from the local tourist office. Shipping regularly navigates the river as far as the port of **Libourne** (K43), junction with the **River Isle**. The most comfortable overnight moorings are to quays on the Isle, which is tidal for 31km to the first lock, No 40, Laubardemont. This and a further two locks (Nos 39, Abzac, K35.1; 38, Penot, K38.6;) are currently workable but their use is at present restricted to a trip boat. As recently as 1936 the Isle continued through 37 more locks to **Périgueux**, 143km above its confluence with the Dordogne. Restoration of all this former waterway is projected.

Libourne is the most convenient place from which to visit the extraordinary town of **St-Emilion**, 10km by bus. It occupies a series of small limestone hills in a famous region of vineyards: these have been excavated to create many caves, one of which was turned into an underground monolithic church between the 9th and 12th centuries.

At **Castillon-la-Bataille** (K78) the English were defeated in the final battle of the Hundred Years War, when the Earl of Shrewsbury was killed in 1453. How much further a boat of reasonable draft can travel will depend greatly on seasonal water levels. **Flaujagues** (K87) is generally regarded as the limit for motor cruisers, although exploration is often possible in small vessels at least to **St-Pierre-d'Eyraud** (K117) and, in ideal conditions, as far as **Bergerac** (K131).

Exploration of the outstandingly beautiful Dordogne Valley beyond Bergerac should be undertaken by car. Itineraries appear in the Michelin Green Guide *Dordogne Berry Limousin*. Hydro-electric barrages obstruct the river upstream of **Argentat**, but a length of 173km from there to **Lalinde** provides water for one of the finest canoe journeys in Europe, normally without any undue hazards. The safest time to go is usually in July and August, when the current is reduced. Various types of boat may be hired, with arrangements for recovery at the downstream end. Such a holiday is the ultimate in back-to-nature waterway travel. The route passes numerous towns and villages, restaurants and ancient *châteaux*. Notable excursions are to the **Padirac Chasm**, 5km south of the river near Castelnau (lifts take you down 75m to an underground cave 99m across, with a subterranean river running for 2,000m – partly negotiated by boat); and to the **Grottes de Lacave**, a network of caves reached by small railway and lift, situated close to the Dordogne between St-Sozy and Souillac.

54 ～ Canal Transaquitain

No Carte Guide available

From the Étang de Cazaux et de Sanguinet to the Étang de Biscarrosse on the Atlantic Coast near Biscarrosse, 5km with 1 lock.

This projected waterway grew out of an ambitious scheme of the early 1970s, but ceased not long after construction began. Further work was abandoned on financial and ecological grounds. The plan had been to link a chain of lakes by lengths of artificial canal, so creating a vast pleasure boating and leisure facility, just inland from the Atlantic, and traversing the pine forests and sand dunes of **Les Landes**. When adopted in 1970, the concept envisaged a waterway extending for about 196km from the estuary of the Gironde to the River Adour downstream of Dax and not far from the

Spanish border. Although only a tiny part was completed, the region offers considerable scope for trailed craft which can be launched into several bodies of sheltered water. One of the most compelling reasons for visiting **Les Landes** is the outstandingly beautiful Atlantic coastline, the **Côte d'Argent**. This is a magnificent 230km continuous beach of fine sand: unlike the Mediterranean, it is subject to considerable tides and sizeable breakers, making it suitable for surfing. As a barrier between the coast and the interior a belt of sand dunes runs along the shore. One dune, **Pilat**, south of the large **Bassin d'Arcachon** natural harbour, may be climbed via a footway and flight of 190 steps. 114m high, it is the biggest dune in Europe and offers a spectacular view over the ocean and the forest.

The most important lakes, all of which are available for boating with ample launching sites and other facilities, are as follows, running north to south: **Lac de Hourtin-Carcans**, 19km long x 3–4km wide; the **Étang**

de Lacanau, 8km long; the Bassin d'Arcachon, connected with the sea at **Cap Ferrat**, much of which dries out at low water; and the **Étang de Cazaux**, inland of **Biscarrosse-Plage**, 10km long and up to 11km wide. Northwards, this is connected with the Bassin d'Arcachon via a little tree-shaded waterway known as the **Canal de Cazaux à la Teste**, 15km long and suitable for the small motor boats widely used in the area. Launching sites around Cazaux include one at a popular sandy beach called **Dune des Places**, with another by a pleasure craft harbour at **Ispe**. The entire lake is surrounded by attractive sandy beaches and pine forests originally planted in the 19th century. Another section of waterway leaves Cazaux at **Navarrosse** (hotel/bar/restaurant) and heads south for 5km through one lock whose rise and fall is about 0.6m. This is worked by boat crews, using a coin-in-the-slot facility. After passing close to the pleasant little town of **Biscarrosse** (shops and restaurants), the canal emerges into the **Étang de Biscarrosse**, 9km long and up to 8km wide.

Equipped with a car and trailed dinghy or cruiser, the lakeland waterways of Les Landes would make an ideal holiday destination. The coast is always within a short driving distance and the splendid beaches are so extensive that overcrowding is never a problem. Outside the limits of the resort towns, naturism is widely practised, especially on the north beach at Biscarrosse, north and south of **Mimizan-Plage** and south of **Contis-Plage**.

55 ⟶ River Adour and Adjoining Waterways

> **No Carte Guide available**

From the Atlantic Coast near the Spanish border at Tarnos to Port de Pouy, upstream of Dax. 76km and mainly tidal with no locks. Navigation in the upper reaches is only practicable when there is a good flow of water. Shortly before World War II, 2,808 barge journeys were recorded on the river each year, horses and oxen being used to haul the vessels. All commercial traffic has long ago vanished. Including several tributaries, this is quite an extensive lock-free system. It is very little used and as it is isolated from the rest of the French network it is only briefly mentioned here in the interests of presenting a complete record. There are about a dozen well-maintained floating pontoons for the use of visiting craft. Several include a water point. Elsewhere, safe moorings can be difficult to locate where banks are muddy and subject to a tidal rise and fall. There are no hire craft, the great majority of pleasure boats being owned by enthusiasts with local knowledge. Once navigable to **St-Sever**, 133km inland from the coast, the Adour's chief towns are **Bayonne** (K6.7, all facilities) and **Dax** (K67).

In downstream order, navigable branches exist as follows:

Gaves Réunis, 9.4km from Peyrehorade to the Adour at Bec du Gave (K40). Tidal.

River Bidouze, 14.9km from a junction with the River Lihoury (which is navigable for 1.5km) to the Adour near Sames (K43). Tidal.

River Aran or **Joyeuse**, 6.2km from Larroque to the Adour near St-Laurent-de-Gosse (K50). Tidal.

River Ardanavy or **Ardanabia**, 2.4km from a railway bridge to the Adour below St-Barthélemy (K55). Tidal.

River Nive, 12.3km from Haïtze to the Adour at Bayonne (K66). Tidal.

A short distance along the coast in the direction of Spain are two further tidal rivers: the **Nivelle**, 7km from Ascain to the sea at St-Jean-de-Luz; and the **Bidassoa**, 9km from Bordarrupia to the sea at Hendaye. Throughout, it marks the Franco-Spanish frontier.

VII • THE RHÔNE VALLEY, GASCONY AND LANGUEDOC

56 ~ River Rhône

> **Carte Guide:** *Rhône*
>
> From a junction with the River Saône in Lyon to the Mediterranean at Port St-Louis, 319km with 12 locks. Additional connections are made with the Petit Rhône near Arles (for the Canal du Rhône à Sète); and the Liaison Rhône-Fos near Salin de Giraud. (Forbidden to pleasure craft. The Canal d'Arles à Fos from Arles is no longer a through route.) There are plans to reinstate a link between the Rhône and the Canal du Rhône à Sète at Beaucaire. About 170km of the Higher Rhône (including a connection to the Lac du Bourget and Aix-les-Bains) exists in varying degrees of navigability: there are 7 locks/boat elevators. For details, see below.

Back in the 1950s, the guide book of the *Canoe Club de France* said of the Rhône: 'Strictly speaking, it is not a river: it is a great torrent'. Far reaching navigation works have since changed all that and this essential link between the Mediterranean and the connected waterways network of the rest of France is available to all but the most under-powered of pleasure craft. At times the current can still run quite swiftly, depending on how much water is being released by the hydro-electric power stations incorporated into each of the first 11 barrages. The flow is considerably reduced when demand for electricity falls, that is, during weekends and at night. Naturally, when there is flood water produced by melting snow pouring down from the Alps, the Rhône navigation demands care and respect, but compared with its wayward behaviour of several decades ago, it is now capable of almost sedate composure. In mid/late summer the flow is often very slight and quite slowing-moving craft should be able to make headway upstream in safety.

Downstream of Lyon the rocks, whirlpools, rapids, shallows and debris-strewn shingle banks of waterway mythology (which I shall always remember from an upstream voyage made in a large motor yacht in the spring of 1975) have gone. Canalisation has greatly improved the look of the Rhône, although in its emasculated form canoeists must regret the passing of one of France's leading long-distance assault courses. Long sections of artificial canal lead to new locks, one of which is among the deepest in Europe. Bankside signs indicate safe canoe portages for those who wish to travel over parts of the original course no longer used for normal navigation.

It is now safe to stop and moor at various points and enjoy the sights, instead of having to apply total concentration to steering a safe course. One hazard to be mentioned, however, is the fierce *Mistral* wind that funnels down the Rhône valley, sometimes for days on end. This can create a sizeable chop on the river and make life difficult in a small cruiser. Some exposed moorings then become dangerous, with waves reaching 2m in height. Never underestimate the potential destructive powers of inland waterways.

Scenically, the 40km below Lyon are the most attractive, with green hills and welcoming banks. Surroundings become ever more rugged and parched as you progress downstream. By way of compensation, there are numerous ruins and fortifications towards the southern end.

Falling 164m from Lyon, the Rhône locks are awe-inspiring but not difficult to negotiate. Keeper's instructions are conveyed by traffic lights and loud speakers. Here, as on other of the larger French navigations, use of the boat's VHF radio telephone is invaluable in advising keepers of your approach and so saving waiting time on arrival. VHF channel numbers are published in the *Carte Guide*. Locks normally function between 05.00hr and 21.00hr. Although capable of passing 1,500-tonne motor barges and 4,500-tonne push-tows, the Rhône is sadly under-used by commercial traffic. Matters would perhaps have been otherwise had creation of the Mediterranean–North Sea Waterway (via the Rhône, Saône, Doubs and Rhine) been carried through to completion. The river is not generally considered suitable for hire boats, so must be explored by private craft, trip boats (the journey from Lyon to Avignon or *vice-versa* takes two days), or by hotel ship.

On many French rivers, it is possible to moor for the night bow-on to a grassy bank. The situation is quite different on the Rhône, where bank protection is frequently of loose rock. Before starting your day's cruise, it is advisable to plan exactly where you expect to moor before the onset of darkness. Some safe and recommended overnight halts include: Lyon, on Saône upstream of Pont Bonaparte; Givors, quay, K18.4; Condrieu, marina, K40.8; Andance, pontoons, K69; Tournon, harbour, K90.9; Valence, marina, K112; Le Pouzin, quay, K133; Viviers, quay on old river course, K166; St-Étienne-des-Sorts, pontoon, K204; Avignon, marina on old river course just upstream of Pont St-Bénezet; Arles, pontoon, K282.7; Port St-Louis, in harbour, K323.

Brief history When the first barge passed through Vaugris Lock in 1980 and the modernisation of the once wild River Rhône was completed, the skipper of *Citerna 18* was presented with a selection of gifts, carrying on a tradition which had been performed at the inauguration of all previous locks on the waterway. These presents included a bottle of *Côtes du Rhône*, a *Saucisson de Vienne*, some walnuts and a terracotta oil lamp. One of Europe's most far-reaching waterway schemes was thus brought to a conclusion. It had taken 47 years.

The Rhône had been in use as a highway since the times of the Greeks and Romans: but it had always been an uncertain navigation, suffering from fierce currents, shallows, floods as the winter snows melted in the Alps and frequent droughts in late summer. There are many reminders of more than 20 centuries of navigation in the form of ancient towns and fortifications. Until the early 19th century, passengers travelled in *coches d'eau* (water coaches), drawn by men, horses or propelled by sail. Such a journey could be very dangerous in times of high winds or floods. Trade on the upper river was conducted in *barques du Rhône*, 75-tonne capacity sailing barges 30m x 3.5m and fitted with a huge rudder and long tiller. Most travelled bearing a painted cross covered with religious symbols as protection against the hazards of the journey. As many as 50 to 80 horses were employed to haul trains of five to seven craft upstream. Goods would be transhipped at Arles into 23m sailing barges known as *allèges d'Arles* for the final run down to the Mediterranean. 30m log rafts brought additional freight down the tributaries, where navigation was equally uncertain (the Isère, Durance, Ardèche, Ouvèze, Arve and the Saône and Higher Rhône). Upstream progress was often out of the question and the craft were broken up when they arrived at their destination.

The Rhône's first experimental steam boat was built at Lyon by Jouffroy d'Abbans in 1783, but regular steam haulage would not be introduced until 1829. It was to last until 1952. Steam passenger vessels 80m–100m long could manage 20kph and were able to tackle the 287km of waterway from Lyon to Arles in a single long day. Among the 19th century steam freight craft were *bateaux-anguilles*, giant cargo boats 157m x 6.35m with paddle wheels amidships; *bateaux crabes*, where paddle wheels were supplemented by a huge toothed 'claw' wheel 6.5m across, designed to grip the river bed in the shallows: acting as tugs, they could haul over 500 tonnes; *bateaux à deux culs* (double backside boats); and a range of single and twin funnelled steam tugs developing up to 1800hp.

In the 20th century powerful motor barges were introduced, such as the *Citerna* fleet, 80m x 8.6m, propelled by diesel engines and with a 1,500-tonne capacity. Some continue in service, together with push-tow convoys 180m long with 4,500 tonnes capacity and the ubiquitous 38.5m *péniches*.

At various times there had been schemes for construction of a lateral canal down the Rhône valley, fed by the river but independent of it. This concept was finally rejected in 1933 when the *Compagnie Nationale du Rhône* was established to tame the waterway itself with a series of locked barrages and canal cuts, with the triple aims of improving navigation, conserving water for irrigation and generating electricity. About 16% of French electricity is now provided by Rhône power stations. Some progress was made in deepening the navigation channel and constructing training walls before World War II brought work to a halt. It began again in 1948 and was to continue for the next 32 years. Completion dates of the barrages and locks were: Donzère-Mondragon, 1952; Montélimar, 1957; Baix-Le-Logis-Neuf, 1960; Beauchastel, 1963; Pierre-Bénite, 1966; Bourg-lès-Valence, 1968; Vallabrègues, 1970; St-Vallier, 1971; Avignon, 1973; Caderousse, 1975; Péage-de-Roussillon, 1977; and Vaugris, 1980.

UPPER RHÔNE

There is much scope for adventurous boating on more than 170km of the river upstream of Lyon. Currently, pending completion of works, pleasure cruising exists only on a very localised basis. Intending boaters are strongly advised to seek local and updated information. Throughout these upper reaches, hydro-electric generating plants have been constructed or are planned; all will eventually be equipped with locks. At the time of writing, 9.6km upstream of Lyon is available to **Villeurbanne** where the Écluse La Feyssine is out of service, as are two further locks (the two-rise **Cusset**, K14 and the Écluse de **Jonage**, K24.3). These are large devices dating from the 1980s, have rarely been used and are to be put back into service by creating smaller chambers within the existing structures. Further upriver, there are mechanised elevators to convey pleasure craft past barrages at **Sault-Brénaz**, K66.5 (lock proposed); **Brégnier-Cordon**, K97.4; and near **Virignin** at the Brens Dam, K115.5. Boats carried on these conveyors are limited to a maximum of five tonnes and a length of 9.5m on a 3.4m beam. Perversely, a further dam at **Chautagne**, K133.9, lacks any elevator. At a number of places, there are marinas each with a range of facilities. From the foregoing remarks it will be evident that boating activity is generally localised rather than long-distance. Pleasure craft harbours include those at **Montalieu**, K71.2; **Briord**, K77.3; **Murs-et-Gélignieux**, K101.9; **Virignin**, K117; **Massignieu**, K123.6; and in **Seyssel**, K146.5, close to the navigation limit.

At **Savières**, K129, is a junction with the 5km Canal de **Savières** which provides a navigable link into the largest natural lake in France, the **Lac du Bourget**. The canal is equipped with a single DIY mechanised lock (admits craft 18m x 5.5m) at Savières and joins the lake close to **Châtillon** (harbour). In delightful alpine surroundings, both canal and lake offer splendid boating possibilities, either by private craft or aboard tripping vessels. There are several marinas including those at **La Châtière, Brison, Aix-les-Bains** and **Charpignat**.

RHÔNE, LYON-MEDITERRANEAN

While the length of this part of the navigation has been reduced to 310km, kilometre posts on the waterway's banks continue to record the former distance of 323km and are thus used as a reference in the *Carte Guide* and the following description.

Lyon. (K0.) For a description of this city at the confluence of the Saône and Rhône, see Chapter 48. In addition to pleasure craft facilities on the Saône, there are moorings at the Rhône's *Maison d'Eau*, left bank (K3.5), before the first lock. The river here is wide and lively, with considerable commercial traffic bound for the many industrial works and fuel depots. The A7 *autoroute* leaves Lyon on the right bank, veering away shortly before arrival at the entrance to the large freight **Port Eduoard-Herriot** (K3, left bank). The first of the hydro-electric barrages appears ahead, with a short cut leading to Pierre-Bénite lock (fall 9.25m) on the left. Looking back upriver, there is a dramatic distant view of Lyon, rising to the hilltop site of *Notre Dame de Fourvière*. 11km of artificial rock-sided channel, with little scenic interest, takes the navigation beneath the *autoroute* and back into the real Rhône at K15. Now the surroundings greatly improve past willow-fringed banks, with sand and gravel works.

Good moorings close to shops will be found on the right bank (K18, pontoon) near the mouth of the River Gier in **Givors**, a manufacturing town specialising in glass making and heavy castings. Here was once a junction with the **Canal de Givors**, a long-lost waterway that had been intended to provide a navigable link of 56km with 99 locks between the Rhône and the Loire at **Andrezieux**. Just 20km with 43 locks to **La Grand-Croix** beyond the industrial town of **Rive-de-Gier** was ever built: it was mostly ready for traffic in 1780. An early victim of the railways, by the 1870s it was little used apart from the extensive port at the junction with the Rhône. Abandoned in 1926, much of the line was obliterated by the A47 *autoroute* in 1971. The motorway returns near **Loire-sur-Rhône** (K22), also industrial and with a commercial harbour. Fuel/gas, right bank, K22.5. Craft wishing to use the quay (K26.5, right bank) just upstream of an *autoroute* viaduct should approach from *below* the bridge. The Rhône makes a broad sweep through **Vienne** (K29), a Gallo-Roman provincial capital grouped around a junction with the River Gère. Although the A7 is uncomfortably evident all the way along the waterfront, the city is well worth a visit for its historical and gastronomic interest. There is a quay with bollards at the start of a public park, below the second bridge; alternatively, try the pontoon on the opposite bank.

Supposedly founded by the Celtic King Allobrox, allegedly a descendant of Hercules, Vienne was at one time governed by Pontius Pilate. From the 4th century AD until 1922 the city's 131m diameter Roman theatre was buried. Now fully excavated, it can be seen in a wonderful state of preservation. Equally fine is the much restored Temple of Augustus. Half an hour's walk leads from the town to *Le Mont Pipet* with a superb view down to the river. Red wines of the *Côte Rôtie* are produced in vineyards that extend a long distance down the waterway. Dating in part from the 13th century is the little waterside church of *Notre Dame de l'Ile*, once an important place for river pilgrims who would throw flowers into the Rhône in memory of early Christians martyred here in AD 177. A further A7 viaduct is followed by **Vaugris** lock (fall 6.7m) at K34, the only one on the navigation designed without approach channels. Downstream is a slipway, east bank.

This area is an important centre of fruit production, with trees smothered in blossom in spring. **Ampuis** (K35.5) mostly lies beyond a railway line and is notable for its waterside Renaissance *château* and sandy beach, a popular swimming place for local children. Newly raised water levels have resulted in numerous trees being flooded along a very lovely reach that extends to **Condrieu** (K41). Craft coming from the Saône with limited time would do well to consider this point as their objective if wishing to explore just a little of the

Rhône. Condrieu, right bank, and **Les-Roches-de-Condrieu**, opposite, are surrounded by vineyards. The main waterfront, with the ancient houses of long-gone Rhône boatmen, is well worth a halt. An excellent large marina with pontoons is situated in a basin near the bridge (water, fuel, repairs, electricity, etc). Shopping and restaurants.

Extensive chemical works line the left bank at **St-Clair-du-Rhône** (K43). Several towns now follow in hilly surroundings that extend virtually without a break to Valence. Access is sometimes rather difficult. **Chavenay** (K47) offers moorings on piles, but the pretty village of **St-Pierre-de-Bœuf** (K51) has been by-passed by the navigation and can no longer be approached by water on account of a barrage at the upper end of the river's natural course with a sill across the channel below Serrières. Between K51 and K63 craft follow the **Péage de Roussillon Canal**; mooring is possible on vertical piling in the cut at K56 and under a bridge above the lock (K58.4). By travelling on to **Sablons** lock (K59.2, fall 14.5m) you can seek permission to moor and walk back to **St-Sornin** and **Serrières** alongside the former navigation. Here, there are shops and an fascinating museum of Rhône life in the 12–14th century chapel of St-Sornin. Exhibits include the highly decorated crosses once carried by vessels as protection from the perils of the river. Slipway in the lower end of the Sablons lock cut, east bank, K62.5.

Between K64 and K69, take care to avoid numerous groynes that extend a considerable distance from each bank towards the centre of the river. A strange stone pillar on the right bank near the village of **Champagne** (K65.5) supported the cable of a former ferry boat. The best moorings in **Andance** (K69) are on pontoons above the bridge, with shops and restaurants close by. Very good slipway, west bank, 100m below the bridge. The smaller town of **Andancette** lies on the opposite side. Scenery in this reach is very fine, encouraging considerable use by local motor cruisers and sailing dinghies.

A boatyard in the broadening of the river at **Laveyron** (K73) offers a variety of services including moorings, slipway and repairs. **St-Vallier** (K76) has moorings on its sloping quays, convenient for good shops and a railway station. Slipway below the bridge, west bank. Diana of Poitiers spent part of her childhood at the *château*. If in doubt about being able to reach a quay a short distance up the River Galaure (headroom under the bridge is very limited), continue for another 2km to the vertical quay, K78.4 left bank, where there is also a slipway. The town is within easy cycling distance. Situations like this make carrying at least one bicycle almost essential, with repeated savings of time and energy.

Splendid views of the St-Vallier Gorge open up ahead, with frequent reminders of the feudal importance of this part of the valley. At the tiny village of **Serves** (K82), the *château* faces a ruined round tower at **Arras** on the opposite shore. Houses with pantiled roofs are clustered at the base of cliffs. Moorings are poor, on a rocky bank. Soon follows the beginning of the Canal de St-Vallier, leading to **Gervans** lock (K86, fall 10.75m); note the Romanesque 11–12th century church on the right bank, where the lock channel rejoins the river. *La Table du Roi* (King's Table) is a menacing rock, marked by buoys at K89, on which St-Louis (King Louis IX) is said to have paused for a meal when bound for the Crusades in 1248. Its historical significance saved it from being blasted away during the Rhône improvements.

Now comes an important wine-production region, famous for *Hermitage* (red), *Larnage* and *Chante-Alouette* (white) at the approach to **Tournon** (K91). Steep-sided vineyards recall parts of the Rhine Gorge. Names of the growers are prominently displayed on stone walls that divide one small terraced field from the next. It is often said that the Rhône Valley wines are the best in southern France. It is certainly very unusual to find a poor *Côtes du Rhône*. Tournon is one of the most interesting towns in the entire course of the river and offers the facilities of a pleasure boat harbour, right bank, upstream of the first of two bridges. Enter with due regard to the current and bearing in mind that the water is not very deep on the downstream end of the quay. The seemingly inviting and deserted walkway fronting the river suffers from an overhanging section, making it impracticable for mooring. Most facilities are available, here or close by. Apart from very convenient shops and restaurants, the 15–16th century *château* offers wide views from its terraces high above the Rhône and across to **Tain l'Hermitage**. Open to the public throughout the summer (not Tuesdays), the interior houses a museum; exhibits include material on the engineer Marc Seguin, builder of the first Rhône suspension bridge, constructed in 1825 and removed 140 years later. The attractions of the town and its situation are a great encouragement to linger. Train enthusiasts can travel on the narrow-gauge **Vivarais** steam railway which passes through a rugged and winding course between Tournon and **Lamastre** along the Doux Valley. Built between 1886 and 1891, the line boasts nine steam locomotives and seven electric units, attracting over 60,000 passengers each year. The journey takes two hours each way, so most of the day should be set aside for the excursion, especially if you wish to spend time in the gastronomic centre of Lamastre. Open daily, July and August; a more restricted service at other times.

Details, tel 04 78 28 83 34. Across the river, Tain still has an altar erected in AD 184 for the sacrificing of bulls.

Limited moorings are available for clients of the *Auberge de Frais Matin* (K95.5, left bank). If time allows, it is worth visiting the remote village of **La Roche de Glun** (K98.5) at the head of an island formed by the Rhône and Bourg-les-Valence lock cut; there are several restaurants, with possible moorings on the left, a short way into the weir stream. **Bourg-les-Valence** lock (K106, fall 11.7m) is followed by the important city of **Valence** (K109), an overnight halt for Rhône passenger vessels. This is a bustling modern place, with a broad tree-lined *boulevard* at its centre where there are many good shops and restaurants. A water point will be found near the bridge. This area tends to be used by commercial craft and you should avoid the quayside painted red and white. The Rhône current can flow swiftly here: a pair of laden breasted-up *péniches* was noted barely able to make headway upstream. Safest moorings, with a capacity approaching 350 berths, are to be found at the *Port de l'Epervière* (K112), offering a wide range of boating facilities but unfortunately a long walk from the city centre. Shopping can be attended to at a huge supermarket within 500m. The Port's clubhouse incorporates a quality restaurant; there is a chandlery and mechanical and repair services. A very useful location where boats may be left quite safely between cruises at much less cost than in Mediterranean marinas.

After a very ruined leaning tower (K116), a broad reach leads to **Beauchastel** lock cut (right bank, alongside a weir). A small port (K120) is convenient for the village of **Charmes**. Beauchastel (K124) lies close to the lock (fall 12.65m), where water may be taken on the right of the chamber.

Once more back on the original river, **La Voulte** (K128) appears on the right bank. There are limited and rather inconvenient moorings on a sloping quay, downstream of the road bridge. Amid a mass of rusty brown pantiles is the 15–16th century *château*, much damaged by German troops in 1944, and an Italianate church. South of the town, an elegant concrete railway viaduct sweeps over the river: it is the longest structure of this type in France. After a confluence with the River Drôme (K131), **Le Pouzin** (K133) appears at a junction with the River Ouvèze. Moorings are just possible near a garage and restaurant, although the vertical quay might be too high for convenience. A further disadvantage is the disturbance created by the railway. Intense cultivation is a feature of the rocky, terraced hillside, for the town occupies a cleft between hills. Mountainous surroundings continue into the Logis-Neuf lock cut which runs parallel to 7km of original Rhône, accessible from the downstream end only,

although navigation is not officially recommended. **Logis-Neuf** lock (K143, fall 13m), is located near the lower end of its canal. A little beyond, at K145, is a most useful harbour, where the sloping quay is well shaded. Close by is **Cruas**, with shops, dating back to a Benedictine foundation in 804. The Romanesque church, in a style similar to that at Tournus on the Saône, is partly 11th century; many of the houses are medieval. Farther downstream is the Cruas nuclear power station, one of several on the Rhône. A concrete quay opposite offers moorings, while the *Port de la Coucourde* commercial boatyard is available for marine repairs, on the left bank, sheltered by a reedy island.

The river has become extremely wide, enabling an artificial commercial harbour to be built in an L-shape, projecting far into the main channel (K152). Once more the navigation divides (K153), the left fork leading to the **Montélimar** cut. Now a modern manufacturing city best known for its nougat industry (started in the 16th century), Montélimar lies too far to the east to be of much interest to boaters. **Ancône** (K154) has useful dolphin moorings, several shops and a restaurant. High on a hillside to the west, the 13–16th century *Château de* **Rochemaure** incorporates a medieval village within its ramparts. Inaccessible to boats, the River Roubion flows across the canal at right angles (K158), followed by the *Port de Montélimar* (K159.5), useful only as a stopping point for there are no town facilities within reach.

The vastness of the Rhône locks is well demonstrated by that at **Châteauneuf** (K164, fall 17.1m), where there is ample space for a 3,000-tonne coal barge, a sizeable passenger vessel and a large twin-engined motor yacht – all at the same time. Buffers prevent craft accidentally hitting the gates at speed. Beyond lies one of the Rhône's most dramatic reaches: the **Donzère Gorge**, whose cliffs rise impressively to a height of about 100m over a length of 3km. At its head, a short distance up the original river course, is the fascinating town of **Viviers** (K166), with an often congested public quay where passenger craft appear to demand priority over private vessels. The adjoining enclosed harbour is too shallow for most pleasure cruisers. Be prepared to anchor and go ashore by dinghy; also, be ready to offer a night's berth alongside to late arrivals who may have no alternative mooring. This has been a seat of bishops since the 5th century, St-Vincent's cathedral dates from the 12th century and there are remains of ancient fortifications. Narrow cobbled streets produce a compelling air of mystery: it is not a place to be missed. Should you have grown weary of the starkness of concrete or rock-sided canal cuts, it makes a pleasant change to divert upstream along the former navigation for about 4km past reedy banks to **Lafarge**.

A prominent statue of St Michael overlooks the upper end of the spectacular Donzère Gorge. This is the last we shall see of the real Rhône for almost 30km, for the navigation now enters the Donzère–Mondragon Canal. Among sites thus bypassed is the famous crossing-point town of **Pont-St-Esprit** whose 1,000m long bridge with 25 arches was built in 1595 and fortified by Vauban in the 17th century. Suitable only for canoes and inflatable craft, and so beyond the scope of this book, the outstandingly beautiful **River Ardèche** flows past limestone cliffs and under the impressive *Pont d'Arc* (a natural stone 'bridge' 34m high). It enters the Rhône above Pont-St-Esprit. Organised canoe trips take participants down 30km of the finest natural river scenery in Europe, with overnight camping stops and opportunities for swimming from sandy beaches. Complete novices are given an initial training, enabling them to tackle the 30 rapids safely. Alternatively, day trips in small boats are possible from **Vallon-Pont-d'Arc**, with transport back to the start.

Sets of radial gates are installed at the upper end of the canal (K171) to protect the channel from floods. Information boards 2–3km above and below the cut entrances inform whether navigation is interrupted: closure during the summer is unlikely. Steel piling here could provide a useful mooring. Scenic interest is somewhat lacking on the straight course of the canal where the most notable features are an atomic energy centre (K183) and a nuclear power station (K184.5). A short distance east of the D204 road bridge (K185) lies the abandoned hilltop village of **Barry**, where cave dwellings were occupied from Neolithic times until the end of the 19th century. The site provides an excellent view of **Bollène** (Donzère–Mondragon) lock (K188) and its adjacent André Blondel hydro-electric power station. With a fall of up to 26m, passage of this lock is a memorable experience, not least for the speed with which the chamber fills or empties in a mere seven minutes. As the first of the Rhône locks, Bollène, completed in 1952, has an architectural style that is now slightly dated, with more than a hint of *Art Deco*. Once believed to be the deepest lock on Earth, it has since been ousted from that position by a lock on Portugal's Douro and since 2003 by an even more massive structure at the start of China's Yangtse Gorges. Bollène was the scene of a tragic accident in February 1998 when a fault caused the upper gate to open at speed, filling the chamber almost instantly, sinking a barge and drowning the lady owner. Although the problem has of course been rectified, regulations now demand that life jackets be worn by those on board craft using Saône and Rhône locks.

By now the river has definitely reached the south, and you instinctively know that Provence and the Mediterranean are at last within easy reach. Coming out of the Donzère–Mondragon Canal (K200.5), note the *Château de* **Mornas** to the east, beyond the A7 *autoroute*. Seized by Catholics in the 16th century, the houses were decorated for the feast of Corpus Christi with the skins of Protestants who had been displaced. In reprisal, a Huguenot force was despatched from Arles and the Catholics driven over the precipitous cliffs on which Mornas stands. The sun-bleached village of **St-Étienne-des-Sorts** (K204, right bank) was once a Rhône boatmen's settlement. There is a pontoon mooring, close to basic shops, small restaurant, slipway and garage. Two great chimneys belong to the **Marcoule** Atomic Energy Centre (K210), in service since 1973 for research and the production of electricity. Visits are possible, with wide views from a terrace. Next feature is the beginning of the **Caderousse** lock cut (K212.5): the concrete of the lock and its approach channel are uncompromisingly severe and a sideways-moving top gate is an unusual feature. On leaving the canal, it is possible to turn back up the former course of the river, running to **L'Ardoise**, where a marina offers comprehensive services and long-stay moorings.

After passing beneath the A9 bridge (K222) a good view of the rocky fortress of *La Tours de l'Hers* (K225)

Bollène lock, deepest on the river with a rise and fall of 26m.

La Tour de l'Hers, near Roquemaure.

appears on the left bank. Opposite is a very ruined *château* and the town of **Roquemaure**, with seemingly ideal moorings on a vertical quay with adjacent slipway. This can be a very dangerous place to lie when the *Mistral* is blowing, as the reach is open for several km in each direction. During a violent August storm in 1994, six pleasure craft over-nighting here were smashed against each other by 2m waves: the damage to craft and personal injuries were extensive. **Châteauneuf-du-Pape** lies a short distance to the east.

A multiplicity of channels at the approach to **Avignon** results from extensive navigation works. The through route is via the **Villeneuve** Canal, in part asphalt-lined and leading to Avignon lock (K234, fall 10.5m). Glimpses of the city appear through the trees

on the left and a detour must be made to get there. Villeneuve (K242) was developed as the Cardinals' City, during the period when Avignon was the City of the Popes. There were no fewer than 15 cardinals' palaces in the town. Various fortifications were constructed by the Kings of France in opposition to the strongholds erected by the Holy Roman Empire on the Avignon side of the river. Rising sheer from the water's edge is the Tower of Philip-le-Bel (14th century and earlier), a defence of the west end of Avignon's bridge. The top is reached by ascending a 176-step spiral staircase. St-André's Fort similarly provides a magnificent view: it remains one of the leading examples of medieval fortification and was constructed by Philip-le-Bel, John the Good and Charles V, in the 14th century. But even greater interest and good mooring facilities will encourage pleasure craft to halt instead in Avignon, reached by heading down river to the railway viaduct

(K244) and then turning upstream along the *Bras d'Avignon*, the former through navigation. Pass under two bridges, with the totally walled city on your right. Four remaining arches of the celebrated *Pont d'Avignon* now appear directly ahead. Just beyond, immediately beneath the city walls and within a short walk of the leading attractions is a marina using floating pontoons. Beware a sometimes fierce current, even in mid-summer. Winter flooding has devastated these installations on a number of occasions. Approaching craft are often met in mid-stream by the harbourmaster's launch and directed to suitable moorings. Facilities are comprehensive.

First impressions of Avignon will be of its very considerable extent: 100,000 people live here in a maze of narrow streets, behind the protection of a massive wall pierced at intervals by gateways. Avignon's golden age began in 1309 when the Pope set up court. The huge fortified Palace was constructed by Benedict XII (1334–42) and Clement VI (1342–52). A masterpiece of medieval architecture, its white stone walls and towers rise more than 45m. The exterior is the best feature; within, there is a lack of furnishings and the hour-long

The Pont d'Avignon.

guided tour may not be to everyone's taste. Gregory XI, last of the true French popes, returned Church rule to Rome in 1377: his successor was so unpopular that a series of anti-popes ruled from Avignon until 1403.

The tourists' centre of the city is the *Place de l'Horloge*, a tree-shaded traffic-free square with numerous restaurants, street musicians and a very animated atmosphere that continues far into the warm summer nights. The Rhône is also busy, with many *péniches* converted into houseboats and other pleasure craft. The old bridge is, of course, Avignon's greatest claim to fame: a mere four arches survive of the original 22 which together spanned a distance of 900m, across an island and over to the far shore at Villeneuve. Legend says that in 1177 a shepherd boy, Bénézet, had a vision commanding him to build a bridge. Previous crossings of the lower Rhône had all been by ferry. When he miraculously lifted a great block of stone single-handed, all scorn and doubts evaporated and funds poured in to complete the task in eleven years. With its chapel of St-Nicolas, the bridge has languished in its present incomplete state since the 17th century. Visitors may walk over the remaining arches on payment of a fee, and those with reduced inhibitions may feel inclined to hold hands in a circle, singing '*Sous le Pont d'Avignon on y danse tous en rond*'. NB '*Sous*' not '*Sur*'.

Restaurant delicacies associated with the city include *Alose à l'Avignonnaise* (shad-fish braised with sorrel and lemon) and *truffes blanches* (white truffles). A favourite eating place is the courtyard restaurant of the splendid *Hôtel d'Europe*.

While in Avignon, a most enjoyable excursion might be made by hiring a car and driving to the 2000-year-old *Pont du Gard*, a Roman aqueduct designed to convey water supplies to the city of **Nîmes**. Restored to its present excellent state under Napoléon III, the three-tiered bridge rises 40m over its river with an uppermost row of 35 arches 275m long. The bravest of visitors can walk over the top.

The speed of the Rhône is now generally reduced: so is the scenic interest, for long reaches have little except reed and willow-fringed banks. While there is a boat-yard offering moorings and other services a short way up the River Durance (K248), the approach channel is in a state of constant change, so it is best reserved for those with local knowledge. At K261, left bank, **Vallabrègues**, is a mooring on floating stages: the approach can be tricky in windy conditions. Adequate shopping and restaurant. One final lock must be negotiated – the Écluse de Vallabrègues (K265, fall 12.15m), whose entrance canal is situated on the left (K262.5) opposite the confluence with the River Gard. As you emerge from the lock, you will see ahead the twin towns of **Beaucaire** and **Tarascon** (K267.5), linked by a road bridge. Most unfortunately, there really is little prospect of being able to moor to explore the superb *châteaux* – and much more – in each place. It is quite astonishing that floating pontoons for visiting boaters have not been installed by the town authorities. Don't they want to welcome travellers arriving by water? Since changing the Rhône water levels in the early 1970s, a former connection with the Canal du Rhône à Sète at Beaucaire has been severed. This point may, however, be reached by boat via the Camargue waterways. It seems probable that the direct link will be reinstated at some future date. Meanwhile, the huge feudal castle of Tarascon, its legendary beast and the sights of Beaucaire are described in Chapter 64, Canal du Rhône à Sète.

Deserted marshland with irrigation canals accompanies the river to a junction with the Petit Rhône (K279.5), the inland route for the Canal du Midi, Canal du Rhône à Sète and the Languedoc Coast (see Chapter 57). The Rhône has one further treasure to offer: the incomparable city of **Arles** (K282), a gateway to the Camargue and one of the chief towns of Provence. Established as a river port by Greeks from Marseille in the 6th century BC, its usefulness was enhanced when the Romans cut a navigation linking it with the Mediterranean at the Golfe de Fos, so avoiding the silted complex of the Rhône Delta. Roman relics include a huge open-air amphitheatre capable of seating 21,000 people. During the Middle Ages it was converted into a circular 'village' of 200 houses and only restored to its present state in the early 19th century. Various public events are regularly staged there.

The Château de Tarascon, near Avignon.

The two great names of Arles are those of painter Vincent Van Gogh (1853–90), who immortalised the region with a frenzy of over 200 pictures in 1888–9; and the Provençal poet Frédéric Mistral (1830–1914). After the coming of the railway in the 19th century, Rhône traffic declined and with it the importance of Arles. Today, it flourishes again thanks to the Camargue rice industry, and as a tourist centre making full use of regional traditions.

Central moorings are on a floating pontoon, right bank, upstream of the *Pont de* **Trinquetaille** (K282.5). Shopping and restaurants are both convenient and excellent. The local tourist office will advise on public transport to nearby places of interest. Car hire is a further possibility. Objectives for day trips include the Camargue marshes and nature reserves (see Chapter 64); **Stes-Maries-de-la-Mer**, with its fortified church where the Camargue meets the sea (good times to visit are during the gypsy celebrations and pilgrimages, held on 24–5 May, the weekend nearest 22 October and the first Sunday of December); and the fascinating rock village of **Les Baux-de-Provence**, 19km NE. All are fully described in the Michelin Green Guide *Provence*.

At the downstream end of Arles, left bank K283.5, the basin of the **Canal d'Arles à Fos** may be reached via a lock. Here is a boatyard where repairs are carried out and arrangements made for long-term moorings. About 2.5km outside Arles, the famous doubled leafed bascule bridge of Van Gogh's paintings spans a former (now level) lock. The wooden structure was replaced by a replica in the 1930s. Opened in 1834, the waterway subsequently formed part of a chain of safe navigations extending to **Marseille**, thus avoiding the problems of the Rhône Delta and the coast. 31km remains available for pleasure craft, with a further gateless (level) lock. Scenery is similar to the Camargue marshlands, with no shade. The terminus is now at **Le Relai**, although of the very small number of craft that use the canal, few ever travel beyond the small village of **Mas-Thibert** (K18.5). Further east, the **Canal de Marseille au Rhône** between Marignane and Marseille has been closed since the collapse of the huge Rove Tunnel in 1963. 7,120m long with a width of 22m and a height of 11.4m, it was probably the largest long distance navigation tunnel in existence. Construction was carried out between 1911 and 1927.

The remainder of the Rhône's course is atmospheric, if featureless, as it follows a wide path along the edge of the Camargue. **Salin-de-Giraud** (K316.5) on the left bank is a small plane-shaded centre of chemical manufacture, connected to the opposite bank by busy car ferries (there are no bridges over the Rhône after Arles). Were it not for a lack of suitable moorings, this would be an ideal place to leave a boat and cycle about 5km past mountains of evaporated sea salt (a sizeable industry) and alongside brackish lakes to one of the finest beaches on France's Mediterranean coast. This is the **Plage de Faraman**, an immense tract of pale sand and dunes a little west of the point where the Rhône finally reaches the sea. Its isolation has prevented any form of development apart from a friendly restaurant in a shack. Vehicles may drive over the firm sand and hundreds of people use the beach as an unofficial camp site in summer. Following widely adopted practice elsewhere in France, nude bathing has become quite acceptable.

In theory, a choice of routes now exists between Salin-de-Giraud and the Mediterranean. Since its completion in 1982, the **Liaison Rhône-Fos** (entrance at K316.5) has offered a 7km canal connection to the new **Port de Fos** and its extensive industrial zone. There is one lock near the Rhône end. Designed for use by 5,000-tonne push-tows, it is not, however, normally available to pleasure craft, which must reach the Mediterranean via Port-St-Louis-du-Rhône.

Port-St-Louis (K323) is entered by making a broad sweep into the Maritime Lock (left bank), beyond which is a large basin. The little town is known for its excellent pleasure boat moorings and facilities for repairs and winter storage. There are shops, restaurants, fuel and water points. From here, the blue Mediterranean is a mere 3km away past commercial docks that line the **Canal St-Louis**. Most pleasure craft that have successfully descended the Rhône will be adequately equipped for a sea passage: but it must be emphasised that the Mediterranean can be extremely rough and is certainly no fit place for river cruisers, except for short trips in ideal conditions. The final 6km of the Rhône, between Port-St-Louis and the sea, are silted and not suited to navigation.

57 ～ Petit Rhône

Carte Guide: *Canaux du Midi or Le Rhône*
From a junction with the (Grand) Rhône at K279.5, upstream of Arles, to the Mediterranean at Grau d'Orgon, west of Stes-Maries-de-la-Mer: 58km with no locks. A junction is made at K299.5 with the short Canal de St-Gilles, which provides a link with the Canal du Rhône à Sète. The lower 38km from there to the sea is little used, except by small fishing boats and cruisers; maximum permitted draft on this section is only about 1m with an air draft of 3m.

Following closure of the Beaucaire connection between the Rhône and the Canal du Rhône à Sète, the first 20km of the Petit Rhône from near Arles to St-Gilles were greatly improved from its former shallow state. It now provides the normal through route for craft using the chain of Midi waterways that link Mediterranean with Atlantic. The channel, while reasonably narrow and winding, is practicable for large commercial vessels and the St-Gilles lock was built to the same dimensions as those on the Rhône. Thick belts of trees and reeds line each bank for the entire distance, with no villages and scarcely any buildings to be seen. The lower 38km to the sea are similarly desolate, although the tree cover decreases nearer to the Mediterranean. Although not especially typical of the Camargue it is all strangely attractive.

Distances along the river are a continuation of the measurements from Lyon: the junction with the Grand Rhône above Arles is K279.5 and the entry to the sea K336.5. Detailed description of the Petit Rhône is not necessary. In the whole course there are a mere five bridges and one ferry crossing; scarcely a hamlet; and in the first 20km not a house to be seen from the water. The sense of isolation is intense and at times it is difficult to be sure where you are. Numerous drainage channels accompany the waterway through the marshes of the Camargue, although little of that fascinating world is evident from a boat. There are no shopping facilities directly on the route. While taking precautions for a slight rise and fall in water levels, there are numerous possible moorings. None is more appealing than a 'desert island' of white sand and tamarisk bushes at K293.3, with swimming beaches offering both deep and shallow water. The nearest contact with civilisation is the Pont de St-Gilles (K297) from which **St-Gilles** is within easy walking distance (see Chapter 64). Just before K300 the Canal de St-Gilles with its large lock appears on the right. Virtually all craft will wish to pass this way, soon joining the Canal du Rhône à Sète.

While there is a clearly marked navigation channel from the Grand Rhône to St-Gilles lock, there is an absence of signs from St-Gilles to the Mediterranean. Although care should be taken to avoid sand banks, this is not difficult water for a small boat: in fact the journey is a very worthwhile excursion, with a good enclosed maritime harbour at **Stes-Maries-de-la-Mer**, reached after a short eastwards coastal passage. This is a lively little seaside resort, noted for its periodic gypsy gatherings.

58 ~ River Garonne

Carte Guide: *Canaux du Midi*

From Bordeaux to a junction with the River Baïse near Buzet, providing a 5km-long connection with the Canal Latéral à la Garonne (Baïse Branch). 132km and 0 locks. In fact, with the exception of very small locally based craft, only the 54km of tideway upstream of Bordeaux is regularly navigated, traffic instead using the Canal Latéral à la Garonne between Castets and Buzet. A small portion of the Garonne between the mouth of the Baïse at St-Léger and the beginning of the River Lot at Nicole is in use as a connection between those two waterways. Entry to the River Dordogne is from the River Gironde (the name of the estuary of the Garonne) at Bec d'Ambès, 26km towards the coast from Bordeaux.

The Garonne rises in the Pyrenees, across the Spanish border. Being tidal throughout what is generally regarded as its navigable length, it demands more careful use than most inland waterways. The portion below Bordeaux is in effect a seaway and is beyond the scope of this book. Forming the western section of the 505km route between Bordeaux and the Mediterranean, the Garonne is a somewhat difficult river and should only be attempted in correctly equipped craft and by people with some experience of tidal waterways. If entering from the Atlantic, use *Service Hydrographique* marine charts 6141, 6139, and 6140. East of Bordeaux there are limited mooring possibilities and it is preferable to make a passage from there to the canal at Castets (or *vice versa*) on one tide. There are rocks to be avoided in places and allowance must be made for a tidal bore which can reach 1m in height for some distance above Bordeaux.

Although there is very considerable interest in the villages associated with many famous Bordeaux vineyards such as Graves, Sauternes and Barsac, they are rarely in evidence from a boat as for much of the time the river banks are lined with a thick belt of trees.

Brief history As recently as 1936, the Garonne was technically navigable for 463km from the Atlantic (including the Gironde from the coast to Bec d'Ambès), but even then, only the section to Castets still carried any traffic. In early times, craft had been able to reach Toulouse with some difficulty: indeed there was no other route for boats travelling from Atlantic to Mediterranean after completion of the Canal du Midi in 1681. Boats and rafts brought stone and lime to Toulouse, all the way from Boussens, about 70km upstream of the city. Passengers aboard the Midi 'water coaches' risked grounding in the river and even the prospect of shipwreck. The poor state of the upper Garonne can be judged from the necessity to transfer the contents of a single Midi freight barge into no fewer than 20 light-draft vessels for the run down river from Toulouse. These difficulties were finally overcome by completion of the Canal Latéral à la Garonne between Castets and Toulouse in 1856. Thereafter, upper Garonne traffic declined and efforts to keep the route dredged were abandoned.

In 1886 it was calculated that there were 1,752km of river navigations in the Garonne basin, comprising 25 individual waterways (excluding artificial canals): these were regularly navigated by 30,952 vessels. Among these lost routes were the Tarn, from above Albi to the Garonne near Moissac (147km with 31 locks); the Lot, (256km with 76 locks); and the Dropt (64km from Eymet to the Garonne at Casseuil with 21 locks). By the earlier part of the 20th century, all these had returned, more or less, to their natural states, although the remains of locks existed. In recent years some of these 'lost' rivers have experienced a remarkable renaissance. An isolated 64km portion of the Lot was reopened to navigation in 1990, while a substantial locked length of the Lower Lot from the Garonne to well beyond Villeneuve has recently been restored (see Chapter 60). Similarly, the once derelict River Baïse is again busy with boats (Chapter 61).

Although 98km inland from the coast, **Bordeaux** is a sizeable and busy port, capable of receiving large ships drawing up to 8.5m. Moorings may be found out of the tideway in the *Bassin à Flot*, between the *d'Aquitaine* and *de Pierre* bridges; or on the river itself in the nearby *Port du Point du Jour* or at the *Port Fluvial* near the Pont St-Jean. Shopping and the city centre are close to the *Port Fluvial*. Water the colour of cocoa, a fierce tide and violent wash from passing traffic are all factors that discourage a long stay.

For two centuries Bordeaux and a sizeable chunk of SW France was under English rule. Eleanor, daughter of the Duke of Aquitaine, married Louis VII of France in 1137, but this union was annulled. Keeping her French lands, Eleanor then married Henry II of England, so providing an eventual cause of the Hundred Years War. Former capital of Aquitaine, the great city is the sixth largest in France. After the Fall of Paris it became seat of Government in 1870 and again in 1914 and 1940; many of its most notable buildings, such as the *Grand Théâtre*, date from the 18th century. Perhaps Bordeaux's greatest claim to fame is as centre of the claret industry. Suggested tours of the vineyards and *châteaux* of the region will be found in the Michelin Green Guide *Atlantic Coast*.

While the river channel lies mostly in the centre, great care should be taken to follow the chart, avoiding sand banks and other hazards. Running with the tide, leave 4–5hr before high water. Depending on the speed of your boat, allow about 6hr for the journey upriver to Castets.

Km posts are numbered from a point upstream of Castets, which is at K17.5. Should you need moorings en route, there are possibilities at the following places, bearing in mind that most pontoons are only in position during the summer months: **Cambes**, pontoon, K56; **Langoiran**, quay, not approachable at times of low water, K49; **Cadillac**, K35.5; and **Langon**, *port de plaisance* projected, K25. All these towns have good shopping facilities. If you decide to explore ashore, Cadillac is possibly the most interesting port of call with fortifications and the *Château des Ducs d'Épernon* (early 17th century and open throughout the year, except Tuesdays). The town's water gate has a flood marker which provides dramatic evidence of the wayward nature of the Garonne. In April 1770 the river rose 12.5m above normal and only a metre less in the famous flood of 1930.

Atlantic weather can bring fog to the lower part of the Garonne. Other characteristics are large 'ring' nets, suspended from cranes on the muddy banks: they are lowered to catch whatever species of fish swims by. Widely advertised specialities include *aloses*, a migratory sea fish known in English as shad and here grilled over vine shoots or stuffed with sorrel; and *lamproies*

A cruiser approaches the first lock of the Canal Latéral à la Garonne at Castets-en-Dorthe.

(lampreys), an eel cooked *à la Bordelaise* sliced with leeks, red wine and garlic. Remember that Henry I paid a high price for eating too much of this dish.

On arrival at the junction with the Canal Latéral à la Garonne at **Castets** (K17.5), approach via the right-hand arch of the road bridge, on the same side as the locks. Should the lock be ready, enter straight away; otherwise anchor in midstream below the bridge or bring up on a bankside mooring, 200m downstream of the bridge. Hoot for the keeper, who is on duty (depending on the state of tides) normally between 05.00hr and 23.00hr. The chamber is worked electrically with another manual lock alongside. Craft leaving the canal for Bordeaux and the Atlantic should time their departure to coincide with high water at Castets.

59 — Canal Latéral à la Garonne

Carte Guide: *Canaux du Midi*

From the River Garonne at Castets to a junction with the Canal du Midi in Toulouse: 193.6km with 53 locks; 5 of these are duplicated by a 'water slope' at Montech which is not available for use by private pleasure craft other than converted *péniches* more than 30m long. Junctions are made at Buzet-sur-Baïse (via a two-rise lock) with the River Baïse; at Moissac (two-rise staircase leading to an attractive reservoir section of the River Tarn); and with the Montauban Branch at Montech. (10.8km with 9 locks, leading to the Tarn. Restoration of the river from that point to Moissac has been proposed.)

It would be preferable to travel from Bordeaux to the Mediterranean and not *vice versa*. For although the Canal Latéral à la Garonne is very pleasant in parts and passes through many places of interest, it would inevitably come as a considerable anti-climax to navigate the Latéral *after* the incomparable Midi. As a work of the mid-19th century, the Latéral features many long straights, compared with its curvaceous 17th century neighbour. You cannot fail, however, to admire the boldness of its engineering. For much of the journey between Agen and Toulouse the railway is close by – sometimes aggressively so. Bridges are utilitarian rather than pretty, many being concrete bow-string structures. On the credit side, the banks of yellow iris provide a remarkable blaze of colour in early summer. Agen is one of the most productive fruit growing regions in France, raising many varieties from strawberries and cherries to apples, pears, plums, peaches and kiwis. Vineyards are rather less in evidence,

although some famous wines include those produced around Buzet.

Locks were lengthened in the 1970s to admit 38m *péniches*; they are mechanised and most are automated for working by boat crews. Controlled by a traffic light system, gates and paddles are set in action by turning a pole (*tirette*) suspended over the water about 300m in each direction. Further controls must be operated when craft are in the chamber. Instructions are displayed in French, German and English. One unfortunate design fault of the locks is the overflow weirs which enable water supplies to run from pound to pound. The inlets and outflows are situated very close to the lock gates, making steering light pleasure boats quite difficult.

Brief history It is said that Pierre Paul Riquet, builder of the Canal du Midi, envisaged an artificial waterway to replace the very uncertain navigation of the Garonne downstream of Toulouse, but work on its construction was not to commence for over 150 years after the Midi was inaugurated. Planned under de Baudré, the Divisional Inspector of the *Ponts et Chaussées*, work started in 1838. By 1843 it was sufficiently advanced for a regular passenger boat service to begin between Montauban and Toulouse. The line had been extended to Agen by 1850 and reached its planned junction with the River Garonne at Castets in 1856. Unfortunately, that was the very year in which the Midi Railway Company completed its connection between Bordeaux and Toulouse. The rival transport concern negotiated a lease (expiring in 1898) for both the Latéral and the Midi and a deliberate policy of canal neglect was adopted. When he cruised between the two seas in his steam yacht *Miranda* (25.9m x 3.35m, 1.42m draft) in 1881, Lord Clarence Paget commented that the railway 'has almost entirely absorbed the traffic'. State control in 1898 brought a change in fortune. By the end of the 1930s all but a few horse boats had been replaced by motorised *péniches* and steel lock gates were standard throughout the route.

In 1939 preliminary Government consent was obtained to construct a ship canal for ocean-going vessels between Bordeaux and the Mediterranean at La Nouvelle. The War intervened and nothing more was to be heard of this plan. Instead, in the 1970s all locks became automated and were lengthened for Freycinet 38m *péniches*. However, enlargement of the adjoining Canal du Midi was only partly carried out, discouraging an increase in freight tonnages. Commercial traffic which was flourishing on the Latéral as recently as the 1980s has now vanished. It is both sad and remarkable that whereas 15 barges passed along the canal each day three decades ago, it is now only used by pleasure craft. Perhaps the most notable innovation was the building of a water-slope for *péniches* in the place of a five-lock flight at Montech. Unique in the world for a decade from 1973, it has since been joined by a similar structure on the Canal du Midi at Béziers.

The great popularity of cruising on nearby waterways such as the Midi and more importantly on the restored Rivers Baïse and Lot has seen a considerable increase in leisure use of the Canal Latéral à la Garonne. This is confidently expected to grow in coming years. There is a proposal to restore navigation on the River Tarn, initially between Montauban and Moissac. Should this happen, the Latéral's Montauban Branch will be given a new lease of life as part of a splendid 68km boating circuit using the Tarn and the canal.

To arrive in the still waters of the canal at **Castets-en-Dorthe** (K0, see Chapter 58) is rather a relief after the turmoil of the tidal Garonne. Not that this waterside settlement is totally safe from the bed-tempered river. Flood marks on the side of the lock house reach up to the *second* storey: at this level the front door is situated, with a magnificent iron stairway sweeping round each side of the building to higher ground at the back. The lock (No 53) consists of a two-rise arrangement, but only the lower chamber seems normally to be used. Consult the keeper for tidal information if preparing to run down to Bordeaux. Castets village hides away up a hillside, overlooked by a huge *château*. Shops and restaurants. There are comprehensive moorings at the *halte nautique* with barbeque facilities, between Écluses 51 and 52.

Many villages lie directly on the canalside and are agreeably agricultural. Some have basic shops, eg **Fontet** (K11, restaurant and moorings) and **Hure** (K14), where there are Gallo-Roman mosaics and an extremely old church. Shortly after passing from the Gironde *Département* to Lot-et-Garonne, we reach a real gem – **Meilhan** (K23). At a point where the Garonne swings in towards the wooded escarpment to the right of its valley, the canal passes beneath a cliff on top of which is a restaurant, public terrace and telescope for admiring the view. To reach this point is an easy uphill walk of perhaps 10 minutes from the canal moorings. Meilhan's look-out offers a rare opportunity to appreciate the Garonne landscape from a high level.

Black-painted wooden barns with open slatted sides will be seen in the fields: they were used for drying tobacco. The sizeable riverside town and former port of **Marmande** is 6km by road from the canal at **Pont des Sables** (K29) where there are hire craft, moorings for private boats and associated facilities such as fuel and slipway. Nearby village shops are adequate with two

Lock house at Castets, junction of the canal and the river. Note the exterior staircase to provide access during flood conditions.

restaurants. Unusually, a rowing club is based here: take care to avoid young people out training. A sad accident is recalled by a stone monument on the bank near **Fourques** (K32). In 1908 all five men aboard steam barge *Le Gascon* were killed when the boiler exploded; it was said that the captain was drunk. Moorings and several shops. **Caumont** (K33) lies near a basin with easy access to the few shops of this small one-street town. At **Le Mas d'Agenais** (K38) a long single carriage-way suspension bridge spans both the canal and the Garonne. This site was occupied by the Romans and among many relics excavated here is the 1st century BC Greek Venus of Mas, now housed in a museum at nearby Agen. Ancient terraced houses with balconies perch on the edge of a tree-covered cliff high above the waterway where there is a major Crown Blue Line hire craft base, also offering facilities to passing boats. Within 500m is the heart of this delightful little town, set around a market square. Shopping is excellent for such a small place – and the church of St-Vincent shelters a Rembrandt *Crucifixion*. Such unlikely discoveries are all part of the fun of travelling in rural France. Do stop to explore: Le Mas is like a thousand other towns in southern France – and yet it is somehow rather special. By a bridge at K40.3 are moorings and a restaurant, with similar facilities and shop in the hamlet of **Villeton** (K45.2). Note a tiny church, occasionally used, on a mound beyond lock 42, La Gaule at **St-Christophe**, K46. **Damazan** (K54) is an old fortified *bastide* town whose years of English domination are recalled by the *Fontaine des Anglais* at an ancient *lavoir*

Cruisers moored at Meilhan, alongside the River Garonne.

(wash-house). There is a pleasure boat halt, adequate shopping, a restaurant, Thursday market and some fine old buildings, especially around the central arcaded square, recently restored to a high standard.

Craft are encouraged to stop at the *halte nautique* in **Buzet-sur-Baïse** (K57), shops, and the excellent *Le Vigneron* restaurant. *Les Caves Co-operatives de Buzet* provide an opportunity for replenishing the ship's wine stores and welcome visitors with a visual presentation and tour (commentary available in English). It is a friendly little town with a market, Fridays. Shortly, there is a junction, via a two-rise lock, with the beautiful River Baïse (see Chapter 61), which in turn provides access to a length of the Garonne leading to the River Lot near Aiguillon (see Chapter 60).

Beyond Écluse 39, Baïse, the canal spans the River Baïse on an aqueduct, soon to arrive near **Feugarolles**

(K64), with a quay and several shops. For the first time the A62 Narbonne–Bordeaux *autoroute* is noticeable on the right. Apart from Écluse 38, l'Auvignon (K68, moorings) and **Sérignac-sur-Garonne** (K77, a gem of a village with moorings and restaurant), there is little of note until the outskirts of the city of Agen. A sharp turn, K83, marks the start of a former 5km branch with two locks, now infilled; this once provided a connection with the River Garonne. Locks 34–37 raise the canal 12.4m, followed by a magnificent 539m stone aqueduct, taking the navigation over the river.

Agen (K86) is the self-styled 'capital of prunes', for of all the fruit grown in the area none is better than the luscious preserved plums to be obtained at various shops in the city, including the *Maison des Pruneaux*, established 1835. To the left of an extended basin a wooded hillside is dotted with elegant villas. There are convenient moorings with hire craft and most boating services very close to the railway station and city centre. Greater Agen has 70,000 inhabitants with a wide selection of restaurants and shops. St-Caprais' 11th century cathedral is disappointingly gloomy: a far more interesting visit is to the *Musée des Beaux Arts*, housed in a series of Renaissance mansions. The leading exhibit is the celebrated Greek marble statue of Venus from Le Mas d'Agenais; displays include furniture, ceramics and paintings by Goya and Sisley.

The waterway that now follows is pleasant but unremarkable. Never far from the banks of the Garonne, it runs straight for considerable distances sometimes bordered by great fields of maize, elsewhere secluded under a canopy of huge plane trees selected for their ability to counteract erosion. Facilities in the nearby towns and villages are as follows: **Boë** (K91.6, moorings and shops); **Lafox** (K94.8, limited shops); **St-Jean-de-Thurac** (K98, restaurant); **Lamagistère** (K107, all services); and **Golfech** (K108, some shops and restaurant). Here, there is an aqueduct over the River Barguelonne, and, downstream of a dammed section of the Garonne, a hydro-electric power station.

An excellent (free) *port de plaisance* in the 13th century *bastide* town of **Valence d'Agen** (K112) is close to most facilities. The splendid circular public *lavoir* (wash-house) is one of three examples here of that peculiarly French facility where architectural styles are often of classical proportions. Many could be seen in use as recently as the 1980s; their popularity has since all but vanished thanks to domestic washing machines. After **Malause** (K120, moorings and town facilities), the canal runs alongside the Garonne, much increased in width by conversion into a huge reservoir up and downstream of the junction with the River Tarn. It may be entered by boat from the Tarn branch canal in Moissac.

Easily the most interesting and agreeable town on the Latéral is **Moissac** (K129). Shortly after Écluse 26, Espagnette, is a convenient roadside garage. Approaching the town centre, it becomes obvious that the canal was built with brick retaining walls down the middle of a wide street. After the *Pont St-Jacques* swing bridge (sound horn) there is a delightful garden gazebo attached to a conservatory: the epitome of 19th century French domestic architecture, it has a slender cone of slates for its roof and an ornate cast-iron balcony. Soon the canal leaves this narrow cutting for a broad basin with plenty of mooring space, water and electricity. Moissac's great treasure is its ancient abbey, founded in the 7th century and preserved in spite of repeated attacks by Arabs, Normans, Hungarians, the English in the Hundred Years War, and during the French Revolution. Having survived thus far, it might have been considered to be safe; but no – there was a quite determined proposal to demolish the structure to create space for the mid-19th century Bordeaux–Sète

A waterside gazebo at Moissac.

railway! The same infamous railway that presented a threat to the Midi canals. Fortunately, the great building was spared. Partly Romanesque and partly Gothic, the abbey church of St-Pierre has a wonderful carved south doorway from the early 12th century, depicting the Vision of the Apocalypse according to St John. The intricacies of this Romanesque stonework are remarkable. Completed towards the end of the 11th century, the abbey cloisters are probably the most outstanding in France, the capitals of each arch decorated with a variety of animal and plant motifs. It seems offensive that a substantial admission charge is made.

Agen is associated with prunes: Moissac has its delicious golden dessert grapes. Shortly before Écluse 25, a branch on the right leads through a two-rise staircase to the **River Tarn**. Although little now remains of the 147km waterway and its 31 locks, once navigable to **Sault-de-Sabo**, upstream of **Albi**, there is currently a proposal to restore the river between Moissac and Montauban, bringing the Montauban branch of the canal back into service. Meanwhile, it is already possible to descend the Moissac locks (silting below may reduce draft to only 1m) and so cruise on a 400 hectare reservoir section of the Tarn where there is a yacht club and swimming pool. Note the remains of a lock on the downstream end of the Promenade du Moulin: it has a gateless diamond-shaped chamber.

The canal now ascends through locks 23–25 on the edge of the town, where trees and grassy banks make a popular waterside walk for local people. Lock 23, **Cacor** (K131), is a delightful haven of peace, the gravel forecourt of the cottage being beautifully maintained for *boules*. Now follows the second of the Latéral's great stone aqueducts, spanning the Tarn for 356m with 13 arches. An extraordinary period in its history followed the great flood of March 1930, during which the adjacent main line railway viaduct was washed away. The aqueduct's towpath was widened sufficiently to enable a single track to be laid along it, and within six weeks of the disaster trains and barges shared the same crossing. This arrangement continued for two years until the opening of the present replacement viaduct. Leakage on the embankment that follows has resulted in the canal bed being lined with asphalt.

Locks 22–19 now intervene before **Castelsarrasin** (K137), a rather dull little town with a full range of shops and market Thursdays and Saturday mornings. Moorings in the basin with a nearby pool. Two more locks, before and after the village of **St-Porquier** (K144), bring the navigator to one of the most fascinating examples of modern waterway engineering in France, the **Montech Water Slope** (K148). In its original form the canal passed (and continues to pass) through Locks 15–11, spread over 2km. Pleasure craft must still use these, while rare barges, trip boats or larger pleasure vessels more than 30m long take the parallel new route leading to a 443m concrete 'flume' or trough; a wedge of water, in which the barge floats is pushed up or down a 3% gradient ahead of a shield propelled by a pair of locomotives. Popularly known as a 'push-puddle' lock, this ingenious concept is best suited to sites with substantial changes in level: here, it is about 14m. The Montech Slope began operating in 1973 and was joined by the world's second water slope at Béziers on the Canal du Midi in 1983. All this modern technology is far removed from the remains of an old wooden Midi barge, decaying in a small dock between locks 11 and 12. Montech town centre lies about 500m away from a basin beyond the top lock. Most shops and an agreeable medium priced restaurant are near the crossroads.

On the canal's other bank is the 11km **Montauban Branch**, with nine locks, which was closed for a number of years before its restoration in 2003. There is a plan to restore navigation on the adjacent River Tarn, at least between Montauban and Moissac. Scenery down the side canal is pleasant with an A61 *autoroute* bridge near the village of **Lacourte St-Pierre**. The branch reaches its terminus at a basin quite close to the middle of

Montauban. Originally, a two-rise staircase lock provided a link with the Tarn Navigation. The ferocity of the well-remembered great flood of 1930 is dramatically recalled by a bust on the riverbank promenade. This depicts a young man named Adolphe Poult. While water swirled through the streets, he used a small boat and saved the lives of no fewer than 317 people before himself being drowned. This is a pleasant city, mainly of pink brick with an early 14th century bridge, a 17th century Archbishop's Palace (now the Ingres Museum) and fine brick arcades surrounding the *Place Nationale* where a flower market is held in the mornings.

Soon after Montech the railway returns to the canal bank and remains a constant and noisy companion all the way to Toulouse. Villages have expanded as a consequence and there are plenty of opportunities for shopping. Surroundings are deeply rural to begin with, through extensive orchards. **Dieupentale** (K162) and **Grisolles** (K167) are both well supplied with shops and restaurants. **Castelnau d'Estrétefonds** (K174) is best approached from Écluse 8. Situated on a ridge with a red brick church and large pedimented *château*, it offers basic facilities. Lock 7 is followed by an aqueduct about 120m long over the River Hers. The last easily approached shopping village before the Toulouse conurbation is **St-Jory** (K178), within 200m of Lock 6. The neighbourhood of the canal now becomes increasingly industrial as five final locks are negotiated before arrival in Toulouse (K193), junction with the Canal du Midi at the *Port de l'Embouchure* (see Chapter 62).

60 River Lot

Carte Guide: *Le Lot* (Éditions du Breil)
From a junction with the River Garonne at Nicole, near Aiguillon, to Lustrac, 68.1km with 6 locks. Upstream of this point is currently being restored over a further 10km with 2 locks to a hydro-electric dam at Fumel. For the present, any navigation on the following section, K78.3 to K128 with 13 locks, is restricted to reaches between locks until the start of an isolated navigable length, Luzech to Crégols, 63.7km with 14 locks. Re-creation of the former navigation upstream of Crégols to Port d'Agrès bridge, is expected to be achieved eventually: 73.4km with 22 locks.

Set in a region rather less known than the neighbouring Dordogne, but displaying equal attractions, the River Lot represents an extraordinary success story in the annals of French waterway restoration. After navigation works had lain derelict for much of the 20th century, a length upstream of Luzech and currently isolated from the rest of the network was reopened to boats in May 1990. It offers plenty of scope for a week's cruise by hire boat; there are a number of firms supplying craft. Alternatively, sufficient slipways exist for the use of private trailed vessels. A long section of the Lower Lot has since been reopened and is presently being extended upstream with the eventual objective of joining the two portions together.

Throughout, scenery varies from very fine to outstanding, placing the Lot high on the list of Europe's most beautiful navigable rivers. Lower reaches feature meadows with extensive fruit farming around Aiguillon and Villeneuve. Otherwise, the banks are thickly wooded. Further upstream in the Cahors area there are spectacular limestone gorges. Virtually all bankside towns and villages will repay exploration; many are based on ancient fortified sites. Hardly any of the river has been affected by modern industrialisation or tourism: generally, this is a deeply rural part of France. Remnants of historic troglodyte castles can be found along the valley. These are the *châteaux des Anglais*, well guarded refuges of the English invaders who were active during the Middle Ages.

Like many French rivers, the Lot is prone to flooding in winter and spring; care should then be exercised in the vicinity of weirs, especially where there are no still-water lock cuts. Under these conditions, when navigating upstream, chamber entrances may be obstructed by a fierce outfall across the channel. Equally, in a downstream boat, it can be difficult to detect a weir and the adjoining lock entrance until the last minute. Such problems are fortunately rare during the main cruising season, but at all times due attention must be paid to the *Carte Guide*. Navigation markers warn of shallow patches of mud, solid rock or even submerged remains of former weirs. For all that, the Lot is not normally a difficult waterway. There are a few regulations specific to the Lot. Speed should not exceed 5kph in artificial cuts or close to the banks; otherwise 12kph is permitted. (Some lengths are set aside for water ski-ing.) Passenger boats must be given priority at locks. Sign boards at locks display three triangles at water levels denoted I, II and III. When the level is below I, available draft may be insufficient for navigation; any point between I and II shows normal conditions. Should the water rise above II, private and hire craft must stop at the nearest lock, wait for the level to drop or contact the river authority for the boat to be conducted to a safe mooring.

In most cases there are adequate landing points above and below locks, enabling boat crews to get ashore. With the exception of two very deep locks (with keepers) alongside hydro-power barrages, gates and paddles are operated by boaters. Those on the lower section are worked electrically, using a 'smart card'. Upstream of Luzech, locks are manual, with fixed windlasses. Here, for reasons described as *sécurité*, it is impossible to operate the gate capstans unless both gate paddles at that end of the lock are fully wound open. If the paddles are not correctly adjusted, the gate-opening mechanisms infuriatingly become disengaged. Low-geared paddle machinery requires about 100 turns, but is not heavy to operate.

There are numerous excursions to be made in the locality, provided you have the use of a car. These include the clifftop pilgrimage city of Rocamadour, the valley of the River Célé (good canoeing), and pre-historic cave dwellings (*Grotte du Pech-Merle*).

Eating local produce is a major preoccupation. Goose, duck, *pâté de foie gras*, many varieties of fungus, freshwater fish (including crayfish), walnuts in salads, crushed for cooking oil or fermented as a sweet *digestif*. Expanses of vineyards around Cahors produce the famous dark red – sometimes almost purple – wine, a favourite with the Russian Tsars.

Brief history Although used with difficulty by small, shallow-draft craft in the 12th century, when 11 flash locks were installed in weirs between Penne-d'Agenais and Fumel, a reliable Lot navigation was not created until Colbert ordered works in the 17th century. By 1776, the river boasted 12 conventional pound locks, some of which replaced earlier time-consuming structures. Still, the Lot had a dangerous reputation. Wreckings were frequent in times of drought and, worse still, during floods.

A complete re-management scheme commenced in 1835, with some 297km being tamed from Le Moulin d'Olt at Entraygues, to the Garonne confluence at Nicole. When rebuilding finished there were 76 locks (including three two-rise staircases), numerous artificial lock cuts and four tunnels varying in length from 139m to 364m: these were cut through high ground to avoid some of the more acute bends. A size-able barge fleet comprised flat-bottomed *sapines* and *gabares* and little swim-ended wooden punts known as *naus*. Typical loads carried were cheese from the Auvergne, Decazeville coal and a wide range of agricultural products chief of which was red wine from Cahors. Greatest tonnage was in a downstream direction, destination Bordeaux, although a substantial quantity of foodstuffs and minerals travelled upriver. During 12 months in 1851/2, nearly 73,000 tonnes of freight was recorded, including 20,000 tonnes of wine.

Railway competition began to exact a savage toll and by 1923 freight figures on the upper and middle river had plummeted to a mere 11,635 tonnes. Late in 1926, the Lot navigation was officially abandoned, all dredging and maintenance on locks and weirs coming to an end. For more than 60 years lock cuts gradually disappeared beneath a tangle of undergrowth and the only boats to be seen were fishing punts and long-distance canoes.

The region suffered economic decline throughout much of the 20th century and with hopes of boosting tourism, M Ricard, *Préfet du Lot*, in 1970 prepared an initial scheme for revitalisation of the river. Little was to come from this. Meanwhile, pleasure boating was increasing rapidly elsewhere in south-west France. A report commissioned from English-born waterways expert David Edwards-May, assisted by Blue Line's managing director, John Riddel, identified nearly 65km of the most scenic portion of the route which could be restored at a cost of about £2.4 million. Financial support was sought from the European Parliament and reconstruction work was carried out at an unusually rapid rate. All was ready to welcome me as the first boat hirer when I made a return journey by water with two friends between Luzech and St-Circq-Lapopie in May 1990. The scheme has been highly successful, with a number of hire companies established on this isolated length, together with several large trip boats. Any upstream extension of this section is unlikely to materialise in the immediate future, for there are two former navigation tunnels now incorporated into hydro-electric schemes and a high dam that will have to be bypassed by construction of a deep lock.

Towards the end of the 1990s, the Lot Aval (Lower Lot) saw the start of a far-reaching restoration programme, so reuniting it with the connected French waterways network. At the time of writing, the rebuilt navigation extends from its junction with the River Garonne, upstream to Lustrac. This length is currently being extended to Fumel, where an 8m-deep lock is to be built to allow navigation past the hydro-electric dam. A further 11 locks are planned so as to link with the isolated section at Luzech. Here, there is another high dam to be circumvented by a new 11.3m-deep lock. The former waterway passed through the centre of Luzech in a deep cutting, now infilled. It is likely that a 250m tunnel will provide the new connection. These works will probably not be completed for a number of years: when they are, the restored Lot will have added 192km of waterway to the system, with the prospect of an additional 74km between Crégols and Port d'Agres. All this is in the interests of pleasure boating and tourism. Remarkable!

LOWER RIVER LOT

Access to the waterway from the interconnected system involves leaving the Canal Latéral à la Garonne at **Buzet-sur-Baïse** (see Chapter 59) and dropping through the two-rise lock into the River Baïse. An electronic card is available from the keeper: this operates DIY locks on the Baïse (see Chapter 61) and the Lot. Following the Baïse for 4.7km downstream through Écluse 2, Buzet, brings you to Écluse 1, **St-Léger**, a two-rise at the Garonne confluence. Because the 4.7km section of Garonne that provides a link with the Lot is considered to be somewhat hazardous in certain circumstances, hire cruisers must be towed by an official tug, with all passengers travelling on board the towing vessel. The current one-way charge, per boat, for this service, is 16 Euros. The Garonne channel is clearly marked and provided they are sufficiently powerful, private boats in the charge of qualified skippers may navigate the river unaided. En route, right bank, you will pass the outfall of the Lot; ignore this and continue to the Écluse de **Nicole**, where you should wait for the tug captain to see you through.

The first stretch of waterway is via a long, leafy and narrow artificial cut (*canalet*), in which mooring is forbidden. A nearby hill, *Pech de Berre*, surmounted by a huge crucifix (at about 15m high, it is among the largest in France) provides a magnificent panorama over the confluence of the two rivers and the fruit farms established in this fertile valley. Nicole has a good value restaurant. The upper end of the cut is spanned by rail and road bridges. Ahead is the Écluse **d'Aiguillon** (K2.6), directly alongside an extremely broad weir with mills at each end. The sandy river bed makes a splendid official bathing beach (supervised, July and August). Cross the bridge to reach the nearby town, set on a hill first occupied by the Romans. Good range of shops and restaurants, supermarket, railway station. Visit the local museum in a former chapel of the river boatmen, the medieval area by the *Château de Lunac* and the open air market (Tuesdays and Fridays) famous for Lot Valley fruit and vegetables. Overnight moorings on a pontoon above the lock are provided with water and electricity. Surrounded by fruit farms and set in its wooded *parc* on the river's left bank at K4.5 is the stone-built 18th century *Chartreuse* manor house *Cul de l'Ilot*, my home since 2004.

The lock at **Clairac** (K9.9) is situated on the right bank, directly alongside a weir and hydro-electric generating station. There are mooring lines hanging inside the chamber. Wooden rails between the lock's upper end and the road bridge prevent boats being drawn onto the weir. Public moorings, hire craft base and a passenger vessel are located on the left bank, downstream of the bridge. All facilities are close by. The moderately-priced *Auberge de Clairac* restaurant is highly recommended. This is a pleasing town with many brick and timber buildings. The former Benedictine abbey has three attractions which will especially appeal to children: the *Musée du Train* (model railways in realistic landscapes); the *Fôret Magique* (animated elves and woodland animals); and *L'Abbaye des Automates*, where lifelike figures recreate activities in the abbey long ago. It is claimed that the monks introduced prunes to the area and brought tobacco from Brazil in 1555. Upstream of the *Château de Poudepé* is a possible mooring, right bank (K13).

Granges-sur-Lot (K19.5) features a real oddity – the Prune Museum. On offer are extensive tours and tastings. Tie up at the nearby pontoon, close to which are several shops. The small town of **Castelmoron-sur-Lot** (K22) comes soon after the site of a vanished weir and lock: take care to follow the navigation markers. Moorings, left by the bridge, are overlooked by a curious Moorish-style *château*, now the *Hôtel de Ville*. Good shopping and restaurants. Each Tuesday in summer there is a *guingette* (open air dance/café) by the river, with barrel organ and entertainments. Castelmoron lock (K22.7) is a recent structure with a 10m rise and fall. It is keeper-operated using signal lights. The 29km reach that now follows to Villeneuve has long been used for aquatic activities and is less prone to fluctuations in water level than some other parts of the Lot. On the edge of town is a leading leisure development at **Port Lalande** (K23.5). This comprises an extensive purpose-built basin, home to a Connoisseur hire fleet. Additionally, moorings are reserved for private craft with a full range of services. Alongside are several dozen small holiday 'lodges'. The whole enterprise will become more visually attractive as it matures and the trees grow. Restaurant a short walk in the upstream direction. On the opposite bank, there are moorings in front of a small chapel. A little beyond this is a former lock house (but no lock).

Le Temple-sur-Lot (K25.2) is a major water sports centre with international standard rowing course and facilities for canoeing and sailing dinghy training. Moorings with water and electricity are situated on the right bank (K25). Basic shopping. The town was founded in the 12th century by the Knights Templar: part of their brick-built *Commanderie* is occupied by an exclusive restaurant; nearby is some outstanding municipal landscaping and a water feature. Painter Claude Monet (1840–1926) stocked his famous lily pools by the Seine at Giverny with plants supplied by Latour-Marliac of Le Temple. The firm, founded in 1875 by Joseph Latour-Marliac (1830–1911), is now

British-owned and their fascinating show ground displays more than 200 varieties of *Nymphaea*, growing in ponds and concrete basins. In spite of this being the only garden centre for which I have ever been charged an entry fee, a visit is essential for anyone even slightly interested in gardening. The blooms are at their best in June and July.

A short distance from the left bank, K27, quay, the delightful village of **Fongrave** has several shops, while the Tuilerie farm sells fruit, vegetables and a speciality local cake called *tourtière*. **Ste-Livrade-sur-Lot** (K32.5) is served by a floating pontoon with convenient shopping and restaurants. Market day is Friday mornings. A really worthwhile port of call is the ancient **Casseneuil** (K39.1), a onetime barge town situated at the confluence of the River Lède. Take a footpath along this stream to the back of the town where historic buildings are perched high above. Market, Sundays and Wednesdays. Quayside moorings are a little downstream of the road bridge. If you walk up the Lot for about 1km, you will reach a barge used by *France Prune* as a prune showroom/sales outlet.

At K43, right bank, a pontoon enables boaters to visit the 13th century *Château de Favols*: advance booking required by phoning the owner, tel 05 53 70 28 19. Now follows one of the river's leading cities, **Villeneuve-sur-Lot** (K50), which stands high on each side of the river's green corridor. Good moorings are found between the first and second bridges, very close to the maze of medieval streets with fortified gateways and towers. Although its origins date back to Gallo-Roman times, the name 'Villeneuve' is fully justified, for it was re-born as a 'new town' *bastide* in 1253. Its present prosperity results largely from fruit farming and particularly from production of prunes. The range of shops and restaurants is extensive. The great *Pont de Cieutats* resulted from destruction by 17th century floods of an earlier bridge. For a long period, navigation and collection of barge tolls provided the town with much useful revenue. Note the tiny chapel at the left-hand bridge approach: it was once used by Lot mariners. Several km SW lies the **Pujols**, fortified and heavily restored; it is regarded as one of the finest villages in France. Note a disused lock, right, K50.6. This is followed by the massive 13m-rise Écluse de Villeneuve, recently built to overcome a hydro-electric barrage. It is keeper-operated. Several further redundant locks will be seen in the following 17km level.

Isolated farm buildings accompany the river to a pair of towns facing each other, downstream of a road bridge. Both have risen splendidly to the opportunities offered by the restored waterway. **Port-de-Penne** (right bank, K59.6) has well managed quays with facilities including showers. Facing it on the other shore is **St-Sylvestre-sur-Lot** with further mooring facilities, a sparkling new waterside shopping complex and restaurants. It is worth taking a taxi for the 2km uphill trip to **Penne-d'Agenais**, a battle-ravaged medieval village now dominated by the 1947-built Sanctuary of *Notre-Dame-de-Peyragude*. Note old lock houses, left bank K61.4, and right bank K63.1.

The Écluse de **Lustrac** (K68.1) where restoration was in progress during the summer of 2003 is flanked on one side by an historic water mill and on the other by a splendid small *château* and its *parc*. Within the very near future, this and the Écluse de **St-Vite** (K75.7) will have been returned to service and the navigation extended to the 7.96m-high **Fumel** barrage. A further 13 locks (including one with a lift of 11.3m and a new tunnel) will have to be constructed or rebuilt before it is possible to reach the upper river at Luzech by boat. A leading attraction in this section is the small hilly town of **Puy l'Évêque** (K98.8), once an important barge centre.

UPPER RIVER LOT

Navigation currently begins upstream of a hydro-electricity barrage immediately north of the small town of Luzech (K128). Old postcard views show that a 200m canal with staircase locks once cut through what is now the market square, bypassing a huge loop of the Lot that nearly describes an entire circle. It was so completely infilled in 1950 that most signs of the waterway have been obliterated, although the *Place du Canal* that replaces it is unusually wide. There is good shopping and other facilities. One indication of Luzech's former importance as a centre of the barge trade is the chapel of *Notre-Dame-de-l'Isle*, where boatmen prayed before setting out on the dangerous loop that formed part of the navigation until 1840. Rock-strewn reedy shallows and a disused lock chamber clearly illustrate the dereliction affecting the unrestored waterway. Nearby are the remains of the prehistoric **Impernal** settlement, later a Roman city. A severe 13th century keep tower dominates the view from a boat. Now begins a level reach of over 12km, fringed by dense woodland with patches of vineyard and walnut groves. On the left (K128.4) is a hire boat base with moorings and facilities: this is the only suitable stopping point for Luzech. A watersports base appears on the left at **Caîx** (K129.4, restaurant): watch out for canoes, swimmers and sailing dinghies. The moorings here are the best place to stop if you wish to visit the 17th century *Château de Caîx*, summer residence of Queen Margrethe II of Denmark.

Mooring is possible at many places; first, carefully check water depths. If in doubt, use sites identified in the *Carte Guide*. One such is the outside wall of the former lock just downstream of the delightful, but seemingly deserted, riverside *Château de Langle*, built in 1500 (K134). Due west, **Parnac** is surrounded by vineyards and fields of tobacco; here you can visit the co-operative cellars for tastings – and purchase – of Cahors wines. Bishop Raimond de Cornil inhabited the *Château de Laroque*, perched on a cliff (K139.6). He was responsible for a 13th century scheme to improve navigation on the Lot. Beyond a camping site (right) and the elegant brick railway bridge of the former Cahors-Fumel line, will be seen the disused chamber of Douelle lock. Soon, **Douelle** appears in the distance, beyond a rocky weir. A direct approach to Cessac lock (K140.5) is not possible, owing to shallows on the right. The course to take is marked by buoys. The small town was once a leading barge port; one reminder of this vanished activity is a votive offering in the form of a boat, suspended from the rafters of the church. I have several times greatly enjoyed the relaxed atmosphere of the cellar-like restaurant *Aux Vieux Douelle*, with steaks grilled over a wood fire. Opposite the town and reached via the suspension bridge is the Crown Blue Line hire cruiser yard with facilities (including a 10-tonne crane) for private use. Local shops cater for all everyday needs. This is exactly the sort of small town that makes people like me want to go boating in France.

Dense tree cover and sheer cliffs characterise the Lot past the 19th century *Château de Carriol* (K143.5) with a somewhat tricky approach to the Écluse de **Mercuès** (K147.8). Rocky shallows are clearly indicated by buoys or stakes. At times of strong flow, there can be a fierce cross-current below the lock. Mercuès village on the left bank and named after a Roman temple to Mercury, is not easily approached by water and access from the quay is difficult. This is unfortunate as high above towers of the 15th century *Château de Mercuès* command a magnificent view along the valley. Formerly a residence of the counts-bishops of Cahors, it was restored in the 19th century and is now a luxury hotel with splendidly palatial furnishings, a range of opulent bedrooms, swimming pool and well manicured terrace gardens. We delayed a visit until reunited with our car at the end of the cruise, arriving for lunch via a vineyard road. A taxi from Douelle would have been equally convenient. The *château* produces and sells excellent wines. Rarely in France have I more enjoyed a meal, served in the central courtyard which was protected by a remarkable wall-to-wall 'umbrella' in the shape of an inverted cone designed to conduct any rainwater into a stone well in the middle of the restaurant. Our food, although expensive, was of the highest quality. We voted this meal one of the highlights of the Lot.

Pradines (right bank, K150.2) faces the river with a jumble of small clifftop houses rising from the remains of earlier fortifications. There is a mooring with shops and a restaurant. The lower approach to the Écluse de Labéraudie (K153.2) presents no problem. However, when leaving the upper end it is essential to remain close to the right bank to avoid remains of a submerged weir. Shortly, we enter a huge loop within which the city of Cahors is bordered by water on three sides. All boating facilities including repairs, moorings and slipway are available at the *Port Ste-Mary* yard, left bank K154.4. Although now a bright and thriving town (there are few better places to buy regional food specialities), its time of greatest glory was long ago. *Divona-Cadurcorum* in the Roman era, by the 13th century it had become one of the most important commercial cities in France. Today, its greatest jewel is the superb *Pont Valentré* (K155.6), probably the finest 14th century fortified bridge in Western Europe. Guarded by three massive stone towers and still carrying road traffic, it overlooks a broad weir. Under the right-hand arch a diamond-shaped lock draws crowds of spectators gazing from the parapets above as a boat works through. At one time there were three similar such bridges in Cahors; astonishingly, one was demolished as recently as 1906. Good moorings are found just beyond: on the right by an elegant stone-built pumping station or opposite. Both are convenient for visits to the city: a little tourist 'train' operates from the left bank, taking in many of the sights. Every tour should include a visit to the mouth-watering indoor food market. Day-long passenger boat trips operate from here to the present head of navigation at St-Cirq-Lapopie. Cruising upriver, sufficient is left of ancient walls and towers to provide a clear impression of how the city must have looked when it was an intact fortress. A day might easily be reserved for full exploration: the leading attractions are listed in the *Carte Guide* or more comprehensively in the Michelin Green Guide *Dordogne Berry Limousin*.

Écluse de Coty, K157.4, like many others on the Lot, is accompanied by an old water mill, one of several in Cahors. Note the impressive stone bollard at the lower entrance to the lock cut. Marker buoys indicate which arch to use at the next bridge, *Pont de Cabessut*, where submerged stone-work must be avoided. Beyond the bridge, left, are moorings convenient for the city centre. A restaurant *péniche* is established opposite.

Be careful to avoid the remnants of an underwater weir upstream of Écluse de Lacombe (K160.8). Beyond, a very pleasant mooring will be found at a small quay in Laroque-des-Arcs (K161.7, shops and restaurants). This friendly little town takes its name from a series of Roman aqueduct arches. Parts of an ancient *château*, seated on a waterside rocky outcrop, are now incorporated into a private residence. Alongside is a water mill. Nearby, a *château des Anglais* occupies a cleft in a tall cliff. A sharply sloping footpath leads to the tiny chapel of St-Roch on top. At the time of the river's reopening, we spoke to the local mayor who, rather than expressing fears at a possible stream of waterborne tourists, assured us that restoration of the Lot was 'the most exciting event round here for many years!'

Moorings with slipway and showers are located on the outskirts of Lamagdelaine (K163.2, restaurant). Then comes the Écluse d'Arcambal, with narrow lock cut. For the village, which has a small number of shops and a traditional brewery (visits), tie up on the right (grassy bank, K166.1) by a slipway opposite Savanac (mooring). Both places have impressive 14th century *châteaux*. Currently the upper river's only completely new lock, Galessie (K167.4), lies on the left bank at a constricted site bordered by a road excavated from cliffs. The original lock can be seen some distance downstream, converted into a small electricity generating station. *Caution*: flow from the weir could make entry from below rather difficult. An infamous hazard, the *Rocher de Tustal*, immediately beyond, left, was in the past regarded with anxiety by Lot boatmen. Traces remain of a capstan erected to assist craft during their passage.

The most impressive gorge scenery so far encountered appears in the reach leading past Le Couzol (K168.7). Surroundings remain equally fine to the Écluse de Vers (K171.7) near the confluence with the little River Vers. The village shopping facilities are good, with a waterside camp site and a very agreeable hotel/restaurant *La Truite Dorée* (swimming pool). You can see the remains of a Roman aqueduct that conveyed pure water to Cahors, a *château des Anglais* and a 14th century castle. Wild and rugged landscape continues through the Écluse de Planiol (K173.9) above which avoid vestiges of an old weir by keeping within a buoyed channel on the right. 50m below the outfall of a hydroelectric station there is a rocky obstruction in mid-river. Now comes a sharp turn in the lee of cliffs to the Écluse de St-Géry (K176.9), succeeded by a long cut providing good views of the weir stream beyond. For shopping in the village, moor to a stone wall halfway along the cut, which, curiously, has a tiny island at its centre. Safe long-term moorings and boat repairs.

One of the potentially most difficult sections is encountered as we pass the disused Écluse de Masseries

(K180.1). Much of its former weir obstructs the navigation, meaning that boats must keep well over to the left bank. This is immediately downstream of a brick and stone railway bridge. The lower end of a channel to the right of Ile aux Chiens (K181.9) above **Port-la-Léque** makes a mildly adventurous navigational diversion, with mooring, although it is not possible to rejoin the main river at the upper end.

Bouziès-Bas and the Écluse de Bouziès (K184.2, ruined lock house) introduce the most spectacular reaches presently available to boats, with sheer cliffs rising directly from the water in a narrow defile. Beyond a suspension road bridge, **Bouziès** (K185.1) has recently developed as a well-patronised riverside resort, with hotel, restaurant, passenger vessel and hire cruisers, directly opposite yet another *château des Anglais* halfway up a cliff, where a winding road dives through a series of tunnels. Moor here for the village which contains medieval buildings. Local produce including wine and *foie gras* is available at the old railway station in **Conduche**, reached by taking the bridge to the left bank.

Almost certainly unique on a European inland waterway and similar to those in China's Yangtze Gorges, 700m of towpath has been carved from the cliff-face at the approach to the Écluse de **Ganil** (K186.4). Best likened to an open-sided tunnel with unsupported roof, this is one of the strangest examples of river navigation in existence. Admirable shelter would have been provided for the barge horses during heavy rain! The lock is followed by a long and narrow cut whose stone banks are piled high with dredgings ablaze with red poppies in early summer. Opposite is a junction with the little River Célé, popular with canoeists but not navigable by larger craft. Places to visit on foot or by taxi are the prehistoric cave dwellings of **Pech-Merle** (4km) – 1,200m of grotto with 600 ancient wall paintings – and the *Ecomusée de Cuzals* (9km), an open air museum displaying reconstructions of 19th century agricultural life and crafts.

St-Cirq-Lapopie (K190.3), self-proclaimed 'prettiest village in France', is certainly special. Perched high over the river, it comprises a series of tiny pedestrianised streets, houses where the roof of one is on the level of its neighbour's front door, open timber balconies, inevitable craft and souvenir shops and a riot of flowers. Historically, the local trade was that of cauldron-making and wood turning. There are wonderful views down to the Lot, especially from the uppermost tiers by the Gardette *château* and fortified church. Food shopping and several restaurants. Access is best from the moorings at the top end of the lock cut. There are further moorings on the left, beyond the road

bridge and close to food shopping and a restaurant in Roucayral.

For the time being, cruising ends below a weir at **Crégols** (K191.7, no facilities) upstream of a lock almost concealed in a tangle of undergrowth. Hopefully, in the not too distant future, further exploration will be possible as new lengths of this spectacular river are returned to navigation.

61 ～ River Baïse

Carte Guide: *Midi Camargue Aquitaine* (**Éditions du Breil**)
From the River Garonne at St-Léger to a terminus at Valence-sur-Baïse: 65.1km with 21 locks, one of which is a 2-rise staircase. Navigation originally continued for a further 21km with another 9 locks to a terminus at St-Jean-Poutge. Normal entry to the waterway is via a short branch (2-rise staircase lock) off the Canal Latéral à la Garonne at Buzet.

A deliciously attractive little river navigation, restored from complete dereliction between 1988 and 1997. The middle reaches pass through the Albret region, with the town of Nérac at its centre. It is justly popular with hire cruisers. Some of the artificial lock cuts are very narrow with little solid bank protection. Until this is remedied, there will be a tendency for the channel to silt up, especially after flooding. Upstream to Lavardac, draft is officially quoted as 1.5m (optimistic at several lock entrances); beyond there, it is only 1.0m. Even this could be reduced in a dry season. Most locks are electrically self-operated by boaters who must insert a 'smart card' in the chamber-side console. Such cards are available from the keeper of the staircase lock at Buzet Junction. This state-of-the-art system is fairly reliable, although a telephone link at each lock will produce an engineer, should the apparatus fail. With its succession of delightful and historic towns and villages, a return trip up the Baïse can easily be stretched into a relaxing week.

Brief history Rudimentary navigation using small flat-bottomed craft on the lower part of the river as far as Lavardac dates from the 13th century. Under Henri IV, five wooden flash locks with associated weirs (Buzet, Vianne, Lavardac, Bapaume and Nérac, 1598–1600) improved matters, although beyond Lavardac the waterway remained extremely shallow for four or five months of the year. Several schemes to extend navigation in the late 18th century came to nothing. In 1830, conditions were described as 'archaic'.

Between 1835 and 1839, new locks were installed to enable craft to reach Condom. In order to increase freight capacity to the river's leading port at Lavardac, locks were enlarged there and at Vianne to 31.4m x 5.2m. A further extension to the St-Jean-Poutge head of navigation had been achieved by 1877. In 1852, construction was completed of the short branch to the new Canal Latéral à la Garonne at Buzet. The final improvement, in 1881, was a junction lock at St-Léger, where the Baïse empties into the Garonne.

By the middle of the 19th century, it was common-place to see up to 90 barges loading or unloading in Lavardac, in addition to those that were passing through. At its peak, the river carried around 130,000 tonnes of freight each year. Payloads of 150 tonnes could reach Vianne; with 100 tonnes to Lavardac. Beyond that point, smaller locks and a draft reduced to 1.0m restricted barges to just 75 tonnes. In 1878, the two leading Baïse barge companies employed about 200 people between them. All traffic was hauled by horses or mules until the introduction of steam power (paddles or propellers) in 1881.

1905 saw the end of flour milling on the waterway and thereafter tonnages declined. By 1930, all horse drawn craft had been replaced by motor barges, which in 1932 conveyed about 40,000 tonnes, including wine, timber, cereals, gravel, sand and flour. The last load on the upper river, a consignment of gravel aboard M René Lorrose's boat *St-Jacques* reached Condom from St-Léger in January 1952. The following month, an unprecedented flood destroyed lock gates throughout the waterway, resulting in abandonment of the navigation above Lavardac.

Utter dereliction over the next 35 years saw lock cuts increasingly choked by silt and vegetation, and several lock chambers were obstructed by small hydro-electric plants. Restoration has not yet reached the uppermost nine locks between Valence-sur-Baïse and St-Jean Poutge. It is doubtful if they will be returned to service, as there are few obvious attractions in these deserted reaches.

A lock marks the junction of the Baïse and the River Garonne at St-Léger. Most craft using this lowest part of the Baïse will be doing so to reach the Lower Lot (see Chapter 60 for regulations relating to the use of hire craft on this link). The Lot/Garonne junction lies a short distance downstream at Nicole. Lock 2 on the Baïse, **Buzet-sur-Baïse** (K4.5) is situated alongside a grim cellulose factory. Moor beyond the lock, right bank, for access to the town (see Chapter 59). Soon after, on the right, a short branch with two-rise locks, provides a connection with the Canal Latéral à la Garonne. If ascending, hoot to alert the keeper who is responsible for supplying the electric cards required for working most Baïse locks. 7km of lonely river now winds through a steep-sided valley, past dense tree growth. Debris caught in branches shows how flooding can raise levels 1–2m. The Baïse passes beneath an aqueduct carrying the Canal Latéral à la Garonne close to its locks 39 and 40. Soon after, limited shopping and a restaurant are 600m from the river in the village of **Feugarolles** (K11, quay beyond the railway bridge). Suitable moorings for the attractive little *bastide* town of **Vianne** (K14.2) are found by a mill, right, below the weir or, more conveniently, on a quay (water and electricity) upstream of the lock. One of four gateways through fortification walls provides access to a large central square with ample shopping facilities (Friday evening market). A glassworks, situated on the upstream outskirts, sells lamps, vases, etc, many items in a distinctive *Art Nouveau* style.

Lavardac (K17.3) lies on the left bank beyond Écluse 4 and a substantial road bridge. There is a good vertical mooring quay, which a century ago would have been packed with dozens of barges. Among the full range of facilities are restaurants and an excellent fish shop where fresh oysters may be obtained at a bargain price. (If you want to buy 18 of them, try saying '*Dix huit huîtres*' very quickly to the assistant: it should produce a smile.) Note the 1838 stone carving of a sailing barge outside the old town hall. Extensive street market Wednesdays. Not far beyond is the confluence with the **River Gélise** (no longer navigable) on which is situated **Barbaste**, notable for its Romanesque bridge and massive 12/13th century fortified mill. A visit on foot from Lavardac (about 30 mins) is recommended. Market, Friday mornings.

Throughout the Baïse, restoration works were planned to retain as many bankside trees as possible, resulting in a dense leaf canopy over the narrow lock cuts, where great care is required to pass other boats. Waiting lay-bys are provided at several points. *La Chaumière d'Albret* restaurant beyond the very fine railway viaduct (K18.7) offers moorings and a good selection of menus.

Écluse **St-Crabary** (K19.5) is the first lock with a width reduced to 4.15m. Its keeper's cottage is a *gîte rural*. Most such buildings on the river have long been in private ownership and considerable opposition was voiced by their owners when restoration plans were announced. Many lengths of bank are private. Boaters should respect their privacy and moor only where invited (see the *Carte Guide*). Views are restricted by dense forest throughout the lower waterway, although several large *châteaux*, in varying stages of dereliction, will be glimpsed in this area.

Locks appear at **Sorbet**, No 6 (K21.3), with a cluster of stone houses, hydro-electricity plant in the mill and caves; and **Bapaume**, No 7 (K23.4). Soon after, we reach the jewel of the Baïse – **Nérac** (K24.9), capital of the Albret and famous for its association with Henri IV, whose *château*, high above the river, has a notable long balcony (local history museum). The waterfront, comprising many restored half-timbered buildings, is really charming. Moorings on both banks between the two bridges. Excursions are available on a replica barge. A maze of narrow streets awaits exploration. Facilities are good, with a thriving street market, Saturday mornings. Beyond the town is the riverside *Parc de la Garenne*, containing a pretty gazebo and a grotto sheltering the Fleurette fountain, a memorial to a young girl who allegedly drowned herself when forced to end a liaison with King Henri.

Écluse 9, **Nazareth** (K26.8), is a magical place with dense vegetation, a cottage built into a cliff and a nearby ruined *château*. Well-groomed goats perch on the lock-side bollards. Note the disused iron/timber capstans, originally installed for working the gates. Hardly a hamlet will be passed in the deep countryside that now follows past Écluse 10, **La Saubole** (K29.4), 11, **Récaillau** (K31.2), 12, **Pacheron** (K34.7), 13, **Lapierre** (K36.6) and 14, **Vialères** (K39.9). After Recaillau, the wooded scenery characteristic of the Baïse since Buzet is gradually replaced by open fields.

It is certainly worth mooring at the bridge-side quay (K42.3, water and electricity) a little beyond lock 15, to walk uphill to the enigmatic small town of **Moncrabeau**, on the border between the Tarn-et-Garonne and Gers *Départements*. As recently as 1995, the lock chamber was completely obstructed by an electricity-generating plant. At least since the 18th century, Moncrabeau has been the self-proclaimed World Capital of Liars. The tradition continues with the annual crowning of the Liar King, (first Sunday of August), a title that is hotly contested as inhabitants vie with each other to invent increasingly fanciful versions of local history. There is much of April Fools' Day (or *Poisson d'Avril*) alive and flourishing here. Unfortunately, some aspects of these tales could quite possibly be true: the visitor will have great difficulty in sorting fact from fiction. Roadside information boards guide you through streets where barges used to moor before river levels fell 50m. Seek the lookout point, from which, on a clear day, it is possible to see the Straits of Gibraltar. Waterways museum, swimming pool and important collection of Impressionist paintings (apply at the *Hôtel de Ville*).

Further locks, 16 **Autiège** (K46.3), 17 **Beauregard** (K48.5), and 19 **Peyroutéou** (K52.4), lead to the sizeable town of **Condom**, with central moorings, hire cruisers and all urban facilities, K53.1. Once a leading river port, Condom remains a centre of Armanac production (museum). It is an agreeable place and the cathedral merits investigation. Tripping boat and small craft for hire. Public park land extends to Lock 19 Gauge (K54.5), where the former mill house is now a welcoming restaurant. Paddles (80 turns to lift halfway) and gates are manually worked by boat crews. The narrow cut beyond is shaded by a 'tunnel' of mature alders.

Unusually for a river navigation, Lock 20 **Graziac** (K58.5) comprises a two-rise staircase, where the stonework of the chambers and bridge has been beautifully restored. As it is manually-operated, requiring a degree of heavy labour, it is perhaps fortunate that the authorities do not trust pleasure boaters to work through unaided: a team of keepers is on hand.

Just before reaching the head of navigation, a halt should be made at a bridge-side quay to visit the well-preserved **Abbaye de Flaran**, an important 12th century Cistercian foundation. The monks have long since departed and the complex is open to public inspection. Among the delights is an authentic herb garden and a large Gallo-Roman mosaic floor.

Every waterway ending in a terminus benefits from having some form of final objective: the Baïse is well served in this respect by the little cliff-top *bastide* town of **Valence-sur-Baïse** (K63.3), founded in the 13th century by the Cistercians. Good moorings with water and electricity immediately before the road bridge. There are ramparts, a Spanish gate and a central square with arcaded buildings. Navigation beyond this point is unwise, as the unrestored river is cluttered with shoals and fallen trees. Exploration by bicycle along farm tracks (pedal hard to avoid grumpy Alsatians) will bring you to **Moulin de Camarade** (K65.1) and the first of the derelict locks, whose chamber has been blocked by an ugly little concrete power station.

62 ～ Canal du Midi

Carte Guide: *Canaux du Midi*
From a junction with the Canal Latéral à la Garonne in Toulouse to the Étang de Thau, an extensive salt lake providing access to the Mediterranean at Sète and to the Canal du Rhône à Sète: 240km and 63 locks of which a number are groups of staircases/risers; the total number of chambers is 91. 1 tunnel. Junctions are made with the La Nouvelle Branch at Cesse: this runs for 37.3km with 13 locks to join the Mediterranean at Port-la-Nouvelle; with the River Hérault Branch at the Round Lock, Agde (for the Lower River Hérault and the Mediterranean at Le Grau d'Agde), 5.2km; and with the Upper River Hérault in Agde, 6.8km to Bessan.

Easily the most popular pleasure boat waterway in France, the Midi forms part of the route from the Atlantic to the Mediterranean. The reasons for its heavy use are easy to understand. For owners of sea-going yachts, it provides a rapid and convenient way from the west coast of France to the Mediterranean or *vice versa*, avoiding the long passage via Gibraltar. But even more important is the very considerable use by hire craft from the very many bases on the canal itself. Almost throughout, the Languedoc scenery is superb, with numerous historical towns and facilities catering for holidaymakers. Sunshine, while not guaranteed, is almost constant throughout the summer: the heat is often such that one is grateful for the lines of giant plane trees that protect much of the route. If your boat has an open steering position, a parasol or more sophisticated sun awning is an idea for which you may be very grateful. A holiday on the Midi can combine canal cruising with visits to the seaside, for at its eastern end there are many opportunities for discovering excellent Mediterranean beaches within walking or cycling distance. Development of the Languedoc coast for leisure purposes is one of the most far-reaching plans of post-war France.

Then there is the grandeur and beauty of the canal itself, with its impressively fine locks, buildings and aqueducts, scarcely changed since they were completed over 300 years ago. These qualities were recognised in 1996 when the canal was classified as a UNESCO World Heritage Site. Commercial traffic declined sharply throughout the 1980s and finally disappeared completely during the drought closure of 1989.

Most of all, this is a languid region: a place for lazing in the sun with no incentive to hurry. There are some yachtsmen who complete the Atlantic–Mediterranean run in a bare week: at such a speed, none of them can possibly enjoy the experience. It is hugely preferable to spend much longer: I have friends who consider that a whole summer does not provide sufficient time!

Although falling short of the gastronomic quality of some other parts of France, the food and wine of the Midi are reason enough to want to holiday there. Much of the agriculture is devoted to vineyards, with opportunities for selecting *Minervois* and *Corbières* wines direct from the producers. Castelnaudary's speciality of *cassoulet* is widely available throughout the region: a stew of haricot beans with various meats – preserved goose, pork and sausage. Nearer the Mediterranean, seafood reigns supreme, with a wide range of fish, shellfish and most importantly oysters from the Étang de Thau.

Brief history The story of the Canal du Midi is better documented than that of any other waterway in France. The best modern account in English, is the late L T C Rolt's masterly *From Sea to Sea* (1973). See also Jean-Denis Bergasse's four-volume illustrated history *Canal du Midi* (J-D Bergasse, Cessenon, 1982–5).

A canal link between the Atlantic and the Mediterranean was considered as far back as Roman times. During the centuries that followed repeated efforts were made to devise a plan, schemes being suggested under Charlemagne (8th century); François I, who had discussions with the celebrated canal designer Leonardo da Vinci in 1516; later in the same century Charles IX and Henri IV; and in 1633, Louis XIII. But no actual construction started. An unusually stable political climate during the long reign of Louis XIV (1643–1715) coupled with the successful building of the world's first substantial summit level canal, the Briare, linking the Loire and the Seine by 1642, were factors that at last made the Canal du Midi a practical proposition. Pierre Paul Riquet (1604–80) was the extraordinary man who achieved this aim.

Riquet was born in Béziers, married into money at the age of 19, and purchased the *château* and estate of Bonrepos, 19km east of Toulouse. He was appointed a collector of the Languedoc salt tax in 1630, a position which demanded extensive travelling throughout the region; he thus gained much detailed knowledge of local topography. A military contracting business helped him earn, in time, a sizeable fortune. Having noticed that water, at what was to be chosen as the canal's summit at Naurouze, flowed both towards the Atlantic and the Mediterranean, he devised an admirable system of feeders: the ultimate key to success in creating a navigation through this arid terrain. François Andreossy (1633–88), lately returned from a tour of

A portrait of the waterway's builder, Riquet. It was commissioned for the canal's tricentenary.

Italian canals, was adopted as Riquet's hydraulic expert and engineer. Remains still exist of the model canal, complete with locks, feeder channels and a tunnel, built as a prototype on the Bonrepos estate. Archbishop de Boulement of Toulouse inspected these works and the site of the reservoir system in the Montagne Noire, and was so impressed that he engaged the interest of the King's minister Jean-Baptiste Colbert (1619–83). After protracted investigations and surveys, Louis XIV proclaimed an edict in October 1666 enabling construction to begin. The chosen design relied on the unlocked course of the River Garonne between Bordeaux and Toulouse, with an artificial canal between there and the western shore of the Étang de Thau near Agde. Six months before canal building commenced, work was inaugurated on the creation of the port of Cette (now 'Sète') where the Étang was linked with the Mediterranean.

Finance came from three sources: Central Government, the Languedoc local authorities and Riquet himself, the undertaker being entitled to profits from canal tolls. Work began on the complicated feeder system and reservoir of St-Ferréol, which was so cleverly engineered that until 1989 the Canal du Midi would remain open to boats even under the most stringent drought conditions; admittedly, an additional Lampy Reservoir was added between 1777 and 1781. For much of 1989 and 1990 a long portion between Toulouse and near Carcassonne was shut through chronic lack of water. It must be said that supplies were then used in support of agricultural interests rather than navigation. Additional reservoirs have since corrected any deficiency. Riquet designed about 60km of feeder channels to bring water down from the Montagne Noire and the addition of 14 locks enabled these to be used for the transport of stone, necessary in the building of the main navigation. Small barges continued to trade on these feeders until 1725. At the same time, work progressed on the canal running eastwards from Toulouse: after the early collapse of a rectangular lock, chambers were built with oval sides, a characteristic feature of the waterway today. With a few exceptions, spill weirs were not provided, surplus water to feed the pound below cascading instead over the wooden lock gates. Intended as a navigation for sea-going craft, the locks were of generous proportions by 17th century standards and admitted two Rhône barges (*caponts*) in one operation. All proceeded well, an inaugural flotilla of three boats travelling from Toulouse to the summit in 1672.

The design of Le Canal Royal, as it was first known, was intended to bring everlasting credit to the reign of Louis XIV, every effort being made to create a grandiose monument to the power of the *Roi Soleil*. This is evident in the high quality of the locks, aqueducts and buildings, all of which display a supreme architectural confidence. With such a novel and extensive enterprise there were innumerable difficulties to overcome: when work had been in progress for 11 years, criticism of escalating costs was widespread. Legend claims (probably wrongly) that Riquet silenced his detractors by completing the 160m Malpas Tunnel in a mere six days. It was 1677: he was an old and tired man. When he died in 1680 the great work was finished but for one league between Agde and the Étang de Thau. Pierre Paul Riquet, Baron de Bonrepos, was buried in Toulouse Cathedral and is celebrated as a hero in Languedoc even now. His waterway transformed the economy of this part of France: more than three centuries later it still benefits tourism and makes a very real contribution to local income.

All was complete for a ceremonial opening of the navigation when a procession of 25 vessels carrying freight and dignitaries departed from Toulouse on May

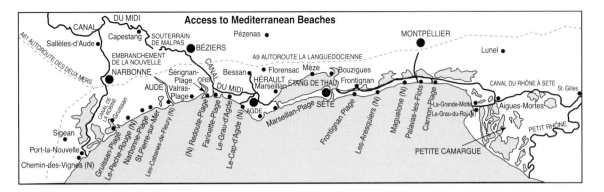

15, 1681, reaching the Étang de Thau on May 25. In spite of its success, the canal failed to provide the Riquet family with a return on their investment until 1724. They lost their rights to proceeds under the Revolution, and when the railway from Bordeaux to Sète was opened in 1857 a period of joint control was established until the lease expired in 1898. Thereafter, the Canal du Midi passed into State ownership. Although never used as a ship canal as had once been intended, much of the freight carried in barges would doubtless have otherwise travelled by sea at vastly greater cost. Matters were not helped by the indifferent state of the Upper Garonne, a problem not finally solved until opening of the Canal Latéral à la Garonne from Castets to Toulouse in 1856.

Initially, the canal appears to have been navigated mainly by small sailing barges with easily lowered masts, bow-hauled by gangs of men. By the middle of the 18th century horse towing had largely taken over. Early in the 19th century the capacity of vessels was increased to 100–120 tonnes: they were about 27m x 5.3m and able to raise a sail for crossing the Étang to Sète; slightly larger boats carrying 145–170 tonnes known as *sapines* were also used, built of timber with an upswept swim-headed bow. Steam tugs to haul trains of craft across the Étang came in 1834 and the use of sailing barges declined. By 1838 there were 273 vessels regularly working on the canal. Smaller 'fast boats' known as *sapinettes* with a load of 50–60 tonnes carried passengers and perishable goods. Packet boats for mail and passengers were fish-shaped in plan with a large cabin and achieved an average speed of 11kph. At first, they avoided working through the thickest congregations of locks, as at Castelnaudary and Béziers, the people taking to the towpath with their luggage to board another vessel. This was eventually regarded as inconvenient and the same boat would be used for a complete journey, working through all locks and taking four days for the run from Toulouse to Sète. Sleeping accommodation ashore was provided at Castelnaudary,

Carcassonne and Le Somail. In the interests of increased speed, day and night working was finally adopted, with a non-stop journey time of just 36 hours. With the opening of the railway in 1857 the era of the passenger boats came to an end.

Arrival of State control in 1898 brought an end to freight tolls. The first motorised barge came into service in 1925. About this time, there were several horse boats in use which towed a strange box-like 'tender' acting as overnight stabling for the horse. The changeover to diesel power was completed by 1935, although horses returned during the fuel shortages of World War II. Some of the old wooden motorised ex-horse boats lasted in operation until the early 1970s after which all freight vessels were purpose-built steel *automoteurs*. Up to the mid-1960s, goods traffic was slightly greater than it had been during the early 19th century. Thereafter, it rapidly declined; by late 1988 there were only two regular barges left. A year later, both had ceased to trade.

During a working life of more than 300 years, the Canal du Midi has experienced remarkably few modifications. Lock gates are now of steel rather than timber; a fine aqueduct was constructed in 1857 to carry the waterway over the River Orb at Béziers, so avoiding the inconvenient crossing of the river on the level; the city of Narbonne was connected with the main line and an alternative route to the Mediterranean opened up in 1776. Perhaps the greatest change of all commenced in 1978, when a programme of lock lengthening was started to enable 38.5m *péniches* to operate instead of 30m Midi barges. One end of each oval-sided lock was modified with an extension of the chamber in parallel-sided concrete. Some two and three-rise staircases were replaced by single, much deeper locks. Inevitably, there was some loss of historic character as at the remarkable Round Lock of Agde, where the perfect symmetry of the stone chamber was brutally altered by partial enlargement in concrete. One exciting development, however, was the building of a 'water slope' (1982–3) enabling boats to avoid the original short chambers of the 6-rise staircase at Béziers. An early failure of the machinery and the resulting enquiry left the water slope disused for the first five years of its life. Fortunately, the adjacent locks had remained in working condition. It briefly returned to service in 1989 but has since degenerated into a semi-derelict white elephant. A 1979 estimate of the cost of all modifications was about £35 million. Only parts of the waterway eastwards from Toulouse and at the Mediterranean end via Agde and down the Narbonne Branch were enlarged before it was realised that commercial traffic was disappearing so rapidly that the whole exercise was now seen as pointless. From a heritage viewpoint, it must be considered fortunate that the greater, central section of the Midi has remained intact, as originally built.

One of the most important events in the canal's recent history occurred on May 30 1969, when a flotilla of seven cruisers arrived in convoy in Toulouse amid publicity that included national television coverage. This was the birth of Blue Line Cruisers (France) Ltd, then one of just two hire boat companies on the entire French network. This British enterprise flourished and after a succession of owners has grown into the world's biggest inland rental fleet. Meanwhile, many other firms have copied Blue Line's example and the hundreds of holiday boats and hotel barges available on the Midi have transformed the economy of bankside towns and villages. Inevitably some commercialism has tainted the waterway fondly remembered by the pioneers of the 1970s. In the early days of the Blue Line fleet, we were offered a chicken by one of the lock keepers. Noting the bird to be fully feathered and alert, we declined, for under these circumstances our meal might have been a somewhat sad affair. Two years later, the same keeper again asked whether we required a chicken for the galley. Laughingly, we reminded him of the earlier encounter. With a flourish, he flung open the door of his cottage to reveal a shining new deep-freeze, filled with oven-ready fowl imported from the local supermarket! Times had changed. By the early 1980s other changes were not so much to our liking: notably a reluctance of many keepers to operate locks until at least two cruisers were present to work through together. Officially, water shortages were blamed, a story difficult to credit while cascades poured over the gates. Quite simply, the staff who used to be delighted to meet a pleasure boat are now conserving their energies. With such frequent delays of up to half an hour, it is almost possible to travel to any kind of schedule. Perhaps this situation applies only in the peak holiday season.

Seventh largest town in France, **Toulouse** is known as the Rose City on account of the pinkish brick used for many of the buildings. A large octagonal basin, the *Port de l'Embouchure*, provides long-term pleasure craft moorings. Until the pleasant and tree-shaded banks of the basin were overtaken by road 'improvements' in the early 1970s, a navigable connection, with a two-rise lock, provided access to the River Garonne: this had formed part of the coast-to-coast route until opening of the Canal Latéral à la Garonne in 1856. A further link with the Upper Garonne, above a river dam, was created with the construction of the short **Canal de Brienne** in 1776; although no longer used by boats, this channel continues to bring water supplies from the river to the basin. The Brienne's junction bridge and the first bridge over the Canal du Midi are known as *Les Ponts Jumeaux* (The Twin Bridges). The brick wall between them is occupied by a large and magnificent bas-relief in white marble where Classical deities represent Atlantic and Mediterranean and canal-building cherubs are busy with picks and shovels. The monument was designed by François Lucas in 1775. A third bridge has since been added, that of the Canal Latéral à la Garonne (see Chapter 59).

As it skirts the city centre the waterway is subject to the full impact of noisy roads on each bank, for traffic is exceptionally fierce. The canal's amenity value is most noticeable, its borders being planted with trees, shrubs, flowers and lawns. By the early 1980s mechanisation and lengthening of locks at this end of the waterway as far as Bazière (K28) was in progress. The original Écluse 4, Matabiau, was removed completely, its change in level being incorporated into former Écluse 5, Bayard (K3.5, fall 6.2m, re-numbered 3): this is a little beyond the very convenient main line rail station. Visiting boats are requested to moor in *Port St-Sauveur* (K5.2, full range of facilities) where there is a colourful collection of converted barges and other pleasure craft. The city centre is only about 800m away. The rich history and leading tourist attractions of Toulouse are well described in the Michelin Green Guide *Languedoc Roussillon Tarn Gorges* whose coverage extends to the whole of the Canal du Midi. Even the briefest stay should provide time to visit the excellent shops and the magnificent Cathedral of St-Étienne, an extraordinary asymmetrical building of mixed brick and stone, combining the Gothic styles of the Midi and the north. At the base of a pillar near the high altar, a black marble tablet mark's Riquet's tomb and honours the man who brought prosperity to Languedoc.

Excursions from Toulouse are available in great variety. The *Syndicat d'Initiative* will advise. Coach tours run to Albi with its great cathedral and Cathar associations (*Musée Toulouse-Lautrec*, with many examples of the artist's paintings and posters); Montségur, where the Catholic Church finally defeated the Cathar heretics in the 13th century; and to the *Montagne Noire* and *Bassin de St-Ferréol* to view the Canal du Midi's extensive water supply system. Canal enthusiasts may also wish to visit the Riquet *Château de Bonrepos*, set in its 150 hectares park at the village of **Verfeil**, east of the city.

For the first 64km of the canal between Toulouse and Castelnaudary scenery is agreeably green and pastoral, but not in any way typical of the Midi country which lies nearer the Mediterranean. A considerable length of the towpath through the suburbs and into the countryside to K50 has been developed as a cycle-way: be aware of fast-approaching bikes. On the outskirts of Toulouse, there are two extensive basins, both offering most boat facilities: **Ramonville-St-Agne** (K11.5, dry dock) and **Port-Sud** (K12.4, restaurant with shopping). At **Castanet-Tolosan** (K15.7) are pleasant overnight moorings, with a tea room in the lock house: shopping centre with market, Tuesday mornings. Close by on the left is the A61 *Autoroute des Deux-Mers*, which is never far from the waterway between here and Carcassonne. Fortunately, thick tree cover shields the canal from this intruder, although the constant drone of traffic might disturb an otherwise idyllic overnight mooring. After Écluse 5, Vic (K17.4, recommended restaurant behind a garage forecourt), scattered houses with the occasional factory finally mark the end of Greater Toulouse, and pleasing wooded countryside with green meadows and hills accompanies the waterway along the valley of the River Hers.

Écluse 6, **Montgiscard** (K24.9), was recently converted to a single deep, lengthened chamber from a two-rise pair. The village is worth a visit, both for its basic shops and the old church offering a good view from the bell tower. Some shops and a market, Sunday mornings. **Aygues-Vives**, Écluse 7 (K28.1), is the last of the modernised locks at this end of the waterway (two chambers replaced by one) with an attractive water mill alongside. Shopping in the village. The *Château de Lastours* at nearby **Baziège** has a well-known restaurant (reservations, tel 05 61 27 87 21) and an up-market antique shop. A hill leads up to the charmingly situated Écluse 9, Sanglier (K29.6, two-rise). A motorway service station (K30.3) can be reached from the towpath and offers the expected facilities.

Montesquieu-Lauragais (K33.3) is notable for its bridge of narrow red bricks dating from the earliest days of the canal: although not the most restricted of the waterway's crossings, it is nevertheless difficult to visualise an unladen barge being able to pass through.

Hire cruiser base with services and moorings. Restaurant in the village. By Écluse 10, **Négra**, a minuscule chapel, inn and stables are all reminders that here was a staging post for the passenger craft of long ago. Restaurant and some shops will be found in **Gardouch**, between two-rise Écluse 12, **Laval**, and Écluse 13 (K38.9). Shore facilities are rather limited until Castelnaudary, so every advantage should be taken of **Villefranche-de-Lauragais** (K41), the largest town since Toulouse and lying 1.5km to the left. It is a 13th century *bastide* (fortified town) with good restaurants and a range of shops; market, Frday mornings. Canalside property had not yet become greatly appreciated in 1982 when a lovely house and barn were for sale at Écluse 16, Emborrel, for a mere £2,400 (3,550 Euros)! From here, left, the village of **Avignonet-Lauragais** is within reach (some shops and several restaurants).

Deep countryside now follows, with a remarkable discovery just before a motorway bridge. This is **Port-Lauragais** (K50, right bank) where a harbour has been created as an integral part of an *autoroute* service station. Facilities shared by road and water transport include fuel, water, shop and restaurant, all at an acceptable distance from the motorway itself. Those in cars may use waterside picnic tables and ponder on which is the more agreeable way to travel. In spring 1983, the *Centre Pierre Paul Riquet* was opened here as a museum devoted to the canal and its builder. Regional products and waterways publications are on sale. All in all, a splendid concept, expertly carried out. The final lock on the ascent from the Atlantic is Écluse 18, Océan (K51.6, start of the summit level), where there is a truly gigantic plane tree. One would assume that many of the planes of the Canal du Midi date from the 17th century: this is not so, and in the early 19th century the canal's four tree nurseries contained 475,000 young plants and seedlings of oak, poplar, larch and ash – but no planes. They were an unknown species in the south of France in Riquet's time. Planes were selected in the mid-19th century for the summer shade they provide and for the manner in which their roots stabilise the banks. With many of them approaching the end of their lives, a programme to replace one in three (about 80,000 trees) over a 15 year period was announced in 2000. New plantings will include oaks and poplars.

A convenient approach to inspect this end of the canal's remarkable water supply system is from Lock 17. Within 500m a fast-flowing feeder will be discovered, having brought water from the far-off *Montagne Noire*. Every devotee of Riquet (it is impossible to travel on his waterway without becoming an admirer) will wish to visit the octagonal basin set amid pine trees and the mysterious stones of **Naurouze**.

Legend tells of a prehistoric giant who was stumbling through the area with a heavy pile of rocks: he slipped and let them fall, whereupon they shattered into many pieces. The stones had been intended for building the city of Toulouse, hence its brick construction instead. These lone boulders have long been the subject of much wonderment. Nostradamus predicted the imminent end of the world if the stones should ever be found joined together again. The site was purchased by Riquet's descendants early in the 19th century and on the mound of stones they erected an impressive obelisk as a memorial to the canal's builder. The monument rises from a group of walnut trees within a walled enclosure and surrounded on the outside by a circle of cedars. If you can find him, ask the canal lengthsman for a key to the gate. Leaving Lock 17, the canal turns through a sharp bend and on the left bank the feeder can be seen pouring into the navigation. Frankly, it lacks the grandeur that might have been expected. Two metal plaques explain the significance of the place. One records the lengths of the feeder canals: 65,242m from a catchment point at Alzau; 52,552m from Lampy Reservoir; 34,436m from the St-Ferréol Reservoir; and 38,121m from the River Sor. The second plaque was erected by British waterways enthusiasts on the canal's tercentenary. It reads (in translation): 'Homage to Pierre Paul Riquet and all those involved in the construction of the Languedoc Canal, opened May 15 1681. This plaque is provided by the Inland Waterways Association of Great Britain in recognition of its deep admiration. May 15, 1981.' It was unveiled by a direct descendant, Mlle Evelyne de Riquet de Caraman.

With the *autoroute* only 200m away from the short summit level, an overnight mooring should be selected with some care. **Le Ségala** (K53.8) is a pretty canalside village with boat hire base and facilities, moorings, shopping, restaurant and rail station. Beyond the canopy of plane trees are lush fields and orchards (the cherries are ripe by late May). This watershed is 189m above sea level and the long descent begins with Écluse 18, Méditerranée (K56.6). Close by is M Not's old pottery, producing terracotta cooking pots in a wood-fired kiln: it is well worth a look. The canal now winds from shallow cutting to embankment, heavily shaded by trees until, after a number of locks, including a double and a triple, it eventually arrives at the quays of the quite large town of **Castelnaudary** (K64.6). Ahead, a hump-backed bridge close to the base of an old windmill leads to *Le Grand Bassin*, a sheet of water whose size initially concealed by a wooded island (*Ile de la Cybelle*). Easiest access to the many shops, railway station and restaurants is from this point. My recommended eating place is the *Restaurant du Centre et du Lauragais*, in the Cours de la République. Huge market, Monday mornings. Soon, the dimensions of the great basin are revealed: totally artificial and acting as a reservoir for the quadruple staircase of locks that follows, it is more than 1km in circumference. There is possibly nothing to equal it on any other European canal. A jumble of houses on the left shore rises towards the elevated town, capped by the church of St-Michel. Fuelling depot for boats is on the left. Opposite, is the celebrated Crown Blue Line hire base, only the second of its kind in France when it was established here in 1970. Facilities with dry dock. Noted for its *cassoulet* (see introduction to this chapter), Castelnaudary is the ideal place from which to drive to the canal's **Bassin de St-Ferréol** (take the road to Revel). Covering 70 hectares, this great reservoir is surrounded by tree-covered rocky hills; its 800m earth-filled stone dam 30m high is believed to be the largest structure of its kind anywhere. Sailing dinghies and tripping launches use the lake and below the dam itself is a network of landscaped footpaths. A constant flow of water emerges from the dam to feed the distant navigation. St-Ferréol is quite rightly a popular tourist attraction with several good restaurants. At least two hours should be reserved for a visit from Castelnaudary, where cars may be hired.

Onwards from this point, the Midi carries the greatest concentration of holiday cruisers. The multiple staircase Écluse 23, St-Roch, has long been an electrically-worked four-rise complex (K65.6). Then follows Écluse 24, Gay, a two-rise (K67.1) and the three-rise Écluse 25, Vivier (K68.7).

In common with virtually all French seaside areas, since the late 1970s the Canal du Midi has adopted the cult of toplessness. Female fashions that might provoke a riot on the Leeds & Liverpool Canal are no longer a cause for comment in the hot and languid south. However, discretion is advised when in towns or villages.

While multiple locks are generally automated, many of the single-chambered ones remain worked by hand and some help with operating the gates is appreciated by the keepers, who generally live on site in delightful cottages as old as the waterway itself. Often, the lock gardens have magnificent flower displays and there may well be polite notices in several languages to 'respect plants and flowers'. **Villepinte** (K76) has a range of shops and restaurant within walking distance of the bridge in the middle of the pound between Écluses 31 and 32. Similarly with shopping and restaurants, **Bram** (K80.8), shortly after Écluse 34, lies 1.5km from a stone quay with facilities. Almost all of these Midi villages are charming little places of faded stone houses, mostly remaining quite unconscious of

The astonishing walled city of Carcassonne.

their attractiveness. Nowhere is this more true than at **Villesèquelande** (K91), where a grassy quay makes an admirable mooring; 500m across a vineyard lies the ancient church and its cluster of buildings. Shopping is very limited, although it comes as a surprise to find any shops at all. Exceptionally sharp bends along this section of canal necessitated the erection of towline guides on the most acute angles of the towpath.

Distant views of the *Montagne d'Alaric* beyond Carcassonne are obtained from the top of Écluse 37, **Lalande** (K98.2), a two-rise. After two further locks the canal enters a deep stone-sided cutting before emerging in a broad basin by **Carcassonne** railway station (K105). Mooring here in the *port de plaisance* is virtually obligatory, for no one should miss a visit to the unique walled 'old' city. In its original form Riquet's waterway avoided Carcassonne altogether, its citizens being unwilling to finance a more costly line. Later, they bitterly regretted this decision, but it was not until 1810 that the present 5.6km deviation was opened to traffic, with a new aqueduct over the diverted River Fresquel.

Shops and restaurants are close to the Carcassonne basin. A longish uphill walk, crossing the River Aude, leads to *La Cité*. (Taxis are available outside the *Hôtel Bristol*.) Occupied by the Romans and the Visigoths (5th century), the hilltop site was developed in the 13th century as Europe's largest and finest fortress. The scale of this splendid town is breath-taking: a double ring of walls with numerous turreted towers encircles large numbers of houses with a substantial resident population. It all looks unreal and like the film set it has frequently been. Some critics complain at the over-thorough restoration carried out by Viollet-le-Duc from 1844, but without his efforts Carcassonne might now have been little more than a ruinous pile of stones. Quite rightly, this astonishing place is listed as a UNESCO World Heritage Site. Inevitably, the narrow cobbled streets are largely devoted to tourist shops, fire-eaters, 21st century troubadours and other attempts to re-create 13th century life. Although over-commercialised, it is all good fun and good value and that includes the restaurants. I was once moored in the basin for 14 July, *Bastille* Day. As the locks were closed there was every opportunity for exploring La Cité at leisure.

Architect and architectural historian, Viollet-le-Duc, who was responsible for the 19th century restoration of many ancient sites. He is best remembered for his work at Carcassonne.

Water sports on the canal included greasy pole contests and a barbaric game in which young men attempted to swim after live ducks (catch it and its yours to take home and eat). At dusk, we climbed to high ground beyond the railway station to see the fortress brilliantly illuminated. Then followed the most lavish fireworks display I have ever witnessed.

The canal runs through the heart of Cathar country and for those prepared to seek there are numerous reminders of the fierce religious wars of 700 years ago. In essence, the Cathars preached a doctrine of reincarnation and rejected the Old Testament and the deity of Christ. Ignored at first by the Catholic Church, the movement spread rapidly throughout Languedoc. Eventually, Pope Innocent III took steps to curb the power of the heretics, but when his Legate was assassinated in Provence, a Crusade was declared in 1208. The following year, the infamous massacre of Béziers took place. In support of the Church, Simon de Montfort seized Cathar castles one by one and was finally killed in the siege of Toulouse in 1218. Later came the Inquisition and Languedoc was annexed to France. By 1244, the last stronghold of Cathar resistance, **Montségur**, had fallen after a prolonged siege; and a famous treasure was lost, never to be recovered. This briefest account of a stormy period of history is best remembered today in the numerous relics of *châteaux* scattered throughout the Aude *Département*. One of them, in the village of **Rennes-le-Château** about 35km south of Carcassonne, is at the centre of an extraordinary mystery of modern times: it has attracted a considerable cult following. Highly involved research points to the existence of knowledge that could undermine the most basic beliefs of the Church. This

might in part explain how the impoverished parish priest of Rennes-le-Château came by a sizeable fortune enabling him to make lavish improvements to the area. The fascinating but complicated tale is recounted in *The Holy Blood and the Holy Grail* by Michael Baigent, Richard Leigh and Henry Lincoln (Cape, 1982).

But back to the canal, where 12km of towpath to Trèbes is a surfaced cycle trail. A very fine avenue of cypress trees lines each bank for 300m after Écluse 41, St-Jean (K108). Then comes the early 19th century aqueduct over the River Fresquel, shortly followed by an unusual arrangement of locks, Nos 42/43. There are, in fact, three chambers: the first pair are arranged as a two-rise and empty into a large oval basin succeeded immediately by another single lock. Gates and paddles are mechanised and supervised by a keeper in a tall steel box planted in the middle of the complex. 150m after Écluse de l'Évêque (K112.6) there is an opportunity for buying wine direct from the producer (right-hand, towpath side). As designed by Riquet, the waterway crossed the River Orbeil near **Trèbes** on the level (K116.7). This proved to be unsatisfactory, as quantities of silt were carried into the canal. Maréchal Sébastien Vauban accordingly designed the present aqueduct, 1686–7; it consists of three arches, each with a span of about 11m. There are good moorings (left) immediately before the busy N610 road bridge, in the centre of the pleasant little town of Trèbes (K117.3) or (right) just afterwards. Connoisseur Cruisers hire base with facilities. A wide selection of small shops is hidden away in a maze of narrow streets. Round the next bend are the three-rise Écluses de Trèbes. Here, the *Auberge du Moulin* is delightfully situated and the food has a good reputation.

One of the last freight barges to operate after more than 300 years of commercial traffic on the waterway. Near Carcassonne, August 1988.

Stop near the third bridge after the locks and you will discover a pleasant settlement of stone buildings, where further local wine may be obtained. This is a very agreeable winding pound, terminating at **Marseillette** (K126.2) with good moorings, two restaurants and limited shopping. All the time, the already glorious scenery is improving as it assumes the true character of the Midi, with cypress trees and distant views over vineyards and rocky hills. Locks occur at Marseillette (K127.2); Fonfile, triple (K130.4); St-Martin, double (K131.6); and Aiguille, double (K133.4). **Puichéric** (K136) is a medium-sized village dominated by the square tower of its church; some shopping with restaurant. Here is a further two-rise lock, whose keeper allowed cruisers travelling in different directions to actually pass each other in the chambers the last time I came through: a fairly odd experience.

La Redorte (K139.5) has a useful quay capable of taking several craft attracted by refuse disposal facilities and two restaurants (it is surprising where your priorities can lie!). Good shopping. It was here that we carefully removed a strange fruit on a branch over-hanging a garden wall. On dissection it proved to be a pomegranate, just one of the exotic plants that flourish in this warm climate. Hire cruisers operate in **Homps** (K145), where there are good moorings, shops, a bulk wine outlet and several restaurants: one of these was so busy serving other customers when we requested the bill at the end of our meal, that we had no alternative but to return to the boat, intending to pay next morning. When we felt compelled to leave at 10 am, all our attempts to wake up M Restaurateur having failed, and now proposing to settle by post, we looked back to see him running down the quayside in night attire, flourishing his *addition*. I understand that the mobile *boucherie chevaline* (horse-butcher) who comes to Homps every Wednesday has the wonderful name of M Selponi. After the single lock of Homps is the two-rise Écluse d'Ognon (K147.1), followed by a small aqueduct over the Ognon River, built in 1826–7 to replace a troublesome level crossing. On the bank is the friendly *Auberge de l'Escale du Canal*, which provides extremely good value.

Pechlaurier Lock (K149.8) is a two-rise staircase where I once saw a scene of amazing chaos. While the upper chamber was packed with five descending cruisers, two uphill boats entered the bottom chamber, unknown to the lock keeper. When the operation was half completed, the keeper noticed the mistake, ordered paddles to be closed and requested that the offending craft back out. It was a case of too many helpers keen to do something. No sooner had the lower gates reopened than someone stupidly raised a paddle on the intermediate set of gates, rapidly washing the two boats into the path of a converted péniche laden with children whose cheers turned into shrieks of alarm at the prospect of the impending collision. Somehow, a catastrophe was averted and we became convinced that lock working should be carried out strictly on the instructions of the resident keeper.

One of the most atmospheric and beautiful villages on the canal is **Argens-Minervois** (K151.3). Others have obviously come to the same conclusion in recent years with a resultant rash of new and not particularly appropriate houses near the waterside. Situated close to the waterway, this once fortified hilltop settlement typifies the timelessness of Languedoc. Dominated by the almost windowless towers of a 14th century *château*, Argens had until the 1980s changed little in many hundreds of years: certainly the residents of the late 17th century would have looked down from the same houses we see today and watched Riquet's men excavating the navigation. A short walk brings you to the cobbled heart of the village: there is little more than a general shop and a bar/restaurant. We were told that the *château* had been reduced to two habitable rooms. Across a courtyard near the main gate, we made a remarkable discovery: a terrace of five deserted cottages,

The highly atmospheric village of Argens-Minervois.

built on the edge of a rocky precipice. Probably, they had housed the castle servants. Although structurally sound, they bore every sign of having been unoccupied for at least half a century. Each consisted of two or three irregularly-shaped rooms with tiled floors, stone fireplaces and a sink draining directly down the cliff face. Quite lacking any concession to modern living, they were utterly medieval in design: a fascinating survival. Back at the canal, a large mooring basin has lately been created: activities include renting cruisers.

The whole of this portion of the waterway is rich in similar little villages: how are you to choose which to visit? Écluse 56, Argens (K152.3), marks the beginning of *Le Grand Bief*, a lock-free pound 54km long with some astonishing windings along the contours. It is probably the longest canal level in France. **Roubia** (K154.8), like many similar villages, is sufficiently canal-conscious to have erected some waterside picnic tables and a sign advertising its few shops. Umbrella pines and palm trees border the grounds of a *château* on the outskirts of **Paraza** (K156.1) where there are basic shops, a restaurant and a direct-sell wine producer. **Ventenac d'Aude** (K160.9) is notable for its huge waterside wine *cave*, where Minervois may be tasted and purchased. Views from the upper windows of this seemingly ecclesiastical building are of vineyards extending to the distant horizon. Bar/restaurant, but the only shops are travelling ones.

Among the former overnight halts for the passenger craft of long ago and port for the city of Narbonne (before it was provided with its direct canal connection) is **Le Somail** (K165.9). It is one of the Midi's prettiest villages, set around an original stone arched bridge. My interest in collecting old canal books has often resulted in my visiting the extensive Gourgues antiquarian book shop, housed in a cavernous barn. Here, I once purchased a splendid leather-bound copy of the fascinating and extremely rare *Des Canaux de Navigation et Spécialement du Canal de Languedoc* by de la Lande (1778); an autographed example of Bischambis' *Narbonne* (1922), containing an extensive history of the La Nouvelle Branch; and a charming 1936 edition of Alphonse Daudet's *La Belle-Nivernaise*, the story of a 19th century canal boat with nostalgic illustrations. My inability to inspect their stock at frequent intervals prompts me to reveal the existence of this treasure house. For food shops, you must rely on mobile ones. Here, I have only had unhappy experiences with restaurants, but hopefully standards have since improved. There is a British-owned hire boat company.

Riquet's solution to the challenge of passing the River Cesse was to construct a level crossing with a 205m dam; this was soon found to be a source of silting

Characteristic scenery on Le Grand Bief *(Long Pound) near Capestang.*

and flooding, and was replaced by Vauban's present three-arched aqueduct of 1686 (K168). Two highly praised restaurants now present themselves: *La Cascade*, on the right bank of the canal; and *Le Bec Fin*, a pleasant 3km walking/cycle/taxi journey away in the village of Mirepeisset. It is generally agreed to offer the best *cuisine gastronomique* on the Canal du Midi. Various boating facilities, including hire craft, fuel and long term moorings, are available at *Port la Robine* (left, K168.6). Shortly after, on the right, follows the junction with the **La Nouvelle Branch**, providing access to the Mediterranean, via Narbonne (details at end of this chapter).

An uncharacteristic industrial estate briefly intrudes, succeeded at K172.6 by moorings for the pleasant little town of **Argeliers**, a little to the east of a long hairpin bend. All shops will be found after a short walk through the vineyards. By the bridge, a long derelict canal lengthsman's house has been skilfully restored to become the *Au Chat qui Pêche* restaurant. Of all places in Europe that the celebrated inland waterways writer Dr Roger Pilkington might have chosen for his retirement home, he selected **Montouliers**, a short distance to the north. Here, he spent his final years, tending grapes and olives, close to his beloved Canal du Midi. He died in 2003 at an advanced age.

Often, the waterway is slightly raised on an embankment, providing good views through the plane trees to a fertile region once covered by a series of shallow lakes, drained at different times up to the 19th century. Here, we have a contour canal *sans pareil*, as the waterway makes an extraordinary series of loops at its approach to **Capestang** (K188.3). I was once moored for the evening several km before the town at a point where the D11 is almost alongside. Wishing to telephone (it was long before the days of mobiles) I cycled down the main road and, having no lights, decided it would be safer to return in the gathering dusk via the towpath. More than an hour later I had still not reached the boat, although the outward trip had taken barely ten minutes. It was intensely dark under the canopy of foliage with the incessant sound of the cicadas (*cigales*). One part of the canal looked just like another and I seriously entertained thoughts that I must somehow have set off in the wrong direction. Eventually, with huge relief, I saw the distant lights of the boat with my friends anxiously awaiting my return. Ever since, I have had good reason to remember this sinuous section of the waterway. At the last bridge before Capestang is the friendly English-run *Le Pourquoi Pas* restaurant. The little town is notable for having one of the lowest and most awkward bridges on the Midi. Although rebuilt in recent years, being historic it was felt necessary to retain all its shortcomings. Large wide-beam motor yachts

may have to resort to flooding their bilges or taking on board up to 30 bystanders in order to pass beneath. Beyond is a long and frequently congested quay. A short walk brings you to the tree-shaded town square with shops and a choice of restaurants. Above a sea of pan-tiled roofs, the 14th century church of St-Étienne soars upwards, topped by a cluster of bells and loudspeakers. These devices, frequently installed throughout the Midi, are for broadcasting public information and sounds of jollification when the town is *en fête*. In November 1766, 42m of canal bank collapsed after heavy rain and snow had flooded the channel: 10,000 workmen toiled in dreadful freezing conditions to repair the breach, completing the task within three months. Automatic siphon sluices were subsequently installed here and at Ventenac, to drain off flood water before it can overflow the bank. When the level has dropped sufficiently, air is admitted to the pipe and the flow ceases. Riquet's position of collector of the Languedoc salt tax is recalled by an old salt store beside the former lake of Capestang.

Closure of locks in the evening normally prevents night navigation on the Canal du Midi. It is banned by the operators of hire craft, and no one cruising for real *pleasure* in his own boat is likely to want to bash on through the dark, oblivious to all but the faint shapes of the plane trees. But it was different for the working boats and every conscientious *batelier* tried to arrange his journey to arrive on the Long Pound shortly before the locks closed. With his knowledge of every bend he could keep moving much of the night. I was once moored under the canopy of trees near Capestang when a furious storm erupted several hours before dawn. It was hopeless to sleep with rain hammering on the cabin roof, so we sat up to enjoy the spectacle as the canal would briefly shine in the brightest green, illuminated by repeated flashes of lightning. Suddenly, the headlight of an oncoming *péniche* could be seen and moments later it was as brilliantly lit as by daylight. The experience was both thrilling and theatrical. And doubtless he was sliding into his first lock before we had cleared away our breakfast.

Poilhes (K194.2) offers good mooring facilities either side of a bridge. The local authority has gone to commendable lengths to make boating visitors welcome: the tap is fitted with a hose and there are public showers and dustbins. Several shops and restaurants. Beyond, is a superb view of distant hills. Another disaster occurred near here in January 1744, when 300m of the waterway was blocked by a landslide. A retaining wall was built and navigation restored within 14 days.

Malpas Tunnel (K198.8), although a mere 160m long, is both wide and high. It has the distinction of being the world's first section of underground navigation canal. Cut through friable sandstone, the western end is badly weathered and much of the inside is lined with stone vaulting. For its date, it is a most impressive structure (one-way working). If you walk NW along the D62 from the tunnel's far end, you will ascend the hill of Ensérune and arrive at the site of **Oppidum d'Ensérune**, an Iberian-Greek settlement founded in the 6th century BC. Depopulated by the 1st century AD, it has been fully excavated and the pre-Roman archaeological museum is open to the public. Nearby, is the curious Lake of Montady, drained for agriculture in the 13th century by monks working for the Archbishop of Narbonne, and displaying an amazing circular pattern of drainage channels radiating from its centre like the spokes of a giant wheel. **Colombiers** (K200.5) is a charming village set around an ancient stone bridge with *lavoir*. There are useful shops and a recommended restaurant at *Le Château*, with tables on a gravelled terrace overlooking the waterway: the building was constructed in the 16–17th centuries on top of 12th century vaulted cellars. Just

around the corner, a large marina, with a range of services, hire boats and a supermarket was created in 1987. In this area – but also at other locations throughout the Canal du Midi – we discovered prolific clusters of wild pheasant's-eye narcissus and the snowdrop-like spring snowflake; an unexpected bonus during a cruise in late March.

Now comes what is perhaps the best-known engineering feature of Riquet's canal: the eight-lock staircase of **Fonserannes** (K206.5). As originally designed, a descent was made to the level of the River Orb in Béziers, the navigation channel using the river bed for 900m until it turned into an artificial canal on the far bank. As might have been expected, floods and silting were regular problems and over the years there were proposals for various designs of aqueduct and even a tunnel *underneath* the river bed. Nothing was achieved, however, until the opening of the present aqueduct in 1856. The new channel is linked with the

The Fonserannes staircase at Béziers.

lock staircase at chamber 7, meaning that boaters now work 6 locks (and not 7 as is generally stated). The total rise and fall is 13.6m. The staircase was mechanised several decades ago. To the right, a 'water slope' was built in 1982–3 for 38m barges, rather than attempt to adapt the shorter, historical locks. Based on the pattern of that at Montech, Canal Latéral à la Garonne, it consists of a concrete flume on a 5° slope. Boats are introduced into a wedge-shaped pool of water which is pushed up or down by an electric traction unit. Inauguration was in the autumn of 1983 and enabled 38m freight craft to navigate from the Rhône to Narbonne, via the Canal du Midi. The cost of all this was estimated at about £3 million. An early failure of the traction unit led to the device being unused until 1989. At the time of writing, it has been again out of service for some years and all traffic is directed through the locks which are a very considerable tourist attraction. These are worked to a timetable, downstream craft having one period in the morning and another in the afternoon; similarly upstreamers have their allocated morning and afternoon passages.

The handsome colonnaded aqueduct designed by Magues provides an excellent view of hilltop **Béziers** (K208.1), surmounted by the 13–14th century Cathedral of St-Nazaire. The city was established about 36 BC and is best known for the Massacre of 1209, for it was here that the first atrocity of the Albigensian Crusade was perpetrated in the name of Pope Innocent III. Between 15,000 and 20,000 townspeople were slaughtered, and as it was difficult to distinguish between heretic and Catholic the victims included many members of the Church of Rome. Bézier's other claims to fame are being the birthplace of Riquet – his statue is in a tree-lined *boulevard* that bears his name – and it is now the capital of the flourishing Languedoc wine industry. Écluses 58 and 59 are situated at each end of a

The River Orb aqueduct at Béziers.

large basin with moorings: this dates from the 19th century. The city lies some distance uphill from here: closer shopping is at the *Intermarché* supermarket in the *Bd de la Liberté*. More convenient still for essential food supplies is **Villeneuve** (K213.8).

From now onwards, the Mediterranean is never far away. **Valras Plage** and **Serignan Plage** are 10km and 8km: follow the D37 from Villeneuve. A naturist beach lies between the two. The closeness of the coast is evident in a change of scenery. Gone are the rocky outcrops of earlier reaches, to be replaced by reed banks and marshes. **Portiragnes** (K218.3) is handy for several shops and a pair of restaurants. The purpose-built hire craft basin at **Port Cassafières** (K222) is another Crown Blue Line base with a restaurant catering almost exclusively for boaters. Moor here or at the nearby bridge for a visit to the sea at **Redoute-Plage** (2km). Everywhere vines are planted on the sandy soil, producing the *vin des sables*. If you fancy a little gentle riding, Camargue style, stables near the Port Cassafières bridge have a selection of amiable horses and ponies for hire. Short conducted treks through the sand dunes are suitable for all abilities.

Where the **River Libron** flows across the canal on its journey to the sea (K225.2) is a curiosity of waterway engineering that is probably unique. When the river is in spate quantities of silt would be poured into the navigation. To prevent this happening, a special barge with high ramps at each end was originally sunk across the river between stone abutments, isolating the canal on each side; when the flood subsided, the barge was raised and navigation allowed to continue. The present arrangement is an improvement in that traffic is never interrupted. A series of chambers is fitted with guillotine gates: the flooding river is allowed to flow first ahead of a boat, and then, as the subsequent chamber is entered, astern of it. Thus both craft and canal are protected. The structure is normally open throughout. The flat nature of the terrain precluded building a conventional aqueduct. **Farinette-Plage** may be reached from here by following a minor road to the sea.

A succession of moored craft along the towpath bank point to the popularity and interest of **Agde** (K231.3). Additional space to tie up is provided in a recently excavated basin, opposite. Note the large and elegant building of the canal authority immediately before Écluse Bassin Rond (The Round Lock). This unusual structure is equipped with three sets of gates: those at 6 o'clock and 12 o'clock are used when working down the waterway from Béziers to the Étang de Thau. The 3 o'clock pair provide access, via a short length of slightly tidal canal, to the River Hérault, the fishing boat quays of Agde and eventually the Mediter-

ranean. It was unfortunate, but unavoidable, that the 1980s lock enlargement programme spoiled the circular symmetry of the chamber with the addition of a new section. Rail links with Sète and Toulouse are provided from the nearby station, a most useful facility if a car is to be collected from the starting point of a one-way cruise such as offered by Crown Blue Line, between Castelnaudary and Port Cassafières. Regular bus services also run from here to Marseillan and the important seaside resort of Cap d'Agde.

Agde itself lies mainly on the far side of the River Hérault. Founded by the Greeks about the 6th century BC, it has a network of hilly narrow streets rising from the waterfront quays and the grim façade of the fortified 12th century Cathedral of St-Étienne, built of black volcanic rock. It is a lively and flourishing town, with shops and boutiques ranging from the trendy to the *chic*, numerous bars and night-clubs, and a sizeable open-air market. Hire cruisers are forbidden to enter the Hérault at this point, but a very pleasant walk of about 5km can be made by following the quayside with its brightly painted fishing boats and craft used for jousting contests, down river to the sea at **Le Grau-d'Agde**. Lovely sandy beaches, **La Tamarissière** and **La Guirandette**, are on either side of the estuary mouth. Access to the lower Hérault and the Mediterranean (for privately-owned craft) is according to a daily timetable: consult the keeper of l'Écluse Ronde. Moorings will be found on the short branch linking canal and river. Suitable stopping places on quays in Agde itself are difficult to locate as the water is often shallow near the banks. Beware of becoming stranded when the slight tide falls. There is, however, ample depth in the centre of the channel at all times.

A little further to the east is the splendid resort of **Cap d'Agde**, constructed since 1969 on a promontory formed by lava flow from the long-extinct Mont St-Loup volcano. Most of the hotels, shops and self-catering accommodation are designed in a low-rise Provençal style, with arcades and red pantiles. More than 70,000 holidaymakers can stay here and 2,000 boats are berthed in a series of harbours. The 500 business premises include more than 100 cafés, restaurants and night-clubs, with cars segregated from the pedestrianised areas. The sandy beaches are excellent, and widespread planting of sweet-scented shrubs and trees has brought about a surprisingly established atmosphere for so new a city. On the eastern side is Europe's largest naturist resort, where hotels, apartments and camping sites cater for up to 20,000 people. Day visitors are welcomed on payment of an entry fee. Nudity is to be found not only on the beach but also in the supermarkets, boutiques and banks: what would seem

The highly unusual Round Lock at Agde.

incongruous in northern climes soon takes on an air of normality under the hot Mediterranean sun. Among the attractions is wind surfing tuition. Cap d'Agde's naturist tradition began in 1940, when German troops came to use the beach alongside the vineyards of the Oltra family. When the war was over, the Germans started to return for nudist camping holidays. Realising the commercial potential, the French Government capitalised on this tradition when development began on the Languedoc coast in the late 1960s. René and Paul Oltra were transformed from peasant farmers into millionaires in a single generation.

After Agde's Round Lock, the canal enters a narrow tree-lined stretch to emerge in the **River Hérault** upstream of the town weir. Through navigation of the Canal du Midi continues up the Hérault for 1km and, right, into the Prades Flood Lock (K233), which is generally open at each end. Alongside is an old-fashioned open air café/bar with dancing – *La Guinguette*. A further 5km of the Hérault is available to boats, as far as the ruins of a mill on the outskirts of **Bessan** (a few shops and market, Sunday mornings). Otherwise, there are no facilities on this excitingly Amazonian passage, past tree-covered banks inhabited by buzzards.

In its final stages the canal undergoes a change, passing through marshland and by the Étang de Bagnas, location of the final lock (K235.3, restaurant at the camp site). Moor near the last road bridge at **Les Onglous** (K238.5) for a visit to **Marseillan-Plage** (2km by road), a very pleasant beach with some shops. 30 minutes' walking along the seashore brings you into Cap d'Agde. Beware local fishermen who are in the habit of stretching nets across the navigation. Even when they are lowered to the canal bed, it is possible to foul your propeller and a rescue operation can be expensive (I know!). The Canal du Midi ends abruptly at Les Onglous Lighthouse, entry to the huge expanse of the Étang de Thau.

LA NOUVELLE BRANCH

Completed in 1776, this comprises the 5.1km Canal de Jonction; a 657m navigable section of the River Aude; and 31.5km of the Canal de la Robine, between the Aude and the sea, a navigation whose origins go back to Roman times. All 13 locks will admit craft up to 38m long. Even if pleasure boaters have no intention of reaching the sea, a return voyage to Narbonne makes a pleasant detour for which two days is sufficient. Locks are automatic and worked by entering the code '1995E' on each control panel. For full instructions, consult the

The 'Roman Bridge' in Narbonne, La Nouvelle Branch.

Carte Guide. Magnificent umbrella pines line the canal at its junction. Five locks lower the Branch to **Sallèles d'Aude** (K3.4); here the 6th lock was until recent times a two-rise staircase, the lower chamber serving also as a dry-dock for barges. Modernisation has destroyed this curiosity, resulting in a single chamber with a fall of 5.4m (a similar arrangement in Béziers has also vanished). The town offers all facilities. You may visit a section of Roman aqueduct and a Roman pottery. Écluse de Gailhousty (K4.9) has a dry dock below, while the ensemble is overlooked by a most elegant 18th century classical-styled keeper's house.

We shortly enter the willow-fringed River Aude. Pay strict attention to the course displayed on a bankside panel. Leaving the canal, remain on the rightand head upriver to a point marked by a cable. Cross to the opposite shore and run downstream, keeping about 4.5m from the side. Deep drafted boats should cross the Aude with extreme care. I have grounded more than once on solid rock with a 1.3m draft: surprising, considering that well laden barges used the waterway with a rather greater depth until the early 1980s. Now drop through the railway bridge, and the first lock of the Canal de la Robine, **Moussoulens** (K5.8), will be

seen ahead. After negotiating Écluse de Raonel (K9.8) and the Écluse de Gua (K14.2) the outskirts of **Narbonne** are reached, with a Connoisseur Cruisers hire base (K15.6). Best visitor moorings will be found beyond the 'Roman Bridge', a picturesque structure supporting houses, but with limited headroom of about 3.3m. Craft with large superstructures may be unable to pass and should therefore select Agde or Sète as their route to or from the Mediterranean. The excellent quayside landscaping makes the centre of Narbonne one of the most attractive and civilised stopping places in any French city. Thanks to the Romans who created the Robine *c* 118 BC, Narbonne was able to develop as a successful sea-port, soon outclassing Marseille as the leading harbour between Spain and Italy. One early governor was the celebrated Marcus Antonius. The Mediterranean subsequently retreated and by the Middle Ages, the city was land-locked. It is now the centre of the Corbières wine area. Its leading attractions are the great slab-sided Archbishop's Palace (12–14th centuries) and the uncompleted Cathedral of St-Just; extensive ramparts were demolished in the 1870s. Excellent shopping is nearby with a spectacular indoor market building, famous for its fresh fish and much more. Museums include one devoted to paintings and ceramics and another containing Gallo-Roman remains. Passenger craft provide short excursions on the water in Narbonne or day-long trips to the main line at Le Somail or the coast at Port la Nouvelle.

The rest of the journey to the sea is along a canal that passes through salt lakes and marshes all very similar to the Camargue, towards the Rhône delta. Here, also, you are likely to see flocks of flamingos, while an African Game Reserve has been established on the west shore of the **Étang de Sigean**. Two final locks must be negotiated: Mandriac (K24.1) and **Ste-Lucie** (K34.3); drinking water available at each. There is evil-smelling black mud below the final chamber: onwards from here allowance must be made for a slight tidal rise and fall. For details of a restored historic barge displayed at Mandriac, see Introduction (under 'Waterways Museums', Canal du Midi). **Port La Nouvelle** (K37.3) is a busy place with real ships and fishing vessels. Best (and perhaps the only) visitor moorings are on the left of the canal immediately before a right-angled turn into the upper maritime harbour. Hire boats should proceed no further. Most otherwise suitable quays and piles are invariably the preserve of local fishing boats, passenger craft or large cargo vessels. *The Restaurant du Port* is a welcoming, family-run concern, noted for seafood and good value. And for real bargain prices, try *Le Casimir*, also on the Quai du Port. Private craft and those bound for the Mediterranean will enjoy the remaining 2.5km to the sea. In calm conditions even the most staid inland vessel will appreciate a few minutes in proper deep water! Fuel and water are available together with cranes for stepping masts. Although the town boasts few tourist attractions, there are several seaside resorts and beaches to be visited by canal holiday-makers.

The entire 180km coastline of Languedoc-Roussillon, between Spain and the Rhône Delta, has been imaginatively developed since the 1960s to cater for half a million tourists. In effect, it is a single continuous sandy beach. While there are several exceptionally well-designed new holiday towns, more than a dozen marinas and numerous camping sites on the dunes, substantial portions remain remote and uncommercialised. Many people find the area more to their taste (and better value) than the sophisticated Riviera, farther along the Mediterranean coast. There are many beaches within easy reach of the Canal du Midi and Canal du Rhône à Sète are shown on the map of the Mediterranean coastline. Toplessness has become universal (but not aggressively obligatory) while nudity (N) is widespread in certain locations, following the introduction of a relaxed official attitude that began in the late 1970s. These areas can, of course, be avoided if you prefer, and in any event the majority of naturist beaches are 'mixed', so newcomers to this form of relaxation have nothing to fear. If the seaside is to your liking, when hiring a cruiser on the canal it is well worth considering reserving a day or two moored at the base: this generally involves availability of your car and freedom to explore coastal or inland places remote from the waterway. However, it is the purpose of this book to mention only those beaches which are within walking, cycling, bus or inexpensive taxi reach of the waterway: the choice is considerable.

A good sandy beach lies a short distance SW of Port la Nouvelle. Continue for less than 1km to reach the official nudist section of **Les Montilles**. **Narbonne Plage** (clothed) lies about 12km from the city centre, via the D168.

63 ～ Étang de Thau

> **Carte Guide:** *Canaux du Midi*
>
> This vast salt-water lagoon extends from the terminus of the Canal du Midi at Les Onglous to the start of the Canal du Rhône à Sète between Sète and Frontignan. Level connections are made with the Mediterranean via the 2km Canal de Pisse-Saumes, near Marseillan-Plage (only suitable for small craft with low air draft) and in Sète.

The Étang de Thau provides inland boating with a distinctly maritime flavour. Once an inlet of the sea, the lagoon was long ago separated from the Mediterranean by a sandbar – *Le Toc*. The 8,000 hectares of water are exceptionally salty and parts are intensively farmed for oysters and mussels. Several colourful small towns with harbours await discovery. For much of the summer the water, sometimes little more than 2m deep, is placid, but when the prevailing strong wind – *Le Mistral* – is blowing from the mussel and oyster beds along the NW shore to the sea, very sizeable waves can develop and craft run the risk of damage or of being blown on to the sand banks of *Le Toc*. The *Mistral* can raise heavy seas surprisingly quickly, out of a fine blue sky. Navigation was simplicity itself during the first four of my many visits, but on the fifth the Étang was in a furious mood when we made a September passage from Frontignan to Marseillan in a hire cruiser. After waiting overnight for the wind to drop we attempted the crossing at dawn only to find visibility reduced to nothing by clouds of spray. Setting out once more in the afternoon, after taking local advice, we experienced a very bumpy passage which literally caused the glass of the saloon windows to burst from the frames. The navigation authority may forbid certain of the Canal du Midi hire cruisers (possibly including narrow boats imported from the UK) to enter the Étang. Much of the time, however, it is difficult to believe that special precautions must be taken.

Use of Maritime Chart 5729, while not essential, is recommended. It shows a navigation channel virtually across the centre of the Étang, for a direct passage between the Canal du Midi and the Canal du Rhône à Sète. From Les Onglous (Canal du Midi) to **Marseillan** is about 2km, running between the lighthouses at each end. Since establishment of a hire cruiser base here in 1970 (now moved elsewhere) this little port has become very popular. Space for visiting craft in the rectangular harbour is often limited, but moorings are generally available in the new port to the left of the twin lighthouses. Recent years have seen an unwelcome growing trend to make a substantial charge for overnight stays in the more popular coastal harbours: this is an established practice throughout the Mediterranean that seems inappropriate on inland waterways. Rates here range up to 34 Euros per night, peak season. Fuel, water and the use of a 2.5-tonne crane. As well as shellfish, Marseillan is devoted to the manufacture of *Noilly Prat*, a vermouth blend of Languedocian white wines with 22 secret herbs. There is also a red version. Both rely on spending a year maturing in the open in oak casks, subjected to weathering by the sun, wind, rain and sea air. Guided tours are available. Much of the five-year process takes place here, before completion at the firm's bottling plant in Marseille. On the quayside is the *Château du Port*, an elegant stone mansion built for a wine merchant and restored since 1965 as a popular boaters' restaurant: there is a wide choice of alternative eating places, but this is the one I habitually return to. In this region, seafood reigns supreme. The nearby town is well equipped with shops. Market, Tuesday mornings. Most convenient is the supermarket just beyond the top of the harbour. When I first visited Marseillan in the early 1970s, deserted waterfront warehouses could hardly be *given* away. They have now all long since been converted into smart holiday accommodation. What a missed opportunity!

From Marseillan it is possible to make a car excursion to the fascinating region of the **Upper River Hérault** (about 36km to **Clermont l'Hérault**). Among places on the itinerary are **Le Lac de Salagou**, a beautiful reservoir with beaches and water sports; **La Grotte de Clamouse**, a series of caves with extraordinary formations and deposits, discovered in 1945 and opened to the public in 1964; the **Cirque de Mourèze**, an ancient rock village with a vast jumble of boulders

in a variety of strange shapes; **St-Guilhem-le-Désert**, the finest Romanesque village in Languedoc; and the **Gorges of the Hérault**, between St-Guilhem and **La Grotte des Demoiselles**. Full details of these attractions appear in the Michelin Green Guide *Languedoc Roussillon Tarn Gorges*.

The next port along the western shore of the Étang is **Mèze**, similar around its harbour to Marseillan but even more lively and colourful. Visitors' moorings are on the right of the entrance and in season are greatly in demand by early evening. Arrive in mid-August and you may find the town *en fête*, with noisy boat jousting contests and the streets filled with fairground rides. Celebrations will continue until well after midnight. Excellent fish restaurants abound and there is a small sandy beach (*plagette*) though the frequent presence of big jelly fish is rather a deterrent to bathing. Quite different in character is **Bouzigues** in the NW corner of the lagoon, a sleepy village of whitewashed stone houses. The small artificial harbour can be difficult to enter in windy conditions, while the draft is limited to about 1.3m. Shopping, restaurants and a fishery museum. It is related that when a band of English landed in Sète in 1710, a single shot was enough to make the inhabitants of Bouzigues run off in terror. Nearby, is the spa resort of **Balaruc-les-Bains**, with outdoor activities and water sports, and the fascinating hilltop village of **Balaruc-le-Vieux** which retains its circular, defensive layout.

In a somewhat forbidding industrial zone, the Canal du Rhône à Sète (Chapter 64) begins its journey across the Camargue at the NE corner of the Étang. It is a short run from here to **Sète** (originally 'Cette') situated at the foot of *Mont-St-Clair*, long ago a Mediterranean island. Little existed here until the site was selected as the seaport for the Canal du Midi in 1666. It has grown into a French 'Salt Lake City': the seventh biggest seaport in the country. There is a temptation to liken the elegant stone façades of buildings lining the main canal to Venice: but Sète does have its own quite distinct character. A friend returned from a visit to the fish market, excitedly exclaiming 'It's just like the Bible down there!' Certainly, for sardines, tunny and a wide range of seafood, this is the centre of the industry in Languedoc. The locals are noisy and Latin in temperament, speaking their own version of French with a strong, almost Spanish accent. This is not the place to improve your facility with the language if you hope to create a good impression in Paris. At various times throughout the summer grandstands appear along the banks of the Canal de Sète for a performance of the chief sporting activity: jousting from galley-shaped rowing boats. Such celebrations were known elsewhere in medieval times,

A jousting contest on a canal in the city of Sète.

and major contests usually honour an event or person. For example, a series of tournaments was staged in 1548–50 in Lyon to mark the accession of Henri II and Catherine de Medici; and the foundation of Sète is remembered each 27 July. Distinct regional styles still to be found include Lyonnaise (Rhône and Loire); Nordist (Merville, Arras, Ors, Étreux and Lille); Parisienne; Isle-sur-Sorgue; Strasbourgeoise; and Languedocienne (from Agde to Grau du Roi). But no one does it with more panache than the Sètoises. The craft are elaborately decorated with painted swags and tassels and carry a small band of Moorish trumpets and drums to encourage the jousters, who attempt to knock their opponents off their platform as the boats are rowed furiously at each other. It is possible that there are rules for this activity. The eventual victor makes a triumphant lap of honour in a speed boat.

Entrance to the town from the Étang is through a pair of opening bridges, lifted early morning and evening to provide access for a mêlée of craft. Many hire cruisers will just be able to pass under at any time. Potential moorings all seem to belong to someone or other (or so they will soon tell you!). A likely space will be found by turning left to the *port de plasaince* (paying) near the rail station. A Canal Maritime, with a further swing bridge,

is the route to follow for the sea. Fine sandy beaches will be found bordering the N108, which runs for 15km along the SE shore of the Étang de Thau and is known as the Plage de la Corniche. In my experience, Sète is an uncomfortable town in which to be afloat for any length of time, the quays being lashed by constant wash from commercial craft or outboard-powered fishing punts that totally ignore any notion of a speed limit. After one night, we could scarcely wait to return to the Étang and lie peacefully at anchor far offshore.

64 ～ Canal du Rhône à Sète

Carte Guide: *Canaux du Midi*

From the Étang de Thau near Sète to Beaucaire on the Rhône (connection with the main Rhône navigation is currently closed): 98km with 1 lock. Junctions are made with the Mediterranean at Frontignan (restricted use for inland pleasure craft); Palavas-Les-Flots, via the Grau de Palavas Branch (headroom limited); Carnon (headroom limited); and at Le Grau-du-Roi via the River Vidourle or the Maritime Channel from Aigues-Mortes. There is a connection with the River Lez near Palavas, leading to Port Ariane on the edge of Lattes, 6km, 1 lock; and with the Petit Rhône via the Canal St-Gilles (Chapter 57).

Some people, and I am one of them, consider this waterway to be fascinating for its wild life, marshland scenery and maritime atmosphere. Others may find it dull and boring with very flat surroundings. Throughout, the canal penetrates an area of saline lakes on the borders of Western Europe's most important wilderness area, the Camargue. Its course from Sète to Aigues-Mortes, is frequently bordered by these *étangs*, a short distance inland from the coast. The navigation channel is provided with stone banks and a towpath. After Aigues-Mortes it heads inland along the northern fringes of the Camargue with tree-lined reaches through St-Gilles, ultimately arriving at its terminus in Beaucaire, on the shores of the Rhône. Features to be long remembered are the sunsets over the *étangs*, teeming with fish; the little wooden houses of fishermen who stretch nets from one side of the canal to the other; a very rich animal and plant life including flamingos, wild white horses and black bulls; and the traditional life-style of the cowboys, *les gardians*. Virtually lock-free, long distances can be cruised in a day if necessary. The more attractive length is the Sète–Aigues-Mortes section, with easy access to many unspoiled beaches. Apart from St-Gilles and the twin towns of Beaucaire and Tarascon, there is reduced interest in the final 49km to wards the Rhône.

Brief history While the Canal du Midi was under construction in the late 17th century, the States of Languedoc began creating a link from the Étang de Thau towards the Rhône by improving medieval channels through the saline lakes to Aigues-Mortes. This navigation was known as the Canal des Étangs. More than a century of vacillation intervened before a plan was adopted in 1777 to build the Canal de Beaucaire as a link between Aigues-Mortes and the Rhône. Work ceased during the Revolution but eventually reached a successful conclusion in 1808. The whole route is now known as the Canal du Rhône à Sète.

Recorded traffic on the waterway in 1936 was 255,000 tonnes, a figure which was maintained until the early 1970s. From 1983 various improvements have been carried out to permit 500-tonne capacity barges (and ultimately 4,500-tonne push tows) to work between the Rhône, the Étang de Thau and Sète. The cost of this work was estimated at £66 million. Completed construction includes bypasses at Frontignan and Aigues-Mortes, widespread channel dredging and bridge raising and removal of some tight bends. As is so often the case with such recent schemes in France, the anticipated freight traffic has failed to materialise. A more secure future for the navigation is likely to come from its huge tourism potential.

Entry to the waterway from the Étang de Thau is at a somewhat desolate spot, with distant views of Sète's industrial zone and boatyard to the left of the groynes of loose rocks. Arriving from the lagoon, home in on a series of silvery storage tanks. Mooring is possible close to the first road bridge (K96.2, distances are measured from Beaucaire). Here, right, is a junction with the **Canal de la Peyrade**, now partly closed, which used to offer a route into Sète, avoiding the Étang. The proprietor of a ramshackle bar/restaurant here once kindly allowed us to use his telephone and we were prompted to book a table for lunch, in anticipation of an experience rather than *haute cuisine*. When we returned, the place was packed with workmen and truck drivers. As can often happen in France, the meal was one of the best of the holiday; including liberal quantities of red wine, the final cost was a fraction of what we had been paying elsewhere. While you are likely to pass flocks of magnificent flamingos in a lake on the left, the ecologists appear not to have been very active, for one pool is being in-filled with wrecked cars.

Extensive refineries provide a dominant first impression of **Frontignan** (K92.2), but the town has much more to offer. Life for boaters centres on the vertical lift bridge which is opened thrice daily at certain times (consult the adjacent notice for details). Good quayside moorings on the left bank each side of this obstacle may be used while waiting. It can be a frustrating experience with a mad mêlée as boats jockey for a prime position as opening time approaches. Shops are close at hand as well as supplies of the famous *Muscat* wine, a sweet brownish liquid for which it is possible to acquire a distinct liking. Worth a visit is the church of St-Paul, rebuilt in Gothic style in the 14th century, and the small town museum nearby. A new large channel on the right serves as a bypass for the infamous Frontignan bridge and connects directly with the coast near Sète. Use is restricted to commercial vessels of which very few appear to travel on it. **Frontignan Plage**, the local beach, is a cycle ride of about 3km. Mainly of fine sand, it is divided into a series of small bays formed by breakwaters.

Take care to avoid becoming ensnared in fishing nets which stretch from one side of the canal to the other; controlled by a pair of winding drums and a dinghy, they will be removed for the passage of craft. One place where they are regularly used is on the outskirts of Frontignan, where the stone-banked waterway passes through the centre of the Étang d'Ingril. Although there are occasional cuts linking the canal with the lagoons, they are shallow and for use by small fishing craft only.

At **Les-Aresquiers** (K86.6) it is possible to moor under a recently built concrete bridge and walk to a beach

400m away. While the seashore restaurant here appears to be attractive, I have several times found it to be closed in the evening; possibly it only serves lunch. A more interesting overnight halt involves continuing across the Étang de Vic and Étang de Pierre Blanche, tying up on the right near the point where a prominent stone gateway stands close to the water. This is **Maguelone** (K78), an ancient settlement on a pine-clad hill by the sea and dating from the 2nd century AD. A great cathedral was erected in the 6th century and a sizeable city grew up around it. The religious settlement was disestablished on the orders of Richelieu in 1622 and every building but the cathedral razed to the ground. Some restoration was carried out in the 19th century and this important but forlorn structure is now open to the public daily. Beyond it lies a splendid beach. The entire coastline between Aresquiers and Palavas-les-Flots is undeveloped apart from a few bungalows and camping sites in the dunes and offers some of the best beaches in Languedoc. Although isolated, they are popular during the summer with holidaymakers who drive in through the rough sandy track from Palavas. Many nudists gather here, especially SW of Maguelone. To approach from the canal, cycle or walk around the southern boundary of the cathedral grounds for about 1km. Back on the canal there is a *bateau* restaurant. A floating pedestrian bridge with motorised opening section enables tourists who have arrived by car from the direction of **Villeneuve-lès-Maguelone**, to cross the waterway and, during the season, journey to the seaside aboard a comic little train. Villeneuve, 2.5km NW, is a pleasant market town with many 14th century buildings.

After crossing the Étang de l'Arnel (left) and the Étang du Prévost (right), the resort town of **Palavas-les-Flots** appears (K75.2). The River Lez flows across the navigation and down to the sea at a four-way junction controlled by lights. Guillotine gates are closed in times of flood to keep surplus water out of the canal. Large boats should moor at the navigation authority depot on the canal, but craft with a headroom of less than 2.4m may turn right under a bridge into the Lez and use the excellent *port de plaisance* pontoons provided for visitors on the left. A large marina, opposite, is for resident boats only. Established as a Customs port and fishing village in the late 18th century, Palavas grew rapidly as a holiday town when a railway link was provided with the nearby city of Montpellier in 1872. Expansion has continued in recent times under the Languedoc-Roussillon Development Scheme. It is a lively and attractive town, very convenient for canal boaters with fuelling facilities and numerous bars, restaurants and souvenir shops lining the banks of the river. Every imaginable variety of seafood is available.

300m below a swing bridge, the river is spanned by the *Transcanal 'Le Mickey'* (a form of chairlift and surely the only example of this form of waterway crossing in France?). Broad, sandy beaches offer safe bathing. Fishing boats and picturesque Mediterranean dories throng the quays. Entertainment includes a large funfair and periodic waterborne jousting contests.

In 1996, 5.5km of the **River Lez** (turn left out of the Canal du Rhône à Sète) were restored to navigation. This potentially torrential stream was canalised by the Marquis de Solas in the late 17th century to provide a port for Montpellier. Total distance from the canal junction to the city basin was 10km with three locks. The route is very pleasant as it winds through the *étangs*. The single lock, La Troisième Écluse, functions remotely when you use the interphone. The present terminus is **Port Ariane**, an exciting marina development combined with waterside housing (hire craft and all boat services except fuel). This is situated on the edge of **Lattes**, where there are good shops and a large number of restaurants. Market, 300m from the port, on Sunday mornings. A short bus ride brings you to the heart of **Montpellier**, fastest-growing city in France where the average age of inhabitants is said to be 25, there being 60,000 university students. Opinion polls suggest that more French people would choose to live here than anywhere else. The city boasts many attractions with much fine architecture, museums and a splendid new tramway system. For full details of the sights, consult the Michelin Green Guide *Languedoc Roussillon Tarn Gorges*. Further restoration of the river towards Montpellier is under consideration.

After its crossing of the Étang de Pérols, the canal arrives at a four-way junction. The left turning leads to a hire boat base and marina (facilities include fuel) in the **Canal du Hangar** (K70.6). This is the recommended mooring for the nearby seaside resort of **Carnon**. A route to an alternative pleasure boat harbour and the sea via the **Canal du Grau de Carnon** is restricted to small craft under 1.2m headroom. The much expanded town has extensive beaches. Market, Wednesdays and Thursdays.

The through route continues bordered on the left by the vast Étang de Mauguio, on whose shores you will see lines of conical fishing nets. Towards the sea, the skyline is dominated by the aggressively modern pyramid-shaped apartment blocks of **La Grand Motte**, a thriving and surprisingly well established 'new' resort. To visit, moor by the transformer station (K64.6) and walk or cycle about 3km.

Pairs of guillotine gates with traffic lights prevent the **River Vidourle** from flooding into the canal (K55). Boats with a headroom of no more than about 2.8m can make a circular diversion by turning under the towpath bridge, right, and following the Vidourle through two *étangs* to the fishing port of **Le Grau-du-Roi**, rejoining the Canal du Rhône à Sète via the Maritime Channel to Aigues-Mortes. In places, the Vidourle is likely to be no more than 1m deep. Pontoon moorings are provided for visitors to Le Grau-du-Roi. Private craft may continue to the sea past numerous seafood restaurants and through a swing road bridge, opened at intervals throughout the day. This part of the waterway is packed with fishing boats. Good sandy beaches are in the town or eastwards (for naturists) at **Les Baronnets**, beyond the Espiguette lighthouse. A short sea passage to the east leads to the admirable aquatic town of **Port-Camargue**, where there are berths for 4,000 craft, waterside holiday homes, shops and restaurants. Although confirmed inland boaters, we thoroughly enjoyed our brief stay there.

Aigues-Mortes (K50.8) is one of the most exciting towns in Southern France. Established in 1240 by King Louis IX (St-Louis), it provided him with a Mediterranean seaport from which to lead a Crusade to Palestine. His fleet of 38 ships set sail in 1248, the King being accompanied by his Queen, two brothers, the Counts of Arles and Anjou, the Cardinal Legate and a large retinue. A second Crusade was launched in May 1270. Louis was never again to see France, for he died of the plague in Tunis. Aigues-Mortes is built in the form of a square and surrounded by stone ramparts about 10m high with a perimeter of 1,750m. There are 10 gates and 14 towers, including the massive Tour de Constance, 33m high with 7m thick walls. From the top are excellent views over the pantiled rooftops to the canals and marshes below. An eight-year-old Protestant girl, Marie Durand, was imprisoned here for 38 years (1730–68). Although now much frequented by tourists (it was nearly deserted in the early 1970s), Aigues-Mortes contrives to retain the atmosphere of a medieval fortified city rather better than Carcassonne. The bustling shops mostly serve the community that still lives here. St-Louis is remembered by a statue in the main square, where the tourist office is housed in a pleasing stone-roomed building. Good moorings (payment demanded) have been provided in the Maritime Channel, along the length of the western

The Tour de Constance at the walled town of Aigues-Mortes.

wall, with a prospect of sailing barges and other craft opposite. If passing through in the direction of the Rhône you should hoot for a railway swing bridge to be opened at the canal junction; much of the time, however, the bridge remains open. Further short-term moorings will be found in the basin beyond, with fuel available from a nearby garage. A canal bypass for large barges was opened to the north of the town in 1994.

An expedition to the heart of the **Camargue** can be arranged from here. Our party of eight once hired the local taxi: we brought a picnic lunch and the driver supplied wine from his own vineyard. The taxi doubled as an ambulance, but we were assured that no one would fall ill while we spent the day enjoying ourselves. This method offered the benefit of acquiring an expert local guide who knew the best locations for sighting flamingos, black bulls and wild horses. Covering about 480m² west of the Rhône Delta, this land of lakes and marshes is one of the most important wetland habitats in Europe. Introduction of fresh water for cultivation of rice in paddy fields and chemical pollution present a threat to the unique wild life. But thanks to the work of conservationists, like Swiss industrialist Dr Luc Hoffman who founded the Tour de Valat biological research station in 1954, the area is now protected from the worst effects of the 21st century. Perhaps you will come closest to the spirit of the Camargue from the saddle: horses can be hired at numerous ranches. Do not be surprised to encounter cowboys more real than their American counterparts; or specimens of the

bright green praying mantis; or great mountains of salt, evaporated from the brackish water. The Camargue is a strange, desolate and utterly captivating world. For further suggestions on places to visit, consult the Michelin Green Guide *Provence*. Aigues-Mortes lies 8km inland via the Maritime Channel. Looking across the lagoons and salt pans, it is easy to understand its name of Dead Waters. Another industry much in evidence here is the Lunel wine company. The sea is reached at the charming fishing port of Le-Grau-du-Roi (see above).

East of Aigues-Mortes, note on the right the entrance lock to the **Canal du Bourgidou**, one of a complicated network of navigable channels intersecting the Camargue that can only be accessed here with portable craft. The Canal du Rhône à Sète now heads inland, away from the coast and the *étangs*. From the level of a cruiser, it may appear rather dull, straight and reedy, but stand on the roof or moor up and you will be rewarded by views of rice fields and the foothills of the Cevennes. Looking back from the bridge at **Gallician** (K39.2), Aigues-Mortes' Tour de Constance can be seen in the far distance. Small marina, shopping, *Costières de Nîmes* wine cellar and the much-extended restaurant *Chez Colette*.

There is little (apart from a convenient mooring at the bridge) to detain you in **Franquevaux** (K35.1).

Fishing nets in the Camargue.

Craft bound for the Rhône must take a right-hand fork (K29) into the **Canal de St-Gilles** (see Chapter 57). Remaining on the route for Beaucaire, we soon arrive at **St-Gilles** (K24), once a seaport served by the Petit Rhône and visited by ships from all corners of the Mediterranean. Now that the canal no longer connects with the Rhône at Beaucaire, commercial traffic is effectively extinct, but there are substantial numbers of hire cruisers based here and at the terminus. One of several self-styled 'Gateways to the Camargue' St-Gilles has modern wine-processing installations (that look more like a petrol refinery) opposite a broad quay with visitors' moorings. Here also is a hire base for Crown Blue Line.

A paving, planting and lighting scheme in 1987 transformed the waterfront, which now presents an animated scene when the locals take their evening stroll in mid-summer. I once spent two weeks here, carrying out boat maintenance and eating at the splendid *Hôtel du Cours*, near the main cross-roads. A bullfight was staged one afternoon in the arena behind the boat yard. As proof that French versions of this barbaric activity can be quite as repulsive as the Spanish variety, a storm drain alongside my mooring was soon bright red with blood. One evening, there was a stage-managed stampede of bulls through the town centre; horsemen were charging in all directions and a number of innocent shoppers came close to being trampled on. St-Gilles is not a place for the faint-hearted!

Restaurants (of which there is a wide choice) serve a local speciality, *Bœuf à la Gardiane*, beef casserole with onions, olives, garlic, tomatoes and red wine: the variety we sampled was unappetising and we dubbed it 'cowboy stew'. The town is said to owe its origins to St Giles, who arrived in Provence during the 7th century from his native Greece aboard a raft. Living as a forest hermit, he struck up a relationship with an albino deer which one day was chased by a large hunting party led by the Visigoth King, Flavius Wamba. Giles intervened and was himself shot in the leg. The King was greatly impressed by this holy man and later persuaded him that an abbey should be built on the site of his dwelling. Giles travelled to Rome to obtain papal recognition for his foundation and was provided with a parting gift of two doors for the new church. These he cast into the Tiber and they duly made their way to the Rhône Delta, timing their arrival to exactly coincide with Giles' return in France! In 1209, the papal legate was assassinated at the very doors of the abbey, resulting in the atrocities of the Albigensian Crusade. The abbey that now stands in St-Gilles dates from the 12th century and has been extensively rebuilt. Its west front features three doorways with Romanesque arches and some wonderful stone carvings depicting the Life of Christ, completed between 1180 and 1240. St Giles' tomb is in the 12th century crypt.

The canal continues in a somewhat featureless but not unattractive way to **Bellegarde** (K13.2), where *Le Restogrill* woodland snack bar is on the waterside by the Pont d'Arles. Basic shops in the town, 1.2km distant. Nourriguier lock (K7.7) is a large chamber, mechanised and operated by boat crews. **Beaucaire** (K0.7) is entered through a briefly industrial area, but it soon becomes evident that this likeable town is well worth the diversion from the through navigation. Good, but crowded, moorings in a broad basin. At the far end, the canal turns sharply to the right before arriving at its terminus by the currently disused Beaucaire lock. A junction with the Rhône has been out of service since the mid-1970s when river levels were altered. It is proposed to open up this important link by reinstating the old lock and adding another to connect with the lock approach channel on the Rhône.

From the 13th century until the coming of the railway in the 19th, Beaucaire staged one of Europe's greatest fairs each July: 300,000 people would crowd into the town, while ships brought goods from throughout the Mediterranean and the Atlantic Coast. All manner of side-shows and performers provided entertainment. These vibrant times are recalled in a Museum of Old Beaucaire in the Rue Barbès and in the annual *Estivales*, for 10 days from 22 July. This festival with a Spanish flavour features dancing, fireworks and various activities inspired by the Camargue. The old and narrow streets are a delight, with stone archways and a wealth of cast-iron embellishment. The castle ruins, surrounded by an 11th century wall, feature a Triangle Tower providing a magnificent view over the Rhône to the mighty fortress of **Tarascon**. Guarding the eastern border of Provence, Tarascon is without doubt one of the finest medieval *châteaux* in France and the tour is a fascinating experience. (Cross the Rhône bridge from Beaucaire.) Enlarged to its present state by Good King René in the 15th century, the castle rises sheer from the rocky river bank. Although unfurnished, the beautifully proportioned rooms give a good impression of the royal lifestyle of 500 years ago. Much later, it was used as a prison; English captives were held here during the Seven Years War and again under Napoléon. Carved stone inscriptions recall these times: for example that by a London river lighterman taken from the sloop *Zephyr* and incarcerated for 16 months from August 1778. Tours are available almost every day of the year. Beaucaire is a convenient centre from which to take a bus to Arles and Avignon. Further excursions are listed under those towns, in Chapter 56.

APPENDICES ~

GUIDES AND MAPS

Carte Guides, which are available from a number of different publishers, are essential for exploration of French waterways, providing detailed maps, tourist information and regularly up-dated information on facilities required by the boater. I personally prefer those from Éditions Grafocarte and unless otherwise stated, these are the publications I mention at the start of each chapter. But the alternatives are also very good. These, and other in-print waterways publications, may be obtained at waterside chandleries in France. Comprehensive mail order catalogues are available from Imray, Laurie, Norie & Wilson Ltd, Wych House, The Broadway, St Ives, Cambs, PE27 4BT, tel 01480 462114. Email Orders@imray.com. An even more comprehensive service is offered in France by Libraire Verte Fluviale, Éditions de l'Écluse, 36 boulevard de la Bastille, 75012 Paris, tel 04 67 50 42 67.

Cruising enjoyment is enhanced by the *Michelin France Tourist and Motoring Atlas*, containing maps of the whole country on a scale of 1:200,000. Published annually. This does not, however, indicate locks, for which larger scale maps are required.

A number of books listed here are long out of print, but it is well worth trying to find second copies either via Google on the Internet, or from specialist water-ways mail order service M & M Baldwin, 24 High Street, Cleobury Mortimer, Kidderminster, West Midlands, DY14 8BY, tel 01299 270110.

Carte Guides Navicarte (Éditions Grafocarte, 125 rue Jean-Jacques Rousseau, BP40, F-92132 Issy-les-Moulineaux Cedex, France). All carry text in French and English, sometimes additionally German and Dutch. Regularly updated.
1. *La Seine. Paris to the Sea*
2. *La Seine. Paris to Marcilly*
3. *La Marne. Paris to Vitry-le-François*
6. *Canaux du Centre. St Mammès to Chalon-sur-Saône*
8. *Champagne-Ardenne. Namur to Burgundy*
9. *Canal de l'Est. Liège to Corre with Belgian Sambre*
10. *La Saône and La Seille*
11. *Les Canaux du Midi. Atlantic to Mediterranean*
12. *Bretagne*
13. *Pays de la Loire*
14. *Nord-Pas-de-Calais. Dunquerque to Valenciennes, etc*
16. *Le Rhône and Petit Rhône*

17. *Canal de la Marne au Rhin with C des Houillères de la Sarre and C du Rhône au Rhin (North Branch)*
19. *Bourgogne Est*
20. *Bourgogne Ouest*
21. *Carte de France. All waterways*
24. *Picardie. Somme, C du Nord, Sensée, St-Quentin, Oise, Aisne, Sambre, etc*
25. *La Charente*
27. *Le Lot. Luzech to St-Cirq-Lapopie*
28. *La Baïse et le Lot aval*
31. *Canal de Bourgogne*
32. *Canal du Rhône au Rhin*
33. *Canal de l'Ourcq*

Carte Guides Vagnon (Les Éditions du Plaisancier, 43 porte du Grand Lyon, Neyron, 01707 Miribel Cedex, France.)
1. *Carte de France des Voies Navigables*
2. *Doubs et C Rhône au Rhin*
3. *C de Bourgogne, Centre, Nivernais*
5. *Le Rhône*
6. *La Saône, La Seille, C des Vosges, La Moselle*
7. *Canaux du Midi. Including Garonne, Gironde, La Baïse, Le Lot aval*
10. *Bretagne. Including Loire Atlantique*
11. *Pays de la Loire. Cher Navigable*
12. *Lorraine Est and Alsace*
13. *Lorraine Ouest and Moselle*

Guides Fluviales (Éditions du Breil, Fitou/Le Breil, 11400, Castelnaudary, France.)
1. *Bretagne*
2. *Loire/Nivernais*
3. *Bourgogne/Franche-Comté*
4. *Alsace/Lorraine*
5. *Le Lot*
6. *La Charente*
7. *Midi/Camargue*
8. *Champagne*
9. *Canal du Rhône au Rhin*
10. *Pays de la Loire*
11. *Bourgogne/Nivernais*
12. *Aquitaine*

Fluviocarte (Libraire Verte Fluvial)
1. *Naviguer en Alsace.* Covers the canalised Rhine, Strasbourg-Rheinfelden, with the Colmar and N Rhône-Rhin Branches.

GENERAL READING

There are many good guides (not specifically navigational) to regions through which the waterways pass. Perhaps the most detailed are the Michelin *Green Guides*, covering the entire country. Available in English editions, relevant volumes are: *Alsace Lorraine Champagne*; *Atlantic Coast*; *Auvergne Rhône Valley*; *Brittany*; *Burgundy Jura*; *Châteaux of the Loire*; *Dordogne Berry Limousin*; *Languedoc Roussillon Tarn Gorges*; *Normandy*; *Northern France and the Paris Region*; *Paris*; *Provence*.

No English-speaking visitor should consider travelling in France without *The A–Z Gastronomique: A Dictionary of French Food and Wine*, by Fay Sharman (Pan/Macmillan, 1992). I have used this dozens of times to translate French restaurant menus and (astonishingly) have never once been able to fault it. Copies are readily available on the Internet.

PERIODICALS

Articles on French waterways and cruising appear in the following English language monthly publications: *Motor Boats Monthly*, *Motor Boat & Yachting*, *Canal Boat & Inland Waterways*, *Waterways World*. But for fullest coverage, see the French language monthly *Fluvial*.

BIBLIOGRAPHY

Limits of space allow for only a small selection of titles here. References to various out of print but highly interesting and desirable books are additionally made throughout the text.

Cooper, Bill & Laurel. *Watersteps Through France*. Adlard Coles Nautical, London, 1996. Travelogue by converted barge.

Edwards-May, David. *Inland Waterways of France*. Imray, St Ives, 2002. Updated with distance tables, maps of each waterway etc.

Liley, John. *France – The Quiet Way*. Stanford Maritime, London, 1983. A wryly amusing and thoughtful description of the French waterways.

Martin, Marian. *The ACN Book of EuroRegs for Inland Waterways*. Adlard Coles Nautical, London, 2004. A pleasure boater's guide to CEVNI rules, navigation markers etc. *The European Waterways*. Adlard Coles Nautical, London, 2003. A manual for first time users.

Massey, Hart. *Travels with Lionel: A Small Barge in France*. Gollancz, London, 1988. Cruising throughout France. Entertaining.

McKnight, Hugh. *The Guinness Guide to Waterways of Western Europe*. Guinness Superlatives, London, 1978. *Slow Boat Through France*. Available from the author, 1991. *Avonbay's* first four years of French travels.

Pilkington, Roger. *Small Boat…series*. Macmillan, 1961–71. Titles relating to France include *Southern France*; *Meuse*; *Upper Rhine*; *France*; *Alsace*; *Luxembourg*. *Small Boat in the Midi*. Pearson, Burton-on-Trent, 1989. *Waterways in Europe*. John Murray, London, 1972.

Rolt, L T C. *From Sea to Sea: The Canal du Midi*. Euromapping, 38170 Seyssinet, France, 1994.

IN FRENCH

Beaudouin, François. *Bateaux des Fleuves de France*. Éditions de l'Éstran, Douarnenez, 1985. Magnificent historical illus. survey of all types of barges.

Didier, Louise (*et al*). *Dictionnaire Marinier*. Bief Édition, BP 96, 21170 St-Jean-de-Losne, France. 1998. 2,400 French waterways terms explained.

Guillet, Jacques. *La Batellerie Bretonne*. Éditions de l'Éstran, Douarnenez, 1989. Massive illustrated history of commercial barge traffic in Brittany.

GLOSSARY OF WATERWAYS TERMS ~

allège, Charente barge

amarrer, to moor

amont, upstream

anneau, mooring ring

argentat, extinct Dordogne sailing barge

ascenseur, vertical boat lift

automoteur, motorised freight barge

autoroute, motorway

aval, downstream

bâbord, port, left side

bac, ferry

bâche, small barge, mainly used for carrying sand, eg on the Saône

bajoyer, bank, or side of a lock

balise, navigation marker

barque, small punt, eg as used in the marshland canals off the Sèvre Niortaise

barrage, weir

barre, steering wheel

bassin de virement, winding hole (widening of canal where long craft can be turned)

bateau-mouche, passenger boat (Paris)

batelier, commercial boatman

batellerie, the commercial boating fraternity

bief (orig. *biez*), pound; a reach of any length between canal locks

bilander, type of dumb barge

bitte, bollard

blin, small punt used in the marshes of the Brière, near Nantes

boulard, bollard

bouée, buoy or lifebelt

boussole, compass

brocante, bric-à-brac or antiques

busc, sill (of a lock)

cabane, extinct passenger barge

cadole, former variety of Saône barge

cale, slipway

canot, boat's dinghy

chaland, barge

chemin de halage, towpath

chômage, stoppage; closure of locks or other part of a waterway for repairs

coche d'eau, water coach, an extinct passenger vessel

congé annuel, French habit of closing shops, restaurants, etc, for a month's holiday and often coinciding with the height of the tourist season when maximum trade might have been expected

conche, small marshland canal in the Marais Poitevin (Chapter 51)

cornet, small flat-bottomed punt with upturned bows, used in the Hortillonnages at Amiens

crêperie, restaurant specialising in savoury and sweet pancakes (mainly Brittany)

cric, lock paddle

darse, dock

déclassé, describing a navigation closed to traffic but still preserved as a watercourse

dérivation, canal section on a river navigation; usually also a lock cut

déversoire, spillway, or side weir at a canal lock

digue, embankment or dike

ducs d'Alba, mooring piles, generally at approach to a lock

écluse, lock

éclusier(e), lock keeper

écoutilles, hatch covers

écran radar, radar screen

flottage, system of floating logs (Chapter 46)

flûte, type of barge of smaller dimensions than a *péniche*

fossé, small marshland canal off the Sèvre Niortaise

Freycinet, the standard *péniche* gauge

gabare, lighter (barge)

galion, small extinct Charente sailing barge

galiot, 19th century passenger boat, eg on Seine

gardian, Camargue 'cowboy'

gouvernail, rudder

grau, channel linking salt lake with the sea, eg on the Canal du Rhône à Sète

gribanne, 19th century Somme barge

grue, crane

haut parleur, loud speaker

hélice, propeller

hirondelle, extinct fast passenger steamer (Loire)

Hortillonnages, market gardens at Amiens, intersected by network of small waterways

inexplosible, 19th century steam passenger craft introduced to allay fears resulting from several spectacular boiler explosions

largeur, beam (width) of a boat

lavoir, public wash-house, often on the banks of rivers or canals or (*bateau-lavoir*) on board a purpose-built barge

longeur, length of a boat

macaron, steering wheel (N France)

manivelle, windlass, or handle to open lock paddles or gates

marinier, boatman, especially on a river

le Mascaret, tidal bore on the lower Seine

mât, mast

nœud, knot

pardon, religious celebration/procession (mainly Brittany); also a barge festival/rally of religious origin

passerelle, footbridge

péniche, standard 38.5m barge of the Freycinet type

pente d'eau, water slope, an alternative to locks for overcoming changes in canal levels, eg Montech and Béziers

pigouille, punt pole (see Chapter 51)

piquet, mooring spike

plage, plagette, bathing 'beach' equally applied to river and coastal situations

plaisancier, pleasure boatman

plan incliné, inclined plane boat lift

point kilométrique, distance marker

port de plaisance, pleasure boat harbour/marina

portes, (lock) gates

portes marinières, navigation weir, staunch or flash lock

poupée, bollard or bitts on a barge

pousseur, pusher (tug) boat

râcle, section of river forming a link between two portions of canal

radié, describing an abandoned navigation

rame, a tow/string of barges

relais nautique, pleasure craft moorings with various facilities

remorqueur, tug boat

rigole, canal feeder; otherwise, waterway in the Marais Poitevin

Roannaise, type of Loire barge

robinet, water tap

rove, steering wheel (Midi)

sablonnier, sand barge

sapine, sapinette, old type of wooden barge

sas, chamber of a lock

sauterelle, small crane on a barge enabling crew to disembark when it is not possible to moor directly alongside the bank

savoyarde, former variety of Saône barge

sentine, extinct Loire barge

seuil, sill of a lock

seysselande, former variety of Saône barge

sondeur, echo-sounder

Syndicat d'Initiative, tourist office

timonerie, wheelhouse

tirant d'air, boat's height above water level; air draft

tirant d'eau, boat's depth below waterline; draft

tirette, pole suspended over a navigation, which, when turned activates a lock

trématage, overtaking (of another boat)

treuil, anchor winch

tribord, starboard; right side

tuyau, water hose

vanne, lock paddle

vedette, passenger launch

ventelle, lock paddle

Voies Navigables de France (VNF), official organisation responsible for most waterways

INDEX